Studies in Scripture

VOLUME FOUR 1 Kings to Malachi

Studies in Scripture

VOLUME FOUR 1 Kings to Malachi

Edited by Kent P. Jackson

Deseret Book Company
Salt Lake City, Utah

Library of Congress Cataloging-in-Publication Data

1 Kings to Malachi / edited by Kent P. Jackson.
    p. cm. — (Studies in Scripture ; v. 4)
    Includes bibliographical references and indexes.
    ISBN 0-87579-789-X
    1. Bible. O.T. — Criticism, interpretation, etc. 2. Church of
Jesus Christ of Latter-day Saints — Doctrines. 3. Mormon Church —
Doctrines. I. Jackson, Kent P. II. Title: First Kings to
Malachi. III. Series: Studies in Scripture (Salt Lake City, Utah) ;
v. 4.
BS1171.2.A15   1993
221.6 — dc20   93-36633
                                    CIP

Printed in the United States of America

10   9   8   7   6   5   4   3   2

CONTENTS

Contents

Contents

PREFACE

The Old Testament is a witness of God at work. It records how he made covenants with his people, delivered them from bondage, blessed them with a promised land, gave them laws and ordinances, challenged them to reject the world and live in accordance with revealed standards, and warned them of the consequences of unrighteous behavior. In the Old Testament, the Lord used the events of history to teach the validity of his covenants, the sanctity of his laws, and the certainty of his word. In it we see demonstrated, in vivid and dramatic fashion, the fulfillment of prophecy. The destructions that decimated Israel and Judah bear testimony that God's word through his prophets is a lifeline for the faithful but a condemnation for those who choose to reject it. That is one of the great messages of the Old Testament, and it is a message that we, in our day, need to learn.

Studies in Scripture, Volume Four: 1 Kings to Malachi has been written to assist Latter-day Saints in their study of the second half of the Old Testament, which for some is the most unfamiliar part of the Standard Works. This book was not written to be a substitute for scripture study. On the contrary, it has been our goal to point readers to the scriptures themselves. We desire that this book will be a helpful resource but that Latter-day Saints will base their understanding of divine things on the revealed word of the Lord.

What we have written in this volume is intended to be our own best insights into the biblical text. Authoritative interpretation of scripture is found only in scripture itself and in the words of our latter-day prophets.

Although we have sought earnestly to write in harmony with the teachings of the scriptures and the leaders of the Church, each contributor is responsible for his or her own conclusions.

This commentary frequently refers to modern revelation, including the Joseph Smith Translation (JST). The Old Testament should not be read without the constant assistance of modern scripture. We encourage readers to use the Church's edition of the King James Version of the Bible, first published in 1979, which in this book is called, for the sake of convenience and brevity, "the LDS Bible." Readers can benefit greatly from its footnotes, which provide inspired readings from the Joseph Smith Translation and cross-references to other Standard Works. Reference is also made to the excellent maps, Topical Guide, and the Bible Dictionary, all of which should be the companions of careful students of the Old Testament.

Finally, I would like to express my thanks to my wife and children, who have been my patient friends during the writing and editing of this book, to my colleagues who contributed to it, to Anthony Rivera, my able and dependable research assistant, and to the staff and management of Deseret Book Company, for their skillful work.

Kent P. Jackson

1

ALL THINGS POINT TO CHRIST

KENT P. JACKSON

As do our other Standard Works, the Old Testament teaches us of God and of our relationship to him. It does that by recounting, in historical books, the record of his interaction with his people and his work to bring about their well-being through the process of history. It also does that by recording the words of the prophets, who served as his messengers and spoke as directed by his Spirit. And it teaches us of God by preserving psalms, poems, hymns, stories, and sayings which describe, praise, and typify his divine character. Through these means, the Old Testament testifies of the Lord Jehovah and brings glory to his holy name.

The Old Testament reveals the character of Jehovah,[1] but it is to modern revelation that we turn to learn more of his identity and the full nature of his work. From the Book of Mormon we learn that he would come into the world as Jesus Christ, that "the Lord Omnipotent who reigneth, who was, and is from all eternity to all eternity, shall come down from heaven among the children of men, and shall dwell in a tabernacle of clay, and shall go forth amongst men. . . . And he shall be called Jesus Christ, the Son of God, the Father of heaven and earth, the Creator of all things from the beginning" (Mosiah 3:5, 8). The knowledge that Jesus is the God of the Old Testament helps us to understand this book of scripture in ways that would not be possible otherwise. We understand, for example, that his mighty acts of deliverance anciently were types of, and bore testimony to, his ultimate act of deliverance, the Atonement. Indeed, all of Israel's religion, law, history,

---

Kent P. Jackson is professor of ancient scripture at Brigham Young University.

[1]For example, see the discussion in Chap. 39 of this volume.

and daily experience bore testimony to this greatest act of salvation. "All things have their likeness, and all things are created and made to bear record of me," the Lord said, "both things which are temporal, and things which are spiritual; . . . all things bear record of me" (Moses 6:63).

The Law of Moses was given to the Israelites when they were found unworthy and unwilling to receive greater things (D&C 84:23–27; cf. Alma 12:10–11). It was "a very strict law" for "a stiffnecked people" (Mosiah 13:29). Still, it bore a forceful testimony of the Atonement by means of what the Book of Mormon calls "types" and "shadows" (Mosiah 3:15). That was done primarily through the teaching power of ordinances. "This is the whole meaning of the law," Amulek said, "every whit pointing to that great and last sacrifice; and that great and last sacrifice will be the Son of God, yea, infinite and eternal" (Alma 34:14). Jacob wrote, "My soul delighteth in proving unto my people the truth of the coming of Christ; for, for this end hath the law of Moses been given; and all things which have been given of God from the beginning of the world, unto man, are the typifying of him" (2 Ne. 11:4).[2]

As with all other scripture, the Old Testament is a testament of Jesus Christ, but it presents special challenges for its readers. Because of the imperfect transmission of the record and the all-too-frequent apostasy of the Israelites, the message of Christ is not as visible in it as in our other scriptures. According to the prophets, the Israelites were a rebellious people, unable to live up to the moral requirements of the Law of Moses.[3] The limitations of their faith are reflected in the nature of the Old Testament. For the most part, it is a book directed to, and recorded for, the Israelite nation in general, not the worthy Saints who were among them. The words of the prophets in it are their public pronouncements to their wayward society, not their private teachings to those who had risen above the sins of their generation. That is why there is a heavy emphasis on judgment and punishment and also why celestial things, "the solemnities of eternity" (D&C 43:34), are not as apparent.

True prophets testify of Christ and proclaim that salvation is brought

---

[2]See Kent P. Jackson, "The Law of Moses and the Atonement of Christ," in *Studies in Scripture, Volume Three: Genesis to 2 Samuel*, ed. Kent P. Jackson and Robert L. Millet (Salt Lake City: Randall Book, 1985), pp. 153–72.

[3]Some examples are JST Ps. 14:2–3; Isa. 1:4–5; Jer. 6:6–7; Ezek. 22:2–4, 8–13; Hosea 4:1–2, 11–18; Amos 2:4, 6–8; Micah 6:10–13, 16; Hab. 1:2–4; Zeph. 1:4–6; 2:1–4.

about through his redeeming love. That is the primary function of their calling. In ancient Israel, the prophets labored under circumstances that required that their message be first and foremost a call for Israel to repent. But they also proclaimed the message of salvation by prophesying of deliverance from temporal foes at the Lord's coming in glory and of deliverance from sin and death through the Atonement. In harmony with the principle of keeping sacred things from the abuse of the irreverent (JST Matt. 7:10), prophecies of the Atonement were generally veiled in types and shadows. Frequently they were written in such a way that only those who understand the plan of salvation or are familiar with the happenings of Jesus' mortal ministry can understand their full meaning. Thus the Old Testament writings and ancient Israel's religion present an invitation not only for the Lord's people anciently but for us as well to look through eyes of faith and see that all things point to Christ.

Modern revelation is the key. I do not hesitate to state that no one can fully understand the Old Testament without the aid of what God has revealed in the latter days through the Book of Mormon, the Joseph Smith Translation of the Bible, the Doctrine and Covenants, the Pearl of Great Price, and the sermons and writings of Joseph Smith. It is from these sources that we learn the true nature of God, the true doctrines of heaven, and the true message of the Lord's prophets. Our study of the Old Testament must be undertaken with a consistent and steady view through the lens of modern revelation.

We are privileged to live in a day in which the gospel is restored, the heavens are open, the Church is on earth, and modern prophets guide the Lord's Saints. But we are especially privileged to enjoy the blessings of the Lord's redeeming work, which has been the message of the prophets and the scriptures in all ages.

2

KINGS AND CHRONICLES

DAVID ROLPH SEELY

The Old Testament contains two separate histories of Israel. The longest and most familiar of the two is found in the books from Genesis through 2 Kings, which recount in sequence the events from the creation of the world in Genesis to the destruction of Jerusalem and the Exile in 2 Kings 25. The second history is found in the books of Chronicles and Ezra and Nehemiah (Ezra-Nehemiah is counted as one book in the Jewish canon). It begins with Adam, in 1 Chronicles, and continues through the return from the Exile, the rebuilding of the temple, and the restoration of Israel recounted in Ezra and Nehemiah. In the Jewish canon, the books of Kings are a part of the Former Prophets, in the same position as in the Christian canon. The books of Chronicles are found in the Writings, at the end of the canon.[1] The Christian canon, reflected in the King James Translation, places all of the historical books together; thus a reader will begin at Genesis and read a continuous historical narrative to the end of 2 Kings and will then start reading the history over again with Chronicles and continue through Nehemiah.

The history preserved in the Bible is sacred history in that it

---

David Rolph Seely is assistant professor of ancient scripture at Brigham Young University.

[1]The Jewish canon is divided into three sections: the Law (or Torah), the Prophets, and the Writings. The Law contains the five books of Moses, or the Pentateuch: Genesis through Deuteronomy. The Prophets is subdivided between the Former Prophets, Joshua through Kings, and the Latter Prophets, Isaiah through Malachi. The Writings contain the poetic books, some historical books, and one prophetic book: Psalms, Job, Proverbs, Ruth, Song of Solomon, Ecclesiastes, Lamentations, Esther, Daniel, Ezra-Nehemiah, and Chronicles. For some reason, in the Jewish canon Ezra-Nehemiah occurs before Chronicles, which is the last book in the Hebrew Bible; however, the last two verses of Chronicles (2 Chron. 36:22–23) are repeated as the first two verses in Ezra (Ezra 1:1–2), demonstrating that the books are to be related in that sequence.

acknowledges the hand of the Lord in human affairs. Biblical history dramatically illustrates many spiritual lessons of value for future generations. It is not known who the authors and editors of these histories were, but it is clear that they understood their story to be one of importance for future Israel. From the Book of Mormon, Latter-day Saint readers are familiar with the process of authorship (as demonstrated by the small plates of Nephi) and the process of editing and abridging by Mormon and Moroni (as demonstrated by Mormon's abridgment from the large plates). In the Book of Mormon, the authors and editors are identified, and a careful reader can identify passages, often introduced by the phrase "and thus we see,"[2] inserted by the authors or editors to indicate, emphasize, and explain the lessons we can learn from the record of the historical events. In contrast, the authors and editors of the biblical histories are almost always anonymous. Although they remain anonymous, their messages, just as in the Book of Mormon, can be examined when we look at what they chose to include in their narrative, the judgments they made about the characters and events they recounted, and the themes that they emphasized throughout. Occasionally a biblical author or editor inserted an explicit passage pointing to the lesson of an event, but more often the spiritual lessons of biblical history are simply imbedded in the narrative itself.

The covenant the Lord made with Israel at Sinai was a conditional one, promising blessings for obedience to the Mosaic law and curses for disobedience (see, for example, Lev. 26; Deut. 27–30). This covenant, of course, is the same kind made later with Lehi and his descendants.[3] The history of Israel from Sinai to the destruction of Jerusalem in 587 B.C. records centuries of Israel's disobedience countered by divinely sent prophetic warnings that were ultimately rejected. There were times of repentance and hope under the reigns of David, Solomon, Hezekiah, and Josiah, but in every case righteousness gave way to apostasy and sin: idolatry, immorality, dishonesty, and oppression of the poor and helpless.

---

[2]See, for example, 1 Ne. 16:29; Alma 28:13–14; Hel. 3:27–30; 12:3–26; Ether 14:25.

[3]Cf., for example, Deut. 11:26–28: "Behold, I set before you this day a blessing and a curse; A blessing, if ye obey the commandments of the Lord your God . . . And a curse, if ye will not obey the commandments of the Lord your God"; and 2 Ne. 1:20: "Inasmuch as ye shall keep my commandments ye shall prosper in the land; but inasmuch as ye will not keep my commandments ye shall be cut off from my presence."

Finally the mercy of the Lord was exhausted, and the promises and prophecies of destruction were fulfilled—first in 721 B.C., when the Assyrians destroyed the Northern Kingdom of Israel and deported her people, and then in 587 B.C., when the Babylonians destroyed Jerusalem and the temple and took the people of the Southern Kingdom of Judah into exile in Babylon. The disastrous consequence of rejecting the covenant is a central theme of the books of Kings and Chronicles, just as it is in the Book of Mormon.

In the original Hebrew, the book of Kings was the longest book in the Bible, followed by the books of Samuel and Chronicles.[4] The translation into Greek, the Septuagint, made these books even longer.[5] For convenience' sake, in the Septuagint the books were each divided in two at a logical break in the text. This practice was, in medieval times, adopted in Hebrew. Thus today we have 1 and 2 Samuel, 1 and 2 Kings, and 1 and 2 Chronicles. In reading these books it should be remembered that because the divisions are artificial, it is best to deal with them as single books.

Kings

The book of Kings (Hebrew *melākîm*, "kings") derives its name from its being an account of all of the kings in the North and the South from the death of David. Kings begins where Samuel leaves off, at the end of the reign of David and the ascension of Solomon to the throne. It then tells the story of the United Monarchy under Solomon, the division of the kingdom into the North and the South (Israel and Judah, or Samaria and Jerusalem) under his son Rehoboam, and the history and destruction of the two kingdoms—the destruction and exile of the North by Assyria in 721 B.C. (2 Kgs. 17) and the destruction of Jerusalem and the exile of the South by Babylon in 587 B.C. (2 Kgs. 24–25). The final passage in Kings (2 Kgs. 25:27–30) inserts a note of hope into the narrative,

---

[4]The longest books in the Old Testament, measured by the number of words, are Kings (25,345 words), Samuel (24,228), and Chronicles (23,801). Then come Jeremiah (21,673), Genesis (20,512), Psalms (19,479), and Isaiah (19,123). These numbers are from Abraham Even-Shoshan, *A New Concordance of the Bible* (Jerusalem: Kiryat Sefer Publishing House, 1985), p. xxxviii.

[5]Hebrew is a more concise language than Greek, and Greek incorporated vowels in the text, whereas Hebrew did not.

recording the death of Nebuchadnezzar in 562 B.C., and stating that Jehoiachin, the Davidic king of Judah, was still alive in exile. A brief outline of Kings may be helpful:

I. 1 Kings 1–11. The reign of Solomon
    A. 1 Kings 1:1–2:11. Death of David; ascension of Solomon
    B. 1 Kings 2:12–4:34. Beginning of Solomon's reign
    C. 1 Kings 5–8. Building of the Temple
    D. 1 Kings 9–11. End of Solomon's reign

II. 1 Kings 12–2 Kings 17. The Divided Monarchy and the end of the Northern Kingdom
    A. 1 Kings 12–14. Kingdom divided: Rehoboam and Jeroboam
    B. 1 Kings 15–2 Kings 17. Kings from North and South and the destruction of the North
        1. 1 Kings 17–2 Kings 2:11. Elijah
        2. 2 Kings 2:12–13:21. Elisha

III. 2 Kings 18–25. The end of the Southern Kingdom

Throughout Kings, emphasis is given to the breaking of the covenant as the theological reason for the downfall of Israel—expressed in 2 Kings 17:6–23 concerning the destruction of Samaria and in 2 Kings 21:1–16, during the reign of Manasseh, about the impending destruction of Judah. Because the language throughout the books of Joshua through Kings is so reminiscent of that in Deuteronomy, scholars often refer to this history as the Deuteronomic history. They point to the possibility of the scroll discovered by Josiah as being all or part of Deuteronomy (2 Kgs. 22)—a discovery that may have influenced the final editing of the entire history. Whatever the case may be, the spirit and the language of Deuteronomy pervade Kings, and a reading of Deuteronomy is helpful for reading Kings. It should be further noted that the narratives in Kings concerning Elijah and Elisha are among the best scriptural accounts of the function of prophets in Israel.

The writer(s) or editor(s) of Kings attempted to preserve a complete account of each king in both the Northern and the Southern Kingdoms and devised an ingenious system that allowed the telling of both histories simultaneously. The system consists of a series of simple formulas that provide the relevant information for each king in both kingdoms and allow both histories to be told in sequence, alternating between the Southern and the Northern Kingdom. The formulas differed slightly for the North and the South, generally including more information from the South. Important historical events are narrated in the reign of the king in which they occurred, and a relative chronology is maintained throughout the book.[6] Recognition of these formulas enhances a reading of Kings. A simplified chart of this system of formulas follows, with reference to one example in each kingdom for illustration.

Southern Kingdom: Judah	*Northern Kingdom: Israel*
Example: Amaziah, in 2 Kings 14	Example: Omri, in 1 Kings 16
1. Reign dated from king in North (v. 1)	1. Reign dated from king in South (v. 23)
2. Data about age, length of reign, name, and queen mother (v. 2)	2. Data about length of reign and place of capital (v. 23)
3. Evaluation of reign, compared with David's (v. 3)	3. Condemnation for following in apostasy of Jeroboam (vv. 25–26)
4. Other sources: "Book of the Chronicles of the Kings of Judah" (v. 18)	4. Other sources: "Book of the Chronicles of the Kings of Israel" (v. 27)
5. Death and successor (vv. 19–21)	5. Death and successor (v. 28)

The results are more than satisfactory, and a conscientious reader following the formulas can easily follow the history of both kingdoms at the same time and be able to master the basic story line. In some ways this formulaic system represents a breakthrough in historiography, producing a method which allowed the editor to preserve the data present in a chronicle and at the same time set up a framework for the narration and interpretation of the events themselves — that is, history proper.

Chronicles

Chronicles begins with Adam and ends, like Kings, with the destruction of Jerusalem and the temple. While much of the story is the same as that in Genesis through Kings, there are many additions,

---

[6]The reigns of the kings in each kingdom are dated from the years of the contemporary kings in the opposite kingdom, thus preserving a detailed relative chronology. Scholars, comparing the relative chronology with known absolute dates of contemporary events, have developed a set of fairly certain B.C. dates for most of the kings. To understand the complexities preserved in this system and possible solutions, see Edwin R. Thiele, *The Mysterious Numbers of the Hebrew Kings* (Grand Rapids, Mich.: Zondervan, 1983).

deletions, and significant differences in the way it is told that make it a very valuable source in the study of biblical history.

In Hebrew the name of the book of Chronicles (*dibrê hayyāmîm*) can be translated "daily events," or perhaps simply as "annals." In the Greek Septuagint it was called "the things left out" (*paraleipomena*) — a title representing an attitude toward this book that persists to this day. The translators of the Septuagint apparently understood Chronicles to be no more than a retelling of the story known in Genesis through Kings, attempting to preserve details that were left out in that account. Chronicles presupposes an understanding of the history and closely follows the text in Genesis through Kings (about half of the text of Chronicles is word for word that in Samuel and Kings). Consequently, most readers read Chronicles only as a supplement to Kings, following footnotes to passages in Kings that direct the reader to more information in Chronicles. Chronicles is an invaluable supplement to Kings, but it is much more than just a supplement.

Kings and Chronicles have much in common, and the story they tell is basically the same. Often, however, they tell the story with significant differences in what each chooses to include and omit, in emphasis given to various periods or people, and in details they include. Chronicles is much more than just a collection of "things left out." It is an independent work vivid in its presentation, rich in detail, and distinctive in perspective. As such it should be read, studied, and appreciated as an independent history of Israel.[7]

The books of Chronicles can be conveniently divided into four units:

1. First Chronicles 1–9. From Adam to David (genealogies)
2. First Chronicles 10–29. The reign of David
3. Second Chronicles 1–9. The reign of Solomon
4. Second Chronicles 10–36. Divided monarchy and destruction of the kingdoms

First Chronicles 1 through 9 covers the period from Adam to David — the same period covered in Genesis through 1 Samuel. The history of

---

[7]A comprehensive yet readable commentary on Chronicles can be found in Jacob M. Myers, *I Chronicles*, Anchor Bible 12 (Garden City, N.Y.: Doubleday, 1965) and *II Chronicles*, Anchor Bible 13 (Garden City, N.Y.: Doubleday, 1965). For the relationship between Chronicles and Ezra-Nehemiah, see Myers, *Ezra-Nehemiah*, Anchor Bible 14 (Garden City, N.Y.: Doubleday, 1965).

this period in Chronicles is told primarily with lists of genealogies, which focus attention on the lineage of the chosen people in general, tracing the descendants of each of the twelve tribes of Israel and the lineage of David in particular. Of special interest in 1 Chronicles are a note that the birthright that belonged to Reuben was given to Joseph (5:1–5), the complete, high priestly lineage from Levi to the Exile (6:1–15), and a passage about the function of the Levites before the Exile (6:31–53) and after (9:26–34), particularly with regard to their participation in the music at the temple (6:31; 9:33–34). There is no formal account of many significant events before David; Chronicles presupposes familiarity with the covenants made with the patriarchs and with the Mosaic law.

First Chronicles 10 through 29 gives a detailed description of the reign of David, beginning with the death of Saul—roughly the same period covered in 2 Samuel. The picture given in Chronicles is an idealistic one, as emphasis is given to the good kings of Judah: David (1 Chron. 10–29); Solomon (2 Chron. 1–9); Jehoshaphat (2 Chron. 17–20); Hezekiah (2 Chron. 29–32); and Josiah (2 Chron. 34–35). The reign of David is particularly glorified, omitting his struggles with Saul (1 Sam. 17–31), his sin with Bathsheba (2 Sam. 11), and the problems in his house including Amnon (2 Sam. 13), Absalom (2 Sam. 13–19), and Adonijah (1 Kgs. 1–2)—all of which are detailed in 2 Samuel and 1 Kings 1 and 2.

Although Chronicles agrees with Samuel that David was not suited to build the temple (2 Sam. 22:1–17; 1 Kgs. 5:3; 1 Chron. 22:8), David is closely associated in Chronicles with the foundation of the temple ritual. In fact, Chronicles records that the pattern of the temple was revealed to David by the Spirit (1 Chron. 28:11–12), which allowed him to make preparations for its building and which he then passed on to his son Solomon. In this connection, Chronicles contains a long and detailed description of David's bringing the ark of the covenant from Kirjath-jearim to Jerusalem (1 Chron. 13–16)—as compared with a shorter version in 2 Samuel (2 Sam. 6:1–5)—and an extensive description of David's preparations for building the temple (1 Chron. 22–29). The emphasis in Chronicles on the temple, the temple ordinances, and the details about the priesthood have led some to speculate that the authors or editors may have been Levites.

Second Chronicles 1 through 9 covers the reign of Solomon—the same period as found in 1 Kings 1 through 11, which the account in Chronicles follows very closely. As with David, the account of Solomon's reign is idealized, and Chronicles omits the sins of Solomon at the end of his life (1 Kgs. 11:4–13) as well as the Lord's appointment during Solomon's reign of Jeroboam as the one who would divide Solomon's kingdom (1 Kgs. 11:26–43).

Second Chronicles 10 through 36 recounts the division of the kingdoms under Solomon's son Rehoboam and the ensuing history of both kingdoms to their respective destructions. Chronicles is primarily interested in the Southern Kingdom. Unlike the account in Kings — which often deals in detail with the kings, prophets, and events in the Northern Kingdom (see for example the long accounts of Elijah and Elisha, prophets in the North) — Chronicles only briefly mentions the kings in Israel when they cross paths with Judah (for example, Ahab's alliance with Jehoshaphat in 2 Chron. 18).

Chronicles contains an explanation of Shishak's invasion and sacking of the temple as the result of Rehoboam's apostasy (2 Chron. 12:1–12), a detail that is missing in the account in 1 Kings 14:21–31. Chronicles also records that Manasseh, the most wicked king in Judah, was captured and sent to Babylon where he repented of his wickedness to return as a righteous king who led a religious reform (2 Chron. 33). In the contrasting account in 2 Kings 21, Manasseh died at the height of his wickedness.

At the end of Chronicles, just as in Kings,[8] there is an appended note of hope from a later period, 539 B.C., indicating the rise of Cyrus the Persian and his proclamation that Judah may return from exile (2 Chron. 36:22–23). These same two verses are found at the beginning of the book of Ezra (Ezra 1:1–3), providing a link between the story in Chronicles and Ezra-Nehemiah,[9] where the story then continues into the Persian period with the restoration of Judah, the rebuilding and rededication of the temple, and the renewal of the covenant in Nehemiah 9 through 13.

---

[8] 2 Kgs. 25:27–30 tells of the death of Nebuchadnezzar and the freeing of the Davidic king Jehoiachin.

[9] There is disagreement whether these verses were original to Chronicles or Ezra-Nehemiah or whether an editor added them to one or the other or both, uniting the books into a continuous historical narrative. Whatever the process, the result indicates that Ezra-Nehemiah is to be read as a sequel to Chronicles.

3

THE REIGN OF SOLOMON

(1 Kings 1–11; 2 Chronicles 1–9)

Terrence L. Szink

Solomon, son of David and Bathsheba, is perhaps the most difficult of Israel's kings to understand. On one hand, he was the paradigm of the wise ruler who built the temple of the Lord and took the kingdom of Israel to new heights economically. On the other, he sowed the seeds for the disintegration of Israel and became involved in the worship of foreign gods, "which thing," we are told in the Book of Mormon, "was abominable" before the Lord (Jacob 2:24), leading one scholar to aptly refer to him as "the wisest of fools."[1]

Solomon Becomes King (1 Kgs. 1–2)

As 1 Kings begins, David had become old and weak. In an effort to invigorate their beloved king, his servants brought him Abishag, a young virgin, to comfort him as a wife or concubine. Adonijah, David's oldest surviving son, sensed his father's decline and moved to take his place on the throne. He assembled "chariots and horsemen, and fifty men to run before him" (1 Kgs. 1:5).[2] In addition to this ceremonial army, Adonijah had the support of Joab, David's nephew and captain of his army, and Abiathar the priest, both of whom had previously been loyal

---

Terrence L. Szink is a doctoral candidate in ancient Near Eastern studies at the University of California at Los Angeles.

[1]George E. Mendenhall, *The Tenth Generation* (Baltimore: Johns Hopkins, 1973), p. 121.

[2]Another son, Absalom, had done the same thing when he tried to wrest the throne from David on an earlier occasion (2 Sam. 15:1).

to David. Thus Adonijah had the backing of important members of both military and religious institutions. A sacrifice was held to which Adonijah invited "all his brethren the king's sons, and all the men of Judah the king's servants" (1 Kgs. 1:9). This was most likely a political-religious ceremony, which had as its purpose the solidifying of Adonijah's power. The list of those who were not invited is interesting: Solomon, Nathan the prophet, Zadok the priest, and several of David's "mighty men," who formed the core of David's personal army.

Informed of this gathering, Bathsheba and Nathan went to David and reminded him that he had promised earlier to make Solomon king (see 1 Chron. 22:5–13). David immediately assented and gave instructions for Solomon to be anointed king by Zadok. When this event took place, at the Gihon spring in Jerusalem (see Map 17, LDS Bible), Solomon was acclaimed by a great crowd (1 Kgs. 1:11–40). Adonijah and his friends heard the noise as they were finishing their feast. When a messenger told them what had happened, Adonijah immediately realized that he had been outmaneuvered and fled to the altar by the sanctuary that preceded Solomon's temple—the tent, or tabernacle.[3] Solomon vowed to spare his older brother, provided he did not turn to "wickedness" (1 Kgs. 1:41–53).

David instructed Solomon to punish Joab and Shimei, who had been disloyal to him, and soon afterward the aged king died (1 Kgs. 2:1–11; see also 2 Sam. 16:5–13). Solomon succeeded to the throne peacefully, but soon thereafter, Adonijah asked Bathsheba to persuade King Solomon to give him Abishag, David's final wife, in marriage. Solomon refused, however, for he assumed that Adonijah would use Abishag to strengthen his claim to the throne, and he took this request as a sure sign that Adonijah was plotting against him.[4] Solomon sent his right-hand military man, Benaiah, to execute Adonijah (1 Kgs. 2:13–25). Solomon also expelled Abiathar from the priesthood and had Benaiah execute Joab,

---

[3]Cf. 1 Kgs. 1:39. The four corners of the altar rose to points, called "horns," which Adonijah grasped; they are especially a symbol of sanctuary and safety. Cf. Amos 3:14; John Gray, *I & II Kings*, 2d ed. (London: SCM, 1970), p. 96.

[4]"The members of the king's harem were considered royal property, to be passed on to the next king"; Herbert G. May and Bruce M. Metzger, ed., *The New Oxford Annotated Bible* (New York: Oxford University Press, 1971), pp. 416–17.

even as he clasped the altar in front of the sanctuary.[5] Zadok became the sole high priest, and Benaiah took Joab's position. Later, Solomon put Shimei on probation—he must stay in Jerusalem; when Shimei left the city to repossess runaway slaves, Solomon had him executed also (1 Kgs. 2:26–46).

So "the kingdom was established in the hand of Solomon" (1 Kgs. 2:46). Though these actions may seem extreme to us, they were perhaps demanded by the harsh politics of the day. In many cases, Solomon gave his enemies mercy, provided they acted circumspectly—which often they did not. The priest Abiathar, however, is an example of an opponent whose life was spared. Still, though Solomon is considered a man of peace rather than a man of war such as his father, David, his reign did not begin without violence.

Solomon's Wisdom and Power
(1 Kgs. 3–4, 10; 2 Chron. 1, 9)

As Solomon commenced his reign, "he began to love the Lord" and "called on the name of the Lord" (JST 1 Kgs. 3:3). His worship included frequent offerings, which were made at the high places (outdoor places of worship), because the temple had not yet been built. Once, when he was at a chief high place at Gibeon, where the tabernacle was then located (2 Chron. 1:3–6; see Map 9, LDS Bible), Solomon spoke with the Lord in a vision. The Lord offered to bless him as he desired; but instead of asking for long life, riches, or power over enemies, Solomon asked for "an understanding heart" to govern the people. The Lord was pleased with this choice, granted him wisdom, and then blessed him with riches and honor in addition (1 Kgs. 3:1–15). Still, he warned the new king: "Thou shalt not walk in unrighteousness, as did thy father David" (JST 1 Kgs. 3:14).

As an example of Solomon's divinely given wisdom, the author of 1 Kings recorded the incident of two women contending over one child. Two prostitutes approached Solomon for judgment, each claiming the

---

[5]Solomon's justification may have been that the Law taught that only a man accused of manslaughter could claim sanctuary, not a murderer (Ex. 21:12–14). For Joab's killing of Abner, see 2 Sam. 3:22–34.

baby to be hers. When Solomon pretended to pick up his sword to cut the baby in half so he could give one piece to each of the women, one woman agreed, but the other was horrified and offered to give up her half of the baby so it could live. Solomon, of course, awarded the baby to the one who wanted to protect the child (1 Kgs. 3:16–28).

Because of that and other incidents, the fame of Solomon's wisdom spread throughout Israel, and even beyond: people from other nations came to visit him and hear his wisdom. The example provided by the author of Kings is that of the queen of Sheba (apparently in south Arabia), who came to Jerusalem to test Solomon's knowledge. When Solomon answered all of her "hard questions" perfectly, she was struck with awe. She was also impressed by his wealth and building projects. She gave Solomon expensive gifts, he reciprocated, and the queen returned to her own country (1 Kgs. 10:1–13; 2 Chron. 9:1–12).[6]

In Solomon's day, according to 1 Kings, his kingdom stretched from the border of Egypt east to the Euphrates, including the land of the Philistines.[7] His subjects lived in prosperity and safety.[8] Solomon's name means "peace"; and God gave him and his people nearly complete peace throughout his life (see 1 Chron. 22:9). Solomon had an extensive royal bureaucracy, household, army,[9] and navy, which a different district supported every month of the year.[10] Trade with other nations was frequent,[11] and the ships of Tarshish brought Solomon gold, silver, ivory, and even apes and peacocks (1 Kgs. 10:22; 2 Chron. 29:25).

Solomon the Builder
(1 Kgs. 5–9; 1 Chron. 28; 2 Chron. 2–8)

In the fourth year of his reign, Solomon began to build the temple, though preparations had been underway since before David had died

---

[6]Solomon's wisdom was so great that he came to be known as the author of Proverbs in the Old Testament (Prov. 1:1); see also, in the apocryphal tradition, "The Psalms of Solomon" and "The Odes of Solomon," in James H. Charlesworth, ed., *The Old Testament Pseudepigrapha*, 2 vols. (Garden City, N.Y.: Doubleday, 1985), 2:639–70, and 2:725–71.

[7]Some scholars feel that the extent of Solomon's empire may have been exaggerated by the biblical historians.

[8]See John Bright, *A History of Israel*, 3d ed. (Philadelphia: Westminster, 1981), pp. 211–28.

[9]For Solomon's large standing army, distinguished by its use of chariots, see Bright, p. 213.

[10]For Solomon's administrative districts, see Map 8, LDS Bible.

[11]For trade under Solomon, see Bright, pp. 214–17.

(1 Kgs. 6:1; 1 Chron. 28).[12] Because he was friendly with Hiram, king of Tyre, he sent Israelites to import cedars from Lebanon (see Map 7, LDS Bible). Hiram also provided craftsmen to help construct the building (1 Kgs. 5:1–18; 2 Chron. 2:1–16). The temple turned out to be ninety feet by thirty feet in length and width and forty-five feet high (1 Kgs. 6:2). It was divided into three rooms: an entrance hall ('*ûlām*; 1 Kgs. 6:3); a main room sixty feet long (*hêkāl*; 1 Kgs. 6:17); and a holy of holies (*debîr*; 1 Kgs. 6:19–20), which was a cube of about thirty feet (1 Kgs. 6:19–20). In the holy of holies (called the "oracle" in the KJV) were placed two cherubim—gold-plated angel figures, perhaps in the shape of sphinxes, whose wings touched (1 Kgs. 6:23–28).[13] Much of the temple was overlaid with gold. Two massive pillars, named Jachin and Boaz, were placed in front of the building (1 Kgs. 7:15–21),[14] as was a molten bronze water basin supported by twelve bronze oxen (1 Kgs. 7:23–26). Inside the main room was a golden incense altar, a table for the bread of presence ("shewbread" in the KJV), and the lamp stands (1 Kgs. 7:48–49; the word "candlesticks" in the KJV is anachronistic).[15]

After seven years of labor, the temple was finished (see 1 Kgs. 6:38). On the day of its dedication, priests took the ark of the covenant and placed it beneath the wings of the cherubim in the holy of holies. When they emerged, a cloud of glory, symbolizing God's presence, filled the building (1 Kgs. 8:1–11; cf. Ex. 40:34–35; Mark 9:7). Solomon blessed the people and then gave the dedicatory prayer for the temple (1 Kgs. 8:22–53). He expressed thanksgiving and then prayed that the Lord would forgive Israel of offenses, providing they repented, and that the Lord would hear the prayers of both Israelites and foreigners. He asked for success in battle, or, if Israel were defeated and taken captive, that they would be restored if they repented.

After this prayer, Solomon blessed the people once more and then

---

[12]On Solomon's temple and its influence, see *The Temple of Solomon*, ed. Joseph Gutmann (Missoula, Mont.: Scholars Press, 1976); W. F. Stinespring, "Temple, Jerusalem," in *The Interpreter's Dictionary of the Bible*, 5 vols., ed. G. A. Buttrick, et al. (Nashville: Abingdon, 1962), 4:534–60.

[13]See May and Metzger, p. 422.

[14]For a discussion of the meaning of these names, see William F. Albright, *Archaeology and the Religion of Israel*, 5th ed. (New York: Doubleday, 1942), p. 139.

[15]See David P. Wright, "The Laws and the Sanctuary," in *Studies in Scripture, Volume Three: Genesis to 2 Samuel*, ed. Kent P. Jackson and Robert L. Millet (Salt Lake City: Randall Book, 1985), pp. 149–52.

offered sacrifice of twenty-two thousand oxen and one hundred twenty thousand sheep. There was a seven-day feast (probably the Feast of Tabernacles; see 1 Kgs. 8:2; Lev. 23:34[16]), and on the eighth day the people returned home rejoicing (1 Kgs. 8:63–66).

The Lord appeared to Solomon in another dream. In it he was told that God had accepted the temple as his own and that if Solomon acted righteously, his throne would be eternal. If Israel stayed righteous, the nation would fare well also, but if there were apostasy in Israel, they would be cut off and plucked out by the roots (2 Chron. 7:20) and the temple would be destroyed (1 Kgs. 9:1–9; 2 Chron. 7:12–22).

To build fortresses, cities, the temple, and other royal buildings, including an elaborate, costly palace, Solomon used forced labor allotted periodically to different districts.[17] But he also used teams of non-Israelite slaves (1 Kgs. 9:20–21). Thus Solomon's glory was at least partially based on the oppression of conquered peoples and native Israelites, and it was deeply resented. When Rehoboam succeeded his father, Solomon, Israel told him that they would not tolerate the "grievous service" of Solomon any more. When he vowed to increase their burdens, he was rejected by the ten northern tribes. He sent them an official as a forced labor leader, and they stoned him. Rehoboam was forced to flee unceremoniously (1 Kgs. 12:1–20). Though this incident took place after Solomon's death, it tells us much about Solomon's reign.

Although the temple was built in response to the Lord's will, had a valid religious motivation, and was of great spiritual value to Israel, Solomon's palace and luxurious court seem to have resulted from other motivations. One thinks of King Noah's elaborate building projects recorded in the Book of Mormon (see Mosiah 11).[18]

Solomon's Apostasy (1 Kgs. 11)

Early in his reign, Solomon married the daughter of the king of Egypt (1 Kgs. 3:1), which was probably a political marriage to protect him from

---

[16]J. Robinson, *The First Book of Kings* (Cambridge: Cambridge University, 1972), p. 113.

[17]See Bright, pp. 220–23.

[18]For archaeological remains from Solomon's era, which confirm the lavish nature of his building projects, see W. F. Albright, *From the Stone Age to Christianity*, 2d ed. (New York: Doubleday, 1957), pp. 291–92. Also, K. M. Kenyon and P.R.S. Moorey, *The Bible and Recent Archaeology*, rev. ed. (Atlanta: John Knox, 1987), pp. 85–107.

invasion by the traditionally powerful and dangerous Egyptians. It was something of an accomplishment for the new Israelite king and probably shows that Israel was strong and somewhat prestigious at this time, but it also shows that Egypt was weak.[19] The Joseph Smith Translation records that "the Lord was not pleased with Solomon" because of this marriage, and thereafter he blessed him "for the people's sake only" (JST 1 Kgs. 3:1). He went on to marry other non-Israelite women, for king Solomon "loved many foreign women" (1 Kgs. 11:1, NIV[20]). The record states that he had seven hundred wives and three hundred concubines (1 Kgs. 11:3).[21] Probably almost all of his wives represented political marriages meant to solidify peace treaties with surrounding nations. The Lord had expressly forbidden marriage with non-Israelites, however, and Solomon paid for his disobedience — his foreign wives led him to worship foreign gods: Ashtoreth of the Sidonians, Milcom of the Ammonites, and Chemosh of the Moabites (1 Kgs. 11:5–8).

The Lord was angry with Solomon and communicated with him once more. He told him that because he had gone astray, the kingdom would be taken from him and given to another after his death. Only one tribe would stay in his kingdom; the rest would secede from it (1 Kgs. 11:9–13).[22]

God also raised up military enemies to harass Solomon: Hadad the Edomite and Rezon of Damascus, who annoyed Solomon during his reign (1 Kgs. 11:14–25). But Solomon's worst fears resulted from an internal threat. He had appointed a man named Jeroboam, son of Nebat, to be overseer of all the forced labor in the tribe of Joseph. While Solomon

---

[19]Solomon's Egyptian wife was probably the daughter of one of the weak kings of the Twenty-first Dynasty, perhaps Siamun. See Bright, p. 212; Martin Noth, *The History of Israel*, 2d ed. (New York: Harper and Row, 1960), p. 216. Cf. "Suppiluliumas and the Egyptian Queen," trans. Albrecht Goetze, in *Ancient Near Eastern Texts Relating to the Old Testament*, 3d ed. with Supplement, ed. J.B. Pritchard (Princeton: Princeton University, 1969), p. 319. Earlier, when Egypt was strong, it would not give princesses even to Babylon or Assyria.

[20]New International Version. The word should be translated "foreign." "Strange" in the KJV has unfortunate modern connotations.

[21]It is possible that the round figure of seven hundred wives and three hundred concubines (total, one thousand) is greatly exaggerated. A concubine, incidentally, is a wife who does not enjoy the legal status of a free woman — she is usually a household servant or a slave captured in war.

[22]The issue involved in the Lord's anger against Solomon was not that he had many wives but that he had married foreign women outside of the covenant (see D&C 132:38).

was still alive, a prophet named Ahijah met Jeroboam once in open country, tore his own garment into twelve pieces, and gave ten of them to Jeroboam. They symbolized the Lord's taking ten tribes away from Solomon because of his apostasy. Out of respect for David, however, they would be taken only after Solomon's death. If Jeroboam would stay close to the Lord, the Lord would preserve him.

When Solomon heard of this prophecy, he tried to have Jeroboam killed,[23] but the future ruler of the Northern Kingdom of Israel escaped to Egypt, where he stayed until Solomon died (1 Kgs. 11:26–40).

Conclusions

Solomon is a troubling figure. It almost seems as if there were two Solomons. The first was a king of great power and glory who gave Israel legendary prestige and a sense of self-worth. He was a ruler of supernatural wisdom who had semiprophetic status, for he had visions and was selected by the Lord to build his temple. He also had a kind of priestly status, for he prayed to dedicate the temple[24] and performed frequent sacrifices. This positive Solomon is emphasized in the account in 2 Chronicles.

The second Solomon (absent in Chronicles) carried out purges to eliminate his rivals. With an extensive court, he lived on a lavish scale and required his people to shoulder the burden. His building projects were vast and impressive but came into being through oppression of the people — foreign slaves and Israelites who were forced to endure temporary slave status. He married foreign women, perhaps because he desired political security or power, and as a result he turned from his piety, his semiprophetic and priestly status, to worship pagan gods. And he sought to kill the man whom the Lord had selected to lead most of Israel after his death — much as Saul had sought to kill Solomon's father, David, whom the Lord had similarly chosen to rule (1 Sam. 19–24; 26).

---

[23]Bright suggests that Jeroboam may have started to plot actively against the king; p. 228.
[24]Cf. Robinson, p. 97.

4

KINGS AND PROPHETS IN DIVIDED ISRAEL

(1 KINGS 12–2 KINGS 10; 2 CHRONICLES 10–22)

ANDREW C. SKINNER

After Solomon's death, long-standing jealousies, antagonisms, and tensions between Judah and Israel (the northern tribes) erupted violently when rebellion against Rehoboam, Solomon's only known child and successor,[1] shattered the unity of the Israelite kingdom. The tensions had been aggravated in Solomon's later years by heavy taxation and forced labor. Hence, the prophesied division of the great Davidic kingdom came to pass: "For thus saith the Lord, the God of Israel, Behold, I will rend the kingdom out of the hand of Solomon. . . . I will take the kingdom out of his son's hand" (1 Kgs. 11:31, 35). The division of the kingdom was the Lord's doing.

The message is subtle but profound. God is not outside the historical process. He is the principal agent in history. He has a plan for Israel and intervenes through his prophets in the affairs of men to bring about his work and purposes. The division of the Davidic kingdom, or house of Israel, was a step preparatory to the scattering of Israel, in which Deity also took a personal role (Jer. 16:13; Ezek. 5:10; Jacob 5:8).

The Division of the Kingdom (1 Kgs. 12; 2 Chron. 10)

When the forty-one-year-old Rehoboam traveled to Shechem to be installed as the new king, he met Jeroboam, the Ephraimite adversary

---

Andrew C. Skinner is assistant professor of ancient scripture at Brigham Young University.

[1]The biblical record mentions no other sons or daughters, though some traditions do.

of Solomon, who had returned from exile in Egypt at the request of the northern tribes of Israel (1 Kgs. 12:1–3; 2 Chron. 10:1–3). It was important for Rehoboam to go to Shechem to be formally recognized as king because Shechem was among the most ancient of the sacred towns of northern Palestine and, thus, a chief city of the northern tribes of Israel (see Map 9, LDS Bible). It was at Shechem that Abraham camped when he first arrived in Canaan (Gen. 12:6). It was at Shechem that the Israelites buried the bones of Joseph when they came out of Egypt (Josh. 24:32). It was at Shechem that Joshua gathered together all the tribes of Israel to give them instructions and establish a special covenant between God and the people.[2] Undoubtedly, the heir apparent to Solomon recognized the need to be confirmed at this important place in order to cement northern allegiance to a united kingdom.

But the people of the North attached conditions to their acceptance of Rehoboam. Before supporting him, they asked for a decrease in the severe financial and labor demands that had been instituted by Solomon (1 Kgs. 12:3–19; 2 Chron. 10:3–19). When the new king made known his decision to increase their burdens instead (the record says he answered roughly or harshly), northern support was effectively destroyed, assuring a divided nation. The author of this section of the biblical narrative puts it succinctly: "So Israel rebelled against the house of David unto this day" (1 Kgs. 12:19).[3]

Rehoboam reacted to the secession by mobilizing an army from Judah and Benjamin to quell the rebellion, force the return of the errant northern territories, and preserve political unity. But the Lord, through the prophet Shemaiah, forbade him to carry out a war (1 Kgs. 12:20–24; 2 Chron. 11:1–4). When war did come a short time later, it proved to be a futile and lengthy enterprise. We are told simply that "there was war between Rehoboam and Jeroboam all their days" (1 Kgs. 14:30). The division between their two kingdoms created two separate nations with separate histories from that time on. It will only be in Christ's millennial kingdom that the two will become one again (Ezek. 37:22).

---

[2] The covenant was one of protection and obedience between God and the people (Josh. 24:1, 24). Shechem is an important city mentioned in many other passages. See "Shechem," Bible Dictionary, LDS Bible.

[3] The phrase "unto this day" is intriguing, but we do not know with certainty how long after the actual events the text was established.

Jeroboam's Perversions (1 Kgs. 12–13; 2 Chron. 11)

Jeroboam the son of Nebat was made king over the Israelites in the North, with their first capital city at Shechem. His kingdom, which consisted of the northern ten tribes, was usually called Israel, or Ephraim. Later, Omri made Samaria its capital (see Map 9, LDS Bible). Rehoboam (922–915 B.C.) became king over the tribes of Judah and Benjamin in the South. His kingdom, Judah, had its capital at Jerusalem (1 Kgs. 12:19–21).[4]

The most significant aspect of Jeroboam's reign in Israel (922–901 B.C.) was his immediate idolatry. By establishing two golden calves (or young bulls) at open-air sanctuaries at Dan and Bethel—opposite ends of his kingdom (see Map 9)—Jeroboam hoped to compete effectively with the Judahite temple in order to strengthen his political position against Rehoboam, expand his religious influence, and solidify the division of the once-unified Davidic kingdom. What he succeeded in doing was to teach his people to shun Jehovah, Jehovah's prophets, and Jehovah's holy temple at Jerusalem. He cleverly manipulated an ancient Near Eastern symbol of strength and divinity (the bull or calf), which was already linked to the northern tribe of Joseph in old prophecy (Deut. 33:17).[5] It appears Jeroboam also hoped that his people had forgotten the idolatrous nature of calf worship (Ex. 32:19–35) and that they would associate his golden calves with the Exodus. In another clever manipulation, he used the Exodus, an event central to the very identity of Israelites and one always to be remembered by them (Ex. 13) as a tool to justify his own schemes and wicked religious reformation. He declared: "It is too much for you to go up to Jerusalem: behold thy gods, O Israel, which brought thee up out of the land of Egypt" (1 Kgs. 12:28). This was an almost verbatim quotation of the people's proclamation at the golden calf incident during the Exodus (Ex. 32:4).

---

[4]The division substantially weakened both kingdoms but especially the North, which exhibited a steady decline politically and militarily. That made it "ripe for plucking" by the Assyrians, who, though wicked and ruthless, were instruments in God's hands (see Isa. 10:5–12).

[5]See also the Hebrew of Gen. 49:24, in which the phrase *'abîr ya'akōb* is used, the literal meaning being "bull of Jacob." The King James Version translates the phrase as "mighty God of Jacob." The bull was a symbol for divine power in the ancient Near East. The earliest dated archeological object of Pharaonic Egypt—the Narmer Palette—depicts the bull as a symbol of the power of the first Pharaoh. The Canaanites of Ugarit worshipped their god El as a bull, and Baal was depicted as mounted on a bull.

In imitation of the Feast of Tabernacles, which was also related to the Exodus, Jeroboam instituted his own perverted feast in the North, created his own priesthood, cast out of his kingdom true priesthood holders, and made unauthorized sacrifices (2 Chron. 11:13–17; 13:9; 1 Kgs. 12:26–31). In all this he sinned greatly (1 Kgs. 12:30), yet in his view these innovations gave the Israelites everything they could want: the god of Joseph, the god of the Exodus, their own holy days, their own priests, and their own sympathetic king. In short, what he hoped the people would believe he was providing was not a new, perverted religious order but rather a new royal administration legitimized by old religious rites that were now being given renewed attention in a new day and age.[6]

Decline of the North and the South
(1 Kgs. 14–16; 2 Chron. 12–16)

Because of Jeroboam's wickedness, the Lord foretold the destruction of his royal house through the same prophet, Ahijah, who had predicted his rise (1 Kgs. 11:28–39). The Lord also foretold the scattering of the

---

[6]Not unexpectedly, the Lord sent another of his prophets to warn Jeroboam of the wickedness he was perpetrating. Yet he "returned [repented] not from his evil way," adding the dregs of society to the ranks of his apostate priesthood (1 Kgs. 13:33). Called simply "the man of God that came from Judah" (1 Kgs. 13), this prophet from the Southern Kingdom was entreated by a northern prophet from Bethel to go against the Lord's instructions. When the prophet from Judah at first refused to enjoy the hospitality of the old prophet from Bethel because God had forbidden it, the latter tested the resolve of the former by telling him that an angel had approved the invitation to dine together. The prophet of Judah acquiesced and then received the prophecy of his own death from the lips of his host. Just as the old prophet had foreseen, when his guest left to return home, a lion slew him and stood guard over the carcass in the roadway until the old prophet mournfully retrieved the body of his younger associate (1 Kgs. 13:23–31).

Perhaps the temptation exists to lay responsibility for the death of the Judahite prophet at the feet of the old prophet from Bethel; however, as Joseph Smith's translation of 1 Kgs. 13:18 makes clear, the old prophet was himself righteous and acting as God's instrument to test the prophet from Judah (JST 1 Kgs. 13:18). Ultimately the Judahite prophet was responsible for his own demise because of his disobedience. That is the broad lesson emphasized by the biblical narrative (see 1 Kgs. 13:21, 26).

Perhaps another important and personalized lesson can be drawn from this episode. Revelation is sometimes given as a test of spiritual maturity just as much as to answer questions or solve problems. To continue to receive personal revelations, we need to act on those we know we have appropriately received and walk by faith. Those alternate voices who might try to divert our attention and commitment away from our callings (even though they may be the voices of well-meaning, well-intended individuals) ought not to be heeded.

northern tribes because of their sins — two hundred years before its occurrence (1 Kgs. 14:15–16). Israel's future was bleak. But Judah in the
South was little better off during the time of northern wickedness, because
they also did evil in the sight of the Lord beyond anything that had been
done by their fathers (1 Kgs. 14:22). Judah's practices included the
worship of the god Baal.

As a consequence of the moral, emotional, social, and physical
weakness that accompanies such behavior among an unfit people, in 918
B.C. a foreign power, Egypt, led by Pharaoh Shishak, invaded Judah and
ravaged the temple in Jerusalem by taking away as booty all "the treasures
of the house of the Lord" (1 Kgs. 14:25–26). A fragment of Shishak's
inscription has been found at Megiddo, and a representation of his victory
over Rehoboam is found at the Temple of Karnak in Egypt. Although
the Bible mentions only Judah, evidence indicates that Shishak invaded
the Northern Kingdom as well. He inscribed the names of many northern
cities on his victory relief at Karnak. Thus, both Israel in the North and
Judah in the South were greatly weakened during and after the reigns of
their respective evil kings, Jeroboam and Rehoboam.[7]

From this point in the historical narrative (1 Kgs. 15) to the account
of the actual fall and deportation of the kingdom of Israel (2 Kgs. 17:6),
the writers of Kings skillfully weave back and forth from one kingdom
to the other to report contemporaneous occurrences in both. It is important to note that the compilers of the biblical text as presently constituted used sources no longer in existence today (1 Kgs. 14:19). Those
missing official records, kept by the kings of both Judah and Israel, are
one more bit of evidence for the actuality of lost scripture and the
importance that was placed on record keeping in ancient times, even
during the reigns of wicked rulers.

The house of David continued on throughout the entire history of
the kingdom of Judah, while a series of kings — some related to each other
and some not — reigned in Israel after the slaughter of all the house of
Jeroboam by Baasha, just as had been prophesied (1 Kgs. 15:29). The
Bible depicts all of Israel's rulers as wicked, and many of Judah's also. A
notable exception was King Asa (third king of Judah; 913–873 B.C.),

---

[7]The North survived as a kingdom until 721 B.C., about one hundred eighty years after Jeroboam.
The South survived longer, until 587 B.C.

whose name comes from the Hebrew root meaning "heal." Indeed, he was able to heal the kingdom spiritually, politically, and economically for a time because his "heart was perfect with the Lord all his days" (1 Kgs. 15:14). Asa had a long and prosperous reign (forty-one years), during which time he saw a number of wicked kings come and go on the throne of Israel in the North. The worst of Israel's kings was Ahab (869–850 B.C.): "And Ahab the son of Omri did evil in the sight of the Lord above all that were before him" (1 Kgs. 16:30). Ahab's reign represents the nadir of both the dynasty of Omri and the Northern Kingdom. The notorious wickedness of the Omride dynasty, including the statutes of Omri and the works of the house of Ahab, was immortalized in later prophetic chastisement (e.g., Micah. 6:16).

Among Ahab's great mistakes was his marriage to a woman whose very name has come to stand for the ultimate in wicked influence. Jezebel was a Phoenician princess who not only promoted Baal worship to the exclusion of true religion but also was personally responsible for slaying the prophets of the Lord and other righteous men (1 Kgs. 18:13). It has been said that more than any other single event, the marriage of Ahab to Jezebel caused the downfall of the Northern Kingdom.[8]

Elijah (1 Kgs. 17–2 Kgs. 2; 2 Chron. 17–19)

It is a true principle that when great evil exists in the Lord's kingdom, there will also be great righteousness manifest alongside it so that truth seekers will not be left to themselves. Hence, it is with the evil reign of Ahab and his wife Jezebel that we are introduced to one of the greatest of the prophets, the man named Elijah (literally, "My God is Jehovah"), who came from Tishbeh in the hill country east of the Jordan River. Elder Bruce R. McConkie wrote: "For dramatic manifestations and the visible exhibition of divine power, the ministry of Elijah the Prophet scarcely has an equal."[9] The very first verse in which Elijah is introduced immediately gives us an idea of his impressive stature and powers: "As the Lord God of Israel liveth, before whom I stand, there shall not be

---

[8]See "Jezebel," Bible Dictionary, LDS Bible.
[9]Bruce R. McConkie, *Mormon Doctrine*, 2d ed. (Salt Lake City: Bookcraft, 1966), p. 222.

dew nor rain these years, but according to my word" (1 Kgs. 17:1). Who can doubt that Elijah, in mortality, stood before the Lord? Certainly his sealing powers were demonstrated when the heavens were sealed shut and a devastating drought ravaged the land of Israel (1 Kgs. 17–18). Apparently, control over the elements is an integral part of the sealing powers of the priesthood; whoever possesses them has power over the earth and the accompanying elements in the heavens, including wind and rain. Nephi the son of Helaman was taught this truth by the Lord when he received the sealing powers (see Hel. 10:6–9; 11:4–13).

But the sealing power of Elijah is greater than having control over the elements. The same Elijah who confronted Ahab appeared to the Savior on the Mount of Transfiguration as a translated being (Matt. 17:1–9) and later stood before Joseph Smith to deliver his powers and authority to redeem the dead (D&C 110:13–16).[10]

The Prophet Joseph Smith taught that "Elijah was the last Prophet that held the keys of the Priesthood" to administer in all its ordinances, including the sealing ordinances.[11] That is why Elijah was translated without tasting death and was chosen to restore those great keys — first to Peter, James, and John, and then, before the Second Coming, to Joseph Smith (Mal. 4:5–6; D&C 2:1; 35:4; 110:13–16; 128:17; 138:46; 3 Ne. 25:5). The Prophet further said:

> The spirit, power, and calling of Elijah is, that ye have power to hold the key of the revelations, ordinances, oracles, powers and endowments of the fullness of the earth; and to receive, obtain, and perform all the ordinances belonging to the kingdom of God, even unto the turning of the hearts of the fathers unto the children, and the hearts of the children unto the fathers, even those who are in heaven. . . . What is this office and work of Elijah? It is one of the greatest and most important subjects that God has revealed. He should send Elijah to seal the children to the fathers, and the fathers to the children . . . this is the spirit of Elijah, that we redeem our dead, and connect ourselves with our fathers which are in heaven, and seal up our dead to come forth in the first resurrection; and here we want the

---

[10]See Robert J. Matthews, "Tradition, Testimony, Transfiguration, and Keys," in *Studies in Scripture, Volume Five: The Gospels*, ed. Kent P. Jackson and Robert L. Millet (Salt Lake City: Deseret Book Co., 1986), pp. 305–8.

[11]Joseph Smith, *Teachings of the Prophet Joseph Smith*, sel. Joseph Fielding Smith (Salt Lake City: Deseret Book Co., 1938), p. 172.

power of Elijah to seal those who dwell on earth to those who dwell in heaven. This is the power of Elijah and the keys of the kingdom of Jehovah.[12]

Ultimately, the power of Elijah is also the power whereby one is sealed up to eternal life, or the power to have one's calling and election made sure.[13]

Of all the mighty works performed by Elijah, including the raising of the widow's dead son (1 Kgs. 17:17–24), no episode in the Old Testament better demonstrates the strength of the prophet's priesthood power than his contest with the priests of Baal, in which he called down fire from heaven, and his opening, or unsealing, the heavens for rain (1 Kgs. 18:17–45). All these things he did that the hearts of the people might be turned to their God (1 Kgs. 18:37), but sadly, no lasting reform of the Northern Kingdom's evil ways could be effected.

It is reasonable to expect that even prophets of God become discouraged, as the experience of Elijah bears out. Having heard of the slaughter of his comrades and fellow prophets and being hunted as a fugitive by Jezebel, who vowed to take his life, Elijah fled the court of Ahab without food or drink and journeyed for a day until circumstances overwhelmed him—whereupon he sat down under a tree and requested to die (1 Kgs. 19:1–4). With great pathos he cried: "It is enough; now, O Lord, take away my life; for I am not better than my fathers" (1 Kgs. 19:4).

But the Lord did not abandon Elijah, either physically or spiritually. It is significant that the first thing that occurred to restore his well-being was the provision for his physical needs—food, drink, and shelter (1 Kgs. 19:5–8). The physical and spiritual natures of our existence must both be fed. Indeed, it requires great spiritual power to remain attuned to the Spirit when one is hurting physically. After Elijah's physical needs were met, the Lord spoke to him to restore his emotional and spiritual welfare also. And, in a great lesson for us, Elijah found the Lord not in earth-shattering signs of power but in the still small voice of the Holy Spirit (1 Kgs. 19:9–12). Those who listen carefully in our day will also hear and should heed the same still small voice.

---

[12]Ibid., pp. 337–38.
[13]Ibid.; see also D&C 131:5.

Encouraged and renewed, Elijah completed his mission, which included the anointing of new kings and a successor prophet, Elisha. The new prophet knew he was chosen when Elijah cast his mantle upon him (1 Kgs. 19:19–21). Elijah's tangible mantle (a coat or cloak) was symbolic of an intangible mantle — the power, authority, light, revelation, and direction given by God to his chosen servants. The casting of the physical mantle was a symbol of the bestowal of the right to succeed the great prophet.[14] Elisha was a man of great loyalty, commitment, and dedication to the work of Jehovah. Though wealthy (as the numerous oxen in his possession testify; 1 Kgs. 19:19), he unhesitatingly rejected the things of the world and "went after Elijah, and ministered unto him" (1 Kgs. 19:19–21). So, too, all true disciples must resolutely reject the world and follow the Lord (Matt. 4:18–20; 8:19–22; 9:9; JST Matt. 16:26).

The last activities of Elijah, before he was taken into heaven in a fiery chariot by a whirlwind, included training Elisha and calling down fire from heaven again — this time to consume soldiers sent to apprehend him (2 Kgs. 1:9–15). He also confronted Ahaziah and Ahab, whose deaths he prophesied (2 Kgs. 1:1–4, 16–17).

Ahab and Jezebel had become participants in, and perpetuators of, one of the very foundational principles of Satan's kingdom: murder to get gain. Their plot to take the life of Naboth the Jezreelite, the owner of a beautiful vineyard which he refused to sell to the covetous king Ahab, surely represents the low point in the royal couple's morally bankrupt existence. The scheme itself was the diabolical concoction of queen Jezebel. She used the ruse of proclaiming a fast day which, in ancient Israelite culture, signaled a grave national emergency brought on by crimes committed by one member which brought the whole covenant community under God's condemnation. Two "sons of Belial" (literally, "worthlessness") were pressed into service as witnesses, as required by Mosaic statute in capital offenses. They perjured themselves to convict Naboth, who was stoned, thus giving the king free access to the vineyard (1 Kgs. 21:1–15).

God sent Elijah to Ahab to remind him in grim fashion that nothing escapes the awareness of the Lord. Elijah laid out in explicit terms the

---

[14]Spencer W. Kimball, "The Mantle of the Prophet," devotional address delivered at the Salt Lake LDS Institute of Religion, 13 Apr. 1973.

consequences of Jezebel's great treachery and the king's complicity in Naboth's murder. In parallelistic Hebrew prose, Elijah prophesied that the Lord would "*consume* [Ahab's] descendants" and cause "dogs [to] *devour* Jezebel by the wall of Jezreel" (1 Kgs. 21:21–23, translation mine). As for Ahab, the Lord said, "In the place where dogs licked the blood of Naboth shall dogs lick thy blood, even thine" (1 Kgs. 21:19). All of these prophecies were fulfilled in due time (1 Kgs. 22:34–38; see also vv. 1–40; 2 Kgs. 9–10).

Elisha and the Sons of the Prophets
(2 Kgs. 2–8; 2 Chron. 20–21)

As the time of Elijah's celestial departure approached, a curious group of men known as the "sons of the prophets" became more prominent in the events surrounding the transition of authority from one prophet to another. Perhaps they are best understood as a group of disciples who followed the prophets, preserved their words, and spread their messages. Since "the testimony of Jesus is the spirit of prophecy" (Rev. 19:10), perhaps we should look upon these individuals (also called "prophets") as the devoted disciples of the Lord in their day. In a time of general apostasy in the kingdom of Israel, it may be that these men and their families were the few who had the light of the gospel, which was largely absent in their generation because of unworthiness. People who live by the Spirit are "prophets" in their own right, and these, who looked on Elijah and then Elisha as their teachers and leaders, were called, symbolically, the sons of their masters. In this regard, Elisha cried out to Elijah, "My father, my father," when he saw the fiery chariot (2 Kgs. 2:12).

How the sons of the prophets were organized is not known. During the time of Elijah and Elisha they were found at various places, including Gilgal, Bethel, and Jericho. We know that some of them had families and that they were not exempt from working for their livelihood. Their families were not unfamiliar with economic misfortune (2 Kgs. 4:1).

The sons of the prophets were spiritually mature and perceptive, as is evident in their recognition that the promised mantle of authority actually rested on Elisha at the time of Elijah's departure (2 Kgs. 2:15).

They also assisted the great prophets in their duties and even officiated when called in the prophetic office themselves, as was the case when Elisha sent one of them to Ramoth-gilead to anoint Jehu king over Israel (2 Kgs. 9:1–10). That young prophet was specifically commanded to use the prophetic formula "Thus saith the Lord" in fulfilling his appointed task (2 Kgs. 9:3).

Elijah, Elisha, and Christ

Elisha's ministry in the Northern Kingdom began in the last years of Ahab's reign and spanned the second half of the ninth century to the first years of the reign of Joash (2 Kgs. 13:14–20). Though there were specific differences between the two, Elisha's ministry greatly resembled and paralleled that of his master, Elijah. That was due in part to Elisha's granted request that he be endowed with a double portion of Elijah's spirit. More importantly, the similar lives and ministries of both men foreshadowed and typified the life of Christ.

Elisha's first miracle — smiting the waters of the Jordan with Elijah's mantle — was also the last miracle performed by his master (2 Kgs. 2:8, 14).[15] Elisha, like Elijah and Christ, had control over the elements (2 Kgs. 3:17; Mark 4:41). Elisha, again much like Elijah, multiplied a widow's oil to sustain her family (1 Kgs. 17:10–16; 2 Kgs. 4:1–7). In an episode foreshadowing one of Christ's great miracles, Elisha even fed one hundred men with only twenty loaves and some grain and had food left over (Mark 6:33–44; 2 Kgs. 4:42–44). Like Christ, he healed the sick, as in the example of the Syrian general Naaman (2 Kgs. 5). Elisha raised a woman's son from the dead in much the same way as had Elijah when he raised the widow's son (1 Kgs. 17:21–22; 2 Kgs. 4:32–35). Raising the dead, especially a widow's son (Luke 7:11–17), was also graphic testimony of Christ's divine power (Mark 5:41–42; John 11:41–46). Finally, Elisha, like both his masters, Elijah and Christ (who was the heavenly Jehovah come to earth), prophesied the future and constantly inveighed against the idolatry of Israel.

---

[15]Elisha's performance of this miracle proved to the sons of the prophets that he had indeed inherited the prophetic powers of Elijah. Both men's miracles showed that they continued the ministries of earlier great prophets: Moses (Ex. 14) and Joshua (Josh. 3–4).

The resemblance between the ministries of Elijah, Elisha, and Christ is attested by the New Testament, especially those references that show that Jesus was mistaken by some for the returning Elijah (see Matt. 16:14). The New Testament also indicates that Christ was keenly aware of and even identified with Elijah's and Elisha's missions (Luke 4:24–27). Truly, the lives and activities of these men were similitudes of the God whom they served.[16]

Jehu's Revolt (2 Kgs. 9–10; 2 Chron. 22)

Elisha presided over the establishment of a new king in Israel, Jehu (842–815 B.C.). Though he did not personally anoint the new king, he specifically commissioned the prophet who did (2 Kgs. 9:1–10). Jehu immediately set out to obliterate the family of Ahab and Jezebel, thus fulfilling the prophecies first made by Elijah and later reiterated by the young prophet at Ramoth-gilead concerning Ahab, Jezebel, and their posterity (1 Kgs. 21:17–29; 2 Kgs. 9:8–10).

After being anointed, Jehu met Joram, king of Israel and son of Ahab, along with Ahaziah, king of Judah, in Naboth's vineyard, where some years earlier Jezebel had had Naboth killed and where Elijah had come to Ahab to prophesy the destruction of his family — the last of the Omride dynasty (1 Kgs. 21:17–21). With prophetic justice it was there in Naboth's vineyard that Joram was killed by Jehu (2 Kgs. 9:14–26; cf. 2 Chron. 22:5–8). Ahaziah, who was a nephew of Ahab, fled but was later wounded and died at Megiddo (2 Kgs. 9:27; cf. 2 Chron. 22:9).

Jehu next turned his attention to Jezebel at Jezreel. Even in her old age Jezebel tried to misuse feminine charm (and lots of makeup) to get Jehu to spare her (2 Kgs. 9:30). Or perhaps she simply wanted to die in style. In any case, she failed. Jehu trampled her on his horse, and when the burial crew went to bury her, only her skull, her feet, and the palms

---

[16]Perhaps the most puzzling episode in Elisha's ministry is that of his cursing of the little children in 2 Kgs. 2:23–24, in consequence of which they were attacked by bears. Footnote 23a in the LDS Bible identifies the mockers as "youths (not little children)." But the Hebrew words clearly identify them as little children: ne'ārîm qetannîm, "little boys" (v. 23), and yelādîm, "children" (v. 24). Whatever the meaning of the words, the account is problematic. Since the prophet's response seems so out of character for a servant of the Lord, it may well be that the story is a fictional tale that was added to the record of Elisha's ministry.

of her hands could be found (2 Kgs. 9:30–35). Thus, we learn that the word of the Lord is sure. The prophecy of Elijah was fulfilled: "The dogs shall eat Jezebel by the wall of Jezreel" (1 Kgs. 21:23; 2 Kgs. 9:36). Jehu then went on to kill all that remained of Ahab's family (2 Kgs. 10:1–14).

Jehu's revolt against the ruling house of Ahab was also a repudiation of Ahab's religion. He destroyed the worship of Baal (2 Kgs. 10:28) and in doing so obtained favor in God's eyes (2 Kgs. 10:30). It was promised him that his posterity to the fourth generation would sit on the throne of Israel. But despite his destruction of Ahab's family and the worship of Baal, Jehu did not continue to keep the Lord's commandments. He "departed not from the sins of Jeroboam, which made Israel to sin" (2 Kgs. 10:31). The Northern Kingdom declined rapidly under Jehu and his son, Joahaz (815–802 B.C.). That which the God of Israel had foreseen long before—the scattering of Israel—began to loom in the distance. The God of history continued to operate and work his design: "In those days the Lord began to cut Israel short" (2 Kgs. 10:32).

A Challenge

After the division of the Davidic empire, the kings of Judah were generally more stable and longer-lived than those of Israel, because they were generally less corrupt. The history of the two kingdoms centers on the Lord's active involvement in the affairs of his people, his purposes, and the prophets through whom he brought about those purposes. It is essentially the history of good confronting evil and of the efforts of prophets and other righteous individuals to promote repentance and bring people to the true religion of Jehovah. One of those prophets, Elijah, issued a challenge in ancient times that still stands as a prod today to those who vacillate between the call of the world and the beckonings of the Spirit: "How long halt ye between two opinions? If the Lord be God, follow him" (1 Kgs. 18:21).

5

ISRAEL AND JUDAH IN THE NINTH AND EIGHTH CENTURIES BEFORE CHRIST

(2 KINGS 11–17; 2 CHRONICLES 23–28)

ANDREW C. SKINNER

During the ninth century before Christ, pagan idolatry became rampant in the kingdoms of both Israel and Judah (2 Kgs. 10:31; 12:3; see Map 9, LDS Bible). This circumstance is confirmed by archaeological evidence.[1] Though the Southern Kingdom of Judah attempted periodically to repent of its evil ways, the Northern Kingdom continued to slide unchecked toward the disaster known as the Assyrian conquest. The accounts in Kings and Chronicles tell the story of both kingdoms before and during that disaster and illustrate variations on the central themes that God is actively involved in the history and destiny of his covenant people, and that Israel's downfall was the result of continual idolatry — a rebuff of Jehovah and his covenant. Thus the historian introduced the events of 842 B.C. (beginning in 2 Kgs. 11) by reminding us that "in those days the Lord began to cut Israel short" (2 Kgs. 10:32).

Athaliah (2 Kgs. 11:1–16; 2 Chron. 22:10–23:15)

Though "Jehu destroyed Baal out of Israel" (2 Kgs. 10:28), the wickedness promoted by Ahab and Jezebel outlived them both and extended beyond their own kingdom into Judah. The exportation of

Andrew C. Skinner is assistant professor of ancient scripture at Brigham Young University.
[1]See, for example, desert way stations and combination religious centers, such as the one unearthed at Kuntilet Ajrud, a site halfway between Beersheba and Elath, where travelers from both Judah and Israel rested, worshiped, and deposited offerings to the deities El, Baal, and Asherah.

northern idolatry was accomplished through the evil designs of Ahab's thoroughly wicked sister (or daughter), Athaliah, queen of Judah.[2]

The Israelite princess Athaliah married King Jehoram (Joram) of Judah (reigned 849–843 B.C.) and introduced Baal worship into the Southern Kingdom, just as the Phoenician princess Jezebel had introduced it earlier into the Northern Kingdom. Chronicles is unequivocal in its condemnation of her profoundly corrupting influence, which she wielded over both her husband (2 Chron. 21:6) and her son, Ahaziah, to whom she acted as counselor when he became king (2 Chron. 22:2–4). She is referred to in stark poignancy as "that wicked woman" (2 Chron. 24:7). A combination of material greed, hunger for political power, and instinct for self-preservation likely led her to murder all the royal heirs to the throne of Judah after she learned of her son's death in the wake of Jehu's destruction of the family of Ahab — her family.

One is hard pressed to think of a more incongruous characteristic associated with motherhood than the premeditated act of murdering one's own children or, as in this case, grandchildren. Yet that is what Athaliah did, so as to seize the throne of Judah unchallenged for herself (2 Kgs. 11:1). She ruled 842–837 B.C. With leadership of this caliber it is no wonder that evil so thoroughly resisted eradication and that God eventually forsook both kingdoms of unrepentant Israelites.

Years ago David O. McKay, ninth president and prophet of the Church, indicated that womanhood was "the living life-fountain from which flows the stream of humanity. She who would pollute that stream . . . is an enemy to the strength and perpetuity of the race."[3] Jezebel and Athaliah were sources of great moral pollution in ancient Israel and Judah. Scripture is unambiguous in its portrayal of these two lives as rotten; both of them corrupted all they touched. In this regard they serve as premier examples of another of President McKay's maxims:

---

[2]2 Kgs. 8:18 and 2 Chron. 21:6 seem to have Athaliah as the daughter of Ahab, though the passages may refer to someone else. But 2 Kgs. 8:26 and 2 Chron. 22:2 explicitly identify her as the daughter of Omri and thus a sister or half-sister of Ahab. John Bright points out: "Since her son was born ca. 864 (2 Kgs. 8:26), she could not have been the daughter of Ahab and Jezebel, who could scarcely have been married over ten years at the time. She may have been Ahab's daughter by an earlier marriage, or . . . a daughter of Omri who was raised by Ahab and Jezebel after the former's death." John Bright, *A History of Israel*, 3d ed. (Philadelphia: Westminster, 1981), p. 242, n. 38.

[3]David O. McKay, *Gospel Ideals* (Salt Lake City: Improvement Era, 1953), p. 449.

"Motherhood is the greatest potential influence either for good or ill in human life."[4] Athaliah emulated Jezebel's ways perfectly, especially in her wanton disregard for human life and perversion of true religion (1 Kgs. 18:13; 2 Kgs. 9:7; 11:1). She then passed these characteristics on to her son: Ahaziah "also walked in the ways of the house of Ahab: for his mother was his counsellor to do wickedly" (2 Chron. 22:3).

Joash (2 Kgs. 11–12; 2 Chron. 23–24)

Athaliah was not completely successful in carrying out her destruction of Ahaziah's children. Jehosheba (Jehoshabeath in Chronicles), half-sister of the late King Ahaziah[5] and wife of Jehoiada the high priest (2 Chron. 22:11), hid Joash (Jehoash), a son of Ahaziah, in the house of the Lord for six years while Athaliah ruled unaware of her grandson's existence. During this period Jehoiada and Jehosheba began the future king's education, teaching him the ways of the Lord while at the same time carefully protecting him until he could be made king (2 Kgs. 11:2–11; 12:2).

The overthrow and execution of Athaliah as well as the coronation of a new monarch only seven years of age were events engineered by the high priest and testify of the close relationship between the political and religious realms in ancient Israel. The new king was crowned and anointed in the temple precinct. As was evidently the custom, the coronation took place by one of the pillars that stood before the porch of the temple (2 Kgs. 11:14), probably to emphasize, if only by locale, the sanctity and covenantal nature of kingship.[6] The tokens of monarchy (symbols of stewardship and authority) given to Joash included something called the "Testimony" (2 Kgs. 11:12) — probably a scroll or document containing the Lord's proscriptions, statutes, and judgments by which he expected his people to live and the king to judge and lead (see Deut. 17:18–20).

---

[4]Ibid., p. 452.

[5]Jehosheba was the daughter of Joram but not by Athaliah.

[6]It seems that many important covenantal events occurred by the temple pillars (2 Kgs. 23:3). When the temple was first built, Solomon had erected two pillars at the porch of the temple and given them names with messianic and covenantal overtones: "And he set up the right pillar, and called the name thereof Jachin [Hebrew, 'He Will Establish']: and he set up the left pillar, and called the name thereof Boaz ['In Him Is Strength']" (1 Kgs. 7:21).

Jehoiada became the power behind the throne. As high priest, he took the lead in enacting a covenant of obedience and recommitment between the Lord, the people, and the king. And he instigated a mass uprising against Baal worship, which culminated in the destruction of the temple of Baal and the killing of the Canaanite priest of Baal (2 Kgs. 11:17–18). Because of Jehoiada's example and instruction, Joash began his reign doing what was "right in the sight of the Lord" (2 Kgs. 12:2; 2 Chron. 24:2). He ruled 837–800 B.C.

Under Athaliah, the temple of Jehovah had been abused and vandalized (2 Chron. 24:7). The new king had the damage repaired and the temple reaccoutred; however, problems persisted in the kingdom of Judah for many years to come, for two reasons. First, even the reforms of Joash and Jehoiada could not eradicate the rival sanctuaries of false gods and deeply entrenched idolatrous worship: "But the high places were not taken away: the people still sacrificed and burnt incense in the high places" (2 Kgs. 12:3; 14:4; 15:4). Second, the king himself eventually turned from righteousness.

While Jehoiada was alive, King Joash lived righteously (2 Chron. 24:2). But as soon as the stalwart high priest died, the king—without the steadying influence of his mentor—could not stand on his own. Joash had been well taught and spiritually nurtured, but unfortunately he caved in to political pressure and worldly influence (2 Chron. 24:17–18). When the Lord sent prophets to call them to repentance, the king and his subjects refused to listen and even went so far as to murder one Zechariah, the son of the very man who had guarded and guided the young king from the days of his infancy. Zechariah had attempted to remind the people that the source of all lasting prosperity is the Lord. But the people "conspired against him, and stoned him with stones at the commandment of the king in the court of the house of the Lord" (2 Chron. 24:20–21).

The rapidity and totality of King Joash's spiritual decline—from complicity with idolatry, to refusal to repent, to murder—provide us with an impressive biblical example of the principle articulated in Alma 24:30: "And thus we can plainly discern, that after a people have been once enlightened by the Spirit of God, and have great knowledge of things pertaining to righteousness, and then have fallen away into sin and transgression, they become more hardened, and thus their state becomes worse than though they had never known these things."

Though 2 Kings omits important details surrounding Joash's ultimate demise, the author of Chronicles makes it clear that the Lord "executed judgment" against him by delivering the rulers of Judah, along with others of the Southern Kingdom, into the hands of the Syrian army and Hazael, king of Syria (2 Chron. 24:24; 2 Kgs. 12:18). To get Hazael to withdraw from Jerusalem, Joash was compelled to send him tribute, which was taken from the temple treasury. By the time the Syrian force left, "all princes of the people" had been destroyed, and the king himself was left severely wounded. Joash's own servants then finished the job the Syrians had begun. They conspired against the king and slew him on his sick bed because he had murdered the sons of Jehoiada (2 Chron. 24:23–25).[7]

Joash fell far. Both he and the princes of Judah rejected a covenant of their own making—a covenant they had entered into freely—and in so doing sinned against light (2 Chron. 23:16; 2 Kgs. 11:17). Joash ended up on the same road his progenitors and relatives (Omri, Ahab, Jezebel, Athaliah, and Ahaziah) had traveled, even though he had been given every opportunity to change the course of his family's spiritual direction.

Four Kings of Judah (2 Kgs. 13–16; 2 Chron. 25–28)

From 800 B.C. to 721 B.C., the year of the Northern Kingdom's destruction, the Southern Kingdom of Judah was led by four kings whose collective reigns swung from wickedness to righteousness back to wickedness. Even during those periods of relative righteousness, however, the persistent and undermining problem of idolatry continued to plague Judah.

Joash was succeeded by his son Amaziah (reigned 800–783 B.C.), who began his rule by slaying the royal servants who had conspired against

---

[7]Note the use of the plural "sons." Perhaps there were other sons of the priest besides Zechariah who met similar fates. We know that the Lord sent several prophets to Joash, and maybe these were related to Jehoiada, who is known to have had two wives as well as "sons and daughters" (2 Chron. 24:3). Another possibility is that the "sons of Jehoiada the priest," whose deaths were avenged by the servants of Joash, were disciples and priesthood followers of the high priest, much like the group known as the sons of the prophets. Perhaps Joash's servants were upset by both the king's willful murder of righteous men and his negligent disbursal of the Lord's property as a bribe to appease the Syrian king (2 Kgs. 12:18).

his father (2 Kgs. 14:5). His reign was one of moral and religious degradation. He provoked a battle with Israel, which, though spiritually worse off than Judah, was stronger militarily. Israel badly humiliated Judah, the temple in Jerusalem was plundered, and Amaziah was taken captive (2 Kgs. 14:8–14).[8] When he was released, he learned of a conspiracy against him in Jerusalem and fled to Lachish (southwest of Jerusalem). But his pursuers killed him there in 783 B.C. (cf. 2 Kgs. 14:19; 2 Chron. 25:27).[9]

Amaziah was succeeded on the throne by his son Uzziah (called Azariah in 2 Kings), who ruled 783–742 B.C. As long as Uzziah sought the Lord, "God made him to prosper" (2 Chron. 26:5). He successfully waged war against Judah's enemies and even restored to the kingdom the southern port of Elath on the Gulf of Aqaba (2 Kgs. 14:21–22).[10] He acquired wealth and property and built up areas all over Judah, especially in the Negeb, as archaeological evidence attests (2 Chron. 26:9–10).[11] His name and fame spread far abroad, "for he was marvelously helped, till he was strong" (2 Chron. 26:15). Like so many others in history, however, Uzziah became proud; he appropriated priesthood authority which was not his to take and was struck with leprosy as a divine punishment. He finished his reign exiled from the temple and the royal palace, with his son Jotham reigning as *de facto* monarch (2 Kgs. 15:1–7; 2 Chron. 26:16–21).[12]

Chronicles again gives a much fuller account of Judah's history at this point than does 2 Kings. The Chronicler skillfully presented the relationship between faithfulness to the covenant and material prosperity in a way that is reminiscent of the Book of Mormon: when we keep the

---

[8]The initial battle occurred at Beth-shemesh in the Shephelah and moved east up the mountains to Jerusalem, where the Israelites broke down part of the city wall.

[9]Lachish was a large city, next to Jerusalem in military and political importance. The conspiracy had been fomenting because the king "turned[ed] away from following the Lord" (2 Chron. 25:27). For the locations of Beth-shemesh and Lachish, see Map 9, LDS Bible.

[10]Elath is Ezion-geber at the bottom of Map 7, LDS Bible.

[11]Several Judean settlements dating from Uzziah's time—equipped with cisterns, irrigation systems, and fortifications—have been found in the southern desert near Mizpeh Ramon. We are told specifically that Uzziah "built towers in the desert, and digged many wells" (2 Chron. 26:10).

[12]A fine but small royal palace two miles south of Jerusalem at Ramat Rachel is thought by its excavator, Yohanan Aharoni, to be the "separate house" (2 Kgs. 15:5) to which Azariah/Uzziah was confined. Several idolatrous symbols removed from its interior are witness of the continual idolatry in Judah (2 Kgs. 15:4).

commandments of the Lord, we prosper in the land (see 2 Ne. 1:7, 9–12).

Jotham (742–735 B.C.) witnessed firsthand what befell his father and resolved to reign in righteousness, becoming "mighty, because he prepared his ways [or 'maintained a steady course'] before the Lord" (2 Chron. 27:6). He also achieved material success, building the high or upper gate of the temple as well as many cities in the mountains of Judah.[13]

It was during the reigns of Uzziah and Jotham that Judah's most eloquent prophet, Isaiah, began his ministry (Isa. 1:1). His task was to inveigh against the pernicious problems weakening Judahite society—idolatry, selfishness, and pride (see Isa. 1; 3:8–26). Another of the writing prophets, Micah, also began his ministry in this period (see Micah 1:1).

Jotham's righteousness was not embraced by his son Ahaz (735–715 B.C.), who was just as evil as his wicked counterparts in the Northern Kingdom: "He walked in the way of the kings of Israel, yea, and made his son to pass through the fire, according to the abominations of the heathen, whom the Lord cast out from before the children of Israel. And he sacrificed and burnt incense in the high places, and on the hills, and under every green tree" (2 Kgs. 16:3–4). Not only did Ahaz revitalize the cult practices of the Canaanites but he also reintroduced into the temple many idolatrous objects and rites of Baal worship (2 Chron. 28:2). Later on he even set up an unauthorized altar after the pattern of a pagan altar he had seen in Damascus (2 Kgs. 16:10–12). Because of this wickedness, the Lord raised up a coalition to wage war against Judah. It consisted of Rezin, the king of Syria, and Pekah, son of Remaliah, king of Israel. These two conspirators attempted to conquer Judah and remove Ahaz from his throne (2 Kgs. 15:37; 16:5; Isa. 7:1–16; 8:1–4). The Lord did not allow them to succeed, but the text makes it clear that they were raised up by him to punish Judah: "For the Lord brought Judah low because of Ahaz" (2 Chron. 28:19).

Syria could not overcome Jerusalem but managed to take Elath from Judah (the same port which Uzziah had built up) as well as carry away "a great multitude" of captives (cf. 2 Kgs. 16:5–6; 2 Chron. 28:5). As a partner in the Syro-Ephraimite alliance against Ahaz, Israel also smote Judah "with a great slaughter," which, according to Chronicles, included

---

[13]This is probably the upper gate of Benjamin mentioned in Jer. 20:2.

one hundred twenty thousand killed in one day and two hundred thousand taken captive (2 Chron. 28:6–8). Attempting to rid Judah of Syrian and Israelite oppression, Ahaz formally acknowledged his vassal status under the king of Assyria, Tiglath-pileser III, ruler of the most terrifying world power to have arisen in the Near East at that time. In return, the Assyrian king forced Syria and Israel to lift their siege of Judah and imposed peace on the area. The rest of Ahaz's reign was spent in an attempt to placate economically, imitate culturally and religiously, and bend politically to the terror-inspiring appetites, whims, and will of the Assyrians (2 Kgs. 16:10–18).[14]

Assyria and Israel (2 Kgs. 17)

The name *Assyria* in the days of Ahaz and Isaiah was synonymous with terrifying military might.[15] By perfecting the latest technology and techniques and pursuing to full advantage policies of terror, the Assyrians fashioned the most fiercely militaristic empire the Near East had ever known. The Assyrian rise to power began innocuously around 1250 B.C. when they established an independent kingdom. Their capital city, Asshur, was named after and dedicated to their god of war, who was the chief god in their pantheon. When Hittite power in Anatolia collapsed around 1200 B.C. a vacuum was created, and the Assyrians began filling the void. For the next few centuries they assembled large forces of chariot-cavalry and infantry to defend their borders, establish a strong political base, and eventually to conquer a huge empire.

Ashurnasirpal II (884–860 B.C.) was among the first Assyrian leaders to resort to systematic terror and mass deportations. He publicized his cruel policies with great effectiveness, depicting in carvings and paintings the atrocities his troops committed against unarmed civilians as well as soldiers.[16] So awesome did the Assyrian reputation eventually become that many nations refused to resist, preferring to "embrace the feet" of the conquerors. Victorious Assyrian kings did not often display mercy.

---

[14]For an overview of this period, see Bright, pp. 247–66.

[15]See Bright, pp. 269–78.

[16]Robert and Helen Howe, *The Ancient World* (White Plains, N.Y.: Longman, 1988), pp. 34–36.

They punctuated the records of their exploits with references to having flayed conquered chieftains, covered the walls of conquered cities with skins of the captured populace, impaled live victims on poles, cut off ears, noses, hands, and legs of prisoners, spanned rivers with corpses to make bridges, mashed victims alive, and fed dead rebels to pigs and vultures. Under Ashurnasirpal and his successors, conquered peoples were put to work on massive building projects, including palaces and monuments. Over time Nineveh became a huge metropolis. By 800 B.C. it boasted arsenals, barracks, palaces, temples, and libraries.

Around this time Jonah was sent from the Northern Kingdom to Nineveh to cry repentance (2 Kgs. 14:25; Jonah 1–4). The book of Jonah reports that for a brief period the people of Nineveh gave up their evil ways. Unfortunately, however, Assyrian contrition was short-lived.

The eighth century also saw the ministries of two great prophets in the North — Amos and Hosea. At this crucial point in history, during the long reign of Jeroboam II (786–746 B.C.), God raised up these men to warn Israel to repent of violation of the covenant. Hosea announced, through the metaphor of divorce, that the covenant relationship between God and Israel was terminated (Hos. 1:1–2:13), thus foreshadowing their destruction at the hand of the Assyrians.

During the reign of Tiglath-pileser III (745–727 B.C.), also referred to in the Bible as Pul (2 Kgs. 15:19),[17] the Assyrians began to incorporate conquered territories into their empire. At its peak, that empire would extend from Iran as far west as the Mediterranean Sea and as far south as Egypt (see Map 10, LDS Bible). Tiglath-pileser's first serious encounter with Israel, during the reign of Menahem (745–737 B.C.), resulted in the payment of a huge sum of tribute money — one thousand talents of silver, or more than thirty-five tons (2 Kgs. 15:19–20). The tribute was collected by levying fifty shekels from every wealthy Israelite citizen (2 Kgs. 15:20).[18] At the time Menahem made his payment, sixteen other kings, including Rezin of Damascus, were put under tribute.[19] It seems

---

[17]The use of Pul(u) for Tiglath-pileser is confirmed by the occurrence of this name for him in the Babylonian King List; D. J. Wiseman and Edwin Yamauchi, *Archaeology and the Bible* (Grand Rapids: Zondervan, 1979), p. 41.

[18]Fifty shekels, the "price of freedom," was the average value of a slave, according to contemporary Assyrian sale contracts; ibid., p. 41.

[19]James B. Pritchard, ed., *Ancient Near Eastern Texts Relating to the Old Testament,* 3d ed. with Supplement (Princeton: Princeton University, 1969), p. 283.

that Menahem was first captured and then released. Tiglath-pileser stated, "As for Menahem I overwhelmed him like a snowstorm and he . . . fled like a bird, alone, and bowed to my feet. I returned him to his place and imposed tribute upon him."[20]

A few years later, Tiglath-pileser began actually absorbing Israel during the reign of Israel's King Pekah (736–732 B.C.) — the same who had made the alliance with Syria and fought against Judah, as described above. These two "firebrands" (Isa. 7:4) together sought to coerce Ahaz of Judah to join a revolt against Assyria, but Ahaz in a panic pleaded for Assyrian assistance. The Assyrians marched west, imposed tribute on Judah, Ammon, Ashkelon, Edom, and Moab, and then took large numbers of people from the Galilee and Gilead areas of Israel into captivity (2 Kgs. 15:29; see Map 9, LDS Bible). This began the deportation of the northern tribes of Israel and was a large part of the scattering that had been foretold by the prophets (see Deut. 4:25–27). The record of these actions included with the tribute list of Tiglath-pileser is impressive evidence of the control he exercised over the entire region.[21]

The year following the Assyrian attack on Israel, Tiglath-pileser stated that he had Pekah replaced by Hoshea on the throne of Israel: "They overthrew their king Pekah and I placed Hoshea as king over them" (cf. 2 Kgs. 15:30).[22] Though this statement may or may not be true, Hoshea (732–724 B.C.) seems to have complied with Assyrian demands for the first part of his reign (2 Kgs. 17:3). But he was the last monarch of the kingdom of Israel.

When Tiglath-pileser died in 727 B.C., many subject peoples believed that the new king would be too weak to control them. Revolts broke out in many parts of the empire. It was against this background that the wary Shalmaneser V of Assyria (726–722 B.C.) found evidence that Hoshea had been in communication with Egyptian authorities and had not sent his annual tribute payment. Thus he attacked Israel and besieged the capital city, Samaria (2 Kgs. 17:4–5). Hoshea the king was captured outside the city before Samaria's fall (2 Kgs. 17:4).

---

[20]Ibid., pp. 283–84. This is in Tiglath-pileser's separate account of his attack on Gaza. Apparently, the Assyrians attacked westward to the coast of the Mediterranean and then moved south.

[21]Ibid., pp. 282–84.

[22]Ibid., p. 284.

Cuneiform texts indicate that Shalmaneser died unexpectedly during the three-year seige of Samaria. His successor, Sargon II, the king mentioned in 2 Kings 17:6, boasted of completing the devastation of Israel and conquering the city (2 Kgs. 17:4–6): "At the beginning of my royal rule . . . the town of the Samarians I besieged, conquered. . . . I led away as prisoners 27,290 inhabitants of it. . . . The town I rebuilt better than it was before and settled therein people from countries which I myself had conquered."[23]

The destruction of Samaria in 721 B.C. was a most important event in scriptural history. It brought to an end the Northern Kingdom and resulted in the deportation of thousands of its inhabitants to other lands. Latter-day Saints of the tribe of Ephraim should take special note of these events and what caused them, for their ancestors were likely among those taken away at that time. Because the scattering was the result of Israel's rebellion, the gathering — now well underway — results when the descendants of those ancient Israelites around the world humbly repent, accept the message of the gospel, and return to the Lord through sacred baptismal and temple covenants (see 1 Ne. 10:14).

The Fall of the North

When speaking to King Ahaz about the Syro-Israelite war against him, Isaiah had prophesied the eventual destruction of the Northern Kingdom: "Within threescore and five years shall Ephraim be broken, that it be not a people" (Isa. 7:8). Though it was foreseen, it could have been avoided. The real cause of Israel's captivity was not Assyrian imperialism or military might but rather decades of unmitigated idolatry and infidelity to Jehovah. The Chronicler proclaimed this fact when he said that just as the worship of false gods was the ruin of Ahaz in Judah, so too was it the ruin "of all Israel" (2 Chron. 28:23).

From the days of the Northern Kingdom's first monarch down to the time of its last, every leader in Israel to one degree or another "did that which was evil in the sight of the Lord" (2 Kgs. 17:2). The wickedness of Jeroboam I was so much supported and promulgated by every one of

---

[23]Ibid.

his successors that the words "the sins of Jeroboam, who made Israel to sin" became a standard phrase used by the historian of this portion of the Bible (e.g., 1 Kgs. 14:16; 2 Kgs. 10:29; 13:2, 11; 14:24; 15:9, 18, 24). It will be remembered that the sins that were initiated at the beginning of divided Israel during the reign of Jeroboam and perpetuated throughout its history included (1) the replacement of Jehovah worship with the worship of false gods (1 Kgs. 12:28); (2) worship at the two golden calves, at Dan and Bethel (1 Kgs. 12:27–30); (3) false feasts and sacrifices in imitation of those that were revealed to Moses (1 Kgs. 12:32); and (4) the rejection of the authorized priesthood of Jehovah and their replacement from the "lowest of the people" (1 Kgs. 13:33; 2 Chron. 11:13–17; 13:7–9).

The Lord sent many prophets to try to turn the Northern Kingdom from errant paths. The list includes Ahijah, Iddo, Jehu, Elijah, Elisha, Micaiah, Hosea, Amos, and Obed. But none of these succeeded in averting Israel's slide toward disaster. With the passing of each unrighteous king, one after another, Israel wallowed in sin, becoming ever more deeply entrenched in the ways of wickedness, until the Lord finally "removed Israel out of his sight, as he had said by all his servants the prophets" (2 Kgs. 17:23).

As both Assyrian and biblical records make clear, after he deported the people of Israel, the king of Assyria imported and resettled other conquered peoples to replace them. These new colonists intermarried with the remaining Israelites, practiced a corrupt combination of Jehovah worship and idolatry (2 Kgs. 17:24–34a, 40), and became the Samaritans of New Testament record.[24]

Instead of becoming the Lord's peculiar treasure (Ex. 19:5; Ps. 135:4), Israel "followed after the worthless thing [Hebrew, *hebel*] and became worthless [Hebrew, *wayyehbālû*]" (2 Kgs. 17:15, my translation). Idolatry is spiritual adultery (see 2 Chron. 21:11; Isa. 57:8; Jer. 2:20; 3:9), and nothing is more worthless or hurtful than false promises of fidelity. Israel was removed because it had played the harlot long enough.

The text of 2 Kings shows the merging and shaping of separate historical accounts by an editor who wanted certain lessons to be unmistakable. Although the author tells us that the people of the northern

---

[24]See "Samaritans," Bible Dictionary, LDS Bible.

tribes were resettled in various locations in the Assyrian empire (2 Kgs. 17:6), where they were taken is not as important as what they did to merit captivity and exile (2 Kgs. 17:7–22) nor as important as the Lord's marked involvement in their destiny (2 Kgs. 17:23, 34–40).[25] Had Israel been humble and honored the true God who had brought them forth from Egypt (2 Kgs. 17:36), he would have fought their every battle and rescued them from every enemy (2 Kgs. 17:39). That God delivers his people *from* their enemies when they obey or *to* their enemies when they disobey is documented in several passages of 2 Kings and ought to be noted, especially by Latter-day Saints (see 10:32; 13:3; 17:20). It is a principle taught in modern revelation: "By hearkening to observe all the words which I, the Lord their God, shall speak unto them, they shall never cease to prevail until the kingdoms of the world are subdued under my feet, and the earth is given unto the saints, to possess it forever and ever. But inasmuch as they keep not my commandments, and hearken not to observe all my words, the kingdoms of the world shall prevail against them" (D&C 103:7–8).

---

[25]Arguing the whereabouts of the so-called "Lost Ten Tribes" from the oft-quoted apocryphal source of 2 Esdras is shaky. The only reliable statements on the location of the descendants of the ancient Israelites come from latter-day revelation. These indicate that Israel is scattered upon the face of all the earth. Consider, for example, 3 Ne. 5:24: "And as surely as the Lord liveth, will he gather in from the four quarters of the earth all the remnant of the seed of Jacob, who are scattered abroad upon all the face of the earth."

6

THE BOOK OF JONAH

DAVID ROLPH SEELY

It is ironic that the profound message of the book of Jonah is often swallowed up in the speculations about the great fish, dwarfed by the debates about the size of Nineveh, ignored because of the image of fasting beasts draped in sackcloth, or diminished by the dramatic growth of a gourd plant. The book of Jonah contains a compelling story of Jonah, an Israelite, and his encounter with foreign men and foreign places replete with all of these wonders. The medium of the message is most often irony — that is, a constant incongruity between what is expected and what actually occurs. But just as the props are not the play, neither is the medium the message; it is only a means to the end. The book of Jonah teaches in its four short chapters much about the nature of God and man and ultimately has something profound to say about relationships, specifically that the relationship between a man and his Maker has profound implications for a man's relationship with his fellow humans. Because we recognize ourselves in Jonah, we initially smile at his humanness — but by the end we are sobered, as we, like Jonah, are humbled by the grace of God and come to recognize our own hidden duplicities.

Jonah, son of Amittai, was a northerner from the village of Gath-hepher[1] and is known elsewhere in scripture as a prophet of the Lord who during the reign of Jeroboam II (786–46 B.C.) accurately prophesied Israel's territorial restoration (2 Kgs. 14:25). The Lord God called Jonah

---

David Rolph Seely is assistant professor of ancient scripture at Brigham Young University.

[1]In Josh. 19:13 Gath-hepher is identified as a border town in the territory of Zebulun that today is identified with Khirbet ez-Zurra, a site three miles northeast of Nazareth; G. W. Van Beek, "Gath-Hepher," in *Interpreter's Dictionary of the Bible*, 5 vols., ed. G. A. Buttrick, et al. (Nashville: Abingdon, 1962–76), 2:356.

on a mission but, as portrayed in chapters 1 and 2 and then 3 and 4, Jonah ended up going on two missions—one on the sea and the other on the dry land. The call was the same in both cases. As recorded in Jonah 1:1–2, "Now the word of the Lord came unto Jonah the son of Amittai, saying, Arise [Hebrew *qûm*], go to Nineveh, that great city, and cry against it; for their wickedness is come up before me." And as recorded in Jonah 3:1–2, "The word of the Lord came unto Jonah the second time, saying, Arise [*qûm*], go unto Nineveh, that great city, and preach unto it the preaching that I bid thee." Jonah's response was prompt, and to each call he "rose up" [*wayyāqām*]—only in different directions. The first time he rose up to disobey, "to flee unto Tarshish [presumably a port in Spain which in the ancient world was approximately the opposite end of the earth from Nineveh] from the presence of the Lord" (Jonah 1:3). The second time, after less-than-subtle persuasion, he finally did obey when he "arose, and went unto Nineveh, according to the word of the Lord" (Jonah 3:3).

There is an inconsistency between what Jonah said he believed and what he did. Although none of us could sufficiently justify it, we all can—from experience—understand his flight. Jonah was finally identified by a casting of lots as the cause of the great storm on the sea (*yām*) that threatened the lives of his fellows. The frightened sailors unleashed a panicked barrage of questions: "For whose cause this evil is upon us; What is thine occupation? and whence comest thou? what is thy country? and of what people art thou?" (Jonah 1:8)—all of which could be answered by Jonah's simple statement, "I am an Hebrew; and I fear the Lord, the God of heaven, which hath made the sea [*yām*] and the dry land [*yabāšâ*]" (Jonah 1:9). The label of *Hebrew* identifies him as one of the chosen people—a member of the covenant community of Israel bound to the Lord and thus to each other by sacred obligations. His "fear" of the Lord God who hath made the "sea and the dry land" (a merism that is tantamount to saying "everything") is a statement of belief—in opposition to the polytheism of his day—in one universal God, who created and thus controls all of creation. The disobedience of a simple Hebrew is enough to bring about this calamity, even in "international waters." How could one professing such a belief ever hope to escape from the presence of such an omnipresent Being? Yet Jonah fled, and on his two missions he would meet this Being on and in the sea and on the dry land.

Jonah demonstrated his selfless charity to his fellowmen by urging them to toss him overboard, while the sailors demonstrated their own charity and fear of shedding innocent blood in attempting to preserve him. In the end the Lord had his way and Jonah was cast overboard, presumably to perish in the sea. The net result of Jonah's first mission was that the sailors, pious Gentiles, feared Jehovah, the Israelite God, and offered sacrifices to him (Jonah 1:16). Jonah, a disobedient Israelite, by the grace of God, was preserved in the belly of a great fish which the Lord had prepared. In the belly of the fish a humbled Jonah prayed for deliverance. The words from his own mouth are "Salvation is of the Lord" (Jonah 2:9). Through his mercy the Lord did deliver Jonah, and the fish "vomited out Jonah upon the dry land [yabāšâ]" (Jonah 2:10) — also the arena of God's creation and power — where the next scene would take place.

After Jonah's second mission call, he arrived at the great city of Nineveh, the capital of the Assyrian empire, which in the day of Jonah was the intellectual, cultural, artistic, and technological center of the ancient civilized world (see Map 10, LDS Bible). At last Jonah bravely began to proclaim the word of the Lord: "Yet forty days, and Nineveh shall be overthrown" (Jonah 3:4). Much to his surprise — and chagrin — all of Nineveh repented, "from the greatest of them even to the least of them" (Jonah 3:5). From the king to the lowliest of beasts, they all humbly repented and fasted in sackcloth and ashes to see "if God will turn and repent, and turn away from his fierce anger, that we perish not" (Jonah 3:9). The merciful God of heaven heard the repentant cries from Nineveh and turned away his anger, as he had preserved his children on the sea. The net result of Jonah's second mission was that the entire city of Nineveh — a "great city of three days' journey" (Jonah 3:4) — repented and turned to God.

Jonah, who on his first mission in time of crisis was willing to give up his own life to save his fellow sailors, now was displeased and very angry at the demonstration of the Lord's mercy to preserve a penitent Nineveh. Whereas Jonah had prayed to the Lord for mercy to be delivered from drowning and praised the Lord with a psalm of thanksgiving that he was delivered (Jonah 2:1–9), now he prayed that the Lord would rescind his mercy from the Ninevites. At last Jonah offered his excuse for not wanting to go to Nineveh in the first place: "Therefore I fled before unto Tarshish: for I knew that thou art a gracious God, and merciful, slow to anger, and of great kindness, and repentest thee of the evil" (Jonah 4:2).[2] The problem is now finally clear. Jonah didn't like Assyrians, a not uncommon position held by many of the Northern Kingdom in the time of Jonah, for they were his enemies. And Israelites were not alone in their resentment of the often cruel and uncompromising rule of the mighty Assyrian empire. While not eager to preach to them in the first place, he found solace in preaching his message only when he could anticipate their ultimate destruction. Though he was eager to proclaim the Lord God of heaven as the Creator of all things and reluctantly admitted that the Lord can control all things on the sea and the earth, he would not allow for a universal application of God's mercy to all of his creatures.

The prophetic calling in Israel often entailed the office of Mediator — even pleading for mercy for the unrighteous.[3] Jonah did the opposite, pleading for judgment against the repentant. Jonah is described as the antithesis of his great northern Israelite predecessor Elijah: Elijah sought the Lord in sorrow over the hardness of the hearts of the people (1 Kgs. 19:4–18); Jonah, in anger at their penitence. Both declared to the Lord that it would be better to die than to live — Elijah out of discouragement and Jonah out of self-righteous despair. On his first mission, in his disobedience, Jonah had prayed for his life; now, in his obedience, he prayed for death. Jonah would rather have died than live to see his enemies receive the mercy of the Lord.

As so often in missionary work, the final convert must be the missionary himself. It was the Lord's turn to preach repentance to his servant. He asked Jonah, "Doest thou well to be angry?" (Jonah 4:4) and then proceeded to teach him a powerful object lesson. While Jonah nurtured his bruised ego with the slight hope that perhaps the Lord would still

---

[2]Note the JST changes at Josh. 3:9–10.

[3]For example, recall Abraham mediating for the wicked cities of Sodom and Gomorrah (Gen. 18), Moses mediating for the children of Israel after the incident of the golden calf (Ex. 32), Samuel intervening for repentant Israel against the Philistines (1 Sam. 7), and Amos for "tiny Jacob" (Amos 7:1–6) — all of which, of course, are a shadow and type of Jesus Christ as Mediator before God for all humankind.

destroy Nineveh (Jonah 4:5), the Lord prepared a gourd plant that provided shade for him "to deliver him from his grief. So Jonah was exceeding glad of the gourd" (Jonah 4:6). At last Jonah was comforted, or at least comfortable, in his grief, and thus he cared about one of God's creations, which so conveniently offered him relief.

But the Lord sent a worm to eat the plant so that it withered. The loss of the shade once again made Jonah angry "even unto death" (Jonah 4:9). Then the Lord said, "Thou hast had pity on the gourd, for the which thou hast not laboured, neither madest it grow; which came up in a night, and perished in a night: And should not I spare Nineveh, that great city, wherein are more than sixscore thousand persons that cannot discern between their right hand and their left hand;[4] and also much cattle?" (Jonah 4:10–11). Thus the Lord's message ended with a rhetorical question, to which the answer is obvious but missing.

The message is clear to the children of Israel, both ancient and modern. As demonstrated by Zenos' allegory of the olive tree, the branches of the wild olives can be grafted into the tree and can bear good fruit (Jacob 5). From the Old Testament we can cite the souls who followed Abraham (Gen. 12:5), the mixed multitude that came out from Egypt with Israel (Ex. 12:38), Rahab (Josh. 2), Naaman (2 Kgs. 5), Ruth (Ruth), and undoubtedly many others who are unmentioned. The gospel net continues to gather of every kind (Matt. 13:47) for the God of heaven who created us all loves us all. "Behold, the Lord esteemeth all flesh in one; he that is righteous is favored of God" (1 Ne. 17:35). Speaking of the doctrine of adoption, John the Baptist warned the children of Israel in his day: "Think not to say within yourselves, We have Abraham to our father: for I say unto you, that God is able of these stones to raise up children unto Abraham" (Matt. 3:9).[5]

---

[4]Some have interpreted this phrase to refer to those of lesser intelligence or religious knowledge or understanding. More likely, however, the image of one not being able "to discern between their right hand and their left hand" refers to innocent children, who like the cattle are to be reckoned in addition to the rest of the population. See a similar phrase in Deut. 1:39 and Isa. 7:16.

[5]Joseph Smith interpreted this passage as referring to the Gentiles, "of these stony Gentiles — these dogs — to raise up children unto Abraham"; *Teachings of the Prophet Joseph Smith*, sel. Joseph Fielding Smith (Salt Lake City: Deseret Book Co., 1938), p. 319. The Prophet further explained the process by which Gentiles are adopted: "As the Holy Ghost falls upon one of the literal seed of Abraham, it is calm and serene; and his whole soul and body are only exercised by the pure spirit of intelligence; while the effect of the Holy Ghost upon a Gentile, is to purge out the old blood, and make him actually of the seed of Abraham. That man that has none of the blood of Abraham (naturally) must have a new creation by the Holy Ghost"; *Teachings*, pp. 149–50.

Near the end of chapter 4 the Lord responded to Jonah with a question: "Doest thou well to be angry for the gourd?" (Jonah 4:9), to which Jonah would have answered in the affirmative. The final statement by the Lord is also phrased in an unanswered question addressed to Jonah as well as to us: "Should not I spare Nineveh?" (Jonah 4:11). For the children of the covenant who profess to "fear the Lord, the God of heaven, which hath made the sea and the dry land," it echoes other such provocative questions posed throughout the scriptures. A certain lawyer once asked, "Who is my neighbour?" (Luke 10:29). King Benjamin queried, "For behold, are we not all beggars?" (Mosiah 4:19). And from the parable of the laborers in the vineyard, the Lord responded to him that would begrudge the latecomer to the covenant a full reward: "Is it not lawful for me to do what I will with mine own? Is thine eye evil, because I am good?" (Matt. 20:15).

7

THE BOOK OF AMOS

D. KELLY OGDEN

Amos, apparently the first of a series of Israelite and Judahite prophets
whose words were committed to writing, prophesied in the Northern
Kingdom in the mid eighth century during the reigns of Jeroboam II of
Israel and Uzziah of Judah.[1] He was, before his call to be a prophet,
"among the herdmen of Tekoa" (Amos 1:1). His hometown of Tekoa
lies about six miles southeast of Bethlehem and twelve miles from Jerusalem (see Map 9, LDS Bible). It was one of the easternmost villages
in Judah and was on the dividing line between cultivated land and
pastureland. It was also on the caravan route which led from Jerusalem/
Bethlehem to En Gedi and beyond to Arabia.

Amos gave a first-person description of his call to Amaziah,

D. Kelly Ogden is associate professor of ancient scripture at Brigham Young University.

[1]Michael Avi-Yonah and Emil G. Kraeling, *Our Living Bible* (Jerusalem-Ramat Gan: International Publishing Co., 1962), p. 229; Richard S. Cripps, *A Critical and Exegetical Commentary
on the Book of Amos* (London: Society for Promoting Christian Knowledge, 1929), p. 9. See also
Andor Szabo, "Textual Problems in Amos and Hosea," *Vetus Testamentum* 25 (1975): 500–501.

On the timing of Amos's ministry, the mention of "Uzziah king of Judah" and "Jeroboam the
son of Joash king of Israel" clearly places the prophet in the mid eighth century B.C. In the
superscription to the book of Amos (Amos 1:1), the prophet's preaching is also dated (beginning)
at "two years before the earthquake." Though seismic disturbances are anything but rare in the land
of Amos, this very earthquake, the only one *explicitly* mentioned in the Old Testament, was apparently
so severe that it was used for some time to date historical events. It was of such unusual intensity
and inflicted such devastation that the memory of it survived for more than two and a half centuries,
and in Zechariah 14:5, this earthquake served as a pattern for extremely intense and destructive
earthquakes: "And you shall flee as you fled from the earthquake in the days of Uzziah, king of Judah."
This earthquake caused damage over a wide area; evidence of it has been discovered in archaeological
excavations from one end of the country to the other, particularly at Hazor in the north, Deir-Alla
in the Jordan Valley, and Beersheba in the south. Yigael Yadin dated the earthquake to approximately
760 B.C.; Yigael Yadin, *Hazor: The Head of All Those Kingdoms* (London: Oxford University, 1972),
pp. 113, 181.

Jeroboam's priest at the Bethel shrine: "I was no prophet, neither was I a prophet's son; but I was an herdman, and a gatherer of sycomore fruit: And the Lord took me as I followed the flock" (Amos 7:14–15). He was called from his pastoral occupations and specifically disclaimed association with professionally trained prophets. He was a *nōqēd*, or sheep-breeder (Amos 1:1). That may suggest that he supervised the work of other shepherds, being a substantial and respected man in his community.[2] Amos also identified himself as a *bôqēr*, a herdman of sheep and goats (Amos 7:14). As a wool-grower in Judah he may have made journeys to markets all over the land, to the Northern Kingdom, and even possibly to Damascus.[3]

In addition to his work as a sheep breeder, Amos was a cultivator, or dresser, of sycomores (Amos 7:14). The biblical sycomore (*Ficus sycomorus*) is not found in the Near East at elevations higher than one thousand feet above sea level. It does not grow near Tekoa, since Tekoa is much more than twice that elevation. Amos's work with sycomore figs, then, would have taken him into the lowland (the Shephelah) of Judah.[4]

Geographical Background of Amos

Amos's geographical milieu figures prominently in his prophetic message. At least ten lands outside the territories of Israel and Judah

---

[2]The only other biblical occurrence of *nōqēd* is in 2 Kgs. 3:4 with reference to Mesha, king of Moab, who had to deliver annually to the king of Israel one hundred thousand lambs and one hundred thousand rams.

[3]Erling Hammershaimb, *The Book of Amos: A Commentary* (New York: Schocken Books, 1970), p. 12; George Adam Smith, *The Book of the Twelve Prophets* (London: Hodder and Stoughton, 1906), p. 74.

[4]*Ficus sycomorus* is a species of fig, or fig-mulberry (the fruit being like a fig and the leaf like the mulberry). The tree is known to grow to great size, sometimes attaining more than fifty feet in circumference, and is evergreen. Its existence, in Israel at least, totally depends on cultivation. The fruit shoots forth on all parts of the stem, several figs on each leafless twig. In the Holy Land it grows in the mild coastal plains and in the Jordan Valley. David considered the sycomore valuable enough that he appointed a special overseer "over the olive trees and the sycomore trees that were in the low plains [Hebrew, *Shephelah*]" (1 Chron. 27:28). Three times scripture mentions that Solomon made cedars as plentiful as the sycomores of the Shephelah (1 Kgs. 10:27; 2 Chron. 1:15; 9:27). From historical and climatic information it is understood that Amos would have nurtured sycomore trees in the Judean Shephelah or in the Jordan Valley.

are referred to in the book of Amos, and the book includes prophetic pronouncements concerning at least twenty-six cities. Amos's writings are replete with images reflecting the agricultural and pastoral background and the breadth of education and life experience of the prophet. There are in his book some highly picturesque figures of speech from the contemporary world of fauna and flora and from phenomena of nature, climate, rainfall, and other meteorological conditions. Amos, like most of the prophet-writers who succeeded him and like the Savior and his apostles, drew many parallels to the human experience from his natural surroundings. Hebrew writers loved to compare the experience of individuals and nations to what was occurring in nature.

Amos expressed his words of rebuke and warning to the northern Israelites in powerful metaphor, as did his contemporaries and successors in the prophetic office. For example, he did not record the Lord's merely saying to his people, "You are a burden to me," but rather, "I am pressed under you, as a cart is pressed that is full of sheaves" (Amos 2:13). Amos uttered his message with illustrations from nature. He called on locusts, lions, bird-traps, cows of Bashan, fish-hooks, cedars, oaks, wormwood, blight, mildew, kings' mowings, fruit baskets, threshing sledges, siroccos, drought, storms, eclipses, and earthquakes to vividly and poignantly prophesy against and warn the people. We might call this the "over-geography" of Amos's prophesying.

Amos saw what was happening to Israelite society and what God was about to do to it by way of chastisement and punishment, and he found the proper expressions in his nature-environment, collocating human actions and divine actions. His visions of locusts and drought-fire devouring the land (Amos 7:1–6) were symbolic of the destruction of Israel as a nation.[5] Amos saw upheaval and disruption in nature as a direct result of upheaval and disruption in society. "You cause the poor of the land to fail" (Amos 8:4); "I'll cause the crops of the land to fail" (Amos 4:9). High society had withheld necessary sustenance from the poor, and God withheld necessary sustenance from the Israelites (Amos 4:6–8). Leaders had swallowed up the needy (Amos 8:4), so God would swallow them up with various catastrophes. Merchants had sold the refuse

---

[5]As the JST changes at Amos 7:3 and 7:6 show, though the nation would be destroyed, a remnant would be preserved for a latter-day repentance and restoration.

of the wheat (Amos 8:6), so God would sell them as refuse into the hands of the enemy (Amos 6:8).

Relationship between Nature and Humankind

Amos saw a cause-and-effect relationship in operation: catastrophe in nature was a direct result of catastrophe in society. He saw evidence of an ethically or morally destroyed society: luxurious living, music-making, reveling while some in society were suffering (Amos 5:23; 6:4–7); prostitution committed in holy sanctuaries (Amos 2:7); shallow, hypocritical festivities and ritual performances (Amos 5:21–22); anticipating the conclusion of holy days so that deceitful business practices and falsifying balances could be resumed (Amos 8:5–6); the wealthy enjoying winter houses and summer "cabins," ivory-decorated houses, cut-stone houses, and palaces, while the poor lived in hovels (Amos 3:15; 5:11; 6:8, 11); treading on the poor, making merchandise of human beings, buying the poor for silver and the needy for a pair of shoes (Amos 5:11; 2:6, 7; 8:6); corrupted court and legal processes, perverted judgment, despising the righteous and afflicting the just (Amos 2:8; 5:7, 10, 12; 6:12). All these practices wrecked or spoiled society. As a result, Amos saw evidence of a destroyed ecosystem and therefore *a physically destroyed society*: rains were withheld, causing famine (Amos 4:6–8); blight and mildew consumed crops (Amos 4:9); earthquakes devastated pasture lands, garden lands, and cities (Amos 1:2; 4:11); locusts devoured the grains (Amos 7:1–2); and drought devoured the land generally (Amos 7:4–5).

Several of the characteristics Amos identified in society he compared with objects in his environment: on the positive side, height and strength were related to the majestic cedar and the mighty oak (Amos 2:9); constancy and consistency in justice and righteousness were related to an ever-flowing stream (Amos 5:24). On the negative side, injustice and unrighteousness were compared to poison and wormwood (Amos 6:12); and pride and vanity were represented in Bashan's full-fed, contented cows (Amos 4:1).

Even the cities and lands cited in the book of Amos were used because of their didactic potential. The corruption capitals of Damascus, Gaza,

Tyre, Bozrah, Rabbah, Kerioth, Jerusalem, and Samaria were condemned because of their offensive behavior in the sight of God and man.[6] Further, Amos called on specific cities and lands from history and current events because of their value as examples in moral instruction. Lo-debar and Karnaim typified arrogance and boasting of strength.[7] Calneh, Hamath, and Gath served as moral comparisons for Samaria (Amos 6:2). Sodom and Gomorrah (Amos 4:11) and the Valley of Aven[8] were selected as examples of sin centers. Bethel, Dan, Gilgal, and Beersheba represented the perversion of true religion.[9] Cush and Caphtor were used to illustrate parental care of all God's children, a strike against the assumed superiority of Israelite society.[10]

---

[6]Damascus (Amos 1:3–5), Gaza (Amos 1:6–7), Tyre (Amos 1:9–10), Bozrah (Amos 1:11–12), Rabbah (Amos 1:13–15), Kerioth (Amos 2:1–3), Jerusalem (Amos 2:4–5; 6:1), and Samaria (Amos 2:6–16). Samaria's (Israel's) crimes continue to be identified throughout the book: violence and robbery (Amos 3:10; 6:3), oppression of the needy, greed, and drunkenness (Amos 4:1; 8:4), hypocrisy in ordinances (Amos 4:4–5; 5:21–23), disdain of honest judges (Amos 5:10), cheating the poor (Amos 5:11), bribery (Amos 5:12), idolatry (Amos 5:26; 8:14), gluttony and revelry (Amos 6:4–7), pride, vainglory, and false sense of security (Amos 6:8, 13), deceitful business practices, and desecration of the spirit of the Sabbath (Amos 8:5–6).

[7]The Hebrew toponyms *Lo-debar* and *Karnaim* can be read as common nouns, as the King James Version's "a thing of nought" and "horns" (Amos 6:13). But *Lo-debar* and *Karnaim* are also names of cities taken in military victories during Israel's recovering control of Transjordan from Syria shortly before the time of Amos (2 Kgs. 14:25).

[8]The Valley of Aven is rendered in KJV Amos 1:5 as "the plain of Aven," meaning the valley of sin, apparently a reference to the Lebanese Beqa'. Compare also Amos 5:5, in which Bethel becomes Beth-aven: the "house of God" had become "the house of sin."

[9]Bethel (Amos 3:14; 4:4; 5:5), Dan (Amos 8:14), Gilgal (Amos 4:4; 5:5), Beersheba (Amos 5:5; 8:14).

[10]Cushites, Nubians, and Ethiopians are the same people, from a biblical point of view. Caphtor is the ancient equivalent of modern Crete. Amos perceived that Israel's pride and self-esteem had become distorted or exaggerated. He humbled them with the cold fact that they were *not* intrinsically more valuable or more important to Jehovah than were the Arameans, or the Philistines, or even the far-off Cushites, and he put the Israelite exodus on the same footing as the migrations of other peoples of antiquity (Amos 9:7). There is no denying that God had entrusted to Israel the precious blessing of laws, statutes, and ordinances under which he wanted all people to live. Jehovah had, in a sense, cared for Israel above all the families of the earth (Amos 3:2), but Israel did not have a privileged position or preferential status before God because of especially deserving behavior. Amos seemed to be pointing out in response to an assertion of spiritual superiority on the part of Israel that Jehovah is God of all peoples, from "beyond Damascus" to the land of Cush, and he warned Israel in unmistakably plain language that "the eyes of the Lord God are upon the sinful kingdom" (Amos 9:8).

Warnings of Captivity

Prophesying approximately a generation before the destruction of the kingdom of Israel, Amos's mission was to warn Israel of its present disastrous state and forewarn it of impending captivity. He pointedly delivered the latter message with such curt exclamations as "I will take you into exile beyond Damascus" (Amos 5:27); "they shall now be the first of those to go into exile" (Amos 6:7); "Israel must go into exile away from his land" (Amos 7:11); and "Israel shall surely go into exile away from its land" (Amos 7:17). But the prophet was not always satisfied with direct statements. He reinforced his message with metaphorical illustrations, which are often more memorable and vivid than literal words. That Israel would be *captured* or *caught* is expressed through the images of a lion devouring an animal and leaving only pieces (Amos 3:12), either the lion, bear, or serpent finally catching up with a fleeing man (Amos 5:19), a bird trapped in a snare (Amos 3:5), sinners carried away hooked as a fish (Amos 4:2), or caught in a sieve (Amos 9:9). There would be no escape from the judgment of God, just as vegetation has no chance of escape before the ravages of the locust-swarm, the sirocco's blasting, or the scorching of drought. The man (Israel) could not escape from the lion, bear, or serpent (enemy nations). The sheep or goat (Israel) could not escape from the lion (God). No one would escape but a righteous few, a remnant (Amos 6:10; 9:1–3, 10).

In due time Amos's prophecies were fulfilled, soon by the Assyrians and then later by other conquerors. The kingdom of Israel was destroyed and taken captive within a few years after Amos warned clearly that such would happen. The Israelites were exiled "beyond Damascus," as he had said (Amos 5:27).[11]

---

[11]Damascus (Amos 1:5) was taken by Tiglath-pileser III in 732 B.C. He did exactly what Amos prophesied: he sent military fire upon and destroyed the house of Hazael and the strongholds of Ben-hadad (Amos 1:4), broke the security-bar of Damascus (Amos 1:5), and cut off inhabitants from the Valley of Aven and officials from Beth-eden by exiling the Syrians (2 Kgs. 16:9). The chief Philistine cities (Amos 1:6–8) were also besieged by Tiglath-pileser in 734 B.C. Amos's promise of punishment on Tyre was only gradually fulfilled. Tiglath-pileser was successfully "bought off," but Tyre was later attacked by Shalmaneser V (a five-year siege), and then by the Babylonian Nebuchadnezzar (a thirteen-year siege). Alexander the Great later laid his causeway, forever connecting the island with the mainland, and marched his armies to destroy the island-city, selling thirty thousand of its inhabitants into slavery, which was the very charge for which Amos had condemned the Tyrians (Amos 1:9–10). Jerusalem was miraculously spared

Although God had *raised up* Israel to perform a special service in the world, its people had *fallen* from their high commission and appointed purpose. The virgin Israel had fallen (Amos 5:2), and the tabernacle of David had fallen (Amos 9:11). Amos warned that sons and daughters would fall (Amos 7:17), worshipers of false gods would fall (Amos 8:14), the altar-horns (symbolic of holiness) and the sanctuary itself would fall (Amos 3:14; 9:1).

Comparison of Agriculture and Society

Amos perceived that God controlled both nature and society and that there must be system and order in both. This sense of order, system, and completeness is evident in Amos's use of metaphor from the cycle of agricultural production: as with agriculture and the produce of the field, so with society and the produce of humankind. The land must be plowed or prepared; God had created or prepared a land for his covenant people. The land would then be planted with the choicest vines, fig trees, and olive trees; God had planted Israel in the good land (Ex. 15:17; 2 Sam. 7:10; Amos 9:14, 15). The husbandman/farmer would water and care for his plants; God had nourished and cared for the people of Israel in their promised land (Deut. 7:6–15; 11:12–17; Amos 3:2). Following a time of careful cultivation, the farmer would expect to reap a bounteous harvest; God expected fruit from Israel (Gen. 35:11; 48:4; Lev. 26:9; Isa. 27:6; Amos 6:12). Upon harvesting his crops, the farmer transported his yield from the fields for storage or consumption; God would transport Israel from their native fields in judgment, where they would be *sifted* through other lands (Amos 9:9) or to exile in enemies' lands where they would be *threshed* and trodden down (Amos 7:11, 17). Then the land might be replowed and replanted, so the cycle would begin anew. What the prophet saw occurring in the fields of Judah and Israel was also occurring in Judahite and Israelite societies — this parallel filtered through into his verbal encounters with the people in Samaria and Bethel.

The "over-geography" is everywhere present in Amos's oracles and

---

destruction by the Assyrians under Sennacherib in 701 B.C. but was burned by Nebuchadnezzar in 587 B.C. — to literally fulfill Amos's prophecy: "I will send a fire upon Judah, and it shall devour the palaces of Jerusalem" (Amos 2:5).

judgments, and only one who had lived with such fauna, flora, agriculture, and natural phenomena could have drawn parallels from them to put flesh on the bare-bones facts of devastation, deportation, and death.

The Vision of Restoration to the Land

Because the last five verses of the book of Amos (the epilogue; Amos 9:11–15) paint a wholly different scene—restoration to the land and prosperity in it, some scholars view those verses as presupposing a different time and situation than that of Amos (mid eighth century B.C.) and consider them the minimasterpiece of a later disciple or redactor, thus denying their authorship to Amos.[12] They also deny the possibility of prophetic preview and see in the description of prosperous times detail which could have been written only by firsthand experience at a later date. Despite these claims, I maintain that the final verses of the book of Amos are not only an acceptable but an essential climax to his writings. The phrase "in that day" (Amos 9:11) in and of itself indicates that a writer living in one time period projects his thoughts into a future time period. Though some would argue that the epilogue is out of harmony with, or even contradictory to, the whole tenor of Amos's pronouncements of ruin, and inconsistent with his condemning voice, it must not be overlooked that there is a pattern visible in Hebrew literature of pronouncing curses, judgments, and destruction followed by a message of hope.

After the catalogue of plagues, desolations, and pestilences recorded in Leviticus 26, hope is held out to Israel (Lev. 26:40–46). Following Isaiah's predicted doom and destruction to Israel and Judah, there is comforting and assuring hope held out for a glorious day of restoration (Isa. 40–66; denied, of course, to Isaiah by the same critics who refuse to credit Amos 9:11–15 to Amos).[13] Following Hosea's recitations of Israel's unfaithfulness and consequent punishment and exile, that prophet

---

[12]Some scholars view the epilogue as presupposing a different time and situation than that of Amos. See William Rainey Harper, A Critical and Exegetical Commentary on Amos and Hosea (Edinburgh: T.& T. Clark, 1936), p. 199. On the other hand, many scholars give credence to its origin in the days of Amos.

[13]But see also Isa. 4; 11; 12; 27; 30; 32; and 35—all with promises of restoration and blessing after the discipline of exile.

records the Lord saying that he will return them to their homeland: "I will heal their backsliding, I will love them freely. . . . I will be as the dew unto Israel. . . . They that dwell under his shadow shall return; they shall revive" (Hosea 14:4–5, 7). Following Micah's forthright iteration of the disgraceful ruin of both Samaria and Jerusalem, he follows up with predictions of future restoration to good fortune (Micah 4–5). Following the great devastation caused by the armies of locusts, Joel reveals God's promises: "I will restore to you the years that the locust hath eaten. . . . Ye shall eat in plenty, and be satisfied. . . . When I shall bring again the captivity [cause the return] of Judah and Jerusalem" (Joel 2:25–26; 3:1).

It may properly be suggested, then, that Amos was perpetuating and cementing a prophetic form as he presented a merciful God who ultimately promises hope and restoration after disciplinary punishment and repentance. Amos is certainly not alone in foreseeing reinstatement, restoration, and recovery.

The message of Amos was the same as the message of other prophets. His was a warning voice; he called people to repentance. Unlike the abstract English word *repent* (which may suggest a passive regret or sorrow for sin), the sense of the Hebrew verb *šûb* is to *return* to God. Just as Moses had raised up a symbolic serpent in the wilderness and promised that as many as would look upon it should live (see Hel. 8:13–15), so now Amos, half a millennium later, actively admonished the nation of Israel to "seek the Lord, and ye shall live" (Amos 5:6).

8

THE BOOK OF HOSEA

S. KENT BROWN

Hosea lived during one of the most prosperous eras of ancient Israel's history and was a contemporary of the prophet Amos. But as his book reveals, his society was deeply marred by depravity and evil. His written record exhibits an extraordinary measure of tenderness and compassion which is combined with a stern resolve against wickedness and, particularly, corruption in high places.

Hosea's name means "deliverance" or "salvation" and, at its root, is connected with the names *Joshua* and *Jesus*. Of his parents and birth we know nothing except the name of his father, Beeri (Hosea 1:1). His prophetic work began before the death of Jeroboam II (746 B.C.) and may well have continued until the eve of the loss of the Northern Kingdom, Israel (721 B.C.), a span of approximately twenty-five years.[1]

The Hebrew text of Hosea's book, unfortunately, is very corrupted, making some passages difficult to grasp. Even so, it is certain that the key for comprehending all of Hosea's words lies in chapters 1 through 3, the report of his marriage to a harlot.

A brief outline of the content of the book of Hosea is as follows:

    I. Hosea's experience in marriage and the Lord's experience with Israel (1:1–3:5)

   II. The Lord's denunciations of Israel (4:1–9:9)

S. Kent Brown is professor of ancient scripture at Brigham Young University.

[1]The length of Hosea's ministry is a matter of discussion. For instance, Bernard W. Anderson, *Understanding the Old Testament*, 4th ed. (Englewood Cliffs, N.J.: Prentice-Hall, 1986), p. 304, holds to a view of a ten-year ministry. Others accept a longer period. See Sidney B. Sperry, *The Voice of Israel's Prophets* (Salt Lake City: Deseret Book Co., 1965), p. 274; and Roland K. Harrison, *Introduction to the Old Testament* (Grand Rapids, Mich.: Eerdmans, 1969), p. 860.

III. The history of divine grace and Israel's apostasy (9:10–13:16)
IV. Future hope for Israel (14:1–9)

Hosea's Marriage (Hosea 1–3)

The stunning sketch of the prophet's marriage consists of three parts: (1) an account in chapter 1 written in the third person, (2) words of the Lord in chapter 2 that draw an analogy between Israel's unfaithful conduct toward him and the infidelity of Hosea's wife, and (3) a second report of Hosea's union in chapter 3 written by the prophet himself, that is, in the first person. Differences among the views of interpreters have focused on how one is properly to understand the connection between the biographical narrative in chapter 1 and the autobiographical sketch in chapter 3. The narrative in chapter 1 reports the Lord's command to Hosea to marry a "wife of whoredoms" to whom were later born three children, whose names symbolized facets of the Lord's ruptured relationship with his people. The narrative in chapter 3 recounts the divine charge to Hosea that he love an adulteress, purchasing her and then confining her to his home, a virtual house arrest (Hosea 3:1–3).

Solutions proposed to explain the ties between the two reports include the hypothesis that Hosea unknowingly married a harlot and, later, retrospectively applied his resulting marital situation to that of the Lord and traitorous Israel. It is clear from the text, however, that the prophet knew beforehand that the woman was a harlot (Hosea 1:2; 3:1). Another interpretation has held that chapters 1 and 3 were to be understood as allegory. On this view, Hosea simply told a story to illustrate a point. But the accounts incorporate details that, if this were the case, remain in the story without function or comment, an unusual feature of allegory. For instance, the name of Hosea's wife, Gomer, does not have special significance for the story or its meaning. In addition, the second child was female and her weaning was specifically noted (Hosea 1:6, 8), but neither detail received further notice. Similarly, in Hosea 3:2 there was no allegorical interest in the price paid for the woman. Moreover, according to both Hosea 1:2 and 3:1, the word of the Lord was directing Hosea's actions.

The explanation that leaves fewer questions unresolved is the view that the two accounts (Hosea 1 and 3) are historical and the events in chapter 1 preceded those of chapter 3.[2] Accordingly, the sequence of events is to be understood as follows. The Lord commanded Hosea to marry a woman with an evil past. The first child born to their union was Hosea's (Hosea 1:3); the other two apparently were not (Hosea 1:6, 8). Even so, at the Lord's behest, all three were given symbolic names. After later abandoning Hosea, Gomer recognized her mistakes and wanted to return; but by then—one must infer—she had become a slave. The Lord directed Hosea to buy her back, a course which he pursued willingly, for he still loved her despite all. The prophet next disciplined Gomer by severely restricting her movements and associations with others before restoring her fully to her former status. On such a view, this sorrowful episode deepened Hosea's appreciation for the Lord's frustration at Israel's infidelity and apostasy, thus fashioning the prophet into an apt spokesman for the messages of divine disappointment and stern warning. In addition, this representation of Hosea's marital troubles fits a wider pattern perceptible in the Lord's dealings with his agents: he leads them through experiences that make them effective messengers for their time and place.[3]

The Lord's Anger and Its Reasons (Hosea 4–10; 12–13)

The ingredients of the prophet's message were tightly fused with his marriage situation and are to be found at the formal beginning of his prophetic remarks: "Hear the word of the Lord, ye children of Israel: for the Lord hath a controversy with the inhabitants of the land, because there is *no truth, nor mercy, nor knowledge of God* in the land" (Hosea 4:1; emphasis added).

The charge that "no truth" existed in the land was a broad incrimination, for it referred not only to the functioning of society on the basis of falsehood but also to the general lack of fidelity and personal integrity.

---

[2]A review of the various proposals for understanding Hosea 1 and 3 is to be found in Harold H. Rowley, "The Marriage of Hosea," in *Men of God* (London: Thomas Nelson, 1963), pp. 66–97. See also Kent P. Jackson, "The Marriage of Hosea and Jehovah's Covenant with Israel," in *Isaiah and the Prophets,* ed. M. S. Nyman (Provo, Utah: Religious Studies Center, Brigham Young University, 1984), pp. 58–60.

[3]See the observations of Abraham Heschel, *The Prophets* (Philadelphia: Jewish Publication Society, 1962), pp. 55–56.

The most serious display of infidelity, of course, consisted of idolatry, which was the rejection of Israel's God. "My people ask counsel at their stocks [of wood] . . . they sacrifice upon the tops of the mountains, and burn incense upon the hills, under oaks and poplars and elms. . . . Ephraim is joined to idols" (Hosea 4:12–13, 17). The spreading blanket of deceit had enveloped even the highest echelons of Israelite society: "They make the king glad with their wickedness, and the princes with their lies" (Hosea 7:3). Moreover, the priesthood had grown seriously corrupt: "And as troops of robbers wait for a man, so the company of priests murder in the way by consent: for they commit lewdness" (Hosea 6:9). Further, society had been convulsed by assassinations in high places (see 2 Kgs. 15:8–31):[4] "They are all hot as an oven, and have devoured their judges; all their kings are fallen" (Hosea 7:7); "they have set up kings, but not by me: they have made princes, and I knew it not" (Hosea 8:4); and "all their princes are revolters" (Hosea 9:15).

The clear evidence of treachery, of course, was linked closely with the second problem identified by Hosea, the lack of "mercy" or steadfast love.[5] For without fidelity or esteem for truth, natural human interactions would be compromised, calculating mistrust would replace trust, and crime supplant respect. "For I desired mercy, and not sacrifice," declared the Lord (Hosea 6:6). "There is [false] swearing, lying, killing, stealing, and committing adultery; they break all bounds and murder follows murder" (Hosea 4:2, RSV[6]). In fact, the situation had deteriorated so severely that all of creation was to be sickened: "Therefore shall the land mourn, and every one that dwelleth therein shall languish, with the beasts of

---

[4]The years following the death of Jeroboam II in 746 B.C. were chaotic. Disaster first struck Jeroboam's son, Zechariah, who reigned six months and was then murdered by Shallum, who himself held the throne for one month. Menahem (745–737 B.C.) murdered Shallum and held onto power by brutally repressing those who opposed him. Although Menahem died in his bed, his son and successor, Pekahiah, after ruling two years, was assassinated by his army commander Pekah, who in turn held the throne for about five years (736–732 B.C.). Pekah's reign was cut short by assassination. Hoshea, Pekah's successor and murderer, ruled during Israel's last few years before dying in Assyrian custody.

[5]The Hebrew term is *hesed*. It is translated variously as "covenant love," that is, love based in a covenant relationship (Henry J. Flanders, Jr., et al., *People of the Covenant*, 3d ed. [Oxford: Oxford University, 1988], pp. 313, 315; see also "Love in the OT," in *The Interpreter's Dictionary of the Bible*, 5 vols., ed. G. A. Buttrick, et al. [Nashville: Abingdon, 1962], 3:165, 167), and as "loving kindness" or "steadfast love." See Anderson, pp. 308–9.

[6]Revised Standard Version.

the field, and with the fowls of heaven; yea, the fishes of the sea also shall be taken away" (Hosea 4:3). To counter this threatened circumstance, the Lord appealed for a return to honorable affections and relationships by saying, "Sow for yourselves righteousness, reap the fruit of steadfast love" (Hosea 10:12, RSV) and "turn thou to thy God: keep mercy and judgment, and wait on thy God continually" (Hosea 12:6).

The Lord's third accusation, the deficiency of "knowing" God, was also linked to Hosea's marital ordeal. The Lord observed, "My people are destroyed for lack of knowledge: because thou hast rejected knowledge, I will also reject thee" (Hosea 4:6). Moreover, "I desired . . . the knowledge of God more than burnt offerings" (Hosea 6:6). The link between knowing God and the prophet's matrimonial predicament is made in Hosea 5:4: "for the spirit of whoredoms is in the midst of them, and they have not known the Lord." Importantly, Hosea was the first of the Old Testament prophets to correlate the covenant of marriage and the Lord's covenant with Israel, a characteristic whose implications have been spelled out by Abraham Heschel.[7] Harlotry, for the Lord, expressed the antithesis of his covenant. In his anger, he asserted that "the spirit of whoredoms hath caused [Israel] to err, and they have gone a whoring from under their God. . . . Therefore your daughters shall commit whoredom, and your spouses shall commit adultery" (Hosea 4:12–13). While the imagery is not enticing, the point is abundantly clear: straying from the covenant of the Lord is tantamount to abandoning one's marriage covenant, deserting one's spouse for a harlot. One additional component is formed by the concept that coming to "know the Lord" is analogous to coming to know one's spouse in a union that is born in a covenant and proven over time with fidelity, love, and mutual trust. Once again, harlotry constituted the opposite.[8]

Because of the seriousness of Israel's crimes, the Lord declared that "their deeds do not permit them to return to their God" (Hosea 5:4, RSV). Clearly, they were doomed. Because they had rejected the word of the prophets, they were as good as sepulchers: "Therefore have I hewed them by the prophets; I have slain them by the words of my mouth" (Hosea 6:5). Even so, there was hope, but not for Hosea's generation.

---

[7]Heschel, pp. 50–51.
[8]See Jackson, p. 60.

The Triumph of Divine Love and Mercy (Hosea 11; 14)

In a most notable passage in scripture, Hosea described the Lord's mixed feelings about his now recalcitrant people. Because Israel was "bent to backsliding from me," the Lord warned that "the sword shall abide on his cities, and shall consume his branches" (Hosea 11:6–7). On the other hand, long ago the Lord had brought an enslaved people out of Egypt (Hosea 11:1), and like a father with a toddler, he had taught Ephraim to walk (Hosea 11:3). His original feelings of parental love still persisted and, although he must punish his people, he vowed that he would check his anger: "How shall I give thee up, Ephraim? how shall I deliver thee, Israel?" (Hosea 11:8). Moreover, he resolved to restore their descendants to their ancestral home: "They shall tremble as a bird out of Egypt, and as a dove out of the land of Assyria: and I will place them in their houses, saith the Lord" (Hosea 11:11).

In his last effort to offer counsel and comfort, even in light of the certain punishment that Israel would experience, the prophet intoned: "O Israel, return unto the Lord thy God; . . . turn to the Lord: say unto him, Take away all [our] iniquity, and receive us graciously" (Hosea 14:1–2). Even though Israel would suffer consequences for wickedness, the Lord promised a blessed future: "I will heal their backsliding, I will love them freely: for mine anger is turned away from him. . . . His branches shall spread, and his beauty shall be as the olive tree. . . . They that dwell under his shadow shall return" (Hosea 14:4, 6–7). Thus would the stage be set for the fulfillment of the Lord's promise of the full flowering of his covenant with his people: "And I will betroth thee unto me for ever; yea, I will betroth thee unto me in righteousness, and in judgment, and in lovingkindness, and in mercies. I will even betroth thee unto me in faithfulness: and thou shalt know the Lord" (Hosea 2:19–20).

This final set of observations leads to a related issue, the emotions or feelings of God. Traditional Christian theology has held that God is not subject to passions or emotions. Although this idea has been challenged by some Christian theologians, it remains a strong tenet of Christian belief.[9] Squarely against this view of God's unemotional character

---

[9]See the summary article "Impassibility of God," in *The Oxford Dictionary of the Christian Church*, 2d ed., ed. F. L. Cross and E. A. Livingstone (Oxford: Oxford University, 1974), p. 694. The notion of God being "free from passions" derived from strands of Middle Platonic thought; see "God" and "Middle Platonism" in the *Encyclopedia of the Early Church*, 2 vols., ed. A. Di Berardino (New York: Oxford University, 1992), 1:355; 1:557–58.

stands Hosea's work. While the Lord threatens chastisement of his people through Hosea's message, he also expresses how he feels about carrying out such threats, using language laden with deep feeling: "How shall I give thee up, Ephraim? how shall I deliver thee, Israel? . . . My heart is turned toward thee, and my mercies are extended to gather thee. I will not execute the fierceness of mine anger, I will not return to destroy Ephraim; for I am God, and not man; the Holy One in the midst of thee" (JST Hosea 11:8–9).

From this passage one readily concludes that it pained the Lord to punish his children, even though they plainly deserved it. One finds similar divine expressions of grief in the prophecies of Jeremiah, spoken more than a century later to the inhabitants of Judah: "For the hurt of the daughter of my people am I hurt; I am black; astonishment hath taken hold on me. Is there no balm in Gilead; is there no physician there?" (Jer. 8:21–22; cf. 4:19–21; 10:19–21). As in the case of Hosea, one fundamental reason for God's threatened punishment in Jeremiah's day was the lack of knowing God: "They know not me, saith the Lord" (Jer. 9:3), and "My people is foolish, they have not known me" (Jer. 4:22). It is in latter-day scripture that the most graphic and memorable scene of God's sorrow over sin is depicted. Enoch described the following in a vision of the heavens: "The God of heaven looked upon the residue of the people, and he wept; and Enoch bore record of it" (Moses 7:28).

In each of these instances, God sorrowed for the wickedness of his children—wickedness which required a tough response on his part. Even so, it is clear from these sources that God has been pained at the prospect of punishing them. Consistently, he has been a God of love and compassion. "When Israel was a child, I loved him, and out of Egypt I called my son. . . . It was I who taught Ephraim to walk, I took them up in my arms; but they did not know that I healed them. I led them with cords of compassion, with the bands of love" (Hosea 11:1, 3–4, RSV).

9

THE BOOK OF MICAH

D. Kelly Ogden

Old Testament prophets are frequently categorized as "Major" or "Minor," according to the size of their writings rather than their quality. Though the book of Micah is relatively short, the prophet's words should not to be relegated to the status of minor importance. Some of his teachings are of major concern and value to us.

The name *Micah* (Hebrew, *mîkâ*) is an abbreviated form of Micaiah (Hebrew, *mîkāyāh* or *mîkāyāhû*), meaning, "Who is like Jehovah?" He was a Morasthite (Micah 1:1; Jer. 26:18), one who came from Moresheth-gath, about twenty-five miles southwest of Jerusalem in the Judahite Shephelah, near the border between Judah and Philistia (near Mareshah; see Map 9, LDS Bible). His ministry was during the reigns of Jotham, Ahaz, and especially Hezekiah, as corroborated in Jeremiah 26:18–19. He was, therefore, a contemporary of the prophets Isaiah and Hosea and somewhat later than Amos. All of their ministries reflect the same social and political backgrounds, and their messages necessarily depict the same social ills in the Israelite kingdoms. Micah's message concerned the capital cities Samaria (Israel) and Jerusalem (Judah). He prophesied the captivity of northern and southern Israelites, their ultimate restoration to the land, and the coming of the Messiah.

The book of Micah is written in polished Hebrew poetry with particular use of parallelism and word-play, a typical form and style for the prophets of Israel and Judah. Bible scholars have proposed various ways

D. Kelly Ogden is associate professor of ancient scripture at Brigham Young University.

to describe the organization of the book.[1] The following outline is, in my view, the most likely structure.

Three prophetic addresses:

Micah 1 through 3 — denunciations and punishments

Micah 4 through 5 — hope

Micah 6 through 7 — combination of doom and hope

Unlike some textual analysts, I can readily assert that the prophets pronounced both doom and hope — that condemnation and devastation were necessarily followed by consolation and restoration.[2]

Condemnation of Samaria and Jerusalem

The first three chapters of Micah contain a catalogue of the crimes of Samaria and Jerusalem. Though the two capital cities were supposed to be spiritual centers, Micah denounced them as sin centers, accusing them of countenancing and even inviting the worship of graven images and idols (Micah 1:7). There could be no greater affront to the God of Israel. The first two of the Ten Commandments that were thundered from Sinai were "No other gods" and "No graven images," yet Jeroboam had set up his golden bulls, and Ahab and Jezebel had erected a house of Baal right in Samaria. Ahab's sister (or daughter[3]) Athaliah married the king in Jerusalem, where the same worship was instituted. Micah continued: Israelites were working evil on their beds (Micah 2:1),

---

[1]See Paul J. Achtemeier, gen. ed., *Harper's Bible Dictionary* (San Francisco: Harper & Row, 1985), p. 633; John Merlin Powis Smith, *International Critical Commentary: A Critical and Exegetical Commentary on the Books of Micah, Zephaniah and Nahum* (Edinburgh: T. & T. Clark, 1911), pp. 8–9; Henry McKeating, *Cambridge Bible Commentary: The Books of Amos, Hosea and Micah* (London: Cambridge University, 1971), pp. 10–11; W. S. LaSor, D. A. Hubbard, F. W. Bush, *Old Testament Survey* (Grand Rapids, Mich.: Eerdmans, 1982), pp. 359–64.

[2]See the discussion of this matter in my treatment of the book of Amos in Chap. 7 of this volume.

[3]2 Kgs. 8:18 and 2 Chron. 21:6 seem to have Athaliah as the daughter of Ahab, though the passages may refer to someone else. But 2 Kgs. 8:26 and 2 Chron. 22:2 explicitly identify her as the daughter of Omri and thus a sister or half-sister of Ahab. John Bright points out: "Since her son was born ca. 864 (2 Kgs. 8:26), she could not have been the daughter of Ahab and Jezebel, who could scarcely have been married over ten years at the time. She may have been Ahab's daughter by an earlier marriage, or . . . a daughter of Omri who was raised by Ahab and Jezebel after the former's death." John Bright, *A History of Israel*, 3d ed. (Philadelphia: Westminster, 1981), p. 242, n. 38.

coveting and violently taking family properties (Micah 2:2), and forbidding true prophets to prophesy (Micah 2:6). Leaders were stripping and devouring the temporal and spiritual possessions of their people: "Hear, I pray you, O heads of Jacob, and ye princes of the house of Israel; Is it not for you to know judgment? Who hate the good, and love the evil; who pluck off their skin from off them, and their flesh from off their bones; Who also eat the flesh of my people, and flay their skin from off them; and they break their bones, and chop them in pieces" (Micah 3:1–3).

Micah accused the Israelites of encouraging false prophets to deceive and misguide the people (Micah 3:5), and he condemned the leaders who abhorred justice and who perverted equity, judging and teaching for money, and prophets who divined for money (Micah 3:9–11). Because of all these spiritual crimes, Micah pronounced specific catastrophes to overtake the two capital cities: "Therefore I will make Samaria as an heap of the field, and as plantings of a vineyard: and I will pour down the stones thereof into the valley, and I will discover [i.e., lay bare] the foundations thereof" (Micah 1:6). "Therefore shall Zion for your sake be plowed as a field, and Jerusalem shall become heaps" (Micah 3:12).

One needs only to visit the site of ancient Samaria to view the literal fulfillment of the prophet's words. The foundations of Samaria were laid bare by the Assyrian conquerors in 721 B.C. — during Micah's ministry — and Jerusalem, though spared for another century, was eventually desolated by the armies of Babylon (and centuries later, the Temple Mount was literally *plowed* by the Roman soldiers of Titus). In the predicted destruction of both cities, Micah used the word *heap,* which in Hebrew means "ruin." Both Samaria and Jerusalem were left a pile of ruins, the latter several times over.

Promise of Restoration

According to the prophetic pattern, Micah then shifted from doom and devastation to a message of hope. Though Zion, or Jerusalem, would certainly become a heap of ruins, yet just beyond that dark cloud that would hang heavy over the city, a ray of hope would shine forth. Zion would "go even to Babylon [but] there shalt thou be delivered; there the Lord shall redeem thee from the hand of thine enemies" (Micah 4:10).

Zion had to return from Babylon; she could not remain in the strange land. Before other great prophecies could be fulfilled she had to be reestablished in her own land. Micah now projected his vision into the latter-day future when the mountain of the house of the Lord (the temple) would be established in the top of the mountains, and many people and nations would flow to it to be taught of the ways of the God of Jacob, when the law would go forth from Zion, and the word of the Lord from Jerusalem (Micah 4:1–2). Micah went on to preview the millennial era, when instruments of war will be turned into implements of agriculture, and nations will not "learn war any more" (Micah 4:3), when "they shall sit every man under his vine and under his fig tree" (Micah 4:4), a figurative and formulaic expression of living comfortably, safely, and securely. We know that almost identical predictions of an era of peace and prosperity were voiced by Isaiah (Isa. 2:1–3). Indeed, the prophets Micah and Isaiah were contemporaries and likely knew each other's writings, but whether one prophet originally gave utterance to this mil-lennial scenario and the other prophet borrowed from those teachings is not known.

Prophecy of the Messiah

Micah again turned his prophetic eye to the future, this time some-what closer to his own day. The Messiah, God's own Son, would come to earth, and it was Micah who specified the location of his birth. All of the prophets wrote and prophesied of the Messiah (Jacob 7:11; Mosiah 13:33), but in the biblical writings of none but Micah do we have preserved the specific prediction of his birthplace: "But thou, Beth-lehem Ephratah, though thou be little among the thousands of Judah, yet out of thee shall he come forth unto me that is to be ruler in Israel; whose goings forth have been from of old, from everlasting" (Micah 5:2). There can be no mistaking: there is only one Bethlehem in Judah and there is only one ruler in Israel whose origins are from eternity. Even the chief priests and scribes understood clearly the prophecy when they quoted it upon Herod's inquiring where the Messiah should be born, and Herod was obviously convinced of the possibility, because he proceeded to issue his infamous order to exterminate the children around Bethlehem: "And they said unto him, In Bethlehem of Judaea: for thus it is written by the prophet, And thou Bethlehem, in the land of Juda, art not the least among the princes of Juda: for out of thee shall come a Governor, that shall rule [Greek, "shepherd," "tend," "nurture"] my people Israel" (Matt. 2:4–6).

Micah Quoted Elsewhere

We may judge some of the most valued parts of Micah's teachings by what was later quoted by others. Besides the possible quotation in Isaiah 2:1–3 and the one in Matthew just cited, we have a note in the book of Jeremiah, a century after Micah's time, affirming that Micah's ministry was effective in deterring the people from their predicted fate: "Micah the Morasthite prophesied in the days of Hezekiah king of Judah, and spake to all the people of Judah, saying, Thus saith the Lord of hosts; Zion shall be plowed like a field, and Jerusalem shall become heaps, and the mountain of the house as the high places of a forest. Did Hezekiah king of Judah and all Judah put him at all to death? did he not fear the Lord, and beseech the Lord and repent? and the Lord turned away the evil which he had pronounced against them" (JST Jer. 26:18–19).

Two passages from Micah were referred to by the Savior when he appeared to the Nephites and Lamanites. The first is from Micah 4:12–13 (cited in 3 Ne. 20:18–19), wherein the Lord, finding other nations gathering against Jerusalem and eyeing her as prey, declared: "But they know not the thoughts of the Lord, neither understand they his counsel: for he shall gather them as the sheaves into the floor. Arise and thresh, O daughter of Zion: for I will make thine horn iron, and I will make thy hoofs brass: and thou shalt beat in pieces many people: and I will consecrate their gain unto the Lord, and their substance unto the Lord of the whole earth."

The Lord was assuring his people that his purposes would be fulfilled. They will return from exile; they will be planted again in their land; they will exert their strength (as iron, brass, "beating in pieces," etc.) with the protection of the Lord, because his people must persist in the land in order to realize the promises to the fathers—for instance, that the Messiah would be born in Bethlehem and would minister to his people in their land.

The other passage is from Micah 5:8–15 (cited in 3 Ne. 20:16–17; 21:12–21), similar in tone to the previous one: "And the remnant of Jacob shall be among the Gentiles in the midst of many people as a lion among the beasts of the forest, as a young lion among the flocks of sheep: who, if he go through, both treadeth down, and teareth in pieces, and none can deliver. Thine hand shall be lifted up upon thine adversaries, and all thine enemies shall be cut off."

In contrast to the threatening, forceful imagery of these verses, the previous verse in Micah states that "the remnant of Jacob shall be in the midst of many people as a dew from the Lord, as the showers upon the grass" (Micah 5:7). In biblical imagery, dew and showers always suggest nourishment, peace, relief, and blessing. Apparently the remnant of Jacob in the latter days will also be a blessing to the Gentiles and promote the righteous life. But in ancient America, the Savior focused on the might and terror which he through the remnant of Jacob (now another branch of the house of Jacob) would strike in the hearts of their adversaries among the Gentiles (see 3 Ne. 20:16–19; 21:12–21).[4]

Great Teachings from Micah

Possibly the most sublime counsel the prophet Micah penned for the benefit of all generations was his rhetorical question of the Lord's expectation for his children, and the prophet's answer: "Will the Lord be pleased with thousands of rams, or with ten thousands of rivers of oil? . . . He hath shewed thee, O man, what is good; and what doth the Lord require of thee, but to do justly, and to love mercy, and to walk humbly with thy God?" (Micah 6:7–8).

Man was expected to emulate his God. Were the people of Judah

---

[4]Many of the predictions of such ancient prophets of Israel as Micah, Isaiah, and others have multiple fulfillment or multiple adaptation. Prophetic utterances are sometimes used in different contexts in different dispensations. Micah's words about the remnant of Israel could very well apply both to antiquity and to futurity. For further discussion of the context of Micah's words in the Book of Mormon, see Joseph F. McConkie, "The Final Gathering to Christ," in *Studies in Scripture, Volume Eight: Alma 30 to Moroni,* ed. Kent P. Jackson (Salt Lake City: Deseret Book Co., 1988), pp. 185–87.

and Israel just and merciful and walking humbly with God? Another catalogue of crimes suggests that they were not: they used wicked balances and deceitful weights (Micah 6:11), rich men were full of violence and lies (Micah 6:12), and they followed the statutes of Omri and the works of the house of Ahab (Micah 6:16).[5] These crimes bring on the punishment of desolation, hissing, and reproach (Micah 6:16).

Notwithstanding the crime and the punishment, God would show his people how to be just and also how to be merciful. Perhaps it is at this point where the name of the prophet *Micah* figures in his message: "Who is like Jehovah?"—for greatness and mercy and compassion? In the end he will fulfill all the Abrahamic covenants, he will bestow all the promised blessings upon Israel. Micah concluded: "Who is a God like unto thee, that pardoneth iniquity, and passeth by the transgression of the remnant of his heritage? he retaineth not his anger for ever, because he delighteth in mercy. He will turn again, he will have compassion upon us; he will subdue our iniquities; and thou wilt cast all their sins into the depths of the sea. Thou wilt perform the truth to Jacob, and the mercy to Abraham, which thou hast sworn unto our fathers from the days of old" (Micah 7:18–20).

---

[5]The "statutes of Omri and the works of the house of Ahab" are partially described in 1 Kgs. 16:25–33. The excesses of these two kings became proverbial in ancient Israel because of their moral and religious perversions, endorsing and sponsoring pagan practices of idolatry.

10

THE REIGN OF HEZEKIAH

(2 Kings 18–20; 2 Chronicles 29–32)

Andrew C. Skinner

The life of Hezekiah, king of Judah, dramatically validates the Lord's declaration in 2 Kings 17 that he delivers his people from difficulties and prospers them when they honor him (2 Kgs. 17:39; 18:11–12). Almost immediately upon ascending the throne, Hezekiah, unlike his father Ahaz, began enjoying the constant help of the Lord. Thus he prospered in all he did (2 Chron. 32:21; 2 Kgs. 18:7). Hezekiah's righteous rule was a repudiation of all that his wicked father had stood for. His twenty-nine year reign (715–687 B.C.) was such that the author of 2 Kings 18 ranked him as the greatest king Judah had ever known or ever would know (2 Kgs. 18:3–5). Chronicles devotes more attention to Hezekiah than any other king since Solomon, including three chapters dedicated to his good deeds and inspired leadership (2 Chron. 29–31).

Hezekiah's Religious Reform (2 Chron. 29–31)

At the heart of the Chronicler's admiration for Hezekiah's rule was the monarch's religious reform. Numerous parallels in Chronicles between Hezekiah and the great king Solomon suggest that the Chronicler may have viewed Hezekiah as a "second Solomon." Wasting no time (beginning in the very first month of his reign, as the text says) Hezekiah reopened, repaired, and repurified the temple (2 Chron. 29:3, 15–19). He revitalized the Levites and Aaronic priests and reestablished proper

Andrew C. Skinner is assistant professor of ancient scripture at Brigham Young University.

sacrificial worship (2 Chron. 29:4–12, 20–36). Last but not least, Hezekiah decreed a Passover celebration that sought to bring together all the tribes of Israel for the first time since Solomon's days, even delaying the date of its celebration one month to coincide with the deferred Passover of the Northern Kingdom's calendar (2 Chron. 30).

Following through with the parallel to Solomon, the Chronicler subtly mentioned the rewards of Hezekiah's loyalty to Jehovah: wealth (2 Chron. 32:27–29), magnified respect in the eyes of all the gentile nations (2 Chron. 32:23), and an expanded dominion — much more than his predecessors had experienced (2 Chron. 30:25). All of these were also enjoyed by Solomon in his righteous days.

While Hezekiah's reforms may not seem like much to modern Saints who live under the gospel covenant, those reforms engendered in the people of Judah far more righteousness than had existed for several years. Hezekiah explained to the priests and Levites that the Lord's past anger against Judah (and hence their political and social woes) were traceable to their forefathers' defilement of God's holy house (2 Chron. 29:6–9). The message, therefore, seems clear for every group in every dispensation which has placed itself in a covenant relationship to God through temple ordinances: community well-being depends on purity and exactness in temple worship (2 Chron. 29:10–11).

The Assyrian Threat (2 Kgs. 18–19; 2 Chron. 32:1–22)

Upon the death of Sargon II in 705 B.C., Hezekiah decided to break altogether from the grasp of Assyria (2 Kgs. 18:7). In 701 B.C. Sargon's son, Sennacherib (704–681 B.C.), invaded Judah to crush the rebellion. Before approaching Jerusalem, he attacked and conquered all the other fortified cities of Judah (2 Kgs. 18:13) — forty-six, according to Assyrian royal records.[1] Judging from the narrative of 2 Kings 18:13–16, things were perilous for Hezekiah. But 2 Chronicles 32 provides additional important information that shows that he was able to face the challenge.

In wise anticipation of a potential Assyrian invasion of Jerusalem,

---

[1]James B. Pritchard, ed., *Ancient Near Eastern Texts Relating to the Old Testament*, 3d ed. with Supplement (Princeton: Princeton University, 1969), p. 288.

Hezekiah consulted with his advisers to carry out life-saving plans. The fortifications of the city were repaired, and a secret tunnel (now commonly called Hezekiah's Tunnel) was dug through solid rock to bring into the city the waters of the Gihon Spring, which bubbled in the Kidron Valley outside the city walls (2 Kgs. 20:20; 2 Chron. 32:4, 30).[2]

As the systematic destruction of the kingdom of Judah reached a crescendo, Sennacherib took personal charge of the siege of Lachish, the last remaining crucial fortified city that guarded the southern route to Jerusalem.[3] During this time, Hezekiah encouraged his military commanders with a message of comfort and courage: "Be strong and courageous, be not afraid nor dismayed for the king of Assyria, nor for all the multitude that is with him: *for there be more with us than with him:* With him is an arm of flesh; but with us is the Lord our God to help us, and to fight our battles" (2 Chron. 32:7–8; emphasis added). The account in 2 Kings reports that Hezekiah also made a bid for peace. He sent tribute to the Assyrian king encamped at Lachish in an attempt to induce the Assyrians to go home. The tribute included the silver from the temple treasury as well as the gold overlay from the temple doors and pillars (2 Kgs. 18:14–16). While it is likely that we do not have the whole story, it appears that Hezekiah sent tribute as a way of stalling for time to complete the last of his preparations for defense against an expected siege.

Hezekiah's tribute payment hardly satisfied Sennacherib. He later sent two officials, his *Rab-saris* or "army commander" and his *Rab-shakeh* or "chief chamberlain,"[4] to intimidate and humiliate both the leaders and the people of Judah into submission. They said, in effect: "We have already destroyed other lands; we have already destroyed your territory; you are the last to hold out. Your feeble god cannot possibly deliver you,

---

[2]Hezekiah's tunnel is an ancient engineering marvel (see Map 17, LDS Bible). It is almost eighteen hundred feet long and was constructed by work crews using hammer, wedge, and pickaxe, digging from opposite starting points three hundred feet beneath the surface of the ground and meeting in the middle. The repository end of the tunnel is the Pool of Siloam. In 1880 an inscription was discovered at the point where the two crews met. Though only six lines long, the inscription is the longest monumental text in early Hebrew and is now preserved in the Instanbul Museum. For a discussion of the text of the inscription and a good translation, see D. Winton Thomas, *Documents from Old Testament Times* (New York: Harper Torchbooks, 1961), pp. 209–11.

[3]There were three great destructions of Lachish. The first occurred during the Israelite conquest under Joshua (Josh. 10:3, 23, 26, 32); the second by Sennacherib in 701 B.C. (2 Chron. 32:9); and the third was completed by the Babylonians in 587 B.C. (Jer. 34:6–7).

[4]These are titles, not names.

just as the gods of other lands could not deliver them. Give up and resign yourselves to the inevitable" (see 2 Kgs. 18:17–36).

Hezekiah turned to what he knew was his only salvation—the Lord. He himself went to the temple and sent messengers to the prophet Isaiah (2 Kgs. 19:1–5). The Lord's word through his prophet was one of assurance: "Be not afraid" (2 Kgs. 19:6). In fervent prayer at the temple, Hezekiah petitioned the Lord for deliverance (2 Kgs. 19:14–19). Isaiah responded again in behalf of Jehovah with a longer oracle against Assyria, rich in powerful poetic imagery (2 Kgs. 19:20–34). Jerusalem could "laugh" Assyria "to scorn," he said, for the invaders had not offended mere mortals; they had "reproached and blasphemed" the Holy One of Israel (2 Kgs. 19:21–22). Concerning Assyria's king, "he shall not come into this city, nor shoot an arrow there, nor come before it with shield, nor cast a bank against it. By the way that he came, by the same shall he return, and shall not come into this city, saith the Lord. For I will defend this city, to save it" (2 Kgs. 19:32–34).

Through divine intervention, Sennacherib did abandon his planned attack on Jerusalem. At night an "angel of the Lord went out, and smote in the camp of the Assyrians an hundred fourscore and five thousand: and when they who were left arose early in the morning" they found the bodies of those who were smitten (JST 2 Kgs. 19:35). Some scholars have proposed that an epidemic struck the Assyrian troops. Others postulate that rumors of revolt back home forced Sennacherib to pull out. An interesting reason for the Assyrian withdrawal was proffered by the ancient Greek historian Herodotus: "[A] number of field mice, pouring in among their enemies, devoured their quivers and their bows, the handles of their shields; so that on the next day, when they fled bereft of their arms, many of them fell."[5] Whatever method the Lord used, the Assyrian demise was an act of God, in clear fulfillment of prophetic promises. It is imperative that its message not be obscured: the Lord delivers his righteous people "out of the hand of all [their] enemies" (2 Kgs. 17:39).

Sennacherib's death also occurred as Isaiah had predicted (2 Kgs. 19:7, 36–37). He was assassinated in 681 B.C. as a result of some palace

[5]Herodotus, *Histories* 2.141; quoted in Robert and Helen Howe, *The Ancient World* (White Plains, N.Y.: Longman, 1988), p. 36.

intrigue, and his son Esarhaddon (680–669 B.C.) came to the throne, followed by Ashurbanipal (668–627 B.C.). After that, Assyria's power was soon eclipsed by that of Babylon.[6]

I Have Heard Thy Prayer
(2 Kgs. 20; 2 Chron. 32:24–33)

The record of Hezekiah in 2 Kings includes an episode in which he learned by revelation of his imminent death (2 Kgs. 20:1–11). With faith he asked the Lord to grant him continued life, and he was promised fifteen more years. "I have heard thy prayer," the Lord said, and "I will heal thee" (2 Kgs. 20:5). Hezekiah was also granted a sign that it would be so.

Along with Hezekiah's many good points, the authors of Kings and Chronicles candidly recorded some things he did wrong (e.g., 2 Chron. 32:25–26). He made a big mistake when he showed his kingdom's wealth to the messengers of Babylon, for in due time, as Isaiah pointed out to him, the Babylonians would return to take possession of it (2 Kgs. 20:12–18; 2 Chron. 32:31).

But even with weaknesses, Hezekiah clearly was one of the greatest — perhaps *the* greatest, as our historian suggested (2 Kgs. 18:5) — of all the kings who ever presided over Israel and Judah, including David and Solomon. He was great because he trusted in the Lord and governed his kingdom in harmony with the divine will, following the guidance of the prophet whom the Lord sent to assist him. Here was a king on the throne of his father David who exemplified righteous kingship. In that way, he foreshadowed to a degree the greatest of all rulers, his future descendant Jesus Christ, who one day would come as King of Kings.

---

[6]For a discussion of some chronological questions concerning Sennacherib's invasion(s) of Judah, see John Bright, *A History of Israel,* 3d ed. (Philadelphia: Westminster, 1981), pp. 278–88, 298–309.

11

AUTHORSHIP OF THE BOOK OF ISAIAH

KENT P. JACKSON

The book of Isaiah has been the subject of intense study by Bible scholars for the past two centuries. As could be predicted, a variety of biases and approaches has yielded a variety of conclusions. One common interpretation among critical scholars is that the book in its present state is not the product of one author but of two, three, or perhaps more.[1] Given the preconceptions of its proponents, this multiple-authorship proposal is inevitable, but the major supposition upon which it is based is clearly false. And for Latter-day Saints, the Book of Mormon provides strong evidence on behalf of the essential unity of the book as we have it.

Approaches to Isaiah

Though several different approaches to dividing Isaiah have been set forth, the following is the most common system:

First Isaiah—chapters 1 through 39: From Isaiah son of Amoz, ca. 740–700 B.C. (chaps. 1–35); plus an extended excerpt from 2 Kings (chaps. 36–39)

Kent P. Jackson is professor of ancient scripture at Brigham Young University.

[1]Good summaries are provided in W. S. LaSor, D. A. Hubbard, F. W. Bush, *Old Testament Survey* (Grand Rapids, Mich.: Eerdmans, 1982), pp. 371–77; R. K. Harrison, *Introduction to the Old Testament* (Grand Rapids, Mich.: Eerdmans, 1969), pp. 764–80; B. W. Anderson, *Understanding the Old Testament*, 4th ed. (Englewood Cliffs, N.J.: Prentice-Hall, 1986), pp. 321–23, 472–75, 502–6.

Second Isaiah—chapters 40 through 55: From an anonymous prophet (often called Deutero-Isaiah) during the Babylonian exile, ca. 540 B.C.[2]

Third Isaiah—chapters 56 through 66: From one or more anonymous disciples of Second Isaiah after the return from exile, ca. 515 B.C. Some commentators include these chapters under Deutero-Isaiah.

According to the proponents of multiple authorship, the anonymous Second and Third Isaiah materials became attached to Isaiah's writings probably because the succeeding prophets were disciples of the first, and the entire collection was viewed as representing one specific branch of prophetic tradition. Scholars who hold to the theory generally do so for the following major reasons:

1. Unlike First Isaiah, the prophecies in Second and Third Isaiah make no mention of Isaiah's name and give no other biographical clues that would link them to him.

2. The historical setting of Second and Third Isaiah is different from that of First Isaiah, as in the following examples: (a) Cyrus, a Persian king who lived more than a century after Isaiah, is mentioned by name; (b) emphasis is placed on the power of the Babylonians, who in Isaiah's day were neither powerful nor very important politically; (c) the cities of Judah are described as already being destroyed, seemingly reflecting circumstances a century after Isaiah; (d) the temple is described as already being in ruins, though it was not destroyed until 587 B.C.; (e) the Israelites are described as already being punished and exiled, which events took place after 587 B.C.

3. The theological perspective is different: there is a shift from judgment to reconciliation. The theme of God's coming judgment is indeed found in the last half of the book, but it does not receive the emphasis there that it does in chapters 1 through 35. Similarly, though forgiveness and reconciliation are found in First Isaiah, in chapters 40 through 66 they predominate.

4. The literary style of chapters 40 through 66 differs from that of the earlier chapters.

These are interesting observations, and for the most part they accurately represent the change in tone that begins in chapter 40. But by

---

[2]Anderson assigns chapters 34 through 35 to Deutero-Isaiah also; p. 322.

no means do they constitute grounds for denying the material in chapters 40 through 66 to Isaiah son of Amoz.

Prophetic Foresight

The fundamental issue in the multiple-authorship theory is whether or not a prophet can see beyond his own time. Those who begin with the supposition that men cannot see beyond their own day *must* logically conclude that Isaiah could not have written those sections of the book that speak to a different historical setting from his own. But those who understand the true nature of revelation and prophetic foresight have no trouble with prophecies of future events. Latter-day Saints are blessed with abundant evidence revealed in the latter days that shows that God can indeed inspire his servants with views of future days and, when appropriate, they impart that vision to others.

Some responses to the question of authorship include the following:

1. It is true that Isaiah's name is never mentioned after chapter 39, but neither do the later chapters ascribe authorship to anyone else. The earliest known translation of Isaiah (the Greek Septuagint, third century B.C.) and the earliest existing manuscript of Isaiah (the Isaiah Scroll from Qumran) both include all the material now found in the book of Isaiah. In fact, no ancient document—including the New Testament and the rabbinic literature—shows any hint that readers in antiquity questioned Isaiah's authorship of the entire book.[3] The fact that the material is found in the book of Isaiah—and has been as far back as the evidence can be traced—clearly places the burden of proof on those who choose to assign it to other authors.

2. The material in chapters 40 through 66 does seem to address, to a degree, historical circumstances different from those of Isaiah's day. In the Book of Mormon we find a similar situation. President Ezra Taft Benson reminded the Church in 1986 that the Book of Mormon "was written for our day,"[4] adding his witness on that topic to those expressed

---

[3]The earliest known suggestion of multiple authorship comes from Rabbi Ibn-Ezra in the twelfth century A.D.

[4]In Conference Report, Oct. 1986, p. 5; or Ezra Taft Benson, "The Book of Mormon—Keystone of Our Religion," in *Studies in Scripture, Volume Seven: 1 Nephi to Alma 29*, ed. Kent P. Jackson (Salt Lake City: Deseret Book Co., 1987), p. 5.

by the book's authors. Moroni explained: "Behold, I speak unto you as if ye were present, and yet ye are not. But behold, Jesus Christ hath shown you unto me, and I know your doing" (Morm. 8:35). Because the Nephite writers saw and understood *our* time, they also wrote to meet *our* needs, not exclusively those of their contemporaries, who would never see the Book of Mormon as we have it. I find in the book of Isaiah a striking parallel: Isaiah saw and understood the circumstances of his countrymen a century and a half after his death, and through the inspiration of heaven he wrote in their behalf, as he also did for his contemporaries. But his scope does not stop there. He also saw our own latter-day setting, and the powerful witness that he left in his record speaks, when appropriately "likened" unto us, to our generation as well (see 1 Ne. 19:23).

3. I, too, perceive a significant shift in tone and subject matter that begins in Isaiah 40, and I believe that the shift was deliberate. In the prophetic books, as a general rule, prophecies of judgment and punishment precede those of blessing and restoration. That organization is true of individual prophecies and chapters as well as of entire books. This order of things mirrors real life, particularly the history of the house of Israel: God's judgment would be the inevitable consequence of Israel's rebellion; but in the latter days Israel would repent, be gathered and restored, and would enjoy full reconciliation with its God. It seems likely that Isaiah's prophecies were meant to follow the same sequence. We should not be surprised if he prepared two collections of revelations (or if his disciples arranged them later) — one, chapters 1 through 39, a "Book of Judgment," and the other, chapters 40 through 66, a "Book of Reconciliation."[5]

4. Even conservative scholars who argue for the unity of the entire book note some stylistic differences between First and Second (and Third) Isaiah. More significant, however, is that even critical scholars who argue for multiple authorship see a great deal of Isaiah son of Amoz throughout the entire collection, pointing to "Isaianic" themes that were carried on by Deutero-Isaiah and his successors.[6] Moreover, almost all of Isaiah was

---

[5]The book of Ezekiel contains an unmistakable shift in tone that begins after the prophet learned that Jerusalem had fallen (Ezek. 33:21). The earlier part of the book is a message of doom for Judah and other nations. The latter part is, for the most part, a message of future hope.

[6]E.g., Anderson, pp. 504–6.

written in poetry, and Hebrew poetry has sufficient flexibility to allow an author a wide range of literary options. Thus arguments for different literary styles are inconclusive, especially since we do not know the history of Isaiah's words once they left his mouth or his pen.

5. Those who believe in the Book of Mormon have additional evidence for the essential unity of the book of Isaiah, at least through chapter 55. When Lehi and his family left Jerusalem, they took with them the plates of brass, which contained, among other things, the writings of Isaiah, who preceded them by about one hundred years. The Nephite authors quoted extensively from Isaiah and included in the Book of Mormon all or part of the following chapters of Isaiah: 2 through 14, 28 and 29, 40, and 48 through 55.[7] The Book of Mormon thus proves that at least those chapters were known to be the writings of Isaiah when Lehi left Jerusalem in 600 B.C. — many decades *before* Second and Third Isaiah were supposed to have been written.[8] This, in my view, is the most important piece of evidence for Isaiah's authorship of later chapters.

An Anthology of Prophetic Thought

Latter-day Saints, who accept the evidence from the Book of Mormon and believe that prophets can write to future generations, should have no difficulty accepting the essential unity of the book of Isaiah as the product of Isaiah son of Amoz from the eighth century B.C. Yet many interesting questions about it remain to be answered.

The noted Old Testament scholar W. F. Albright pointed out that the prophetic books are not books but "anthologies of oracles and sermons."[9] This description certainly fits the book of Isaiah. Like the Bible itself, it is not a book but a collection. And, as with the Bible itself, the circumstances under which it was written and compiled are not clearly known. Did Isaiah record his prophecies himself, or did he dictate them to scribes? If they were dictated, was Isaiah responsible for their final

---

[7]Monte S. Nyman, *"Great Are the Words of Isaiah"* (Salt Lake City: Bookcraft, 1980), pp. 283–87.

[8]Since nothing from "Third Isaiah" is contained in the Nephite record, the Book of Mormon argument cannot be used to prove Isaiah's authorship of chapters 56 through 66.

[9]William F. Albright, *From the Stone Age to Christianity*, 2d ed. (Garden City, N.Y.: Doubleday/Anchor, 1957), p. 275.

poetic structure, or were others? Did Isaiah gather and compile the revelations himself, or did others do it? Were they collected in his lifetime, or later? Were they edited or reworded by later scribes?[10] Though the answers to these questions are not critical for our understanding of Isaiah's message, they may explain such things as changes in emphasis, organization, and literary style of the revelations that make up the book of Isaiah.[11]

---

[10]A rabbinic tradition (*Baba Bathra* 15a) states that the book was compiled by "Hezekiah and his company." Hezekiah was the king of Judah during a significant portion of Isaiah's ministry.

[11]An interesting parallel is *Teachings of the Prophet Joseph Smith*, the standard collection of sermons and writings of the Prophet. It was compiled and edited by Elder Joseph Fielding Smith almost one hundred years after the Prophet's death. He used as his sources documents collected both during and after the Prophet's lifetime, some of which had been edited substantially. No one would argue that Joseph Smith was responsible for the final form of *Teachings of the Prophet Joseph Smith*, even though he was the author of its content.

12

GOD IS WITH US

(ISAIAH 1–17)

KEITH A. MESERVY

Through the Nephites, the Savior challenged us to search the prophecies of Isaiah with diligence, because his words are so "great" (3 Ne. 23:1). They inspire visions, open vistas, challenge laborers, enlighten thinkers, give courage, instill faith, encourage repentance, inspire compassion, and lead ultimately to God. Thus, says the divine Literary Critic, Isaiah's words are *great*.[1]

Isaiah's ministry overlapped the reigns of "Uzziah, Jotham, Ahaz, and Hezekiah, kings of Judah" (Isa. 1:1; approximately 742–700 B.C.[2]). He appeared at a point in history when God's work seemed about to collapse. The chosen people had forsaken the Lord to worship idols, and they were imitating the ways of the world and doing wicked things. Both kingdoms, Israel and Judah, consequently felt of God's wrath: citizens of the Northern Kingdom along with many of the Southern Kingdom were carried into Assyrian captivity; the land of promise was made desolate, and so few people remained that Isaiah could lament that had God not left them "a very small remnant," they would have been as Sodom and Gomorrah (Isa. 1:9). The covenant people were not carrying out their

---

Keith A. Meservy is professor emeritus of ancient scripture at Brigham Young University.

[1]Latter-day Saint commentaries on Isaiah include Victor L. Ludlow, *Isaiah: Prophet, Seer, and Poet* (Salt Lake City: Deseret Book Co., 1982); and Monte S. Nyman, *"Great Are the Words of Isaiah"* (Salt Lake City: Bookcraft, 1980). Other helpful (and conservative) commentaries include Edward J. Young, *The Book of Isaiah*, 3 vols. (Grand Rapids, Mich.: Eerdmans, 1965); and Homer Hailey, *A Commentary on Isaiah, with Emphasis on the Messianic Hope* (Grand Rapids, Mich.: Baker, 1985).

[2]A rabbinic tradition dates Isaiah's death to the reign of Hezekiah's son Manasseh, in which case he would have died no earlier than 687 B.C.

mission to bless the nations of the earth and were resisting all of God's efforts to reclaim them.

It was at this point that Isaiah was called to remind the Lord's people of fundamental truths: God knows the end from the beginning, his purposes are fixed, he had known the Israelites from the first and knew how well they would serve his purposes. He would yet fulfill the promises he had made to Abraham, Isaac, and Jacob, for in the last days he would reconstitute Israel as his people in their land of promise, and again they would teach all nations about God and his ways. In the meantime, each rising generation would know from reading Isaiah's prophecies why they had been separated from their land and why they must never despair of enjoying the blessings that God had promised their forefathers. Isaiah's vision of God at work in bringing about his just and righteous purposes builds faith and hope in the hearts of his readers, and that has caused his prophecies to be recognized as a magnificent message of consolation.

Isaiah's Call (Isa. 6)

Isaiah's call to be a prophet came in a vision of the Lord in the temple. Standing in the presence of his holy Lord caused him to feel keenly how unworthy he was (Isa. 6:5). But in words reminiscent of the Savior's, his "Here am I; send me" (Isa. 6:8) shows how quickly he responded to whatever call the Lord might give him (cf. Abr. 3:27). The Lord cleansed Isaiah symbolically by using a burning coal to take away his sins (Isa. 6:6–7). Obviously, the searing action was a visionary experience, but Isaiah's personal sense that he had been purified from his sins would have strengthened his own witness that scarlet sins can be made white (Isa 1:18).

Isaiah was introduced to a key aspect of his ministry when he was charged to tell the people, "Hear ye indeed" and "See ye indeed" (Isa. 6:9). But, as the superior reading in the Book of Mormon indicates, "they understood not" and "they perceived not" (2 Ne. 16:9). He was charged to "make the heart of this people fat, and make their ears heavy, and shut their eyes; lest they see with their eyes, and hear with their ears, and understand with their heart, and convert, and be healed" (Isa. 6:10). That did not mean, of course, that Isaiah was to make seeing people become blind. The blindness referred to in this book and by Jesus in his ministry refers to people who have eyes to see but who prefer to walk in darkness. When Isaiah provided revelation and light from God for that generation and they chose to walk in darkness, they, not God, inflicted blindness upon themselves (cf. John 9:40–41; see also Alma 29:4–5; D&C 93:31–32, 38–39; John 3:19–20).

Isaiah's generation loved darkness and hated light. He called them "rebellious," "lying" people who refused to "hear the law of the Lord: Which say to the seers, See not; and to the prophets, Prophesy not unto us right things, speak unto us smooth things, prophesy deceits: Get you out of the way, turn aside out of the path, cause the Holy One of Israel to cease from before us" (Isa. 30:9–11; cf. John 12:46). When Isaiah offered them light and they preferred darkness — to be spiritually blind — they were bringing upon themselves God's judgments.

Isaiah and his contemporary Micah were not privileged to work the whitened fields (see Micah 7:1–7); rather, they prepared a fallen people for the judgments at hand. According to the general sense of all scripture, a loving and merciful God encourages sinners to repent and return to him; he encourages rather than discourages repentance and conversion. Thus there must be something wrong with a translation or text that suggests that God wanted the Israelites to fail, so that they would not "see with their eyes, and hear with their ears, and understand with their heart, and convert, and be healed" by God (Isa. 6:10).

But after the judgments were meted out, just as surely as foliage returns to a tree when spring returns, so surely will a tenth of the remnant of Israel return (Isa. 6:13). This major theme of Isaiah explains one reason why he gave his son the name of Shear-jashub, "a remnant will return" (Isa. 7:3; 8:18).

The Great Arraignment (Isa. 1)

Leviticus 26 and Deuteronomy 28 through 30 provide the covenant background for understanding all the book of Isaiah. When the Lord gave the land of promise to the Israelites, he promised that they would stay free because he would not permit the sword of the enemy to penetrate their land. But this promise was based on a very big "if": if they would

keep the covenant they had made to serve him and keep his commandments (Ex. 24:3–8; Deut. 29, esp. vv. 10–15). If, however, they failed
to serve him, he would give the enemy power over them.

In Isaiah's time, when the Israelites were no longer faithful to their
covenant commitments, their country had already been overrun by the
Assyrians, their land devastated, and their people carried into captivity.
Thus Isaiah wondered why they would want to continue in their evil
ways and "be stricken any more" (Isa. 1:5; see Lev. 26:14–32, esp. vv.
18, 21, 24, 28).

Isaiah 1 is Israel's great arraignment before God — a courtroom scene
in which Israel is the accused and God is the prosecutor and the judge.
It introduces us to Isaiah's audience and shows us, especially in verses
21 through 25, what Nephi called "the manner of the Jews," which
means the manner of Jewish life. Nephi insisted that the works of the
Jews "were works of darkness, and their doings were doings of abominations" (2 Ne. 25:2). Their deeds revealed their evil hearts. Isaiah
characterized them as being a "sinful nation, a people laden with iniquity,
a seed of evildoers, children that are corrupters: they have forsaken the
Lord, they have provoked the Holy One of Israel unto anger, they are
gone away backward" (Isa. 1:4; see also 1:15; 59:3–7). They were a lying
and a violent generation that murdered to satisfy the proud, covetous
demands of their hearts. Justice, truth, and equity, all building-blocks
of civilization, were personified as being alien to them: "Judgment is
turned away backward, and justice standeth afar off: for truth is fallen
in the street, and equity cannot enter. Yea, truth faileth" (Isa. 59:14–
15). Israelites, called to be exemplars and lights to that generation, were
negative models (see Isa. 2:5–9; 5:4; 59:1–4; Micah 7:1–4). Consequently, "Your country is desolate, your cities are burned with fire: your
land, strangers devour it in your presence, and it is desolate, as overthrown
by strangers. . . . And when ye spread forth your hands [in prayer], I
will hide mine eyes from you: yea, when ye make many prayers, I will
not hear" (Isa. 1:7, 15).

Like Jesus, the prophet-poet Isaiah used metaphor to express his
divinely inspired perception of Israel and its needs. In chapter 1, he
portrayed Israel as being mortally ill but having neither means nor helpers
to provide healing, even while rejecting divine remedies. Again, it was
a matter of pride — trusting self-sufficient remedies that were inadequate

while excluding divine remedies that would have worked (Isa. 1:5–9; cf. Lev. 26:14–18). They trusted in their own wisdom and power rather than in the living God. They rejected the light and power that came from God while worshipping the silent, impotent idols created in human minds and formed by finite hands.[3] Though idolatrous, they still performed aspects of Mosaic temple worship, causing Isaiah to wonder "to what purpose" they were doing it. Did they think they could walk away from God to live in darkness, to lie and do violent deeds, and then come to God's holy house and perform some rites that would reconcile them to him? "To what purpose is the multitude of your sacrifices unto me? saith the Lord" (Isa. 1:11; see vv. 11–14).

Isaiah offered Israel the chance to be healed. His remedies were simple: "Cease to do evil; Learn to do well; seek judgment [i.e., justice], relieve the oppressed, judge the fatherless, plead for the widow." Then God would come back into their lives: "Though your sins be as scarlet, they shall be as white as snow; though they be red like crimson, they shall be as wool" (Isa. 1:16–18).

Old Testament prophets used the treatment of widows and orphans within the community as a litmus test of how righteous the community itself was (e.g., Isa. 1:23). If society respected the rights of those who were most vulnerable, the society was good. On the other hand, if powerful people bribed the judge, twisted judgment, and overrode the rights of the defenseless to satisfy their own ambitions, then society was in trouble with the God of justice (Isa. 10:1–4). Only Zion-like people, that is, pure-hearted people, dwell in the presence of a pure-in-heart God (see Matt. 5:8; D&C 93:1). This truth was illustrated when Enoch and his people became pure in heart: a pure and holy God came to dwell in their midst (Moses 7:16–19). God is holy and likes company. He called Israel to be holy, promising them that if they would become holy, he would live among them (Lev. 19:2; Ex. 22:31; 25:8; 29:42–46).

In this light, God's sacred covenants with Israel were likened by the prophets to a marriage covenant wherein God and Israel, the marriage partners, were committed by covenant to be faithful to each other, even

---

[3]See Isa. 44:10–19, especially v. 17. Cf. also chap. 40, in which the majesty, intelligence, and power of God (vv. 1–31) are contrasted with things made by human hands (vv. 19–20). How could God be likened to any of them? (vv. 18–25).

as a husband and wife are faithful to each other. Thus, Jerusalem, the temple-based center of Israel for the people who had covenanted to love and be faithful to God, was also thought of as God's wife. By Isaiah's time, however, she had broken her vows and was then chasing after her other lovers, the false gods. The once pure-hearted bride had become a harlot (Isa. 1:21). Her inhabitants were murderers, her aristocracy was aligned with the underworld, and her citizens bribed judges, causing her widows and orphans to mourn that justice was no longer attainable (Isa. 1:21–23). But God, looking beyond that day, invited her to repent (Isa. 1:16–18), promising to refine her and purge away her sins. She would yet become "the city of righteousness, the faithful city" (Isa. 1:24–26).

The Day of the Lord (Isa. 2)

People who ignore God and his commandments must somehow be warned that the day of God's judgment is coming. It is the day of the Lord, a day which symbolizes all other times of judgment in history. It is a day when the unrighteous receive their reward, and the worthy receive theirs as well. Thus for some it will be a day of rejoicing, while for others it will be a day of sorrow and regret.

Judgments will begin at the Lord's house (cf. D&C 112:25–26) with the purification of Israel, who will be restored as God's people to their full covenant privileges. Something of that day is described in Isaiah 2 and 3: flashes of light pierce the darkness, leading to the dawning of the day of judgment. After that judgment, Israel will be renewed, as Isaiah described in chapter 4.

While Jerusalem for the present was a harlot (Isa. 1:21), in the day to come God will sanctify her and establish his residence once more in his holy mountain. Then divine light will come from Zion, and all nations will come to gain light, knowledge, and instruction in God's ways: "And it shall come to pass in the last days, that the mountain of the Lord's house shall be established in the top of the mountains, and shall be exalted above the hills; and all nations shall flow unto it. And many people shall go and say, Come ye, and let us go up to the mountain of the Lord, to the house of the God of Jacob; and he will teach us of his ways, and we will walk in his paths: for out of Zion shall go forth the law, and the word of the Lord from Jerusalem" (Isa. 2:2–3).

In that day, the Lord will bring true justice to the world. The image of swords being beaten into plowshares is a powerful metaphor to describe the peace that will exist in the world where "nation shall not lift up sword against nation, neither shall they learn war any more" (Isa. 2:4). That is how it will be when God rules the whole world.

Having painted this idyllic picture of what will be in the Millennium, when God's will is done on earth as it is in heaven, Isaiah invited Israel: "Come ye, and let us walk in the light of the Lord" (Isa. 2:5). Isaiah knew that his own generation was wicked and that for them, only the prophecies of destruction would be fulfilled. They would experience the great and dreadful day of the Lord in their own time as a foretaste and type of God's judgments at the end of the world. Isaiah frequently spoke of the imminent judgments on his people in the same breath with the last-days judgments on all the world. Each is a type of the other.

The prophet warned that all high and elevated things based on human pride and wisdom will fall. High things, such as mountains, trees, towers, even "lofty looks," will all come down, when God alone is exalted in that day (Isa. 2:7–17). Idols, man's substitute for God, made by human wisdom and human powers out of wood and stone, are among the greatest evidences of human pride. In the day of God's judgment, men will try to conceal their embarrassment at having resorted to such incapable sources (Isa. 2:18–22).

Anarchy, Pride, and Purification (Isa. 3–4)

Isaiah foresaw a time when Jerusalem would lie in ruins and Judah be fallen (Isa. 3:8). The kingdom of Judah would reap as it had sown (Isa. 3:10–11). The leaders would fail in their leadership (Isa. 3:12; cf. Ezek. 34:1–8), and the Lord would hold them responsible for the national tragedy (Isa. 3:13–15; Ezek. 34:9–10). The prophet knew that Zion would be purged of those men and women who had polluted it, just as in the latter days it must be purified by a refining process so the ultimate Zion might be established in righteousness. Isaiah detailed the haughtiness and vanity of Zion's women, who in due time would be stripped of all the external things that had been used to enhance their beauty (Isa. 3:16–24). He foresaw that Jerusalem's men would fall by the sword (Isa. 3:25). The leaders of the people would be taken (Isa. 3:1–4), and conditions would be so anarchic and pathetic that anyone with a suit of clothes would be enlisted to lead, pressed upon with the plea, "Be thou our ruler, and let this ruin be under thy hand" (Isa. 3:6; see also vv. 7–9). These pitiful circumstances describe well the condition of Jerusalem's citizens after the city's destruction in 587 B.C. The prophet Jeremiah, an eyewitness to Judah's fall, recorded it vividly (Jer. 40–42).

Ultimately, the refining will produce a purified people. Whoever survives — those who "are escaped of Israel," "he that is left in Zion," and "he that remaineth in Jerusalem" (Isa. 4:2–3) — will be "holy" and prepared for the arrival of the Lord, making it possible for God in that day to live in the midst of a pure-in-heart people.[4] Purged by judgments, including the spirit of burning (Isa. 4:4), Zion will be glorious, and its glory will be its defense (Isa. 4:5–6; see D&C 45:66–67, 70; Moses 7:13–17). In that day, each dwelling place and every public building ("assembly") will shine gloriously, showing that God is present wherever his people are, whether they are at home or in their assemblies. How gloriously this prophetic picture compares and contrasts with that special time in Israel's earlier history when God was present in their camp but only in his tabernacle. *All* citizens of Zion will be holy then (Isa. 4:5–6).

The Parable of the Vineyard (Isa. 5)

Though its perspective is more limited, the parable of the vineyard in Isaiah 5 (vv. 1–7) reminds us of Zenos' allegory recorded in Jacob 5. God, the husbandman, worked to make the lives of his children productive and fruitful. Righteous deeds were the good fruits that came from righteous lives; bitter fruit came from covetous, violent, and lying deeds. The house of Israel was the vineyard, the promised land was the fruitful hill, and Judah was the choice vine ("pleasant plant"; Isa. 5:7). By

---

[4] 3 Ne. 10 illustrates how God can cause righteous people to survive when the world around them is being destroyed. See also D&C 35:13–14; 63:34; 101:12; 115:6.

acquiring good ground (Isa. 5:1), by getting the choicest kind of plants, by bestowing his best work, God, the farmer, believed he could expect to harvest good fruit. In anticipation, he prepared the winepress, set up his watchtower to guard his crop so no one would steal it, and waited for his bountiful harvest. But despite his careful preparation, he harvested bitter-tasting wild grapes (behavior such as murder, violence, and deceit), rather than sweet-tasting fruit. In his amazement he wondered why his effort was so poorly rewarded.

People are not plants; they have agency. So there is no adequate answer for God's question about why his vineyard brought forth wild grapes. When he laments, "What could have been done more to my vineyard, that I have not done in it?" (Isa. 5:4), we see him revealed as a very concerned Father who strives with all the powers at his command to bring good into the lives of his children. Jesus wondered why careless chicks refused to gather under his all-protective wings (Luke 13:34; Matt. 23:37). The allegory of Zenos extends the meaning of Isaiah's allegory by showing that God does not give up his saving work, despite temporary crop failure. Rather, he continues his work until he produces a good crop. Still, Isaiah was left to prophesy the devastation of the land and the end of the nation (Isa. 5:5–6; 6:11–12).

In the rest of chapter 5, Isaiah detailed some of the wickedness of his people. Joining one house to another refers to building up great landed estates by oppressive means, as the context of this prophecy shows. Even the most beautiful of their houses would be "desolate" and "without inhabitant" (Isa. 5:8–9). Contrasting the smallness of their harvest with the large amount of land and seed they had sown, Isaiah showed how much they were missing from their lives by trying to live without God (Isa. 5:10; cf. Lev. 26:14–26). As materialistic and sensual people, they banqueted and paid absolutely no regard to God, and neither did they consider his work (Isa. 5:11–12). Having come to earth to show their obedience to the Lord, they chose rather to show their lack of interest. Indeed, they called "evil good, and good evil"; they placed "darkness for light, and light for darkness"; they were "wise in their own eyes, and prudent in their own sight" (Isa. 5:20–21). Thus they were being carried into captivity and their land was being depopulated, just as Moses had predicted (Isa. 5:24–30; cf. Lev. 26:27–34; Deut. 28:45–50).

The Sign of Deliverance (Isa. 7–8)

God's promise to give Israel power over their enemies if they would serve him and keep his commandments (Lev. 26:6–8; Deut. 28:7) was put to the test as Assyrian dreams of empire rose. The Assyrians would eventually conquer Syria, Palestine, and even Egypt, but those conquests lay in the future as chapters 7 through 10 of Isaiah's record begin. At that point, Rezin, king of Syria, and Pekah, king of Israel (Ephraim), became allies and pressured Ahaz, king of Judah, to join their coalition (see Map 9, LDS Bible). When he refused, they agreed to conquer Judah and install someone named ben-Tabeal on Ahaz's throne (Isa. 7:1–6). In this threatening predicament, God tried to teach Ahaz that he should turn to Him for deliverance in times of need.

Not only did Ahaz refuse to believe in the Lord but he even sacrificed his children in his zeal to serve pagan gods. Moreover, he tried to eliminate any faith in Jehovah that remained in Judah by closing Solomon's temple and erecting altars throughout the country for his people to worship other gods (see 2 Chron. 28:2–4, 22–25).

With two enemies allied against him, Ahaz needed powers superior to his own. The Lord stood ready to help. So Isaiah asked Ahaz what kind of sign, either one from heaven or one from earth, would convince him that the hand of the Lord would be manifest in his forthcoming victory (Isa. 7:10–11). But apparently, if God granted Ahaz some kind of personal sign that he might request, Ahaz would be obliged to believe in Jehovah rather than in foreign gods. So Ahaz refused God's gracious offer. It was as though he were saying that nothing the Lord could do would convince him; his mind was made up (Isa. 7:12).

In spite of Ahaz's refusal to put God to the test, the Lord specified his own sign: the fall of Judah's enemies before a special baby, yet to be born, would be old enough to know the difference between good and evil. The two lands feared by Ahaz (Syria and Ephraim) would both lose their kings (Isa. 7:14–16). This sign was given when a baby was born to the prophet Isaiah, as a careful comparison of Isaiah 7:14–16 and 8:1–4 shows.

7:14 Behold, a virgin shall conceive, and bear a son	8:3 And I went unto the prophetess; and she conceived, and bare a son

7:14 And shall call his name Immanuel [God is with us]	8:3 Then said the Lord to me, Call his name Maher-shalal-hash-baz [The plunder hurries, the spoil hastens]
7:15 Butter and honey shall he eat, that he may know to refuse the evil, and choose the good	8:3 (No parallel)
7:16 For before the child shall know [Hebrew, kî beṭerem yēdaʻ hannaʻar]	8:4 For before the child shall have knowledge [Hebrew, kî beṭerem yēdaʻ hannaʻar]
7:16 To refuse the evil, and choose the good	8:4 To cry, My father, and my mother
7:16 The land that thou abhorrest	8:4 The riches of Damascus and the spoil of Samaria
7:16 Shall be forsaken of both her kings	8:4 Shall be taken away before the king of Assyria

From these prophecies we learn that—

1. The birth of a baby is the sign of deliverance (Isa. 7:14; 8:18).

2. The baby is a boy (Isa. 7:14; 8:3).

3. His name is divinely given (Isa. 7:14; 8:3).

4. The name suggests deliverance ("God is with us," or "The plunder hurries, the spoil hastens," meaning the plunder of Judah's enemies is hastening; Isa. 7:14; 8:3).

5. Ahaz's enemies will be overthrown, and their cities will be plundered (Isa. 7:16; 8:4).

6. Both of these results will occur before the baby reaches the age of accountability or cries "Mommy" and "Daddy" (Isa. 7:16; 8:4).

7. What the two kings had determined concerning Jerusalem and its king will not take place, for God will defend Ahaz against this threat (Isa. 7:7–9; 8:4).

From the earliest times, God has used deliverance from specific earthly threats to signify the ultimate deliverance through his Son. "All things have their likeness, and all things are created and made to bear record of me, both things which are temporal, and things which are spiritual; things which are in the heavens above, and things which are on the earth, and things which are in the earth, and things which are under the earth, . . . all things bear record of me" (Moses 6:63). Thus, "many signs, and wonders, and types, and shadows showed he unto them, concerning his coming" (Mosiah 3:15). "All things which have been given of God from the beginning of the world, unto man, are the typifying of him" (2 Ne. 11:4). Whenever people sacrificed the blood of the firstlings of their flocks, they typified how God would shed the blood of his Firstling; when they shed the blood of goats and bullocks for remission of sins, they signified how remission of sins would come through the shedding of Christ's blood (Lev. 17:11, 14; Heb. 9:22). When they daubed blood on the posts and lintels of their doors to be saved from the destroying angel (Ex. 12:21–23, 27), they showed how Christ, the real Passover, would save them from death, the ultimate destroying angel (1 Cor. 5:7). When Moses lifted up the serpent in the wilderness (Num. 21:4–9), they learned that "even so must the Son of man be lifted up: That whosoever believeth in him should not perish, but have eternal life" (John 3:14–15; Hel. 8:14–15).

Thus, within the prophetic context, any act of divine deliverance foreshadows God's ultimate deliverance — salvation. Therefore, there should be no problem in seeing how God used the birth of a baby in Isaiah's time to foretell deliverance for that generation, while focusing attention on the birth of another baby, through whom all the world will be delivered (Isa. 9:6). And Isaiah himself was chosen by the Lord to be the father, just as the faithful witness recorded (Isa. 8:1–3, 18). How honored Isaiah must have felt when his own son was called to typify the birth of God's own Son. "I and the children whom the Lord hath given me are for signs and for wonders in Israel from the Lord of hosts," Isaiah said (Isa. 8:18). Indeed, the Lord's message of deliverance is contained in their names: "Isaiah," Hebrew yeša'yāhû, means "Jehovah saves." "Maher-shalal-hash-baz" (Isa. 8:1) represents an earthly deliverance that points to salvation, and "Shear-jashub" (Isa. 7:3) means "a remnant will return."

But, ever the rebel, Ahaz rejected God's deliverance while proudly carrying out his own plan to seek help from the enemy of his enemies, the Assyrian king Tiglath-pileser. He said, "I am thy servant and thy son: come up, and *save me* out of the hand of the king of Syria, and out of the hand of the king of Israel, which rise up against me" (2 Kgs. 16:7; emphasis added).

Isaiah had warned Ahaz that if he did not believe the Lord, he would not be established (Isa. 7:9). In Moses' day, some had refused to look at the sign by which they could be saved. "Therefore they perished. Now the reason they would not look is because they did not believe that it would heal them" (Alma 33:20). Thus, in Ahaz's day, "the Lord brought Judah low because of Ahaz king of Israel; . . . And Tilgath-pilneser [variant spelling] king of Assyria came unto him, and distressed him, but strengthened him not" (2 Chr. 28:19–20), just as Isaiah had predicted (Isa. 7:9). Ahaz needed what God could give. God had offered it. Ahaz had ignored the offer for one of his own devising, but by ignoring God, he suffered the failures he had sought to avoid.

In the sequel, Ahaz's failure to believe in the Lord led to the devastation of his land by the Assyrians, the same source to which he, in his twisted wisdom, had looked for deliverance. In fact, Isaiah said that God sent the Assyrians against his people to humble them (Isa. 10:5–11). The account of this appears in Isaiah 36–37 and 2 Kings 18–19, in which the writer explains: the "king of Assyria came against all the defenced cities of Judah, and took them" (Isa. 36:1). Sennacherib, the Assyrian king, boasted in his own records about how he conquered forty-six fortified cities plus innumerable smaller cities in their environs and carried their inhabitants into captivity.[5] The kingdom of Judah was devastated. Of its cities, only Jerusalem survived.

The Advent of the Messianic King (Isa. 9)

In Isaiah 9 a poem of rejoicing celebrates Israel's future deliverance. "The people that walked in darkness have seen a great light: they that dwell in the land of the shadow of death, upon them hath the light shined" (Isa. 9:2). The cause of that deliverance would be the baby who would come to reign: "For unto us a child is born, unto us a son is given: and the government shall be upon his shoulder: and his name shall be called Wonderful, Counsellor, The mighty God, The everlasting Father, The Prince of Peace. Of the increase of his government and peace there shall be no end, upon the throne of David, and upon his kingdom, to

---

[5]James B. Pritchard, ed., *Ancient Near Eastern Texts Relating to the Old Testament,* 3d ed. with Supplement (Princeton: Princeton University, 1969), p. 288.

order it, and to establish it with judgment and with justice from henceforth even for ever" (Isa. 9:6–7).

We know that the government was not placed on Christ's shoulders during his first coming, but it will be when he comes the second time to fulfill his complete messianic role. When he came as a baby, it was important for his believers to know what his overall role would be. As Gabriel told Mary, "the Lord God shall give unto him the throne of his father David: and . . . of his kingdom there shall be no end" (Luke 1:32–33; reiterated by Zacharias in Luke 1:69–74). Inspired people have always kept Christ's overall ministry in mind to comprehend the full nature of his earthly mission (see Luke 1:33, 68–71).

Isaiah frequently used an interesting phrase when discussing Judah's sins and God's continued acts of judgment against her: "For all this his anger is not turned away, but his hand is stretched out still" (Isa. 5:25; 9:12, 17, 21; 10:4). Despite repeated punishments, Isaiah's people refused to repent. This reminds us of the words of Amos, Isaiah's contemporary, when he repeated after a whole series of devastating experiences, "Yet have ye not returned unto me" (Amos 4:6, 8, 11). These phrases imply that God uses judgments as chastening tools to accomplish his divine purpose. As Mormon wrote, "And thus we see that except the Lord doth chasten his people with many afflictions, yea, except he doth visit them with death and with terror, and with famine and with all manner of pestilence, they will not remember him" (Hel. 12:3).[6]

"O Assyrian, the Rod of Mine Anger" (Isa. 10)

Judah was the hypocritical nation referred to in Isaiah 10:6. It would be brought down, for "the eyes of the lofty shall be humbled" (Isa. 5:15). In Isaiah 10, we see how God's divine purpose was accomplished, even though the principal agent by which it was done was evil. God used the Assyrians to bring about his judgments on Judah. The Assyrians intended to conquer and plunder (Isa. 10:7–11, 13–14), but God intended to humble his hypocritical, proud, and rebellious people (Isa. 10:5–6). They

---

[6]Hel. 12:3 and Lev. 26 show that the divine hand that is stretched out would be stretched out in anger and not in mercy, although an angry hand works to bring about mercy and salvation.

both intended to devastate Judah, though their reasons differed. Still, God empowered the Assyrians to do it (cf. Deut. 28:47–52).

Ahaz's successor was the faithful king Hezekiah, who vainly tried to turn his people back to God after his father had led them astray (see Isa. 36–37; 2 Kgs. 18–19). The Assyrian king Sennacherib rightly claimed that God had called him to attack Judah (Isa. 36:10). Thus, he "came up against all the defenced [fortified] cities of Judah, and took them" (Isa. 36:1).[7] Isaiah knew by revelation that that would happen: "Now therefore, behold, the Lord bringeth up upon them the waters of the river, strong and many, even the king of Assyria, and all his glory: and he shall come up over all his channels, and go over all his banks. And he shall pass through Judah; he shall overflow and go over, he shall reach even to the neck; and the stretching out of his wings shall fill the breadth of thy land" (Isa. 8:7–8). But Sennacherib glorified himself by crediting his mighty armies and superior leaders for his victory over Judah; he boasted, "By the strength of my hand I have done it, and by my wisdom; for I am prudent" (Isa. 10:13).

The Lord had foretold what would happen if the Assyrians took the honor to themselves: "When the Lord hath performed his whole work upon mount Zion and on Jerusalem, I will punish the fruit of the stout heart of the king of Assyria, and the glory of his high looks" (Isa. 10:12). In response to Assyrian arrogance, the Lord asked whether an inanimate tool should brag against the man who works it: "Shall the axe boast itself against him that heweth therewith?" (Isa. 10:15). The Lord humbled Sennacherib by devastating his army and preserving Jerusalem intact, in answer to the faith of Hezekiah and his people (Isa. 37:33–37).[8]

In chapter 10 (vv. 20–27), Isaiah again referred to the day when a remnant would escape and return, a theme reflected in the name of his son Shear-jashub (Isa. 7:3; 10:21–22).

The Millennium (Isa. 11–12)

A revelation in the Doctrine and Covenants identifies the subject of Isaiah 11:2–5 as the Stem of Jesse and teaches us that he is Jesus Christ

---

[7]Pritchard, p. 288.
[8]For a fuller discussion, see Chap. 10 of this volume.

(D&C 113:1–2). David was a son of Jesse, and his sons were promised the right to Israel's throne in perpetuity. Identifying Jesus as the Son of David mentioned in these verses shows him to be the legitimate, messianic heir to the throne of Israel.

Isaiah dramatically contrasted the righteous government that the Messiah will establish with those set up by men, whose nature and disposition is to rule unrighteously. He identified some of the characteristics of Christ as our millennial king: with the Spirit of God that leads to "wisdom," "understanding," "counsel," "knowledge," "fear of the Lord," and "quick understanding in the fear of the Lord," he will rule with "equity" (Isa. 11:1–5). With righteousness in the land, the earth, after six thousand years of tension, will finally know peace (see also Moses 7:48–49, 61–64). What a dramatic contrast there is between Isaiah's millennial vision and the happenings of his contemporary world, where human desires went unchecked. For those who long for the day when might does not make right, Isaiah holds out hope.

In the millennial day, men and women will be instructed in divine programs and actions, making the Millennium into God's great finishing school, in which he will prepare his faithful children to rule and reign in the eternities. Nothing will be withheld. They will learn about the powers and dominions of the Gods, how and why they make worlds, and the laws that govern the universe. Thus, as foreseen by Isaiah, the earth will be enveloped in "the knowledge of the Lord," as fully "as the waters cover the sea" (Isa. 11:9; see also D&C 101:25–34; 121:26–32; Jer. 31:31–34; 2 Ne. 27:7–11; Ether 3:21–28; 4:6–8; Rev. 5:1).

The peace that will exist among all creatures on the earth is exciting. Flesh-eating and plant-eating animals will be at peace with each other, because all living creatures in that day will be herbivorous, as they were in the Garden of Eden. Truly, "the wolf also shall dwell with the lamb, and the leopard shall lie down with the kid; and the calf and the young lion and the fatling together; and a little child shall lead them" (Isa. 11:6; see also 11:6–9; Abr. 4:29–30; D&C 101:26, 29).

In our day, the Church is the kingdom of God that has been established on earth to prepare the world for the coming of God's heavenly kingdom (see D&C 65:1–2, 6). The vision of Isaiah 11 prepares our minds for that coming. Moroni's four-fold repetition of this prophecy to

Joseph Smith (JS–H 1:40, 45–46, 49) shows how important it was that he understand what Isaiah was saying, here and in other related scriptures.

We understand Isaiah 11 by turning to modern revelation:

SYMBOL – ISAIAH 11	IDENTIFICATION – D&C 113
Isaiah 11:1 Stem of Jesse	D&C 113:1–2 Jesus Christ
Isaiah 11:1 Rod or twig from the stem	D&C 113:3–4 Servant of Christ, descendant of Jesse and Joseph, blessed with much power
Isaiah 11:10 Root of Jesse	D&C 113:5–6 Descendant of Jesse and Joseph, with a right to the priesthood and its keys for the gathering

It appears that Joseph Smith is both the "rod" and the "root" of which Isaiah wrote. The images of the rod in Isaiah 11:1 and the root in Isaiah 11:10 define similar, perhaps identical, roles. Because Joseph Smith is the leading holder of priesthood keys of this dispensation, the man who undertook the work of gathering, who presides over the preparatory work, who has great priesthood power (2 Ne. 3:11; D&C 112:15, 32), and who is a servant of Christ, it is therefore likely that he is both the rod and the root, both of whom are servants in the hands of Christ to carry out crucial work in preparation for his millennial reign on earth. That suggests why it was so important for Joseph Smith (and then all others) to understand this prophecy and to know that God's prophecies are being fulfilled and through what means they are being fulfilled.

Joseph Smith was the first one in this dispensation to receive the keys of the priesthood and the keys of the gathering of Israel (D&C 128:20; 110:11–16). According to revelation, he had a legal right, by lineage, to the blessings of the priesthood (D&C 86:8–10). While he descended from Joseph (as 2 Nephi 3:7, 15 shows), we have no scriptural knowledge of his descent from David, other than what we conclude from these verses. If Joseph Smith had mixed Israelite heritage, as seems totally probable, he could easily have been both of Joseph as well as of Judah, thus fulfilling the prophecy of Isaiah.[9]

---

[9]President Joseph Fielding Smith wrote, "The Book of Mormon states that Joseph Smith the Prophet was a descendant of Joseph, son of Jacob. By revelation we learn also that he is of the tribe of Ephraim, but it is evident that he also had some Gentile blood in him, for it is written in

The gathering of God's people is a major theme of Isaiah 11, because it is a basis on which God's work will succeed in the last days. Joseph Smith testified that the gathering was a matter of greatest importance.[10] Thus, if the stem (Jesus the Christ, whose work is defined in vv. 2–5) is to do his work, then the rod must do his also. The intimate relationship between the two roles is implied in the metaphor of a rod, or better, a "branch" or a "twig," that grows out of the stem. Jesus used a similar metaphor in describing himself and other apostolic servants: "I am the vine, ye are the branches" (John 15:5). The latter-day gathering is the second gathering (Isa. 11:11–12), whereas the first was the gathering of Israel out of Egypt, making Moses the official holder of the gathering keys (see D&C 110:11). Not only will Israel be gathered, but many among the Gentile nations will also join the gathered remnant to learn of God (see Isa. 11:10, 12; 14:1; Jer. 16:14–16). The Church and the restored gospel will be the rallying standard, or "ensign," to which Israel and these others will come (cf. 2 Ne. 6:14; 25:17; 29:1).

It is important to know biblical history in order to understand how significant it is that Judah and Ephraim will be at peace in that day (Isa. 11:12–13). In biblical times, Ephraim, the Northern Kingdom (also called Israel), and Judah, the Southern Kingdom, often fought each other (Isa. 11:13), as we have seen (Isa. 7–8). Things will be otherwise in the Millennium, when they will come together amicably. As the scattered bones of a body will be reunited into one body, so scattered Israelites will become one nation under one king (see Ezek. 37:1–14).

Isaiah 11 (vv. 14–15) shows the Lord's power over Israel's traditional enemies in that coming day. To bring his people home, he will provide the way or means for them to return—a "highway for the remnant of his people" (Isa. 11:16; cf. D&C 133:27). The "highway" metaphor represents the divinely provided means of return. As God provided a

---

the Book of Mormon, that it came forth, 'by way of the Gentile' (1 Ne. 13:35, 39), and it came by Joseph Smith. It is reasonable, therefore, to understand that we one and all have come through a mixed relationship, and that the blood of Ephraim and also of Manasseh could be in the veins of many of us, likewise the blood of others of the twelve tribes of Israel, and that none of us had come through the ages with clear exclusive descent from father to son through any one of the tribes." *Answers to Gospel Questions,* 5 vols. (Salt Lake City: Deseret Book Co., 1957–66), 3:63–64; see also 3:61–63.

[10]See, for example, *Teachings of the Prophet Joseph Smith,* sel. Joseph Fielding Smith (Salt Lake City: Deseret Book Co., 1938), pp. 83, 92, 101, 163, 183, 307–8, 310, 312.

"highway" for the first gathering out of Egypt, he will in the last days provide a way for his people to return from their scattering among the nations. Whether it takes a seaway, airway, or roadway to convey his people back home, he will provide it (see D&C 45:9; Isa. 11:15–16). The full gathering and the miraculous means will both be provided in conjunction with the Lord's arrival on the earth. Ephraim, which is gathering first, will take a preparatory role in being ready to administer blessings to his brothers (see D&C 133:25–35; cf. Jer. 31:6–8).

In the millennial day, the song in Isaiah 12 will honor the Lord Jesus Christ, who has worked his wonders and whose great and mighty deeds have been established for the benefit of his covenant children. It rightly follows chapter 11 and forms a fitting conclusion to the marvelous work predicted in that chapter. It praises God for the arrival of his kingdom on earth and expresses Israel's joy in being redeemed, in being in favor with God once more, and in receiving of the rich bounties of his Spirit (Isa. 12:1–6).

The Fall of Babylon (Isa. 13–14)

Isaiah 13 through 23 consists of oracles against the nations: Babylon (Isa. 13:1–14:23), Assyria (Isa. 14:24–27), Philistia (Isa. 14:28–32), Moab (Isa. 15–16), Damascus (Isa. 17:1–3), Israel (Isa. 17:4–14), Ethiopia (Isa. 18), Egypt (Isa. 19), Egypt and Ethiopia (Isa. 20), Babylon (Isa. 21:1–10), Edom (Isa. 21:11–12), Arabia (Isa. 21:13–17), Judah (Isa. 22), and Tyre (Isa. 23).[11] What conditions evoked these messages or how they were delivered is not stated, but they are a meaningful part of the scriptural record. A discussion of their collective purpose and message is found in Chapter 13 of this volume.

Isaiah 13 and 14 constitute for the most part a prophecy against Babylon, beginning with the characteristic phrase, "the burden of Babylon, which Isaiah the son of Amoz did see" (Isa. 13:1). The term "burden," Hebrew massa', is used frequently in prophetic writing to represent a prophecy of doom.

---

[11]Other large collections of prophecies against the nations are found in Jer. 46–51 and Ezek. 25–32. Note how Israel and Judah are included in Isaiah's list.

The city of Babylon was a major power through much of biblical history, though in Isaiah's day it was under the domination of Assyria (see Map 10, LDS Bible). Isaiah prophesied that the city would fall, and he foretold the role of the Medes in the process (Isa. 13:17). Babylon was overthrown in 539 B.C. when Cyrus, king of the Medes and Persians, took the city. It never regained its prominence thereafter.

Though Isaiah's prophecy deals with the fall of a city and its ruler, it deals with a much greater event as well—the fall of the wicked world, its ruler, and all that they represent. In scriptural imagery, Babylon is the enemy of God and the antithesis of Zion, the friend of God. Zion is the chaste, heavenly bride, while Babylon is the wicked, worldly prostitute, the one who entices men away from their love and loyalty to God by promising them all the seductive advantages that the world offers—materialism, power, glory, and sensualism—all of which appeal to one's pride.

Lucifer is the king of Babylon and the arch-rebel who typifies all other rebels. A son of the morning, he aspired to ascend above the stars of God and be like the Most High (Isa. 14:13–14; D&C 76:25–27). With pride and arrogance, he promised to do what God himself would not do—save all men[12]—and thus laid claim to God's glory (D&C 29:36–37; Moses 4:1–4). Thus God's heavenly arch-rival became the type or model for all earthly rivals. When Babylon, the wicked world, presumes to fight against God, it follows Satan's model and becomes the antithesis of everything God represents.

It is crucial that the Saints know that Babylon, with all her allurements, will eventually fall, as Isaiah prophesied. That sustains their hopes when they are criticized, persecuted, and hated by all those identified with Babylon because they live so differently from Babylon (see 1 Ne. 22:22–23).[13]

Isaiah 13 describes the destruction of the wicked in the day of the Lord (Isa. 13:9; see also 1 Ne. 11:35–36), that great and terrible day spoken of by the prophets. "I will punish the world for their evil, and the wicked for their iniquity; and I will cause the arrogancy of the proud

---

[12]Smith, *Teachings*, p. 357.

[13]Isa. 2; 13; 24; and 34 are examples of chapters that deal with the end of the wicked world. See also Ezek. 38–39; Zech. 12; 14; Rev. 11; 16–18; D&C 29:21–22, to cite a few others.

to cease, and will lay low the haughtiness of the terrible" (Isa. 13:11). On the Lord's side will be the "sanctified ones," God's all-powerful force before whom no enemy can stand. The sanctified ones are those who "rejoice in [God's] highness" (Isa. 13:3) and who are set apart to his service (Isa. 13:2–5).

In Isaiah 14, the fall of Lucifer is a type for the fall of the king of Babylon. The pride and arrogance of Lucifer, when he rebelled in heaven, provided food for thought anciently, as many nations have stories of war among the gods. Lucifer's pride and fall are alluded to in verses 12 through 14. Likening the fall of the king of Babylon to that of Lucifer evokes images of his arrogance, but it also shows how futile his work will be when it all fails: "Thou shalt be brought down to hell, to the sides of the pit" (Isa. 14:15). The nations will look upon this fall with amazement and disgust (Isa. 14:16–20), "for I will rise up against them, saith the Lord of hosts" (Isa. 14:22). Whatever is not built up by the Lord will fall in those days. Just as surely as Lucifer fell, so also will all kingdoms and powers that are based on pride and rebellion against God (Isa. 14:26–27; cf. 2:10–17).

Prophecies against Moab, Damascus, and Ephraim (Isa. 15–17)

The prophecy against Moab in Isaiah 15 and 16 is typical of others in prophetic writing. It describes the mourning that will prevail in Moab after it is "laid waste" and "brought to silence" (Isa. 15:1). Several cities are mentioned (see Map 9, LDS Bible, for some of them). Moab is condemned for its "pride," "haughtiness," "wrath," and "lies" (Isa. 16:6), for which sins its people will "howl" and "mourn" (Isa. 16:7). The survivors among them will be "very small and feeble" (Isa. 16:14).

The one ray of hope in this oracle is a millennial prophecy, which focuses a messianic contrast on the depravity of the contemporary world. The "extortioner," the "spoiler," and the "oppressors" will be destroyed. But "in mercy" a throne will be established, and one from the tent of David will rule, "judging, and seeking judgment, and hasting righteousness" (Isa. 16:4–6; cf. 11:3–5).

Damascus (Syria) and Ephraim (Israel) are the subjects of the prophecy of judgment in Isaiah 17 (chaps. 7 and 8 provide a context for understanding this revelation; see above). Damascus will become "a ruinous heap" (Isa. 17:1). The "glory of Jacob" (the kingdom of Israel) will fade, and his flesh will grow lean, like a harvested field (Isa. 17:4–5). But as in an orchard of harvested olives, two or three remain "in the top of the uppermost bough" and four or five remain in the "outmost" branches (Isa. 17:6). Not only will a remnant survive, but, as Isaiah foretold previously, Shear-jashub, "a remnant will return" (Isa. 7:3; 8:18; 10:21–22).

Conclusion

The Saints do not need to wallow through every one of life's mires to find what is most important to do and to avoid. The Lord tells us how we can succeed with him and how the world, known as Babylon, built on human values and standards, will fail. When Babylon exercises her full usurped powers, the Saints may grow weary, but reading the scriptures by the light of the Spirit will cause them to take heart and endure in faith. They are called to build Zion and oppose Babylon, even when Babylon seems to be all-powerful and ever-present. Since the Lord knows the end from the beginning and his purposes do not fail, members of his Church can find courage to live their lives with faith and hope, looking patiently for that day to come when the Lord, having finished the building of Zion, will dwell among his Saints. How privileged we are to live in a day when we can see prophecies being fulfilled—when we can see the hand of the Lord and his plan being unveiled.

13

THE LORD IS OUR JUDGE AND OUR KING
(ISAIAH 18–33)

DAVID ROLPH SEELY

"The Lord is our judge, the Lord is our lawgiver, the Lord is our king; he will save us" (Isa. 33:22). Commenting on this passage, and on the people who had it as their motto, Joseph Smith said, "Happy is that people, whose God is the Lord."[1] Isaiah was addressing a people who had accepted by covenant the Lord God as their judge, lawgiver, king, and — according to their obedience — their savior.[2] Yet the people of Isaiah's day were not happy. Because of apostasy, the house of Israel was personified by the Lord in Isaiah's introductory chapter as sick and wounded. Through his prophet the Lord pleaded, "Why should ye be stricken any more? ye will revolt more and more: the whole head is sick, and the whole heart faint. From the sole of the foot even to the head there is no soundness in it; but wounds, and bruises, and putrifying sores: they have not been closed, neither bound up, neither mollified with ointment" (Isa. 1:5–6). The remedy prescribed by the Lord was not a "multitude of sacrifices" (Isa. 1:11), nor "vain oblations" (Isa. 1:13), nor

---

David Rolph Seely is assistant professor of ancient scripture at Brigham Young University.

[1] In quoting this verse, Joseph Smith emphasized the aspect of the Lord as lawgiver and went on to say about ancient Israel: "Their government was a theocracy; they had God to make their laws, and men chosen by him to administer them; He was their God, and they were his people." *Teachings of the Prophet Joseph Smith*, sel. Joseph Fielding Smith (Salt Lake City: Deseret Book Co., 1938), p. 252.

[2] The root of the Hebrew verb "to save" is yšʻ, the same root from which the names *Isaiah* and *Joshua* are derived, both of which mean "Jehovah is salvation." The Savior would be named *Joshua* (more fully *Yehoshua;* Aramaic *Yeshua*), which rendered in Latinized Greek became *Jesus*. Thus the verb "to save" and its nominal form "salvation" in Isaiah have many connections and theological ramifications beyond their simple meaning.

"many prayers" (Isa. 1:15) — but repentance: "Wash you, make you clean; put away the evil of your doings from before mine eyes; cease to do evil" (Isa. 1:16).

Chapters 18 through 33 span three distinct units in the book of Isaiah: chapters 18 through 23 are part of the Oracles against Foreign Nations in chapters 13 through 23; chapters 24 through 27 form a single unit of last-days prophecies often called the The Apocalypse of Isaiah; and chapters 28 through 33 are a collection of more loosely related prophecies also involving latter-day events of judgment and restoration. Some of the prophecies are well known to Latter-day Saints — such as that in chapter 29, a detailed prophecy about the coming forth of the Book of Mormon — but most of the chapters in this section are relatively unfamiliar. For example, although about one-third of the entire book of Isaiah is directly quoted and interpreted in the Book of Mormon, apart from chapter 29 (which is cited and commented on at length by Nephi in 2 Ne. 26–27), only one verse of Isaiah from chapters 18 through 33 is cited in the Book of Mormon (Isa. 28:10, in 2 Ne. 28:30).[3]

The unifying theme of these chapters is the Lord as lawgiver and judge sending judgment on his disobedient children, in Israel as well as in other nations. Many of the prophecies refer to identifiable events in Isaiah's day, and many more refer to the last days — the day of the Lord — when judgment will be universal and destruction cosmic. In the words of Amos, "Woe unto you that desire the day of the Lord! to what end is it for you? the day of the Lord is darkness, and not light" (Amos 5:18). When the king returns in the "day of the Lord," he will bring judgment because of the wickedness of the children of men. But darkness and destruction are balanced by restoration and rebuilding. For the righteous the day of the Lord is a day of light, vindication, healing, and salvation. With the return of the king — the light of the world (John 8:12) — "the light of the moon shall be as the light of the sun, and the light of the

---

[3]The appendices in Monte S. Nyman, *"Great Are the Words of Isaiah"* (Salt Lake City: Bookcraft, 1980), pp. 253–302, are an invaluable reference to the citation and interpretation of Isaiah. Nyman has compiled several verse-by-verse lists citing the references where Isaiah is quoted in ancient (New Testament) and modern scripture (Book of Mormon, Doctrine and Covenants, Pearl of Great Price) as well as prophetic commentary by Joseph Smith and other General Authorities. Another excellent LDS commentary is Victor L. Ludlow, *Isaiah: Prophet, Seer, and Poet* (Salt Lake City: Deseret Book Co., 1982).

sun shall be sevenfold, as the light of seven days, in the day that the Lord bindeth up the breach of his people, and healeth the stroke of their wound" (Isa. 30:26).

Oracles against Foreign Nations (Isa. 18–23)

Isaiah 18 through 23 is only a part of the collection of oracles against foreign nations in Isaiah 13 through 23.[4] In all, these prophecies of judgment include eleven sets of oracles against ten nations: Babylon (Isa. 13:1–14:23), Assyria (Isa. 14:24–27), Moab (Isa. 15:1–16:14), Damascus (Isa. 17:1–3), Ephraim (Isa. 17:4–14), Egypt (Isa. 18:1–20:6), Babylon (Isa. 21:1–10), Edom (Isa. 21:11–12), Arabia (Isa. 21:13–17), Jerusalem (Isa. 22:1–25), and Tyre (Isa. 23:1–18).

The Old Testament prophets viewed their mission and responsibility in a worldwide setting, and the oracles against foreign nations are an important, though often neglected, part of the prophetic corpus demonstrating this fact. Even among the former prophets, whose writings are not preserved, we have evidence that the prophets saw themselves in this universal setting. For example, in 1 Kings 19:15–18, Elijah was commissioned to participate in international affairs by anointing a new king over Syria—a job finally carried out by his successor, Elisha.[5] In addition to the isolated statements that occur throughout the prophetic writings, Isaiah (Isa. 13–23), Jeremiah (Jer. 46–51), and Ezekiel (Ezek. 25–32), as well as Amos (Amos 1–2) and Zephaniah (Zeph. 2:4–15), have significant collections of oracles against nations. The entire books of Obadiah and Nahum are oracles against Edom and Assyria, respectively.

In general terms, five points can be made about the significance of the Oracles against Foreign Nations in the prophetic writings:

---

[4]The term *oracle*—from Latin *oraculum*, "oracle" or "prophecy"—is a noun derived from the verb *orare*, "to speak." It refers to a prophet delivering from his mouth the word of the Lord.

[5]Other instances of former prophets include a man of God who came to Israel during Ahab's war with Syria and delivered an oracle condemning the enemy (1 Kgs. 20:26–30). And Elisha uttered a prophecy against Syria as well (2 Kgs. 13:14–17). In the Pentateuch, Balaam, a foreigner himself, when asked to curse Israel, actually blessed them but is recorded as having uttered threats against Amalek (Num. 24:20), the Kenites (Num. 24:21–22), and the invaders from Kittim (Num. 24:23–24).

1. *The oracles against nations clearly demonstrate that the sovereignty of the Lord God is universal and that he participates in the history of all of his children, not just of Israel.* In a polytheistic world where the worship of gods was often confined to their native local realms, this is a significant theological point. It is emphasized throughout the Bible, from the account of the Creation, in which it is recorded that the Lord God created all things (see Gen. 24:3; Ps. 121:2; 124:8), to the prophecies about the end-time when he will redeem and gather all the nations. And though the focus of much of the Bible is God's dealings in his relationship with his covenant people, there is ample evidence that he is mindful of the rest of the world and participates in history on their behalf as well. Two good examples of this understanding are Zenos' allegory of the olive trees (Jacob 5), in which the wild olive trees — the Gentiles — play an important role in divinely directed history, and Amos' revealing statement to Israel: "Are ye not as children of the Ethiopians unto me, O children of Israel? saith the Lord. Have not I brought up Israel out of the land of Egypt? and the Philistines from Caphtor, and the Syrians from Kir?" (Amos 9:7).

This theme of the sovereignty of God over all nations is particularly important for Isaiah. In the oracle against Assyria the Lord declares, "This is the purpose that is purposed upon the whole earth; and this is the hand that is stretched out upon all the nations. For the Lord of hosts hath purposed, and who shall disannul it? and his hand is stretched out, and who shall turn it back" (Isa. 14:26–27). And just as the Lord is the God of all the earth, so the prophets are his representatives to the world.

2. *As demonstrated by the oracles in Isaiah, the central message to the nations is one of divine judgment and destruction.* Although it is often supposed that Israel could gain solace from the promised destruction of her enemies and neighbors, the sobering fact remains that often Israel is included in these lists of nations to be punished. For example, in Amos 2:4–5 and 2:6–16, Judah and Israel, respectively, are the final two nations to be targeted for destruction — a literal as well as rhetorical culmination of the judgments of the Lord. And in Zephaniah 3:1–7, after the oracles against nations in Zephaniah 2:4–15, Jerusalem is condemned. In the oracles against the nations in Isaiah, Ephraim is condemned in 17:4–14 and Jerusalem in chapter 22. In those books that have collections of oracles not including Israel, large sections of material against Israel or

Judah speak of the same judgment. The destruction promised to the foreign nations is very like that promised to Israel, showing that God is concerned about wickedness everywhere. So, although covenant Israel is unique, the uniqueness is not to be found in an exemption from the Lord's judgments.

3. *The distinction between the punishment of the nations and the punishment of the covenant people is in the nature of the crimes for which they are to be punished.* Whereas the foreign nations are judged for pride, excessive violence, and gloating over the destruction of Israel, Israel is held accountable for the more specific commandments contained in the covenant: forsaking the Lord, idolatry,[6] immorality, and especially neglecting the poor. The Lord, in Isaiah, often cites pride as the cause for the destruction of Israel and her neighbors: all men (2:11); Samaria/Ephraim (9:9; 28:1, 3); Assyria (10:5–19); Babylon (compared with Lucifer; 14:12–14); Moab (16:6; 25:11); Tyre (23:9). This same principle has been enunciated to the latter-day covenant people: "For of him unto whom much is given much is required; and he who sins against the greater light shall receive the greater condemnation" (D&C 82:3).

4. *Some of the oracles of destruction against the nations, like the oracles promising the destruction of Israel, are closely connected with future promises of comfort and restoration—some even containing promises that these foreigners will be converted to the covenant.* Not only does the Lord render judgment on the whole earth but also restoration. The Lord loves and is mindful of all his children. There are specific prophecies of restoration in some of the oracles against nations in Isaiah: for example, Isaiah 18:3 says all the inhabitants of the world will see the ensign raised on the mountain and will come to the mountain of the Lord; Isaiah 19:23–25 prophesies the restoration of Egypt and Assyria with Israel; and Isaiah 23:17–18 concerns the restoration of Tyre. More important is the universalism found throughout the book of Isaiah, in which the gospel in the last days is promised to all peoples: "all nations shall flow unto it [the mountain of the Lord's house]" (2:2); "all ye inhabitants of the world . . . see ye . . . an ensign on the mountains" (18:3); the strangers and eunuchs "will I bring to my holy mountain" (56:1–8); "the Gentiles shall come to thy light" (60:3); "all flesh [shall] come to worship before me" (66:23).

---

[6]Although idolatry is rarely cited as a reason for the destruction of foreign nations, there is much mention of these pagan gods (or "no gods"; Isa. 37:13; Jer. 2:11; 5:7) being conquered and destroyed by the Lord, thus emphasizing his omnipotence.

5. *Although the Lord issues the decree that these nations be conquered, quite often a specific human agent is designated (and rarely ever Israel) to carry out the actual destruction.* This principle is most clearly articulated in the Book of Mormon, in which the Lamanites are to be a "scourge" to the Nephites (1 Ne. 2:24; 2 Ne. 5:25; Jacob 3:3), and at the end of Nephite history when Mormon wrote, "Behold, the judgments of God will overtake the wicked; and it is by the wicked that the wicked are punished; for it is the wicked that stir up the hearts of the children of men unto bloodshed" (Morm. 4:5). This principle helps us to understand how the Lord operates and involves himself in history. For example, in Isaiah 10:5, Assyria is a rod in God's hand for punishing Israel.

Prophecies against Egypt (Isa. 18–20)

Throughout the history of Israel, the Lord continually told his people they must put their trust in him and not in foreign alliances (Isa. 7:9). Political conditions at the time of Isaiah made this a true test of faith and a difficult political decision for the leaders of Israel and Judah. In Isaiah's lifetime, Assyria was the dominant world power. All other nations had either to submit and pay tribute or to rebel by making alliances with neighbors, hoping that together they would be powerful enough to stand against Assyria and maintain their autonomy. Early in Isaiah's lifetime, the Northern Kingdom made a pact with Syria to revolt against Assyria (2 Kgs. 16:1–9) and to force Judah to join with them. The Lord commanded Judah not to join but rather to trust in his power to deliver them (Isa. 7:1–9). The other major power during this period was Egypt. Judah was greatly tempted at various times to make alliances with that nation in hopes of being delivered from Assyrian domination and being relieved of tribute. The oracles of destruction against Egypt in Isaiah 18 through 20 may have been given to further discourage God's chosen people from unwise alliances with the world—a theme that is continued and elaborated in chapters 30 through 31.

Isaiah 18 seems to refer to Egyptian ambassadors sent to Judah to encourage her to join an anti-Assyrian confederacy. Evidence of such coalitions against Assyria exists in historical sources.[7] If that interpretation is correct, then chapter 18 can be read with the following two chapters (19–20) as a prophecy against Egypt. In Isaiah's day, Egypt was ruled by Shabako, a pharaoh from an Ethiopian dynasty. Thus here, as in several other prophecies, the terms *Egypt* and *Ethiopia* are used interchangeably. Even with this interpretation, however, the oracle presents difficulties.[8] Verses 5 and 6 may describe the destruction of this ill-fated coalition against Assyria or perhaps the destruction of Assyria itself.

At the end of the oracle is an optimistic vision of restoration (Isa. 18:7). Scholars note that if this is an oracle against Assyria, then it spells deliverance for Egypt. If so, the KJV rendering of the first word as "Woe" may be misleading. The Hebrew word *hôy*, considering the context of the chapter, could be rendered as a greeting or word of encouragement, such as "Ah" (RSV).[9] On the other hand, some in the Church have interpreted Isaiah 18 as foretelling missionary work that will proceed from the Americas to the world.[10] If this interpretation is correct, chapter 18 would not be considered an oracle against Egypt.

Several of the prophecies against the nations begin with the phrase "the burden of," followed by the name of the nation targeted.[11] The precise meaning of the term "burden" (Hebrew *maśśā'*) is debated. Literally, the Hebrew word means "burden," suggesting that the prophecy of doom is a "heavy load" for Isaiah to deliver. Others derive meaning from the verbal root *nś'*, "to raise," and suggest that the word means "to raise one's voice" in an oracle or prophecy.

In Isaiah 19, verses 1 through 15 constitute an obvious prophecy of doom against Egypt presented in vivid poetic images of social and environmental chaos. Neither their arms, their gods, nor the wisdom of

---

[7]Scholars place this prophecy "either in the period of the Philistine revolt in the year 713–711, or in the year after the death of Sargon in 705 in which Hezekiah played the decisive role in southern Palestine in the movement of revolt against Assyria. The implication is that the ambassadors mentioned in v. 2 are in Jerusalem at the behest of the Ethiopian Pharaoh Shabako in order to discuss common action against the Assyrians with Hezekiah." Otto Kaiser, *Isaiah 13–39*, The Old Testament Library (Philadelphia: Westminster, 1974), pp. 90–91.

[8]A summary of scholarly views on this issue can be found in Kaiser, pp. 89–97.

[9]This term is often used in the context of a prophetic threat, "Woe," but is also attested as a simple interjection, "Ah" (Revised Standard Version) or "Ho."

[10]For a full discussion of this interpretation, see Nyman, pp. 89–90, and Ludlow, pp. 204–10.

[11]E.g., Babylon (13:1); Moab (15:1); Damascus (17:1); Egypt (19:1); and Tyre (23:1).

their people would be able to save them. The message should have been clear for the citizens of Judah: do not turn to Egypt for help, which will not be able to save itself, let alone anyone else. Isaiah foretold that the Egyptians would be given over "into the hand of a cruel lord; and a fierce king shall rule over them" (Isa. 19:4). The precise historical fulfillment of these events is debated. During the lifetime of Isaiah, Egypt was conquered in 714 B.C. by the Ethiopian pharaoh Shabako and defeated in battle by Sargon II of Assyria in 711; later, probably after Isaiah's death, Egypt was again conquered, by Esarhaddon in 671 B.C. and by Ashurbanipal in 663. Each of these conquests was accompanied by civil disorder such as that described in Isaiah 19:2.

The remainder of Isaiah 19 is punctuated by the phrase "in that day," a prophetic idiom which almost always points to a setting in the latter days. "In that day," Egypt will recognize the Lord's power among his people (Isa. 19:16–17); Israel's language will be spoken in cities of Egypt, and the Lord will be worshiped there (Isa. 19:18); an altar to the Lord will be built there—a reference to a temple—and "the Lord shall be known to Egypt, and the Egyptians shall know the Lord" (Isa. 19:19–21). Though he once punished the Egyptians, now "he shall be intreated of them, and shall heal them" (Isa. 19:22). "In that day," Egypt and Assyria, mortal enemies and rival superpowers in Isaiah's time, will be brought together with the Lord's people in a common bond and will together enjoy his favor: "Blessed be Egypt my people, and Assyria the work of my hands, and Israel mine inheritance" (Isa. 19:23–25).

In Isaiah 20, Egypt's inability to withstand Assyrian power is again the topic. The Lord commanded Isaiah to strip himself as an impoverished exile and walk around "naked and barefoot" (Isa. 20:2). Isaiah's attire was to symbolize the plight of the Egyptians, who would be overpowered and taken captive by Assyrian forces. The message, of course, was to Judah, whose reliance on Egypt would be to no avail. In despair they would say, "See what has happened to those we relied on, those we fled to for help and deliverance from the king of Assyria! How then can we escape?" (Isa. 20:6, NIV).[12] Fortunately, Judah's king, Hezekiah, wisely chose to follow Isaiah's counsel and trusted in Jehovah for deliverance (Isa. 36:1–37:38).

[12]New International Version.

Prophecies against Judah and Other Nations
(Isa. 21–23)

Five prophecies in Isaiah 21 through 23 complete the Oracles against Foreign Nations and demonstrate with specific examples the universal nature of the Lord's judgments. They are a bridge between the prophecies of destruction, many of which were fulfilled in ancient times, and the last-days prophecies in chapters 24 through 27, which foretell judgment being poured out on the whole world.

Isaiah 21:1–10 is a prophecy directed against Babylon, called "the desert of the sea" because of its arid setting at the head of the Persian Gulf: "Babylon is fallen, is fallen; and all the graven images of her gods he hath broken unto the ground" (Isa. 21:9). Babylon was conquered by the Assyrian king Sennacherib in 691–89 B.C. and again by Cyrus of Persia in 539 B.C. But perhaps here, as in other places, Babylon is used as a type of the world, and its fall typifies the universal destruction of wickedness. The Lord spoke in similar words to Joseph Smith of the latter-day manifestation of Babylon: "Every man walketh in his own way, and after the image of his own god, whose image is in the likeness of the world, and whose substance is that of an idol, which waxeth old and shall perish in Babylon, even Babylon the great, which shall fall" (D&C 1:16).

Isaiah 21 concludes with two short prophecies. Verses 11 and 12 seem to foretell alternating periods of light and darkness for Edom.[13] Verses 13 through 17 prophesy doom for the tribes of Arabia.

The following prophecy, Isaiah 22, is directed against Jerusalem, a city of hills and valleys that is referred to here as "the valley of vision" (Isa. 22:1). Just as Ephraim was counted among the nations for destruction in Isaiah 17, now Jerusalem is also included. The setting of the prophecy seems to reflect the circumstances of Sennacherib's invasion of Judah in 701 B.C. The Assyrian king successfully conquered all of the country but Jerusalem, which was saved in a miraculous way when King Hezekiah and his people put their trust in Jehovah's power to deliver them, reversing Judah's former policy of trusting in misguided alliances with foreign kings.

---

[13]Edom (or Greek, "Idumea"), like Babylon, is sometimes a type of the world in ancient as well as modern scripture. See D&C 1:36, and see the discussion of Isa. 34 in Chap. 14 of this volume.

When Sennacherib invaded, the people of Jerusalem turned to their weapons, fortified their defensive walls, and stored water inside the city (Isa. 22:8, 10–11). But these measures, which would have been no match for Assyria's power, were not needed. God intervened, as he promised he would, and defended Jerusalem himself (Isa. 36–37; 2 Kgs. 18:13–19:37).

The miraculous deliverance was to be seen as another opportunity to repent, but instead of repenting, the people celebrated: "In that day did the Lord God of hosts call to weeping, and to mourning, and to baldness, and to girding with sackcloth: And behold joy and gladness, slaying oxen, and killing sheep, eating flesh, and drinking wine: let us eat and drink; for to morrow we shall die" (Isa. 22:12–13). For that response, Isaiah wrote, they would eventually be held accountable: "And it was revealed in mine ears by the Lord of hosts, Surely this iniquity shall not be purged from you till ye die" (Isa. 22:14).

This same attitude of arrogance is also identifiable in two of Jerusalem's public servants. Shebna, a court official, had in his self-assurance built himself a splendid sepulchre in a high place (Isa. 22:16) and rode in a glorious royal chariot (Isa. 22:18). The Lord promised to bring down all of that: Shebna would fall from his high position, and captivity would be his reward. Another man, Eliakim, would be given authority and power. "The key of the house of David" would be laid on his shoulders (Isa. 22:22). He would be as secure as "a nail in a sure place" (Isa. 22:23), but eventually he too would "be cut down, and fall" (Isa. 22:25). Some have read the imagery in this passage messianically. But much caution is required: Eliakim failed in his calling, but the Messiah did not.

The last in this series of prophecies, Isaiah 23, foretells the destruction of the Phoenician port city of Tyre. Tyre, the marketplace of the nations (Isa. 23:3), was one of the most important and prosperous cities of the world, because it controlled much of the trade in the eastern Mediterranean. Its wealth had led to pride, which is abhorrent to the Lord. In Isaiah's day, Tyre was an island off the Phoenician coast (see Map 9, LDS Bible).[14] Although the city was forced to pay tribute several times during the Assyrian and Babylonian periods, it was not captured or destroyed until almost four centuries after Isaiah, when in 332 B.C. it

---

[14]The word Tyre (Hebrew, ṣûr) means something like "rock."

fell to Alexander the Great.[15] The oracle concludes with the prophecy that Tyre will one day be dedicated to the work of the Lord: "Her merchandise and her hire shall be holiness to the Lord" (Isa. 23:18).

The Apocalypse of Isaiah (Isa. 24–27)

The word *apocalypse* literally means "from hiding" and refers to prophetic discourse or revelation in general. The common definition of this word, however, is derived from the New Testament, in Revelation 1:1, in which it refers to the vision given to John the Beloved on the Island of Patmos concerning the events surrounding the latter days, the Second Coming, and the end of the world. Today *apocalyptic* is used as a virtual synonym of *eschatology* (Greek, "teachings about last things") and also denotes visions and revelations about events of cosmic destruction and the end of the world.[16] The absolute nature and the finality of the language in Isaiah 24 through 27 is clearly eschatological, and the fulfillment of these prophecies is best looked for in the last days.

This section provides a climax to the book of Isaiah up to this point. Isaiah begins with prophecies of destruction and restoration for Israel in chapters 1 through 12, followed by the Oracles against Foreign Nations in chapters 13 through 23, each directed against a specific nation. Chapters 24 through 27 then move to the universal destruction.

Isaiah 24 depicts the end of the world as the reversal of creation. The Creation, recorded in Genesis, is a cosmic event: "In the beginning God created the heaven and the earth" (Gen. 1:1). The Lord, through his word ("And God said . . . and it was so"), made the earth, set the lights in the firmament, filled the earth with life (first animal and then humans), and then "planted a garden eastward in Eden; and there he put the man whom he had formed" (Gen. 2:8). At the end of each phase of creation, the Lord "saw that it was good."

As portrayed in Isaiah 24, the judgment of the Lord, at the end of time, will also be of cosmic proportions. The Lord, through his word,

---

[15]Nebuchadnezzar unsuccessfully besieged Tyre for thirteen years until he resolved the conflict by treaty. Alexander built a causeway out to the island, thus connecting it permanently to the mainland, and his combined sea and land assault captured the city after only seven months.

[16]See "Apocalyptic Revelation," in Chap. 28 of this volume.

will declare destruction on his creation, which, though once good, has now become corrupt: "Behold, the Lord maketh the earth empty, and maketh it waste, and turneth it upside down, and scattereth abroad the inhabitants thereof" (Isa. 24:1); "the earth shall reel to and fro like a drunkard" (Isa. 24:20); "then the moon shall be confounded, and the sun ashamed" (Isa. 24:23). The catastrophes that will afflict a world that "lieth in sin, and groaneth under darkness and under the bondage of sin" (D&C 84:49) include earthquakes (Isa. 24:1, 18–20), drought (Isa. 24:4), a curse that devours the earth (Isa. 24:6), burning (Isa. 24:6), desolation and destruction (Isa. 24:12), and flood (Isa. 24:18).

In short, the end of the world is a reversal of creation: "The land shall be utterly emptied, and utterly spoiled: for the Lord hath spoken this word" (Isa. 24:3). The reason for such drastic action is clear: "The earth also is defiled under the inhabitants thereof; because they have transgressed the laws, changed the ordinance, broken the everlasting covenant" (Isa. 24:5).[17] All of the inhabitants will suffer: people and priests, servant and master, maid and mistress, buyer and seller, lender and borrower, and taker and giver of usury (Isa. 24:2).[18] After the burning, only a few will be left (Isa. 24:6). One prominent image is that of the harvest—"the shaking of an olive tree, and as the gleaning grapes when the vintage is done" (Isa. 24:13).

At the end of judgment, the Creator will return in his glory—"the Lord of hosts shall reign in mount Zion, and in Jerusalem, and before his ancients [elders] gloriously"—with which the sun and the moon will pale in comparison (Isa. 24:23).

The reversal of creation through destruction when the "earth mourneth and fadeth away" (Isa. 24:4) is the Lord's preparation for the

---

[17]Jewish tradition often interprets the "everlasting covenant" as the covenant given to Noah—called the "everlasting covenant" in Gen. 9:16—which was made between God and the whole human race and which included a basic moral law about the sanctity of life and the seriousness of murder (Gen. 9). The Lord in D&C 1:15 uses similar language about those in the world who will perish with Babylon: "For they have strayed from mine ordinances, and have broken mine everlasting covenant." Joseph Smith interpreted this verse as the covenant brought by Christ that was offered to the Jews and rejected but then taken to the Gentiles, who at first accepted it but through the apostasy finally rejected it as well; *Teachings*, p. 15.

[18]Each of these expressions is a merism, a rhetorical device in which two members of a set (often opposites, as in "buyer and seller," "lender and borrower") are juxtaposed to mean a whole. In other words, *everyone* will suffer.

new creation, described at length in Isaiah 40 through 66[19] (especially 60–66), when the Lord will create "the new heavens and the new earth" (Isa. 65:17; 66:22) and will form a new people (Isa. 43:21), with whom he will make an everlasting covenant (Isa. 61:8).

Isaiah 25 contains a psalm of praise and thanksgiving to the Lord God, who has been a "strength to the poor, a strength to the needy in his distress, a refuge from the storm, a shadow from the heat, when the blast of the terrible ones is as a storm against the wall" (Isa. 25:4). The Lord upon his return will celebrate a great feast, called the messianic banquet, when he will "make unto all people a feast of fat things, a feast of wines on the lees, of fat things full of marrow, of wines on the lees well refined" (Isa. 25:6). Feasting is a powerful symbol, incorporating imagery from the sacrament of the Lord's supper and the partaking and eating of the tree of life, as well as imagery of communal meals and fellowship. This feast is to be understood literally as well as spiritually as an occasion that has been prepared for the rich and mighty but is also attended by the poor and humble, an occasion for rejoicing in the richness and fellowship of the Saints with their king (see Zech. 14:16–19; Matt. 8:11; 22:1–10; Luke 14:15–24; 22:18; Rev. 19:9; D&C 58:8–12). At this day the Lord will remove "the vail that is spread over all nations. He will swallow up death in victory; and the Lord God will wipe away tears from off all faces; and the rebuke of his people shall he take away from off all the earth" (Isa. 25:7–8).

Isaiah 26 teaches that God's righteous judgment is a reversal of the ways of the world. "Like as a woman with child, that draweth near the time of her delivery, is in pain, and crieth out in her pangs; so have we been in thy sight, O Lord" (Isa. 26:17). Throughout history, the Saints in the world have uttered such laments. When the judge and king returns, he will come in judgment and restore justice, for which the righteous have longed and the wicked feared (Isa. 26:8–9). Justice entails a reversal of the ways of the world: the Lord "bringeth down them that dwell on high; the lofty city, he layeth it low; he layeth it low even to the ground; he bringeth it even to the dust. The foot shall tread it down, even the

---

[19]For a complete discussion of this theme in Isaiah, see Carroll Stuhlmueller, *Creative Redemption in Deutero-Isaiah*, Analecta Biblica 43 (Rome: Biblical Institute, 1970).

feet of the poor, and the steps of the needy" (Isa. 26:5–6).[20] Then will "the inhabitants of the world learn righteousness" (Isa. 26:9), and the earth will be full of peace (Isa. 26:3, 12). The Lord answers his Saints with the promise of resurrection—through the Atonement the consequences of the Fall can be reversed: "Thy dead men shall live, together with my dead body shall they arise. Awake and sing, ye that dwell in dust: for thy dew is as the dew of herbs, and the earth shall cast out the dead" (Isa. 26:19).

Throughout the scriptures, covenant Israel is often depicted in horticultural terms (Ps. 80:8–13; Jer. 2:21; Ezek. 15; Hos. 10:1; Matt. 21:33–43; Mark 12:1–11; Luke 20:9–17; Jacob 5, etc.). In Isaiah 5:1–7 the Lord addressed his beloved Israel as a vineyard that in spite of his constant care had brought forth wild grapes and was thus ready for destruction. Just as the destruction of the people had been couched in the images of harvesting, so restoration and gathering is expressed as planting a vineyard, watering it, and weeding it (Isa. 27:2–4). Through the care of the Lord, "Israel shall blossom and bud, and fill the face of the world with fruit" (Isa. 27:6).[21] When "the iniquity of Jacob be purged" and Israel cleansed of idolatry (Isa. 27:9), the Lord will "thresh" (KJV, "beat off") his people—separate the wheat from the chaff—and gather his people "one by one" (Isa. 27:12). Eventually the harvest will be gathered from Egypt and Assyria (perhaps symbolic of the whole world), and they "shall worship the Lord in the holy mount at Jerusalem" (Isa. 27:13).

The Six Woes (Isa. 28–33)

Isaiah 28 through 33 is a collection of many diverse prophecies, mostly eschatological, in a framework of six Woes, each illustrating a timeless lesson as relevant today as it was to ancient Israel.

1. *"Woe to the crown of pride, to the drunkards of Ephraim"* (Isa. 28). The prophecy of the destruction of Ephraim—the Northern Kingdom,

---

[20]See also Ps. 147:6, "The Lord lifteth up the meek: he casteth the wicked down to the ground"; the New Testament in the Sermon on the Mount, Matt. 5:5, "Blessed are the meek: for they shall inherit the earth"; Luke 1:51, "He hath put down the mighty from their seats, and exalted them of low degree."

[21]See also Isa. 28:23–29, where the care of the Lord for his people is portrayed in terms of planting and harvesting.

Israel, or Samaria—was undoubtedly given in the first half of Isaiah's ministry, because the promised destruction occurred at the hands of the Assyrians in 721 B.C. and the ten northern tribes were carried into captivity. Before it was destroyed, Samaria was wealthy, prosperous, arrogant, and overindulgent, as reflected by the indictments pronounced by the prophets to the North (Hosea and Amos) and the archaeological evidence. Samaria is thus personified in Isaiah 28:1 as a city on a hill surrounded by a towered wall (1 Kgs. 16:24) resembling a "crown of pride." And the crown (a garland of fading flowers) is sitting upon the drunkard Ephraim[22] at the head of "fat valleys," representing the rich agricultural resources in the North. All of this is ephemeral. It will soon "be trodden under feet" (Isa. 28:3) "and as the hasty fruit before the summer" will be eaten up by the conqueror (Isa. 28:4).

The condition of the Northern Kingdom is also the condition of Judah in the south (Isa. 28:7, "but they also"), where the drunkenness is spiritual as well. A stupor is upon priest and prophet, which renders them incapable of discernment either in vision or in judgment (Isa. 28:7). The vomit and filthiness of their parties are unclean (Isa. 28:8). One sophisticated and scornful drunkard sarcastically questions the prophet (or the Lord): "Whom shall he teach knowledge? and whom shall he make to understand doctrine? them that are weaned from the milk, and drawn from the breasts?" He mimics the simplicity of the prophet's message, "For precept must be upon precept, precept upon precept; line upon line, line upon line; here a little, and there a little" (Isa. 28:9–10).[23] The prophet responds by repeating their mocking lines. Indeed the message is simple—precept by precept, line upon line—but deceptively so; if not followed, it will lead to their destruction (Isa. 28:13).

Isaiah 28:10 is quoted as the word of the Lord in 2 Nephi, without the sarcasm, as a demonstration that the mastery of the word of the Lord is a simple yet gradual process. A promise is added: "And blessed are those who hearken unto my precepts, and lend an ear unto my counsel,

---

[22]Amos indicted Israel for wanton drunkenness and described a drinking party in Samaria (Amos 6:1–6).

[23]The Hebrew of the first part of this passage reads *saw lāsāw saw lāsāw qaw lāqāw qaw lāqāw*—syllables in Hebrew that are either abbreviations of intended words, denoting perhaps a common proverb, or, as some have suggested, a teacher teaching his young students the alphabet. See Kaiser, pp. 243–46.

for they shall learn wisdom; for unto him that receiveth I will give more; and from them that shall say, We have enough, from them shall be taken away that which they have" (2 Ne. 28:30; see also D&C 98:12; 128:21).

2. *"Woe to Ariel, the city where David dwelt"* *(Isa. 29:1–14)*. This Woe is addressed to Ariel—a word that probably means "hearth of God," referring to the altar at the temple.[24] It is used here as a personification of Jerusalem, the city where David dwelt. The message is that destruction will befall Ariel, a prophecy that was fulfilled in 587 B.C. by the Babylonians and again in A.D. 70 by the Romans. But though Ariel shall be brought down to the ground, in the future its voice will be heard from the dust, as the voice of the dead speaking to the living (Isa. 29:4).

Isaiah 29:3–24 is quoted extensively, with significant changes and additions, in 2 Nephi 26:15 through 27:35.[25] In the Book of Mormon, Nephi applies the prophecy of destruction to his own people and identifies the voice from the dust as the Nephite record, the Book of Mormon, which will speak from the dust. This is clearly an example of a prophecy that is best understood by those who live in the time of its fulfillment (2 Ne. 25:7), and we in the latter days have witnessed a detailed fulfillment of this prophecy. The promised apostasy occurred: "For the Lord hath poured out upon you the spirit of deep sleep, and hath closed your eyes: the prophets and your rulers, the seers hath he covered" (Isa. 29:10). The "words of a book that is sealed" (the golden plates) were delivered to the "one that is learned" (Charles Anthon) who could not read it and then delivered back to "him that is not learned" (Joseph Smith; 29:11–12), as recounted in Joseph Smith–History 1:63–65. And today the Book of Mormon speaks "low out of the dust" (in the words of Nephi, "I speak unto you as the voice of one crying from the dust"; 2 Ne. 33:13; see also Moro. 10:27). The circumstances of the coming forth of the Book of Mormon through the unlearned demonstrate that the Lord is able to do his own work in his own due time (2 Ne. 27:21).[26] We have seen the "marvellous work and a wonder" (Isa. 29:14) as the restored gospel goes forth to the world.

---

[24]The word occurs in Ezek. 43:15–16, describing the altar at the temple.

[25]JST Isa. 29 corresponds with the version in 2 Ne. For a more complete discussion, see Nyman, pp. 112–17, and Ludlow, pp. 268–77.

[26]See the treatment of 2 Ne. 27 in Robert J. Matthews, "Two Ways in the World: The Warfare between God and Satan," in *Studies in Scripture, Volume Seven: 1 Nephi to Alma 29,* ed. Kent P. Jackson (Salt Lake City: Deseret Book Co., 1987), pp. 152–55.

3. *"Woe unto them that seek deep to hide their counsel from the Lord"* (*Isa. 29:15–24*). In the beginning, God, the father of our spirits, "formed man of the dust of the ground" (Gen. 2:7). Because the Hebrew verb *yṣr* ("to form") is often used to describe pot-making, the original image intended may have been the Lord shaping man out of the clay.[27] Those who seek to hide their counsels from their Creator rationalize, "Who seeth us? and who knoweth us?" (Isa. 29:15). The Lord responds to such people, "Surely your turning of things upside down shall be esteemed as the potter's clay: for shall the work say of him that made it, He made me not? or shall the thing framed say of him that framed it, He had no understanding?" (Isa. 29:16). The irony and ultimate futility of the creation's impudence towards its Creator is one of Isaiah's favorite themes. In Isaiah 45:9 there is a similar image: "Woe unto him that striveth with his Maker! Let the potsherds strive with the potsherds of the earth. Shall the clay say to him that fashioneth it, What makest thou? or thy work, He hath no hands?" And in Isaiah 10:15 the Lord says, "Shall the axe boast itself against him that heweth therewith? or shall the saw magnify itself against him that shaketh it?" In its context, Isaiah 29:15–24 is directed against those who would resist, based on the wisdom of men, God's marvelous work and wonder.

4. *"Woe to the rebellious children . . . that take counsel, but not of me"* (*Isa. 30*). This Woe continues, "and that cover with a covering, but not of my spirit, that they may add sin to sin" (Isa. 30:1). It is specifically directed against those who "walk to go down into Egypt, and have not asked at my mouth; to strengthen themselves in the strength of Pharaoh, and to trust in the shadow of Egypt!" (Isa. 30:2). The historical circumstance is Judah's constant attempts to make political alliances with Egypt (Isa. 18, 31). In the larger context of chapter 30, the immediate enemy is identified as the Assyrians (Isa. 30:27–33). Not only has Judah demonstrated lack of faith in the Lord but has not even sought his counsel in time of need. The Lord's response, as illustrated in the oracles against Egypt in Isaiah 18 through 20, is that Egypt will not stand, and "the Egyptians shall help in vain, and to no purpose" (Isa. 30:7).

The Lord commanded Isaiah to preserve a record of his prophecies

---

[27]For other imagery of God as a potter, see Isa. 64:8; Jer. 18:1–6; and Rom. 9:20–24.

as a witness against the people in the day of their fulfillment (Isa. 30:8; 8:16). Then the Lord indicted the house of Israel on several counts: they are rebellious children who "will not hear the law of the Lord" (Isa. 30:9), and they deny the visions of the seers and only want to hear "smooth things" from the prophets (Isa. 30:10). Indeed, they are a people who "hear but understand not, and see but do not perceive" (Isa. 6:9). In addition, this is a people who trust in the speed of their horses—their military might—rather than in the Lord (Isa. 30:11–12, 15–16). They will discover that without the Lord they are no match for their enemies, who will pursue and destroy them until they are "left as a beacon upon the top of a mountain, and as an ensign on an hill" (Isa. 30:17).

This oracle of doom is balanced by one of hope in Isaiah 30:18–26. The Lord promised that after "the bread of adversity, and the water of affliction" (Isa. 30:20), deliverance will come, which will include rain, abundance, light, and healing (Isa. 30:23–26)—all imagery pointing to the Millennium. This suggests that the oracle of destruction against Assyria in Isaiah 30:27–33 is a type of the cosmic destruction of Satan in the last days. Deliverance is not to be found in foreign alliances but in the arm of the Lord, which will once more be turned against Israel's enemies (Isa. 30:30). The king of Assyria will be defeated and laid on a pyre, which "the breath of the Lord, like a stream of brimstone, doth kindle" (Isa. 30:33).

5. *"Woe to them that go down to Egypt for help" (Isa. 31–32).* Just as in Isaiah 30, this Woe is directed against those who turn to Egypt for help "and stay on horses, and trust in chariots, because they are many; and in horsemen, because they are very strong; but they look not unto the Holy One of Israel, neither seek the Lord!" (Isa. 31:1). The Lord's response is simple, logical, and prophetic: "Now the Egyptians are men, and not God; and their horses flesh, and not spirit. When the Lord shall stretch out his hand, both he that helpeth shall fall, and he that is holpen shall fall down, and they all shall fail together" (Isa. 31:3).

The Book of Mormon expression of this principle is found in a Woe uttered by Nephi against those who say, "We have received the word of God, and we need no more of the word of God, for we have enough!" (2 Ne. 28:29). Then Nephi wrote, "Thus saith the Lord God: I will give unto the children of men line upon line, precept upon precept," a quotation of Isaiah 28:13 (2 Ne. 28:30). Nephi continued echoing Isaiah's injunction in Isaiah 30:1: "Cursed is he that putteth his trust in man, or maketh flesh his arm, or shall hearken unto the precepts of men, save their precepts shall be given by the power of the Holy Ghost" (2 Ne. 28:31; see also 4:34).

Isaiah 32 is a messianic prophecy looking forward to the many years of hardship that remain for the covenant people "until the spirit be poured upon us from on high, and the wilderness be a fruitful field, and the fruitful field be counted for a forest" (Isa. 32:15). Then with the Messiah will come justice, righteousness, and peace (Isa. 32:16–18).

6. *"Woe to thee that spoilest, and thou wast not spoiled"* (Isa. 33). In Isaiah's day, this Woe could well have been addressed to Assyria, who achieved its day of glory and conquest but ultimately would suffer the same treachery that it dealt to others (see Isa. 10:5–19). The message is a timeless warning to all seeking wealth, power, and glory who would justify the means by the end. Judgment will be terrible for the wicked and glorious for Zion. The righteous anxiously await their king (Isa. 33:2), at whose return the "highways lie waste" (Isa. 33:8), "the earth mourneth and languisheth" (Isa. 33:9), "and the people shall be as the burnings of lime: as thorns cut up shall they be burned in the fire" (Isa. 33:12). Just as ancient Israelites seeking entrance to the temple asked at the doors: "Who shall ascend into the hill of the Lord? or who shall stand in his holy place" (Ps. 24:3–6; 15:2–5), so in the face of destruction "the sinners in Zion are afraid; fearfulness hath surprised the hypocrites" (Isa. 33:14). They cry out the same questions: "Who among us shall dwell with the devouring fire? who among us shall dwell with everlasting burnings?" (Isa. 33:14). The Lord's response to such questions as to who is worthy and able to endure his presence reveals much about Israel's sins: only he is worthy "that walketh righteously, and speaketh uprightly; he that despiseth the gain of oppressions, that shaketh his hands from holding of bribes, and stoppeth his ears from hearing of blood, and shutteth his eyes from seeing evil" (Isa. 33:15).[28]

Isaiah's message to Israel from beginning to end is simple: repent or be destroyed. It is a message of hope for the humble and of doom for the disobedient. The Lord told Israel at the outset: "Come now, and let us reason together, saith the Lord: though your sins be as scarlet, they shall

---

[28]The Lord's definitions of worthiness in Ps. 15:2–5 and 24:3–6 contain similar elements and provide an interesting comparison.

be as white as snow; though they be red like crimson, they shall be as wool" (Isa. 1:18). Isaiah 33 looks to the time when the Lord as judge and lawgiver will return as king and Savior (Isa. 33:22) to usher in the Millennium. Israel, who in chapter 1 was stricken, sick, and wounded (Isa. 1:5–6), will finally, after she has received her punishment, be healed and forgiven: "And the inhabitant shall not say, I am sick: the people that dwell therein shall be forgiven their iniquity" (Isa. 33:24).[29]

---

[29]The language of Isa. 33:24 appears to be a deliberate echo and *inclusio* of Isa. 1:5–6.

14

COMFORT MY PEOPLE

(ISAIAH 34–50)

KENT P. JACKSON

As a general rule, when Latter-day Saints use the word *restoration* they think of the restoration of the gospel – the process by which the true Church, true priesthood, and true doctrine were brought back to the earth through the ministry of Joseph Smith. In Old Testament prophecy, the idea of restoration adds upon those things to include the restoration of the house of Israel to its covenant status, the restoration of its people to their promised lands, and the restoration of the Lord himself to his rightful position as Israel's king. Also included in the prophetic vision are the restoration of justice to the world, the restoration of the earth to the status it enjoyed prior to the Fall (see A of F 10), and the restoration of peace and happiness to God's faithful children. God's justice is a major theme in the book of Isaiah. When the Lord restores justice, all people will receive what they justly deserve, whether good or bad.[1] It is the totality of these blessings that readers should have in mind as they study the words of Isaiah, who saw and recorded the marvelous latter-day circumstances that would make the restoration process complete.

The Lord's Vengeance and Recompense (Isa. 34–35)

Isaiah 34 and 35 constitute a single prophecy of two parts. The first part, chapter 34, is a warning of the judgment which God will bring

---

Kent P. Jackson is professor of ancient scripture at Brigham Young University.

[1]Almost always in the Old Testament of the KJV the word *judgment* is used to translate the Hebrew word *mišpāt*, which would more accurately be translated as "justice."

upon the world because of its wickedness. The second, chapter 35, is a promise of the earth's subsequent millennial renewal.

In expressing his anger against "all nations" (Isa. 34:1–4), the Lord gave us a glimpse into the cataclysmic circumstances that will attend his second coming: the "host of heaven," presumably the stars,[2] will be "dissolved," the heavens will be "rolled together as a scroll," and "all their host shall fall down," like autumn leaves (Isa. 34:4). The exact nature of this cosmic occurrence cannot be determined now, but its reality is well attested in the scriptures (see Matt. 24:29; D&C 29:14; 34:9; 45:42; see also Joel 2:31).

The Lord singled out Edom (Isa. 34:5–6; "Idumea" in the KJV)[3] as being a specific object of his wrath and vengeance. In Isaiah's day Edom bordered the kingdom of Judah on the southeast, south of Moab. According to the biblical genealogies, the Edomites were descendants of Jacob's brother Esau (see Gen. 25:30; 36:1). They are frequently the object of God's anger in the Old Testament (see Jer. 49:7–22; Ezek. 25:12–14; Obad. 1), so seeing them specified here as a nation to be destroyed by the Lord's justice is not surprising. But in this context it appears that Edom has a broader meaning as well. In the writings of the Old Testament prophets, the names of unrighteous nations are frequently used typologically to represent the wickedness of the world in general. As the references to Edom are part of a larger prophecy that deals with the destruction and later glorification of the whole world, it is likely that in this passage Edom represents the entire earth. This extended symbolism finds a distinct parallel in Doctrine and Covenants 1:36, in which the Lord uses the term *Idumea* to represent the world.

So great will be the destruction of the world in Isaiah's depiction that it will become a desolate wilderness, devoid of human habitation, the home of thorns, brambles, and the "wild beasts of the desert" (Isa. 34:11–17).[4]

---

[2]This passage is the only occurrence of the term "host of heaven" in Isaiah. Elsewhere in the Bible it is used with reference to stars (e.g., Deut. 4:19; 17:3; 2 Kgs. 23:5; Jer. 8:2), or heavenly beings (e.g., 1 Kgs. 22:19; 2 Kgs. 17:16). In several of these passages the term may refer to both, given the popularity of astral deities in the ancient Near East.

[3]Also in Ezek. 35:15; 36:5. *Idumea* is the Greek form of the name *Edom*. It was known as Idumea during the Hellenistic period, including the New Testament period, when Greek was the common language of the Near East.

[4]Two of these "wild beasts" are of special interest. The KJV translates the Hebrew word for

There can be no question that Isaiah's words, as given him by the spirit of prophecy, were intended to evoke deep feelings in the hearts of his ancient and modern readers. The day of the Lord is the day of the Lord's recompense; it is the day in which he will measure out to individuals and nations alike the fruits of their deeds — rewards or punishments that suit, in God's just judgment, their actions. Those nations or individuals whose actions reveal pride, vanity, and hatred will receive a just reward that is characterized by many of the dreadful punishments listed in Isaiah 34. It will be by these that the earth will be cleansed to become the inheritance of the Lord's Saints in Zion: "For it is the day of the Lord's vengeance, and the year of recompences, for the [cause] of Zion" (Isa. 34:8).

Isaiah 35 presents a much different scene — a scene of the earth restored after the cleansing process described in the previous chapter. In its millennial renewal the earth will be restored to the state it enjoyed before the Fall (A of F 10), which will include the revival and revitalization of its landscape. The desert, Isaiah wrote, will "blossom as the rose. It shall blossom abundantly, and rejoice even with joy and singing" (Isa. 35:1–2). Waters will "break out" where once only desert was found (Isa. 35:6); "the parched ground shall become a pool, and the thirsty land springs of water." The arid range of jackals (KJV, "dragons") will be covered with "grass with reeds and rushes" (Isa. 35:7). Isaiah likened the millennial earth's fruitfulness with that of areas famous in his day for their forests and fertility: the Lebanon and Carmel mountains and the Plain of Sharon (Isa. 35:2).

The millennial renewal will not be limited to the earth; its beneficiaries will also include the Lord's people, both as individuals and as a nation. When the Lord returns with vengeance and recompense, the blind, the deaf, the lame, and the mute will enjoy the healing power of his presence. Although the healing of physical impairments is a common metaphor for spiritual healing (e.g., Isa. 29:18), there is good reason to look forward to a very literal fulfillment of these words as well. As Christ's mortal ministry included the restoration of sight, hearing, mobility, and

---

"wild oxen," *re'ēmîm* (Isa. 34:7), as "unicorns." Joseph Smith, in the JST, removed the word "unicorns" and transliterated the Hebrew word to "reem." The KJV word "dragons" in v. 13 (Hebrew, *tannîm*) means "jackals."

speech, so also will his millennial service to those who believe in his name (Isa. 35:5–6).

The "ransomed of the Lord" will be established in Zion, the perfect Christ-centered society that will characterize the Millennium. Isaiah described their coming as a safe return along a highway—the "Way of Holiness"—free of danger from the unrighteous and the unclean (Isa. 35:8–9). His Saints will "come to Zion," he wrote, "with songs and everlasting joy upon their heads: they shall obtain joy and gladness, and sorrow and sighing shall flee away" (Isa. 35:10).

Trusting in the Saving Power of the Lord (Isa. 36–39)

One important theme of the book of Isaiah is the need to trust in the Lord's power to save. Several passages teach this principle and emphasize the futility of putting faith either in the false gods of the nations or in the armaments of war. Because Jehovah is the true king of Israel and Judah, his people—when properly equipped and fortified with righteousness—can rely on his power to save them. He will fight their battles (Josh. 10:11; 2 Chron. 20:15–17; Ps. 44:3–8), as Isaiah taught with repeated emphasis (Isa. 7:1–16; 8:1–10; 10:24–34; 51:4–8). His faithful people need not fear, "for God is with us" (Isa. 8:10).

Perhaps the most dramatic example of this principle is found in Isaiah 36 through 39, which is a copy of 2 Kings 18:13 through 20:19 with some modifications. No indication is given why this material is included in the book of Isaiah (it starts and ends without editorial comment), but readers can readily see why its inclusion is appropriate. It contains an important episode from Isaiah's career that bears testimony to his work as God's spokesman. It also includes some important revelations that otherwise would have been left out of his prophetic record.

Because a discussion of the corresponding chapters from 2 Kings is found elsewhere in this volume,[5] it will be necessary here only to make a few brief observations.

The issue in Isaiah 36 through 39 concerns the Lord's desire that we place our trust in him, that we put him to the test by exercising faith

---

[5]See Chap. 10 of this volume.

in his promises. The Rabshakeh, speaking in behalf of Sennacherib, king of Assyria (704–681 B.C.), taunted Hezekiah and the people of Jerusalem: Do not trust your king Hezekiah (Isa. 36:14), and do not trust your god (Isa. 36:15; 37:10–13). No other nation's god has been able to deliver it from Assyrian conquest. Neither can yours; nothing can save you from the power of the king of Assyria.

In response to this display of arrogance, the Lord responded through his prophet with a biting announcement that Sennacherib had now taken on a foe much too powerful for him: "Whom hast thou reproached and blasphemed? and against whom hast thou exalted thy voice, and lifted up thine eyes on high? even against the Holy One of Israel" (Isa. 37:23). To Hezekiah the assuring word came: "He shall not come into this city, nor shoot an arrow there, nor come before it with shields, nor cast a bank against it. By the way that he came, by the same shall he return, and shall not come into this city, saith the Lord. For I will defend this city" (Isa. 37:33–35). Because Hezekiah and his people were willing to turn to the Lord for deliverance, Jerusalem was saved.

Chapters 38 and 39 record other events in which Isaiah's prophecies came true. Through Hezekiah's faith and fervent prayer, the Lord extended his life by fifteen years, delivering him from the effects of illness (Isa. 38:1–8). Chapter 39 ends on a less happy note, as Isaiah foretold that one day Babylon would plunder Jerusalem and take some of its population into exile (Isa. 39:6–7).

The Book of Reconciliation

Isaiah 40 begins a new and significant section (chaps. 40–66) that I call the "Book of Reconciliation" (see the explanation in Chap. 11 of this volume). Some significant features of this part of Isaiah include the following:

1. The political reality of Judah and Israel (Ephraim) as separate peoples is no longer mentioned. Instead, the whole family is known by the name *Israel* or by the synonymous name *Jacob.*

2. The Millennium is stressed, because the emphasis is on God's reconciliation with his people and their future blessing.

3. There is emphasis on God's power to foretell the future (e.g., Isa.

41:22–23; 42:9; 44:7–8, 26; 45:21; 46:10, 11; 48:3–7, 14). It is ironic that this part of Isaiah stresses God's capacity to give knowledge of the future to his prophets—the very point that causes some to deny its authorship to Isaiah.

4. The work of God's "Servant" is foretold.

Good Tidings for Zion (Isa. 40–41)

Perhaps no chapter better sums up the spirit and message of Isaiah's "Book of Reconciliation" than chapter 40. It is a chapter of annunciation—the announcement that Israel's day of trial and sadness is over and that the Lord has come to save and heal the world. Three beautiful passages in the first half of the chapter express joy in the announcement of the good news of salvation (Isa. 40:1–2, 3–5, and 9–11):

1. *"Comfort ye, comfort ye my people."* Verses 1 and 2 of Isaiah 40 foretell the consoling message that the sorrows and horrors of Jerusalem's probation are over: "her warfare is accomplished," "her iniquity is pardoned," and she has "received of the Lord's hand double for all her sins." Up to that yet-future time, Jerusalem's history will have been one of all too frequent sadness, brought about because its inhabitants refused to obey the laws that would have guaranteed its peace (Luke 13:34–35). As the Old Testament prophets foretold, Jerusalem was destroyed at the hands of the Babylonians in 587 B.C., climaxing a four-hundred-year vain experiment of mortals replacing Jehovah as king of Israel. Sorrow continued for Jerusalem's later inhabitants under the oppressive rule of succeeding foreign powers, down to the time of Jesus. "How often would I have gathered thy children together," the Savior lamented, "and ye would not!" (Matt. 23:37). Even greater sorrows would follow. Foretelling Jerusalem's destruction by the Romans in A.D. 70, Jesus taught, "For then, in those days, shall be great tribulation on the Jews, and upon the inhabitants of Jerusalem, such as was not before sent upon Israel, of God, since the beginning of their kingdom until this time" (JS–M 1:18).

Sorrow would continue to be Jerusalem's lot, even into the latter days, as its inhabitants would continue to refuse Jesus' message of salvation. John characterized the latter-day Jerusalem as "Sodom and Egypt" (Rev. 11:8), and Ether foretold yet another destruction (Ether 13:5).

Isaiah's announcement in Isaiah 40:1–2 proclaims the end of these tragedies and the end of the circumstances that brought them about. Jerusalem's rebellion will end, its inhabitants will be converted to Christ, and it will be restored to what Ether called "a holy city unto the Lord. . . . And the inhabitants thereof, blessed are they, for they have been washed in the blood of the Lamb; and they are they who were scattered and gathered in from the four quarters of the earth, and from the north countries, and are partakers of the fulfilling of the covenant which God made with their father, Abraham" (Ether 13:5, 11).[6]

2. *"Prepare ye the way of the Lord."* Isaiah 40:3–5, presented in the words of a messenger, announce the coming of the Lord in glory and challenge us to be prepared for his arrival.[7] At his coming the earth will undergo a dramatic transformation, characterized by the elevation of valleys, the sinking of mountains, and other profound changes (Isa. 40:4). Recall that at Christ's coming to the children of Lehi—a pattern for what will transpire at his second coming—"the whole face of the land was changed" (3 Ne. 8:12; see also vv. 5–18). Ether, foretelling this transition to millennial splendor, wrote that it would be "a new heaven and a new earth; and they shall be like unto the old save the old have passed away, and all things have become new" (Ether 13:9).[8] When "the glory of the Lord shall be revealed," Isaiah wrote, "all flesh shall see it together" (Isa. 40:5), consistent with Jesus' own words that his coming will be so obvious and conspicuous that it will be like the light of the sun coming up in the east, moving across the sky to the west, and covering the whole earth (JS–M 1:26).

In the New Testament, all three of the Synoptic Gospels refer to

---

[6]Perhaps the words are Moroni's, because Moroni was paraphrasing Ether.

[7]It appears that a more accurate translation of the Hebrew of Isa. 40:3 would be:
A voice is calling:
"Clear in the desert
 a way for the Lord;
Straighten in the wilderness
 a highway for our God."

[8]Terms such as "new heaven" and "new earth" are sometimes used to describe the final state of the earth when it becomes a celestial globe (Rev. 21:1; D&C 29:23–24). It is clear, however, that Ether was using these terms to refer to the millennial earth, when it "will be renewed and receive its paradisiacal glory" (A of F 10; other examples are Isa. 65:17; 66:22; 2 Pet. 3:13). The changes mentioned by Ether will take place *before* the coming of the New Jerusalem in America (Ether 13:10) and the restored Jerusalem in Palestine (Ether 13:11).

Isaiah 40:3 in connection with the mission of John the Baptist as fore-runner (Matt. 3:3; Mark 1:2–3; Luke 3:4–6). Like the messenger(s) who would be sent to prepare the way for Christ's millennial work, John was sent to prepare for his mortal coming; thus this passage can be appro-priately applied to John's ministry. John announced that the kingdom of heaven was "at hand" and that those who would take part in it would need to be found worthy (Matt. 3:2).[9]

3. *"Good tidings."* Isaiah 40:9–11 rejoices at the announcement that Jerusalem's God has come. Isaiah called for Jerusalem to "get thee up into the high mountain," to lift her voice "with strength," and to pro-claim, "Behold your God!" (Isa. 40:9). His coming is characterized both by his strength, "His arm shall rule for him" (Isa. 40:10), and his tend-erness, "He shall feed his flock like a shepherd: he shall gather the lambs with his arm, and carry them in his bosom" (Isa. 40:11).[10]

The rest of Isaiah 40 contains a discussion of God's incomparable wisdom and power. Those who reject it and rely on their own strength "shall faint," "be weary," and "utterly fall" (Isa. 40:30). Those who hope in the Lord, however, "shall renew their strength; they shall mount up with wings as eagles; they shall run, and not be weary; and they shall walk, and not faint" (Isa. 40:31).

In chapter 41 the Lord emphasized his special relationship with his people, calling Israel "my servant," the one "whom I have chosen," and "my friend" (Isa. 41:8). Because the family of Israel stands in that cov-enant relationship to God, it has important obligations to him, but it also receives the promise of his love and protection.[11]

---

[9]For more on messengers sent to prepare for the Lord's coming, see Kent P. Jackson, "The Appearance of Moroni to Joseph Smith," in *Studies in Scripture, Volume Two: The Pearl of Great Price*, ed. Robert L. Millet and Kent P. Jackson (Salt Lake City: Randall Book, 1985), pp. 348–49, and n. 25.

[10]Readers often notice that some of the numbers from George Frideric Handel's *Messiah* come from Isaiah 40: "Comfort Ye My People" (Isa. 40:1–3); "Every Valley Shall Be Exalted" (Isa. 40:4); "And the Glory of the Lord" (Isa. 40:5); "O Thou That Tellest Good Tidings to Zion" (Isa. 40:9; see also 60:1); "He Shall Feed His Flock like a Shepherd" (Isa. 40:11). Also coming from Isaiah are the following: "Behold! A Virgin Shall Conceive" (Isa. 7:14); "For Behold, Darkness Shall Cover the Earth" (Isa. 60:2–3); "The People That Walked in Darkness" (Isa. 9:2); "For unto Us a Child Is Born" (Isa. 9:6); "Then Shall the Eyes of the Blind Be Opened" (Isa. 35:5–6); "He Was Despised" (Isa. 53:3; Isa. 50:6); "Surely He Hath Borne Our Griefs" (Isa. 53:4–5); "And with His Stripes We Are Healed" (Isa. 53:5); "All We like Sheep Have Gone Astray" (Isa. 53:6); "He Was Cut Off Out of the Land of the Living" (Isa. 53:8).

[11]Latter-day Saint readers will recognize the promises in Isa. 41:10 as underlying verse 3 of the hymn "How Firm a Foundation."

The prophecy of the earth's millennial restoration in Isaiah 41:17–20 is similar to that in Isaiah 35:1–2, 6–7, discussed above. In the place of desert and parched land will be water and vegetation in abundance. And all will recognize "that the hand of the Lord hath done this, and the Holy One of Israel hath created it" (Isa. 41:20).

One of the important topics in the second half of Isaiah is God's capacity to foretell the future, a power which he refused to concede to the false gods that others worshiped (see Isa. 42:8).[12] The Lord challenged idol worshipers to bring forth their idols "and shew us what shall happen. . . . Shew the things that are to come hereafter, that we may know that ye are gods" (Isa. 41:22–23). The outcome of the challenge is obvious: "Ye are of nothing, and your work of nought: an abomination is he that chooseth you" (Isa. 41:24). In contrast, "Behold, the former things are come to pass, and new things do I declare: before they spring forth I tell you of them" (Isa. 42:9).

The Lord's Servant in Isaiah

One characteristic of Isaiah's "Book of Reconciliation" is the emphasis on the work of the Lord's "servant." Several passages in this section speak of a servant whom the Lord has chosen to do his will, but the servant's identity is not made clear. Perhaps more than one interpretation is valid.

1. When God made covenants with Abraham, Isaac, and Jacob, he called them to bless the world through their service. They and their descendants became "chosen people." Too often members of the house of Israel have looked upon this "chosen" condition as an elite status—a status that gives them automatic advantage in the eyes of God over others (e.g., Matt. 3:9–10). It is true that membership in the covenant family is a blessing, but it is important that we understand what it means to be "chosen." The scriptures make it clear that Israel is chosen to *serve* (e.g., Abr. 2:9–11). Much as one is chosen for callings in the Church today, members of the house of Israel are called to represent the Lord in service to others. On the most basic level, Israel itself seems to fit the

---

[12]See the discussion in Chap. 11 of this volume.

description of the Lord's chosen servant in Isaiah: "Thou, Israel, art my servant, Jacob whom I have chosen, the seed of Abraham my friend" (Isa. 41:8); "Yet now hear, O Jacob my servant; and Israel, whom I have chosen" (44:1).[13] Jesus taught his disciples how they should serve: "Ye are the salt of the earth" (Matt. 5:13); "Ye are the light of the world" (Matt. 5:14); "Feed my sheep" (John 21:16).

2. Just as the Lord has called Israel collectively to be his servant, some individuals within Israel have been called to a more specific level of service. Some of Isaiah's servant passages may find more appropriate application to the mission of the prophets rather than to Israel at large. The prophets are servants within God's servant nation.

3. Finally, Jesus Christ himself is *the* Servant; it is in him that Isaiah's servant passages find their most complete fulfillment. Jesus is the source of all the good gifts with which his servants minister. He is the light of the world in the fullest way; the light that the prophets and the house of Israel possess simply reflects his character and glory—the source of all true light. Whatever priesthood, virtue, or wisdom his servants may be found to possess comes from him. Similarly, though his servants have been called to feed his sheep (John 21:16), he himself is the Good Shepherd (John 10:14). Jesus stated, "The Son of Man came not to be ministered unto, but to minister" (Matt. 20:28). Appropriately, then, Isaiah's prophecies identify him in that role.

Because all good things and all good people are types of Christ and reflect his nature, perhaps we can identify the servant of whom Isaiah wrote on different levels, depending on the information provided: the house of Israel collectively, the prophets, and the Lord himself. Some of the passages seem to apply to more than one of these.[14]

Redeemer of Israel (Isa. 42–44)

Isaiah 42 begins with a servant passage (vv. 1–7) that seems to refer to the Savior in both his mortal and postmortal roles. In all meekness

---

[13]In both of these passages, "Jacob" and "Israel" are used synonymously and refer to the same people.

[14]A good summary of the "Servant" issue is found in W. S. LaSor, D. A. Hubbard, F. W. Bush, *Old Testament Survey* (Grand Rapids, Mich.: Eerdmans, 1982), pp. 392–95.

he will bring justice[15] to the nations of the world (Isa. 42:3–4), as "a covenant of the people, for a light of the Gentiles" (Isa. 42:6). His mission will include opening blind eyes and bringing "out the prisoners from the prison, and them that sit in darkness out of the prison house" (Isa. 42:7). For those whose spiritual vision is impaired, he "will make darkness light before them, and crooked things straight" (Isa. 42:16). The message of freeing those who are imprisoned bears a striking similarity to Jesus' work among the spirits of the dead, as recorded by the Apostle Peter and President Joseph F. Smith: "Being put to death in the flesh, but quickened by the spirit: by which also he went and preached unto the spirits in prison" (1 Pet. 3:18–19); "From among the righteous, he organized his forces and appointed messengers, clothed with power and authority, and commissioned them to go forth and carry the light of the gospel to them that were in darkness, even to all the spirits of men; and thus was the gospel preached to the dead" (D&C 138:30). Christ's message is one of liberation from the bondage of spiritual impairment and the prison of sin, both for the living and for the dead.

In Isaiah 43 the Lord made clear to his covenant people that he is their Savior, reminding them of some of the things that he had done in their behalf and would yet do for them (Isa. 43:1–21). But Israel responded to his goodness with ingratitude and unfaithfulness (Isa. 43:22–28), for which he gave "Jacob to the curse, and Israel to reproaches" (Isa. 43:28). Although their rebellion could only lead to sorrow and scattering, still the Lord promised their descendants a latter-day restoration: "I will bring thy seed from the east, and gather thee from the west; I will say to the north, Give up; and to the south, Keep not back: bring my sons from far, and my daughters from the ends of the earth" (Isa. 43:5–6).[16]

Chapter 44 continues the theme of blessings for future Israelites: "I will pour my spirit upon thy seed, and my blessing upon thine offspring: And they shall spring up as among the grass, as willows by the water courses" (Isa. 44:3–4). Repentant Israel will be identified as Jehovah's

---

[15]KJV, "judgment," in Isa. 42:1, 4; see n. 1, above.

[16]According to Oliver Cowdery, Isaiah 43:6 was quoted by Moroni to Joseph Smith when he appeared to him on the night of 21–22 September 1823; *Messenger and Advocate*, Apr. 1835, p. 111. Other Isaiah passages quoted by Moroni on that occasion, according to Oliver Cowdery, are Isaiah 1:7, 23–24, 25–26; 2:1–4; 4:5–6; 11:15–16; 29:11, 13, 14. Of these, the Prophet himself mentioned only Isaiah 11 (presumably the entire chapter; JS-H 1:40). See Jackson, pp. 359–61.

own people, signifying the reestablishment of their covenant relationship with him: "One shall say, I am the Lord's; and another shall call himself by the name of Jacob" (Isa. 44:5). "Still another will write on his hand, 'The Lord's,'[17] and will take the name Israel" (Isa. 44:5, NIV[18]).

One temptation to which the Israelites all too frequently fell prey was to worship other gods. In the ancient Near Eastern society of Isaiah's day, the existence of a variety of deities was taken for granted. Worshipers would have favorites among them (usually based on cultural and political identity), but few would doubt the existence even of the gods of their enemies. But Israel's God, Jehovah, not only demanded that his people worship only him but also proclaimed that no other deities existed: "Thus saith the Lord the King of Israel, and his redeemer the Lord of hosts; I am the first, and I am the last; and beside me there is no God" (Isa. 44:6). Following this passage comes a powerful rebuke of idol worship — the worship of nonexistent gods in the form of metal, stone, and wooden images (Isa. 44:9–20). Isaiah pointed out in biting, satirical, words what a folly the worship of manmade objects is. How vain it is, he wrote, that a man can chop down a tree, use part of the wood to build a fire to warm himself and roast his meat, and then use what is left to construct a god to which he bows down and worships! Is the poor fool not bright enough to ask, "Is there not a lie in my right hand?" (Isa. 44:20).

The Lord at Work in History (Isa. 45–48)

Cyrus the Great became ruler of Persia in 550 B.C. It is not without reason that he is considered to be one of the great men of the ancient world. It was he who brought to an end, in 539 B.C., the Neo-Babylonian empire that Nebuchadnezzar had built up about fifty years earlier. The Persian Achaemenid empire that Cyrus founded in its place showed little resemblance to the empires of Babylon and Assyria that had preceded it. Unlike his predecessors, Cyrus did not treat his subject nations as an inexhaustible plundering ground. Instead, he set up a well-organized

---

[17]Meaning "belonging to Jehovah" — used to designate ownership.

[18]The NIV (New International Version) is one of the very best English-language Bible translations, in my opinion. Written in beautiful contemporary English, it has the sense of reverence and devotion that plays such an important role in the King James Translation.

imperial structure that almost universally was considered to be a blessing compared to the atrocities of previous conquerors. Cyrus allowed the Jews who had been deported by Nebuchadnezzar to return from their Babylonian exile to their ancestral homeland and to rebuild their temple and cities there (2 Chron. 36:22–23; Ezra 1:1–11).

The importance of Cyrus in the book of Isaiah lies in that he is mentioned by name — more than a century before he was born.[19] Speaking of future things as though they had already transpired — a style common in the writings of the prophets (see Mosiah 16:6) — the Lord spoke of Cyrus as his agent in bringing to pass the rebuilding of Jerusalem and its temple (Isa. 44:28). Though Cyrus was unaware, the God of Israel was prospering his work and blessing him with success: "I have even called thee by thy name: I have surnamed thee, though thou hast not known me" (Isa. 45:4; see also vv. 1–14). God is at work in history, as the Old Testament and the Book of Mormon attest. Because he knows the future, he can also make it known to his servants — even to the point of describing the missions of individuals not yet born and calling them by name: "Yea, I have spoken it, I will also bring it to pass; I have purposed it, I will also do it" (Isa. 46:11).

Isaiah 47 is a lengthy prophecy against Babylon, which in Isaiah's day was under the domination of the Assyrian empire, the great super-power of the eighth and seventh centuries B.C. In Isaiah's day, Babylon was not a threat to his homeland, Judah, nor would it be for another one hundred years (Assyria did not fall until 609 B.C., at which time Babylon ascended to rule the Near East). Yet soon it would be known for its wealth and wickedness, and the very mention of its name would bring such things to mind.

Babylon is depicted in Isaiah 47 as a spoiled and pampered queen whose fall would quickly reduce her to the status of a peasant (Isa. 47:1–3). Though she had boasted that she would be a lady forever, to God she was a "wanton creature" (Isa. 47:8, NIV), and he made her both childless and widowed in a single day (Isa. 47:9). Neither her magic nor her astrology could help her now, as the Lord said — "None shall save thee" (Isa. 47:12–15).

This revelation deserves our attention for two important reasons:

---

[19]See the discussion in Chap. 11 of this volume.

1. Given the historical setting, a revelation concerning the fall of Babylon was clearly not as important for Isaiah's own time as it would be for readers several generations later. Perhaps this revelation, like the Book of Mormon, was written not for his contemporaries but for later people whom the prophet foresaw and whose circumstances he knew.[20]

2. As elsewhere in prophetic writings, the circumstances of contemporary nations often serve as types for latter-day things. The degrading fall of Babylon prefigures the fall of those unholy things that are characterized by it: lust, opulence, the political machinations of the world, and pride. As Babylon falls—both the ancient kingdom literally and its latter-day counterpart figuratively—God commands his people to flee: "Depart ye, depart ye, go ye out from thence, touch no unclean thing; go ye out of the midst of her; be ye clean" (Isa. 52:11; see also 48:20).

The Lord reminded his people in Isaiah 48 that he can see and foretell the future (Isa. 48:1–7), which is one of many mighty acts that he has done to bless their lives. He desired to give them every chance; he even deferred his anger from them (Isa. 48:9), but they remained rebellious. Thus, in words that are as moving poetically as they are spiritually, the Lord lamented: "I am the Lord thy God which teacheth thee to profit, which leadeth thee by the way that thou shouldest go. O that thou hadst hearkened to my commandments! then had thy peace been as a river, and thy righteousness as the waves of the sea: Thy seed also had been as the sand, and the offspring of thy bowels like the gravel thereof; his name should not have been cut off nor destroyed from before me" (Isa. 48:17–19). Yet "there is no peace," the Lord reminds us, "unto the wicked" (Isa. 48:22).

A Day of Salvation (Isa. 49–50)

Isaiah 49 is a very important chapter, because we see in it the servant in a significant role that seems to find fulfillment in the latter days. In the first part of the chapter we learn something of the servant's call: he was foreordained, set apart, and prepared to show forth God's glory (Isa. 49:3). Yet in spite of his call and his qualifications, he felt, as have others

---

[20]See Chap. 11 of this volume.

in the Lord's service on occasion, that his work was to no avail—"I have laboured in vain, I have spent my strength for naught" (Isa. 49:4). Verse 5 reveals the nature of his service: he was called to restore the house of Israel, "to bring Jacob again to him."[21]

The restoration of the house of Israel is one of the great events of the last days, and the servant could rejoice in his role in it (Isa. 49:5b). That restoration includes not only the gathering to promised lands but especially the reestablishment of covenants between God and his people, both as a nation and as individuals. Jeremiah looked upon the latter-day restoration as being far greater than the Lord's gathering his people the first time, from Egypt. So great would be this new latter-day exodus that the old one in the days of Moses would soon be forgotten (Jer. 16:14–15).

But this would not be all for the Lord's servant. He learned that the gathering of Israel would be too small a task.[22] The Lord had something more for him to do: "I will also give thee for a light to the Gentiles, that thou mayest be my salvation unto the end of the earth" (Isa. 49:6). In other words, the servant's mission is even greater than simply to restore the house of Israel. It also includes a work on behalf of the Gentiles— those who are not descendants of Israel[23]—to bring salvation to them as well. The scriptures bear consistent testimony to the dual mission of the latter-day gathering, both of Israel and of the Gentiles. Even the Gentiles, Jeremiah wrote, "shall come unto thee from the ends of the earth" (Jer. 16:19), and Isaiah foresaw an "ensign" to which "the outcasts of Israel," "the dispersed of Judah," and "the nations" will gather (Isa. 11:12; see also D&C 86:11; Abr. 2:9–11).

The essence of the gathering is the gathering to the covenants of the gospel of Jesus Christ, as Nephi taught (1 Ne. 10:14)—the same

---

[21]The KJV is difficult in Isa. 49:5, as is the Hebrew manuscript on which it is based: "to bring Jacob again to him, Though Israel be not gathered." A seemingly better-preserved Hebrew original in the Qumran Isaiah Scroll (1QIsa^a) provides a more likely translation: "to bring Jacob back to him and gather Israel to himself."

[22]The KJV phrase "a light thing" (Isa. 49:6) means "a *small* thing" or "an *insignificant* thing." The word *light* also appears later in the same verse, but there it is translated from a different word and means something entirely different.

[23]This is the Old Testament definition of *Gentiles*. The Book of Mormon definition is usually different. There the term seems to be defined culturally, not genealogically: those who are not Lamanites or Jews are Gentiles, regardless of their lineage.

covenants that God made with Israel's great ancestors, Abraham, Isaac, and Jacob. Because such phrases as "the gathering of Israel" usually refer to joining the Church, the idea of a physical return in the scriptures may often be a metaphor for returning to the covenants, accepting the gospel, and joining Christ's church. Geographical relocation plays a lesser role. Today the gathering of Israel is taking place as individuals from all over the earth are gathering to the Church in their own lands.[24] And Gentiles — those who are not of literal Israelite descent — are equally welcome.

These verses point to Christ, as do all of Isaiah's servant passages. At the same time, the work of the servant in these verses seems to embody the gathering mission of the Church in the latter days. Thus it seems reasonable to see a fulfillment in the work of the Church, the tribes of Joseph who are now gathering others, and specifically the Prophet Joseph Smith.[25]

Isaiah 49 continues with a poetic description of the return of the scattered sheep of Israel (Isa. 49:8–13): "They shall not hunger nor thirst; neither shall the heat nor sun smite them: for he that hath mercy on them shall lead them, even by the springs of water shall he guide them" (Isa. 49:10).

Zion, in the next section of chapter 49, is depicted as a mother bereaved of her children, "forsaken" and "forgotten." But just as a mother cannot forget her child, the Lord cannot forget his chosen one; her memory is ever before him (Isa. 49:14–15) and he will bless her according to her desire. The return of her lost children will be so dramatic that she will hardly be prepared to receive them. In her joy, excitement, and bewilderment she will ask, "Who hath begotten me these, seeing I have lost my children, and am desolate, a captive, and removing to and fro?

---

[24]President Spencer W. Kimball taught: "The gathering of Israel consists of joining the true church and their coming to a knowledge of the true God. . . . Any person, therefore, who has accepted the restored gospel, and who now seeks to worship the Lord in his own tongue and with the Saints in the nation where he lives, has complied with the law of the gathering of Israel and is heir to all of the blessings promised the Saints in these last days." *The Teachings of Spencer W. Kimball*, ed. Edward L. Kimball (Salt Lake City: Bookcraft, 1982), p. 439.

[25]For more specific suggestions, see Monte S. Nyman, *"Great Are the Words of Isaiah"* (Salt Lake City: Bookcraft, 1980), pp. 175–78; Victor L. Ludlow, *Isaiah: Prophet, Seer, and Poet* (Salt Lake City: Deseret Book Co., 1982), pp. 408–10; Kent P. Jackson, "Revelations Concerning Isaiah," in *Studies in Scripture, Volume One: The Doctrine and Covenants*, ed. Robert L. Millet and Kent P. Jackson (Salt Lake City: Randall Book, 1984), pp. 326–30.

and who hath brought up these? Behold, I was left alone; these, where had they been?" (Isa. 49:21).

An important revelation follows: "Behold, I will lift up mine hand to the Gentiles, and set up my standard to the people: and they shall bring thy sons in their arms, and thy daughters shall be carried upon their shoulders. And kings shall be thy nursing fathers, and their queens thy nursing mothers" (Isa. 49:22–23). This is one of several prophecies that show the nations no longer oppressing the Lord's people but serving them. The Book of Mormon provides important interpretations. Nephi, who recognized that Isaiah's prophecies are fulfilled in "temporal and spiritual" ways (1 Ne. 22:3), foresaw the Gentiles contributing to the temporal blessing of his descendants and others of the house of Israel (1 Ne. 22:6). He also saw them contributing in an even more important spiritual way. According to Nephi, the fulfillment of this prophecy will be "the making known of the covenants of the Father," "in bringing about his covenants and his gospel unto those who are of the house of Israel." The bringing of the gospel of Jesus Christ to the house of Israel is the great blessing from the Gentiles and the great fulfillment of this prophecy. It began with the restoration of the gospel and continues as missionaries from Gentile nations take the gospel to Lehi's descendants and others of the house of Israel. Being "brought out of obscurity and out of darkness," the covenant people are thus learning "that the Lord is their Savior and their Redeemer, the Mighty One of Israel" (1 Ne. 22:9, 11–12). The Lord revealed to Jacob a yet-future temporal fulfillment of Isaiah 49:23. When the Jews believe in him, that he is Christ, then he will fulfill the covenant to their fathers that they will be restored "unto the lands of their inheritance" and will be "gathered in from their long dispersion. . . . And the nations of the Gentiles shall be great in the eyes of me, saith God, in carrying them forth to the lands of their inheritance. Yea, the kings of the Gentiles shall be nursing fathers unto them, and their queens shall become nursing mothers" (2 Ne. 10:7–9).[26]

Isaiah 50 continues the theme of God's unceasing desire to save his people. He asked, "Is my hand shortened at all, that it cannot redeem? or have I no power to deliver?" (Isa. 50:2). Sadly, some will reject his

---

[26]My discussion here is necessarily very brief. A more detailed analysis can be found in Nyman, pp. 182–84.

invitation to salvation and will prefer to walk in the light of their own fire. "This shall ye have of mine hand," the Lord promised them, "ye shall lie down in sorrow" (Isa. 50:11).

Isaiah 50:4–9 is a servant passage that is often regarded as messianic, i.e., foretelling the mission of Christ. In it the servant submits himself to all things, including the derision and physical abuse of others; "I hid not my face from shame and spitting" (Isa. 50:6). Yet knowing that he was justified by God, he set his "face like a flint," firm in the confidence of his vindication (Isa. 50:7–8).

It seems likely that Isaiah himself is the servant in this passage. Although righteous King Hezekiah (715–687 B.C.) ruled in Isaiah's day, so also did his wicked father Ahaz (735–715 B.C.) and perhaps also his equally wicked son Manasseh (687–642 B.C.).[27] It is not unlikely that Isaiah's career included persecution and abuse from evil men, and perhaps this passage reflects such things. At the same time, the servant's experience clearly parallels that of the mortal Christ. Even if it is indeed Isaiah who is called the servant here, he, like others of the Lord's ministers, typified the life of his Master and reflected his nature.

---

[27]According to Jewish tradition, Isaiah was executed by being cut in half with a saw during the reign of Manasseh. But the superscription to the book (Isa. 1:1) does not mention Manasseh as ruling during the days of Isaiah.

15

THE LORD WILL BRING SALVATION

(ISAIAH 51–66)

DAVID ROLPH SEELY

The name *Isaiah* (Hebrew, *yeša'yāhû*) means "Jehovah saves," and salvation is a major theme of the book that bears his name. Although salvation is a term that has many nuances and manifestations in Isaiah, it ultimately refers to the Atonement. Israel receives the full blessings of the plan of salvation—implemented in the premortal existence—through the Abrahamic covenant and later through the Mosaic covenant received at Sinai. The Messiah would be named Jesus (Hebrew, *yehôšûa'*), which means "Jehovah is salvation." His mission would be to conquer death and sin and bring spiritual as well as temporal salvation to the world.[1] Because Israel did not keep the covenant, they were scattered, a process by which many lost the knowledge and blessings of the plan of salvation. To scattered Israel, salvation is manifested through the preaching of the gospel and their eventual gathering to Zion. At the end of time, the Redeemer will return in judgment, bringing vengeance to the wicked and vindication for the righteous. Isaiah 51 through 66 contains prophecies regarding all phases of this endeavor to bring salvation to the children of men: the first coming of the Messiah, when God came down to earth; the preaching of the gospel and the gathering of Israel; and the return of the Messiah at his second coming, bringing about the establishment of his millennial kingdom.

David Rolph Seely is assistant professor of ancient scripture at Brigham Young University.

[1]A primary meaning of the Hebrew root *yš'* is "deliver" or "be victorious" in battle, which is consistent with the metaphor common in Isaiah of God as the Divine Warrior.

"Look unto Abraham Your Father" (Isa. 51)

"Hearken to me, ye that follow after righteousness, ye that seek the Lord: look unto the rock whence ye are hewn, and to the hole of the pit whence ye are digged. Look unto Abraham your father, and unto Sarah that bare you: for I called him alone, and blessed him, and increased him" (Isa. 51:1–2).

The Lord admonishes the seekers of righteousness to look to Abraham their father and Sarah their mother. The Lord covenanted with Abraham that his seed would be blessed with land and posterity and that "in thy seed after thee . . . shall all the families of the earth be blessed, even with the blessings of the Gospel, which are the blessings of salvation, even of life eternal" (Abr. 2:11). Thus salvation is promised to the worthy seed of Abraham, along with the responsibility of preaching and administering the plan of salvation. But who is the seed of Abraham? The Lord blessed Abraham that "as many as receive this Gospel shall be called after thy name, and shall be accounted thy seed" (Abr. 2:10). Throughout Isaiah 51 through 66 the Lord constantly reminds covenant Israel that the gospel, with all of its attendant blessings, is for everyone.

The remainder of Isaiah 51 talks about the return of the Lord, the gathering of his people, and the building of the millennial Zion. That the Lord will ultimately save and comfort his people is the main theme. The establishment of Zion is seen as a new creation: "For the Lord shall comfort Zion: he will comfort all her waste places; and he will make her wilderness like Eden, and her desert like the garden of the Lord" (Isa. 51:3). Before the re-creation of the millennial earth and the salvation and comfort of the righteous, there must first be a destruction of the old: "Lift up your eyes to the heavens, and look upon the earth beneath: for the heavens shall vanish away like smoke, and the earth shall wax old like a garment, and they that dwell therein shall die in like manner" (Isa. 51:6).

As part of the judgment to precede the Second Coming, the Lord will cause the nations to drink from the "cup of his fury" (Isa. 51:17), which will result in destruction. This destruction will involve the forces of nature as well as the forces of nations: "These two things are come unto thee; who shall be sorry for thee? desolation, and destruction, and the famine, and the sword: by whom shall I comfort thee?" (Isa. 51:19).

In conjunction with these trials the Lord includes a short prophecy: "Thy sons have fainted, they lie at the head of all the streets, as a wild bull in a net: they are full of the fury of the Lord, the rebuke of thy God" (Isa. 51:20). In its context in Isaiah this prophecy is enigmatic, but elsewhere in scripture it is explained in greater detail.

The reading of these verses in the Joseph Smith Translation and in 2 Nephi changes the passage significantly. There the text reads: "These two sons are come unto thee, who shall be sorry for thee — thy desolation and destruction, and the famine and the sword — and by whom shall I comfort thee? Thy sons have fainted, save these two; they lie at the head of all the streets; as a wild bull in a net, they are full of the fury of the Lord, the rebuke of thy God" (2 Ne. 8:19–20; JST Isa. 51:19–20 is only slightly different).

Revelation 11:1–12 further expands and clarifies the event alluded to in Isaiah 51. According to the passage in Revelation, the Lord will give to two of his witnesses in the last days power over their enemies, as well as over the elements — accounting for destruction and famine. They will have power to withstand the enemy for a period of twelve hundred and sixty days, until "they shall have finished their testimony" (Rev. 11:7), at which point they will be killed by the forces of evil. Their bodies will lie in the street for three and one-half days while their enemies rejoice. Then they will be resurrected and will ascend to heaven in glory.[2] The book of Revelation further associates these two witnesses with the symbolism of two olive trees and two candlesticks mentioned in Zechariah 4:11–14 (Rev. 11:4). In the Doctrine and Covenants the Lord identified these two witnesses as "two prophets that are to be raised up to the Jewish nation in the last days, at the time of the restoration, and to prophesy to the Jews after they are gathered and have built the city of Jerusalem in the land of their fathers" (D&C 77:15).

"How Beautiful upon the Mountains" (Isa. 52)

Isaiah 52:1–2 contains a call to Zion:

Awake, awake; put on thy strength, O Zion;

---

[2]For a complete discussion of this passage in Revelation, see Richard D. Draper, *Opening the Seven Seals: The Visions of John the Revelator* (Salt Lake City: Deseret Book Co., 1991), pp. 118–27.

>put on thy beautiful garments, O Jerusalem, the holy city:
>for henceforth there shall no more come into thee
>>the uncircumcised and the unclean.
>Shake thyself from the dust;
>>arise, and sit down, O Jerusalem:
>loose thyself from the bands of thy neck,
>>O captive daughter of Zion.

These verses are interpreted by modern revelation, which provides a solid foundation for a discussion of the rest of the chapter. In Doctrine and Covenants 113 some questions are posed to the Lord about these verses, which he answers:

>Q: What is meant by the command in Isaiah, 52d chapter, 1st verse, which saith: Put on thy strength, O Zion — and what people had Isaiah reference to?
>
>A: He had reference to those whom God should call in the last days, who should hold the power of priesthood to bring again Zion, and the redemption of Israel; and to put on her strength is to put on the authority of the priesthood, which she, Zion, has a right to by lineage; also to return to that power which she had lost (D&C 113:7–8).
>
>Q: What are we to understand by Zion loosing herself from the bands of her neck; 2d verse?
>
>A: We are to understand that the scattered remnants are exhorted to return to the Lord from whence they have fallen; which if they do, the promise of the Lord is that he will speak to them, or give them revelation. See the 6th, 7th, and 8th verses. The bands of her neck are the curses of God upon her, or the remnants of Israel in their scattered condition among the Gentiles (D&C 113:9–10).

"How beautiful upon the mountains are the feet of him that bringeth good tidings, that publisheth peace; that bringeth good tidings of good, that publisheth salvation" (Isa. 52:7). In Hebrew, "how beautiful" is *mah nā'wû*. From this phrase the Prophet Joseph Smith derived the name *Nauvoo*, which he interpreted as "place of rest" or "beauty."[3] The phrase "him that bringeth good tidings" (Hebrew, *mebaśśēr*), is based on the Hebrew root *bśr*, meaning "announce" or "proclaim." This phrase occurs in Isaiah seven times (40:9, twice; 41:27; 52:7, twice; 60:6; 61:1) in key passages in which it means "proclaiming the tidings of salvation." Isaiah

---

[3] *Teachings of the Prophet Joseph Smith*, sel. Joseph Fielding Smith (Salt Lake City: Deseret Book Co., 1938), p. 182.

40:9; 52:7; and 61:1 particularly refer to messengers proclaiming the coming of the Messiah and the message of salvation through the atone- ment that he brings. The Greek Septuagint translated this word with the verb *euangelízomai,* literally "to bring a good message" (root of the English word *evangelize*). The writers of the New Testament, presumably on account of the occurrence of this word in the Septuagint passages in Isaiah, used the same term throughout, referring to the "good tidings" of the coming of the Savior (Luke 1:19; 2:10). The noun form *euangélion* (Matt. 4:23; 24:14; 26:13; Mark 1:1, 14; 8:35; 13:10; etc.) was rendered in Latin as *evangelium* and was then translated into Anglo-Saxon as *god-spell,* meaning "good-news." This led to the modern English *gospel.* Hence the occurrence and meaning of the term *gospel* in the New Testament is based on these very important passages in Isaiah, which refer to the coming of the Messiah and the Atonement.

One of the priests of Noah asked Abinadi the meaning of Isaiah 52:7–10 (Mosiah 12:20–24). Abinadi did not answer the question im- mediately, but after his scathing rebuke of the priests for their wickedness, he taught them about the coming of the Savior as the Suffering Servant, reading them Isaiah 53 in its entirety. He interpreted chapter 53 that "God himself should come down among the children of men" (Mosiah 17:8) — the teaching for which Abinadi would be put to death. Finally he returned to the original question and gave a prophetic interpretation of Isaiah 52:7–10. He explained that those who follow Christ and the prophets are the seed of Christ, who as servants "are *they* [changing the singular "him" of Isa. 52:7 to a plural] who have published peace, who have brought good tidings of good, who have published salvation; and said unto Zion: Thy God reigneth" (Mosiah 15:14). Abinadi further explained that these servants are only doing what they have seen *the* Servant do: "And behold, I say unto you, this is not all. For O how beautiful upon the mountains are the feet of *him* that bringeth good tidings, that is the founder of peace, yea, even the Lord, who has redeemed his people; yea, him who has granted salvation unto his people" (Mosiah 15:18). Thus those who accept the gospel become the seed of Abraham and the seed of Christ, and their responsibility is to look to the "rock from whence they are hewn" and to do as Abraham and Christ have done — to proclaim the good tidings, to preach the gospel.[4]

---

[4]For further discussion of the servant theme, see Kent P. Jackson, "The Lord's Servant in Isaiah," in Chap. 14 of this volume.

Jesus quoted several of the verses from Isaiah 52 in his address to the Nephites in 3 Nephi 20:36–46, but he quoted the verses in a significantly different order: 1–3, 7, 11–15, interpreting the events as relating to the latter days, the restoration and preaching of the gospel, and the Second Coming.

Some scholars read the passage in Isaiah 52:13–15 about the servant whose "visage" was to be "marred" together with Isaiah 53, referring to the same suffering servant. The Book of Mormon never places it in this context; rather, the resurrected Jesus appears to have read this passage as referring to a servant who was yet to come (3 Ne. 20:43–45). He explained the passage in the context of the latter days, referring to a future servant who will be marred but healed (3 Ne. 21:9–10). Some have seen this as a prophecy referring to the coming of the Savior himself, who has been marred but preserved through the resurrection. Others see it as a reference to Joseph Smith or some other latter-day servant.[5]

"He Is Despised and Rejected of Men" (Isa. 53)

The bringer of salvation in Isaiah is the Servant, Jesus Christ. While Christ is the Suffering Servant who through the Atonement would bring salvation to all, servant imagery is developed throughout Isaiah in many passages where the servant is a type that can be variously applied to Israel, Cyrus, Isaiah, and all of the servants of the Lord as they participate in bringing salvation, through Jesus Christ, to the children of men. The type of the servant powerfully demonstrates how we, in some small way through sharing the attributes and calling of Christ, can also function as servants in the administration of salvation to the children of men. There are, however, some aspects of the servant typology that only Jesus Christ could do—namely, suffer for the sins of others and conquer death through the resurrection.

After reading Isaiah 53 in its entirety to the priests of Noah, Abinadi said, "Ye should understand that God himself shall come down among the children of men, and shall redeem his people" (Mosiah 15:1). Isaiah

---

[5]See Victor L. Ludlow, *Isaiah: Prophet, Seer, and Poet* (Salt Lake City: Deseret Book Co., 1982), pp. 439–41.

53 is a prophecy of the ministry of the Messiah Jesus Christ and the Atonement, which he performed. The meaning of the rich imagery in this chapter can be illuminated by many scriptural references. Links can be found to many Old Testament messianic prophecies, the New Testament writers often cited passages in this revelation as they related to Christ's mortal ministry, and Abinadi gave us a rich doctrinal exposition on some of the images in Mosiah 15:1–12.

The following lists some of the significant scriptural citations and allusions to various passages in Isaiah 53 that illuminate the imagery in that chapter.

Isaiah 53	*Other Passages of Scripture*
1. Who hath believed our report? and to whom is the arm of the Lord revealed	John 12:37–38 quoted Rom. 10:16 quoted
2. For he shall grow up before him as a tender plant, and as a root out of a dry ground	Rev. 22:16 I am the root and the offspring of David D&C 93:13 And he received not of the fulness at first, but continued from grace to grace, until he received a fulness See also Isa. 11:1; Jer. 23:5; Ezek. 17:6, 22; Zech. 3:8
3. He is despised and rejected of men	Matt. 13:57 A prophet is not without honour, save in his own country Luke 4:24 No prophet is accepted in his own country
3. And we hid as it were our faces from him	John 1:5 And the light shineth in darkness; and the darkness comprehended it not John 1:11 He came unto his own, and his own received him not
4. He hath borne our griefs, and carried our sorrows	Mosiah 15:5 Suffereth himself to be mocked, and scourged, and cast out, and disowned by his people Matt. 8:16–17 quoted Mark 9:12 quoted

5. With his stripes we are healed	2 Ne. 25:13 They will crucify him; and after he is laid in a sepulchre for the space of three days he shall rise from the dead, with healing in his wings
	Rom. 4:25 quoted
	1 Pet. 2:24 quoted
6. All we like sheep have gone astray	1 Pet. 2:25 quoted
6. We have turned every one to his own way	Jer. 17:5 Cursed be the man that trusteth in man, and maketh flesh his arm
	D&C 1:16 Every man walketh in his own way, and after the image of his own god
7. He is brought as a lamb to the slaughter	Mark 14:24 This is my blood of the new testament, which is shed for many
	Acts 8:32 quoted
9. And he made his grave with the wicked, and with the rich in his death	Matt. 27:38 Then were there two thieves crucified with him, one on the right hand, and another on the left
	Matt. 27:57–60 There came a rich man of Arimathaea, named Joseph, . . . and begged the body of Jesus . . . and laid it in his own new tomb
10. He shall see his seed	Mosiah 15:11 All those who have hearkened unto their words, and believed that the Lord would redeem his people . . . these are his seed, or they are the heirs of the kingdom of God
	John 1:12 But as many as received him, to them gave he power to become the sons of God, even to them that believe on his name

12. Therefore will I divide him a portion with the great, and he shall divide the spoil with the strong

John 14:2 In my Father's house are many mansions . . . I go to prepare a place for you

D&C 76:20 And we beheld the glory of the Son, on the right hand of the Father, and received of his fulness

D&C 84:37–38 And he that receiveth me receiveth my Father; And he that receiveth my Father receiveth my Father's kingdom; therefore all that my Father hath shall be given unto him

12. And he was numbered with the transgressors

Luke 22:37 quoted

12. He bare the sin of many, and made intercession for the transgressors

Mosiah 15:9 Standing betwixt them and justice; having broken the bands of death, taken upon himself their iniquity and their transgressions, having redeemed them, and satisfied the demands of justice

Mark 10:45 And to give his life a ransom for many

The prophecy in Isaiah 53 expresses with precision some of the details of the mission of Christ, providing evidence for the Saints of all ages that the prophets foresaw the coming of the Messiah. At the same time, the poetic images are powerful in communicating to us the drama of the events of the Atonement, as well as their significance. In the words of Abinadi: "For behold, did not Moses prophesy unto them concerning the coming of the Messiah, and that God should redeem his people? Yea, and even all the prophets who have prophesied ever since the world began — have they not spoken more or less concerning these things? Have they not said that God himself should come down among the children of men, and take upon him the form of man, and go forth in mighty power upon the face of the earth? Yea, and have they not said also that he should bring to pass the resurrection of the dead, and that he, himself, should be oppressed and afflicted?" (Mosiah 13:33–35).

"With Great Mercies I Will Gather Thee" (Isa. 54–55)

In Isaiah 54:1–3 the Lord addresses his barren bride Israel: "Sing, O barren, thou that didst not bear." Marriage as a metaphor for the covenant—the Lord being the groom and Israel the bride—occurs frequently in the Old Testament (e.g., Hosea 1–3; Jer. 2–3; Ezek. 23). Israel, as the unfaithful spouse, is guilty of adultery and is a harlot. Certainly these are grounds for divorce, and the penalty for adultery is death. The Lord punished Israel with death, destruction, and scattering by the Assyrians in 721 B.C., by the Babylonians in 587 B.C., and by the Romans in A.D. 70. Many suffered the penalty of death, but the Lord in his mercy spared Israel's posterity and scattered them throughout the earth. In Isaiah's metaphor, there was no divorce ("where is the bill of your mother's divorcement"; Isa. 50:1) but a separation. The Lord explained, "For thy Maker is thine husband . . . for a small moment have I forsaken thee . . . in a little wrath I hid my face from thee for a moment; but with everlasting kindness will I have mercy on thee" (Isa. 54:5–8). The Lord in his love and mercy, as dramatized by Hosea when he forgave his unfaithful wife (Hosea 1–3), will take back his bride, and her barrenness will be replaced with productivity as the Lord begins to gather their posterity (Isa. 54:7).

The gathering of Israel will necessitate the enlarging of the family tent, the lengthening of the cords, and the strengthening of the stakes (54:2)—an image aptly used in the latter days for the gathering of Israel and the growth of the Church (D&C 82:14; 96:1; 133:9). This same imagery was quoted by the Lord in the Doctrine and Covenants as he described to the members of the Church their obligation to build Zion: "For Zion must increase in beauty, and in holiness; her borders must be enlarged; her stakes must be strengthened; yea, verily I say unto you, Zion must arise and put on her beautiful garments" (D&C 82:14). Israel will be restored, and Zion will be built upon foundation stones of beautiful colors and sapphires, with windows of agates, gates of carbuncles, with borders of precious stones (Isa. 54:11–12). And Israel's children will be taught of the Lord (Isa. 54:13).

In Isaiah 55 the Lord pleads, "Incline your ear, and come unto me: hear, and your soul shall live" (Isa. 55:3); "seek ye the Lord while he may be found, call ye upon him while he is near" (Isa. 55:6). The gathering of Israel occurs when God's children hearken to his word, come to their Redeemer, and enter into the covenant (Isa. 55:3). It occurs when the children of men recognize that the "thoughts" and "ways" of the Lord are higher than the thoughts and ways of men (Isa. 55:8–9). The Lord promises, "For ye shall go out with joy, and be led forth with peace: the mountains and the hills shall break forth before you into singing, and all the trees of the field shall clap their hands" (Isa. 55:12).

Israel's Transgressions (Isa. 56–59)

Isaiah 56 through 59 contain a list of the transgressions that Israel must overcome before they can build Zion. The nature of these sins makes these passages timely for Israel in any period but especially for those at the time of Isaiah who would attempt to avert the impending disaster brought on by disobedience, to those who faced the challenge of rebuilding Zion after the return ordered by Cyrus in 539 B.C., and to the Saints at the time of Christ who attempted to build Zion. Ultimately, of course, it is directed to Israel in the latter days as they undertake the building of Zion to usher in the Millennium.

Isaiah 56:1–6 promises great blessing to each individual "that keepeth the sabbath from polluting it, and keepeth his hand from doing any evil" (Isa. 56:2). These blessings are not confined to Israel but are extended to the stranger and the eunuch, representing the extension of the gospel to all nations. Under the Law of Moses, Israel was obligated to be civil to the strangers, or foreigners (Ex. 22:21; Deut. 10:19), who could attain full membership in the community by becoming converts, but eunuchs were excluded from the "congregation of the Lord" (Deut. 23:1; see also Lev. 21:20). The point of Isaiah's imagery is that with the fulfillment of the Law of Moses, membership and participation in the covenant of the Lord are not based on lineage or lack of physical deformity but rather on faithfulness. John the Baptist reminded the Pharisees, "And think not to say within yourselves, We have Abraham to our father: for I say unto you, that God is able of these stones to raise up children unto Abraham" (Matt. 3:9). Those who accept the gospel by entering into the covenant and keep the sabbath will be given a place in Israel and an everlasting name in the house of the Lord (Isa. 56:3–5). They will have a place in temple ordinances, and the house of the Lord "shall be called an house of prayer for *all* people" (Isa. 56:7; emphasis added). Jesus quoted part of Isaiah 56:7, along with part of Jeremiah 7:11, when he cleansed the temple in Jerusalem: "My house shall be called the house of prayer; but ye have made it a den of thieves" (Matt. 21:13).

The Lord condemned the corrupted leaders in Judah, portraying their uselessness as blind watchmen, sleeping watchdogs, greedy dogs, and self-serving shepherds who pursue their own concerns (Isa. 56:10–11). When Jesus proclaimed, "I am the good shepherd" (John 10:14), he dramatically set himself in contrast to these unrighteous leaders (see also Ezek. 34:11–19, in which the shepherd who seeks out, gathers, and feeds his sheep is the Lord God).

Isaiah 57 addresses the issue of idolatry—a prominent theme in Isaiah (2:8, 18–20; 10:11; 31:7; 45:16). The Lord referred to idolatrous Israel as "sons of the sorceress, the seed of the adulterer and the whore" (Isa. 57:3). Such allusions may have a two-fold reference. First, in the metaphor of the covenant as marriage, leaving the worship of the true God to worship other gods is unfaithfulness to marriage vows and is therefore adultery. In addition, the worship of Canaanite gods may have involved cultic immorality (1 Kgs. 14:23–24; Jer. 2:23–27; 3:2; Ezek. 16:16), which could be considered the physical acting out of Israel's adultery.[6] In Isaiah 57:9 ("thou wentest to the king"), the word "king" should be rendered "Melech" or "Molech," a Canaanite god associated with child sacrifice (see n. 9a, LDS Bible). Israel's unfaithfulness expressed by her adoption of Canaanite religious practices extended even to this hideous act, and children were sacrificed in biblical times at Tophet in the Hinnom Valley, near Jerusalem (Lev. 18:21; 20:2–5; 2 Kgs. 23:10; Jer. 32:35).

Isaiah 58 is an extraordinary lesson on the correct way to fast. The chapter consists of a dialogue between the Lord and Israel. Israel asks the Lord why their regular and stringent fasting has gone unheeded (Isa. 58:3a). The Lord then rebukes them and in the process defines what true fasting consists of: "Is not this the fast that I have chosen? to loose

---

[6]It has long been assumed that ritual prostitution was a common practice of Canaanite religion. The allusions to such practices, however, are nearly all found in the Old Testament rather than in Canaanite texts and in contexts of idolatry as "metaphorical adultery." Therefore many scholars question whether such allusions are to be taken literally as cultic prostitution or simply as metaphors for being unfaithful to the Lord through idolatry.

the bands of wickedness, to undo the heavy burdens, and to let the oppressed go free, and that ye break every yoke? Is it not to deal thy bread to the hungry, and that thou bring the poor that are cast out to thy house? when thou seest the naked, that thou cover him; and that thou hide not thyself from thine own flesh?" (Isa. 58:6–7). Fasting is not a passive act, for in order to be efficacious it must be accompanied by righteous living and charity demonstrated not only through fast offerings but through daily living and interaction with our fellowmen.

Isaiah 1 indicts Israel for her failure to live up to the covenant. The Lord said to Israel, "When ye spread forth your hands, I will hide mine eyes from you: yea, when ye make many prayers, I will not hear: your hands are full of blood" (Isa. 1:15). When the children of Israel spread forth their hands in prayer the Lord will not listen, for they are full of iniquity. In Isaiah 59 the Lord returns to this image: "But your iniquities have separated between you and your God, and your sins have hid his face from you, that he will not hear. For your hands are defiled with blood, and your fingers with iniquity; your lips have spoken lies, your tongue hath muttered perverseness" (Isa. 59:2–3). The sins of Israel are portrayed with vivid imagery: "they conceive mischief, and bring forth iniquity" (Isa. 59:4); "their feet run to evil, and they make haste to shed innocent blood" (Isa. 59:7); "we grope for the wall like the blind, and we grope as if we had no eyes: we stumble at noonday as in the night; we are in desolate places as dead men" (Isa. 59:10; see also D&C 95:6).

Judgment is imminent. Salvation comes from the Lord (Isa. 59:16). He will return as the Divine Warrior dressed with a breastplate of righteousness, the helmet of salvation, the garments of vengeance, and a cloak of zeal (Isa. 59:17)[7] — an image that applies to the Redeemer both as he conquered sin and death and also as he returns to judge the world at the end of time. Vengeance will come upon the wicked, and the Spirit of the Lord will rise up against the enemy. "And the Redeemer shall come to Zion, and unto them that turn from transgression in Jacob, saith the Lord" (Isa. 59:20). The gathering of Israel prepares the world for the return of the Redeemer of Israel and sets the stage for the ushering in of the Millennium.

---

[7]Paul, in his letter to the Ephesians, teaches the Saints to gird themselves with the armor of the Divine Warrior, using much of this same imagery (Eph. 6:11–18; see also D&C 27:15–18).

"Thy Light Is Come" (Isa. 60–62)

Isaiah 60 through 62 describes the building of the glorified Jerusalem/ Zion and the reign of the Lord. These prophecies were partially fulfilled by the return of Judah beginning in 539 B.C. and the rebuilding of Jerusalem and the temple and also in many ways spiritually with the coming of the Messiah in the meridian of time. But the prophecies will only be completely fulfilled in the latter days, with the restoration of the gospel, the events leading up to the Second Coming, and the Millennium, when Christ will reign on the earth. Finally the earth will fulfill the measure of its creation and become the celestial kingdom (D&C 88:17–20), giving an added spiritual dimension to the promise of land in the Abrahamic covenant. (Isa. 60–62 should be read with Isa. 2 and 11 as well as Ezek. 40–48, Zech. 14, and Rev. 21.)

Isaiah gives a comprehensive description of the mission and message of the Messiah as well as the Atonement that he would perform. His prophecies do not always delineate precisely between what was to be fulfilled in Christ's first coming and what would be fulfilled by his second coming. Hence we speak of the "dual nature" of prophecy, meaning that a prophecy will be partially fulfilled in the meridian of time but not completely until the Messiah returns in glory. For example, part of Isaiah's messianic prophecy, "unto us a child is born, unto us a son is given" (Isa. 9:6), was fulfilled with the mortal birth of the Savior. But the continuation, "and the government shall be upon his shoulder . . . of the increase of his government . . . there shall be no end . . . to establish it with judgment and with justice from henceforth even for ever" (Isa. 9:6–7), will not be fulfilled until the Second Coming. As Nephi observed, a precise understanding of Isaiah's prophecies is apparent only to those who live in the time of their fulfillment (2 Ne. 25:7). Because we live after the first coming of Jesus Christ, with an understanding of the basic events of his mission, it is much simpler for us to distinguish between what has already occurred and what must still come to pass.

The establishment of Zion in the fullest sense consists of the coming of the Messiah, his reign on the earth, and the gathering of Israel and the nations of the earth who accept his gospel and come to worship him. The presence of the Lord is characterized throughout scripture by the presence of light and glory. His guiding presence among his children as he delivered them from Egyptian bondage was attested by a pillar of fire by night and a cloud by day. This light and glory was symbolized in the tabernacle by the great lamp-stand and was present as the Lord accepted his dedicated temple at the time of Solomon. In Isaiah, light is also an important motif of the presence of the Lord: "Arise, shine; for thy light is come, and the glory of the Lord is risen upon thee. For, behold, the darkness shall cover the earth, and gross darkness the people: but the Lord shall arise upon thee, and his glory shall be seen upon thee" (Isa. 60:1–2). This passage is reminiscent of Isaiah 2:5, "O house of Jacob, come ye, and let us walk in the light of the Lord," as well as Isaiah 60:19, "The sun shall be no more thy light by day; neither for brightness shall the moon give light unto thee: but the Lord shall be unto thee an everlasting light, and thy God thy glory" (see also Isa. 62:1).

Jesus read the messianic prophecy in Isaiah 61:1–2 in the synagogue at Nazareth at the outset of his ministry. He declared to the people, "This day is this scripture fulfilled in your ears" (Luke 4:16–32). The people immediately understood his identification of himself as the Messiah and attempted to kill him for blasphemy, exclaiming, "Is not this Joseph's son?" (Luke 4:22). The language of this prophecy has many allusions to other messianic prophecies in Isaiah:

Isaiah 61	Elsewhere in Isaiah
61:1 The Spirit of the Lord God is upon me	42:1 I have put my spirit upon him
	44:3 I will pour my spirit upon thy seed
	59:21 My spirit that is upon thee
61:1 The Lord hath anointed me (Hebrew, *māšaḥ*; the Hebrew for "anoint" is the root from which the word *Messiah* is derived)	45:1 Thus saith the Lord to his anointed (Cyrus as a type of the Messiah)
61:1 To preach good tidings	40:9 O Zion, that bringest good tidings
	41:27 I will give to Jerusalem one that bringeth good tidings
	52:7 How beautiful upon the mountains are the feet of him that bringeth good tidings

61:1 Unto the meek	11:4 And reprove with equity for the meek of the earth
	29:19 The meek also shall increase their joy in the Lord
61:1 To bind up the brokenhearted	25:8 He will swallow up death in victory; and the Lord God will wipe away tears from off all faces (see also Rev. 7:17; 21:4)
61:2 To proclaim the acceptable year of the Lord	49:8 In an acceptable time have I heard thee

The liberty proclaimed to the captives and the opening of the prison (Isa. 61:1) can refer to the preaching of the gospel to those in spirit prison (1 Pet. 3:19). But in a larger sense it refers to the victory of the Atonement over sin and death. It is noteworthy that Jesus deleted the ending of Isaiah 61:2, "and the day of vengeance of our God," as a description of his mortal ministry (see Luke 4:19). This prophecy, like many messianic prophecies in Isaiah, was only partly fulfilled in the meridian of time and will be completely fulfilled with the Second Coming, when the Messiah returns in his glory as the judge of the earth.

The gathering of Israel is to be facilitated in part by the Gentiles (starting with Cyrus and concluding with the final gathering of Israel in the latter days), who would join Israel in coming to the Lord (Isa. 60:3, 5, 10–11, 16; 61:5, 9; 62:2). Interestingly, Midian, Ephah, and Sheba (Isa. 60:6), counted among the Gentiles, are descendants of Abraham by his wife Keturah (Gen. 25:1–4). Kedar and Nebaioth (Isa. 60:7) are descendants of Abraham through Ishmael (Gen. 25:13), coming to receive their inheritance in Zion. That they bring offerings of gold and incense was seen by early Christians as an allusion to the coming of the Magi to acknowledge and celebrate the mortal birth of Jesus.[8] Elsewhere they come from all over the world, bearing the wealth of the earth to help build the eternal city. "The Lord hath proclaimed unto the end of the world . . . Behold, thy salvation cometh" (Isa. 62:11), and "they shall call them, The holy people, The redeemed of the Lord" (Isa. 62:12).

---

[8]Matthew himself does not note a connection between the wise men and Isa. 60:6. The early Christian Fathers, beginning with Justin Martyr, began this interpretation. See W. F. Albright and C. S. Mann, *Matthew*, Anchor Bible 26 (Garden City, N.Y.: Doubleday, 1971), pp. 13, 16.

"Mighty to Save" (Isa. 63–64)

Isaiah 63 contains a dramatic poem describing the return of the Lord, in his glory, bringing judgment and salvation to his people (63:1–6). The image is that of the Divine Warrior destroying the enemies of his people. He is returning triumphantly from Edom, where he has wrought his vengeance with the blood of the vanquished on his garments. Edom is a type of the world (D&C 1:36; "Idumea" is the Greek form of *Edom*). It is a fitting type. The Edomites are descendants of Esau (Gen. 36:1), and although their forefathers Esau and Jacob eventually made up, the enmity of these people started with the disputed birthright and continued throughout history.

Edom was Israel's neighbor to the south and to the east in the rocky desert and mountainous country. When Judah fell to the Babylonians in 587 B.C., the Edomites rejoiced, took part in the pillage of Jerusalem, and encroached upon Judah's territory in the south (Ezek. 25:12–14; Obad. 1:10–16). Israel's prophets constantly denounced them (Amos 1:6, 9, 11; 2:1; Ps. 137:7; Isa. 11:14; 34:5–17; Jer. 49:7–22; Ezek. 35; Mal. 1:2–4). Obadiah prophesied their doom because of the pride of their hearts and their impudence (Obad. 1:3). Isaiah 34 portrays universal judgment and destruction focusing on Edom, as a type of all the world. In the same way that Edom is a type of the world, the city of Bozrah represents all of Edom. In prophetic oracles, the almost impregnable mountain fortress of Bozrah is the symbol of Edom's strength, and its destruction signifies the destruction of all of Edom (Isa. 34:6; 63:1; Jer. 49:13, 22; Amos 1:12).

A key word in Isaiah 63:4 is "vengeance." The Hebrew root *nqm* signifies retribution. The "day of the Lord" brings divine judgment to the world—great and terrible for the wicked but a time of vindication and reward for the faithful. Isaiah 63:2 reads: "Wherefore art thou red in thine apparel, and thy garments like him that treadeth in the winefat?" There is a pun here. The word for "red" in Hebrew is *'ādom*, from the same root as Edom (*'edôm*). The word-play is continued in verse 3: "and their blood shall be sprinkled upon my garments." The Hebrew word for "blood" is *dām*, and it is the blood that makes the garments red. The image of red in this passage is thus that of the blood of the vanquished. Of course, it is through the Atonement that Christ assumes the role of judge, and the imagery of the blood of the sins of the world staining his garments points both to the Atonement as well as to the Judgment at the day of vengeance. (This chapter should be read with Isa. 34; D&C 133:46–56; Rev. 19:11–17; see also D&C 76:107; 88:106.)

Isaiah 63:7–9 reminds Israel that the judgment is accompanied by loving kindness (Hebrew, *ḥesed*). Justice is tempered with mercy, and in the past the Lord had heard the afflictions of his children and delivered them: "In his love and in his pity he redeemed them; and he bare them, and carried them all the days of old" (63:9).

Isaiah 63:15–64:12 contains a prayer, presumably by Isaiah speaking for his people, petitioning the Lord that he might "look down from heaven" (Isa. 63:15), to "come down, that the mountains might flow down at thy presence" (Isa. 64:1). The Lord is asked to show mercy: "Be not wroth very sore, O Lord, neither remember iniquity for ever: behold, see, we beseech thee, we are all thy people" (Isa. 64:9).

The passage in Isaiah 64:1–5 is cited in Doctrine and Covenants 133:40–45 in the context of the preaching of the gospel to all the nations (as prophesied in Rev. 14:6–7, paraphrased in D&C 133:37–39). A reference is made to the Creation: "But now, O Lord, thou art our father; we are the clay, and thou our potter; and we all are the work of thy hand" (Isa. 64:8). The image is reminiscent of the allegory of the potter in Jeremiah 18 but goes back to the creation of man in Genesis 2:7: "And the Lord God formed man of the dust of the ground." The verb in Hebrew for "formed" is *yṣr*, a term used for the shaping of pottery. In Isaiah the image of the creation of man, from the hands of the Lord, is extended to mean that through the covenant the Lord has created not just individuals but the whole nation (Isa. 29:23; 45:9–11; 60:21).

"New Heavens and a New Earth" (Isa. 65–66)

In Isaiah 65 and 66 the Lord responds to the prayer recorded in Isaiah 63:15–64:12. First the Lord reminds his people that he had always been there—it was they who had forsaken him (see the same image in Isa. 50:1; 54:7–8 about the bill of divorcement). He had stretched out his hand to his children, but they had responded with rebellion rather than repentance (Isa. 65:3–7). At last the Day of Judgment has arrived. The "day of the Lord is darkness" (Amos 5:18), and the destruction of the wicked will be terrible indeed. In Isaiah the Second Coming is seen as the beginning of a new creation; finally the darkness will give way to light, chaos to creation; and the Lord declares, "Behold, I create new heavens and a new earth: and the former shall not be remembered, nor come into mind" (Isa. 65:17; 66:22).

This new creation will be a reversal of the normal course of mortality. The Lord describes in Isaiah 65:19–25 the conditions during the Millennium: joy; end to infant mortality; building, planting, and eating; enjoyment of the labor of one's hands; and peace on earth — symbolized by the coexistence of the wolf and the lamb (see Isa. 11:7–8; 2:4). Contrasted with the fire and the sword by which the Lord will answer the wicked (Isa. 66:15–16), he will look with favor on the man "that is poor and of a contrite spirit" (Isa. 66:2). Finally the Lord will comfort Israel, "as one whom his mother comforteth" (Isa. 66:13; see the same theme in Isa. 40:1, "Comfort ye, comfort ye my people"). His glory shall be declared to the Gentiles (Isa. 66:19), who will bring the remnant of Israel as an offering to the Lord (Isa. 66:20). Then "shall all flesh come to worship before me, saith the Lord" (Isa. 66:23). The final verse is a sober reminder of the reward for those who transgress against the Lord, "for their worm shall not die, neither shall their fire be quenched" (Isa. 66:24).

The salvation of the Lord is thus completed. The Lord God of Israel is the Creator, Redeemer, and finally the Judge of the world. In the end he brings justice: salvation and vindication for the righteous and punishment for the unrepentant. As he had the power to create the world in the beginning, so at the end will he create it again. The earth, having "filled the measure of its creation," will be sanctified and crowned with glory (D&C 88:18–19) and prepared to receive the seed of Abraham, who through their faithfulness to the covenant will finally inherit the promised land.

16

THE FALL OF THE KINGDOM OF JUDAH

(2 Kings 21–25; 2 Chronicles 33–36)

Gary Lee Walker

Few examples in recorded history equal the dramatic and sudden reversal of national fortune that befell the kingdom of Judah during the last century before the fall of Jerusalem. During this one-hundred-year period recorded in 2 Kings 21 through 25 and in 2 Chronicles 33 through 36, seven kings reigned in Judah, only one of whom, Josiah, was righteous and found favor in the eyes of the Lord. From 697 to 597 B.C.[1], Judah plummeted toward the abyss of destruction, as foretold by the prophets of God.

For the twenty-nine years preceding the final century before Jerusalem's fall, however, the righteous Hezekiah reigned as king of Judah. Encouraged by the prophet Isaiah, he desired to achieve two goals: to gain independence from Assyria, and to purify his kingdom's religion and abolish the worship of foreign deities. He achieved the latter goal, for he suppressed idolatry and reestablished pure temple service. Although he never achieved independence from Assyria, Hezekiah generally listened to the counsel of the Lord given through Isaiah and saw his nation delivered from its enemy through divine intervention (2 Kgs. 19:35).

Gary Lee Walker teaches history at Brigham Young University and at Utah Valley State College.

[1]An excellent discussion of problems in dating can be found in William S. LaSor, David A. Hubbard, and Frederic W. Bush, *Old Testament Survey* (Grand Rapids, Mich.: Eerdmans, 1982), pp. 288–97.

Manasseh (2 Kgs. 21; 2 Chron. 33)

Sometimes faithful and worthy parents have children who choose unrighteousness. Such was the case with Hezekiah, whose son Manasseh (687–642 B.C.) can certainly be considered among the most wicked of all the kings of Judah. The Bible confirms that in an extremely long reign he had many years in which to accomplish his restitution of idolatry in Judah. He sat on the throne for forty-five years, among the longest reigns of any of the sons of David. The Lord's displeasure with him is vividly recalled at the time of the fall of Jerusalem, when the writer of Kings states: "Surely at the commandment of the Lord came this upon Judah, to remove them out of his sight, for the sins of Manasseh, according to all that he did; And also for the innocent blood that he shed: for he filled Jerusalem with innocent blood; which the Lord would not pardon" (2 Kgs. 24:3–4).

Manasseh collaborated with Assyria and succeeded in becoming a faithful vassal of that powerful nation.[2] He may have had little choice in submitting, for the Assyrian empire was at the apex of its power and its authority reached far and wide (see Map 10, LDS Bible). Totally reversing the policies and accomplishments of Hezekiah, his father and predecessor, Manasseh successfully introduced every form of idolatry and pagan worship back into the religion of his kingdom. This action earned for him the scathing rebuke and denunciation: "And he did that which was evil in the sight of the Lord, after the abominations of the heathen, whom the Lord cast out before the children of Israel" (2 Kgs. 21:2; see also 2 Chron. 33:2, 9).

Manasseh rebuilt the high places which his father had destroyed (2 Kgs. 21:3). These were hilltop areas where images and altars to Baal and other foreign gods were erected. In addition, the account states that an Asherah (called a "grove" in the KJV) was set up. An Asherah was a tree or pole, symbolizing the female side of nature worship—the Canaanite goddess Asherah. In 2 Kings 21:3, the writer states that "all the host of heaven" were worshipped, indicating that the king reintroduced the polytheistic deities of the Near East into Judah's religious practices.

---

[2]LaSor, Hubbard, and Bush, p. 283; and John Bright, *A History of Israel,* 3d ed. (Philadelphia: Westminster, 1981), pp. 311–12.

Astrological cults and magic were also introduced, as noted in 2 Kings 21:6, for Manasseh "observed times, and used enchantments, and dealt with familiar spirits and wizards."

To complete his reintroduction of wickedness and idolatry into Judah, Manasseh desecrated the temple by building altars in it for the worshipping of gods other than Jehovah (2 Kgs. 21:4–5). Flagrantly defying the wrath of God, he placed the image of Asherah within the walls of the temple proper (2 Kgs. 21:7). The capstone of Manasseh's reign of idolatry and sin was the introduction of the practice of child sacrifice, for we are told that "he made his son pass through the fire" (2 Kgs. 21:6; 2 Chron. 33:6).[3]

It was common for vassals to submit to the worship and religious practices of their overlords. But a careful reading of the accounts of Manasseh makes it clear that he went much further than was necessary in appeasing his Assyrian masters. The author of 2 Kings surely recognized his evil intent when he summarized Manasseh's accomplishments: "And Manasseh seduced them to do more evil than did the nations whom the Lord destroyed before the children of Israel. . . . Moreover Manasseh shed innocent blood very much, till he had filled Jerusalem from one end to another; beside his sin wherewith he made Judah to sin, in doing that which was evil in the sight of the Lord" (2 Kgs. 21:9, 16). It should be noted that 2 Chronicles 33:12–20 tells of a brief period in Manasseh's reign that would indicate a change of heart. According to that narrative (which is absent from 2 Kings), he was taken in chains to Babylon (2 Chron. 33:11–13), where in his afflictions he "humbled himself greatly before the God of his fathers" (2 Chron. 33:12). In attempting to at least show some outward sign of submitting to the Lord's will, Manasseh undertook some purifying restorations. The records indicate that his efforts, if indeed even sincere, went unnoticed and unheeded by his people, for they were now steeped in idolatry. Manasseh had succeeded in influencing Judah to become a wicked nation.

Upon the death of Manasseh, his twenty-two-year-old son Amon ascended the throne of Judah (2 Kgs. 21:18–26; 2 Chron. 33:20–25). The brief two-year reign (642–640 B.C.) saw a continuation of his father's

---

[3]In 2 Chron. 33:6, the writer notes that Manasseh "caused his *children* to pass through the fire in the valley of the son of Hinnom" (emphasis added).

policies: "And he did that which was evil in the sight of the Lord, as his father Manasseh did. And he walked in, and served the idols that his father served, and worshipped them: And he forsook the Lord God of his fathers, and walked not in the way of the Lord" (2 Kgs. 21:20–22). Political assassination by "servants" ended Amon's reign, possibly the result of anti-Assyrian feelings among political factions in the kingdom.[4] In turn, "the people of the land" hunted down and assassinated the murderous conspirators and placed Amon's son Josiah on the throne (2 Kgs. 21:24).

The Political Situation in the Near East

The final drama in Judah was being played against a backdrop of political intrigue and decay in the Near East. Although at the height of her power, Assyria was overextended and maintained her status only by sheer terror and force. Enemies in the form of Babylonia, Egypt, Persia, various others pressing upon her northern frontier, and Arab tribes of the Syrian desert, were threatening to overcome the stranglehold of the Assyrian empire on the nations. Under the leadership of Ashurbanipal, king of Assyria (668–627 B.C.), enemies to the empire remained subjected as vassals. Upon his death, however, internal strife overtook his government, thus weakening the hold Assyria had maintained on her neighbors. In less than twenty years, Assyria was overthrown by some of her former vassals. The Babylonians, also known in the scriptures as the Chaldeans, became the dominant force in the Near East, crushing all who stood in their way. By 609 B.C., Assyria was no more.

Josiah (2 Kgs. 22:1–23:30; 2 Chron. 34–35)

As the grip of Assyria weakened, Judah once again found herself a free country. Josiah's thirty-one-year reign (640–609 B.C.) began when he was but eight years of age. Our ancient historian tells us that "he did that which was right in the sight of the Lord, and walked in all the way

---

[4]Bright, p. 316.

of David his father, and turned not aside to the right hand or to the left" (2 Kgs. 22:2). We can assume that righteous advisers administered the affairs of state during the childhood of the king. A passage in 2 Chronicles, however, indicates the nature of the young monarch: "For in the eighth year of his reign, while he was yet young, he began to seek after the God of David his father: and in the twelfth year he began to purge Judah and Jerusalem from the high places, and the groves, and the carved images, and the molten images" (2 Chron. 34:3).

Josiah's reforms should be viewed in light of the rapid decline of the Assyrian empire. As the conquering empire released her grip on Judah and her other vassal nations, the decision to rid the country of the idolatrous religion of the Assyrians and other foreign cults could be made and executed.

The religious reforms of this young and righteous king were among the most consistent and thorough in his country's history. The writer of Chronicles tells us that he removed all of the pagan idols, Asherah pillars, and altars from throughout the land of Judah (2 Chron. 34:3–7). His desire to remove any corrupt religious object from Judah was so profound that he made dust from the idolatrous images and had it sprinkled on the graves of those who had sacrificed before them (2 Chron. 34:4). Further, he exhumed the bones of the pagan priests and had them burned on their own altars (2 Chron. 34:5).

According to the account in 2 Kings, Josiah's purge of idolatrous religious practices continued through the eighteenth year of his reign, when he was twenty-six years old. At that time, he turned his attention to the sacred temple in Jerusalem, which had fallen into disrepair through misuse and pagan worship. There are discrepancies in the chronology of events between 2 Kings and 2 Chronicles at this point, but it is safe to conclude that Josiah's purges were an ongoing enterprise that preceded and continued on after the discovery of the "book of the law" (2 Kgs. 22:8; 2 Chron. 34:14–15). This is supported by the account in 2 Chronicles, for Josiah's reforms are pictured as a series of steps.

The discovery of the "book of the law" can be considered the most important event of Josiah's reign. Apparently uncovered by the high priest Hilkiah, the book was brought before the king. Upon hearing the words of the book, Josiah, now profoundly moved and disturbed by its content, "rent his clothes" (2 Kgs. 22:11). The book that was found within the walls of the temple is generally considered to be some form of the book of Deuteronomy.[5] Scholars have pointed to some of Josiah's reforms as reflecting things that are found only in Deuteronomy, namely the centralization of the religion in Jerusalem and the integration of religious leaders outside of Jerusalem with the temple officiators (see Deut. 12:13–14, 17–18; 18:6–8).

Josiah instructed Hilkiah and others to seek the word of the Lord concerning the book through a prophetess named Huldah (2 Kgs. 22:12–14). He recognized that if the book was indeed a sacred volume, his people were already under great condemnation for not obeying the laws of God. Huldah's prophecy testified to the sacred nature of the book and also confirmed that the people of Judah were indeed under condemnation for their idolatrous practices. Through Huldah, the Lord offered no consolation or optimistic future for his chosen people: "Behold, I will bring evil upon this place, and upon the inhabitants thereof, even all the words of the book which the king of Judah hath read: Because they have forsaken me, and have burned incense unto other gods, that they might provoke me to anger with all the works of their hands: therefore my wrath shall be kindled against this place, and shall not be quenched" (2 Kgs. 22:16–17). Elsewhere in 2 Kings, the writer recorded that the sins of Manasseh had brought destruction upon the people of Judah (2 Kgs. 23:26; 24:3–4).

But the Lord, through Huldah, made the following promise to the humble and tender-hearted Josiah: "I will gather thee unto thy fathers, and thou shalt be gathered into thy grave in peace; and thine eyes shall not see all the evil which I will bring upon this place" (2 Kgs. 22:20).

Concerned for the welfare of his erring people, Josiah gathered them to the temple area and read the words of the book so that all could hear. After the reading, Josiah and his people covenanted "before the Lord, to walk after the Lord, and to keep his commandments and his testimonies and his statutes with all their heart and all their soul to perform the words of this covenant that were written in this book. And all the people stood to the covenant" (2 Kgs. 23:3; 2 Chron. 34:31). The purging of idolatrous images and practices then took on new meaning and continued with consistency and force. Now the temple was purified by the removal

---

[5]Bright, p. 319; LaSor, Hubbard, and Bush, p. 284, n. 16.

of Canaanite altars and the Asherah pillar, which had been placed there by Manasseh, and by the destruction of the cultic prostitution centers adjacent to the temple (2 Kgs. 23:3–8). Topheth, the center for child sacrifice, was desecrated so "that no man might make his son or his daughter to pass through the fire to Molech" (2 Kgs. 23:10).

Although the chronology again appears to be somewhat distorted, the records indicate that a great Passover feast was held during the eighteenth year of Josiah's reign (2 Kgs. 23:23). It was to be kept "as it is written in the book [the book of the law] of this covenant" (2 Kgs. 23:21), which would indicate that the feast was part of Josiah's intense desire for the reinstitution of God's laws and ordinances in Judah. In addition, as the Passover celebrated the deliverance of the children of Israel from the Egyptians, Josiah's great feast could well have reminded the people of their developing freedom from Assyrian oppression. The authors of both Kings and Chronicles note specifically that the great feast was the most elaborate and magnificent in the history of all of Israel (2 Kgs. 23:22; 2 Chron. 35:18). In 2 Chronicles 35:1–19, the great detail and elaborate preparations that went into the execution of this Passover are outlined.

The last years of Josiah's reign are not recorded in scripture. With the Assyrian grip on the Near East ending, we can assume Josiah's kingdom was somewhat secure. He apparently retook some of the northern sections once occupied by the kingdom of Israel, as well as other areas adjacent to Judah. Further, because Josiah had reinstituted the covenant law, it can be assumed that overall public morality and government were vastly improved.

The last recorded account of Josiah deals with his battle and subsequent death at the hands of the Egyptians under the leadership of Necho II (610–594 B.C.; 2 Kgs. 23:29–30; 2 Chron. 35:20–24). The year was 609 B.C., and international affairs were confused and tenuous. For centuries Egypt had opposed Assyrian control of the Mediterranean seaboard. For whatever reason, Necho now decided to support severely wounded Assyria and her fight against the coalition of Babylonians and Medes. Perhaps a weakened Assyria appeared better in the international scheme of politics than a strong Babylonia, strengthened even more by her allies. The importance of this event lies in its relationship to the death of Josiah. The reason for Josiah and his army rushing out to stop the Egyptian army is unclear. Perhaps he saw an Egypto-Assyrian victory as a threat to his kingdom's security and independence. Regardless, Josiah and his troops marched to Megiddo and engaged Necho's army in battle. Disguised as a soldier, Josiah went into the thick of battle and was fatally wounded by Egyptian archers (2 Chron. 35:22–23). The dying king was placed in a chariot and taken back to Jerusalem.

The prophecy of Huldah had come to pass. Josiah was taken away before he could witness the final scenes of destruction in Jerusalem. When the Lord, through his prophetess, uttered the words, "And thou shalt be gathered into thy grave in peace" (2 Kgs. 22:20), the people could not have expected their righteous king to be killed in a bloody battle. Few probably discerned that the peace the Lord had spoken of was the peace revealed to Alma: "And then shall it come to pass, that the spirits of those who are righteous are received into a state of happiness, which is called paradise, a state of rest, a state of peace, where they shall rest from all their troubles and from all care, and sorrow" (Alma 40:12).

The righteousness of Josiah is unquestioned, for we are told that the great prophet Jeremiah "lamented for Josiah" (2 Chron. 35:25). A young Jeremiah began his ministry during Josiah's reign and perhaps had an influence on the king and his reformation. His respect for Josiah's character and work can be noted in Jeremiah 22:15–16. Zephaniah also prophesied during the administration of this righteous king, probably prior to or in the early days of the reform period.[6] Other prophets — Nahum, Habakkuk, Obadiah, and Lehi — were perhaps influenced during their youth by Josiah's faithful rule.

Despite the great reformation executed by Josiah, the judgments of the Lord were not turned away from an erring Judah. His reforms seem to have changed his kingdom on the surface, but the hearts of many of his people still reflected the works of Manasseh. Moreover, Josiah was Judah's last righteous king. Those who followed after him led their kingdom to destruction: "The Lord turned not from the fierceness of his great wrath, wherewith his anger was kindled against Judah, because of all the provocations that Manasseh had provoked him withal. And the Lord said, I will remove Judah also out of my sight, as I have removed Israel,

---

[6]Bright, pp. 320–21.

and will cast off this city Jerusalem which I have chosen, and the house of which I said, My name shall be there" (2 Kgs. 23:26–27).

The First Siege of Jerusalem
(2 Kgs. 23–30–24:16; 2 Chron. 36:1–10)

In a little more than twenty years Jerusalem would fall. With Necho's victory over Josiah, Judah again became a tributary, this time to Egypt. Josiah's twenty-three-year-old son, Jehoahaz, was anointed king. Following in the evil footsteps of his great-grandfather, Manasseh, Jehoahaz ruled only three months (609 B.C.) before being removed by Necho and deported to Egypt (2 Kgs. 23:31–33). A puppet ruler named Eliakim, another son of Josiah, was then installed. Necho changed his name to Jehoiakim (609–598 B.C.) and forced him to exact massive tributes from the people of Judah (2 Kgs. 23:33, 35). Jehoiakim also followed in the footsteps of Manasseh, squandering funds and subjecting the people to forced labor (Jer. 22:13–19).

Egypt's dominance of Judah ended in 605 B.C., when Nebuchadnezzar of Babylon defeated Necho and his army at Carchemish, thus becoming the master of the Near East. Jehoiakim was now forced to submit to the Babylonian monarch and "became his servant three years: then he turned and rebelled against him" (2 Kgs. 24:1). The rebellion was a fatal error for Jehoiakim and Judah, even though retaliation was not immediate. Nebuchadnezzar had returned home to reorganize his armies after a battle with Egypt in 601 B.C. in which both sides sustained heavy losses. The Babylonian king did not march with his armies until December, 598 B.C., the same month in which Jehoiakim's eleven-year reign, declared "evil in the sight of the Lord" (2 Kgs. 23:37), ended with his death.[7] Josiah's reforms had long since collapsed, and idolatrous worship returned along with the deterioration of public morality. Jeremiah, whose ministry overlapped with the reigns of Judah's last five kings, bore testimony of his country's degeneration (see Jer. 5:26–29; 7:1–18; 11:9–14).

Jehoiakim's eighteen-year-old son, Jehoiachin, also denounced as an

---

[7]Note Jer. 22:18–19 and 36:30. The description of what was to occur with Jehoiakim's body after his death leads one to believe that he could well have been assassinated, rather than dying of natural causes.

evil ruler, was placed on the throne in 598 B.C. (2 Kgs. 24:9). The first Babylonian siege of Jerusalem occurred three months later, with the city surrendering to Nebuchadnezzar on 16 March 597 B.C.[8] At this time, Jehoiachin, his mother, and the entire royal household were taken hostage and transported to Babylon (2 Kgs. 24:12). Along with the royal family, thousands of Judah's leaders, craftsmen, soldiers, and people of influence were carried away (2 Kgs. 24:14–16). This was the beginning of what is called "the Exile," the period in which the Jews were exiled from their homeland to Babylonia. It was the deportation which took Ezekiel, and probably also Daniel, to later begin prophetic ministries among the exiled Jews. The account states that "none remained, save the poorest sort of the people of the land" (2 Kgs. 24:14). We learn later, however, that a few people of status and leadership must have remained, for the weak character of Jehoiachin's successor would be no match for the stronger wills of some of the survivors. Nonetheless, Nebuchadnezzar's actions show that he did not want to leave anyone who might organize or carry out a rebellion.

The Final Days of Jerusalem
(2 Kgs. 24:17–25:30; 2 Chron. 36:11–23)

The Babylonian ruler appointed Mattaniah, Josiah's son and Je-hoiachin's uncle, to be king of Judah in 597 B.C. and changed his name to Zedekiah (2 Kgs. 24:17). Though Zedekiah was declared an evil king (2 Kgs. 24:19), there is evidence in the book of Jeremiah that he may have had some good intentions (Jer. 37:17–21; 38:7–28). He was a weak monarch, however, fearful of the people and unable to stand up to the nobles and his underlings (Jer. 38:5, 19). It was during the first year of his reign that Lehi and his family left Jerusalem (see 1 Ne. 1:4).

The ten years of Zedekiah's reign (597–587 B.C.), before the final siege and destruction of Jerusalem, were filled with strife, sedition, and continual agitation. Unrest was probably inflamed by the exhortations of self-appointed prophets who gave false hope to the leaders and people of Judah (Jer. 28:1–17; 29:8–9). Some of these were later executed by

---

[8]Bright, p. 327.

Nebuchadnezzar (Jer. 29:21–23). Jeremiah's denunciation of these un-inspired prophets apparently fell on deaf ears (Jer. 27; 28; 29). So also did his warnings to Zedekiah to submit to the yoke of bondage under Nebuchadnezzar, for the unrighteous king openly rebelled (2 Chron. 36:12–13). Along with his condemnation of the false prophets, Jeremiah also wrote a letter to the exiled people, counseling them to prepare for a seventy-year stay in captivity (Jer. 29).

In January of 588 B.C., Jerusalem was placed under a blockade.[9] Surrounding areas were taken over one by one until the city was encircled by the armies of Nebuchadnezzar (Jer. 34:7). The people of Jerusalem held out until July of 587 B.C., when the conquering armies prevailed "and the city was broken up" (2 Kgs. 25:1–2, 4). By this time the people of Jerusalem were in a desperate state because of famine (2 Kgs. 25:3). Zedekiah and his army fled under the cover of darkness toward the plain of Jordan but were overtaken by the army of the Chaldeans and brought before Nebuchadnezzar (2 Kgs. 25:4–6).

The sacking, spoiling, looting, burning, and physical cruelty to po-litical prisoners by ancient Near Eastern conquerors is aptly illustrated in 2 Kings 25:7–21, as well as in the book of Jeremiah and other scriptures touching upon the final scenes in Jerusalem. No mercy was shown to the rebellious Zedekiah: he first was forced to witness the execution of his sons,[10] then his eyes were put out, and finally he was bound in chains and transported to Babylon, where he remained until his death (2 Kgs. 25:7). A month later, Nebuzar-adan, commander of Nebuchadnezzar's guard, arrived in Jerusalem, torched the city, and leveled its walls (2 Kgs. 25:8–10), putting to an end not only Jerusalem but also the kingdom of Judah.

Much of the remaining population was deported to Babylon (2 Kgs. 25:11–12, 18–21). Nebuzar-adan only "left of the poor of the land to be vinedressers and husbandmen" (2 Kgs. 25:12). The final blow to the defeated people, a witness that God had forsaken them in their wicked-

---

[9]Jer. 52 also recounts the last days of Jerusalem and records additional details of the sacking of the city and the dispersion of the people.

[10]We know from the Book of Mormon that Mulek, one of the sons of Zedekiah, did not share the fate of his brothers but journeyed to the Americas. From him and his group descended the Mulekites. See Omni 1:15; Mosiah 25:2; Hel. 8:21. See also John L. Sorenson, "The 'Mulekites,' " *BYU Studies*, Summer 1990, pp. 6–22.

ness, was the sacking and destruction of the temple, built by Solomon three and one-half centuries earlier (2 Kgs. 25:13–17; Jer. 52). The once sacred and glorious temple and city of Jerusalem were reduced to rubble.

Gedaliah, a nobleman,[11] was appointed governor over the remaining poor peasants. Even a puppet ruler was not safe in those turbulent times, for he was soon assassinated by Ishmael, a distant member of the royal family, with the assistance of other conspirators (2 Kgs. 25:25–26; Jer. 40:7–41:15). The murderers subsequently fled to Egypt, forcing the prophet Jeremiah to go with them (Jer. 41:16–43:7).

Second Kings concludes by telling of an event some thirty-seven years later. Nebuchadnezzar's son, Amel-marduk (562–560 B.C.), the Evil-merodach of the King James Version, ascended the throne of Babylon. For reasons that are unclear, he released the former king of Judah, Jehoiachin, from his long captivity in prison. He was subsequently treated very kindly, recognized as a legitimate ruler, though still a captive, and given a pension, "a daily rate for every day, all the days of his life" (2 Kgs. 25:30; see 25:27–30). It was through him that the royal lineage was preserved until the time of Jesus (Matt. 1:11–16).

The Future: "One of a City, and Two of a Family"

The people and leaders of Judah had been counseled constantly and warned for hundreds of years by authorized servants of the Lord to seek after righteousness in order to avoid the wrath of a God who would not be mocked or defied. Among the known Old Testament prophets shortly before Jerusalem's fall were Zephaniah, Huldah, Nahum, Habakkuk, and, of course, Jeremiah, whose difficult and lonely life was a testimony and a witness to the tragic events that culminated in the fall of Jerusalem and the exile of the people of Judah.

The story of a contemporary of Jeremiah is found in the Book of Mormon. Lehi, a native of Jerusalem, began his prophetic work when Zedekiah ascended the throne of Judah (1 Ne. 1:4). Blessed with a vision of things to come, Lehi faithfully preached repentance to the wicked people, but like his contemporaries, he met with violent resistance

---

[11]Bright, p. 331.

(1 Ne. 1:19–20). Favored of the Lord, he and his family were commanded to leave Jerusalem prior to its fall. Under inspiration they would eventually travel to the American continent, where great nations would descend from them. Eventually, their descendants would be blessed with a personal visitation from the Savior (3 Ne. 11–28).

The people of Judah had felt the full wrath of God. If any single lesson can be learned from the fall of Jerusalem, it is that the Lord will not tolerate sin in any form and that repentance must be complete and sincere, not merely an exercise in lip service. Even with the tragedy of Jerusalem, however, the prophets foretold a great day when Israel and Judah would be gathered and redeemed. For the righteous of those times, as well as for those of the latter days, there is great comfort in the word of the Lord through his prophet, Jeremiah: "I will take you one of a city, and two of a family, and I will bring you to Zion: And I will give you pastors according to mine heart, which shall feed you with knowledge and understanding" (Jer. 3:14–15).

17

THE BOOK OF ZEPHANIAH

RULON D. EAMES

His writings relegated to the back of the Old Testament, it seems strangely appropriate that Zephaniah's name should be interpreted "The Lord has hidden."[1] Yet the first commentary on any book of the Bible written by an LDS Church leader was Oliver Cowdery's treatise on the book of Zephaniah in 1834.[2] The reason behind Elder Cowdery's fascination with this small book is clear. From the early years of the Restoration, modern prophets have seen in the visions of Zephaniah a vivid picture of the last days.

Very little is known about Zephaniah the man. The only solid information about him is in the superscription that opens his book (Zeph. 1:1). He is described as "the son of Cushi, the son of Gedaliah, the son of Amariah, the son of Hizkiah," or, as this last name is more commonly rendered in English, Hezekiah (Zeph. 1:1). On the basis of this genealogy, it has been proposed that Zephaniah was a descendant of King Hezekiah of Judah (715–687 B.C.), a suggestion that remains a matter of conjecture. Noting the lack of detail regarding Zephaniah's personal background, one scholar has observed: "His own person apparently played no role; the message was the totally dominating feature."[3]

Rulon D. Eames is an instructor at the LDS Institute of Religion in Salt Lake City, Utah.

[1]See Maria Eszenyei Szeles, *Wrath and Mercy: Habakkuk and Zephaniah* (Grand Rapids, Mich.: Eerdmans, 1987), p. 62.

[2]*Evening and Morning Star*, Feb. 1834, pp. 132–33; Mar. 1834, pp. 140–42; Apr. 1834, pp. 148–49.

[3]Arvid S. Kapelrud, *The Message of the Prophet Zephaniah* (Oslo, Norway: Universitetsvorlaget, 1975), p. 46.

Beyond the names of Zephaniah's ancestors, the only biographical datum provided by the superscription is the statement that the word of the Lord came to Zephaniah "in the days of Josiah the son of Amon, king of Judah." The reign of Josiah is typically assigned to the years 640 to 609 B.C. Internal clues in the book of Zephaniah suggest that the prophet's ministry may have taken place during the first half of Josiah's reign. Arguing from that evidence, "it seems reasonable to conclude that the prophet Zephaniah preached in Jerusalem in the years between 635 and 625 B.C."[4]

The Day of the Lord

The book of Zephaniah is a prophecy of divine judgment and redemption, expressed in powerful images. Acknowledging that Zephaniah may not rank with Isaiah or even Hosea in his skill as a poet, one scholar has explained: "He had an imperative message to deliver and proceeded in the most direct and forceful way to discharge his responsibility. What he lacked in grace and charm, he in some measure atoned for by the vigour and clarity of his speech. He realised the approaching terror so keenly that he was able to present it vividly and convincingly to his hearers. No prophet has made the picture of the day of Yahweh more real."[5]

Careful analysis of Zephaniah reveals an underlying structure that highlights the mercy and redemptive power of Jehovah. This effect is achieved through a thematic progression from scenes of total annihilation at the beginning of the book, to scenes of triumphant salvation in the closing verses. As in the writings of other Old Testament prophets, the prophecies of doom precede those of salvation and restoration. The contrast between Jehovah's fierce justice and his ultimate and enduring mercy is further emphasized by the direct juxtaposition of a prophecy of global judgment and an oracle of redemption in the book's final chapter (Zeph. 3:8–20).

Zephaniah's major theme was the day of the Lord, a term used in

---

[4]Kapelrud, p. 42.

[5]John M. P. Smith, William H. Ward, and Julius A. Bewer, *A Critical and Exegetical Commentary on Micah, Zephaniah, Nahum, Habakkuk, Obadiah, and Joel*, The International Critical Commentary (New York: Scribner's, 1911), p. 176.

the scriptures for the time when the Lord will recompense all according to what they deserve.[6] For Zephaniah's unrepentant nation, the kingdom of Judah, the day of the Lord came when the Babylonians destroyed their cities and took their people into forced exile. These events took place within a few decades of Zephaniah's warnings. For the world as a whole there will be a similar day of reckoning, on a global scale, when wickedness will be cleansed from the earth at Christ's second coming. For the faithful it will be a great day of blessing and mercy. For the unrepentant it will be a dreadful day of judgment and sorrow. In Zephaniah's writings, the earlier day of the Lord's recompense is used as a type to foreshadow the latter-day judgment on all the earth. Although the day of the Lord will end in redemption, it must commence with judgment. The first chapter of Zephaniah presents a panorama of violent and unrelenting destruction that would be poured out upon the entire human and animal creation and particularly upon the treacherous inhabitants of Judah and Jerusalem. The language employed by the prophet seems deliberately evocative of the wording of the Flood narrative (Zeph. 1:2–3; cf. Gen. 6:17; 7:21–23). The result is a reversal of the Creation; the earth returns to the primordial chaotic darkness that prevailed "in the beginning" (Zeph. 1:15; cf. Gen. 1:2; Jer. 4:23–28).[7]

The opening chapter also contains the Lord's indictment against the kingdom of Judah. The catalog of trespasses includes idol and astral worship (Zeph. 1:4–5; cf. 2 Kgs. 21:1–7, 19–21), spiritual cynicism and indifference toward religious duties (Zeph. 1:6, 12), adoption of foreign fashions and superstitions (Zeph. 1:8–9), and the acquisition of wealth through "violence and deceit" (Zeph. 1:9). These odious practices provoked the Lord to declare a holy war against his own people.[8] The graphic imagery of divine warfare against Judah gives way to a picture of universal desolation as the whole earth is "devoured by the fire of his jealousy" (Zeph. 1:10–18). Thus the very real and imminent destruction of Judah would prefigure the universal destruction in the last days.

The book's second chapter begins on a hopeful note as the prophet

---

[6]See E. A. Leslie, "Zephaniah," in *The Interpreter's Dictionary of the Bible*, 5 vols., ed. G. A. Buttrick, et al. (Nashville: Abingdon, 1962), 4:952.

[7]Paul R. House, *Zephaniah: A Prophetic Drama* (Sheffield: Almond, 1988), p. 75.

[8]Ralph L. Smith, *Micah–Malachi*, Word Biblical Commentary, vol. 32 (Waco, Texas: Word Books, 1984), p. 132.

pleads with Judah to seek the Lord. Still, Zephaniah cannot ensure the safety of even the penitent. One scholar has pointedly observed: "The word 'perhaps' [Zeph. 2:3; "it may be," KJV] speaks volumes. The prophet would not presume on the prerogative of Yahweh to determine who would or would not be hidden. Zephaniah, like Amos (cf. Zeph. 5:15), knew that not even righteousness nor humility could guarantee a person's safety. That was all in the hand of Yahweh."[9]

All the writing prophets of the eighth and seventh centuries, except Hosea, pronounced oracles against foreign nations. Thus, in the second chapter of Zephaniah the anger of Jehovah shifts from Judah to her traditional enemies at each of the points of the compass: Philistines to the west, Moab and Ammon on the east, Egypt on the south (the reference to Ethiopians seems to be a taunt based on Ethiopian domination of Egypt[10]), and Assyria on the north (Zeph. 2:4–15). The same punishments that would bring destruction to Philistia, Moab, and Ammon would yield blessings of wealth and prosperity for Judah, for "the residue of my people shall spoil them, and the remnant of my people shall possess them" (Zeph. 2:5–10).

Jehovah's wrath is focused on Jerusalem once again in the final chapter (Zeph. 3:1–7). Those whom the prophet condemned were the leaders of Judahite society: the rulers (Zeph. 3:3), the false prophets, and the priests (Zeph. 3:4). It hardly seems coincidental that the prophet's denunciation of high-level wickedness and corruption in Jerusalem comes immediately after his attack on Nineveh, capital of the arrogant and tyrannical Assyrian empire (Zeph. 2:13–15). Jerusalem is no better than Nineveh. In fact, because Jerusalem was the repository of Jehovah's law, her crimes were far worse than those of pagan Nineveh. Of the once holy city of Jerusalem he said: "Woe to her that is filthy and polluted, to the oppressing city! She obeyed not the voice; she received not correction; she trusted not in the Lord; she drew not near to her God. . . . I said, surely thou wilt fear me, thou wilt receive instruction . . . but they rose early and corrupted all their doings" (Zeph. 3:1–2, 7). Consequently, the wicked in Judah would be consumed just as would the transgressors from every nation. Jehovah would assemble all of them for destruction,

[9]Smith, p. 132.
[10]Smith, p. 136.

"for all the earth shall be devoured with the fire of my jealousy" (Zeph. 3:8).

With the next verse (Zeph. 3:9), the prophetic tone is dramatically transformed. The ensuing promises of Jehovah to the righteous are like rays of pure sunlight piercing the smoke of the global holocaust. The linguistic and spiritual confusion of Babel will be undone as all people worship Jehovah in a pure speech (Zeph. 3:9; cf. Gen. 11:6–9; Moses 6:6; Isa. 6:5–7). The Lord will reign in the midst of his people (Zeph. 3:15, 17), sorrow will turn to rejoicing (Zeph. 3:14, 18), and the shame of Israel's long dispersion will be swallowed up in anthems of praise— from "all people of earth" (Zeph. 3:19–20). As the third chapter closes, the transition from destruction to redemption is complete. The judgments of Jehovah must come upon the wicked in every nation; yet it is his exaltation of the righteous that will be the final and enduring reality.

Latter-day Judgments and Gathering

From the time of Joseph Smith, modern prophets have seen in the visions of Zephaniah a multilayered view of the future with great significance for Latter-day Saints. Citing Zephaniah's declaration that "the great day of the Lord is near" (Zeph. 1:14), Elder Bruce R. McConkie declared: "He is speaking of our day. We live in the last days, when the day of the Lord is near."[11] Zephaniah described the day of the Lord as a "day of trouble and distress, a day of wasteness and desolation, a day of darkness and gloominess, a day of clouds and thick darkness" (Zeph. 1:15). Elder Neal A. Maxwell applied this prophecy to the wickedness and resultant misery of the latter days, observing that the "coming decades will be times of despair."[12] Zephaniah saw the destruction of the kingdom of Judah in the larger context of the ultimate and climactic judgments that must precede the Second Coming. The fall of wicked cities and nations in Zephaniah's day portended the final collapse of Satan's kingdom at the end of the world. President Joseph Fielding Smith interpreted the visions of widespread devastation as a picture of the judgments that will

---

[11]Bruce R. McConkie, *The Millennial Messiah* (Salt Lake City: Deseret Book Co., 1982), p. 497.

[12]Neal A. Maxwell, in Conference Report, Oct. 1982, p. 96.

precede the Savior's return.[13] In harmony with this view, Elder McConkie identified Zephaniah 1:14–18 and 3:8 as warnings of latter-day judgments in the form of "premillennial wars,"[14] and President Spencer W. Kimball cited Zephaniah 1:17–18 to illustrate the severity of God's impending vengeance.[15]

Another subject of great importance in the prophecy of Zephaniah is the gathering and restoration of disgraced and scattered Israel. While Zephaniah hinted that this gathering could commence prior to the great day of the Lord with its attendant devastation (Zeph. 2:1–3), he seemed to assign a major part of that gathering to the period *after* the Savior's return (Zeph. 3:15–20). The Lord's presence among his gathered Saints will be the cause of much happiness: "The Lord thy God in the midst of thee is mighty; he will save, he will rejoice over thee with joy; he will rest in his love, he will joy over thee with singing" (Zeph. 3:17).

Although Zephaniah does not rank among the best-known books of the Old Testament, its message is one of tremendous importance for latter-day Israel. In three short chapters, Zephaniah depicted not only the judgments that would come upon Judah and Jerusalem in the sixth century B.C. but also the latter-day redemption of Israel and the global turbulence that will herald Jehovah's return. Impressed by the clarity and the power of his vision of the future, modern seers have used the words of Zephaniah to support and amplify their own teachings concerning the coming day of the Lord. To all who long for that day, the book of Zephaniah is a priceless treasure.

[13]Joseph Fielding Smith, *Doctrines of Salvation*, 4 vols., sel. Bruce R. McConkie (Salt Lake City: Bookcraft, 1954–56), 3:19, 47.
[14]McConkie, pp. 497–98, 543.
[15]Spencer W. Kimball, in Conference Report, Oct. 1975, p. 8.

18

THE BOOK OF NAHUM

D. Kelly Ogden

Nahum was a prophet of the kingdom of Judah who prophesied late in the seventh century B.C., perhaps shortly before the fall of Nineveh in 612.

The book of Nahum may not appear to be very inspirational or uplifting. Its three brief chapters present a harsh description of the destruction of the Assyrian capital of Nineveh. Its tone is accusing and vengeful, seemingly bereft of ethical and theological empathy. Nahum's words almost burn with anxiety to see judgments poured out on the barbarous Assyrians.

Jonah and Nahum have something in common. Both were called to pronounce a burden, or message of doom, on Nineveh, to lift the warning voice to those children of Heavenly Father. The brutality and violence of the Assyrian warlords was widely known and widely deprecated. They were famous for atrocities committed upon conquered peoples, such as forcing prisoners to parade through the streets with freshly decapitated heads around their necks, or, as depicted on the Lachish siege panels from Sennacherib's palace at Nineveh, capturing and impaling prisoners on sharpened poles.[1]

D. Kelly Ogden is associate professor of ancient scripture at Brigham Young University.

[1]James B. Pritchard, ed., *Ancient Near Eastern Texts Relating to the Old Testament,* 3d ed. with Supplement (Princeton: Princeton University, 1969), pp. 276, 288, and 291.

These lines from Ashurnasirpal II (883–859 B.C.) are a further example of the brutality of the conquering Assyrians: "I built a pillar over against his city gate and I flayed all the chiefs who had revolted, and I covered the pillar with their skin. Some I walled up within the pillar, some I impaled upon the pillar on stakes, and others I bound to stakes round about the pillar . . . And I cut the limbs of the officers, of the royal officers who had rebelled. . . . Many captives from among them I burned with fire, and many I took as living captives. From some I cut off their noses, their ears

Jonah at first wanted nothing to do with the assignment to preach repentance to such people. He was bitter toward Israel's enemy and was reticent about the thought of giving them opportunity to repent and be spared (see Jonah 1:1–3; 4:1–3). We do not know about Nahum's personal attitude toward the Assyrians, but it seems to be intentional that his prophecy does not fit the usual pattern of doom followed by hope. Nineveh would be destroyed forever. Unlike Israel and Judah, it would never enjoy a later restoration, so there was no hope to prophesy about in Nineveh's case (Nahum 1:9).

After the Assyrians' cruelties perpetrated on Israel and Judah during the decades prior to Nahum's ministry, the prophet was called to pronounce the Lord's condemnation on the Ninevites. The God of Israel and of all the earth was about to unleash his fury and vengeance on his adversaries (Nahum 1:2). The word of the Lord is always strong and harsh against wickedness. Nahum's high and polished poetry, his fiery figures and white-hot images, graphically depict the deserved destruction in the streets of Nineveh. The reader vividly conjures up the clashing chaos: the chariots raging in the streets, jostling one against another and running like lightning, the noise of whips, of rattling wheels, of prancing horses and jumping chariots, horsemen with bright swords and glittering spears; then numberless carcasses, no end of corpses, stumbling on corpses (Nahum 2:4; 3:2–3).

The destruction of Nineveh that Nahum envisioned was brought about by the combined forces of Babylon and Media in 612 B.C. The destroyers were the armies of Nebuchadnezzar's father, Nabopolassar.

The third chapter of Nahum addresses the question, Why was Nineveh's fate deserved? "Because of the multitude of the whoredoms of the wellfavoured harlot, the mistress of witchcrafts, that selleth nations through her whoredoms, and families through her witchcrafts" (Nahum 3:4). The Lord asked, "Art thou better than populous No?" (Nahum 3:8). The Egyptian city called No, or No-Amon, or ancient Thebes — one of the greatest, most splendid cities of antiquity — was sacked by the

---

and their fingers, of many I put out their eyes. I made one pillar of the living and another of heads, and I bound their heads to tree trunks round about the city. Their young men and maidens I burned in the fire. Twenty men I captured alive and I immured them in the wall of his palace. . . . The rest of their warriors I consumed with thirst in the desert of the Euphrates." Daniel David Luckenbill, *Ancient Records of Assyria and Babylonia*, vol. 1, nos. 433, 445, 455, and 472.

Assyrian king Ashurbanipal in 663 B.C., a few decades before Nahum's vision of Nineveh's own fall. And what had the Assyrians done to Thebes? "Her young children also were dashed in pieces at the top of all the streets: and they cast lots for her honourable men, and all her great men were bound in chains" (Nahum 3:10). The message is unmistakable: Nineveh would suffer a similar fate.

One of the foremost messages of Nahum is a warning to all nations against strident militarism, seeking to conquer and get gain. Jesus later taught, "All they that take the sword shall perish with the sword" (Matt. 26:52). The message was clear to Assyria: "Behold, I am against thee, saith the Lord of hosts; and I will discover [i.e., uncover] thy skirts upon thy face, and I will shew the nations thy nakedness, and the kingdoms thy shame. And I will cast abominable filth upon thee, and make thee vile, and will set thee as a gazingstock. And it shall come to pass, that all they that look upon thee shall flee from thee, and say, Nineveh is laid waste: who will bemoan her? . . . There is no healing of thy bruise; thy wound is grievous: all that hear the [report] of thee shall clap the hands over thee: for upon whom hath not thy wickedness passed continually?" (Nahum 3:5–7, 19).

The vision of the destruction of Nineveh is another illustration of the Book of Mormon teaching that "the words of truth are hard against all uncleanness" (2 Ne. 9:40) and the word of God "speaketh harshly against sin" (2 Ne. 33:5).

Nahum's message, however, does not end there. It is clear from his writings that Nineveh is a type of things to come, just as Babylon and other cities were types (see Isa. 13–14; 1 Pet. 5:13; Rev. 14:8; 17; 18; D&C 1:16; 133:5, 7, 14). The Lord declared several times in modern scripture, "What I say unto one I say unto all" (D&C 61:18, 36; 93:49). The hard message of Nahum to Nineveh is a hard message to nations and peoples in all ages, particularly in these last days preceding the Second Coming (Nahum 1). As Rudyard Kipling pleaded poetically: "Lo, all our pomp of yesterday is one with Nineveh and Tyre!" "Lord God of Hosts, be with us yet, lest we forget, lest we forget."[2] Nahum's three recorded chapters stand as a forceful warning to people everywhere to repent and walk in the path of the Lord—or suffer the vengeance of a just God.

[2]*Hymns of The Church of Jesus Christ of Latter-day Saints* (Salt Lake City: The Church of Jesus Christ of Latter-day Saints, 1985), no. 80.

19

THE BOOK OF HABAKKUK

Victor L. Ludlow

Habakkuk was a Judahite prophet who lived during the time when Jeremiah, Lehi, Nahum, Zephaniah, and other prophets taught in Jerusalem (see 1 Ne. 1:4). Habakkuk questioned the Lord about the decadence of his people and the power which the wicked seemed to have over the righteous (Hab. 1:1–4). He was also concerned about the ominous Babylonian (also called Chaldean) threat which the people of Judah were experiencing, and he was even more worried about the promised destruction of his country by Babylon. Very little is known about his life and background, although scholars are united in dating his pronouncements around 600 B.C.[1]

The three brief chapters of Habakkuk are easily outlined as follows: the first dialogue between Habakkuk and the Lord (Hab. 1:1–11), the second dialogue (Hab. 1:12–2:5), a taunt song against Babylon (Hab. 2:6–20), and a prayer-psalm (Hab. 3:1–19).

The First Dialogue between Habakkuk and the Lord (Hab. 1:1–11)

The book of Habakkuk in the King James Translation begins on a heavy note by describing the writings of Habakkuk as a "burden" which he saw (Hab. 1:1). The Hebrew word translated "burden," *maśśā'*, is commonly rendered as "oracle." Usually the word refers to prophecies

---

Victor L. Ludlow is professor of ancient scripture at Brigham Young University.

[1]See, for example, O. Palmer Robertson, *The Books of Nahum, Habakkuk, and Zephaniah* (Grand Rapids, Mich.: Eerdmans, 1990), pp. 34–38.

of doom. Thus the book of Habakkuk contains the ominous prophecy or revelation that the prophet saw and which was later recorded.

Reflecting on conditions around 605 B.C., the prophet began with some weighty concerns as he asked the Lord why He had not responded to his outcries against the wickedness surrounding him. The people of Judah had not internalized the religious reforms of King Josiah (640–609 B.C.). Instead, they were quickly reverting to the evil practices fostered by King Manasseh (687–642 B.C.), including idolatry, rampant immorality, human sacrifice, and social corruption (see 2 Kgs. 21:1–15; 23:26–27). Habakkuk had witnessed many acts of violence and injustice, and although he had petitioned the Lord concerning them, the wicked were overpowering the righteous, and evil seemed to be prevailing. He asked if the Lord were going to do anything about the deteriorating situation.[2]

Starting in Habakkuk 1:5, the Lord answered Habakkuk's question, telling the prophet to expect the unusual, something unbelievable, as a response to his prayers for justice. The unbelievable is that the Lord would raise up the Chaldean horde from Babylon to deliver justice upon the wicked citizens of Judah. Instead of calming Habakkuk's fears, however, the Lord's message generated even more anxiety as he described the awesome power and speed of the Chaldean forces. They are "terrible and dreadful," as described in Habakkuk 1:7–10. This Babylonian judgment would be much more disastrous than ever expected. Habakkuk's Judahite audience may have wondered how any people could stand up to the Chaldean juggernaut. But the Lord revealed a fatal flaw in the Babylonian attitude in verse 11. As this conqueror marched swiftly on, he offended the Lord either by giving credit for his conquests to his strange, foreign, idol god (KJV) or by relying so much on his own power that his own might and strength became his god (NIV; RSV).[3] The independent power and arrogance of the Babylonians is suggested in verse 7, as they "proceed of themselves," without any divine help or power.

---

[2]This concern for why the wicked prosper and the righteous suffer is frequently found in the Old Testament. An appeal to God for an explanation of his apparent injustice or indifference is expressed more fully in Job, and the question is also raised by Habakkuk's contemporary prophet, Jeremiah (see Jer. 12). It is also addressed at various times in Psalms, as various psalmists wondered why the wicked prevailed and the Lord did not seem to respond (see Ps. 13; 73–74; 79; 89:46–52; 94).

[3]New International Version; Revised Standard Version.

By verse 11 it is clear that they had taken too much credit for themselves and in their misplaced pride had become guilty. The implication is that the Lord, and not any nation, would bring about Babylon's downfall.

The Second Dialogue between Habakkuk and the Lord (Hab. 1:12–25)

Habakkuk protested that an everlasting, holy God would not allow the wicked Babylonians to gain power over God's own people, unrighteous as they might be. After all, Habakkuk complained, how could the wicked heathens prevail over those who are more righteous? Habakkuk asserted that even the wicked Judahites were better than the Chaldeans. He reminded the Lord, You are pure and they are evil, so why do they have power over the more righteous? (see Hab. 1:13).

There are some reasons why this condition may have existed. In absolute terms, the Babylonians were likely more wicked than the Israelites. Yet God also measures wickedness in relative terms, according to the level of light and truth that a people have. Thus, lesser sins by Israelites, who should have known better because of their rich prophetic and scriptural background, would bring greater condemnation than the gross wickedness of a people who lacked the revealed light. The real question was not as much an evaluation of the external moral behavior of a people as a measurement of how large the gap was between public behavior and private accountability. That is, God is able to judge the difference between one's actions and one's knowledge and understanding of right and wrong.

Another possible explanation is that God can choose whatever resource he wants as an instrument of judgment upon his wicked children, much as he allowed the more wicked Lamanites to chasten and punish the somewhat rebellious but more accountable Nephites at one point in Book of Mormon history (2 Ne. 5:19–25). Habakkuk 1 is very similar to Isaiah 10, in which the Assyrians, who are first called the instrument of the Lord's anger, are later spoken of in terms of chastisement and judgment (Isa. 10:5–20). Vengeance is the Lord's, and although the Babylonians would have temporary power over Judah, eventually the Babylonians would receive retribution for their own wickedness.

Habakkuk continued his questioning complaint as the picture of the marauding power resumed (Hab. 1:14–17). With hooks and nets the enemy would harvest his prey and rejoice over his conquests. Echoing the Lord's comments in verse 11, the prophet also mentioned their misplaced pride, telling how the Chaldeans sacrificed to their nets and offered incense to their dragnets, as though these things were the source of their power. Regardless, their power seemed unending, and Habakkuk asked how long they would continue to mercilessly slay the nations (Hab. 1:16–17).

Finally, in a mood of desperation and resignation similar to that of Elijah (1 Kgs. 19:1–14), Job (Job 31), and Mormon (Morm. 3:9–16), Habakkuk stepped aside, retreated to his watchtower, and awaited the Lord's response. Like Abraham (Gen. 18:32), Habakkuk had pushed the Lord as far as he dared and sensed that he might even have gone too far. So he now waited for the Lord's answer or reproval (Hab. 2:1).

The marvelous pronouncement Habakkuk received is of such importance that he was commanded to write it succinctly and plainly on tablets in large enough letters that even a runner could see and read it without stopping (Hab. 2:2). The Lord's response was that Habakkuk should be patient, because the Chaldeans would eventually meet their own doom. The righteous, in contrast, would be preserved by their "faith."[4] The promise that "the just shall live by his faith" was probed by Paul in his New Testament epistles (Rom. 1:17; Gal. 3:11) and was amplified in Hebrews 10:36–38, in which the principle of national deliverance for a righteous people was applied to spiritual salvation for the faithful. This phrase of the just living by faith later became a rallying cry of the Protestant Reformation.

The Lord continued characterizing Babylon's arrogance, which was comparable to death, hell, and its legions (Hab. 2:5). He explained that Babylon's tyranny would lead to self-destruction, portrayed in a taunt song containing five "woe oracles." These five divine judgments could apply to all wicked people and societies.

---

[4]More accurately, "faithfulness." The New Testament references change the emphasis from the intent of the Hebrew word—"faithfulness," "firmness," "steadfastness."

A Taunt Song against Babylon (Hab. 2:6–20)

The taunt song comprises two parts, each of ten Hebrew lines (Hab. 2:6–14, 15–20). Both conclude with a significant, positive theological statement (Hab. 2:14, 20). Three "woes" are in the first part, and two are in the second. Together, the five oracles provide a picture of how the wicked would bring about their own demise.

First, Babylon's oppression and selfishness would breed selfishness and insurrection from her subjects (Hab. 2:6b–8; cf. Isa. 5:8–22; Esth. 5:9). Second, greed and loftiness would be no security, because the inner core and foundation of their society were corrupt (Hab. 2:9–11; cf. Isa. 14:13–15; Prov. 8:36). Third, cruelty begets cruelty, and the wicked would ultimately destroy themselves until only those recognizing the Lord's glory would remain on the earth (Hab. 2:12–14; cf. Micah 3:10–12; Isa. 11:9). Fourth, those who seek to degrade others would bring about their own degradation (Hab. 2:15–17; cf. Nahum 3:5; D&C 109:29). And finally, idols and false gods would be worthless, whereas the living God would rule the earth from his holy temple (Hab. 2:18–20; cf. Isa. 44:9–20). The song ends with the same counsel that is recorded in Habakkuk 2:3: Wait patiently and silently and you will see what the Lord is going to do (see Ps. 46:10; Zech. 2:13).

The Prayer-Psalm of Habakkuk (Hab. 3:1–19)

Perhaps relieved that he had not been chastised by the Lord and grateful that God would vindicate the righteous, Habakkuk composed a prayer-psalm of praise to God for his glory and might. It comes complete with musical instructions (Hab. 3:1, 19) and functions as a hymn.

Other ancient and modern prophets have also composed psalms or hymns. The Old Testament contains examples attributed to Moses (Deut. 32; Ps. 90), Isaiah (Isa. 42; 49; 50; 53), and Jeremiah (Lam. 1–5). The contemporary Latter-day Saint hymnbook contains inspirational words from a variety of modern General Authorities. Many of God's servants have used music or verse as a means of expression.

Habakkuk's psalm is a hymn of praise to God for his deliverance of his people in times of oppression. The prophet recounted the redemptive acts of the Exodus as an example of the Lord's power for future deliverance. In the context of his questions and dialogue with the Lord about the problem of suffering, this psalm expresses Habakkuk's trust in God during a time of anxiety. The psalm is easily divided into four segments:

1. *Introduction (Hab. 3:1–2)*. In memorable words, the prophet appealed to the Lord to renew his awesome work of salvation and mercy for his people.

2. *The divine manifestation (or theophany) in the past (Hab. 3:3–7)*. In ancient times, God came out of the southern desert to deliver his people (cf. Deut. 33:2; Judg. 5:4–5).

3. *The conflict between God and the forces of the earth (Hab. 3:8–15)*. God comes to defeat his enemies and the foes of his people, represented by the elements, especially the waters. The purpose of the storm is to subdue the earth, overthrow the enemy, and rescue God's people.

4. *An affirmation of faith in the Lord (Hab. 3:16–19)*. The prophet's fear changed to faith, and he knew he would experience joy despite the adversity he was facing. Verses 17 through 19 are memorable phrases, expressing joy in God's salvation and confidence in his strength.

The book of Habakkuk raises a universal question of humankind: Why do the wicked seem to prosper while the righteous suffer? Our response should include the realization of two things: first, the wicked sow seeds of self-destruction with their prideful behavior, and second, God's deliverance in past times brings faith in his future salvation. As Habakkuk delivered a magnificent expression of the victory of faith over the unrighteous aggression of evil, he presented this issue in a compact, poetic message that finds relevance in our modern society.[5]

---

[5]For additional insights, see Robertson, pp. 133–248, and relevant passages in pp. 1–52. See also Ralph L. Smith, *Micah–Malachi,* Word Biblical Commentary, vol. 32 (Waco, Texas: Word Books, 1984), pp. 91–117. For historical background on Habakkuk's day, see John Bright, *A History of Israel,* 3d ed. (Philadelphia: Westminster, 1981), pp. 310–30.

20

THE MINISTRY OF JEREMIAH

(JEREMIAH 1, 25–29, 32–45, 52)

DAVID ROLPH SEELY

The opening words of the book of Jeremiah (1:1) tell us that the prophet was the son of Hilkiah from a priestly family of Anathoth (modern Anata), a village about three miles northeast of Jerusalem.[1] It is likely that this family descended from the Aaronite Abiathar—a descendant of Eli, the custodian of the ark of the covenant at Shiloh in the time of Samuel—who served as high priest in the last years of David's reign and was exiled to Anathoth by Solomon because he had supported the attempt of Adonijah, Solomon's half-brother, to gain the throne (1 Kgs. 1–2). This proposed connection between Jeremiah's family and the old high priestly line that had once resided in the Northern Kingdom may be supported by Jeremiah's vivid recollections of the fate of the temple at Shiloh (Jer. 7:14; 26:6), his interest in the restoration of the Northern Kingdom, and perhaps by his seeming familiarity with the writings of the northern prophet Hosea, whose themes are often found similarly expressed in Jeremiah.

Jeremiah received his call in 627 B.C., in the thirteenth year of the reign of Josiah (Jer. 1:2). The superscription notes that his ministry lasted

---

David Rolph Seely is assistant professor of ancient scripture at Brigham Young University.
    [1]Iron Age remains of the biblical city are found at Ras el-Kharrubeh, a mile southwest of modern Anata. See S. Cohen, "Anathoth," in *The Interpreter's Dictionary of the Bible*, 5 vols., ed. G. A. Buttrick, et al. (Nashville: Abingdon, 1962–76), 1:125.

through the reigns of Judah's last five kings until 587, the eleventh year of the reign of Zedekiah — a period of forty years.[2]

Jeremiah's Call (Jer. 1)

Each prophet can trace the origin of his prophetic calling to a specific encounter in which the Lord called him as his representative and revealed the nature of his prophetic mission. Prophets are frequently called in the course of their normal daily lives: Enoch was journeying in the land (Moses 6:26), Moses was herding sheep (Ex. 3:1), Samuel was asleep in his bed (1 Sam. 3:3), Amos was following his flocks (Amos 7:15), and Ezekiel was sitting beside the river Chebar (Ezek. 1:3). Most expressed humility and some a certain reluctance to undertake a lifetime calling that would cause them to be scorned and abused by men and require them to exercise faith beyond the capacities of most mortals.

Jeremiah simply noted, "The word of the Lord came unto me" (Jer. 1:4). The Lord introduced Jeremiah's call with an extraordinary revelation of his premortal preparation and foreordination for such a calling: "Before I formed thee in the belly I knew thee; and before thou camest forth out of the womb I sanctified thee, and I ordained thee a prophet" (Jer. 1:5).

Like Enoch, Moses, and Isaiah before him, Jeremiah expressed his inadequacy: "Ah, Lord God! behold, I cannot speak: for I am a child" (Jer. 1:6). To Enoch's reply that he was young, hated, and slow of speech, the Lord had promised, "Open thy mouth, and it shall be filled, and I will give thee utterance" (Moses 6:32; see also 6:33–36). To Moses' complaint that he too was "slow of speech," the Lord had promised that he would be with his mouth but finally promised in addition to provide for him a spokesman, his brother Aaron (Ex. 4:10–16). Isaiah felt unworthy to be in the presence of the Lord and answered, "I am a man of unclean lips" — to which the Lord sent a seraph with a live coal from the altar to touch Isaiah's mouth and promise, "thine iniquity is taken away, and thy sin purged" (Isa. 6:5–7). Just as he had to Enoch, Moses,

---

[2]Besides the three kings mentioned in the superscription — Josiah, Jehoiakim, and Zedekiah — two other kings ruled for only a few months each: Jehoahaz, who ruled for three months until he was exiled to Egypt in 609 B.C.; and Jehoiachin, who ruled for three months before being exiled to Babylon in 598.

and Isaiah, the Lord responded to Jeremiah with a promise followed by a distinctive symbolic act. He said, "Say not, I am a child: for thou shalt go to all that I shall send thee, and whatsoever I command thee thou shalt speak. Be not afraid of their faces: for I am with thee to deliver thee, saith the Lord" (Jer. 1:7–8). With that admonition and promise, the Lord, in the words of Jeremiah, "put forth his hand, and touched my mouth. And the Lord said unto me, Behold, I have put my words in thy mouth" (Jer. 1:9). This gesture would serve Jeremiah throughout his mission as a sober reminder of the divine origin and urgency of the words that he would be asked to deliver and as a comfort that the Lord was with him to deliver him from his enemies. It also serves to remind us that the words in his book are of God.

The Lord then designated Jeremiah's far-reaching audience as well as the essential outline of his message: "See, I have this day set thee over the nations and over the kingdoms, to root out, and to pull down, and to destroy, and to throw down, to build, and to plant" (Jer. 1:10). Jeremiah was called to be a prophet to the nations, and his mission was to proclaim destruction as well as restoration. Obviously the prophecies of doom would make Jeremiah unpopular and would lead to much persecution, even to the point of threatening his life. Yet the Lord promised that he would protect him: "For, behold, I have made thee this day a defenced city, and an iron pillar, and brasen walls against the whole land" (Jer. 1:18). This imagery is ironic, for though Jeremiah would be protected as a mighty city, his people and the holy city they inhabited would not be. But protection from his enemies did not lessen the burden of suffering that Jeremiah would be called upon to bear.

Jeremiah lived in turbulent times. During his ministry he witnessed the solemn rededication to the covenant and the religious reforms of Josiah, the ensuing optimism and political independence shattered by Josiah's untimely death, the decline of the kings of Judah as vassals of Egypt and then Babylon, and ultimately rebellion, the destruction of the temple, and exile. He shared these times with several other prophets, including Zephaniah, Habakkuk, Nahum, Lehi, and Ezekiel—all of whom bore solemn witness that Jerusalem must repent or be destroyed. Like Mormon, Jeremiah would address a hard-hearted people, and his message would fall on deaf ears. But at the end of forty years of alternately pleading and threatening, he would be an eyewitness to the truthfulness of his words and an eyewitness to the destruction of his people.[3]

The Book of Jeremiah

From the narrative itself we learn something about the process through which the book of Jeremiah came into existence. Many, if not all, of the words of Jeremiah that have survived were copied and collected by his friend and scribe, Baruch. In 605 B.C. Jeremiah commissioned Baruch to record his prophecies from the days of Josiah until the present on "a roll of a book" (Jer. 36:2). He then instructed the scribe to take the scroll and read it in the temple, where the words were received with a clamor that reached the king. When Jehoiakim heard about it, he ordered one of his servants to bring the scroll and read it to him and his court. Baruch was advised to escape and hide himself and Jeremiah (Jer. 36:19). As the servant read three or four columns of the scroll, Jehoiakim derisively cut them off and cast them into the fire. Such a rejection of the word of the Lord is noted, "Yet they were not afraid, nor rent their garments, neither the king, nor any of his servants that heard all these words" (Jer. 36:24).[4]

Jeremiah then took another roll and had Baruch rewrite the words, "and there were added besides unto them many like words" (Jer. 36:32). That such a collection of Jeremiah's words was distributed, at least to some, is demonstrated by the note in 1 Nephi 5:13 that the plates of brass contained "many prophecies which have been spoken by the mouth of Jeremiah."

In Hebrew, the book of Jeremiah contains almost 22,000 words and is the longest book of the Prophets.[5] The material collected in it appears to be rather loosely organized with attempts to arrange the material first

---

[3]For more on Jer. 1, see the discussion in Chap. 21 of this volume.

[4]Contrast his father Josiah's reaction in a similar situation, recorded in 2 Kgs. 22:10–11.

[5]This compares to about 17,000 words in Isaiah, 19,000 in Ezekiel and 20,500 in Genesis— the second longest single book in scripture. The only books in the Bible larger than Jeremiah are the combined books of 1 and 2 Samuel (about 24,000), 1 and 2 Kings (25,000), and 1 and 2 Chronicles (24,000). A convenient list of the lengths of the biblical books can be found in Abraham Even-Shoshan, *A New Concordance of the Old Testament* (Jerusalem: Kiryat Sepher, 1985), p. xxxviii.

topically and within each topic chronologically.[6] Some of the prophecies are dated to a specific year in the reign of one of the kings of Judah, but it is impossible to determine the chronological order of much of the material. For our purposes, however, a general understanding of the content and structure is sufficient:

Jeremiah 1 through 25	Prophecies of Judgment against Judah and Jerusalem
	A. Jeremiah 1 through 6 Time of Josiah
	B. Jeremiah 7 through 20 Time of Jehoiakim
	C. Jeremiah 21 through 25 Time of Zedekiah
Jeremiah 26 through 35	The Restoration of Israel and Judah
Jeremiah 36 through 45	Baruch's Biography of Jeremiah
Jeremiah 46 through 51	Oracles against Foreign Nations
Jeremiah 52	Historical Appendix: The Fall of Jerusalem, Exile, and Aftermath

For convenience of discussion in this and the following two chapters, I have organized the material in the book of Jeremiah into three groupings: biographical material, prophecies against Jerusalem and Judah, and prophecies against the nations and of destruction and restoration — particularly from the time of Zedekiah. The biographical material (Jer. 1, 25–29, 32–45, 52) is discussed in Chapter 20 of this volume, the prophetic material from the time of Josiah and Jehoiakim (Jer. 2–20) in Chapter 21, and the prophetic material from the time of Zedekiah, including prophecies of destruction and restoration (Jer. 21–24, 30–31) and oracles against foreign nations (Jer. 46–51), in Chapter 22.

We have a significant amount of biographical material concerning Jeremiah, but only a small portion of it can be examined here. Although biographical material is scattered throughout the book, some have suggested that chapters 36 through 45, because of their common theme, cohesiveness, and style, may represent Baruch's biography of the prophet he served. Certainly the location of the touching personal note to Baruch in chapter 45 would support such an observation. I will attempt to note the major historical events and correlate them with the biographical material about Jeremiah in chronological sequence as they relate to the

---

[6]Several scholars argue that the structure and organization of the book may be more sophisticated than meets the eye at first glance. For a discussion of some of these problems, see John Bright, "The Book of Jeremiah: Its Structure, Its Problems, and Their Significance for the Interpreter," *Interpretation* 9 (1955): 259–78.

three kings mentioned in the superscription: Josiah, Jehoiakim, Zedekiah, and the aftermath of the destruction of Jerusalem.

Jeremiah in the Time of Josiah, 627–609 B.C.

Because Jeremiah called himself a "child" at the time of his call (Jer. 1:6) it is generally assumed that he was born sometime between 650 and 640 B.C., in the final years of the reign of Manasseh. Manasseh ruled 687 to 642 B.C., a period in which the mighty Assyrian empire under such rulers as Sennacherib, Esarhaddon, and Ashurbanipal ruled the Near East with an iron fist. Manasseh departed from the policy of his father Hezekiah—who had followed the prophet Isaiah in this regard—of avoiding foreign alliances. He promptly allied Judah with Assyria and sent tribute,[7] rebuilt the high places that his father had destroyed, practiced many forms of idolatry, including child sacrifice, and shed much innocent blood. He was followed on the throne by his son Amon (642–40), who continued his father's policies and practices. Amon was assassinated after only two years and replaced by his son Josiah—a boy of only eight years, perhaps about the same age as Jeremiah—who would become known as the most righteous of the kings of Judah (2 Kgs. 23:25).

The Chronicler noted that in the eighth year of Josiah's reign, "while he was yet young, he began to seek after the God of David his father: and in the twelfth year he began to purge Judah and Jerusalem from the high places, and the groves, and the carved images, and the molten images" (2 Chron. 34:3). Josiah's religious reform followed in earnest (2 Chron. 34:3–7), including the purification of cities once part of the Northern Kingdom (2 Chron. 34:6). In 627, the same year Jeremiah received his call, Ashurbanipal died, and his son Sin-shar-ishkun, having put down a serious civil war, sat precariously on the Assyrian throne. Then in 626 the Babylonian king Nabopolassar successfully evicted Assyria from Babylon. Thus the world sat on the threshold of the fall of

---

[7]Although the biblical account is silent on these matters, the Assyrian annals note Manasseh as a vassal who sent tribute to Nineveh to build the king's palace. For a translation of this text, see D. Winton Thomas, *Documents from Old Testament Times* (New York: Harper & Row, 1961), pp. 73–75.

Assyria and the rise of Babylon, and hopes for independence of the subordinate entities, including both Egypt and Judah, were aroused.

Josiah's reforms came to a climax in 622 with the discovery of the book of the law in the process of renovating the temple. He carried out a program of rigorous religious purification of the temple and the land in strict accordance with Mosaic injunctions, and the covenant was formally renewed among the people (2 Kgs. 22–23). In 612 Nineveh, the Assyrian capital, fell to the Babylonians and the Medes, and Egypt, fearing a victorious Babylon more than an aged Assyria, marched north under Necho II to aid the Assyrians in their last gasp against Babylon. Josiah, perhaps fearing an Assyrian victory and a more powerful Egypt, or perhaps under an alliance with Babylon, moved to stop the Egyptians at Megiddo, where he was defeated and killed (2 Kgs. 23:29). In 605 the Babylonians defeated both the Assyrians and the Egyptians at Carchemish. Before Babylon could consolidate her new empire in the west, Judah fell to Egypt. Necho promptly exiled the new king, Jehoahaz the son of Josiah, to Egypt and put another of Josiah's sons, Jehoiakim, on the throne (2 Kgs. 23:34). Jeremiah uttered judgment against Jehoahaz (occasionally called Shallum in the text) that he would die in exile in Egypt (Jer. 22:10–12). Thus ended Judah's short period of political independence.[8]

Jeremiah admired Josiah, remembering him as one who "judged the cause of the poor and needy" (Jer. 22:15–16), and he lamented his death (2 Chron. 35:25). We do not have a great deal of material clearly dated to the time of Josiah, but it is odd that Jeremiah is silent about Josiah's reforms. Some have interpreted this silence as a tacit approval; others suggest that Jeremiah was cautiously optimistic; and still others conclude that perhaps any such references may simply have been lost. Certainly the themes from the early prophecies in Jeremiah 1 through 6 of the apostasy and unfaithfulness of Judah to her God would be sympathetic with Josiah's attempts at reform. In these chapters Jeremiah maintained the hope of a reunited and restored Israel, which would correlate with the hopes of the time of Josiah, but he foresaw first judgment and destruction and prophesied restoration only in the future.

---

[8]For more on the history of these kings and the times in which they lived, see Chap. 16 of this volume.

Perhaps our best evidence for the results of Josiah's reform can be found in Jeremiah's temple sermon in chapters 7 and 26, dated to the first year of Josiah's successor Jehoiakim. Here it appears that despite Josiah's best efforts, his reforms succeeded only superficially at best. Jeremiah addressed a self-righteous people who had experienced religious reform and were full of confidence that the newly cleansed temple rendered them invincible. But he noted that the people had already begun idolatrous worship (Jer. 7:17–19). The defeat and death of Josiah at Megiddo and the ensuing Egyptian domination put an end to political independence and should have served as a warning against such feelings of invincibility.

Jeremiah in the Time of Jehoiakim, 609–598 B.C.

Jehoiakim submitted to Egypt and eventually, in 604 B.C., to the Babylonians under their new king Nebuchadnezzar (2 Kgs. 24:1). As noted by the author of Kings, "he did that which was evil in the sight of the Lord, according to all that his fathers had done" (2 Kgs. 23:37). In 601, sensing Babylonian vulnerability in their war against Egypt, he rebelled. Nebuchadnezzar was not able to address the rebellion in Judah until 597, when he besieged Jerusalem to punish the rebels. Just before Jerusalem fell Jehoiakim died; some speculate that the timing of his death suggests either that he was killed in battle or that he was assassinated by pro-Babylonian factions. He was replaced by his son Jehoiachin (in Jeremiah called Jeconiah or Coniah), who reigned in Judah only three months. Nebuchadnezzar subdued Judah with restraint and exiled their king along with many others, including Ezekiel and possibly Daniel. Nebuchadnezzar then put Zedekiah—Jehoiachin's uncle and Josiah's son—on the throne (2 Kgs. 24:17).

Jeremiah had nothing good to say about Jehoiakim and vigorously denounced him, comparing him unfavorably with his father Josiah (e.g., Jer. 22:13–19). It was Jehoiakim who banned Jeremiah from the temple and upon hearing the prophetic words recorded on his scroll cut them up and burned them—as recorded in Jeremiah 36. Jeremiah prophesied that the king's death would not be lamented and that he would be "buried with the burial of an ass" (Jer. 22:18–19).

Jeremiah suffered much rejection and persecution during those years, resulting in the threat on his life by officials after the temple sermon (Jer. 7; 26). Even his fellow citizens of Anathoth and his family turned against him (Jer. 11:21; 12:6). In this period he recorded: "The word of the Lord came also unto me, saying, Thou shalt not take thee a wife, neither shalt thou have sons or daughters in this place" (Jer. 16:1–2), apparently indicating that he would not be allowed to have a normal family life. It was probably in this period that he wrote many of his personal laments found interspersed in chapters 7 through 20.

Some Warnings (Jer. 25–26)

Jeremiah 25 is dated to the fourth year of the reign of Jehoiakim, 605 B.C. Jeremiah reminded the people that he had spent twenty-three years warning them about the consequences of their apostasy. Drawing heavily on phrases and images found in his temple sermon in 609 (chaps. 7, 26),[9] Jeremiah identified the enemy from the north — of whom he had been warning Judah from the beginning — as Nebuchadnezzar of Babylon. He announced that because the people had not repented they would be destroyed and taken into captivity.

In the first part of chapter 25 Jeremiah predicted, "And this whole land shall be a desolation, and an astonishment; and these nations shall serve the king of Babylon seventy years" (Jer. 25:11). Because the return from exile began in 539, the precise time-frame indicated by this number is debated. A passage in Zechariah 1:12 seems to apply the number to the years between the destruction of the temple in 587 and its rebuilding in 520–15, but in any case, it was an indication that the Exile would be a long one.

The second part of Jeremiah 25 involves the image of the Lord giving to Jeremiah the divine cup of wrath, which the prophet was to deliver to all nations, spreading destruction over the whole world — a fulfillment of his calling to be a prophet to the nations (Jer. 25:15–38). This passage will be examined in conjunction with Jeremiah 46 through 51.[10]

---

[9]See, for example, the parallels Jer. 25:3–4 and 7:25; 25:10 and 7:34.
[10]See Chap. 22 of this volume.

Jeremiah 26 is an account of Jeremiah's temple sermon, in which he warned the inhabitants of Judah that they would find no divine protection on account of the temple unless they would repent. In response to these words, the enraged audience demanded that he be executed for what they considered blasphemy and treason. This attempt on his life was thwarted by a plea to remember that King Hezekiah had allowed Micah to speak such words and live and by the intervention of Ahikam, a high government official. This sermon was recorded in full in Jeremiah 7.[11]

The Example of the Rechabites (Jer. 35)

Jeremiah 35 is dated simply to "the days of Jehoiakim." It is clear from verse 11 that Nebuchadnezzar and the Babylonians were then in the land, suggesting a date late in Jehoiakim's reign after he had rebelled against Babylon (see 2 Kgs. 24:1–2).

As an object lesson to Judah, the Lord instructed Jeremiah to summon a group of Rechabites to the temple to appear before some of the temple officials. The Rechabites called themselves after a certain Rechab, a descendant of the Kenites (1 Chron. 2:55), a people who lived in the desert of Sinai and are listed in Genesis 15:19 as indigenous to the land of Canaan.[12] The Rechabites followed the words of their ancestor Jonadab son of Rechab (Jer. 35:6, 14) and continued to live in a desert tradition. They built no houses, living in tents, avoided agriculture of all sorts, and drank no wine (Jer. 35:7–10). Perhaps this lifestyle was a response to the idolatry practiced by sedentary Israel and an effort to imitate the model of the children of Israel in the wilderness. As noted in Jeremiah 35:11, they had come to Jerusalem only for protection from the Babylonians who were in the land. The Lord commanded Jeremiah to present the Rechabites before the Judahite officials and set before them cups of wine, which Jeremiah instructed the Rechabites to drink. They, of course, staunchly refused, citing their commitment to the words of their ancestor Jonadab. This simple refusal condemned Judah. The Lord declared, "The words of Jonadab the son of Rechab, that he commanded his sons not

---

[11]I have discussed the temple sermon in greater detail in Chap. 21 of this volume.

[12]According to Judg. 1:16 and 4:11, Moses' father-in-law, Jethro, a priest of Midian (Ex. 2:15–16; Num. 10:29), was also identified as a Kenite.

to drink wine, are performed; for unto this day they drink none, but obey their father's commandment: notwithstanding I have spoken unto you, rising early and speaking; but ye hearkened not unto me" (Jer. 35:14). So while a small desert group continued to be faithful to the words of their forefather for two hundred years, the covenant people would not hearken to the words of the Lord God of Israel as delivered repeatedly through his prophets. The Lord blessed the Rechabites for their faithfulness, promising, "Jonadab the son of Rechab shall not want a man to stand before me for ever" (Jer. 35:19).

Jeremiah in the Time of Zedekiah, 597–587 B.C.

Zedekiah was only twenty-one when he became king (2 Kgs. 24:18). His years were the last for Judah and Jerusalem. Jeremiah had much to say about Zedekiah — that he was well-intentioned (Jer. 37:17–21; 38:7–28) but weak, vacillating, and fearful of public opinion (Jer. 38:5, 19). Throughout his reign he occasionally sought Jeremiah's counsel. The word of the Lord was clear: submit to Babylon. But his advisers, who no doubt looked to the glorious past of political independence, constantly urged rebellion. Zedekiah, contrary to Jeremiah's advice, finally succumbed to this pressure in 593, joining an alliance then and once again in 589 when he noted significant unrest in Babylon. This time, in 588, Nebuchadnezzar moved with vengeance to lay siege to Jerusalem. In 588 the hopes of Judah were briefly sparked when the Egyptians came to their rescue (see Jer. 34 and 37). Nebuchadnezzar left the siege of Jerusalem only briefly to smash this Egyptian resistance, and then he returned.

Just before Jerusalem fell, king Zedekiah and his "men of war" escaped from the city and fled into the wilderness eastward. The Babylonians overtook him and sent him to Nebuchadnezzar, who apparently had remained at headquarters in Riplah in Syria. There Zedekiah's sons were killed before his eyes — all but Mulek, who was taken by the hand of the Lord to America (Omni 1:15–16; Hel. 6:10; 8:21). Then Nebuchadnezzar had Zedekiah's eyes put out and sent him to Babylon where he died (Jer. 39:4–7; 52:7–11), the last of the mortal kings of Judah to sit on the throne of David.

At the beginning of Zedekiah's reign the Lord called Lehi along with "many prophets, prophesying unto the people that they must repent, or the great city Jerusalem must be destroyed" (1 Ne. 1:4). Like the other prophets, Lehi was rejected, and some "sought his life, that they might take it away" (1 Ne. 1:20; 2:1–2). It was revealed to Lehi that he and his descendants would be preserved from impending disaster if he would obey the Lord and take his family into the wilderness, from which he would be led to a new promised land.

But though Lehi was allowed to leave, it was Jeremiah's task to remain with the people until the end and deliver the word of the Lord to submit to Babylon rather than face destruction. Because of this message, Jeremiah was accused of treason, thrown into a dungeon (Jer. 37:13–16), and finally entrusted to the "court of the prison," under a sort of house arrest, until the time when the Babylonians destroyed Jerusalem (as recorded in 2 Kgs. 25; Jer. 52). While Jeremiah was in prison, Zedekiah secretly sent for him, seeking from him the word of the Lord but not having the courage to obey it by submitting to Babylon (Jer. 37:16–21).

The Yoke of Babylon (Jer. 27–29)

Although the heading in Jeremiah 27:1 gives a date in the reign of Jehoiakim (apparently in error), I will discuss the related events in chapters 27 through 29 in the context of the reign of Zedekiah.[13] Chapters 27 and 28 record the symbolic act performed by Jeremiah when he wore a yoke around his neck representing the word of the Lord, urging the people to submit to Babylon. The Lord revealed his will on the matter, "And now I have given all these lands into the hand of Nebuchadnezzar the king of Babylon, . . . and it shall come to pass, that the nation and kingdom which will not serve the same Nebuchadnezzar . . . will I punish" (Jer. 27:6–8). But at the same time there were prophets who said, "Ye shall not serve the king of Babylon" (Jer. 27:14). Others said, "Behold, the vessels of the Lord's house shall now shortly be brought

---

[13]Jer. 27:1 indicates that these events occurred in the reign of Jehoiakim, but Jer. 28:1, which seems to be closely connected, indicates the fourth year of the reign of Zedekiah. The discussion in Jer. 27 also concerns the period of Zedekiah (see, for example, Jer. 27:2, 20) rather than Jehoiakim, leading to the conclusion that Jer. 27:1 should read *Zedekiah* rather than *Jehoiakim*. The passage in question, Jer. 27:1, is not found in the Septuagint. But the Peshitta, the Syriac text, reads *Zedekiah* rather than *Jehoiakim*.

again from Babylon" (Jer. 27:16). Hananiah, one of the prophets bearing the latter message, came to Jeremiah and dramatically broke the yoke off his neck, proudly proclaiming that in this same way the yoke of Babylon would soon be removed (Jer. 28:10–11). Of both these kinds of prophets the Lord proclaimed, "They prophesy a lie unto you" (Jer. 27:14, 16; see also 14:13–15).

This was truly a test for Judah to see if they could determine the word of God and his will and then have the courage to obey. Whereas the word of the Lord to Isaiah had warned of the danger of an alliance with Syria and Israel or with the Assyrians (Isa. 7–8), the word of the Lord to Jeremiah was to submit. The most reliable way to discern the words of the Lord from the words of men is through the power of the Spirit (D&C 18:34–35; 68:3–4), but another reliable key to prophecy was to be found already in the Law of Moses: "When a prophet speaketh in the name of the Lord, if the thing follow not, nor come to pass, that is the thing which the Lord hath not spoken, but the prophet hath spoken it presumptuously" (Deut. 18:22; see also Jer. 28:9). Jeremiah rebuked Hananiah: "The Lord hath not sent thee; but thou makest this people to trust in a lie. Therefore thus saith the Lord; Behold, I will cast thee from off the face of the earth: this year thou shalt die, because thou hast taught rebellion against the Lord" (Jer. 28:15–16). The following terse note should have demanded the attention of any who had witnessed this dramatic confrontation, even without the power of the Spirit: "So Hananiah the prophet died the same year in the seventh month" (Jer. 28:17).

In Jeremiah 29 we find a letter in which Jeremiah delivered the word of the Lord to those already in exile in Babylon. To the exiles the Lord said, "Build ye houses, and dwell in them; and plant gardens, and eat the fruit of them" (Jer. 29:5), all language reminiscent of Jeremiah's call "to build, and to plant" (Jer. 1:10). The point is that the Exile would be long, and therefore the people should live their lives, taking husbands and wives and begetting sons and daughters, with an understanding that Babylon would be home for them. In part this letter was a response to those false prophets in Babylon who apparently were raising the hopes of the people for a quick return (Jer. 29:7–9). The Lord even noted that two of those false prophets of the Exile would be turned over to Nebuchadnezzar and killed (Jer. 29:21). In a real sense, the scattering of Israel that had begun on a large scale with the deportation of the Northern

Kingdom in the eighth century was being continued. Jeremiah's letter served to remind exiled Judah that though they should not become part of the world, they should learn to live in the world.

A Promise of Restoration (Jer. 32–33)

Jeremiah 32 and 33 can be read together with chapters 30 and 31 as parts of the Book of Consolation, because they contain prophecies of the restoration of Israel. In fact, the chronological notation in Jeremiah 32:1 (the tenth year of the reign of Zedekiah, 588 B.C.) would place this event between chapters 37 and 38. During Nebuchadnezzar's siege of Jerusalem, Jeremiah was imprisoned on account of his prophecies of destruction against the city (see Jer. 37:21) and his prophecies of the capture and exile of King Zedekiah. While Jeremiah was in prison, the Lord told him that his cousin Hanameel would come to him with an offer to allow him to purchase a piece of land in Anathoth that belonged in the family. According to the Law of Moses, land should always be kept in the family (Lev. 25:25), and any land that was in danger of being sold outside the family should be offered to another member of the family first. Hanameel came and the king allowed Jeremiah to leave prison long enough to go to Anathoth and complete the transaction. This purchase, by the prophet who had for years prophesied the destruction of Jerusalem and the exile of her people, became a symbolic act of the Lord's intention to one day restore the people to their land. In this act Jeremiah was symbolically fulfilling his call to build and to plant with the outward show of confidence that the return would occur. At the end of the chapter the Lord said, "Like as I have brought all this great evil upon this people, so will I bring upon them all the good that I have promised them. And fields shall be bought in this land . . . for I will cause their captivity to return" (Jer. 32:42–44).

The Siege of Jerusalem (Jer. 34–38)

In the course of the siege of Jerusalem (588–587 B.C.), Zedekiah had by a covenant with the people (Jer. 34:8) implemented the release of

Hebrew slaves, who were to be freed at the end of seven years according to the Mosaic law (Ex. 21:2; Deut. 15:12). This covenant had been confirmed with a solemn oath ceremony in the temple (Jer. 34:15).[14] But the people had broken their oath and forced the slaves back into submission (Jer. 34:11).[15]

The Lord pointed out to the people that they had taken a step toward repentance with the declaration of liberty to their slaves—a repentance that could have led to their own deliverance. In response to their unwillingness to keep their recent covenant, the Lord responded with sarcasm: "Behold, I proclaim a liberty for you, saith the Lord, to the sword, to the pestilence, and to the famine" (Jer. 34:17). Jeremiah warned the people that the Babylonians would return (Jer. 34:22; 37:5–10) after defeating the Egyptians and would punish them for their unfaithfulness. The penalty of death was pronounced upon those who had broken this covenant: "Their dead bodies shall be for meat unto the fowls of the heaven, and to the beasts of the earth" (Jer. 34:20).

Following the incident of the Rechabites (Jer. 35), the burning of the scroll (chap. 36), and Jeremiah's promise of the Babylonian return (chap. 37), Jeremiah was delivered to the king and charged with treason and weakening the morale of the people under siege with his prophecies of doom (Jer. 38:1–5). The vacillating Zedekiah first turned him over to the princes who wished to kill him, saying, "He is in your hand" (Jer. 38:5). They cast him into a dungeon full of mire until his noble friend Ebed-melech, an Ethiopian eunuch, saved him and delivered him to better conditions in the court of the prison. There Zedekiah once again secretly consulted him, promising him his life if he would but tell him

---

[14]The ceremony consisted of passing through the parts of a calf cut in two (Jer. 34:18). The supposed implication of such symbolism is that of imprecation—that the fate of the calf would be visited upon any who did not fulfill the oath. A similar ritual associated with an oath is found in Gen. 15:9–17, in which the Lord confirmed to Abraham the promises of the covenant. For a discussion of the symbolism of such oath rituals, see M. H. Pope, "Oaths," in *The Interpreter's Dictionary of the Bible*, 3:575–77; and George E. Mendenhall, "Ancient Oriental and Biblical Law," and "Covenant Forms in Israelite Tradition," in *The Biblical Archaeologist Reader 3*, ed. Edward F. Campbell and David Noel Freedman (Garden City, N.Y.: Doubleday, 1970), pp. 3–53.

[15]The events of Jeremiah 34 apparently occurred—according to a note in verse 22 that the Lord would cause the Babylonians to *return* to the siege—in 588 when the Egyptians marched into Judah, presumably to aid Zedekiah (Jer. 37:5), and Nebuchadnezzar left the siege to meet this threat. It was probably at this point—when the immediate danger was past—that the people broke their oath and took back their slaves (Jer. 34:11).

the word of the Lord. Wearily Jeremiah, perhaps for the last time, de-livered the same message to Zedekiah: "Thus saith the Lord . . . If thou wilt assuredly go forth unto the king of Babylon's princes, then thy soul shall live, and this city shall not be burned with fire" (Jer. 38:17). Zedekiah refused the word of the Lord, excusing himself, "I am afraid of the Jews that are fallen to the Chaldeans, lest they deliver me into their hand, and they mock me" (Jer. 38:19) — a king who feared men more than the Lord.

The Fall of Jerusalem and Its Aftermath (Jer. 39–41)

In Jeremiah 39 and 52 we find recorded one of the major events of the history of Israel (see also 2 Kgs. 25). The destruction of the covenant people warned about by Moses (Deut. 27–28) and by each of the suc-ceeding prophets finally came to pass. The cup of the wrath of the Lord (Jer. 25:15–38) was poured out upon his own people through the in-strument of the enemy from the north (Jer. 1:13–16) — Nebuchadnezzar and the Babylonians.

A month after Jerusalem fell, Nebuchadnezzar ordered Nebuzar-adan, captain of the guard, to burn the temple, the royal palace, and the rest of the city, and to prepare all but the poorest of the land for exile to Babylon. Nebuchadnezzar appointed one Gedaliah as governor over Ju-dah. From a prominent family of Jerusalem, his father Ahikam and grandfather Shaphan had both served in King Josiah's court (2 Kgs. 22:3, 14). Gedaliah moved the capital north of Jerusalem to Mizpah (see Map 9, LDS Bible). Gedaliah promised his people that he would represent them well before the Babylonians if they would submit, and he urged them to begin immediately to harvest what they could of their crops (Jer. 40:9–10). In the seventh month[16] a malcontent from the royal family, Ishmael (2 Kgs. 25:25), conspired against Gedaliah and killed him, along with the Jews and the Babylonians present at the court in

---

[16]It is not clear how long Gedaliah was governor before being assassinated. According to Jeremiah, the "seventh month" seems to refer to the same year that he began his rule. A note in Jer. 52:30 indicates that there was another deportation in the twenty-third year of Nebuchadnezzar, 582 B.C., which some interpret as the Babylonian response to Gedaliah's assassination and would therefore argue that Gedaliah governed for six or seven years before his death.

Mizpah (Jer. 41:1–4). Ishmael then proceeded to slaughter ruthlessly another seventy men before fleeing with hostages from Mizpah to the Ammonites (Jer. 41:10).

Because Jeremiah had been an advocate of submission to Babylon, the Babylonians released him from the court of the prison, according to one account (Jer. 39:14), or from Ramah, according to another, where he was chained with the rest of the captives awaiting removal to Babylon (Jer. 40:1).[17] The Babylonians invited Jeremiah to move to Babylon or to remain in his land as he wished. He decided to remain in Judah and immediately went to Mizpah to his friend Gedaliah, whose father Ahikam had once saved Jeremiah from death (Jer. 26:24). How Jeremiah escaped the slaughter by Ishmael is unknown. A short time after the death of Gedaliah, Jeremiah was forced against his will to accompany a group of Judahites to Egypt. Sometime in this period, if the tradition of authorship is correct, he would have written one of his final laments found in the book of Lamentations.

Jeremiah in Egypt (Jer. 42–44)

A group of Judahites, apparently worried about Babylonian retaliation for the assassination of the governor, besought Jeremiah to pray and obtain the word of the Lord for them and promised to obey this word "whether it be good, or whether it be evil" (Jer. 42:6). After ten days the Lord responded, "If ye will still abide in this land, then will I build you, and not pull you down, and I will plant you, and not pluck you up" (Jer. 42:10). The Lord went on to warn them that if in fact they did proceed to Egypt, as they had evidently been planning to do, "the sword, which ye feared, shall overtake you there in the land of Egypt, and the famine, whereof ye were afraid, shall follow close after you there in Egypt; and there ye shall die" (Jer. 42:16). The people, after consulting with "all the proud men," responded to Jeremiah, the prophet of the

---

[17]John Bright, *Jeremiah,* Anchor Bible 21 (Garden City, N.Y.: Doubleday, 1981), p. 246, suggests that these two accounts can be reconciled: "It is quite possible that Jeremiah, after having been released from confinement by the military government upon the city's fall, was picked up on the streets by Babylonian soldiers as they were rounding up civilians for deportation and herded along with the rest into the stockade at Ramah, only to be released again on Nebuzaradan's orders."

Lord, "Thou speakest falsely: the Lord our God hath not sent thee to say, Go not into Egypt to sojourn there" (Jer. 43:2). After all of Jeremiah's forty years of prophesying had been vindicated by actual events, these men still could not recognize the word of the Lord.

For some reason this group forced Jeremiah and his scribe Baruch to accompany them to Egypt, where they settled in Tahpanhes, a frontier city in the northeastern delta. There Jeremiah prophesied that Nebuchadnezzar would come and "smite the land of Egypt" (Jer. 43:11), a prophecy that was fulfilled in 568, when, according to a fragmentary historical text "in the 37th year, Nebuchadnezzar, king of Babylon marched against Egypt to deliver a battle."[18]

In chapter 44 of his book we find Jeremiah, the prophet to the nations, delivering the word of the Lord for the last time, addressing all the Jews in Egypt. The message was a familiar one: "Ye provoke me unto wrath with the works of your hands, burning incense unto other gods in the land of Egypt, whither ye be gone to dwell" (Jer. 44:8). In a sense the children of Israel had returned home to the Egypt from whence Moses brought them, and they had taken their idolatry back with them. The Lord pleaded, "Have ye forgotten the wickedness of your fathers?" (Jer. 44:9). Apparently they had. Jeremiah faced a new generation, in another place, who because they would not listen to the same word would learn from the cup of the Lord's wrath, "For I will punish them that dwell in the land of Egypt, as I have punished Jerusalem, by the sword, by the famine, and by the pestilence" (Jer. 44:13).

A Message to Baruch (Jer. 45)

Jeremiah 45, out of chronological sequence, identifies itself as the words of the Lord delivered by Jeremiah to Baruch his scribe in the fourth year of Jehoiakim, after Baruch had completed writing, or rather re-writing, the words of Jeremiah (see Jer. 36). Baruch is often in the background of the book, and in this short prophecy we get our only poignant, personal glimpse of Baruch's own sacrifice and suffering as he

---

[18]For this translation, see James B. Pritchard, ed., *Ancient Near Eastern Texts Relating to the Old Testament*, 3d ed. with Supplement (Princeton: Princeton University, 1969), p. 308.

realized that Jeremiah's words of doom to Israel would affect his own life. The Lord said that he could offer no immediate comfort or relief from the terrible things that were then happening and that were soon to come about (Jer. 45:4). Those "great things" that Baruch would like to pursue for himself in his personal life would not be attainable. The only consolation the Lord could offer was that his life would be spared (Jer. 45:5).[19]

Baruch remained faithful to Jeremiah to the end. The last we hear of him he was in Egypt, still recording the word of the Lord through Jeremiah. Perhaps the placement of this oracle at the end of the biographical material is the work of Baruch, who copied and edited those words, attaching his own personal oracle at the end as proof that the Lord had indeed spared his life and as evidence of his hand in the biographical section.

Historical Appendix (Jer. 52)

It is fitting that the chapter describing the siege, capture, and destruction of Jerusalem and her temple and the ensuing exile is found at the end of the book of Jeremiah. Indeed, the Lord had "hastened his word to perform it" (Jer. 1:12). The destruction that Jeremiah had prophesied finally came about. Jeremiah 52 is almost a duplicate of 2 Kings 25 but adds some significant details to the historical events. Of particular interest is the account of a deportation in the twenty-third year of Nebuchadnezzar's reign (582 B.C.), presumably following the rebellion that resulted in the murder of the Babylonian-appointed governor Gedaliah (Jer. 52:30).

Throughout his ministry Jeremiah pronounced prophecies of comfort and hope for restoration. Although he told those in Babylon to prepare for a long stay, he promised that in seventy years there would be a return. The final note in Jeremiah 52:31–34 is dated "in the seven and thirtieth

---

[19]In the phrase "thy life will I give unto thee for a prey," the Hebrew word translated "prey" is *šālāl*. It can also have the sense of "booty." It occurs in this idiom several times in Jeremiah (21:9; 38:2; 39:18) and clearly means that one's life will be preserved. Bright suggests that perhaps the phrase originated in the military, where it meant to get booty in war. In the case of defeat, a soldier fortunate to survive might say something like "my life was all the booty that I was able to bring home." See Bright, *Jeremiah*, pp. 184–85.

year of the captivity of Jehoiachin" and the first year of the reign of the
Babylonian king Evil-merodach—a tactful reference to the death of Nebuchadnezzar in 562 (Jer. 52:31). It is recorded that Nebuchadnezzar's
successor Evil-merodach, in the first year of his reign, released Jehoiachin,
the exiled king of Judah, out of prison and restored him to a respectable
lifestyle. This foreshadowing of the restoration of Judah in 539 would
serve as a type of the establishment of the "new covenant" (Matt. 26:28)
and finally the new and everlasting covenant (D&C 1:22).

A Lifetime of Commitment

Jeremiah exemplifies for us many important aspects of a prophet. He
was a servant of the Lord called to deliver his word. Therefore, he had
to remain throughout his life worthy to receive the word and be willing
to deliver it. From the time of his call when the Lord first delivered his
word to him until we last hear of him in Egypt, he faithfully represented
his Master before his people. Throughout his life he delivered the word
of the Lord to kings, princes, priests, prophets, his neighbors, the exiles
in Babylon and Egypt, and to all nations. The message was two-fold:
destruction and restoration—"to pull down, and destroy" and "to build,
and to plant" (Jer. 1:10). To those children of the covenant who were
unfaithful to the Lord, hope and mercy were extended on the condition
of repentance. Unfortunately they rejected that message, and for the
unrepentant there remained only judgment.

Forty years is a short time in the history of the world, but for Jeremiah
it was a commitment of his whole life. Because of his faithfulness he
suffered many trials and much affliction, and his entire life stands as an
example of faith, obedience, and sacrifice.

The Lord promised Jeremiah from the beginning that he would "hasten" to perform his word (Jer. 1:12), and Jeremiah witnessed the fulfillment of many of his prophecies in his own lifetime—including the
destruction of Jerusalem and the exile of his people. The fulfillment of
these prophecies stands as a solemn witness to the certain fulfillment of
the word of the Lord regarding building and planting in the days to come
(Jer. 31:27–28), including the restoration of the "new covenant" (Jer.
31:31) and the gathering and reuniting of Israel and Judah (Jer. 30:3).

At one point in his life Jeremiah recalled the joy he once had found in his calling: "Thy words were found, and I did eat them; and thy word was unto me the joy and rejoicing of mine heart; for I am called by thy name, O Lord God of hosts" (Jer. 15:16). He then lamented the persecution and loneliness that resulted from delivering the words: "I sat not in the assembly of the mockers, nor rejoiced; I sat alone because of thy hand" (Jer. 15:17). The Lord responded with the promise he had made at the beginning: "I will make thee unto this people a fenced brasen wall: and they shall fight against thee, but they shall not prevail against thee: for I am with thee to save thee and to deliver thee, saith the Lord" (Jer. 15:20–21). The Lord protected and preserved Jeremiah until his mission was completed. As we study the life of Jeremiah, we begin to understand a man who trusted in the Lord rather than in the arm of flesh (Jer. 17:5–8) and one whose call was to sacrifice the approval of men in order to gain the presence of God.

21

I AM WITH THEE, TO DELIVER THEE

(JEREMIAH 1–20)

DAVID ROLPH SEELY

When Jeremiah received his call, the Lord delivered to him his word, both symbolically when he touched his young mouth, and also literally when he spoke with Jeremiah and revealed to him his will. From then on Jeremiah could deliver with authority the phrase "Thus saith the Lord" with the attendant message.

Along with the word, the Lord gave Jeremiah two symbolic visions when he called him.[1] In the first vision (Jer. 1:11–12) the Lord asked Jeremiah to look at the rod of an almond tree — in Hebrew, *šāqēd* — and delivered his message to Jeremiah through a pun: "I will hasten — *šōqēd* — my word to perform it" (Jer. 1:11–12). This symbol would remind Jeremiah that the words he would be asked to deliver would indeed come to pass. The second vision contained the essence of the Lord's warning to Judah. Jeremiah looked at a "seething pot" tipping from the north southward,[2] presumably about to spill out its contents. The Lord explained that it would be from the north that the promised destruction would come upon the cities of Judah on account of their forsaking the covenant. The Lord declared, "I will utter my judgments against them touching all their wickedness, who have forsaken me, and have burned incense unto

---

David Rolph Seely is assistant professor of ancient scripture at Brigham Young University.

[1]It is possible that both of these object lessons were not visions at all but were actually real objects within Jeremiah's field of vision and the Lord simply directed his attention to them to make his point.

[2]The Hebrew phrase rendered by the KJV "and the face thereof is toward the north" is probably better translated "facing away from the north." It is clear that the phrase was intended to convey to Jeremiah that the enemy would come from the north; see, for example, Jer. 4:6; 6:1, 22–23.

other gods, and worshipped the works of their own hands" (Jer. 1:16). Although Babylon is located due east of Judah, the Babylonian armies would march up the Euphrates River Valley and around the fertile crescent through Syria and Lebanon, rather than taking the almost impossible route across the Arabian desert, and they would thus invade Judah from the north (see Map 10, LDS Bible).

Needless to say such a message would not be a popular one. The Lord informed Jeremiah that he would set him up to "root out, and to pull down, and to destroy, and to throw down" (Jer. 1:10). What the Lord demanded he tell the inhabitants of the land would be difficult; thus he exhorted, "Thou therefore gird up thy loins, and arise, and speak unto them all that I command thee: be not dismayed at their faces, lest I confound thee before them" (Jer. 1:17). He told Jeremiah he would find himself pitted "against the kings of Judah, against the princes thereof, against the priests thereof, and against the people" (Jer. 1:18) — in short, against everyone. "They shall fight against thee," the Lord said, "but they shall not prevail against thee; for I am with thee, saith the Lord, to deliver thee" (Jer. 1:19).

Throughout Jeremiah's forty-year ministry, his task would require of him almost more than he could bear. His ministry would require courage, humility, perseverance, patience, charity, and an uncompromising intolerance of sin, all of which would result in a spiritual maturity that he eloquently and poetically expressed in his writings. Jeremiah would suffer rejection, persecution, loneliness, isolation, and injustice. He would be arrested, threatened, beaten, and imprisoned. Yet in the face of all adversity, he maintained a dynamic and meaningful relationship with the Lord to whom he freely expressed the depths of his emotions — his grief, anger, and despair — as well as his spiritual triumphs. At times the Lord responded, sometimes sharply and sometimes gently; at other times he listened. But as he promised, he was always there.

In the collection of prophecies in Jeremiah 1 through 19 are only two chronological points of reference. The first is found in Jeremiah 3:6, "in the days of Josiah," and the other can be deduced for the Temple Sermon in chapter 7, assuming that this sermon is the same as that alluded to in chapter 26 in the biographical material. In chapter 26 the date of this sermon is given "in the beginning of the reign of Jehoiakim the son of Josiah" (Jer. 26:1), which would be 609 B.C.[3] From these two notations, as well as thematic unity and other internal evidence pointing to known historical events, chapters 1 through 6 appear to contain prophecies largely from the early part of Jeremiah's ministry in the time of Josiah (627–609). Chapters 7–20 contain prophecies from the time of Jehoiakim (609–598). The assumption that these chapters can be treated as a unit is supported by an echo of the womb imagery from Jeremiah's call (Jer. 1:5) in his lament (Jer. 20:14–18), perhaps functioning as a rhetorical device indicating the unity of chapters 1 through 20.[4] In contrast to the uncertainties of dating and organization, the themes and messages of these prophecies are for the most part clear and straightforward.

Prophecies from the Time of Josiah (Jer. 2–6)

In chapters 2 and 3 the Lord revealed to Jeremiah the covenantal lawsuit he was bringing against his people on account of their disobedience. The legal imagery of the Lord charging his people — a covenantal lawsuit — is a common feature in biblical prophecy, and good examples can be found in Deuteronomy 25, Hosea 4, Isaiah 1, Micah 6, and Psalm 50.

The stipulations of the Mosaic covenant — the Law — were from the beginning inseparably connected with specific promises of blessings and curses, depending on obedience to the commandments. These blessings and curses were specified in Deuteronomy 27 and 28. This connection between obedience and blessing is well known to Latter-day Saint readers, as it is repeated throughout the Book of Mormon in regard to the promised

---

[3]The Hebrew expression berē'šît mamlekût, "in the beginning of the reign," is most likely a technical term referring to the period between the king's accession and the following New Year. See John Bright, *Jeremiah*, Anchor Bible 21 (Garden City, N.Y.: Doubleday, 1965), p. 169.

[4]The organization of the material in the book of Jeremiah has been discussed for centuries. Some have concluded that the book is only loosely organized; others have found evidence of sophistication in the ordering of the material. See John Bright, "The Book of Jeremiah: Its Structure, Its Problems, and Their Significance for the Interpreter," *Interpretation* 9 (1955): 259–78. One interesting study in which the echo in Jer. 1:5 and 20:14–18 is noted is J. R. Lundbom, *Jeremiah: A Study in Ancient Hebrew Rhetoric*, Society of Biblical Literature Dissertation Series 18 (Missoula, Mont.: Scholars Press, 1975).

land: "Inasmuch as ye shall keep my commandments, ye shall prosper" (1 Ne. 2:20; 4:14). The corresponding curse is likewise expressed, "But inasmuch as ye will not keep my commandments ye shall be cut off from my presence" (2 Ne. 1:20). The eternal nature of this principle is reiterated in modern revelation: "There is a law, irrevocably decreed in heaven before the foundations of this world, upon which all blessings are predicated—And when we obtain any blessing from God, it is by obedience to that law upon which it is predicated" (D&C 130:20–21).

The specific punishments pronounced on Israel for disobedience to the Law are spelled out in detail in Deuteronomy 28. They include pestilence, drought, and ultimately destruction by the sword and scattering:[5] "The Lord shall send upon thee cursing, vexation, and rebuke, in all that thou settest thine hand unto for to do, until thou be destroyed, and until thou perish quickly; because of the wickedness of thy doings, whereby thou hast forsaken me" (Deut. 28:20). "And the Lord shall scatter thee among all people, from the one end of the earth even unto the other; . . . And among these nations shalt thou find no ease, neither shall the sole of thy foot have rest: but the Lord shall give thee there a trembling heart, and failing of eyes, and sorrow of mind" (Deut. 28:64–65).

In Jeremiah 2 and 3 the covenant lawsuit, like much of the biblical imagery of covenant, is based on one of the most tender and moving of biblical images—the covenant between God and his people as a marriage. The Lord portrays Israel as a young bride who was espoused in the wilderness and married at Sinai. This imagery shows remarkable similarity both in general as well as in specific phrases with the language of Hosea 1 through 3 (which is followed by the imagery of a lawsuit in Hosea 4). The imagery of the covenant as a marriage was carried on in Ezekiel 16 and in the New Testament, where it is found in the parable of the ten virgins (Matt. 25:1–13; see also Luke 14:16–24; Rev. 19:7, 9).

The Lord led his young bride "out of the land of Egypt, . . . through the wilderness, through a land of deserts and of pits, through a land of drought, and of the shadow of death, through a land that no man passed through, and where no man dwelt" (Jer. 2:6). He brought her to "a

---

[5]In Jeremiah, these curses are categorized as sword, famine, and pestilence (see Jer. 14:12; 21:9; 24:10; 29:17; 34:17; 38:2; 44:13; etc.).

plentiful country, to eat the fruit thereof and the goodness thereof" (Jer. 2:7). But when Israel arrived she "defiled" the land and followed other gods. The charge against Israel is thus infidelity—in the imagery of the covenant as marriage, it is adultery. As demonstrated by the reign of Manasseh, seeking after foreign gods was also an integral part of foreign political alliances, which included accepting their gods and their images into the temple. The Lord placed the blame for such apostasy on the priests ("they that handle the law"), the shepherds ("pastors," perhaps a reference here to the kings and princes indicted in Jer. 1:18)[6], and the prophets (Jer. 2:8).

In addition to portraying the Lord as husband, Jeremiah portrayed him as father. He referred to Israel as the "firstfruits" (Jer. 2:3), perhaps an allusion to Exodus 4:22, in which the Lord called Israel his firstborn son. The imagery of the Lord as father calling his son Israel out of Egypt is also found in Hosea 11:1–4. This image of the fatherhood of God is continued in Jeremiah 2:27, in which the Lord accused his children of seeking for their paternity elsewhere—in a "stock," a reference to the wood used to make an idol or perhaps the wooden Asherah, and a "stone," probably referring to the stone images that played a part in Canaanite religion. In Jeremiah 3:9 the marriage and paternity images are combined as these idols become the partners of adultery. The Lord laments, "My people have committed two evils; they have forsaken me the fountain of living waters, and hewed them out cisterns, broken cisterns, that can hold no water" (Jer. 2:13). "Living water" is a phrase used to refer to running water, a spring, which would be pure. Jeremiah later explicitly used this image to describe the Lord: "They have forsaken the Lord, the fountain of living waters" (Jer. 17:13). The Savior in his ministry used this image in reference to the power of the Atonement as a "well of water springing up into everlasting life" (John 4:10–14).

Not only has Israel left her husband but in terms of worshiping other gods she has become an insatiable harlot. This theme is well developed in Hosea 1 through 3 as well as Ezekiel 16. Under the Law of Moses the

---

[6]The image of the shepherd is for obvious reasons an apt one for leaders of the people. In the Bible it is used to refer to both spiritual and political leaders (Jer. 10:21; 23:1–4; 25:34–38; Ezek. 34:1–10; Zech. 10:3; 11:4–17). It is also used of the Lord in Ps. 23 and Ezek. 34, both of which uses add richness to Christ's sermon in John 10:1–29 in which he proclaimed, "I am the good shepherd: the good shepherd giveth his life for the sheep" (v. 11).

punishment for adultery was death (Lev. 20:10), a sentence that hangs over Israel. The Lord reminded Israel: "If a man put away his wife, and she go from him, and become another man's, shall he return unto her again? . . . but thou hast played the harlot with many lovers" (Jer. 3:1). Under the law a divorce is in order. Yet this is no ordinary husband who instead pleads, "Return again to me, saith the Lord" (Jer. 3:1). As an illustration of the potential disaster of apostate behavior, the Lord reminds Judah of her sister Israel, the Northern Kingdom. Because of her adultery the Lord gave her a bill of divorce, and the result was destruction and deportation by the Assyrians in 721 B.C. "Yet for all this her treacherous sister Judah hath not turned unto me with her whole heart, but feignedly, saith the Lord" (Jer. 3:10).

Jeremiah's assignment was to plead for the Lord: "Return, thou backsliding Israel, saith the Lord; and I will not cause mine anger to fall upon you: for I am merciful, saith the Lord, and I will not keep anger forever" (Jer. 3:12). "Return, ye backsliding children, and I will heal your backslidings" (Jer. 3:22). What the Lord envisioned is expressed in terms of marriage and fatherhood—a reuniting of the spouses, the gathering and restoration of scattered Israel and Judah, and the return of the children of Israel who will call, "My father; and shalt not turn away from me" (Jer. 3:14–19).

In Jeremiah 4 through 6 the Lord continued the lawsuit, after offering Judah the chance to return to the marriage, pronouncing judgment on an unrepentant, adulterous Judah. The Lord decreed, just as in Jeremiah's call, "I will bring evil from the north, and a great destruction. . . . to make thy land desolate; and thy cities shall be laid waste, without an inhabitant" (Jer. 4:6–7). The destruction from the north is also referred to in Jeremiah 5:15–18 and 6:22–23). The vivid terror of destruction can be felt in Jeremiah's description of the feelings he felt as he witnessed the terrible vision: "My bowels, my bowels! I am pained at my very heart; my heart maketh a noise in me; I cannot hold my peace, because thou hast heard, O my soul, the sound of the trumpet, the alarm of war" (Jer. 4:19). "For my people is foolish, they have not known me; they are sottish children, and they have none understanding: they are wise to do evil, but to do good they have no knowledge" (Jer. 4:22). Destruction is described in cosmic terms as Jeremiah reported, "I beheld the earth, and, lo, it was without form, and void [a reversal of creation]; and the heavens, and they had no light" (Jer. 4:23). The Lord taunted his adulterous bride: "And when thou art spoiled, what wilt thou do? Though thou clothest thyself with crimson, though thou deckest thee with ornaments of gold, though thou rentest thy face with painting, in vain shalt thou make thyself fair; thy lovers will despise thee, they will seek thy life" (Jer. 4:30).

The threat of destruction was tempered by the promise that the destruction would not be total: "Nevertheless in those days, saith the Lord, I will not make a full end with you," but a remnant would be sent into exile where, just as they had forsaken the Lord and worshiped strange gods in their own land, they would "serve strangers in a land that is not yours" (Jer. 5:18–19).

Once again the blame was placed not just on the corrupt political and religious authorities but on everyone: "A wonderful and horrible thing is committed in the land; the prophets prophesy falsely, and the priests bear rule by their means; and my people love to have it so" (Jer. 5:30–31).

Prophecies from the Time of Jehoiakim (Jer. 4–20)

Because only a few of the diverse themes and images of the many prophecies recorded in Jeremiah 7 through 20 can be discussed here, I will concentrate on four of them: first, Jeremiah's Temple Sermon in chapter 7, which contains a comprehensive overview of what the Lord perceived to be the problems in Judah and the proposed solutions; second, three symbolic acts in which the word of the Lord was dramatized; third, a prophecy of the scattering and the gathering; and fourth, Jeremiah's laments, which are interspersed throughout these chapters and reveal the depths of Jeremiah's personal struggles and suffering as he went about the work of the Lord.

The Temple Sermon (Jer. 7)

The description of the Temple Sermon in the biographical chapter 26 is so close to the account of the actual sermon in chapter 7 that it is almost certain that the event described is the same. The date is 609 B.C., the first year of King Jehoiakim. The circumstance is similar to Jesus' cleansing of the temple (Matt. 21:12–13; Mark 11:15–18; Luke 19:45–48), and in fact, Christ even quoted Jeremiah's charge of a "den of robbers" (Jer. 7:11; Matt. 21:13; Mark 11:17; Luke 19:46). Jeremiah faced a hard-hearted and self-righteous people who did not wish to hear his message of repentance. This people had developed a self-righteous assurance that the Lord would protect and preserve them. It was based on the existence of the temple — the house of the Lord — combined with the recent reforms of Josiah, which succeeded in reforming the external practices of religion to the Mosaic prescriptions. The people were certain that these would preserve them.

Jeremiah responded to the first of these false notions with the warning, "Trust ye not in the lying words, saying, The temple of the Lord, The temple of the Lord, The temple of the Lord" (Jer. 7:4). To the second false notion, perhaps revealing that he considered the net result of Josiah's reforms to be superficial at best, Jeremiah cited compliance with the moral injunctions of the Mosaic covenant as the only safety, not an outward adherence to the laws of sacrifice alone: "If ye throughly amend your ways and your doings; if ye throughly execute judgment between a man and his neighbour; If ye oppress not the stranger, the fatherless, and the widow, and shed not innocent blood in this place, neither walk after other gods to your hurt: then will I cause you to dwell in this place, in the land that I gave to your fathers, for ever and ever" (Jer. 7:5–7).

This language was certainly familiar to those at the temple that day, because this same injunction to the people to care for the defenseless among them — widows, orphans, and foreigners — is found in Exodus 22:21–22, where it is followed by the stern warning: "If thou afflict them in any wise, and they cry at all unto me, I will surely hear their cry; and my wrath shall wax hot, and I will kill you with the sword; and your wives shall be widows, and your children fatherless" (vv. 23–24).

Jeremiah's message reminds us of the message of the Savior in his ministry and the self-righteous hypocrisy of the outwardly religious, which should serve as a solemn reminder to all of the covenant children who are favored in having the temple in their midst. We are reminded of such statements as "Woe unto you . . . hypocrites! for ye pay tithe of mint and anise and cummin, and have omitted the weightier matters of the law, judgment, mercy, and faith" (Matt. 23:23) and of the comparison to "whited sepulchres, which indeed appear beautiful outward, but are within full of dead men's bones, and of all uncleanness" (Matt. 23:27). The Savior outlined the criterion for final judgment: "For I was an hungred, and ye gave me meat: I was thirsty, and ye gave me drink: I was a stranger, and ye took me in: Naked, and ye clothed me: I was sick, and ye visited me: I was in prison, and ye came unto me" (Matt. 25:35–36).

In addition, Jeremiah cited the sins of the people as stealing, murder, adultery, false swearing, burning incense unto Baal, and walking after other gods — six of the Ten Commandments (Ex. 20:3–17). A similar list is found in the lawsuit in Hosea 4:2. Indeed, the temple had "become a den of robbers" (Jer. 7:11).

As an object lesson, Jeremiah reminded them of what happened to the house of the Lord at Shiloh (1 Sam. 1:7). If Jeremiah was indeed a descendant of Eli, custodian of the tabernacle at Shiloh (1 Sam. 1:9), this story would have been a vivid recollection in Jeremiah's family. The Lord asked Judah, "But go ye now unto my place which was in Shiloh, where I set my name at the first, and see what I did to it for the wickedness of my people Israel" (Jer. 7:12). In contrast to the well-documented capture of the ark of the covenant when unrighteous Israel was delivered into the hand of the Philistines in 1 Samuel 4 through 7, an account of the destruction of Shiloh where the ark had been kept is only preserved here (see also Ps. 78:60).

The Lord in his wrath ordered Jeremiah not even to attempt to intercede for such a people as they had become (Jer. 7:16; see also 14:11–12). Apparently idolatry was still rampant in the land, and while the children collected the wood, the fathers made the fire and the mothers baked the cakes to the queen of heaven (Jer. 7:18).[7] The Lord, probably as hyperbole, stated that he had never ordered sacrifice in the first place

---

[7]In Jeremiah, as in other books, the Lord condemns idolatry. Idols are manmade, cut from a tree, and nailed by hammers (Jer. 10:3–4). They cannot move, they cannot speak, they must be carried, and they cannot walk. They can do nothing — neither bad nor good (Jer. 10:4–5). But God, in contrast, is powerful, as these verbs of action demonstrate: he made the earth, he established the world, he stretched out the heavens, he places water in the sky, he creates clouds, lightning, rain, and wind; he has power, wisdom, and discretion (Jer. 10:12–13). Indeed, he is the maker of "all things" (Jer. 10:16).

but rather would have obedience. Such a sentiment, also found in Amos (5:21–25), Hosea (6:6), Isaiah (1:10–17), and Micah (6:1–8), is probably meant not as a polemic against all sacrifice but rather as a way of emphasizing the importance of obedience to the moral injunctions as opposed to only the strict adherence to ritual.[8] The importance of obedience over sacrifice was dramatically taught by Samuel to Saul in the incident of Agag the Amalekite in 1 Samuel 15.

Throughout Israel's history the Lord reminded them of their commitment to obedience, "but they hearkened not, nor inclined their ear, but walked in the counsels and in the imagination of their evil heart [see D&C 1:16], and went backward, and not forward" (Jer. 7:24). He constantly sent his prophets, "yet they hearkened not unto me, nor inclined their ear, but hardened their neck: they did worse than their fathers" (Jer. 7:26), a phenomenon that Jeremiah would personally witness and experience throughout his life. The result would be as prophesied by the Lord to Moses, "My wrath shall wax hot, and I will kill you with the sword; and your wives shall be widows, and your children fatherless" (Ex. 22:24) — slaughter, destruction, and exile — "then will I cause to cease from the cities of Judah, and from the streets of Jerusalem, the voice of mirth, and the voice of gladness, the voice of the bridegroom, and the voice of the bride: for the land shall be desolate" (Jer. 7:34).

In chapter 26 we learn that after this sermon the people, in conjunction with the priests and prophets, took Jeremiah before the rulers of Judah, saying, "Thou shalt surely die" (Jer. 26:8–10). They charged him before the rulers as prophesying against the holy city. Jeremiah's defense was simple: "The Lord sent me to prophesy against this house and against this city all the words that ye have heard. Therefore now amend your ways and your doings, and obey the voice of the Lord your God, and repent, and the Lord will turn away the evil that he hath pronounced against you" (JST Jer. 26:12–13). In the ensuing debate

---

[8]Note, for example, the important place of sacrifice in the restoration of Judah as prophesied by Jeremiah (Jer. 33:11). See also Ps. 51:16–19, which echoes a similar sentiment and then explains: "For thou desirest not sacrifice; else would I give it: thou delightest not in burnt offering. The sacrifices of God are a broken spirit: a broken and a contrite heart, O God, thou wilt not despise. Do good in thy good pleasure unto Zion . . . Then shalt thou be pleased with the sacrifices of righteousness, with burnt offering and whole burnt offering: then shall they offer bullocks upon thine altar."

"certain of the elders" argued that Jeremiah should be spared, citing the example of Micah, who also had prophesied against the city and had been spared by King Hezekiah. It was probably only the intervention of Ahikam, the son of Shaphan,[9] a high court official, that saved Jeremiah's life. The danger of being killed for delivering such a message was real, as evidenced by a note at the end of chapter 26 about an otherwise unknown prophet Urijah of Kirjath-jearim, who, like Jeremiah, prophesied against Jerusalem during the reign of King Jehoiakim. The king sought to put him to death, but he fled to Egypt. The relentless king then had him hunted down, extradited, convicted, and finally killed (Jer. 26:20–23).

Jeremiah's Symbolic Acts

Many important oracles of judgment are recorded in memorable imagery throughout the book of Jeremiah. I will concentrate on three prophecies that were accompanied by symbolic acts or allegories. The symbolic act, a dramatization of a prophetic message, was already a well-known phenomenon associated with the prophets, as, for example, the prophet Zedekiah's donning a set of iron horns (1 Kgs. 22:11), Hosea's marriage with Gomer (Hosea 1–3), Isaiah's naming his sons (Isa. 7–8), and Isaiah's walking around Jerusalem naked and barefoot (Isa. 20). Likewise the ministry of Ezekiel was characterized by several significant symbolic acts: lying on his side for a prescribed period (Ezek. 4), digging a hole through a wall (Ezek. 12), and refraining from mourning for his wife (Ezek. 24:15–27). Jeremiah participated in three such symbolic acts, one involving a linen girdle (Jer. 13:1–11), another a potter at his wheel (Jer. 18), and still another a potter's earthen bottle (Jer. 19–20), which the Lord interpreted for him allegorically.[10] A brief look at these incidents can give us a further taste of the nature of Jeremiah's prophecies.

---

[9]Both of these men, Ahikam and Shaphan, served in the court of Josiah (2 Kgs. 22:12). Ahikam's son Gedaliah would be appointed governor of Judah by Nebuchadnezzar after the fall of Jerusalem, and Jeremiah would go to his court at Mizpah, suggesting that the friendship between Jeremiah and this family continued through the years.

[10]Elsewhere in the book of Jeremiah he wore a yoke (chaps. 27–28) and used the Rechabites in an object lesson (chap. 35).

The Linen Girdle (Jer. 13:1–11)

The Lord commanded Jeremiah to put a linen girdle on his loins and journey to the Euphrates, a distance of between three and four hundred miles, and hide the girdle in a hole in a rock. This Jeremiah did.[11] After many days the Lord then told him to go and retrieve his girdle. Jeremiah discovered when he dug it up that "the girdle was marred, it was profitable for nothing" (Jer. 13:7). The Lord explained: "After this manner will I mar the pride of Judah, and the great pride of Jerusalem" (Jer. 13:9). At one level the meaning is clear: if Judah were to be involved with the Euphrates it would be to her downfall. The Lord went on to explain that Israel and Judah were like the girdle in that they were wrapped around the Lord as the girdle had been wrapped around Jeremiah (Jer. 13:11). Perhaps this is a reference to the fact that when Israel or Judah were no longer faithful to the Lord—symbolized by being wrapped around the waist—then they really were worthless and would eventually be destroyed. A nation that refused to hearken to the Lord and worshiped other gods was to the Lord God of Israel just like the girdle—useless. Some have seen in the reference to the Euphrates an allusion to the eventual exile of the people there.

There is no record that anyone witnessed this event other than Jeremiah, and we can only speculate what kind of an impact this had on his prophetic understanding. Certainly it would have illustrated the close relationship between the Lord and his people and the need for them to remain pure in order to be of any use or value to the Lord.

The Potter's Wheel (Jer. 18)

In another of the most well-known images in Jeremiah, the Lord commanded him to go to the house of a potter and watch him work. The image of the work of the potter as an act of creation is well known throughout the Bible. In the statement in Genesis 2:7, "the Lord God formed man of the dust of the ground," the verb used is ysr, the same verb used to mean forming a pot. This same image of the Lord "forming" individuals is used elsewhere, as in Jeremiah's call "before I formed thee

---

[11]Some have suggested, in light of the great distance involved, that this symbolic act occurred in a vision or was simply to be understood as a parable. It is not out of the question that it was fulfilled literally.

in the belly" (Jer. 1:5), and "shall the clay say to him that fashioneth it, What makest thou?" (Isa. 45:9; see also 44:21, 24), and as a reference to the Lord's "forming" his people Israel (Isa. 27:11; 43:1, 21).

As Jeremiah watched the potter, who was probably molding a pot on a potter's wheel, the pot "was marred in the hand of the potter: so he made it again another vessel, as seemed good to the potter to make it" (Jer. 18:4). The Lord explained: "O house of Israel, cannot I do with you as this potter? saith the Lord. Behold, as the clay is in the potter's hand, so are ye in mine hand, O house of Israel" (Jer. 18:6). The Lord reaffirmed his power to intervene in history with the same verbs known from Jeremiah's call—that he has the power to "pluck up, and to pull down, and to destroy" (Jer. 18:7). At this time there was still hope for repentance, and the Lord promised those who would repent and return that he would "build" and "plant" them (Jer. 18:8–9).

Apart from being a memorable image of the omnipotence of God, this image of the potter reinforces the covenantal relationship of the Lord with his people. He has the power to form them as individuals and as a nation and to then destroy them and start over again. In history, when the pot has become marred, the Lord has destroyed it and started over again. He has done this on several occasions throughout scriptural history, such as the Flood, the destruction of the Nephites, and the Apostasy and the Restoration. Once again, we have no account that this revelation was witnessed or experienced by any other than Jeremiah, suggesting that it may have been for his own spiritual understanding.

The Potter's Earthen Bottle (Jer. 19–20)

The third symbolic act is related to the imagery of the potter at his wheel, but the vessel destroyed is the finished product. Of these three incidents, this is the only one that was apparently done for the public; their reaction is most interesting. Jeremiah was instructed to take an earthen bottle and go with some of the elders and priests to the Hinnom Valley, just south of Jerusalem. There he proclaimed: "Hear ye the word of the Lord, O kings of Judah, and inhabitants of Jerusalem; Thus saith the Lord of hosts, the God of Israel; Behold, I will bring evil upon this place, the which whosoever heareth, his ears shall tingle" (Jer. 19:3). Jeremiah enumerated their acts of idolatry, many of which had become localized in the Hinnom Valley and Tophet.[12] He then uttered the threats of the Lord of a great "slaughter" (Jer. 19:6), destruction by the sword, their carcasses to be carrion (Jer. 19:7), the city to become desolate (Jer. 19:8), and the besieged in the city forced to eat the flesh of their sons and daughters (Jer. 19:9). All this is reminiscent of the graphic prophecies in Deuteronomy 28 that were directed against the covenant people if they broke the covenant. Symbolic of this destruction, Jeremiah broke the earthen bottle and declared: "Thus saith the Lord of hosts; Even so will I break this people and this city, as one breaketh a potter's vessel, that cannot be made whole again" (Jer. 19:11). Unlike the clay on the potter's wheel (Jer. 18:1–6), the individuals represented by the finished vessel that was broken would not have a second chance but would be buried in Tophet until there was no more room.

This symbolic act was a public event, and the implications were immediately understood by those present. Jeremiah 20 recounts the persecution that Jeremiah endured for delivering the word of the Lord to those who found the truth offensive. Pashur, the chief governor in the house of the Lord—a temple official who undoubtedly had heard about the Temple Sermon—had Jeremiah beaten and put into stocks (Jer. 20:1–2). Jeremiah prophetically pronounced upon this man a new name, Magor-missabib ("Terror all around"), and prophesied that Pashur himself would witness the death of his friends and the capture of Jerusalem by the Babylonians and that he would go into exile where he would die with all of his friends "to whom thou hast prophesied lies" (Jer. 20:3–6). This is the last we hear of this particular official in Jeremiah, perhaps because he was one of those sent in the deportation of 597 B.C.

The Scattering and the Gathering (Jer. 16)

Jeremiah 16 contains a series of prophecies that foretold both sorrow and joy. The message in verses 1 through 13 is one of doom for Jeremiah's

---

[12]Tophet was a place in the Hinnom Valley. The name *Tophet* itself was derived from the consonants of an Aramaic word meaning "hearth" (*tpt*) and the vowels of the Hebrew word for "shame" *bōšet*), because it was a place where Israelites were known to have offered sacrifices, most notably child sacrifices, to the gods Baal and Molech (2 Chron. 28:3; 33:6; 2 Kgs. 16:3; 21:6). Josiah had attempted to wipe out such atrocities, but the Bible tells us that these practices were reinstituted after his death (2 Kgs. 23:10).

people. "I have taken away my peace from this people, saith the Lord" (Jer. 16:5), because, the Lord said, "your fathers have forsaken me" and "ye have done worse than your fathers" (Jer. 16:11–12). As a result, the people of Judah would be deported to a foreign land, where they would serve foreign gods and receive no favor from the God of Israel (Jer. 16:13).

At this point the prophecy of future sorrow is interrupted by a prophecy of future joy (Jer. 16:14–15). The imminent deportation will be followed by a latter-day return. And that return will be one of the great events of Israel's history, eclipsing even the deliverance of the children of Israel from the bondage of Egypt. The Lord will bring Israel "from the land of the north, and from all the lands whither he had driven them." And he will restore them "into their land that I gave unto their fathers" (see also Jer. 23:7–8).

Jeremiah 16:16 is often understood as a prophecy of latter-day gathering, but the context seems to identify it as part of God's relentless punishment of Judah. None of his rebellious children would be able to escape his wrath and the punishment that he had decreed for them. Their iniquity was not hidden from him, and they would pay double for it. They had defiled his land, and they had filled his inheritance "with the carcases of their detestable and abominable things" (Jer. 16:18). The chapter ends with a beautiful reference to the gathering of non-Israelites to the Lord and his covenants (Jer. 16:19–21). They will come to the realization that they have inherited falsehood from their progenitors and that their gods are "no gods." With this understanding, they will be ready to learn the truth, and they will know the Lord (see also Isa. 2:1–3; Zech. 8:20–23).

Jeremiah's Laments

"When I would comfort myself against sorrow, my heart is faint in me. . . . The harvest is past, the summer is ended, and we are not saved. For the hurt of the daughter of my people am I hurt; I am black; astonishment hath taken hold on me. . . . Oh that my head were waters, and mine eyes a fountain of tears, that I might weep day and night for the slain of the daughter of my people" (Jer. 8:18–9:1). With these words

Jeremiah revealed to us that he was a man with much emotion and compassion about the events that he witnessed in the past, present, and through his prophetic gift, the future. We are reminded of the prophet Mormon, who also spent his life's work crying repentance to his unrepentant people, only to witness their destruction: "My soul was rent with anguish, because of the slain of my people, and I cried: O ye fair ones, how could ye have departed from the ways of the Lord! O ye fair ones, how could ye have rejected that Jesus, who stood with open arms to receive you! Behold, if ye had not done this, ye would not have fallen. But behold, ye are fallen, and I mourn your loss" (Morm. 6:16–18).

Jeremiah the prophet saw life from the human perspective and at the same time was compelled to view it from God's perspective through the message that he bore. On the one hand, he viewed the coming disaster with compassion and sorrow; on the other hand, he felt righteous indignation as he considered the unfaithfulness of his people, which he longed to escape: "Oh that I had in the wilderness a lodging place of wayfaring men; that I might leave my people, and go from them! for they be all adulterers, an assembly of treacherous men. And they bend their tongues like their bow for lies: but they are not valiant for the truth upon the earth; for they proceed from evil to evil" (Jer. 9:2–3). In short, he understood that they deserved the impending judgment. Such laments reveal his mixed feelings about his people.

At the same time, we are presented throughout the book of Jeremiah with a series of personal laments—termed by many the "confessions," which are quite unlike anything else in the biblical prophecies—in which Jeremiah revealed the personal struggles and suffering that he as servant of the Lord was called to endure. Through these laments Jeremiah sought for an understanding of many of life's most difficult questions. They remind us of the probing of Job in his trials and of Joseph Smith in Liberty Jail. For some of the laments we are presented with a historical context; for others, we can only imagine. To some of these complaints the Lord responded; to others, he was silent. A look at these haunting poetic passages helps us to appreciate better the great human drama of prophets, the burden of the uncompromising call of the Lord, and most of all, the importance of a dynamic relationship with our Maker which can help us all to "endure to the end." There are at least six examples of personal laments, each of which we will examine, identifying the issues that Jeremiah discussed and the divine answers to such questions.

Like a Lamb to the Slaughter (Jer. 11:18–12:6)

The Lord revealed to Jeremiah the sins of his people as well as the judgment that was to come. Jeremiah recorded: "And the Lord hath given me knowledge of it, and I know it: then thou shewedst me their doings" (Jer. 11:18). Because Jeremiah had faithfully delivered this message, it was he who would suffer, and in fact, there were those who sought his life. He pleaded his innocence: "But I was like a lamb or an ox that is brought to the slaughter" (Jer. 8:19) — words that remind us of the image of Christ as the Suffering Servant (Isa. 53:7) and that were quoted by the Prophet Joseph Smith as he went to Carthage (D&C 135:4).[13] It was Jeremiah's own community that was most indignant. He cried to the Lord for "vengeance on them: for unto thee have I revealed my cause" (Jer. 11:20). The Lord assured him that divine justice would prevail, and in this case it would be in the not-too-distant future: "The men of Anathoth, that seek thy life, saying, Prophesy not in the name of the Lord, that thou die not by our hand: . . . Behold, I will punish them: the young men shall die by the sword; their sons and their daughters shall die by famine: And there shall be no remnant of them: for I will bring evil upon the men of Anathoth, even the year of their visitation" (Jer. 11:21–23).

But Jeremiah's complaint did not end there, and he asked the Lord, just as did Job and the psalmist (Job 21; Ps. 73), the age-old question: "Wherefore doth the way of the wicked prosper? wherefore are all they happy that deal very treacherously?" (Jer. 12:1). The Lord responded, much as he did to Job, with questions, two enigmatic proverbs: "If thou hast run with the footmen, and they have wearied thee, then how canst thou contend with horses? And if in the land of peace, wherein thou trustedst, they wearied thee, then how wilt thou do in the swelling of Jordan?" (Jer. 12:5).

The answer is clear, though the implications not comforting: for Jeremiah the challenges and trials had just begun.

---

[13]"I am going like a lamb to the slaughter; but I am calm as a summer's morning; I have a conscience void of offense towards God, and towards all men" (D&C 135:4).

Called by Thy Name (Jer. 15:10–21)

Jeremiah recounted his reception of the words of the Lord in much the same image as did Ezekiel (Ezek. 3:1–3) and John the Revelator (Rev. 10:9–10): an act of eating. "Thy words were found, and I did eat them; and thy word was unto me the joy and rejoicing of mine heart: for I am called by thy name, O Lord God of hosts" (Jer. 15:16). And yet the results were persecution, rebuke (Jer. 15:15), isolation, and loneliness: "I sat not in the assembly of the mockers, nor rejoiced; I sat alone because of thy hand: for thou hast filled me with indignation. Why is my pain perpetual, and my wound incurable, which refuseth to be healed? wilt thou be altogether unto me as a liar, and as waters that fail?" (Jer. 15:17–18).

The Lord responded sharply to the accusation, reminding Jeremiah of the privilege of his station and of his need to repent and be converted to his calling: "Therefore thus saith the Lord, If thou return, then will I bring thee again, and thou shalt stand before me: and if thou take forth the precious from the vile, thou shalt be as my mouth" (Jer. 15:19). Repeating the promise he gave to Jeremiah from the beginning at his call, the Lord reminded him of whom he was serving: "I will make thee unto this people a fenced brasen wall: and they shall fight against thee, but they shall not prevail against thee: for I am with thee to save thee and to deliver thee, saith the Lord" (Jer. 15:20). Indeed, without the help of the Lord such a calling would be unthinkable.

Heal Me (Jer. 17:14–18)

"Heal me, O Lord, and I shall be healed; save me, and I shall be saved: for thou art my praise" (Jer. 17:14). When it is read in sequence with the previous lament, this passage reveals a more humble Jeremiah praying in faith for the continued protection and inspiration promised by the Lord. At the same time he prayed for divine justice—a double dose: "Let them be confounded that persecute me, but let not me be confounded: let them be dismayed, but let not me be dismayed: bring upon them the day of evil, and destroy them with double destruction" (Jer. 17:18). To this plea there was no divine response.

Forgive Not Their Iniquity (Jer. 18:18–23)

In Jeremiah 18 we learn more about those who were persecuting Jeremiah. Their statement that in spite of what they did to him, "the law shall not perish from the priest, nor counsel from the wise, nor the word from the prophet" (18:18), reveals that they considered the official religion of the land to be in good hands. Jeremiah again pleaded for judgment against his enemies. He reminded the Lord that at one time he had acted as mediator for his people: "Remember that I stood before thee to speak good for them, and to turn away thy wrath from them" (Jer. 18:20). No longer would he plead for those who sought his life: "Yet, Lord, thou knowest all their counsel against me to slay me: forgive not their iniquity, neither blot out their sin from thy sight, but let them be overthrown before thee; deal thus with them in the time of thine anger" (Jer. 18:23). To this plea also came no divine response.

As a Burning Fire (Jer. 20:7–13)

In a lament recorded in Jeremiah 20, we learn of the unwilling human nature of the prophet in submitting himself to the will of the Lord in delivering an unpopular message. At the same time we find a marvelous image of a man of God who could not contain the word of the Lord in his heart: "O Lord, thou hast deceived me, and I was deceived: thou art stronger than I, and hast prevailed: I am in derision daily, every one mocketh me. For since I spake, I cried out, I cried violence and spoil; because the word of the Lord was made a reproach unto me, and a derision, daily. Then I said, I will not make mention of him, nor speak any more in his name. But his word was in mine heart as a burning fire shut up in my bones, and I was weary with forbearing, and I could not stay" (Jer. 20:7–9).

Jeremiah, perhaps comforted by his own admission of weakness, went on to reaffirm his faith and to praise the Lord, who is "with me as a mighty terrible one . . . that triest the righteous, . . . [and] delivered the soul of the poor from the hand of evildoers" (Jer. 20:11–13).

Cursed Be the Day (Jer. 20:14–18)

Another lament recorded in Jeremiah 20 provides a climax to the unit of chapters 1 through 20. In these verses Jeremiah expressed a grief as profound as any in scripture:

> Cursed be the day wherein I was born:
>> let not the day wherein my mother bare me be blessed.
> Cursed be the man who brought tidings to my father, saying,

A man child is born unto thee; making him very glad.
And let that man be as the cities which the Lord overthrew,
    and repented not:
And let him hear the cry in the morning,
    and the shouting at noontide;
Because he slew me not from the womb;
    or that my mother might have been my grave,
        and her womb to be always great with me.
Wherefore came I forth out of the womb to see labour and sorrow,
    that my days should be consumed with shame (Jer. 20:14–18).

The references to the womb are poignant echoes of the glorious foreordained mission of Jeremiah, which was bestowed even before he was in the womb—ironic references to the Lord's call in Jeremiah 1:5. These wretched cries as recorded are unanswered and serve as a solemn reminder of the lifetime of sacrifices that Jeremiah made to serve his God and his fellowmen.

To those of us who have cried out in despair to the Lord in laments like Jeremiah's, the answer of the resurrected Lord to Joseph Smith in a dark moment in Liberty Jail provides a humbling but comforting appreciation that the Lord with whom we are invited to share our sorrows truly understands:

If thou art called to pass through tribulation;
If thou art in perils among false brethren;
If thou art in perils among robbers;
If thou art in perils by land or by sea;
If thou art accused with all manner of false accusations;
If thine enemies fall upon thee;
If they tear thee from the society of thy father and mother and brethren
    and sisters; . . .
And if thou shouldst be cast into the pit, or into the hands of murderers,
    and the sentence of death passed upon thee;
If thou be cast into the deep;
If the billowing surge conspire against thee;
If fierce winds become thine enemy;
If the heavens gather blackness, and all the elements combine to hedge
    up the way;
and above all, if the very jaws of hell shall gape open the mouth wide
    after thee,
know thou, my son, that all these things shall give thee experience,
and shall be for thy good.

The Son of Man hath descended below them all.
Art thou greater than he? (D&C 122:5–8).

In the dark times of self-doubt, loneliness, and despair, Jeremiah could reflect on the moment when the Lord lovingly touched his mouth and said, "Behold, I have put my words in thy mouth" (Jer. 1:9) or on the Lord's promise at his call: "They shall fight against thee; but they shall not prevail against thee; for I am with thee, saith the Lord, to deliver thee" (Jer. 1:19). Perhaps in a quiet moment the Lord spoke to him further words of comfort, as he did to the Prophet Joseph Smith, reminding him that the trials of mortality can only be endured with an eternal perspective:

> Therefore, hold on thy way, and the priesthood shall remain with thee;
> for their bounds are set, they cannot pass.
> Thy days are known, and thy years shall not be numbered less;
> therefore, fear not what man can do,
> for God shall be with you forever and ever (D&C 122:9).

22

A PROPHET OVER THE NATIONS

(JEREMIAH 21–24, 30–31, 46–51)

DAVID ROLPH SEELY

The relationship between the Lord and his people has from the very beginning been defined and regulated by covenant, established first with Adam and his posterity and then after the Flood with Noah and his posterity. At a certain point in time the descendants of Noah, because of their presumption, built the notorious Tower of Babel—the Hebrew word for Babylon[1]—an act for which they were punished by being scattered throughout the world and having their language confounded. It was after this event that the Lord called Abraham out of the world, from Ur of the Chaldees to the promised land, and made a covenant with him. The promises of the covenant were accompanied by the simple yet all-encompassing obligation, "Be thou perfect" (Gen. 17:1). The accounts of Abraham demonstrate that he understood all of the implications of this injunction and sought to become perfect in every way.

Throughout the rest of the Old Testament, the mercy and grace of the Lord toward his people is remembered in the miraculous events of the Exodus, when the Lord heard the cries of his covenant people in Egypt, delivered them from bondage, met them at Sinai where he established a new covenant with them, and led them into the promised land. The accompanying obligations of the Mosaic covenant were explicitly set forth in detail, both in terms of ethical behavior as well as ritual, in the Law of Moses. The Lord defined the relationship thus:

David Rolph Seely is assistant professor of ancient scripture at Brigham Young University.

[1]The Hebrew word *bābel* is rendered by translators as "Babel" in the story of the tower but as "Babylon" (from the Greek) throughout the rest of the Bible.

"And I will take you to me for a people, and I will be to you a God" (Ex. 6:7; Jer. 31:33) and explained the accompanying obligations, "Ye shall be holy; for I am holy" (Lev. 11:44; 19:2; 20:26). To the Mosaic covenant were attached blessings and curses: obedience would bring prosperity and protection, whereas disobedience would bring death and destruction. The sacred history of Israel recounts centuries of Israel's struggle to understand, remember, and keep the conditions of the covenant—a struggle that most often ended in apostasy. To regulate the covenant, the Lord sent prophets to his people. Their message was always the same: repent or face the acknowledged consequences. Through the conditions of the covenant, disobedience warranted the justice of God, which meant judgment and destruction. Yet the prophets always reminded the people that ultimately, through God's mercy, restoration and rebuilding would come.

The Lord defined Jeremiah's mission in his call to be prophet when he touched his mouth and said, "Behold, I have put my words in thy mouth. See, I have this day set thee over the nations and over the kingdoms, to root out, and to pull down, and to destroy, and to throw down, to build, and to plant" (Jer. 1:9–10). Thus Jeremiah's message was twofold: judgment and destruction on the one hand[2] and restoration and rebuilding on the other. And just as his audience was not limited to Israel but extended to "the nations" (see also Jer. 1:5, "I ordained thee a prophet unto the nations"), so his message extended beyond the immediate future to the end of time. The three sections of the book of Jeremiah discussed in this chapter illustrate the full scope of Jeremiah's message: chapters 21 through 24 contain prophecies of the destruction and the scattering of Judah in the immediate future; chapters 30 and 31 contain prophecies of hope and consolation for a future, latter-day, renewal of the covenant, and the gathering and restoration; and chapters 46 through 51 contain oracles directed against Israel's neighbors, some of which are types of the destruction awaiting the world in the last days.

---

[2]Note that there are four terms for destruction ("root out," "pull down," "destroy," and "throw down") and only two for restoration ("build" and "plant"), signifying a double portion of destruction. The prophecies throughout the book reflect the same proportion of destruction, which must precede the restoration.

A Prophecy against Zedekiah (Jer. 21:1–10)

During Nebuchadrezzar's[3] siege of Jerusalem in 587 B.C., King Zedekiah sent two messengers, Pashur and Zephaniah, to Jeremiah with the request that he inquire of the Lord on behalf of the king and all of Judah "if so be that the Lord will deal with us according to all his wondrous works, that he may go up from us" (Jer. 21:2). The phrase "wondrous works" (Hebrew, *niple'ōt*) is used throughout the Old Testament to refer to the "mighty acts" that the Lord performed in the deliverance of Israel from Egypt.[4] Zedekiah hoped that the Lord God of Israel would deliver his people now through his miraculous power as he had at the time of Moses from the Egyptians and most recently from the Assyrians at the time of Hezekiah (2 Kgs. 18–19; Isa. 36–37). The Lord's reply was grim. Not only would he not aid Judah in her defense (Jer. 21:4) but, he said, "I myself will fight against you with an outstretched hand and with a strong arm, even in anger, and in fury, and in great wrath" (Jer. 21:5). The phrase "mighty hand and a stretched out arm" is another key formula used in reference to the Lord's strength in defeating Pharaoh's army, whose destruction is portrayed as a military encounter during the Exodus (Deut. 4:34; 5:15; 7:19; 11:2; 26:8).[5] In Jeremiah, though, the adjectives of the formula are switched, "outstretched hand and strong arm" indicating the reversal that has come about through Judah's transgressions.

---

[3]The proper name of the Babylonian king is found in its correct form here, as also elsewhere in Jeremiah and Ezekiel. As indicated in the cuneiform sources, his name was Nebuchadrezzar, not -nezzar. The change from r to n may be simply an error in transcription, as the letters in ancient Hebrew are very similar, but recently some have argued that the change to Nebuchadnezzar may be attributed to a deliberate pun on his name. In Babylonian the name *Nabu-kudurru-uur* means something like "Nabu [a Babylonian god] protect the crown prince!" Changing *kudurru* to *kudanu* "mule" (accounting for the -n- in Nebuchadnezzar) renders a name that means "Nabu, protect the mule!" See A. van Selms, "The Name Nebuchadnezzar," in *Travels in the World of the Old Testament,* ed. M. van Voss, Philo Houwink ten Cate, and N. A. van Uchelen (Assen, Netherlands: Van Gorcum, 1974), pp. 223–29. I thank Paul Y. Hoskisson for bringing this reference to my attention.

[4]For example, see Ex. 3:20 referring to the plagues; Ex. 34:10; Deut. 34:11; Ps. 106:7 about the deliverance from Egypt; and the same word used by Joshua (Josh. 3:5) about the miraculous events surrounding the entry into the promised land. A form of this same root is found in the well-known passage in Isa. 29:14, "I will proceed to do a *marvelous work* (Hebrew, *haplî'*) among this people, even a *marvelous work and a wonder*" (Hebrew, *haplē' wāpele'*). In this passage the phrase describes the Lord's activities in the latter-day restoration in terms of the Exodus.

[5]The normal Hebrew formula is *beyād hazāqâ ûbizrôa' netûyâ.* The King James translators translated *hazāqâ* as "strong" in the normal formula but as "mighty" in Jeremiah. The Hebrew word is the same in both cases.

Whereas before the Lord fought *for* Israel against her enemies, now the Lord will join the enemy and fight *against* his people.[6] In addition to this grim tiding, the Lord said through Jeremiah: "He that abideth in this city shall die by the sword, and by the famine, and by the pestilence: but he that goeth out, and falleth to the Chaldeans that besiege you, he shall live, and his life shall be unto him for a prey" (Jer. 21:9). The only chance for survival is surrender, a message for which Jeremiah would be branded a traitor (Jer. 38:2–4).

Prophecies against the Kings of Judah
(Jer. 21:11–22:30)

The passage in Jeremiah 21:11 through 22:9 is a call to the kings in the house of David to be faithful to the ethical imperatives of the covenant to ensure social justice: to execute judgment (Jer. 21:12) and righteousness and to "deliver the spoiled out of the hand of the oppressor: and do no wrong, do no violence to the stranger, the fatherless, nor the widow, neither shed innocent blood" (Jer. 22:3). If they failed to do this, as they had in the past, then destruction would come. After the destruction, many of the world would pass by Jerusalem, asking, "Wherefore hath the Lord done thus unto this great city? Then they shall answer, Because they have forsaken the covenant of the Lord their God, and worshipped other gods, and served them" (Jer. 22:8–9).

Chapter 22 contains several short prophecies directed against three successive kings of Judah: Jehoahaz, Jehoiakim, and Jehoiachin. Each of these kings is judged against the standard of the covenant and is found wanting.

Jeremiah 22:10–12 prophesies the captivity of Shallum, another name for Jehoahaz (1 Chron. 3:15) son of Josiah, which was fulfilled when he was removed from the throne and taken to Egypt by Pharaoh Necho in 609 B.C. (2 Kgs. 23:33–34).

Jeremiah 22:13–19 is directed against Jehoahaz's successor, Jehoiakim, who attempted to justify his unjust reign by the props of a new and magnificent palace instead of judging the cause of the poor and

---

[6]See Lam. 2:4–5 as well, where this image is described in retrospect after the destruction.

the needy (vv. 13–16). His reward will be an ignominious death and "the burial of an ass, drawn and cast forth beyond the gates of Jerusalem" (v. 19). This prophecy is expanded in another prophecy, in which Jeremiah declared, "His dead body shall be cast out in the day to the heat, and in the night to the frost" (Jer. 36:30). The account of his death in 2 Kings 24:6 simply says that he "slept with his fathers." But the situation surrounding his untimely death in the face of the punitive expedition that was shortly to be sent from Babylon because of his revolt against Nebuchadnezzar—a situation that resulted in the siege and capture of Jerusalem and the exile of his son—has led some to suspect that he may have been assassinated.[7]

Jeremiah 22:20–30 contains an oracle against Coniah, another name for Jehoiachin, son of Jehoiakim. His punishment will be like that of a useless, broken pot, to be cast off by the Lord to join his countrymen in exile to Babylon. This prophecy is accompanied by the promise that his seed would not sit upon the throne of Judah. It was fulfilled when he was replaced by the conquering Babylonians with his uncle Mattaniah, whose name was changed to Zedekiah. Jehoiachin is mentioned as being still alive in Babylon—the king in exile—as late as 562 B.C., when Nebuchadnezzar died (2 Kgs. 25:27–30; Jer. 52:31–34).

A Prophecy of Restoration (Jer. 23)

Jeremiah 23 may be best categorized as a messianic oracle. Verses 1 through 4 pronounce doom on the "pastors" (shepherds) of Israel, a metaphor often referring to Israel's spiritual and political leaders—prophets, priests, and kings (Ezek. 34; John 10). Instead of caring for the sheep, these leaders had scattered them. It would take the Lord, the Good Shepherd, to gather his sheep and "set up shepherds over them which shall feed them" (Jer. 23:4). If applied to the first coming of the Messiah, this prophecy would refer to a spiritual gathering made possible through the Atonement. A completion of its fulfillment is to be found in the

---

[7]See H. B. Maclean, "Jehoiakim," in *The Interpreter's Dictionary of the Bible*, 5 vols., ed. G. A. Buttrick, et al. (Nashville: Abingdon, 1962–76), 2:813–14. The problems of reconstructing the events surrounding his death are further compounded by the passage in 2 Chron. 36:6, which says that Nebuchadnezzar "bound him in fetters" to take him into captivity.

Second Coming, when God will "raise unto David a righteous Branch, and a King shall reign and prosper, and shall execute judgment and justice in the earth" (Jer. 23:5). When those days come, "they shall no more say, The Lord liveth, which brought up the children of Israel out of the land of Egypt; But, The Lord liveth, which brought up and which led the seed of the house of Israel out of the north country, and from all countries whither I had driven them; and they shall dwell in their own land" (Jer. 23:7–8).

Jeremiah 23:9–40 continues the denunciation of the wicked shepherds, specifying the wickedness of the false prophets and priests. This section provides a key for distinguishing and dealing with false, as opposed to true, prophets. Their sins are grievous: "They commit adultery, and walk in lies: they strengthen also the hands of evildoers, that none doth return from his wickedness" (Jer. 23:14). This description brings to mind Christ's injunction given in the Sermon on the Mount and repeated to the Nephites: "Beware of false prophets, who come to you in sheep's clothing, but inwardly they are ravening wolves. Ye shall know them by their fruits" (Matt. 7:15–16; 3 Ne. 14:15–16). Because these false prophets have come on their own accord, the Lord said, "I have not sent these prophets, yet they ran: I have not spoken to them, yet they prophesied" (Jer. 23:21); "I have heard what the prophets said, that prophesy lies in my name, saying, I have dreamed, I have dreamed. How long shall this be in the heart of the prophets that prophesy lies? yea, they are prophets of the deceit of their own heart; Which think to cause my people to forget my name by their dreams which they tell every man to his neighbour, as their fathers have forgotten my name for Baal" (Jer. 23:25–27). Consequently they speak their own words and not the words of the Lord; "they speak a vision of their own heart, and not out of the mouth of the Lord" (Jer. 23:16). They were popular because their message was what the people wanted to hear: "The Lord hath said, Ye shall have peace; and they say unto every one that walketh after the imagination of his own heart, No evil shall come upon you" (Jer. 23:17).[8] Following such

---

[8]This is exactly the kind of prophet that Samuel the Lamanite told the Nephites they would accept: "But behold, if a man shall come among you and shall say: Do this, and there is no iniquity; do that and ye shall not suffer; yea, he will say: Walk after the pride of your own hearts; yea, walk after the pride of your eyes, and do whatsoever your heart desireth—and if a man shall come among you and say this, ye will receive him, and say that he is a prophet" (Hel. 13:27).

prophets is nothing less than idolatry — attempting to find divine approval for selfish interests — and the Lord accused them of such, characterizing these false prophets as those "which think to cause my people to forget my name . . . as their fathers have forgotten my name for Baal" (Jer. 23:27).

The same image of "one that walketh after the imagination of his own heart" (Jer. 23:17) occurs in the Doctrine and Covenants and is applied to our day. The people of this generation are likewise accused of idolatry: "They seek not the Lord to establish his righteousness, *but every man walketh in his own way,* and after the image of his own god, whose image is in the likeness of the world, and *whose substance is that of an idol,* which waxeth old and shall perish in Babylon, even Babylon the great, which shall fall" (D&C 1:16; emphasis added).

Two Baskets of Figs (Jer. 24)

After Nebuchadnezzar captured Jerusalem in 597 (2 Kgs. 24:10–16), he took the young king Jehoiachin and many leading citizens into exile in Babylon. Among these were Ezekiel and Daniel. Nebuchadnezzar then replaced Jehoiachin with his father's brother, Mattaniah, changing his name to Zedekiah. In response to those in Jerusalem who continued to believe they had been preserved from total destruction because of their righteousness, the Lord showed Jeremiah the vision of the two baskets of figs. The Lord revealed that the good figs represented the fate of those who had been taken to Babylon, and the bad represented the fate of those who had been left behind. To the good figs in Babylon the Lord spoke of hope: "I will bring them again to this land: and I will build them, and not pull them down; and I will plant them, and not pluck them up. And I will give them an heart to know me, that I am the Lord: and they shall be my people, and I will be their God: for they shall return unto me with their whole heart" (Jer. 24:6–7). The restoration and return to the promised land is phrased in the same language as the original covenant: "They shall be my people, and I will be their God" (Jer. 24:7). The evil figs would be delivered to the kingdoms of the earth and would be consumed by the sword, famine, and pestilence (Jer. 24:8–10). That prophecy was fulfilled in 587 B.C. with the destruction of Jerusalem and the temple and the capture of King Zedekiah (2 Kgs. 25). Lehi, a good fig, was delivered by the Lord from this fate and taken to a new promised land, a land given by covenant.

The Book of Consolation (Jer. 30–31)

Jeremiah's heavy burden of destruction and sorrow is balanced by equally weighty prophecies of restoration and consolation, collected in chapters 30 and 31. Hope is found in the promise of a restoration and renewal of the covenant — a new covenant — and a gathering and return to the promised land. These two chapters can be divided into three sections: chapter 30, prophecy of hope directed to Judah and Israel; 31:1–21, prophecy to Ephraim; 31:22–40, prophecy to Judah and Ephraim.

Chapter 30 looks to a day when Israel and Judah, referred to together with the name of their father Jacob, will be released from the yoke and bonds of their captivity (Jer. 30:3, 8), return to the land of their inheritance (Jer. 30:3), and "serve the Lord their God, and David their king" (Jer. 30:9). The imagery of return and restoration in this chapter is that of healing. The wounds had been caused by the Lord, "For I have wounded thee with the wound of an enemy, with the chastisement of a cruel one, for the multitude of thine iniquity; because thy sins were increased" (Jer. 30:14). Just as the wounds will be healed, so will the relationship be resumed: "Their children also shall be as aforetime, and their congregation shall be established before me" (Jer. 30:20). As in past days, the wrath of the Lord will be reserved for those who oppress his people (Jer. 30:20), and "it shall fall with pain upon the head of the wicked" (Jer. 30:23), who are the enemies of Israel, rather than fall on Israel herself.

The first part of chapter 31 contains a prophecy about the gathering of Israel. Parts of this prophecy are directed specifically to Ephraim, one of the ten tribes that were lost and scattered after the destruction of the kingdom of Israel by the Assyrians in 721 B.C. Clearly this vision is intended for the latter days. Once again, the key words from Jeremiah's call occur (Jer. 1:10): "build," in regard to the "virgin of Israel," an appellation often used for a city, and "plant," referring to the vines of Samaria (Jer. 31:4–5). Oliver Cowdery, in his summary of the things the angel Moroni taught Joseph Smith, quoted Jeremiah 31:6:[9] "For there shall be a day, that the watchmen upon the mount Ephraim shall cry, Arise ye, and let us go up to Zion unto the Lord our God." The central event of this prophecy is the gathering: "Behold, I will bring them from the north country, and gather them from the coasts of the earth" (Jer. 31:8); and "Hear the word of the Lord, O ye nations, and declare it in the isles afar off, and say, He that scattered Israel will gather him, and keep him, as a shepherd doth his flock" (Jer. 31:10).

A New Covenant

The second half of Jeremiah 31 contains a prophecy directed to Judah and Israel — one of the most significant of all of the prophecies in Jeremiah (see a similar prophecy in Ezek. 11:19; 36:26–27). Several passages from this prophecy, according to Oliver Cowdery, were quoted or paraphrased to Joseph Smith by Moroni.[10] In Jeremiah 31:28, the Lord recounted the call of Jeremiah and noted that as the destruction had and would occur, so also would the rebuilding: "And it shall come to pass, that like as I have watched over them, to pluck up, and to break down, and to throw down, and to destroy, and to afflict; so will I watch over them, to build, and to plant, saith the Lord" (Jer. 31:28). The final answer to the destruction that comes upon Israel through the breaking of the covenant is the making of a new covenant: "Behold, the days come, saith the Lord, that I will make a new covenant with the house of Israel, and with the house of Judah: Not according to the covenant that I made with their fathers in the day that I took them by the hand to bring them out of the land of Egypt; which my covenant they brake, although I was an husband unto them, saith the Lord" (Jer. 31:31–32).

---

[9]This particular passage was quoted by Oliver Cowdery between passages of Isaiah in the *Messenger and Advocate*, Apr. 1835, p. 111. The particular passages of scripture included in Oliver Cowdery's account of Moroni's discourses to Joseph Smith in the *Messenger and Advocate* have been identified in Kent P. Jackson, "The Appearance of Moroni to Joseph Smith," in *Studies in Scripture, Volume Two: The Pearl of Great Price*, ed. Robert L. Millet and Kent P. Jackson (Salt Lake City: Randall Book, 1985), pp. 360–62.

[10]*Messenger and Advocate*, Apr. 1835, pp. 110–11. A list of these citations, as well as other latter-day commentary on these passages, can be found in Monte S. Nyman, *The Words of Jeremiah* (Salt Lake City: Bookcraft, 1982), pp. 83–95.

The fulfillment of this prophecy occurred in stages. First, in the universal sense, this prophecy was fulfilled by Christ. On the eve of his arrest, at the Last Supper, Jesus and his disciples celebrated, through the symbolism of the Passover meal, the miraculous deliverance from the bondage of Egypt and the destruction of Pharaoh's army at the Red Sea — events that are types of the Atonement, which delivers us from the bondage of sin and death. At the end of that Passover meal, when the events leading up to the covenant at Sinai were symbolized and the Passover lamb was eaten, Matthew records: "And as they were eating, Jesus took bread, and blessed it, and brake it, and gave it to the disciples, and said, Take, eat; this is my body. And he took the cup, and gave thanks, and gave it to them, saying, Drink ye all of it; For this is my blood of the new testament ['covenant'[11]], which is shed for many for the remission of sins" (Matt. 26:26–28). In the meridian of time, Christ literally fulfilled what had been symbolically celebrated through the law of sacrifice for millennia and meticulously observed through the Mosaic law for centuries. Jesus instructed his disciples that from that day forth the symbols of bread and wine would replace those of blood sacrifice as contained in the Passover. Whereas the blood sacrifice looked forward with faith and hope to the time when Christ would come and accomplish the Atonement, so the sacramental meal would look back. The symbolism of the historical event of the deliverance from Egypt and the miracle at the Red Sea was replaced by the symbolism of the historical event against which the Exodus pales in comparison: the Atonement and the conquest of sin and death. Christ, through his sacrifice, laid the foundation for the new covenant, by which men could implement the gospel in their lives, return again to God, and gain immortality and eternal life. It is from Christ's reference to "the new covenant" of Jeremiah 31:31 in Matthew 26:28 ("the new testament") that we have derived our designation of the "new covenant" as the New Testament, and thus "the old covenant" as the Old Testament.

Joseph Smith, in a letter in 1833,[12] taught that in a more specific

---

[11]The Greek word *diathēkē* is the word used throughout the Septuagint to translate Hebrew *berît*, "covenant." As an extension of the meaning "covenant," the Greek word also has the meaning of "last will and testament," which was the sense translated by the Latin *testamentum*, preserved in KJV "testament."

[12]Joseph Smith, *Teachings of the Prophet Joseph Smith*, sel. Joseph Fielding Smith (Salt Lake City: Deseret Book Co., 1938), pp. 13–18.

sense the "new covenant" was not completely fulfilled in the meridian of time: "Christ, in the days of His flesh, proposed to make a covenant with them, but they rejected Him and His proposals, and in consequence thereof, they were broken off, and no covenant was made with them at that time. But their unbelief has not rendered the promise of God of none effect: no, for there was another day limited in David, which was the day of His power; and then His people, Israel, should be a willing people;—and He would write His law in their hearts, and print it in their thoughts; their sins and their iniquities He would remember no more."[13]

Jeremiah described the nature of this new covenant in the language of the Exodus known throughout Jeremiah: "But this shall be the covenant that I will make with the house of Israel; After those days, saith the Lord, I will put my law in their inward parts, and write it in their hearts; and will be their God, and they shall be my people" (Jer. 31:33). The "heart" and "inward parts" represent an internalization of the covenant in the souls of those who accept it. Paul discussed the nature of this covenant, written "not in tables of stone, but in fleshy tables of the heart" (2 Cor. 3:3) and explained that this process of internalization can only occur through the power of the Spirit. The fulfillment of this prophecy is in process with the establishment of the new and everlasting covenant. It is "new" because, as the Lord said, "all old covenants have I caused to be done away in this thing"; and it is "everlasting" because it is "that which was from the beginning" (D&C 22:1).

Oracles against Foreign Nations (Jer. 46–51)

The book of Jeremiah contains prophecies against nine foreign nations in chapters 46 through 51.[14] These oracles, as in the other major prophets, are grouped together. They appear in no obvious chronological or geographical order: Egypt (chap. 46), Philistia (chap. 47), Moab (chap. 48), Ammon (49:1–6), Edom (49:7–22), Damascus (49:23–27), Kedar (49:28–33), Elam (49:34–39), and Babylon (chaps. 50–51). The oracles

---

[13]Ibid., pp. 14–15.
[14]For an introduction to the Oracles against Foreign Nations, see Chap. 13 of this volume.

follow closely, though not exactly, the order of cities and nations listed in the passage about the cup of wrath in Jeremiah 25:15–38.[15] They are also connected thematically with the imagery of the prophecy in that passage.[16] There the Lord told Jeremiah to "take the wine cup of this fury at my hand, and cause all the nations, to whom I send thee, to drink it. And they shall drink, and be moved, and be mad, because of the sword that I will send among them" (Jer. 25:15–16). Jeremiah took the cup and dispensed this judgment and destruction, starting with Jerusalem and then to all the nations of the world (Jer. 25:17–38). In a prophetic sense, the oracles in chapters 46 through 51 fulfill this injunction as Jeremiah pronounced the judgment of God on these nations. Although only two of the oracles have specific dates (Egypt, Jer. 46:2; Elam, Jer. 49:34), many are fulfilled in events recorded from the time just preceding and just following Nebuchadnezzar's destruction of Jerusalem in 587 B.C.

A Prophecy against Egypt (Jer. 46)

Jeremiah 46 is dated to the fourth year of Jehoiakim (605 B.C.) and consists of three poems:[17] verses 1 through 12, 13 through 24, and 27 through 28, with a short prose section in verses 25 and 26. The Lord's specific agent of destruction is Babylon (Jer. 46:2, 13, 26). The reasons cited for the destruction are the vengeance of the Lord (Jer. 46:10) and the shame of Egypt (Jer. 46:12).

The first poem, Jeremiah 46:1–12, most likely deals with the battle at Carchemish in Syria on the northern Euphrates, where the Egyptians

---

[15]The order of cities and nations in Jeremiah 25:15–38 is Egypt (v. 19); Uz (v. 20); Philistia: Ashkelon, Gaza, Ekron, and Ashdod (v. 20); Edom (v. 21); Moab (v. 21); Ammon (v. 21); Tyre, Sidon (v. 22); Arabia: Dedan, Tema, Buz (vv. 23–24); kings of Zimri (v. 25); Elam (v. 25); Medes (v. 25); Sheshak, which is Babylon (v. 26).

[16]In the Greek Septuagint the oracles that occur in chapters 46–51 of the Masoretic Text are placed after the passage about the cup of wrath in Jer. 25:13 and in a totally different order from that of the Hebrew tradition. Hebrew versions closely resembling the texts behind both the Masoretic Text and the Septuagint have been found at Qumran, suggesting that the differences are not necessarily due to the translation into Greek. For a complete discussion of this problem, see J. Gerald Janzen, *Studies in the Text of Jeremiah* (Cambridge, Mass.: Harvard University, 1973).

[17]It should be noted that the poetry in this section in particular, as well as the Oracles against Nations as a whole, is regarded by scholars as some of the best in the book of Jeremiah. See John Bright, *Jeremiah*, Anchor Bible 21 (Garden City, N.Y.: Doubleday, 1965), pp. 307–8.

led by Necho II were soundly defeated by the Babylonians led by Nebuchadnezzar in 605 B.C. This battle marked the turning point in the control of the west. With the defeat of Egypt, which was the major opposition, the way was open for Babylonian incursion and conquest. The severity of the Egyptian defeat is described in Jeremiah 46:6. "Let not the swift flee away, nor the mighty man escape; they shall stumble, and fall toward the north by the river Euphrates." That is very much like the description preserved in the Babylonian Chronicle[18] of the same event: "He [Nebuchadnezzar] defeated them (smashing) them out of existence. As for the remnant of the Egyptian army which had escaped from the defeat so (hastily) that no weapon had touched them, the Babylonian army overtook and defeated them in the district of Hamath, so that not a single man [escaped] to his own country."[19]

The second poem, Jeremiah 46:13–24, refers to the second stage of Nebuchadnezzar's advance through the west and alludes to the imminent conquest of Egypt itself (see Jer. 43:8–13 for another allusion to the conquest of Egypt). The Babylonian Chronicle records a confrontation on the Egyptian frontier sometime around 601 or 600 B.C. between Nebuchadnezzar and Necho, which ended in a stalemate.[20] According to the best sources, the Babylonian conquest of Egypt occurred in 568/7 B.C.[21]

In the prose passage of Jeremiah 46:25–26, the Lord declared that he would punish the Egyptians and their gods, kings, and all that trusted them by delivering them into the hands of the Babylonians. In a sense that is the conclusion to the great contest between the Lord God of Israel and the divine Pharaoh along with his gods and magicians that was begun at the time of Moses. In verse 26 the Lord promised eventual restoration

---

[18]The Babylonian Chronicle is a series of Neo-Babylonian tablets preserving contemporary accounts from 626 B.C., the death of Ashurbanipal, to 539 B.C., the fall of Babylon to the Persians. Unfortunately, the extant tablets cover only the years 626–22, 610–594, 556 and 555–39 B.C. The standard English edition with text, translation, and notes is D. J. Wiseman, *Chronicles of Chaldean Kings* (London: British Museum, 1961). A more popular version, with translations by Wiseman of passages relevant to Old Testament history, can be found in D. Winton Thomas, *Documents from Old Testament Times* (New York: Harper Torchbooks, 1961), pp. 75–83.

[19]Thomas, pp. 78–79; Wiseman, pp. 67–69.

[20]Wiseman, p. 71.

[21]James B. Pritchard, ed., *Ancient Near Eastern Texts Relating to the Old Testament*, 3d ed. with Supplement (Princeton, N.J.: Princeton University, 1969), p. 308.

of their nation "as in the days of old." Similar promises of restoration occur in Jeremiah 48:47 in regard to Moab, in Jeremiah 49:6 in regard to Ammon, and in Jeremiah 49:39 in regard to Elam.

The third poem, an oracle addressed to Israel in Jeremiah 46:27–28, is God's assurance that although they would be delivered into the hands of nations that would be destroyed, "I will not make a full end of thee, but correct thee in measure; yet will I not leave thee wholly unpunished" (Jer. 46:28).

Prophecies against Philistia and Moab (Jer. 47–48)

The oracle in Jeremiah 47 is directed against Philistia, Judah's long-time neighbor on the southwestern coast of Palestine. For many years, the Philistines had attempted to expand their territory by conquest of Israel. Their power had been broken by David (2 Sam. 5:17–25), but the individual city states continued. It is not specified who the human agent of God's destruction was to be, but Jeremiah 47:2 says that destruction would come from the north. It is likely that this reference indicates the Babylonians. Any invading army from the east would come to the west along the established roads, thus confronting most of the nations of Palestine from the north. No specific crimes are cited. The reference to the Phoenician cities of Tyre and Sidon in verse 4 may refer to an alliance they made with Philistia in the face of the Babylonian threat. The Babylonian destruction of Philistia for allying itself with Egypt took place in 604/3 B.C., when, according to the Babylonian Chronicle, Ashkelon fell after a long siege.[22]

The oracle against Moab in Jeremiah 48 is either one long and rather complicated poem or a series of smaller units that have been juxtaposed and in some cases linked by prose portions. It shows similarities with other oracles against Moab but most particularly with the oracle against Moab in Isaiah 15 and 16. Ever since the Exodus, Israel and Moab had been enemies (Num. 22–24). The animosity was undoubtedly heightened in 600–598 B.C. when the Moabites helped the Babylonians put down the rebellion of Jehoiakim as recorded in 2 Kings 24:2. The crimes cited

---

[22]Wiseman, p. 69.

David Rolph Seely

are pride and arrogance (Jer. 48:7, 29–30) and the Moabites' derision of Judah (Jer. 48:26–27). Also, the existence of high places is noted (Jer. 48:35) as well as the defeat and exile of the Moabite god Chemosh (Jer. 48:7, 13). The specific human agent of destruction is not cited but is likely the Babylonians: in 582 and 581, Nebuchadnezzar, in response to further rebellion, invaded Judah again and deported more of its population (Jer. 52:30). Josephus noted that Nebuchadnezzar also invaded Moab and Ammon.[23] Soon afterward, Moab was further attacked by the neighboring Arab tribes. The oracle against Moab also ends with a promise of restoration (Jer. 48:47).

Prophecies against Ammon, Edom, and Other Nations (Jer. 49)

There had been a longstanding dispute between Israel and Ammon over the territory of Gilead, which was claimed by Israel after defeating Sihon and Og and had been a point of contention ever since the time of Jephthah (Judg. 11) and Saul (1 Sam. 11). The human agent is not specified, and the crime of arrogance may be referred to in Jeremiah 49:4. The exile of the Ammonite god Milkom is also probably mentioned in Jeremiah 49:3 (Hebrew, *malkām*; KJV "their king" is usually read by modern translations as "Milkom"). The fulfillment of this prophecy presumably occurred along with the fulfillment of the prophecy against her neighbor Moab. Restoration is also promised to Ammon in Jeremiah 49:6.

The oracle against Edom in Jeremiah 49:7–22 shows similarities to the oracle against Edom in Obadiah. No human agent is specified, and the crime cited is pride (Jer. 49:16). As demonstrated in Ezekiel 25:12–14, Psalm 137:7, and Obadiah, Edom fully cooperated with the Babylonians against Judah. Edom was finally destroyed near the end of the sixth century B.C. by incursions of Arab tribes.

In the oracle against Damascus in Jeremiah 49:23–27, the human agent is specified as Babylon, but no specific crime is mentioned. The historical fulfillment is problematic. If it was spoken early in Jeremiah's

---

[23]*Antiquities* 10.9.7; see Flavius Josephus, *Jewish Antiquities*, The Loeb Classical Library, trans. Ralph Marcus (Cambridge, Mass.: Harvard University, 1978), 6:257–61.

career, this prophecy could have had fulfillment in 605 B.C. at the Battle of Carchemish, when Egypt was defeated in this region, which would have spelled doom for the cities in the area. It is recorded that Syrian troops assisted the Babylonians against Jehoiakim's revolt sometime around 600 B.C. (2 Kgs. 24:2–4).

Kedar and Hazor are discussed next (Jer. 49:28–33). Kedar is an area east of Ammon and Moab in the Arabian desert. Babylon is mentioned as the human agent of destruction. Although many of the tribes may have been wanderers, there are also indications that the Kedarites lived in villages (Gen. 25:13–16; Isa. 42:11), one of which must have been called Hazor. The fulfillment may be seen in the Babylonian Chronicle, which records that in 599/8 B.C. the Babylonians "scouring the desert . . . took much plunder from the Arabs, their possessions, animals and gods."[24]

An oracle against Elam concludes Jeremiah 49 (vv. 34–39). Elam was a state to the east of Babylon, in present-day Iran. This oracle's general date is the beginning of the reign of Zedekiah. No human agent is cited, and no specific crime is mentioned. A reconstruction of a fragmented portion of the Babylonian Chronicle[25] may allude to an invasion of Nebuchadnezzar in 596/5 B.C., which could be a fulfillment of this oracle. A future restoration is promised (Jer. 49:39).

A Prophecy against Babylon (Jer. 50–51)

Throughout Jeremiah, Babylon is portrayed as the instrument in the hand of the Lord, the cup of wrath in his hand by which he has dispensed judgment. But Babylon too would be punished for her crimes. As in the oracle against Egypt, the vengeance of the Lord is cited (Jer. 50:15), and here the list of crimes includes the capture of Judah (Jer. 50:17; 51:49), the destruction of the temple (Jer. 50:28), and the Exile (Jer. 50:33). The defeat and destruction of their false gods and images (Bel and Marduk) is mentioned (Jer. 50:2; 51:44, 47, 52). The historical fulfillment of this prophecy occurred in 539 by Cyrus and the Persians.

---

[24]Wiseman, p. 71.
[25]Wiseman, p. 72.

The city itself was captured but not destroyed by the Persians, nor later yet by Alexander the Great. Babylon's demise was gradual. During the Hellenistic period a city named Seleucia was built nearby, and most of the population moved there. The city of Babylon eventually disappeared. And true to Jeremiah's prediction (Jer. 50:38–40), it remained for many centuries desolate and uninhabited. Its spiritual namesake, Babylon as the world, on the other hand, has grown and prospered throughout the ages.

The destruction of spiritual Babylon — the world — still remains to be fulfilled, making this prophecy a timely one. Much of the imagery of this oracle occurs throughout the book of Revelation. Jeremiah described Babylon: "O thou that dwellest upon many waters, abundant in treasures, thine end is come, and the measure of thy covetousness" (Jer. 51:13). The angel showed John the Revelator a woman as a "great whore that sitteth upon many waters" (Rev. 17:1) and defined the waters as the "peoples, and multitudes, and nations, and tongues" (Rev. 17:15) and the woman as "that great city, which reigneth over the kings of the earth" (Rev. 17:18). Just as in Jeremiah's day "Babylon hath been a golden cup in the Lord's hand, that made all the earth drunken" (Jer. 51:7), so Babylon the harlot in Revelation 17:4 holds in her hand a golden cup "full of abominations and filthiness of her fornication." In the latter days the Lord once again used this image of the destructive influence of Babylon as "the same which has made all nations drink of the wine of the wrath of her fornication" (D&C 35:11; see also 86:3).

The short prose ending records that Jeremiah sent a copy of this oracle to Babylon with Seraiah, a court official and probably the brother of Baruch, since they are both the sons of Neriah (Jer. 51:59–64). In Babylon Seraiah was to read these words, bind a stone to the book, and throw them into the Euphrates, reciting these words of the Lord: "Thus shall Babylon sink, and shall not rise from the evil that I will bring upon her" (Jer. 51:64). Likewise the angel in the book of Revelation, symbolic of the end of the world, "took up a stone like a great millstone, and cast it into the sea, saying, Thus with violence shall that great city Babylon be thrown down, and shall be found no more at all" (Rev. 18:21).

The history of the covenant people now has gone full cycle: from Babel to Babel, Babylon to Babylon. And the Exile — the end of the story in Jeremiah 52 — aptly provides the setting for a new beginning. As the

Lord commanded the patriarch Abraham to leave his land, Ur of the Chaldees, so the Lord at the time of Jeremiah commanded his people to flee Babylon, the land of the Chaldeans: "My people, go ye out of the midst of her, and deliver ye every man his soul from the fierce anger of the Lord" (Jer. 51:45). Their destination is the promised land, a land given by covenant. This same commandment has been given in the latter days — as part of the new and everlasting covenant — to us who are born into the world. And the promised land, by covenant, is Zion. The Lord has commanded: "Go ye out from Babylon. Be ye clean that bear the vessels of the Lord" and "flee unto Zion" (D&C 133:5, 12). "For verily I say, tomorrow all the proud and they that do wickedly shall be as stubble; and I will burn them up, for I am the Lord of Hosts; and I will not spare any that remain in Babylon" (D&C 64:24).

23
LAMENTATIONS

Jo Ann H. Seely

The lament, an ancient poetic form found in Sumerian, Akkadian, and Egyptian traditions, records defeat or loss. In the Sumerian laments over ruined cities, the patron god of the city is overwhelmed by other gods and the residents are left helpless.[1] Judah's lament in Lamentations delineates the desolation of the city of Jerusalem, but it reminds its readers that the Lord still reigns. This is a case not of foreign gods overpowering a weaker deity but of the Lord chastening his own people. Lamentations is Judah's response to the whys of their misery and destruction. Why must we suffer? Why is the Lord turned against us? Why must we wait for deliverance? Why must Israel be in captivity? Why is Zion destroyed? It is a painful explanation to the elect people of how and why they have fallen.

The name "Lamentations" comes from the Greek *thrēnoi*, translated from the Hebrew *qînōt*, meaning "laments." In the Hebrew Bible the book of Lamentations is called *'êkâ* — "How?" — following the practice of using the first word of a book for its title. In English translations the title is often expanded, as it is in the Greek Septuagint and the Latin Vulgate, to ascribe authorship to Jeremiah. The historical accuracy and intensity with which the author wrote concerning the destruction of Jerusalem and the absence of details concerning the end of the Exile suggest that the composition of Lamentations was sometime between the fall of Judah in 587 B.C. and the return from exile in 538 B.C. The

---

Jo Ann H. Seely is a part-time instructor in ancient scripture at Brigham Young University.

[1]Samuel Noah Kramer, trans., "Lamentation over the Destruction of Ur" and "Lamentation over the Destruction of Sumer and Ur," in *Ancient Near Eastern Texts Relating to the Old Testament*, ed. James B. Pritchard (Princeton: Princeton University, 1969), pp. 455–63, 611–19.

descriptions are vivid, as an eyewitness account would be. Many have suggested that Jeremiah wrote Lamentations (as the title reflects), because he fits all the requirements and is known to have written other laments (2 Chron. 35:25).[2]

Lamentations is written in acrostics, that is, it is organized by starting each stanza or line with a successive letter of the Hebrew alphabet—a feature unfortunately lost in translation.[3] The acrostic form does not distract from the beauty of the poems but adds a sense of completeness, as if the poet had covered all that needed to be said from beginning to end.[4]

There Is No Comfort for Zion (Lam. 1–2)

The initial word "how" of three of the poems in Lamentations poses unanswerable questions and expresses the utter inability of the poet to articulate the agonies that had befallen Jerusalem: "How doth the city sit solitary . . . how is she become as a widow! . . . how is she become tributary!" (Lam. 1:1). It expresses the afflicted's disbelief: "How hath the Lord covered the daughter of Zion with a cloud in his anger" (Lam. 2:1). In chapter 1 the poet personifies the city of Zion as a widow, a pitiful woman in pain. As frequently noted in the Bible, widows are the symbol of the distressed and disenfranchised element of society who are bereft of protectors. Israel the bride of the Lord has now become a widow, as the Lord has withdrawn and even become her afflicter (Lam. 1:5). Once

---

[2]Lamentations is one of the Megillot—five short scrolls read at different Jewish festivals. It is read on the ninth of Ab, commemorating the destruction of the temple. See Delbert R. Hillers, *Lamentations*, Anchor Bible 7A (Garden City, N.Y.: Doubleday, 1982), pp. xl–xli, for comments concerning liturgical use of Lamentations. Christian Bibles follow the Septuagint and the Vulgate in placing it after Jeremiah.

[3]In Lam. 1, 2, and 4, the first word in each successive stanza begins with the successive letter in the Hebrew alphabet. In Lam. 3 each line within the stanza begins with the same letter. Lam. 5 is the exception in that it has twenty-two lines but the initial word of each line is not in alphabetical order—an "alphabetless acrostic."

[4]Most of the lines are written in bicola with three stresses in the first colon and two in the second, producing a lamenting or "qinah" meter. The "qinah" meter gives a falling sense to Lamentations, distinguishing it from other Hebrew poetry and adding to the mood of the poems. See Hillers, pp. xxx–xxxvii, for discussion of Budde's discovery of "qinah" meter ("Das hebräische Klagelied," *Zeitschrift für die alttestamentliche Wissenschaft* 2 [1882]: 1–52) and a survey of other theories concerning Hebrew meter.

great among the nations, Zion now sits alone weeping. She has been deserted by all her lovers, friends, and the Lord: "There is none to comfort her" (Lam. 1:17). This theme is repeated throughout the lament (Lam. 1:2, 9, 16, 17, 21): her streets are empty during the appointed feasts (Lam. 1:4), and "her children are gone into captivity" (Lam. 1:5). Zion the weeping woman is a tragic figure; even death would bring her solace.

How will Judah preserve faith in God when they have been conquered? The Lord has not been defeated by the gods of Babylon; rather, it was the Lord who destroyed Jerusalem. Lamentations 2:1–9a delineates in detail the destruction caused by the Lord: leveled strongholds (vv. 2, 5); ruined temple, altar, and holy places (vv. 6–7); razed walls and gates (vv. 8, 9a). Verse 14 suggests the cause of this calamity: "Thy prophets have seen vain and foolish things for thee: they have not discovered thine iniquity, to turn away thy captivity, but have seen for thee false burdens and causes of banishment." The people have caused their own plight through their disobedience and through listening to pleasing but false prophets. The destruction was in fulfillment of prophecy: "The Lord hath done that which he had devised; he hath fulfilled his word that he had commanded in the days of old: he hath thrown down, and hath not pitied: and he hath caused thine enemy to rejoice over thee" (Lam. 2:17). Israel has seen the fruition of her works; the curses of the covenant have been confirmed (see Deut. 28:15–68).

A Personal Lament and Prayer (Lam. 3)

Lamentations is not only a personification but a personalization of the suffering the poet is trying to convey. It is a first-person experience of a survivor. We can feel with him and with what he has endured. In Lamentations 3, between his laments in chapters 1 and 2 and 4 and 5, the poet has placed his message. The Lord "doth not afflict willingly nor grieve the children of men" (Lam. 3:33); "though he cause grief, yet will he have compassion according to the multitude of his mercies" (Lam. 3:32). The poem moves from the personal lament of the first verses to the expression of hope for society.

"This I recall to my mind, therefore have I hope," wrote the man of sorrow (Lam. 3:21). Hope emerges when one recognizes that the Lord will not only fulfill what he has "devised" but also bring to pass what he promised long ago. The Lord promised Abraham: "I will make nations of thee" (Gen. 17:6); "I will give unto thee . . . all the land of Canaan, for an everlasting possession" (Gen. 17:8); and "in thee shall all families of the earth be blessed" (Gen. 12:3). Covenant Israel will not be forgotten, but they must be patient. "It is of the Lord's mercies that we are not consumed, because his compassions fail not" (Lam. 3:22). And in that compassion, he has offered them the opportunity for repentance. "It is good that a man should both hope and quietly wait for the salvation of the Lord" (Lam. 3:26). Zion has felt the depths of despair, but she will yet see the salvation of her Savior.

The final verses of chapter 3 contain a familiar prayer—calling out from the "low dungeon" (v. 55), reminiscent of Jonah calling from the belly of the fish (Jonah 2:1–10) or the psalmist calling from the pit of hell for salvation (Ps. 18:5, 6; 88:3–12). The Lord responds, "Fear not" (Lam. 3:57), and the supplication continues that he be Israel's redeemer and judge. "O Lord, thou hast pleaded the causes of my soul; thou hast redeemed my life. O Lord, thou hast seen my wrong: judge thou my cause" (Lam. 3:58–59).

The Suffering of Zion's People (Lam. 4–5)

In the fourth chapter of Lamentations, the "dominant figure of speech is comparison,"[5] illuminating the disparity between past and present. The precious sons of Zion who were once fine gold are now earthen pitchers (Lam. 4:2), the rich are heaped on dunghills (Lam. 4:5), and Nazarites whiter than milk now are blacker than coal (Lam. 4:7, 8). The severity of Israel's punishment is worse than that of Sodom: "For the punishment of the iniquity of the daughter of my people is greater than the punishment of the sin of Sodom, that was overthrown as in a moment and no hand stayed on her" (Lam. 4:6). Israel must endure misery and captivity to atone for her sins.

A vivid image concerns the prophets and priests—symbols of Judah's

---

[5]Francis Landy, "Lamentations," in *The Literary Guide to the Bible*, ed. Robert Alter and Frank Kermode (Cambridge, Mass.: Harvard University, 1987), p. 332. Landy gives a literary analysis of the book of Lamentations.

uniqueness. Prophets, the champions of the poor, "have shed the blood of the just" (Lam. 4:13). Priests, the guardians of purity and cleanliness, are unclean and wandering to derisive shouts of defilement (Lam. 4:15). The picture is completed in verse 20 with the king—"the breath of our nostrils, the anointed of the Lord"—taken and cast into the pits of the enemy.

The final lament (chap. 5) begins with an appeal: "Remember O Lord what is come upon us" (Lam. 5:1), followed by a recitation of the terrible state of Zion. They are as orphans, widows, and servants; they suffer hunger, the women are ravished, the princes are hanged. "The crown is fallen from our head: woe unto us, that we have sinned!" (Lam. 5:16). Judah has brought tribulation upon herself; she has lost the blessings of the Lord's elect people. The poem concludes with an entreaty to the Lord: "Turn thou us unto thee, O Lord, and we shall be turned; renew our days as of old" (Lam. 5:21). The poet recognized that Judah was dependent upon the Lord's mercy to repent and regain her status.

Through painful images and poignant words, the book of Lamentations poetically expresses the grief of a people in a sorrowful state. The woeful account recalls in different voices the various aspects of what has occurred. The grisly details of the terrible destruction of Jerusalem and the fate of the king, prophets, priests, and people are recorded. Lamentations illuminates the relationship of the Lord with his people. "And I myself will fight against you with an outstretched hand and with a strong arm, even in anger, and in fury, and in great wrath" (Jer. 21:5). The Lord's hand in the devastation is a reminder of disobedience and the need for repentance.

The children of Zion must have faith that as they have experienced justice and destruction, so they will also experience mercy and restoration. The Lord has not forsaken his children but has given them the chance to return: "I will make a new covenant with the house of Israel, and with the house of Judah. . . . I will forgive their iniquity, and I will remember their sin no more" (Jer. 31:31, 34). The poet concluded: "Wherefore dost thou forget us for ever, and forsake us so long time?" (Lam. 5:20). Judah must believe that their defeat is a sign that the Lord has not forgotten them; now their faith is required to remember him: "Let us search and try our ways, and turn again to the Lord. Let us lift up our heart with our hand unto God in the heavens" (Lam. 3:40–41).

24

OLD TESTAMENT PROPHETS IN THE BOOK OF MORMON

(Lehi, Zenock, Neum, Zenos, Ezias)

Terry B. Ball

As a preface to a revelation in 1832, the Prophet Joseph Smith recorded, "From sundry revelations which had been received, it was apparent that many important points touching the salvation of man had been taken from the Bible, or lost before it was compiled."[1] Nearly two and one-half millennia earlier an angel of the Lord bore similar witness. This messenger from God explained to the prophet Nephi that the covenants and prophecies that would be contained in the latter-day Bible would be fewer than those then available on the plates of brass to the Book of Mormon peoples (1 Ne. 13:23). The angel further warned that there would be those who, in order to "pervert the right ways of the Lord," would take away from the Bible "many parts which are plain and most precious; and also many covenants of the Lord" (1 Ne. 13:26–27).[2]

Although the amount of scripture missing or removed from the Bible cannot be known, the Book of Mormon is helpful in restoring the names and some teachings of several prophets whose writings have not been preserved in the Old Testament. These prophets include Lehi, Zenock, Neum, Zenos, and Ezias. All of these deserve recognition as Old Testament prophets. They prophesied in Old Testament lands, during Old

---

Terry B. Ball is assistant professor of ancient scripture at Brigham Young University.

[1]Joseph Smith, *History of The Church of Jesus Christ of Latter-day Saints*, 7 vols., 2d ed. rev., edited by B. H. Roberts (Salt Lake City: Deseret Book Co., 1957), 1:245.

[2]For more discussion on missing scripture, see Robert A. Cloward, "Lost Scripture," in *The Encyclopedia of Mormonism*, ed. Daniel H. Ludlow (New York: Macmillan, 1992), pp. 845–46.

Testament times, to Old Testament peoples, and about Old Testament themes, especially the Messiah and his covenant people.

Lehi

Lehi is the first of these prophets to be mentioned in the Book of Mormon. In an abridgment of his father's record, Nephi wrote that around 600 B.C. "many prophets" came to warn of the impending destruction that awaited the people of Jerusalem if they did not repent (1 Ne. 1:4). The Old Testament indicates that among these prophets were men such as Jeremiah (e.g., Jer. 5–9), Zephaniah (Zeph. 1:3–6), and Habakkuk (Hab. 1:5–9).

The warnings of the prophets moved Lehi to fervent prayer on behalf of the people. His petition was answered with a powerful revelation in which "there came a pillar of fire and dwelt upon a rock before him; and he saw and heard much" (1 Ne. 1:5–6). In a subsequent vision, Lehi "saw God sitting upon his throne," and was given a prophetic book by "one" who had descended "out of the midst of heaven" and whose "luster was above that of the sun at noon-day" (1 Ne. 1:8–11). The message of the book echoed the warnings of the prophets that Lehi had heard: "And he read, saying: Wo, Wo, unto Jerusalem, for I have seen thine abominations! Yea, and many things did my father read concerning Jerusalem—that it should be destroyed, and the inhabitants thereof; many should perish by the sword, and many should be carried away captive into Babylon" (1 Ne. 1:13).

After receiving the vision, Lehi "went forth among the people, and began to prophesy and to declare unto them concerning the things which he had both seen and heard" (1 Ne. 1:18). Like his contemporaries, Lehi testified of the destruction of Jerusalem, the wickedness of the people, and of the coming of the Messiah to redeem the world. Lehi's message of doom was likely a threat to the tenuous morale and political stability of the time, and the people resented being reminded of their iniquities.[3] Consequently, the Jews responded to Lehi as they did to other prophets

---

[3]As was the case with his contemporary, Jeremiah (Jer. 38:2–4). See also Hugh Nibley, *Since Cumorah,* 2d ed. (Salt Lake City: Deseret Book Co. and the Foundation for Ancient Research and Mormon Studies, 1988), pp. 276–77.

of his time. They "did mock him because of the things which he testified of them," and they "sought his life, that they might take it away" (1 Ne. 1:19, 20).

Lehi's tenure as a prophet in Judah proved to be short lived. Before the people could harm him, he was instructed by the Lord to "take his family and depart into the wilderness," eventually to be led to the new promised land on the American continent (1 Ne. 2:2).[4]

Zenock, Neum, Zenos, and Ezias

While listing prophets who had testified of the Messiah, Nephi introduced the names of three other pre-Exilic prophets: Zenock, Neum, and Zenos (1 Ne. 19:10). Later, Nephi, son of Helaman, added the name of Ezias to the list (Hel. 8:20). Although these prophets are not mentioned in the Bible, their teachings and prophecies were apparently included on the plates of brass (1 Ne. 19:21).

The number of years by which these men predated Lehi cannot be determined. Nephi, son of Helaman, listed Zenock, Zenos, and Ezias as prophets who had testified since the days of Abraham (ca. 1900 B.C.), but he also spoke of prophets who foretold of Christ "a great many thousand years before his coming" (Hel. 8:19–20). Mormon seems to imply that Zenock and Zenos were both descendants of Joseph and ancestors to the Book of Mormon peoples, which would place them later than ca. 1600 B.C. (3 Ne. 10:16–17).

The prophecies of these men are, for the most part, reported in plain and simple language, more resembling the Book of Mormon prophets than the biblical prophets, who preferred to couch their messages in poetic imagery.[5] Whether Zenock, Neum, Zenos, and Ezias themselves actually delivered their messages in such plain language, or their teachings

---

[4]For more on Lehi's ministry, see S. Kent Brown, "Lehi's Personal Record: Quest for a Missing Source," *BYU Studies*, Winter 1984, pp. 19–42; and chaps. 3, 4, 6, 8, and 9 in Kent P. Jackson, ed., *Studies in Scripture, Volume Seven: 1 Nephi to Alma 29* (Salt Lake City: Deseret Book Co., 1987).

[5]The "Allegory" and "Thanksgiving Hymn" of Zenos being notable exceptions (Jacob 5; Alma 33:3–15). In these passages, Zenos used typology and poetic style very similar to those of other biblical prophets.

were interpreted into simpler rhetoric by the Book of Mormon authors who cited them, cannot be ascertained.

Zenock

The teachings of Zenock are referred to five times in the Book of Mormon. In each case, his message centers on the Messiah. Zenock taught that the Son of God would come to redeem his people (Alma 34:7; Hel. 8:18–20). He spoke of the Lord's anger with the covenant people for their refusal to understand the mercies which had been bestowed upon them because of the Son (Alma 33:14–17). He prophesied that the Savior would be crucified (1 Ne. 19:10) and that great destruction would accompany his death (3 Ne. 10:14–16). Both Mormon and Nephi, son of Helaman, mentioned that Zenock was martyred. Alma explained why and how to the Zoramites: "Because the people would not understand his words they stoned him to death" (Alma 33:17).

Neum

Neum, also a messianic prophet, finds mention only once in the Book of Mormon. As Nephi reviewed the teachings of prophets who foretold the mission and message of the Messiah, he explained that the Savior would come "to be crucified, according to the words of Neum" (1 Ne. 19:10). Thus Neum deserves to be classified with the prophets Jacob referred to when he taught that all the holy prophets which were before the Nephites knew of Christ and "had a hope of his glory" (Jacob 4:4).

Zenos

Elder Bruce R. McConkie called Zenos "one of the greatest prophets in Israel."[6] Support for Elder McConkie's statement can be found in the fact that next to Isaiah, Zenos is the most quoted Old Testament prophet in the Book of Mormon. In addition to several brief references, there are two long quotations of Zenos' teachings found in the Nephite text.

In an effort to help his brethren understand the responsibility and

---

[6]Bruce R. McConkie, A New Witness for the Articles of Faith (Salt Lake City: Deseret Book Co., 1986), p. 588. See also "The Doctrinal Restoration," in The Joseph Smith Translation: The Restoration of Plain and Precious Things, ed. M. S. Nyman and R. L. Millet (Provo, Utah: Religious Studies Center, Brigham Young University, 1985), p. 17.

future of the covenant people, the prophet Jacob quoted what is often referred to as Zenos' allegory of the olive tree (Jacob 5). Constituting the longest single chapter in the Book of Mormon,[7] this allegory chronicles the apostasy of Israel, the subsequent scattering, the Gentiles' adoption into the covenant people, the latter-day gathering of Israel, the millennial reign of the Messiah, and the end of the mortal world.[8] The second longest quotation from Zenos was offered by Alma as he taught the more humble Zoramites about when and where to pray (Alma 33:3–15). In this passage Zenos used poetic style reminiscent of the biblical psalmist to praise God for hearing his prayers wherever and whenever he cried unto him in "afflictions" and "sincerity." He further rejoiced in the mercy and protection that the answers to those prayers afforded him and the recognition that judgment had been turned away from him because of the Son of God (see also Alma 34:7).

In addition to these lengthy quotations, Nephi, son of Lehi, referred to Zenos' prophecies concerning the burial of the Messiah in a sepulchre and the three days of darkness that would accompany his death (1 Ne. 19:10–17). Mormon wrote to remind future Book of Mormon readers that Zenos had also prophesied of the destruction that took place on the earth at the death of the Savior (3 Ne. 10:14–17). Nephi, son of Helaman, listed Zenos as yet another Old Testament prophet who was slain for his testimony of the coming Messiah (Hel. 8:19).

Ezias

Like Neum, the teachings of the prophet Ezias are referred to only once in the Book of Mormon. Little can be known of his life, but Nephi, son of Helaman, taught that the message of Ezias was like that of other prophets who foretold the Savior's coming "that even redemption should come unto them" (Hel. 8:18–20).

---

[7]Daniel H. Ludlow, "Zenos," in Ludlow, *Encyclopedia of Mormonism*, pp. 1623–24.

[8]See Kent P. Jackson, "Nourished by the Good Word of God," in Jackson, *Studies in Scripture, Volume Seven*, pp. 186–95; Paul Y. Hoskisson, "Explicating the Mystery of the Rejected Foundation Stone: The Allegory of the Olive Tree," *BYU Studies*, Summer 1990, pp. 77–87. See also L. Gary Lambert, "The Allegory of Zenos," in Ludlow, *Encyclopedia of Mormonism*, pp. 31–32.

Recognition

Nephi son of Lehi was instructed by an angel that in the latter days the Book of Mormon would help establish the truth of the biblical books "and shall make known the plain and precious things which have been taken away from them; and shall make known to all kindreds, tongues, and people, that the Lamb of God is the Son of the Eternal Father, and the Savior of the world; and that all men must come unto him, or they cannot be saved" (1 Ne. 13:40). The prophecies of Lehi, Zenock, Neum, Zenos, and Ezias preserved in the Book of Mormon help accomplish its divine mission. For their teachings to the Old Testament peoples and their willingness to surrender their lives to and for the Messiah and his covenant people, each of these men deserves recognition among the great Old Testament prophets.

25

THE BOOK OF OBADIAH

DARRELL L. MATTHEWS

The book of Obadiah is the shortest book of the Old Testament. It consists of one chapter of only twenty-one verses. The greater part of the book is a warning to Edom that the wrath of God will come upon its people for their participation in destroying Jerusalem. Much about the book remains uncertain. We do not possess any biographical information about the prophet Obadiah, and there is no clear historical information on exactly when to date the book. And because the name *Obadiah* itself means "servant of the Lord," some have suggested that it is a title instead of a name. Since other individuals with this name are attested in the Bible, however, there is no reason to reject it as the prophet's actual name.

The date of the book has also been debated, with proposals ranging from 850 B.C. to about 200 B.C. The main criteria for dating this book are the mention of the destruction of Jerusalem and the similarity of several verses to passages in Jeremiah.[1] Undoubtedly the destruction mentioned is the 587 B.C. fall of Jerusalem at the hands of the Babylonians during the time of King Zedekiah and the prophet Jeremiah. There is no mention of the Exile in Babylonia.

A few verses in this book have close parallels in the book of Jeremiah. If this book was written soon after the destruction of Jerusalem, Obadiah and Jeremiah would have been contemporary prophets and likely would have known each other. We know from the Book of Mormon that there

Darrell L. Matthews is a librarian at the Eisenhower Library at Johns Hopkins University.
[1]Compare Obad. 1:1–4 with Jer. 49:14–16, and Obad. 1:5–6 with Jer. 49:9–10.

were many prophets during the time immediately preceding the fall of Jerusalem (1 Ne. 1:4), one of whom was Lehi.[2]

As already mentioned, Obadiah's vision consists mainly of a warning to the Edomites on account of their participation in the destruction of Jerusalem. The Edomites were neighbors to Judah and lived in the area south of the Dead Sea. We are told that they were the descendants of Esau, the brother of Jacob (Gen. 36:1; 1 Chron. 1:35–43) and were therefore blood relatives of the Israelites. During the early part of Israel's existence, it appears that there were peaceful relations between the two nations, but with time hostilities developed, especially after David and his army attacked Edom (2 Sam. 8:13–14).

In Obadiah's revelation, the Edomites were told that they were "greatly despised" (Obad. 1:2). In their pride they believed that they were secure and that no one would harm them. This false security was about to end. In verse 5 we learn that their destruction would be complete. They were told that if a robber were to come he would only take until he had enough. If the grapegatherers came, they would always leave a few grapes for the poor. But when the judgment of the Lord comes it will be complete, and nothing of the Edomites would remain to be salvaged. By the second century B.C. there was no longer an Edomite state.

Beginning in verse 10 we are told why this judgment would come upon Edom. They had betrayed their brothers of the house of Israel and thus would "be cut off for ever." Apparently they had assisted the Babylonians in carrying away the captives of Jerusalem and destroying the city. The authors of Psalm 137 and Lamentations both wrote about the involvement of the Edomites in the downfall of Jerusalem (Ps. 137:7; Lam. 4:21–22). Verses 12 through 14 of Obadiah contain the Lord's witness against the Edomites. We are told that they had rejoiced over their brother Judah's destruction and took great pride in their participation. Even worse, they attacked those who tried to escape. As the Lord stated: "Neither shouldest thou have stood in the crossway, to cut off those of his that did escape; neither shouldest thou have delivered up those of his that did remain in the day of distress" (Obad. 1:14).

---

[2]It is likely that Jeremiah, Lehi, Obadiah, Nahum, Habakkuk, Zephaniah, and Huldah (2 Kgs. 22:11–20) were all contemporary prophets.

God's judgment would be decisive. The Edomites would be treated as they treated Judah. They would be destroyed and carried captive. The Lord said, "Thy reward shall return upon thine own head" (Obad. 1:15).

The last five verses of Obadiah prophesy that the house of Israel will once again prevail and gain possession of the land of its inheritance. It will be as if the house of Jacob were a fire and Esau were stubble. Esau would be burned, and Jacob would be restored to its possession (Obad. 1:18–20). Deliverance will be in Zion (Obad. 1:17), where a righteous remnant[3] "shall come up on mount Zion to judge the mount of Esau." And "the kingdom shall be the Lord's" (Obad. 1:21).

From this book we learn important lessons. Among the most significant is that pride is a destructive element that should be eliminated from our lives. President Ezra Taft Benson emphasized that truth.[4] Pride leads to the destruction and downfall of nations, as both the Bible and the Book of Mormon testify. The Edomites were an example of this.

God watches over his people and will avenge them of their wrongs. That does not mean that his people will not have trials and problems; in fact, it often seems to mean the opposite. But in the Lord's justice — and in his due time — all will receive what they deserve, whether good or bad, and God's plan will prevail.

---

[3]The intention of the difficult Hebrew word here, translated "saviours" in the KJV, is not clear. Some translations follow the ancient Greek Septuagint (3d century B.C.) and read it as a passive participle, "saved ones," i.e., *mûšā'îm*, which seems to make good sense in this context. But "saviors" (or "deliverers") also works well, since those who are saved out of the world then have the calling to stand as deliverers for others. Joseph Smith used the term "saviors on Mount Zion," though not in the context of Obadiah, to refer to "the remnant which was left"—"the 'ministers of our God' "—who would in turn bless the lives of others; Andrew F. Ehat and Lyndon W. Cook, *The Words of Joseph Smith* (Provo, Utah: Religious Studies Center, Brigham Young University, 1980), pp. 73–74. Later he used the term consistently with specific reference to proxy work for the dead; ibid., pp. 77, 318, and 368; see also *Teachings of the Prophet Joseph Smith*, sel. Joseph Fielding Smith (Salt Lake City: Deseret Book Co., 1938), p. 223.

[4]Ezra Taft Benson, "Beware of Pride," *Ensign*, May 1989, pp. 4–6.

26

A WATCHMAN TO THE HOUSE OF ISRAEL

(EZEKIEL 1–24)

STEPHEN D. RICKS

No themes so thoroughly pervade the writings of the prophets as judgment and hope. Of the sixteen canonical "writing prophets," ten — Amos, Hosea, Micah, Isaiah, Zephaniah, Jeremiah, Obadiah, Ezekiel, Zechariah, and Joel — wrote about Israel's punishment and exile as well as future hopes of return. Without exception, each of these prophets who wrote in the pre-Exilic period reflected on Israel's exile. Among the Exilic and post-Exilic prophets — Jeremiah, Obadiah, Ezekiel, Zechariah, and Joel — the "scattering of Israel" was already an accomplished fact. Thus, if their works contain no explicit mention of Israel's exile, that is doubtless because it was presupposed by them. Unlike the Exilic and post-Exilic prophets Obadiah, Zechariah, and Joel, none of whom explicitly commented on the fact of the Exile, Ezekiel frequently reflected on the causes of the Exile and on Israel's future hope (Ezek. 1–24, e.g., 6:8–10; 11:16–21; 12:15–16). Indeed, the entire book of Ezekiel hinges on these two themes, and the book as a whole is divided, roughly speaking, between prophecies of judgment (1–24) and prophecies of Israel's future hope (25–48).

Unlike the two other major "writing prophets," Isaiah and Jeremiah, nothing is recorded about Ezekiel in the historical writings that have been preserved in the Old Testament (Kings and Chronicles), but few prophets have been more highly personal in their writings than Ezekiel. According to Ezekiel's own record, he was descended from priestly lines

---

Stephen D. Ricks is professor of Hebrew and Semitic languages at Brigham Young University.

and was the son of Buzi, who is otherwise unknown (Ezek. 1:3), was born in the kingdom of Judah in the seventh century B.C., was taken by Nebuchadnezzar into exile with King Jehoiachin in 597 B.C., and was active in his prophetic calling in captivity in Babylon. If he was already functioning as a priest before being taken into Babylon as a captive, he must have been at least thirty years old at the time. Ezekiel's prophecies in chapters 1 through 24 reflect deeply on the theological implications of the Exile as well as on the religious situation of those who remained in Judah and Jerusalem. Following is an outline of the book of Ezekiel:

    I.   1–3 Ezekiel's Prophetic Call
   II.   4–24 Prophecies against Disobedient Judah and Jerusalem
 III.   25–32 Prophecies against Foreign Nations
 IV.   33–37 Restoration
  V.   38–39 Gog and Israel
 VI.   40–48 A New Jerusalem and a New Temple

Ezekiel's Vision, Prophetic Call, and Commission (Ezek. 1–3)

Ezekiel 1 through 3 contains an account of Ezekiel's call to be a prophet. Like the commissions of many of the prophets in scripture and in noncanonical writings (e.g., the Pseudepigrapha, Jewish writings dating primarily from the period between the two testaments), Ezekiel 1 through 3 contains a record of a remarkable "throne-theophany" vision of the heavenly realms, as well as several other regularly recurring features: a historical introduction, a divine confrontation, the reaction, the throne-theophany, the prophetic commission, divine reassurance, and the conclusion of the call. The prophetic call of Ezekiel in chapters 1 through 3 shows particularly close parallels to the calls of Lehi in 1 Nephi 1 and 2 and of Isaiah in Isaiah 6 and will be considered in conjunction with them. This call pattern may be schematized as follows (in the interest of space, only the examples from Ezekiel will be cited in the discussion):

	Ezek. 1–3	Isa. 6	1 Ne. 1–2
1. Historical Introduction	1:1–3	6:1a	1:4
2. Divine Confrontation	1:4–28a	6:1b–4	1:6a
3. Reaction	1:28b	6:5	1:6b–7
4. Throne-Theophany	1:20–26a	6:1b–4	1:8
5. Commission	2:3–8	6:9–10	2:1
6. Reassurance	2:9–3:2	6:6–7	
7. Conclusion	3:22–27	6:11b–13b	1:18–20[1]

1. The "historical introduction" usually contains short introductory remarks providing such background details as the time, place, and historical setting of the prophetic call. The "historical introduction" to Ezekiel's call provides not merely the year, but also the day and month of the vision: "Now it came to pass in the thirtieth year, in the fourth month, in the fifth day of the month, as I was among the captives by the river Chebar, that the heavens were opened, and I saw visions of God. In the fifth day of the month, which was the fifth year of king Jehoiachin's captivity, the word of the Lord came expressly unto Ezekiel the priest, the son of Buzi, in the land of the Chaldeans by the river Chebar; and the hand of the Lord was there upon him" (Ezek. 1:1–3). Similar dating is to be found in Ezekiel 3:16; 8:1; 20:1; 24:1; 26:1; 29:1, 17; 30:20; 31:1; 32:1; 32:17; 33:21; 40:1 (cf. Hag. 1:1; 2:1, 20).[2]

2. In the "divine confrontation" either God, an angel, or some other manifestation of the divine appears to the individual. The "divine confrontation" (Ezek. 1:4–28a) unfolds in a manner unique in scripture, through a symbolic vision of the chariot with four wheels and of "the likeness of the glory of the Lord." This highly ornate, difficult, and puzzling passage has probably engendered more commentary than any other chapter in the Old Testament and has spawned a whole genre of

---

[1]This chart, and some of the subsequent discussion, is based on the perceptive study by Blake T. Ostler, "The Throne-Theophany and Prophetic Commission in 1 Nephi: A Form-Critical Analysis," *BYU Studies,* Fall 1986, p. 72, though it diverges from that of Ostler at several points. I have eliminated one of the features given by Ostler in his chart, the "objection," which follows the "commission" in Isa. 6 but is absent from both the calls of Lehi and Ezekiel. Similarly, I have not included Jeremiah on this chart, because it represents an "auditory" rather than a "throne-theophany" type of prophetic commission; cf. Stephen D. Ricks, "The Narrative Call Pattern in the Prophetic Commission of Enoch (Moses 6)," *BYU Studies,* Fall 1986, pp. 97–105.

[2]See Moshe Greenberg's detailed discussion of dates in Ezekiel in *Ezekiel 1–20,* Anchor Bible 22 (Garden City, N.Y.: Doubleday, 1983), pp. 7–11.

mystical literature in later Judaism known as *merkavah* (chariot) mysticism.[3]

3. In the "reaction" section the prophet reacts to his confrontation with the divine through words or actions reflecting awe, fear, or unworthiness. Thus, following his vision, Ezekiel reports that "when I saw it, I fell upon my face, and I heard a voice of one that spake" (Ezek. 1:28b).

4. In the course of the "divine confrontation," the prophet has a "throne-theophany" vision in which he sees God seated on his throne. In Ezekiel, the image of God seated on his throne is less direct than it is in the visions of Lehi and Isaiah: "above the firmament" is "the likeness of a throne, as the appearance of a sapphire stone: and upon the likeness of the throne was the likeness as the appearance of a man" (Ezek. 1:26).[4]

5. In the "commission," the individual recipient is commanded to perform a given task and assume the role of prophet to the people. Ezekiel's commission is accompanied by a description of the people to whom he was being sent: "And he said unto me, Son of man, I send thee to the children of Israel, to a rebellious nation that hath rebelled against me: they and their fathers have transgressed against me, even unto this very day. For they are impudent children and stiffhearted. I do send thee unto them; and thou shalt say unto them, Thus saith the Lord God. And they, whether they will hear, or whether they will forbear, (for they are a rebellious house,) yet shall know that there hath been a prophet among them" (Ezek. 2:3–5).

6. In the "reassurance" section of the prophetic call passages, God or his representative promises the prophet that he will be protected so that he can fulfill his call. Sometimes combined with the "reassurance" is some act that symbolizes God's protecting power. The prophetic "reassurance" in Ezekiel contains such a supernatural, symbolic act. Ezekiel was handed a book containing "lamentations, and mourning, and woe" (Ezek. 2:10), which he was commanded to eat. Amazingly, despite the book's content, it was like honey in taste, perhaps symbolizing that God's gifts, of whatever sort they may be, are sweet.

---

[3]Cf. David J. Halperin, *The Faces of the Chariot: Early Jewish Responses to Ezekiel's Vision* (Tübingen: Mohr, 1988).

[4]This element distinguishes the "throne-theophany" prophetic commission from the primarily auditory commissions, e.g., Jer. 1:4–10.

7. The prophetic call generally concludes with a statement indicating that the prophet begins to execute his commission. As we shall see below, although Ezekiel was disposed to preach to the people, he was constrained from doing so because of their wickedness.

The Watchman on the Tower (Ezek. 3:16–21)

After his initial call, Ezekiel sat overwhelmed for seven days (Ezek. 3:15). Ezekiel was called to be a watchman in the service of God, whose chief task it was to warn his people in accordance with the words God had given him (Ezek. 3:16–21; cf. 33:1–9). The image of the watchman derives from the role of the watchman on the wall of the city and refers to his role in warning against the approach of an enemy. Besides his role in guarding against the incursions of enemies, he was obliged to watch constantly for signs of fire or civil disturbance within the city (cf. 2 Sam. 18:24–27; 2 Kgs. 9:17–20). In Doctrine and Covenants 124 the image of the watchman is also used. There, the Nauvoo House is commanded to be built as "a resting place for the weary traveler, that he may contemplate the glory of Zion, . . . that he may receive also the counsel from those whom I have set to be as plants of renown, and as watchmen upon her walls" (D&C 124:60–61).

Ezekiel's main task as a watchman was to announce the imminent judgment of God upon Judah and Jerusalem, which then loomed on the horizon. Just as the watchman of a city is liable when he fails to warn its inhabitants, so Ezekiel would be responsible if he failed to warn Israel. If he warned the wicked of the house of Israel that they would die, or the righteous who turned from their righteousness that they would die, and they did not turn from their ways and died, Ezekiel had fulfilled his duty and was innocent of their death. On the contrary, if he failed to warn the righteous or the wicked so that they died without having been duly warned, then Ezekiel would be responsible for the spilling of their blood, and he would die ("their blood required at his hand," cf. 2 Sam. 4:5–12; Ezek. 18:20–32; 33:1–20; Judg. 9:24). Accountability for properly fulfilling one's stewardship was clear. The false prophets (about whom Ezekiel had much to say later) who failed in their responsibility to warn

Israel, proclaiming "Peace" when there was no peace, would suffer the consequences of God's judgment of death (Ezek. 13:1–23; 14:9–11). Similarly, Jacob, in the Book of Mormon, wished to preach to his people in order that their blood "might not come upon [his] garments" (Jacob 1:19). Personal deliverance from punishment depends in part on whether others have been aided in being delivered as well: "Nevertheless if thou warn the righteous man, that the righteous sin not, and he doth not sin, he shall surely live, because he is warned; also thou hast delivered thy soul" (Ezek. 3:21).

From the time of his call until the fall of Jerusalem, Ezekiel was a virtual recluse in his house for what appears to have been seven and one-half years (Ezek. 3:24–27; 24:25–27; cf. 33:22). His dumbness seems to refer to a silence enforced by circumstances: "But thou, O son of man, behold, they shall put bands upon thee, and shall bind thee with them, and thou shalt not go out among them" (Ezek. 3:25). "They" and "them" in this verse seem to refer to other Jews in exile with him. Having been forced to silence, he was not responsible for their wrongdoing. The elders and people came to him to inquire from the Lord (cf. Ezek. 8:1; 14:1; 20:1; 33:30–33), and then he spoke only when the Lord opened his mouth to proclaim, "Thus saith the Lord God" (Ezek. 3:27).

Symbolic Acts (Ezek. 4–5)

Ezekiel 4 and 5 contain a series of acts symbolic of God's judgment on the city of Jerusalem. These symbolic acts follow a pattern: a command to carry out the symbolic act; a report of carrying out the symbolic act; and the interpretation of the symbolic act. Ezekiel 4:1–3 contains the first and third elements, the command and the interpretation:

Command Thou also, son of man, take thee a tile, and lay it before thee, and pourtray upon it the city, even Jerusalem: And lay siege against it, and build a fort against it, and cast a mount against it; set the camp also against it, and set battering rams against it round about. Moreover take thou unto thee an iron pan, and set it for a wall of iron between thee and the city: and set thy face against it

Interpretation and it shall be besieged, and thou shalt lay siege against it. This shall be a sign to the house of Israel.

Other symbolic act passages in Ezekiel that contain a command and the interpretation of the command include 4:8–9, 9–17; 5:1–17; 12:17–20; 21:11–12, 23–29; 24:1–14; 37:15–28. The passages in Ezekiel that contain a command, the report of the carrying out of the command, and the interpretation of the command are 12:1–11 and 24:15–24.[5]

In the first symbolic act (Ezek. 4:1–3), Ezekiel took a tile, drew on it Jerusalem, and then sketched in forts, mounds, and battering rams — much as a Babylonian military commander might do. Thereafter, Ezekiel took an iron plate and placed it between himself and the tile with Jerusalem sketched on it, apparently as a symbol of the separation between God and the people in the city. The command for Ezekiel to "lay siege against it" (Ezek. 4:3) probably symbolizes the siege against Jerusalem. In the following verses (Ezek. 4:4–8), Ezekiel was told to lie on his left side for 390 days, corresponding to the number of years that the house of Israel would be punished. Thereafter, he was to lie on his right side for forty days, possibly to represent the forty years of captivity and exile of Judah. Others suggest combining the two numbers to make the sum of 430 years, which, if calculated from the time of Jehoiachin's exile in 597 B.C., would end at 167 B.C., approximately the year that the Maccabean revolt began and the Jews again exercised rule over the land of Canaan for the first time since 597 B.C.[6] Details of the conditions that would prevail during the siege of Jerusalem are given in the next section (Ezek. 4:9–17), where bread is made with a mixture of grains, since there was no single grain in sufficient supply to make bread. Ezekiel was then commanded to take a sharp sword and use it as a barber's razor to shave his beard (Ezek. 5:1–13). A third of the beard was to be burned in the middle of the city that was portrayed on the brick (Ezek. 4:1–2), a third he was to strike with the sword all around the city, and a third was to be scattered to the wind. From the latter number he was to save a few hairs in his garment, presumably to symbolize members of exiled communities such as the one in which Ezekiel himself lived. Its interpretation is given later: "A third part of thee shall die with the pestilence, and with famine shall they be consumed in the midst of thee: and a third

---

[5]Georg Fohrer, *Die symbolischen Handlungen der Propheten*, 2d ed. (Zürich: Zwingli, 1968), p. 18.

[6]Ralph Alexander, *Ezekiel* (Chicago: Moody Press, 1976), p. 23.

part shall fall by the sword round about thee; and I will scatter a third part into all the winds and I will draw out a sword after them" (Ezek. 5:12). Cutting off the hair itself represents the loss of personal identity associated with exile (cf. Isa. 7:20).[7]

Judgment upon the Mountains of Israel (Ezek. 6–7)

Whereas Ezekiel's words in chapters 4 and 5 were directed primarily to the community in exile in Babylon, now in chapters 6 and 7 Ezekiel's attention is focused on those who still remained in the land of Judah. Significantly, it is the mountains, hills, valleys, and stream beds that are addressed, the primary sites of the high places, incense altars, and idols of Canaanite worship to which errant Israelites were devoting themselves. In an act of divine poetic justice, God would slay before those very altars, high places, and idols the Israelites who had broken faith with him by worshiping there (cf. Deut. 29:16–28; 30:15–20). But though God promised death and destruction to the many, escape would be vouchsafed a few: "Yet will I leave a remnant, that ye may have some that shall escape the sword among the nations, when ye shall be scattered through the countries" (Ezek. 6:8).

In chapter 7, it is no longer the single community but the whole of the people who are addressed. "Over and over the prophet repeats his devastating message until his words pound the reader like a hammer. Disaster approaches. An end has come upon the land. Doom is near. God will not spare any of the people and will not pity them. The people are helpless against the approaching enemy. Prophets, priests, elders, and king are terrified and can do nothing. God will be known to Israel only in the irreversible judgment that will repay the people for their sins."[8] This section is redolent of the terror of the "Day of the Lord" prophecies found in other prophets, perhaps most notably Amos (5:18–20; 8:1–14) and Isaiah (chap. 13), in which God would approach Israel, for good or ill, in judgment.

---

[7]Robert R. Wilson, "Ezekiel," in James L. Mays, ed., *Harper's Bible Commentary* (San Francisco: Harper and Row, 1988), p. 665.

[8]Ibid., p. 666.

The Departure of the Lord's Glory from the Temple
(Ezek. 8–11)

In Ezekiel 8 through 11, the picture of aberrant worship was reinforced when the prophet was shown an idol being worshiped in the temple,[9] men praying toward the sun (forbidden in Deut. 4:19) with their backs to the temple (Ezek. 8:14–16),[10] and women participating in mourning rites for Tammuz (Dumuzi), the ancient dying and rising fertility god of Mesopotamia, whose annual journey to the underworld was the occasion for wailing among his worshipers. When Tammuz died in the fourth month of the year (at the summer solstice), he descended into the netherworld, taking all his rain clouds with him. He needed to be resurrected in the autumn, in time for the beginning of the rainy season. Meanwhile, his consort descended after him to call him back from death.[11]

The visionary judgment against the temple began when God called six armed executioners of the city, who approached the temple from the north, the traditional invasion route of enemy armies and the direction from which divine judgment was usually thought to come. They were accompanied by a scribe clothed in linen, the traditional garb of priests (Ex. 28:29–42) and angels (Dan. 10:5; 12:6). The Lord commanded the scribe to put a mark (the Hebrew letter *taw*, which originally had the appearance of our X) on all of the people in Jerusalem who mourned over the abominations being committed there. To the six executioners, the Lord gave the order to kill all of the men, women, and children in the city except those who had the mark on their forehead, beginning at the temple. Ezekiel, in distress at the carnage, asked the Lord if he would

---

[9]Morton Smith, "The Veracity of Ezekiel, the Sins of Manasseh, and Jeremiah 44:18," *Zeitschrift für die Alttestamentliche Wissenschaft* (1975): 11–16.

[10]Franz Dölger, in his lengthy and brilliant *Sol Salutis* (Münster: Aschendorff, 1925), discusses the practice of prayer toward the sun, including in the Judeo-Christian tradition. H. W. F. Saggs, "The Branch to the Nose," *Journal of Theological Studies* 11 (1960): 318–29, claims that "branch to the nose" in Ezek. 8:17 was a ritual gesture in the Mesopotamian worship of the sun. On sun worship in Judah during the late monarchic period, see Nahum Sarna, "Psalm XIX and the Near Eastern Sun-god Literature," *Fourth World Congress of Jewish Studies I* (Jerusalem: World Union of Jewish Studies, 1967), pp. 171–75.

[11]Samuel N. Kramer, *The Sacred Marriage Rite* (Bloomington, Ind.: Indiana University Press, 1969); Thorkild Jacobsen, *Toward the Image of Tammuz and Other Essays* (Cambridge, Mass.: Harvard University Press, 1970), p. 100; Oliver Gurney, "Tammuz Reconsidered: Some Recent Developments," *Journal of Semitic Studies* 7 (1962): 147.

not relent. In reply, the Lord said that the sin of the people was very great, since they had said, "The Lord hath forsaken the earth, and the Lord seeth not" (Ezek. 9:9). Thereafter, Ezekiel had another vision of God in the temple at Jerusalem (chap. 10) that is reminiscent of the "throne-theophany" in chapter 1. Here, as the prophet looked on, the cherubim of the temple became the divine throne borne by the heavenly cherubim. As they departed from the temple, so also did the glory of the Lord (Ezek. 10:18–19; 11:22–23; cf. 43:1–5). God commanded the scribe to take coals from between the cherubim to spread over Jerusalem in order to destroy it. Before the scribe could do so, however, one of the cherubim handed the coals to him (Ezek. 10:6–8). The section ends with a series of prophecies of judgment and hope directed to Judah and Jerusalem (Ezek. 11:16–20).

The theological significance of this section is considerable. Many at Jerusalem at this time (some six years before its final destruction by Nebuchadnezzar) still believed that God would not allow the city and the temple to fall to any enemy. Ezekiel's message was unmistakable, however: God's presence had departed from Jerusalem, the temple was no longer inviolate, and the city itself was doomed because of the people's wickedness. Nevertheless God had not altogether forgotten his people: although he "cast them far off among the heathen," still the Lord would "be to them as a little sanctuary in the countries where they shall come" (Ezek. 11:16). Eventually, too, they would be gathered again in the land of Israel itself.

Symbols and Prophecies of Exile (Ezek. 12–14)

In sight of the exiles in Babylon, Ezekiel was commanded to pack up his knapsack by day and to depart by evening while they still watched. This pantomime was to symbolize the fate of those who were yet in Jerusalem and other parts of the land, who would be taken captive and forced to become vagabonds in order to sustain themselves (Ezek. 12:1–10). This pantomime reflects, in fact, what happened to some of those at the time of the destruction of Jerusalem by the Babylonians. Even King Zedekiah attempted to escape from Jerusalem by night but was captured by the Babylonians and blinded (2 Kgs. 25:3–7; Jer. 39:4–7; 52:6–11).

Then the interpretation of the pantomime is given, and the entire act is interpreted as a type of what would happen to the people: "Like as I have done, so shall it be done unto them: they shall remove and go into captivity" (Ezek. 12:11). The symbolic acts of the prophets are similar to the simile curses found in the ancient Near East,[12] in which a curse is dramatized by some kind of symbolic action.[13]

Such "simile curses," explicit or implied, are to be found in the Book of Mormon as well as elsewhere in the Old Testament. In Alma 46, Moroni called upon the people to take up arms against Amalickiah, in response to which they rent "their garments in token, or as a covenant, that they would not forsake the Lord their God; or, in other words, if they should transgress the commandments of God . . . the Lord should rend them even as they had rent their garments" (Alma 46:21). Similarly, one of Moroni's soldiers "smote off the scalp of Zerahemnah" and then "took up the scalp from off the ground by the hair, and laid it upon the point of his sword, and stretched it forth unto them, saying unto them with a loud voice: Even as this scalp has fallen to the earth, which is the scalp of your chief, so shall ye fall to the earth except ye will deliver up your weapons of war and depart with a covenant of peace" (Alma 44:13–14).

Ezekiel attacked all false human hopes (Ezek. 12:21–28; cf. 33:23–29), thereby preparing the ground for a hope based on God's own purposes (Ezek. 36:16–38). The people would no longer be able to repeat the proverb, as they had in the past, "The days are prolonged, and every vision faileth" (Ezek. 12:22). Ezekiel affirmed that God's words would be fulfilled and that there would not be a long delay in their fulfillment. Ezekiel also attacked the false prophets and diviners — men and women —

[12]As noted by Georg Fohrer, *Die symbolischen Handlungen*, p. 57.

[13]For example, "Treaty between Ashurnirari V of Assyria and Mati'ilu of Arpad," trans. Erica Reiner, in *Ancient Near Eastern Texts Relating to the Old Testament*, 3d ed. with Supplement, ed. James B. Pritchard (Princeton: Princeton University, 1969), p. 532.; see also Stephen D. Ricks, "Oaths and Oath Taking in the Old Testament," in *A Symposium on the Old Testament* (Salt Lake City: The Church of Jesus Christ of Latter-day Saints, 1983), pp. 140–41; Johannes Pedersen, *Der Eid bei den Semiten* (Strassburg: Trübner, 1914), pp. 110–18, in which curse elements in oaths are taken into consideration; Delbert Hillers, in *Treaty Curses and the Old Testament Prophets* (Rome: Pontifical Biblical Institute, 1964), pp. 8–10.

who, through their lying oracles (which one commentator referred to as "whistling in the dark"[14]), had given Judah hope that had ultimately failed. False prophets are mentioned several times in the Old Testament. Ahab had his own prophets, some four hundred of them, who "prophesied" according to their own wishful thinking (1 Kgs. 22:6). Zedekiah also had such court prophets, who opposed Jeremiah violently but were ultimately discomfited by him (see Jer. 27:12–18; 28:1–17).

Ezekiel's writing is suffused with a strong sense of the sovereignty of God and his direction of human history. God's activity in history includes judgment as well as salvation and is intended to bring the house of Israel and the nations to know that Jehovah is God. Because of Judah's repeated failure and sin, God had now resolved to destroy the nation. That decision was irrevocable (Ezek. 14:12–20; 21:1–7), and even Noah, Job, and Daniel (or Danel) would not be able to protect them from famine, dangerous animals,[15] sword, and pestilence. Noah and Job were chosen as examples here because of their righteousness in their own generations. Noah, at least, was, through his righteousness, able to save his sons, his wife, and his daughters-in-law. Job, according to one tradition, brought his children back to life at the end of the story.[16] The Daniel referred to here most likely is not the same individual who is mentioned in the book of Daniel, because he was roughly a contemporary of Ezekiel; however, this could be the Danel mentioned in the Ugaritic materials that have been discovered and translated during this century. According to the Aqhat legend from Ugarit, Danel was a wise and good king who pleaded with the gods, coupled with sacrifice and prayer, for a son. Finally, Baal was moved to relay his request to the supreme god El, and Danel's request was granted. When his son, Aqhat, attained manhood, he was given a bow by Kothar, the Canaanite blacksmith deity. Anat, the Canaanite goddess, desired the bow and asked Aqhat for it. He demurred, and Anat, in her rage, indirectly brought about his death. Although the

---

[14]William H. Brownlee, *Ezekiel 1–19,* Word Biblical Commentary, vol. 28 (Waco, Texas: Word, 1986).

[15]Hillers, pp. 54–56, indicates devouring animals mentioned in the Near Eastern treaty literature and in the Old Testament.

[16]Shalom Spiegel, "Noah, Danel and Job: Touching on Canaanite Relics in the Legends of the Jews," *Louis Ginzberg Jubilee Volume* (New York: American Academy for Jewish Research, 1945), pp. 305–55.

Ugaritic tale is sketchy at this point, it appears likely that Danel, by his prayers, was able to restore his son to life.[17] The point of these three figures that Ezekiel cited as examples would be that even if there were righteous men who had been able to preserve other generations, they would not be able to do so here.

Three Prophetic Allegories (Ezek. 15–17)

To strengthen in the minds of his readers the certainty of God's judgment against Judah, Ezekiel summarized the judgment and its reasons in three allegories. The first of these (chap. 15) concerns a wild vine. When compared with other trees of the forest, the wild vine has little use except as fuel for fire (Ezek. 15:1–5). Just as the wild vine was suitable only for the fire, so also was Israel suited only for the consuming flame of God's fire. God's determination and his faithfulness to his judgments would be shown in the destruction of Jerusalem and the desolation of the land, "because they have committed a trespass" (Ezek. 15:6–8).

With striking, graphic, sometimes shocking language, Ezekiel described Jerusalem and Judah as a harlot (chap. 16). Although carelessly treated at her birth in Canaan, she was treated kindly by God, who "spread his skirt" over her — a symbol of intention to marry (Ezek. 16:8). In preparation for that marriage, God said: "Then washed I thee with water; yea, I thoroughly washed away thy blood from thee, and I anointed thee with oil. I clothed thee also with broidered work, and shod thee with badger's skin, and I girded thee about with fine linen, and I covered thee with silk" (Ezek. 16:9–10). Washing, anointing, and clothing in preparation for marriage are mentioned elsewhere in the Old Testament (Ruth 3:3) and in other parts of the ancient Near East as well.[18] Despite

---

[17]John Day, "The Daniel of Ugarit and Ezekiel and the Hero of the Books of Daniel," *Vetus Testamentum* 30 (1980): 174–84; H. H. P. Dressler, "The Identification of the Ugaritic Dnil with the Daniel of Ezekiel," *Vetus Testamentum* 29 (1979): 152–55; Baruch Margalit, "Interpreting the Story of Aqht: A Reply to H. H. P. Dressler," *Vetus Testamentum* 29 (1979): 152–61; *Vetus Testamentum* 30 (1980): 361–65.

[18]Jack M. Sasson, *Ruth: A New Translation with a Philological Commentary and a Formalist-Folklorist Interpretation* (Baltimore: Johns Hopkins University Press, 1979), pp. 67–68; Samuel Greengus, "Old Babylonian Marriage Ceremonies and Rites," in *Journal of Cuneiform Studies* 20 (1966): 55–72, includes details from cuneiform sources that parallel the biblical passages; Moshe Greenberg, *Ezekiel 1–20*, p. 278, doubts the ritual connection of the acts of washing, anointing, and clothing.

the marriage of the Lord and Judah, Judah proved herself constant only in her profligacy and unfaithfulness. For her adulteries, she would be punished.

By means of a third allegory (chap. 17), an explanation is given for God's judgment on Judah and Jerusalem. The allegory is presented in Ezekiel 17:1–10 and explained in 17:11–21. The historical background for the allusions in this chapter may be found in 2 Kings 24:6–20; 2 Chronicles 36:8–16; and Jeremiah 37; 52:1–7. An eagle (Nebuchadnezzar) broke off the top of the cedar (Jehoiachin of Judah) and brought it to the land and city of merchants (Babylon). The eagle (Nebuchadnezzar) took some of the seed of Judah and planted it, causing a vine to sprout (Zedekiah and those remaining in Judah). Soon, however, the vine began to incline toward a second eagle (Egypt) for nourishment. In the second part of the chapter a detailed explanation is given: the king of Babylon went to Jerusalem, bringing back the rightful king and nobles with him. In the absence of King Jehoiachin, the king of Babylon made a treaty with Zedekiah, one of the members of the royal family. Zedekiah soon rebelled against Nebuchadnezzar by sending his envoys to Egypt for an army. In response, the Lord declared that the Pharaoh will be of no value to Zedekiah, who will die in captivity in Babylon.

"Turn Yourselves, and Live" (Ezek. 18–19)

Ezekiel 18 refutes the idea implicit in the proverb: "The fathers have eaten sour grapes, and the children's teeth are set on edge" (v. 2), meaning, "Our own acts are immaterial, because we are reaping the effects of the acts of our fathers anyway." The hereditary principle as the cause of wickedness or righteousness is invalid. Several important principles are laid out in this chapter concerning responsibility for one's actions: (1) if the son does what is lawful, he will live, despite what his father may have done; (2) the transgressor will die; (3) the righteous will be rewarded for his righteousness, the wicked will be punished for his wickedness; (4) the wicked who repents will be forgiven; and (5) conversely, the righteous who turns from his righteousness to wickedness will be punished. In sum, the Lord says through Ezekiel, "Is not my way equal? are not your ways unequal? . . . I have no pleasure in the death of him that dieth, saith the Lord God: wherefore turn yourselves, and live" (Ezek. 18:25, 32).

Chapter 19 contains a lament against the "princes of Israel" (v. 1), given through two metaphors: the lioness and her whelps (vv. 1–9) and the vine and its branches (vv. 10–14). In the first figure, Judah, portrayed as a lioness (cf. Gen. 49:9; Num. 23:24; 24:9), brought up one of her cubs, who learned to catch prey and devour men. Finally, however, he was captured in a pit and taken in chains to Egypt (Ezek. 19:1–4). This figure refers to Jehoahaz, the son of Josiah, who became notorious for his wickedness and was finally seized by Pharaoh Necho and taken in chains to Egypt, where he died (cf. 2 Kgs. 23:30–34; 2 Chron. 36:1–4). To continue the figure, when the lioness saw that "her hope was lost" (Ezek. 19:5), she made another of her cubs a young lion. Like the first whelp, he too "learned to catch the prey, and devoured men. . . . And he knew their desolate palaces, and he laid waste their cities" (Ezek. 19:6–7). Finally, the nations captured him and brought him in chains to the king of Babylon, "that his voice should no more be heard upon the mountains of Israel" (Ezek. 19:9). This figure appears to refer to Jehoiachin, who was placed on the throne of Judah after Jehoahaz and Jehoiakim (who is not mentioned here) and was finally taken captive to Babylon where he was freed many years later (2 Kgs. 24:8–15; 25:27–30).

The second metaphor used in the chapter is that of Judah as a vine, with branches (representing her rulers) that had been dried up by the east wind (probably Babylon) and lost their strength. Eventually they would be transplanted to the "wilderness, in a dry and thirsty ground" (Ezek. 19:13; probably also Babylon). The point of this can surely not be missed: because of the wickedness of the last kings of Judah, the strength of the land was destroyed.

The Consequences of Israel's Rebellion (Ezek. 20–21)

Unlike Hosea and Jeremiah, who viewed Israel's history as one of initial faithfulness followed by disobedience, Ezekiel described Israel's entire existence from Egypt on as one of disobedience and rebellion (Ezek.

20:1–38). This description was coupled with promises of ultimate restoration.

The book of Ezekiel contains a succinct summary of the Lord's reasons for exiling his people as well as his grounds for allowing their return. The Exile "profaned" the Lord's name because of the disrepute into which it had fallen. Thus, the Lord says, "I withdrew mine hand, and wrought for my name's sake, that it should not be polluted in the sight of the heathen, in whose sight I brought them forth" (Ezek. 20:22). Later, in chapter 36, Ezekiel told the people that the reassembled nation would be purified in heart and spirit and there would be one flock with one shepherd. Thus the Lord promised his people: "For I will take you from among the heathen, and gather you out of all countries, and will bring you into your own land" (Ezek. 36:24). This restoration would include a renewal of the land and its products (Ezek. 36:34–35). Just as vital, the Lord promised a chastened Israel a new covenant: "Then will I sprinkle clean water upon you, and ye shall be clean: from all your filthiness, and from all your idols, will I cleanse you. . . . And I will put my spirit within you, and cause you to walk in my statutes, and ye shall keep my judgments, and do them" (Ezek. 36:25, 27). The same pattern that is described in Ezekiel of righteousness/blessing, and unrighteousness/punishment, including the expulsion from the land, is a pattern also to be found in the books of Deuteronomy and Judges, as well as in the Book of Mormon.[19]

Ezekiel's writing is suffused with a strong sense of God's sovereignty and of his direction of history. The divine direction of history includes both blessing and salvation for righteousness and judgment and punishment for wrongdoing, all of which is designed to bring Israel and the nations to the true knowledge of God. Now, because of Israel's repeated failure and sin, God had resolved to destroy the nation. Chapters 20 and 21 contain several pronouncements against the land and people of Judah and Jerusalem. One of the pronouncements involves a symbolic act: Ezekiel was to mark out two roads for the king of Babylon to take. Ezekiel was also to mark signposts to direct the king of Babylon, one to Rabbah, capital of the Ammonites, the other to Judah and Jerusalem. There at

---

[19]See Donald W. Parry and Stephen D. Ricks, "The Judges of Israel," in *Studies in Scripture, Volume Three: Genesis to 2 Samuel,* ed. Kent P. Jackson and Robert L. Millet (Salt Lake City: Randall Book, 1985), pp. 239–47.

the crossroads the king would divine by arrows which of the roads to take.[20] Such divination usually included marking names on the arrows, placing them in the quiver, and whirling them around. The first arrow to fall out would indicate the will of the gods.[21] Further divination would take place through consultation of idols and livers. In this case, Jerusalem would be chosen first for attack; war against the Ammonites would be pressed later (Ezek. 21:18–32).

God's Judgments on His Unfaithful People (Ezek. 22–24)

Ezekiel 22 contains three unrelated pronouncements against Jerusalem. The first pronouncement (vv. 1–16) accuses Jerusalem of bloodshed "in the midst" of it (cf. Ezek. 24:7) and of idolatry, besides a list of violations of Mosaic injunctions: dishonoring father and mother (cf. Ex. 21:17; Lev. 20:9); oppressing strangers, widows, and orphans (cf. Ex. 22:21–22; Deut. 14:29); desecration of Sabbaths (cf. Lev. 19:30); and a whole range of prohibited sexual practices (cf. Lev. 18; 20). Because of these practices, Jerusalem and Judah would be disinherited and dispersed (Ezek. 22:15).

In the next pronouncement (Ezek. 22:17–22), the inhabitants of Jerusalem are likened to dross that will be heated until it is completely dissipated. Unlike other passages that also speak of a smelting process that purifies and purges the dross (Isa. 1:22, 25; Mal. 3:2–3), here Ezekiel speaks of the people as being nothing but dross. As a result, the heating process will leave nothing.

The final pronouncement is against those individuals and leaders in Jerusalem who should have acted to forfend judgment but failed to do so. The princes, who should have protected the rights of the citizens, have shed blood instead. The priests, whose responsibility was to preserve purity and promote the observance of the law, "have violated my law, and have profaned mine holy things: they have put no difference between the holy and profane, neither have they shewed difference between the

[20]As Martin Puhvel, *The Crossroads in Folklore and Myth* (New York: Peter Lang, 1989), pp. 49–57, makes clear, the choice of the crossroads as a site of divination is significant, because it was traditionally perceived as being suffused with the supernatural.

[21]Alexander, p. 70.

unclean and the clean, and have hid their eyes from my sabbaths" (Ezek. 22:26). False prophets among the people "have devoured souls" (Ezek. 22:25) and "have daubed them with untempered mortar, seeing vanity, and divining lies unto them, saying, Thus saith the Lord God, when the Lord hath not spoken" (Ezek. 22:28). As a result, the Lord has executed judgment against them (see also Zeph. 3:3–4; Micah 3:11).

Again, in chapter 23, Ezekiel returned to the harlotry metaphor, already developed in such explicit detail in chapter 16. Here he presented the allegory of the two sisters, Aholah and Aholibah, who represent Samaria and Jerusalem (i.e., Israel and Judah), respectively (Ezek. 23:4). According to the allegory, although the two sisters had already "committed whoredoms in Egypt" (Ezek. 23:2), the Lord still took them in "marriage." Exactly what these "whoredoms" consisted of is not made clear, although it is likely that it refers to Israel's rebellion in the desert even before the covenant ("marriage") at Sinai – or Israel's state of apostasy in Egypt before the Exodus (cf. Ex. 14:10–18; 15:19–26; 16:1–26; 17:1–6). Thereafter, Aholah played the prostitute with Assyria, probably referring to the many treaties made between Samaria and Assyria before the fall of the Northern Kingdom (2 Kgs. 15:19–22; 17:1–6). As a result, said Ezekiel, God gave Samaria into the hand of her lovers. Aholibah, who should have learned from the sorry example of her sister, actually redoubled her crime: not only did she commit adultery with Assyria (a likely reference to Judah's alliances with Assyria; cf. 2 Kgs. 16:7–9; 18:1–36) but with Babylon as well (cf. 2 Kgs. 20:12–21). For these wrongdoings, Judah would suffer the same punishment as had Samaria: defeat, death, and exile.

Ezekiel began chapter 24 with the allegory of the pot. Here, God commanded Ezekiel to record the date – the ninth year, the tenth month, and the tenth day of the month (i.e, 10 January 588 B.C.) – whose significance becomes apparent in the following verse, for "the king of Babylon set himself against Jerusalem this same day" (Ezek. 24:2). In the allegory, someone was told to fill a pot with choice pieces of meat and bones and to place a fire under it to cook the contents of the pot. Two interpretations are then given. In the first, the pot, "whose scum is therein, and whose scum is not gone out of it" (Ezek. 24:6), is likened to Jerusalem "the bloody city . . . for her blood is in the midst of her" (Ezek. 24:6, 7), apparently referring to innocent blood that has been shed within her walls. In the second interpretation, Jerusalem is likened to the pot, which will be placed over a fire so violent that it will completely consume the impurities that are in the pot. This time, the Lord said, he will complete the process: "I will not go back, neither will I spare, neither will I repent; according to thy ways, and according to thy doings, shall they judge thee" (Ezek. 24:14). As the exiles in Babylon would soon learn from direct reports from Jerusalem, God had, through the Babylonians, begun the process of burning and purifying Jerusalem on the very day that Ezekiel had received this word.

In the second part of chapter 24, Ezekiel was told that his wife would die suddenly but that he was not to mourn her. When asked concerning this peculiar—and, in the light of the importance of mourning rites, highly inappropriate (cf. Jer. 16:1-7)[22]—behavior, Ezekiel was to explain that it was a symbol for Jerusalem, whose inhabitants and temple would be so suddenly destroyed that there would be no time for mourning. The sudden death of his wife and his inability to mourn for her according to custom became a symbol of the sudden destruction of God's sanctuary in Jerusalem (Ezek. 24:15-18). The temple and the city would soon fall.

---

[22]Fohrer, pp. 35-38, 64-65.

27
I WILL BE YOUR GOD
(EZEKIEL 25–36)

KENT P. JACKSON

The second half of the book of Ezekiel begins with a collection of prophecies against foreign nations. Almost all of Judah's immediate neighbors are mentioned.[1] As we have seen in other books, the prophets of Israel and Judah recorded scores of warnings and prophecies directed against other countries. Although Jehovah had selected the house of Israel as his people with whom he had a unique covenant relationship, still he was sovereign over all the earth, and all nations were subject to his will. Because all people are endowed at birth with the light of Christ that teaches them the difference between right and wrong, all will be held accountable to some degree and will receive the justice of Israel's God, even those who never knew him.[2]

Prophecies against Ammon, Moab, Edom, Philistia, and Tyre (Ezek. 25–28)

As is frequently the case, God's complaint against the nations includes references to how they treated his covenant people (see Ezek. 28:24–26). Ammon (Ezek. 25:1–7) and Moab (Ezek. 25:8–11) were denounced for rejoicing over Judah's fall.[3] Because of this, Ammon would be given

---

Kent P. Jackson is professor of ancient scripture at Brigham Young University.

[1]Syria (Damascus) is the only exception.

[2]See the introduction to the Oracles against Foreign Nations in Chap. 13 of this volume.

[3]The revelation in this chapter is not dated, but obviously it came after the fall of Jerusalem in 587 B.C.

over to the "men of the east." No longer would it be "remembered among the nations" (Ezek. 25:10), and its capital city, Rabbah (modern-day Amman, Jordan), would be destroyed and become "a stable for camels" (Ezek. 25:5). Moab would suffer a similar fate, and both nations "shall know that I am the Lord" (Ezek. 25:7, 11).[4]

Edom (Ezek. 25:12–14) and Philistia (Ezek. 25:15–17) were condemned for taking revenge on Judah. "They shall know that I am the Lord," he said, "when I shall lay my vengeance upon them" (Ezek. 25:17; see Map 9, LDS Bible, for the locations of all these places).

Ezekiel 26 through 28 is dedicated to the condemnation of one of the chief cities of the ancient Near East. Tyre, whose name may mean something like "rock," or "fortress," was built on a small island one-half mile off the Phoenician coast (see Map 9, top). Its maritime location made it almost impregnable and guaranteed its role as the premier trading city in the eastern Mediterranean. In chapter 26, received in the eleventh year of Ezekiel's exile, or about 587 B.C., the prophet foretold that Nebuchadnezzar, king of Babylon, would conquer Tyre: "With the hoofs of his horses shall he tread down all thy streets: he shall slay thy people by the sword, and thy strong garrisons shall go down to the ground. And they shall make a spoil of thy riches, and make a prey of thy merchandise: and they shall break down thy walls, and destroy thy pleasant houses: and they shall lay thy stones and thy timber and thy dust in the midst of the water" (Ezek. 26:11–12). So terrible would be the slaughter in Tyre that the other kings of the coast would sit on the ground and lament, "Now shall the isles tremble in the day of thy fall; yea, the isles that are in the sea shall be troubled at thy departure" (Ezek. 26:18).

Chapter 27 continues the prophecy. Verses 1 through 24 recount her great prosperity as an economic power of the ancient world, whose trading partners came from all over the Mediterranean and the Near East. From her profits she had become fabulously wealthy and, in her own estimation, "of perfect beauty" (Ezek. 27:3). But all this would end:

---

[4]In the Oracles against Foreign Nations, this phrase appears at 25:5, 7, 11, 17; 26:6; 28:22, 23, 24, 26; 29:6, 9, 21; 30:8, 19, 25, 26; 32:15; 35:4, 12, 15. God's great manifestations of power demonstrate clearly that he is sovereign of the earth. Eventually, all nations and all people will know that he is the Lord (see Isa. 11:9).

"In the time when thou shalt be broken by the seas in the depths of the waters thy merchandise and all thy company in the midst of thee shall fall" (Ezek. 27:34). Her fall would be so dramatic that the merchants would ask, "What city is like Tyrus, like the destroyed in the midst of the sea? . . . The merchants among the people shall hiss at thee; thou shalt be a terror, and never shalt be any more" (Ezek. 27:32, 36).

In chapter 28 the king of Tyre is singled out for specific condemnation, though he probably represents here all that is presumptuous about his city. In the pride of his heart he proclaims, "I am a God, I sit in the seat of God, in the midst of the seas" (Ezek. 28:2). The Lord foretold that his fall would be commensurate with the loftiness of his self-image: "I will cast thee to the ground, I will lay thee before kings, that they may behold thee. . . . All they that know thee among the people shall be astonished at thee." And again, "Never shalt thou be any more" (Ezek. 28:17, 19).

Sidon, another Phoenician city, is also doomed (Ezek. 28:20–23). And, like the other nations condemned to destruction, her inhabitants "shall know that I am the Lord" (Ezek. 28:23).

Prophecies against Tyre and Egypt (Ezek. 29)

Ezekiel 29 through 32 contains a collection of prophecies of conquest and doom for Egypt, Judah's most prominent neighbor. Apparently because they share the same subject matter, these four chapters were placed together in one section of Ezekiel, though they were received over the course of several years.

Chapter 29 consists of two prophecies that announce Egypt's destruction at the hands of Nebuchadnezzar (vv. 1–16 and vv. 17–21). Like Tyre, Egypt is condemned for its arrogance; its king said, "My river [the Nile] is mine own, and I have made it for myself" (Ezek. 29:3, 9). But God would bring down Egypt's pride: "I will make the land of Egypt utterly waste and desolate," he declared (Ezek. 29:10). A recurring theme in the prophetic books is the Lord's insistence that his covenant people rely only on him for protection and not seek alliances with pagan nations. During the years of the Assyrian and Babylonian threats, Judah was often tempted to seek aid from Egypt, a temptation which the Lord consistently challenged his people to resist (e.g., Isa. 20:1–6; 30:1–3, 7; 31:1–3). They learned the hard way that Egypt could offer them no support: "They have been a staff of reed to the house of Israel. When they took hold of thee by thy hand, thou didst break, and rend all their shoulder: and when they leaned upon thee, thou brakest" (Ezek. 29:6–7; see also Isa. 36:6). Egypt "shall be no more the confidence of the house of Israel," the Lord foretold, but will be a reminder of Israel's sin in turning to her for help (Ezek. 29:16). The fall of Egypt would remove it from the ranks of the ancient superpowers, making it instead a "lowly" kingdom; "neither shall it exalt itself any more above the nations: for I will diminish them, that they shall no more rule over the nations" (Ezek. 29:15).

In some ways, the short prophecy in Ezekiel 29:17–21 is among the most interesting of the prophecies in the Bible. Although it foretells the fall of Egypt, its greatest revelation has to do with the prophecies in Ezekiel 26 through 28 that Tyre would be destroyed and plundered by Nebuchadnezzar of Babylon. Those prophecies were not fulfilled as announced.

Nebuchadnezzar apparently attempted for thirteen years[5] (ca. 586–573 B.C.) to conquer Tyre but with less than satisfactory results. The offshore fortress city was extraordinarily difficult to take with the conventional means by which the Babylonians had prevailed elsewhere—siege warfare involving massive deployment of land troops and siege machinery. Historical sources are silent about how the long siege came to closure, but it must have ended in some kind of negotiated settlement. It appears that afterward a Babylonian governor was stationed in Tyre and presided alongside a new Tyrian king.[6] In any case, Ezekiel 29:18–20 makes it clear that the plunder promised to the Babylonians by Ezekiel's prophecy was not forthcoming. Their efforts in that regard were in vain.

The prophecy in Ezekiel 29:17–21 is the last-dated passage in the entire book of Ezekiel and appears to be the last revelation Ezekiel recorded, coming in about 571 B.C.[7] It concedes that Nebuchadnezzar failed to destroy and plunder Tyre as prophesied, but it points out that

---

[5]Josephus, *Antiquities of the Jews* 10.11.1.

[6]For a fine discussion of the sources and issues, see Walther Zimmerli, *Ezekiel 2* (Philadelphia: Fortress, 1983), pp. 22–24, 118–19.

[7]The long revelation at the end of the book, encompassing Ezek. 40–48, dates to two years earlier.

he and his warriors would not go away unrewarded. For their efforts the Lord would give them Egypt instead:

> Nebuchadnezzar king of Babylon drove his army in a hard campaign against Tyre; every head was rubbed bare and every shoulder made raw. Yet he and his army got no reward from the campaign he led against Tyre. Therefore this is what the Sovereign Lord says: I am going to give Egypt to Nebuchadnezzar king of Babylon, and he will carry off its wealth. He will loot and plunder the land as pay for his army. I have given him Egypt as a reward for his efforts because he and his army did it for me, declares the Sovereign Lord" (Ezek. 29:18–20, NIV).[8]

The graphic figure of heads "rubbed bare" and shoulders "made raw" is "derived from the burden-bearing laborer who works in bondage,"[9] and it represents the efforts expended by the Babylonians in their unsuccessful attempt to sack Tyre. Where Nebuchadnezzar failed at the task, a later conqueror succeeded. Alexander the Great, recognizing that extraordinary measures were needed to bring down Tyre, constructed a causeway two hundred feet wide from the mainland one-half mile to the island. This causeway enabled him to combine a sea attack with a land siege. Tyre fell after a seven-month effort in 333 B.C. (not a very long campaign by ancient standards). Alexander sold thirty thousand of its people into slavery, hanged two thousand of its leading citizens, and destroyed the city. Never again would Tyre proclaim, "I am a God, I sit in the seat of God, in the midst of the seas" (Ezek. 28:2).[10]

Prophecies against Egypt (Ezek. 30–32)

Ezekiel 30 contains two prophecies of Egypt's doom (vv. 1–19 and 20–26). According to Ezekiel, Egypt's fate would be certain: "The sword shall come upon Egypt, and great pain shall be in Ethiopia, when the slain shall fall in Egypt, and they shall take away her multitude, and her foundations shall be broken down" (Ezek. 30:4). In this period the terms *Egypt* and *Ethiopia* (also called Cush) were frequently used synonymously

---

[8]New International Version.
[9]Zimmerli, p. 119.
[10]Alexander's causeway still connects Tyre to the mainland today.

in poetic parallelism (e.g., Isa. 20:3, 5; 43:3; Nahum 3:9). Once again, Nebuchadnezzar would be God's agent to bring about his justice against the wicked nation: "I will also make the multitude of Egypt to cease by the hand of Nebuchadnezzar king of Babylon" (Ezek. 30:10).

In chapter 31 the prophet foretold the destruction of lofty Egypt by means of an allegory concerning the fall of the Assyrian empire. This revelation came in about 587 B.C., two decades after Assyria's demise. In the allegory Assyria is described as a tall tree, a cedar of Lebanon without parallel — "envied by all the trees of the Garden of Eden" (Ezek. 31:9). So imposing was it that all the great nations lived in its shade. Yet because of the great cedar's loftiness, "his heart is lifted up in his height" (Ezek. 31:10). Thus the Lord decreed that it would be chopped down.

In the allegory the tree is brought down by foreign powers: "strangers, the terrible of the nations" (Ezek. 31:12), who are not identified by name but clearly represent the forces of Persia and Babylonia, who combined to end Assyria's control of the Near East. They "cut him off, and have left him: upon the mountains and in all the valleys his branches are fallen, and his boughs are broken by all the rivers of the land; and all the people of the earth are gone down from his shadow, and have left him" (Ezek. 31:12).

But the message of this chapter is to Pharaoh and his country, not to the Assyrians, who had already met their fate. Just as Assyria had arrogated itself above God's creations, so now did Egypt. The outcome would be the same: "To whom art thou thus like in glory and in greatness among the trees of Eden?" the Lord asked Egypt. "Yet shalt thou be brought down. . . . This is Pharaoh and all his multitude, saith the Lord God" (Ezek. 31:18).

In about 585 B.C., Ezekiel received from the Lord instructions to take up a lament against the king of Egypt (Ezek. 32:1–16). The mocking poem that follows describes him as a sea monster pulled out of the water in a net and thrown onto the land. "The beasts of the whole earth" will gorge themselves on him (Ezek. 32:4), following which the Lord will scatter the remains of his carcass and blood all over the landscape. The interpretation of this metaphor is presented as follows: "The sword of the king of Babylon shall come upon thee. By the swords of the mighty will I cause thy multitude to fall, the terrible of the nations, all of them:

and they shall spoil the pomp of Egypt, and all the multitude thereof shall be destroyed" (Ezek. 32:11–12).

In a revelation that apparently followed the previous one by two weeks (Ezek. 32:17–32), the Lord informed Ezekiel what would become of Pharaoh and his forces. He instructed the prophet to wail for Egypt and to cast its hosts down "unto the nether parts of the earth, with them that go down into the pit" (Ezek. 32:18). "Out of the midst of hell," the rulers of other fallen nations will mark Egypt's coming (Ezek. 32:21). Assyria is there, as are Elam, Meshech and Tubal, Edom, and Sidon and the "princes of the north" — all with their armies and their slain in graves (Ezek. 32:22–30). Perhaps because misery enjoys company, Pharaoh "shall see them, and shall be comforted," consoling himself in the idea that others shared his ignominious fate (Ezek. 32:31).[11]

The Watchman (Ezek. 33)

Chapter 33 repeats themes that were first introduced in Ezekiel 3:17–21 and 18:20–32. Ezekiel was called to be a "watchman" for his people, a metaphor that is explained clearly in 33:2–9. A watchman's responsibility was to warn his people of the coming of invading armies. If he fulfilled his responsibility and warned them, he would be guiltless if they fell to the sword. But if he failed to warn them, God would require their blood "at the watchman's hand" (Ezek. 33:6). The Lord told Ezekiel that his prophetic call carried the same weight of responsibility. If he warned the people with God's message and they refused to listen, he would be innocent of the consequences that they would bear. If, however, he failed to warn them as commanded, God would require their blood at Ezekiel's hand (Ezek. 33:7–8). Because of this responsibility that comes to those who are called to serve, Lehi's sons Jacob and Joseph magnified their

---

[11]In 1842 Joseph Smith referred to this episode, stating that it provides "a pattern to this generation, and the nations now rolling in splendor over the globe, if they do not repent, that they shall go down to the pit also, and be rejoiced over, and ruled over by Old Pharaoh, King Devil of mobocrats, miracle rejecters, saint killers, hypocritical priests, and all other fit subjects to fester in their own infamy." Andrew F. Ehat and Lyndon W. Cook, eds., *The Words of Joseph Smith* (Provo, Utah: Religious Studies Center, Brigham Young University, 1980), p. 122.

callings, lest they "would not be found spotless at the last day" (Jacob 1:18–19).[12]

The Lord cares much less about whom he should blame for our wrongdoings than that we overcome them and be blessed. "I have no pleasure in the death of the wicked," he said, "but that the wicked turn from his way and live: turn ye, turn ye from your evil ways; for why will ye die, O house of Israel?" (Ezek. 33:11). Powerful lessons in repentance and enduring to the end follow. One who abandons a life of evil and turns to good will be rewarded in accordance with his repentance and his final disposition to do right: "None of his sins that he hath committed shall be mentioned unto him" (Ezek. 33:16; see also vv. 14–15, 19). On the other hand, one who forsakes a life of faithfulness and becomes unrighteous cannot count on prior good acts to save him when he dies in his sins: "All his righteousnesses shall not be remembered" (Ezek. 33:13; see also vv. 12, 18).

The last section of chapter 33 (vv. 21–33) begins with the announcement that Jerusalem had fallen, an event that was accompanied by a huge slaughter and the deportation of most of the city's remaining population. Yet these catastrophes would not be the end of Judah's sorrows, Ezekiel announced. Those who remained in the ruins would "fall by the sword," those who had escaped to the countryside would be devoured by animals, and those still hiding would die of plague (Ezek. 33:27). Like the other nations chastened by God's hand, Judah too would "know that I am the Lord" (Ezek. 33:29).[13]

Had the people not been warned? Had Ezekiel and other prophets not been watchmen to let them know that these disasters would come? Indeed they had been warned, but their rejection of God's prophets was one of the causes of their sorrows. As the Lord told Ezekiel, "they hear thy words, but they will not do them" (Ezek. 33:31). Because the watchman had raised his voice and the people had not obeyed, they would carry the full burden of their sins. Ezekiel had foretold the consequences of their behavior, and when they would be forced to the realization that

---

[12]This does not mean that the negligent watchmen, prophets, parents, or teachers will be held responsible for the sins of the individuals they fail to warn. Those individuals will be responsible for their own behavior (see Ezek. 18:20; 33:6, 8), but those who had been charged to warn them will be accountable for not providing them every opportunity to avoid danger.

[13]See n. 4, above.

his prophecies had come true — as they surely would — then they would know "that a prophet hath been among them" (Ezek. 33:33).

The Good Shepherd and His Flock (Ezek. 34)

In Ezekiel the powerful metaphor of sheep and shepherds is developed only in chapter 34 (cf. Jer. 23:1; 31:10; 50:6, 17). The Lord condemns the shepherds of Israel for their gross neglect of the flock: "Should not the shepherds feed the flocks?" (Ezek. 34:2); "they were scattered, because there is no shepherd" (Ezek. 34:5); "yea, my flock was scattered upon all the face of the earth, and none did search or seek after them" (Ezek. 34:6).

Nowhere are the shepherds of Israel defined, but the meaning seems quite clear. Shepherds are leaders, those to whose care God's children have been entrusted. In ancient Israel the leaders included the prophets, the priests, and the kings. With callings of prophecy, priesthood, and royalty, these individuals had been charged with the responsibility of presiding in the house of Israel and providing leadership within their respective spheres. Unfortunately, the Bible shows evidence for all-too-frequent corruption in each of these areas: most of the kings were wicked,[14] many priests defiled themselves, and false prophets were popular. A few passages, in fact, list these three as a triad of wickedness: "Her priests have violated my law. . . . Her princes in the midst thereof are like wolves. . . . And her prophets have daubed them with untempered morter, seeing vanity, and divining lies unto them" (Ezek. 22:26–28). "Her princes within her are roaring lions. . . . Her prophets are light and treacherous persons: her priests have polluted the sanctuary" (Zeph. 3:3–4). "The heads thereof judge for reward, and the priests thereof teach for hire, and the prophets thereof divine for money" (Micah 3:11).

These shepherds were not worthy of their callings, the Lord told Ezekiel, so God himself would become Israel's shepherd and gather his flock:

---

[14]The Old Testament identifies *all* of the kings of Israel and twelve of the twenty kings of Judah as wicked. See Andrew E. Hill, *Baker Handbook of Bible Lists* (Grand Rapids, Mich.: Baker, 1981), pp. 206–7.

Behold, I, even I, will both search my sheep, and seek them out. As a shepherd seeketh out his flock in the day that he is among his sheep that are scattered; so will I seek out my sheep, and will deliver them out of all places where they have been scattered in the cloudy and dark day. And I will bring them out from the people, and gather them from the countries, and will bring them to their own land, and feed them upon the mountains of Israel by the rivers, and in all the inhabited places of the country. I will feed them in a good pasture, and upon the high mountains of Israel shall their fold be (Ezek. 34:11–14).

The message of the gathering of Israel is clear in this passage. The lost sheep of Israel will be brought back to the fold, gathered "out from the people" and "from the countries." They will be restored to the covenants of the gospel with Jehovah as their shepherd. He is their *true* prophet, priest, and king.

When Jesus proclaimed himself to be the "good shepherd" (John 10:11, 14), he was drawing upon the divine shepherd imagery familiar to the Jews from the Old Testament. Thus he was saying much more than "Follow me." Israel's Good Shepherd was Jehovah himself, as the Jews knew, and Jesus' pronouncement was a statement of that fact. In saying it, he was proclaiming that he is God: "I Am Jehovah." As he punctuated the announcement with the phrase, "I and my Father are one," the Jews "took up stones again to stone him" (John 10:30–31).

In Ezekiel 34:17, the prophet's metaphor takes a sudden and surprising turn. Though the shepherds will be condemned for their abuse or neglect of the flock, the sheep themselves are also accountable. They too will be judged, and the judgment against them will not be easy. Some of them ate the good pasture and trampled what was left. They drank the water and dirtied the rest with their feet, leaving those identified as the Lord's own flock to drink foul water. They pushed away the weaker among them and "scattered them abroad" (vv. 18–21). The Lord will intervene: "Therefore will I save my flock, and they shall no more be a prey" (v. 22).

The next passage is a powerful revelation about the Lord's millennial rule among his people: "I will set up one shepherd over them, and he shall feed them, even my servant David; he shall feed them, and he shall be their shepherd. And I the Lord will be their God, and my servant David a prince among them" (Ezek. 34:23–24). In another revelation the Lord said, "David my servant shall be king over them; and they all shall have one shepherd. . . . And my servant David shall be their prince for ever" (Ezek. 37:24, 25).

There is no mystery about the identity of the "David" mentioned here. These passages refer to Jesus Christ, who was a descendant of David in the flesh and who is and ever will be the true Shepherd and King of Israel. To the ancient Israelites, David embodied the very essence of kingship for several reasons: he was appointed by revelation from God, during his reign Israel and Judah were united as one nation under one king, he ruled as a powerful and popular monarch, he defeated all enemies and introduced a period of peace and prosperity, and the Lord's sanctuary was among the people in his day.[15] These things came to mind whenever David's name was mentioned, and they provided for later Israelites not only the reminiscence of a past golden age but also the longing for a future age that would be even more glorious. Thus the name David took on symbolic significance and was applied to Israel's millennial King. He would be, as it were, a second King David, who would restore the glories of the past to which later generations of oppressed Israel looked with longing.

Who will be the second David, the millennial King of Israel? The scriptures are quite clear on this point: the Lord Jehovah, Jesus Christ, will be Israel's millennial king. "The Holy One of Israel," wrote Nephi, will "reign in dominion, and might, and power, and great glory" (2 Ne. 22:24). His name, Jeremiah foretold, would be "Jehovah, our Righteousness" (Jer. 23:5–6). "The king of Israel, even the Lord," reported Zephaniah concerning the Millennium, "is in the midst of thee" (Zeph. 3:15), and to Zechariah God said, "The Lord shall be king over all the earth: in that day shall there be one Lord, and his name one" (Zech. 14:9; see also vv. 16–17). The New Testament also identifies Israel's millennial king as Christ, who will rule at his Second Coming as "King of kings, and Lord of Lords" (Rev. 19:16). "For the Lord shall be in their midst," the Prophet Joseph Smith learned, "and his glory shall be upon them, and he will be their king and their lawgiver" (D&C 45:59). As the Prophet summarized, "Christ will reign personally upon the earth" when it is renewed in "paradisiacal glory" (A of F 10).[16]

---

[15]Later Israelites seem to have overlooked or forgotten David's fall and the tragedies that resulted from it in the latter part of his reign. In their tradition he always remained the ideal king.

[16]For additional references to Christ as Israel's millennial king, see "Jesus Christ, Millennial Reign," and "Jesus Christ, King," Topical Guide, LDS Bible. See also Bruce R. McConkie, *The Millennial Messiah* (Salt Lake City: Deseret Book Co., 1982), pp. 589–611.

Who then is the "one shepherd," "even my servant David" in Ezekiel 34:23? Once again, it is the Lord Jesus Christ. "I am the good shepherd," the Lord proclaimed—a doctrine that is repeated in many passages (John 10:14; see also Heb. 13:20; 1 Pet. 5:4; Alma 5:38, 39, 41, 57, 60; D&C 50:44). Nephi learned from an angel that there is but "one Shepherd over all the earth" (1 Ne. 13:41), and many have testified that there will be "one fold and one shepherd" (1 Ne. 22:25; Hel. 15:13; 3 Ne. 15:17, 21; 16:3).

With Christ as Shepherd and King, the day of Israel's redemption will be a day of peace, safety, and well-being for the Lord's people. If the time of David's rule was a golden age, then the time of Christ's millennial rule will be one of transcendent happiness and order. The rain will fall in its season, the vegetation of the earth will yield its fruit, and hunger and shame will be things of the past (Ezek. 34:25–29). "I will make with them a covenant of peace," the Lord said (Ezek. 34:25); "thus shall they know that I the Lord their God am with them, and that they, even the house of Israel, are my people" (Ezek. 34:30).

A Prophecy against Edom (Ezek. 35)

Chapter 35 would seem to be more at home among the other oracles against foreign nations in chapters 25 through 32. No explanation regarding its placement here is given, nor is there a reference to the date of the revelation. It is a prophecy against Edom (KJV, "Idumea"), called in this chapter "Mount Seir." Like the other nations, God proclaimed, Edom would "know that I am the Lord" (Ezek. 35:4, 15) when his judgments would come upon it. Edom's offense was hostility against the kingdom of Judah—"a perpetual hatred"—which was manifest at the time of Judah's destruction. In response, the Lord would make Mount Seir "most desolate," a "perpetual desolation" (Ezek. 35:7, 9). As in other places where individual nations represent the evils of all humankind, Edom, especially, is used by the prophets to represent the world and its ways (D&C 1:36). Perhaps the placement of this revelation here, in the midst of two great prophecies of restoration (Ezek. 34; 36) is meant to remind readers that the day of the Lord's redemption of his people will also be the day of his cleansing the world of all that is evil in it.

A New Heart and a New Spirit (Ezek. 36)

The first fifteen verses of Ezekiel 36 contain a prophecy addressed to the mountains, hills, ravines, valleys, and ruined cities of Israel, which had long suffered the scorn of the nations around them. This passage shows the fulfillment of the prophecy of destruction in Ezekiel 6:1–14, but it also announces that the Lord would restore what was lost: a new day would come in which the land's productivity and population would return. This would include the gathering of the house of Israel — "even all of it" (Ezek. 36:8–10). "Yea, I will cause men to walk upon you, even my people Israel; and they shall possess thee, and thou shalt be their inheritance" (Ezek. 36:12).

In the second revelation in chapter 36 (vv. 16–38), the Lord explained to Ezekiel why he had expelled the house of Israel from its promised land: "When the house of Israel dwelt in their own land, they defiled it by their own way and by their doings. . . . Wherefore I poured my fury upon them for the blood that they had shed upon the land, and for their idols wherewith they had polluted it: And I scattered them among the heathen [i.e., the nations[17]], and they were dispersed through the countries" (Ezek. 36:17–19). Unfortunately, their scattering did not induce them to repent, and they continued to profane the Lord's holy name wherever they went in their dispersion (Ezek. 36:20–23). Despite that, however, the Lord would yet be glorified through the mighty work that he would bring to pass in the latter days. He would gather the dispersed of Israel back to him: "I will take you from among the heathen, and gather you out of all countries, and will bring you into your own land" (Ezek. 36:24). There they would be purified and come into harmony with the Lord's will, a process that is described in a series of metaphors that are clearly reminiscent of spiritual rebirth: "sprinkled clean," "new heart," "new spirit," "cleansed" (Ezek. 36:25–27, 33; cf. Alma 5:14, 19, 26).

To these promises the Lord added the crowning pronouncement: "Ye shall be my people, and I will be your God" (Ezek. 36:28). This phrase,

---

[17]The words *heathen, nations,* and *gentiles* are synonymous in the Old Testament, being translated (inconsistently in the KJV) from the synonymous Hebrew words *'ammîm* and *gôyîm.* These terms refer to the non-Israelite nations.

in my view, is one of the most significant statements in the entire Old Testament. It is found frequently, and it always signifies that the covenant relationship between Jehovah and his people is intact.[18] It shows the fulfillment of the Lord's intention as he established his covenant with the house of Israel: "I will take you to me for a people, and I will be to you a God" (Ex. 6:7). In times of apostasy the covenant relationship was nullified—"Ye are not my people, and I will not be your God" (Hosea 1:9)—but the prophetic promise foretold a day in which it would be established again, this time forever: "I will say to them which were not my people, Thou art my people; and they shall say, Thou art my God" (Hosea 2:23).[19]

When the Lord takes back his repentant people and renews the covenant that bound them to him, he will also endow them richly with the blessings of the earth. The land will produce as never before, cities will be built, and desolate areas will be tilled (Ezek. 36:29–38). In that millennial setting, countryside that once lay waste and desolate will "become like the garden of Eden" (Ezek. 36:35), and, as Joseph Smith promised, "the earth will be renewed and receive its paradisiacal glory" (A of F 10).

---

[18]In addition to the passages cited in this discussion, the phrase is also found in Lev. 26:12; Jer. 7:23; 11:4; 24:7; 30:22; 31:33; 32:38; Ezek. 11:20; 14:11; 37:23, 27; Zech. 8:8; D&C 42:9.

[19]For a similar discussion centered on the metaphor of marriage, see my "The Marriage of Hosea and Jehovah's Covenant with Israel," in *Isaiah and the Prophets*, ed. Monte S. Nyman (Provo, Utah: Religious Studies Center, Brigham Young University, 1984), pp. 57–73.

28

THE LORD IS THERE

(Ezekiel 37–48)

Kent P. Jackson

When news came to Ezekiel in Mesopotamia that Jerusalem had fallen (Ezek. 33:21), the Jews who were with him in exile should finally have realized "that a prophet hath been among them" (Ezek. 33:33). For years he had foreseen Jerusalem's destruction, and now that it had taken place, the focus of his revelations naturally turned to other things. Thus, from chapter 34 to the end of his book, Ezekiel's message shifted to a focus on the latter days, emphasizing things that were far into the future from his own time. These include the restoration of the house of Israel, the reunion of the kingdoms of Israel and Judah, the efforts of the ungodly in their opposition to the Lord's people and the Lord's work, the destruction of the wicked prior to Christ's coming, and his glorious reign as Israel's millennial king.[1]

The last chapters of Ezekiel are among the most symbolic, dramatic, and intriguing in all of scripture. As a result, unfortunately, they have often been misused to create doctrinal and historical mischief. All Latter-day Saints should realize that no prophecy in the Old Testament can be fully understood independently of modern revelation. A careful application of this principle is good insurance against misinterpretation. Modern revelation provides the perspective and the context that are necessary for understanding the revelations of the past, making it an indispensable

---

Kent P. Jackson is professor of ancient scripture at Brigham Young University.

[1]Interestingly, these are the very topics that Moroni taught to Joseph Smith when he appeared to him on 21–22 September 1823 to introduce him to his mission and that of the Church in the dispensation of the fulness of times. See Kent P. Jackson, "Moroni's Message to Joseph Smith," *Ensign*, Aug. 1990, pp. 13–16.

tool for which we will always be thankful.[2] We should have this ever in mind as we explore Ezekiel's prophecies of things yet to come.

Bones and Sticks (Ezek. 37)

Ezekiel 37 records two highly symbolic revelations, each of which describes in powerful images the restoration of the house of Israel. Although that is their central focus, they also teach other things that are of significant value to latter-day readers.

At the beginning of chapter 37, Ezekiel was shown a vision of a valley full of dry bones. In response to the Lord's command, he prophesied to the bones that they would come back to life. With a rattling sound "the bones came together, bone to his bone" (Ezek. 37:7). Tendons, flesh, and skin covered the reassembled bodies in due course, and "breath came into them, and they lived, and stood up upon their feet, an exceeding great army" (Ezek. 37:10).

As is common in Ezekiel's revelations, the symbolic activity or vision is followed by a clear interpretation. "These bones are the whole house of Israel," the Lord said. The metaphor of scattered bones well describes Israel's pitiful condition: they had been destroyed as a nation, their temple and holy city lay in ruins, thousands of their number had been killed in the Babylonian invasion (and earlier invasions as well), and their Davidic monarch and thousands of their countrymen had been taken into exile. They lamented, "our bones are dried, and our hope is lost: we are cut off for our parts" (Ezek. 37:11).

Ezekiel's vision of the dry bones announced to ancient and modern Israel that their scattering would not be forever. The Lord would bring them out of their graves, assemble their scattered parts, give them life, and reestablish them in their own land (Ezek. 37:12–14). The image of resurrection in this passage shows that though the house of Israel were dead, it would be restored again—to life and to a renewed covenant with God.

---

[2]In practical terms, this means that if something seems to be foretold in an Old Testament prophecy that is nowhere to be found in modern revelation, one should withhold judgment on it, at the very least. More likely, the passage probably means something other than one supposes— something that is clearly revealed in modern revelation.

The following section of the chapter, Ezekiel's vision of the uniting of the two sticks (Ezek. 37:15–28), is one of the Bible's best-known prophecies for Latter-day Saints. But most are aware only of its secondary message, the joining of scriptural records, and not of the primary focus of the revelation: the restoration of the house of Israel with Christ as king.

As the revelation began, the Lord commanded Ezekiel to take in hand two "sticks." The Hebrew word translated "stick," '*ēṣ*, has as its primary meanings "tree" and "wood."[3] The most likely meaning in this context is a piece of wood, a board. One well-known interpretation in the Church proposes that Ezekiel envisioned a writing board called a "diptych," which consisted of two pieces of wood hinged together to fold like the covers of a book. The inside surfaces of the boards were coated with wax, providing a convenient and reusable writing medium.[4] Although this explanation is not certain, it is reasonable and could well approximate what Ezekiel saw.[5] In any case, the boards in the revelation were symbols meant to represent greater things, and thus their exact nature is not as significant as the message conveyed through them.

Ezekiel was commanded to write on the first board, "Belonging to Judah and the children of Israel his companions." On the second he was commanded to write, "Belonging to Joseph—the stick of Ephraim—and all the house of Israel his companions" (Ezek. 37:16, my translations). These are phrases of identification that were very commonly used in ancient Israel to designate ownership. The message is clear: one board belonged to Judah and the other to Joseph.

As the revelation continued, Ezekiel was instructed to place the two boards together in one: "and they shall become one in thine hand" (Ezek. 37:17). This revelation is one of several in which the Lord commanded Ezekiel to engage in highly symbolic actions.[6] As "visual aids," they were

---

[3]Current English-language translations render the word here in a variety of ways: "stick" (Jewish Publication Society Bible; Revised Standard Version), "stick of wood" (New International Version), "leaf of a wooden tablet" (New English Bible; Revised English Bible).

[4]See Keith A. Meservy, "Ezekiel's Sticks and the Gathering of Israel," *Ensign*, Feb. 1987, pp. 4–13. Excellent photographs of a diptych can be seen in *National Geographic*, Dec. 1987, pp. 730–31.

[5]Meservy's writing board interpretation, which he proposed originally in the 1970s (*Ensign*, Sept. 1977, pp. 22–27), is adopted in the footnote to Ezek. 37:16 in the LDS Bible.

[6]Some others include Ezek. 2:9–3:4; 4:1–8, 9–17; 5:1–5, 12; 12:3–12, 17–19; 24:16–26.

meant to convey messages of importance to the house of Israel, and they were almost always followed by explanations of their purpose and meaning. In this case the explanation follows, in verses 18 through 28. When we add to the material provided in those verses some significant things that we learn through modern revelation, we gain a clear understanding of the truths Ezekiel taught by means of the two "sticks."

As is apparent in Ezekiel 37:21–27, the central message of Ezekiel's revelation is the restoration of the house of Israel. For Latter-day Saints the word *restoration* usually evokes thoughts of Joseph Smith and the restoration of lost truth and authority in the latter days. But the restoration, in its greatest sense, involves much more than that. As Ezekiel reported, it includes the gathering of the dispersed of Israel (Ezek. 37:21), their reestablishment in promised lands (Ezek. 37:21–22, 25), the restoration of Judah and Israel into one nation (Ezek. 37:22), the restoration of their status as a worthy covenant people before the Lord (Ezek. 37:23–24, 26–28), and the restoration of the Lord himself to his rightful position as Israel's divine king (Ezek. 37:22, 24–25). These constitute the central focus of Ezekiel 37 and of many other important prophecies as well. For all of these the Lord provided a sign: the bringing together of the two inscribed pieces of wood—the "stick of Judah," and the "stick of Joseph, which is in the hand of Ephraim" (Ezek. 37:19).

Our distinctive Latter-day Saint point of view regarding Ezekiel's sticks came in a revelation to the Prophet Joseph Smith in August 1830, in which the Lord spoke of Moroni, "whom I have sent unto you to reveal the Book of Mormon, containing the fulness of my everlasting gospel, to whom I have committed the keys of the record of the stick of Ephraim" (D&C 27:5). Ezekiel's visionary stick of Joseph in Ephraim's hand thus represents Joseph's scriptural record, the Book of Mormon. It follows therefore that Judah's stick represents the scriptural record of Judah, the Bible.

Ezekiel was not the only prophet who knew of the coming together of the two scriptural records. Almost a thousand years earlier, ancient Joseph received a revelation in which he learned of the joining of the record of his descendants with that of the tribe of Judah. That would be done under the ministry of the great latter-day seer, Joseph Smith, who would be an instrument in the Lord's hand to bring to pass the restoration of Israel. Lehi, who found this revelation on the plates of brass, considered it to be significant enough to give it special emphasis for his family, and Nephi recorded it on his small plates (2 Ne. 3:4–24). The Lord told ancient Joseph: "Wherefore the fruit of thy loins shall write, and the fruit of the loins of Judah shall write; and that which shall be written by the fruit of thy loins, and also that which shall be written by the fruit of the loins of Judah, shall *grow together* unto the confounding of false doctrines, and laying down of contentions, and establishing peace among the fruit of thy loins, and bringing them to a knowledge of their fathers in the latter days; and also to the knowledge of my covenants, saith the Lord" (JST Gen. 50:31; 2 Ne. 3:12; emphasis added; see also 1 Ne. 13:41).

The coming together of the two records is thus a central event in the restoration of the house of Israel. Indeed, it is an essential ingredient in the Lord's latter-day work, for the gospel message thus produced will confound false doctrine, lay down contentions, establish peace between the two estranged halves of the house of Israel, and bring them to a knowledge of God's covenants (cf. Ezek. 37:22–23, 26–27).[7] It is no wonder, then, that Ezekiel would view the bringing together of the two records, the sticks of Joseph and Judah, as being the very symbol of the restoration of Israel.

Other prophets also foretold this event as the sign of Israel's restoration. The Savior himself did when he ministered to the children of Lehi following his resurrection. While teaching them of the restoration of Israel, he spoke of the coming forth of their record, the Book of Mormon. He called it a *sign:* "I give unto you a sign, that ye may know the time when these things shall be about to take place — that I shall gather in, from their long dispersion, my people, O house of Israel, and shall establish again among them my Zion" (3 Ne. 21:1). The sign would be the coming forth of their record, by which both they and the Gentiles would know that they are "a remnant of the house of Jacob" (3 Ne. 21:2;

---

[7]The Lord told ancient Joseph that the great latter-day seer's ministry would include "convincing them of my word, which shall have already gone forth among them" (JST Gen. 50:30; 2 Ne. 3:11). As the Lord revealed in 1820 when the Church was organized, one important purpose for the coming forth of the Book of Mormon was to bear testimony to the truth of the Bible (D&C 20:11; see also 1 Ne. 13:39–40). The coming together of the records of Joseph and Judah enables each to bear testimony to the message of the other and both together to bear testimony to the Lord and his work. In Nephi's words, "they both shall be established in one" (1 Ne. 13:41).

see also vv. 3–6). "And when these things come to pass that thy seed shall begin to know these things—it shall be a sign unto them, that they may know that the work of the Father hath already commenced unto the fulfilling of the covenant which he hath made unto the people who are of the house of Israel" (3 Ne. 21:7).

Mormon, who compiled the record of Joseph, also saw its publication as a sign of Israel's restoration: "When the Lord shall see fit, in his wisdom, that these sayings shall come unto the Gentiles according to his word, then ye may know that the covenant which the Father hath made with the children of Israel, concerning their restoration to the lands of their inheritance, is already beginning to be fulfilled" (3 Ne. 29:1; see also vv. 2–9). Because the Bible was already known when the Book of Mormon was first published in 1830, the appearance of the Book of Mormon was, in effect, the coming together of the two records—the sign that the reunion of the branches of the house of Israel and their reestablishment in the covenants would soon take place.[8]

The latter-day restoration of the house of Israel, according to Ezekiel, would involve not only the gathering of the dispersed to their promised land (Ezek. 37:21, 25), but it would also entail the reunification of the two rival nations, Israel and Judah (Ezek. 37:22). The united monarchy of David and Solomon split into two separate countries shortly after Solomon's death (1 Kgs. 12), with the northern ten tribes as the kingdom of Israel and the tribes of Judah and Benjamin as the kingdom of Judah. Since that time they had been rival kingdoms with separate histories, separate ruling families, and separate destinies. Israel—which was frequently called "Joseph" or "Ephraim"[9]—was destroyed by the Assyrians a century and a half before Ezekiel received this revelation. Most of its

---

[8]The mere availability of the two companion records does not necessarily mean that their union is complete. Elder Boyd K. Packer pointed out in 1982 that the newest editions of the scriptures are a part of the bringing together of the "sticks" foreseen by Ezekiel: "The stick or record of Judah—the Old Testament and the New Testament—and the stick or record of Ephraim—the Book of Mormon, which is another testament of Jesus Christ—are now woven together in such a way that as you pore over one you are drawn to the other; as you learn from one you are enlightened by the other. They are indeed one in our hands" (in Conference Report, Oct. 1982, p. 75; see also pp. 73–76).

[9]For Joseph, see Ezek. 37:16, 19; Obad. 1:18; Zech. 10:6. For Ephraim, see Isa. 7:2, 5, 8, 9, 17; 11:13; 17:3; Jer. 7:15; 31:6, 9, 18, 20; Ezek. 37:16, 19; Hosea 4:17; 5:3, 11–14; 6:4, 10; 8:9, 11; 9:3; 10:6, 11; 11:3, 8, 9, 12; Zech. 9:10, 13. It is likely that several other more ambiguous references to Joseph and Ephraim also refer to the entire kingdom of Israel. See Zimmerli, p. 274.

people who survived the warfare were deported to other parts of the Assyrian empire (2 Kgs. 17:1–24), from which their descendants now have lost their identity and have become assimilated into the nations of the world. By the time of this revelation, Judah had been beaten by the Babylonians. Its capital city, Jerusalem, lay in ruins, and much of its population (including Ezekiel) had been deported to Mesopotamia or had been scattered or directed elsewhere (including Lehi).

Under these circumstances, Ezekiel's revelation of the reunification of Israel and Judah was remarkable. Like the two inscribed boards, they would be brought together again and would become "one nation . . . , and they shall be no more two nations, neither shall they be divided into two kingdoms any more at all" (Ezek. 37:22).

This is a prophecy of greatest importance that still has not been fulfilled. But we know who the two nations are today, and we know what must be done before they will be brought together. Judah consists of the Jews, who are scattered in most of the nations of the earth. Aside from the very few who have accepted the gospel, they are still outside the covenants which the Lord established with their fathers in biblical times. Israel is The Church of Jesus Christ of Latter-day Saints, the vast majority of whose members belong, either by birth or by adoption, to the chief northern tribes of Ephraim and Manasseh.[10] The prophesied reunification of the two groups will come when the descendants of Judah accept the covenants of the gospel of Jesus Christ and join with their brothers and sisters of Israel in the Lord's Church. It appears that the complete fulfillment of this prophecy will not be seen until after Christ's second coming.

Ezekiel's prophecy of the restoration of Israel's kingship is also remarkable. As in chapter 34, he used the name *David* for the messianic ruler: "And David my servant shall be king over them; and they all shall have one shepherd. . . . And my servant David shall be their prince for ever" (Ezek. 37:24–25). Jesus Christ is the latter-day "David," the "King," the "Shepherd," and the "Prince" of Israel. In the Millennium, the time in which all of Ezekiel's promises will find their ultimate realization, he "will reign personally upon the earth," as Joseph Smith prophesied (A

---

[10]See Kent P. Jackson, "The Abrahamic Covenant: A Blessing for All People," *Ensign*, Feb. 1990, pp. 50–53.

of F 10). As I have explained elsewhere (see the discussion at Ezek. 34:23–24 in Chap. 27 of this volume), we need not look to anyone else but Christ as Israel's millennial king, because the scriptures clearly identify him in that role.

The restored Israelite nation, in its several millennial locations, will be Zion, a community of faithful individuals who have overcome sin and have joined the Lord in covenants. They will be those, as Moroni wrote, "whose garments are white through the blood of the Lamb . . . , for they have been washed in the blood of the Lamb; and they are they who were scattered and gathered in from the four quarters of the earth, and from the north countries,[11] and are partakers of the fulfilling of the covenant which God made with their father, Abraham" (Ether 13:10–11). When the covenant is renewed and the relationship restored between Jehovah and his people, it will be "a covenant of peace . . . an everlasting covenant" (Ezek. 37:26). And again the Lord will affirm, "I will be their God, and they shall be my people" (Ezek. 37:27; see also v. 23).

Apocalyptic Revelation

There are several sections of the scriptures in which visions are presented in a highly symbolic revelatory style called "apocalyptic."[12] An understanding of this kind of writing will enhance our study of the remainder of the book of Ezekiel. Apocalyptic vision is the mode of revelation in which the observer is withdrawn from the earthly sphere with its normal circumstances of time and space and is moved, as it were, into the realm of the divine. In this realm he sees things no longer from an earthly perspective but from the perspective of the visionary sphere. Most often what he sees there cannot be described in earthly terms and

---

[11]The terms "four quarters of the earth" and "north countries" both represent the various locations throughout the earth where the house of Israel was scattered. Since north was the direction to which the deportees of Israel and Judah were taken, their return is often described as being from the north.

[12]Because definitions of apocalyptic literature vary, no universally accepted list exists. D. S. Russell includes only the book of Daniel from the Old Testament in his list of fully developed apocalyptic literature; see *The Method and Message of Jewish Apocalyptic* (Philadelphia: Westminster, 1976), pp. 36–39. He includes Ezek. 38–39, Zech., Joel 3, and Isa. 24–27 in a transitional category that later developed into full apocalyptic.

can only be characterized with the use of vivid, dramatic symbols, most of which transcend our understanding of "normal" space, logic, time, and the rules of science as we understand them. Ezekiel's visions in chapters 1 and 10 are excellent examples of this, as are Daniel's revelations in chapters 7 through 12.[13]

Apocalyptic vision is characterized by what is called "dualism" — the idea of the universal struggle between the forces of evil and good. In the here-and-now the forces of evil usually prevail. But there will be an end-of-the-world time in which the forces of good, God and his chosen Saints, will triumph over the forces of evil, Satan and his hosts. The victory of right over wrong will not take place as a result of the natural flow of history. Instead, there will be a dramatic break with the past, as God and his forces will stop the course of history to defeat the powers of darkness and bring the world into the final age of peace and glory. God's ultimate victory is sure; it is predetermined.

This kind of revelation is highly typological — it abounds in vivid symbols, or "types." The types frequently are patterns that represent more than one specific thing; often they represent whole categories.[14] Apocalyptic prophecies are "fulfilled" whenever the categories that are depicted exist. In other words, they can be "fulfilled" more than once and with different individuals or nations involved. At the same time, however, they point to a grand and *ultimate* fulfillment, on a universal scale, in a last-days setting.

The symbolism in apocalyptic vision is thus much different from metaphor, the literary imagery that is used so abundantly throughout the Old Testament. Metaphor is meant to be understood. For the most part it is easily comprehended by those who are familiar with the culture,

---

[13]Although they lack the bizarre imagery of the visions of Ezekiel and Daniel, Lehi's and Nephi's visions of the tree of life exhibit apocalyptic characteristics. In their visions, Lehi and later Nephi were transported into a world of symbols. It seems safe to suggest that the tree, the rod of iron, the great building, and other things they saw never actually existed except as symbols in the vision (see 1 Ne. 8–14). The apocalyptic nature of the latter part of the vision is even more apparent. See Stephen E. Robinson, "Early Christianity and 1 Nephi 13–14," in *First Nephi, The Doctrinal Foundation*, ed. M. S. Nyman and C. D. Tate (Provo, Utah: Religious Studies Center, Brigham Young University, 1988), pp. 177–91.

[14]For example, the scenes depicted in the tree of life vision did not represent a specific event in the experience of Lehi's family but a lifelong process by which they chose to follow either God or the ways of the world.

history, language, geography, and social circumstances in which the scripture arose.[15] Apocalyptic vision, in striking contrast, is meant to be understood fully only with the help of other revelation. The vision usually requires an angelic interpreter or a companion revelation to unlock its meaning.[16] Joseph Smith taught this principle:

> When the prophets speak of seeing beasts in their visions, they saw the images — types to represent certain things. And at the same time they received the interpretation as to what those images or types were designed to represent. I make this broad declaration, that where God ever gives a vision of an image, or beast, or figure of any kind, he always holds himself responsible to give a revelation or interpretation of the meaning thereof, otherwise we are not responsible or accountable for our belief in it. Don't be afraid of being damned for not knowing the meaning of a vision or figure where God has not given a revelation or interpretation on the subject.[17]

Nephi was accompanied through the symbolic world of the vision of the tree of life by a heavenly messenger, who translated its symbols for him (1 Ne. 8–14). Modern readers can understand its meaning because of the interpretation the messenger provided. In several other apocalyptic visions, however, the Lord has not yet seen fit to provide an interpretation in the scriptures. Thus we must read them with caution and recognize that we will not fully understand them until the Lord makes their meaning known.

Gog's Invasion of Israel (Ezek. 38–39)

Ezekiel 38 and 39 contain a vision that exhibits some important traits of apocalyptic revelation.[18] The vision depicts an invasion of "Israel" by

---

[15]As Nephi wrote, the Jews could understand the writings of their prophets because they were intimately familiar with these things (2 Ne. 25:5–6). See Kent P. Jackson, "Nephi and Isaiah," in *Studies in Scripture, Volume Seven: 1 Nephi to Alma 29*, ed. Kent P. Jackson (Salt Lake City: Deseret Book Co., 1987), pp. 134–39.

[16]An example of the latter is D&C 77, which interprets passages from John's revelation.

[17]Discourse of 8 April 1843, recorded by William Clayton; Andrew F. Ehat and Lyndon W. Cook, eds., *The Words of Joseph Smith* (Provo, Utah: Religious Studies Center, Brigham Young University, 1980), p. 185; punctuation and spelling modernized. Also in Joseph Smith, *Teachings of the Prophet Joseph Smith*, sel. Joseph Fielding Smith (Salt Lake City: Deseret Book Co., 1938), p. 291.

[18]Scholars generally see Ezek. 38–48 as not fully developed apocalyptic literature, which they

a foreign power called "Gog" of the land of "Magog," the "chief prince of Meshech and Tubal" (Ezek. 38:1). Gog and his forces will attack the "mountains of Israel," whose people will have been "brought forth out of the nations" and will be dwelling safely (Ezek. 38:7–8). Like "a cloud to cover the land," he and his allies—"a great company, and a mighty army"—will advance on the Lord's people (Ezek. 38:15–16). But the Lord will not allow them to succeed. With earthquake, sword, pestilence, blood, rain, hailstones, fire, and brimstone the Lord will intervene to stop Gog's attack; he and his armies will be slaughtered (Ezek. 38:19–39:8). So massive will be Gog's armies and so thorough their defeat that for seven years the people of Israel will gather the weapons of their defeated enemies and use them for fuel. Their corpses will be so abundant that it will take seven months to bury them. Even after that, individuals will be employed to go through the land to find the bodies not yet buried (Ezek. 39:9–16). Next is depicted a huge feast, in which the birds and the animals will gorge themselves on the blood and flesh of the slain (Ezek. 39:17–20; see also D&C 29:20).[19]

Apocalyptic elements are readily apparent in this vision, suggesting that it is an apocalyptic scene and not necessarily a literal transcript of one specific future event. The latter-day setting of the prophecy seems clear. The Lord's people are called "Israel," and they have been "gathered out of many people" and "brought forth out of the nations" (Ezek. 38:8). It seems likely that Israel here does not represent a latter-day political entity, country, or geographical location, but the Lord's people, wherever they may be found. As President Spencer W. Kimball taught, "the gathering of Israel consists of joining the true church and their coming to a knowledge of the true God."[20] Israel thus represents the Lord's Saints, the members of his Church who have gathered to the covenants of his gospel throughout the nations of the world.

In the symbolic vision, Gog, coming with vast armies from distant unknown lands, sets as his goal the devastation and plunder of the Lord's

---

feel is best manifested in documents from the second century B.C. Instead, Ezek. 38–48 is called "proto-Apocalyptic," or "the 'stuff' from which apocalyptic is made." See Russell, pp. 88–91.

[19]The destruction of the wicked is depicted as a sacrificial feast also in Isa. 34:5–8 and Zeph. 1:7.

[20]Spencer W. Kimball, *The Teachings of Spencer W. Kimball*, ed. Edward L. Kimball (Salt Lake City: Bookcraft, 1984), pp. 439–40.

people. In apocalyptic fashion, the figure "Gog" here probably does not represent a real person or nation who will attack the Saints with military force. Instead, he and his hosts seem to represent the powers of evil that are arrayed against the Saints, manifested in a variety of ways, places, and times. Satan is the very embodiment of this evil and the archenemy of the Lord and his followers. As the vision depicts, the forces of evil will not be allowed to prevail. With a mighty act so characteristic of apocalyptic scenes, the Lord himself will intervene to put an end to evil and its consequences.

When will this prophecy be "fulfilled"? As stated above, this kind of apocalyptic typology often represents entire categories rather than specific individuals or events. But there are enough close parallels between this prophecy and others (both apocalyptic and predictive), that the time-frame for its fulfillment seems apparent.

In the period in which we now live, the gathering of the house of Israel and the establishment of Zion have commenced. Satan's forces, in a variety of manifestations, are engaged in relentless battle against Israel, that is, against individual Saints and the Church collectively. As other scriptures teach us, their efforts will increase in intensity as the coming of Christ draws near (see 1 Ne. 14:11–14). Like the hosts of Gog, however, they will not succeed in their efforts to destroy the Lord's Church. Instead, all forms of wickedness will be wiped from the earth in preparation for the Savior's coming in glory, which will usher in a thousand-year era of millennial peace.

The Book of Mormon prophet Nephi recorded a revelation similar to that of Ezekiel, in which he described this same effort of Satan and his followers to destroy the Saints (1 Ne. 14:11–17). Whereas Ezekiel used the image of a mysterious "Gog" from the land of "Magog," Nephi chose the image of a "great whore" — "the mother of abominations," "the mother of harlots" — to represent the same things that Ezekiel foretold. As Nephi described it, the Church will be found "upon all the face of the earth" (1 Ne. 14:12). The forces of evil will muster their resources "among all the nations of the Gentiles" in order to "fight against the Lamb of God" (1 Ne. 14:13). But "the power of the Lamb of God" will descend on the Saints throughout the world, and they will be "armed with righteousness and with the power of God in great glory" (1 Ne. 14:14). In his wrath, the Lord will punish the enemies of his people by subjecting them to "wars and rumors of wars among all the nations and kindreds of the earth" (1 Ne. 14:15; see also v. 16). Nephi's vision in 1 Nephi 14 is thus an additional witness for what Ezekiel foretold, but more importantly, it enables us to understand Ezekiel's message. Additional insight from modern revelation is provided in a passage in the Doctrine and Covenants describing the destruction of the wicked: "And the great and abominable church, which is the whore of all the earth, shall be cast down by devouring fire, according as it is spoken by the mouth of Ezekiel the prophet, who spoke of these things, which have not come to pass but surely must, as I live, for abominations shall not reign" (D&C 29:21).[21]

Almost all Old Testament prophecy focuses on these latter-day events: the restoration of the house of Israel, the destruction of wickedness, the coming of the Lord, and the Millennium. It should not surprise us, then, if these are the very themes alluded to by Ezekiel in the important apocalyptic scene recorded in Ezekiel 38 and 39. The emphasis is on the efforts of the adversary to overcome the Saints, followed by his destruction and the end of his evil works when the Lord intervenes to save his people. Ezekiel's conclusion bears testimony to these truths: "Now will I bring again the captivity[22] of Jacob, and have mercy on the whole house of Israel. . . . I have gathered them unto their own land, and have left none of them any more [in captivity]. Neither will I hide my face any more from them: for I have poured out my spirit upon the house of Israel, saith the Lord God" (Ezek. 39:25–29).[23]

---

[21]Footnotes at D&C 29:20–21 identify Ezek. 38–39 as the Ezekiel prophecy referred to in the D&C passage. Though the wording is not identical, the identification is most likely correct, as it is the closest thing in Ezekiel to the content of D&C 29:21. If this is the case, then Gog's battle against Israel is the same thing as the great whore's battle against the Saints in 1 Ne. 14.

[22]The Hebrew that underlies the KJV phrase "bring again the captivity" means either "bring back from captivity" or "restore the fortunes."

[23]John used the names "Gog" and "Magog" in his apocalyptic prophecy of the great battle at the end of the Millennium. In Rev. 20:7–10, "Gog and Magog" are used to personify those whom Satan will induce to rebel against God in his final effort to derail God's work. They attack Zion, but God intervenes with fire from heaven that devours them. Satan is then "cast into the lake of fire and brimstone" (cf. Jacob 5:76–77). These are typical apocalyptic images that reflect the vocabulary of Ezekiel's vision.

The Envisioned Temple and Its Surroundings
(Ezek. 40–48)

The last nine chapters of the book of Ezekiel record another great apocalyptic vision. In it are depicted, among other things, a temple with its priesthood and sacrifices, the division of the land among the tribes, and the dimensions of the land and the city.

This vision, received in the twenty-fifth year of Ezekiel's exile, or 573 B.C., is like nothing else in the Old Testament. Its apocalyptic nature is evident. As we learn from the introductory verses, Ezekiel was transported "in the visions of God" from Babylonia to a "very high mountain" which overlooked Jerusalem and its temple to the south (Ezek. 40:2). There he was met by a man whose appearance was like bronze,[24] who accompanied him and guided him through the vision. These elements of the revelation—transported in vision, placed on a very high mountain, nonexistent mountain north of the temple, strange angelic guide—are recognizable characteristics of apocalyptic literature. As discussed earlier, apocalyptic vision is characterized by the use of vivid symbolic scenes that can only be understood fully with the help of additional revealed information. It seems that much more needs to be made known concerning this vision before all of its symbols can be understood. Still, its general message of a renewed house of Israel in a renewed promised land is clear.

In the vision, Ezekiel's guide gave the prophet a detailed tour of a temple in Jerusalem, including all its surrounding structures. The guide carried with him a measuring stick with which precise measurements were provided throughout the vision (cf. Rev. 21:9–10, 15–17).[25] The first part of the temple complex observed and measured was the area from the east gate to the outer court. After that, Ezekiel and his guide saw the outer court, the north and south gates, the gates to the inner court, rooms for the preparation of sacrifices, rooms for the priests, and the temple itself (Ezek. 40:5–42:20).

Ezekiel was next brought to the gate facing east, from which he saw the glory of God approaching the temple. With radiant light and the

---

[24]KJV "brass"; more accurately, bronze.

[25]See Ezek. 40:5 and fn. 5c in the LDS Bible for an explanation of the "long cubits" used in this vision.

roar of rushing waters, the glory of the Lord entered through the gate where the prophet stood and filled the Lord's house with its splendor (Ezek. 43:1–5; 44:4). Almost two decades earlier Ezekiel had experienced a similar apocalyptic vision in which he saw God's glory depart (Ezek. 9:3; 10:18–19; 11:22–23). In that earlier vision an angelic guide showed him the temple in its time of wickedness (Ezek. 8–11). In graphic detail he saw symbolic figures and actions that represented its apostasy and the evil works that were done in it. Now, years later and after the destruction of the temple and the exile of the Jews, he saw in striking symbols a vision of the temple in a purified state. Whereas Ezekiel's first temple vision represented all that was corrupt and degenerate about Israel's relationship with God, his later visionary temple represents all that will be holy and glorious about that relationship when the house of Israel is purified.

The next stop in Ezekiel's visionary tour was at the altar, where he was given instructions for the direction of the priests in their sacrifices (Ezek. 43:13–27). In chapter 44 he learned of the roles of the priests and the Levites in the temple. Of these, only the "sons of Zadok" would be allowed to enter the sanctuary (Ezek. 44:15–16).[26] Through their actions and their appearance, they would teach the Lord's people the difference between the "holy" and the "profane" and "the unclean and the clean" (Ezek. 44:23). Ezekiel was shown the division of the land and the sacred precinct that would result from it. The priests and the Levites would each receive an inheritance 25,000 cubits long and 10,000 cubits wide. The sanctuary would be located in the priests' portion. The property of the city, which would belong to the whole house of Israel, would be 25,000 cubits by 5,000 cubits. Adjacent to these portions would be the property of the prince (Ezek. 45:1–12).[27] Ezekiel found out more about these special allotments at a later stage in his vision (Ezek. 48:8–22).

Ezekiel next learned, in some detail, of the offerings and holy days that would be observed in the temple. Everything was to be administered according to a prescribed plan (Ezek. 45:13–46:23).

A new scene of the vision opened as Ezekiel's guide took him to the

---

[26]Zadok was the high priest during the reign of King David. The lineage of Israel's legitimate high priests descended from his line, through which John the Baptist came into the world.

[27]For a drawing of these divisions, see Zimmerli, p. 535.

entrance of the temple, from which he saw water flowing from under the threshold toward the east. He and his guide followed the flow of water and measured its depth along the way. A thousand cubits from the source it was ankle deep. A thousand cubits farther it was knee deep. After another thousand it was up to his waist, and after another it was a river, deep enough to swim in (Ezek. 47:1–5). The water continued its flow to the Dead Sea, which became a freshwater lake on contact with the river from the temple. Ezekiel saw that swarms of living things would live wherever the river flowed, and varieties of fish would inhabit the lake which had once been hostile to life (Ezek. 47:6–10). Fruit trees of all kinds would adorn the banks of the river. "Their leaves will not wither, nor will their fruit fail. Every month they will bear, because the water from the sanctuary flows to them. Their fruit will serve for food and their leaves for healing" (Ezek. 47:12, NIV[28]).

The next part of Ezekiel's vision focuses on the division of the land among the tribes (Ezek. 47:13–48:29). All thirteen of the tribes are mentioned, and each would receive an inheritance.[29] The list includes Levi, which in Old Testament times did not receive a tribal allotment but was settled in special cities throughout the territories of the other tribes. Even non-Israelites would receive an inheritance. Those who would dwell among the children of Israel would be considered as native-born Israelites and would receive an inheritance among them (Ezek. 47:21–23).

In the last segment of the vision, Ezekiel learned the names of the gates of the holy city. On each of the four sides of the city—which would be 4,500 cubits square—there would be three gates, each one named for one of the tribes (Ezek. 48:30–34). In this case Ephraim and Manasseh are not mentioned, but one gate is named Joseph and one is named Levi.

A Millennial Temple in Jerusalem

It appears that Ezekiel's vision represents the millennial condition of the house of Israel, in which they will enjoy the blessings of their

---

[28]New International Version.

[29]For a map, see Zimmerli, p. 537.

promised land, their holy ci'y, and their temple. The centerpiece of the vision is a house of God that will be built at some future time. Some have suggested that Ezekiel foresaw Jews in Palestine building a temple independently of the Church and without a knowledge of the gospel of Jesus Christ. If they did, it would not be in fulfillment of divine prophecy (Ezekiel's or anyone else's), for the Lord's house is a house of order, and the keys of temple building are found only in The Church of Jesus Christ of Latter-day Saints (D&C 110:13–16).[30] If there is to be a true temple built by members of the house of Judah someday, it will not be a temple of Judaism but of Mormonism, built by Jewish Latter-day Saints to the glory of their Savior, Jesus Christ.[31]

As in other apocalyptic visions, the symbols often are not meant to portray literally the events, people, or things, but to characterize or idealize them. It seems that such is the case with this vision. It depicts the future glories of Israel's restoration in the most idealized images. Everything about the millennial day—including the land, the city, and the temple—would exceed by far the best of what had existed in earlier times. But the vision was limited by the level of doctrinal understanding of its readers, who were still under the Law of Moses without a comprehension of the gospel of Christ and still rejected the words of living prophets, as is so evident in the book of Ezekiel. Thus the vision showed a temple of the Law of Moses, patterned after the temples of ancient Israel. Officiating in it was the Aaronic priesthood, as in biblical times (Ezek. 43:13–27; 44:10–31), and burnt offerings, sin offerings, and fellowship ("peace") offerings are depicted (Ezek. 43:18–27).[32]

But the scriptures make it clear that the Law of Moses and its sacrifices by the shedding of blood were ended with the atonement of Christ (Alma 34:13–14; Heb. 10:18). Given this fact, it seems unlikely that a temple for the performance of Mosaic animal offerings will ever again be built, especially during the Millennium, when there will be no death. Future

[30]Elder Bruce R. McConkie taught: "There is only one place under the whole heavens where the keys of temple building are found. There is only one people who know how to build temples and what to do in them when they are completed. That people is the Latter-day Saints" *Millennial Messiah* (Salt Lake City: Deseret Book Co., 1982), p. 279.

[31]See ibid., pp. 279–80.

[32]Of these, it appears that only burnt offerings predate the Law of Moses. Sin offerings and fellowship offerings were part of the Mosaic system.

temples, both before and after the Second Coming, will presumably be similar to those with which we are familiar in the Church now, in which ordinances of the Melchizedek Priesthood will be performed for the living and the dead. Joseph Smith taught that to make the Restoration complete, "all things had under the Authority of the Priesthood at any former period shall be had again." He included the restoration of sacrifice in his discussion, though not of those sacrifices that were revealed with the Law of Moses.[33] Given the clear message from the scriptures that animal sacrifice ended with Christ (Alma 34:13–14), perhaps we can view the sacrifice of which the Prophet spoke as a short-term or one-time event in fulfillment of Malachi 3:3 and 4, to signal that the Levites are again in the covenant and have assumed their rightful priesthood function in the house of Israel.[34]

Ezekiel's vision portrayed the future temple by means of familiar Old Testament temple images because his readers would not have recognized or comprehended a temple like ours today. The Lord communicates with people in their own language and according to their level of understanding (D&C 1:24). In this vision he taught ancient Jews transcendent millennial things by using images drawn from their own time and experience. The design, purpose, and ordinances of modern temples would have made no sense to them (just as they make no sense to Jews and other Christians today). The real millennial temple will be much different from its visionary symbol — more glorious and with a more profound purpose. In it, worthy Saints will enter into covenants and participate in sacred ordinances — all designed to help them prepare to enter the presence of God in the highest degree of glory.

Who will build this temple? When? And where will it stand? Because Ezekiel's immediate ministry was to Jews recently exiled from their homeland, who had experienced the destruction of their kingdom, their city, and their temple, it is likely that the scene he witnessed has its focus in the restoration of Judah and Jerusalem. As other passages of scripture teach, a temple will yet be built in that city. Whether or not it will

---

[33]Ehat and Cook, p. 42; see also pp. 43–44.

[34]See also Joseph Fielding Smith, *Doctrines of Salvation,* 3 vols., sel. Bruce R. McConkie (Salt Lake City: Bookcraft, 1954–56), 3:93–94; Bruce R. McConkie, *Mormon Doctrine,* 2d ed. (Salt Lake City: Bookcraft, 1966), p. 666; *The Mortal Messiah,* 4 vols. (Salt Lake City: Deseret Book Co., 1979–81), 1:128.

stand on the same spot as the ancient temples is not important. What is important, however, is that one day the inhabitants of Jerusalem will again be worthy to have a house of God in their midst. Ezekiel's images suggest that it will be built in a day when Israel is gathered and its people sanctified—conditions which can only follow the time when they will lay aside the false religions and traditions of their ancestors and join the Church of Jesus Christ through baptismal covenants. It appears that for the people there in general, it will be only after the Second Coming that those conditions will exist. Those who will participate in its construction will be the Saints of God who will reside in that area—Jews who will have gathered again to the covenants, Arabs who will have likewise joined the Lord's Church, and others who will dwell among them.

"The Lord Is There"

Other symbols in Ezekiel's vision convey additional insights. The scene of the division of the land depicts the restoration of all the tribes of Israel to allotted territory in Palestine (Ezek. 47:13–48:29). Modern revelation explains, however, that whereas Judah will one day be restored in righteousness to the Holy Land, the descendants of Manasseh and Ephraim will receive their inheritance in the New World (see 3 Ne. 15:13; 16:16; 21:22; Ether 13:8). And it is not unlikely that diverse parts of the world will be provided as gathering places for others of the covenant people. Perhaps Ezekiel's symbolic division of the land represents a future presence for members of all the tribes in their ancestral homeland. Or perhaps it represents all the millennial gathering places worldwide in which faithful covenant people will dwell. In that millennial day when all the world is Zion, the location and extent of one's real estate is likely to be of minor interest. And perhaps prophecies of gathering to promised lands have more to do with gathering to covenants than with geographical matters.

The vision depicts a river of water flowing from beneath the temple and bringing life to everything it touches (Ezek. 47:1–12). Similar scenes are found in Joel 3:18, Zechariah 14:8, and Revelation 22:1. In the apocalyptic contexts of all three of these passages, the symbolic waters seem to convey the idea of truth, life, and healing emanating from the

Lord's house to fill the world. "Whosoever drinketh of the water that I shall give him shall never thirst," Jesus said, "but the water that I shall give him shall be in him a well springing up into everlasting life" (John 4:14). In the Millennium, Isaiah wrote, "the earth shall be full of the knowledge of the Lord, as the waters cover the sea" (Isa. 11:9). Truth and eternal life will flow freely in that day, and a literal transformation of the planet will take place as well: the parched places will become green, the deserts will blossom as a rose (Isa. 35:1–7), and "the earth will be renewed and receive its paradisiacal glory" (A of F 10).

In Ezekiel's earlier vision he witnessed the glory of the Lord leaving the temple, which had become unworthy of the divine presence (Ezek. 10:18–19; 11:22–23). In this vision of millennial things he saw it return, this time to usher in a thousand years of Christ's reign (Ezek. 43:1–5; 44:4). Holiness and glory will be the watchwords in that day, for they will fill the earth and characterize all that is done in it. As Zechariah foretold, even the pots and pans and the bells on the horses will be inscribed with "Holiness unto the Lord" (Zech. 14:20–21), just as our temples are today. "For the Lord shall be in their midst, and his glory shall be upon them, and he will be their king and their lawgiver" (D&C 45:59). We look forward with anticipation to the glorious Millennium and hope to be worthy to be citizens of Zion then, when Christ's presence will sanctify the earth and those who will be privileged to dwell on it. That will be the day in which Jerusalem will at last become a Holy City — so appropriately renamed in Ezekiel's vision: "The Lord is there" (Ezek. 48:35).

29

THE BOOK OF DANIEL

RICHARD D. DRAPER

Judah's perplexity and fear due to the Babylonian Exile provided the driving force leading to the content of the book of Daniel. With its focus on one of the great seers of all time, it was written to ignite faith in Israel's God and to instill courage and patience in the hearts of uprooted exiles. The society in which they lived—Babylon, also called Chaldea— was at best antagonistic to their religion and at worst outright hostile to it. The author's objective in recording Daniel's experiences seems to have been to teach his people that not only could they live their religion in this alien and spiritually inhospitable land but they could also find a close relationship with God in doing so. In other words, God had not abandoned his people and would, therefore, continue to be their God even in Babylon.

Daniel had a message that complemented and confirmed the testimony of other prophets, such as Ezekiel and Jeremiah. The Exile was not to be permanent. The present distress was only for a moment. If it were endured with faith, Judah would see the great day of deliverance. Babylon could not prevent it. No nation, not even this mighty colossus, could withstand God's designs. Indeed, Daniel bore witness to the unimaginable: the powerful nation that had taken Judah and other nations captive would in due time lose all control over its captives and pass from the scene of history.

Daniel could appreciate as few others could what it would take for Babylon to fall. He came personally to control a good deal of the power

---

Richard D. Draper is assistant professor of ancient scripture at Brigham Young University.

of that great nation and also of the Persian empire that succeeded it. These were no weak, backwater states. Babylon and Persia each in turn controlled most of the Near Eastern world (see Maps 11 and 12, LDS Bible). But through profound revelations, Daniel knew that God had begun to winnow the nations, and this process would continue beyond the time of Babylon and Persia. No matter how great any one nation would become, another nation, great and terrible, would rise to take its place, only to fall in its turn. Finally, near the end time, God would bring forth his kingdom, which would eventually encompass the whole earth and never be thrown down. Thus, each of these seemingly formidable empires was little more than a footnote to the real history of the world. They represented impotent aberrations occupying only for a moment the stage of history. None of these, Daniel testified, was the actual driving force of history. God is.

This truth rested upon another less obvious but equally important reality. Daniel's book, like much of apocalyptic literature, insists that God has preordained history. According to this view, God is both sovereign and ultimate. He has set the course of the nations and determined the final outcome of world history.[1] With this principle in mind, Daniel taught his people an important lesson: even though the people of God were in captivity, the Lord controlled their destiny. The indispensable lesson the prophet urged upon them was anchored in the reality that God was master and that his kingdom would come. Therefore, they must be faithful to the Lord's commandments and work in concert with him. God would not force their allegiance. They were agents who could choose for themselves, but they must be prepared to fall with the kingdoms of the world if they were not willing to maintain their citizenship in the kingdom of God.

But Judah was not the only people who had to learn that God ruled supreme. Daniel's book shows that the rulers of the nations who temporarily controlled the fate of Judah also had to learn an important lesson: their false gods were nothing; Israel's God was everything.

---

[1]Apocalyptic literature does not concern itself with the problem between agency and predestination. Both are believed to be simultaneously operating causes. Men are free to act, but so is God. He has foreordained the order of things and they will come out as he has determined, but he acts in harmony with the principle of free will.

Authorship

This book of scripture is named after its major character, the prophet Daniel. The first six chapters were written about him and his associates in the third person, suggesting that the events may have been recorded by someone else. But chapters 7 through 12 are clearly first-person autobiographical records of his visions. Thus the book consists of some episodes from his life (whether written down by him or by someone else) collected with his own record of his visions. There is no way to know if the compilation was made during his own lifetime or later on.

But the book contains some difficulties that suggest that it may not have been transmitted carefully or accurately through the generations.[2] There are some apparent chronological problems, such as the statement that Darius conquered Babylon (Dan. 5:30–31), and the apparent placing of Darius earlier than Cyrus (Dan. 1:21; 6:28).[3] Some scholars also see references and vocabulary in the text that they believe reflect a date of authorship centuries after Daniel's time. While some use these questions to date the book very late (second century B.C.), a wiser conclusion would be that the text of Daniel carries some scars from the process of translation and transmission before it reached its final form. But even so, the problems are minor; its message has been preserved with complete fidelity, and modern revelation confirms the accuracy of its major doctrinal sections (see D&C 65:1–6; 116; 138:44).[4]

The book of Daniel easily divides into two sections, each of which deals with the same basic theme: God's dominion is over all nations. The first half of the book (chaps. 1–6) deals with the experience of Daniel and his associates and shows the supremacy of Jehovah over gods, kings, and nations. Tied to this is the idea that God will not abide the prideful

---

[2]One puzzle concerning its transmission is that Dan. 1:1–2:4a and 8:1–12:13 are preserved in Hebrew, whereas the rest is inexplicably in Aramaic.

[3]Darius I Hystaspes (see Ezra 4:5, 24; 6:14–15; Hag. 1) gained the throne of the Persian empire in 522 B.C., some years after Cyrus conquered Babylon in 539 B.C. Scholars who date the book of Daniel late believe, based on some historical sources, that it was Nabonidus, not Nebuchadnezzar, who went insane, as described in Dan. 4. See Georges Roux, *Ancient Iraq*, 2d ed. (Harmondsworth, England: Penguin, 1980), p. 352.

[4]For brief surveys of the dating arguments, see W. S. LaSor, D. A. Hubbard, and F. W. Bush, *Old Testament Survey* (Grand Rapids, Mich.: Eerdmans, 1982), pp. 662–68; and A. E. Hill and J. H. Walton, *A Survey of the Old Testament* (Grand Rapids, Mich.: Zondervan, 1991), pp. 349–51.

arrogance of those who take credit for the things of God. The second portion of the book (chaps. 7–12) deals with God's dominion over later nations and, finally, with the establishment of his kingdom in the latter days.

A God of Gods (Dan. 1–2)

The first task of Daniel was to teach Israel that great blessings follow faith in God and obedience to his commandments. Daniel knew personally of what he spoke, but he did not underplay the difficulty of being faithful. From the beginning, the book stresses that it is not easy to show fidelity to Jehovah while living in Babylon.

Daniel was probably a youth when he was taken into exile by Nebuchadnezzar's forces.[5] Though he lived a long life, at least until the third year of the reign of Cyrus (ca. 536 B.C.; see Dan. 1:21; 10:1), he never again saw his homeland. Instead, he served in the Babylonian and Persian courts. As the Bible points out, his rise to high position was nothing short of providential.

It was apparently Babylonian custom to train promising captive young men to serve in the royal court. Officials carefully screened the boys, looking for those who were "skilful in all wisdom, and cunning in knowledge, and understanding science, and such as had ability in them to stand in the king's palace, and whom they might teach the learning and the tongue of the Chaldeans" (Dan. 1:4). Daniel and some of his friends showed great promise. For this reason they came to the attention of a ranking officer. The record makes it clear this was not by chance, for "God had brought Daniel into favour" (Dan. 1:9). From the outset, Jehovah was with his servants, and the book never lets its readers forget that the omnipresent power of God was ever working with and for the faithful.

---

[5]Dan. 1:1 states that Daniel was taken with exiles in Jehoiakim's third year, after Nebuchadnezzar besieged Jerusalem. The date would be ca. 606 B.C. No known siege or deportation took place that year, but it is known that Nebuchadnezzar, who did not become king until a year later, conducted a campaign to the west at that time. Whether it took him as far to the south as Jerusalem is not known. If the date in Dan. 1:1 was a later, inaccurate addition to the text, then it is more likely that Daniel was taken with the first wave of exiles in 597 B.C., when Ezekiel, King Jehoiachin, and many others were deported. See LaSor, Hubbard, and Bush, p. 662 and n. 7.

The book of Daniel assists its readers in understanding why the prophet found such favor with Jehovah. Three times angels declared to him that he was beloved by God (Dan. 9:23; 10:11, 19). The Hebrew word translated "greatly beloved" could be translated just as readily "very desirable," thus suggesting that Daniel possessed qualities that allowed him to find favor in God's eyes.[6] As the angel Gabriel explained to him: "I am come to shew thee; for thou art greatly beloved: therefore understand the matter, and consider the vision" (Dan. 9:23). Note that it was because Daniel was beloved that he was given to understand the visions both he and others had. The qualities that caused him to find special favor with God were mentioned briefly by an angel: "From the first day that thou didst set thine heart to understand, and to chasten thyself before thy God, thy words were heard, and I am come for thy words" (Dan. 10:12). Determined obedience and humility were two qualities that marked Daniel throughout his ministry. It was this close association with the Spirit that allowed him to understand the deepest mysteries of God.

The book shows that Daniel was determined to keep himself pure from the beginning: he "purposed in his heart that he would not defile himself" (Dan. 1:8). His first challenge came with being chosen as a potential minister within the court. During his training period he was to eat the same food as that prepared for the king. Daniel refused. The issue was not so much that he feared the food violated the Mosaic dietary code as that he knew of the pagan practice of consecrating the king's meals to Babylonian deities. Such meals then became a sort of sacrament through which the king partook of the power of the gods. For Daniel to have eaten the king's food would have been tantamount to idol worship, an admission that these gods had something to offer. Daniel's request that he and his Jewish colleagues be permitted instead to eat vegetables ("pulse," consisting primarily of legumes) for the brief period of ten days was, in reality, little less than a challenge to the notion that one gained power from eating food consecrated to an idol. That the Jewish boys' countenances were noticeably different after such a short period proved the prophet's point; strength came not from idols but from the true and living God (Dan. 1:8–18).

---

[6]The Hebrew word here does not derive from *'hb* or *dwd*, the usual verbs expressing deep affection. It is *hamûdôt*, meaning "highly desired."

The power of the Spirit augmented Daniel's native abilities, which were already considerable. The young prophet soon gained a reputation in the Babylonian court as a "wise man." As one of that group—which included astrologers, magicians, soothsayers, and counselors—whatever befell them as a class also befell him. It was because of this that he brought himself to the attention of the king and became directly involved in the lesson that God was to teach the monarch (see Dan. 2:12–16).

Chapter 2 contains the core of the first half of the book of Daniel. It testifies that God will bring about his work in a specified period of time, and nothing and no one can stop him. The way the revelation came forth both heightens its importance and confirms its truthfulness. The king had a dream that "troubled" his spirit (Dan. 2:1). It appears that he knew precisely the content of the dream but wished to have the interpretation verified through a proof: a clear description of the vision. The confession of the court magicians is all-important: "There is none other that can shew it before the king, except the gods, whose dwelling is not with flesh" (Dan. 2:11). Through this admission the writer set the stage to make two points. First, God, through Daniel, was able to do what the gods of the wise men could not. The inability of the wise men effectively showed that their claimed source of power was nonexistent. Second, Daniel's God did associate with those in the flesh and was very willing to manifest his will. One other point should not be overlooked. Daniel's ability to retell the dream did what the king designed it to do; it gave proof to the validity of Daniel's interpretation. Also important is the king's reaction to Daniel's prophetic ability. Falling before him the king proclaimed: "Of a truth it is, that your God is a God of gods, and a Lord of kings, and a revealer of secrets, seeing thou couldest reveal this secret" (Dan. 2:47). The king's confession did not acknowledge that Jehovah was the supreme God, let alone the only God, but it did make the Lord a recognized member of the Babylonian pantheon. Having Jehovah become just one of the gods was not the objective, however. So the king had more to learn.

The content of the dream, in harmony with Daniel's message throughout the book, teaches us that for the present the government of the world is in the hands of the kingdoms of men. But a future day will come when God's kingdom will prevail. Daniel perceived that the "great image" which the king saw in his dream was a chronological time line that extended from his own time to the last days. The kingdoms of the world would come and go: one would replace another, only in turn to be replaced by another, and so forth (Dan. 2:31–43). It would be in the latter-day setting that God would create his own kingdom—"without hands," i.e., not of human construction—which would supplant the kingdoms of men, "that no place was found for them." Eventually, God's kingdom would fill "the whole earth" (Dan. 2:34–35), but unlike the other kingdoms, "it shall stand forever" (Dan. 2:44).

"The Church of Jesus Christ of Latter-day Saints was restored in 1830 after numerous revelations from the divine source," said President Spencer W. Kimball, "and this is the kingdom, set up by the God of heaven, that would never be destroyed nor superseded, and the stone cut out of the mountain without hands that would become a great mountain and would fill the whole earth. . . . There was purpose for this unveiling of the history of the world so that the honest in heart might be looking forward to its establishment, and numerous good men and women, knowing of the revelations of God and the prospects for the future, have looked forward to this day."[7]

None Can Stay His Hand (Dan. 3–4)

Chapter 3 contains the next lesson that Nebuchadnezzar needed to learn. Again the details are listed in such a way as to highlight a point. The text is clear that Shadrach, Meshach, and Abed-nego refused to worship the new Babylonian image, knowing full well that the consequence was death (Dan. 3:1–12). Explaining that they were worthy of death because they had disobeyed his decree, the king ended his sentencing with a question that was nothing less than a challenge: "And who is that God that shall deliver you out of my hands?" (Dan. 3:15). The king's ill-disguised boast revealed his belief that his great idol was supreme; nothing could overmaster this god.

The prisoners responded, "If it be so, our God whom we serve is able

---

[7]Spencer W. Kimball, in Conference Report, Apr. 1976, p. 10; see also pp. 9–12; D&C 65:2, 5–6. For additional interpretation of the dream, see Kent P. Jackson, "May the Kingdom of God Roll Forth," in *Studies in Scripture, Volume One: The Doctrine and Covenants*, ed. Robert L. Millet and Kent P. Jackson (Salt Lake City: Randall Book, 1984), pp. 251–57.

to deliver us from the burning fiery furnace, and he will deliver us out of thine hand, O king. But if not, be it known unto thee, O king, that we will not serve thy gods, nor worship the golden image which thou hast set up" (Dan. 3:17–18). The response cast no doubt on God's ability to save; the men responded that if God desired to save them he could. But whether or not he did, the idol was still nothing and they would not worship it. That God did save them proved their point—both Nebuchadnezzar and his image were powerless.

The details of the attempted execution magnify the power of God and the helplessness of the king. The text states that the furnace was heated seven times hotter than usual and that the guards who threw the Jews into the fire died before they could get away from the heat. No one could withstand that heat even for a few seconds. Thus, nothing short of divine intervention could save a mortal. But the writer pushed the idea further, noting that when the men were released they did not even smell of smoke (Dan. 3:19–27). Nebuchadnezzar was not slow to get the point when he saw the men walking unharmed amidst the flames in the company of one "like the Son of God" (Dan. 3:25).[8] "There is no other God," he exclaimed, "that can deliver after this sort" (Dan. 3:29). Not only was the king's idol nothing but Jehovah emerged as the great savior God. Now Nebuchadnezzar was ready to acknowledge him as "the high God" (Dan. 4:2). The confession did not mean, however, that the king was ready to follow him as Lord and God. But God's hand was upon him, and the king would learn firsthand of Jehovah's power.

The vision recorded in chapter 4 emphasized God's controlling power over the great king (Dan. 4:1–18). There is a point here that should not be overlooked. The book of Daniel emphasizes the position of Jehovah not only as the God of the Jews but also as the God over the Babylonian king and, thus, over the whole nation as well. Indeed, Jehovah is the God of all nations. Daniel knew immediately upon hearing the dream recorded in Daniel 4:4–18 that the king had come under Jehovah's censure and that judgment would follow (Dan. 4:19–27). The curse had a purpose:

[8]The translators of the KJV identified the one "like the Son of God" (Dan. 3:25) with Christ, as shown by the capital letter on "Son" (Hebrew and Aramaic have no capital letters). More likely, it was an angel, because the Aramaic term, bar-'elāhîn, was used commonly in ancient literature for subordinate gods, angelic beings, members of the heavenly council, etc.

it would remain, said Daniel, "till thou know that the most High ruleth in the kingdom of men, and giveth it to whomsoever he will" (Dan. 4:25). That one verse summarizes the major thesis of the book. Both the visions of Nebuchadnezzar and those of Daniel all teach that lesson.

Daniel is careful to point out the specific sin that brought the curse from God — Nebuchadnezzar's pride — and at the same time show that he tried to prevent it. "Break off thy sins by righteousness," the prophet pleaded, "and thine iniquities by shewing mercy to the poor" (Dan. 4:27). But the arrogant king refused. The text reveals the king's insolent pride, quoting his boast, "Is not this great Babylon, that I have built for the house of the kingdom by the might of my power, and for the honour of my majesty?" (Dan. 4:30). Thus was fully exposed the king's self-centered refusal to recognize the hand of God, in spite of personal revelation. God's punishment was swift and full. As predicted, the king went mad (Dan. 4:31–33). The curse lasted until, eventually, the king turned to heaven for help. Then came peace. Nebuchadnezzar was humbled at last. "I blessed the most High," he declared, "and I praised and honoured him that liveth for ever, whose dominion is an everlasting dominion, and his kingdom is from generation to generation: And all the inhabitants of the earth are reputed as nothing: and he doeth according to his will in the army of heaven, and among the inhabitants of the earth: and none can stay his hand" (Dan. 4:34–35). The lesson was learned. God will not long put up with pride. He and he alone rules the nations and sets their course.

The Living God (Dan. 5–6)

Chapter 5 emphasizes God's supremacy by showing that the same kind of arrogance seen earlier brought immediate punishment to the next generation. Belshazzar, the son of Nabonidus, served as a coregent with his father for a time. Revelry heightened by drunkenness lowered his inhibitions and allowed his arrogant impudence to express itself. His decision to drink from the captured wares of Jehovah's temple was, in effect, an attempt to show that he, not just his gods, was superior to Jehovah (Dan. 5:1–4). His vision (Dan. 5:5), like those of Nebuchadnezzar, showed clearly that God controls the destiny of nations. The message written by the divine hand in Aramaic on the wall of the palace constituted a kind of riddle. It was for this reason that the ruler and his court could not figure out its meaning (Dan. 5:7–16). MENE means "a numbering" which, according to Daniel, meant that the number of days determined by God for Babylon's duration was up (Dan. 5:26). TEKEL is a measure of weight. Belshazzar had been weighed on a scale and was found wanting (Dan. 5:27). UPHARSIN can be rendered "(and) separations," "divisions." Daniel linked the singular form, PERES ("a separation," "a division") by a play on words with the name of the nation which would conqueror Babylon — PARAS, the Persians: "Thy kingdom is divided, and given to the Medes and Persians" (Dan. 5:28).

Babylonian rule was to cease. God's will would be done. Further, it would continue to be done. That is the point made in Daniel's harrowing experience of being thrown into the lion's den (Dan. 6:1–28). The author shows the continuity of God's hand over yet another generation, this time with a king of the succeeding empire, Persia. As in each of the other cases, circumstances arose by which Daniel was able to teach the faithful how the name of Jehovah was exalted among the nations. The enemy in this case was not the monarch but officials of the court jealous of Daniel's influence. Darius, the king, seems to have already understood that Daniel's God was the saving God.

A key to this event is that the king "set his heart on Daniel to deliver him: and he laboured till the going down of the sun to deliver him" (Dan. 6:14). But he could not persuade the court. Therefore, the mighty king, shown to be powerless, had to rely on God to do what he himself could not. That Daniel was unharmed proved to all that God was mightier than any mortal or combination of mortals. Darius's proclamation to all parts of his kingdom stated the point clearly: Daniel's God "is the living God, and stedfast for ever, and his kingdom that which shall not be destroyed, and his dominion shall be even unto the end" (Dan. 6:26). The rest of the book of Daniel shows the reality of this statement. God's will is ultimate and his dominion never-ceasing.

The Visions of Daniel (Dan. 7–12)

The second half of the book of Daniel contains the prophet's visions of the history of the earth to the coming of the Son of Man, albeit told in apocalyptic terms (see "Apocalyptic Revelation" in Chap. 28 of this volume). This portion of the book, for the most part, can be treated only in the broadest of outlines, assisted by the thesis of the book as a whole. It is premature to be dogmatic on specifics. Daniel makes repeated references to time, but they are very oblique. The various time frames that add up to three and one-half seem consistently to symbolize the period when evil will dominate. The number seven is associated with the eventual triumph of the Lord.

The reason no detailed commentary can be given for the whole section is that the full understanding of the book has been sealed up. Daniel was told expressly that he was to "shut up the words, and seal the book, even to the time of the end" (Dan. 12:4). In other words, it was deliberately preserved in such a way that its meaning could not be fully known. Further, some of the information contained in his dreams would be kept even from him. "And I heard, but I understood not: then said I, O my Lord, what shall be the end of these things? And he said, Go thy way, Daniel: for the words are closed up and sealed till the time of the end" (Dan. 12:8–9). Thus, the Lord would not explain all the details even to his mighty prophet.

The book of Daniel has remained sealed to this day. The Prophet Joseph Smith counseled the elders, saying, "Never meddle with the visions of beasts and subjects you do not understand."[9] He was obedient to his own counsel, speaking only on very rare occasions about the beasts in Daniel and Revelation, primarily to set straight misunderstandings.[10] The Prophet taught an important principle concerning this kind of revelation:

> When the prophets speak of seeing beasts in their visions, they saw the images — types to represent certain things. And at the same time they received the interpretation as to what those images or types were designed to represent. I make this broad declaration, that where God ever gives a vision of an image, or beast, or figure of any kind, he always holds himself responsible to give a revelation or interpretation of the meaning thereof, otherwise we are not responsible or accountable for

---

[9]Andrew F. Ehat and Lyndon W. Cook, eds., *The Words of Joseph Smith* (Provo, Utah: Religious Studies Center, Brigham Young University, 1980), p. 186.

[10]Joseph Smith, *Teachings of the Prophet Joseph Smith*, sel. Joseph Fielding Smith (Salt Lake City: Deseret Book Co., 1938), pp. 287–94.

our belief in it. Don't be afraid of being damned for not knowing the meaning of a vision or figure where God has not given a revelation or interpretation on the subject.[11]

Thus we must await further revelation to understand these visions clearly. One such inspired insight was provided by Joseph Smith himself: "When God made use of the figure of a beast in visions to the prophets He did it to represent those kingdoms which had degenerated and become corrupt, savage and beast-like in their dispositions, even the degenerate kingdoms of the wicked world." Further, he noted, Daniel's figures "are spoken of to represent the kingdoms of the world, the inhabitants whereof were beastly and abominable characters; they were murderers, corrupt, carnivorous, and brutal in their dispositions. The lion, the bear, the leopard, and the ten-horned beast represented the kingdoms of the world."[12]

Chapter 7 records a vision of a series of four kingdoms (Dan. 7:17), each depicted as a beast with very strange features: a lion, a bear, a leopard, and an undefined beast with iron teeth and ten horns (Dan. 7:2–8). Replacing them, the Ancient of Days took his place, after which the Son of Man appeared. "And there was given him dominion, and glory, and a kingdom, that all people, nations, and languages, should serve him: his dominion is an everlasting dominion, which shall not pass away, and his kingdom that which shall not be destroyed" (Dan. 7:14; see also vv. 9–13).

Of this event we do have some prophetic understanding. Joseph Smith revealed that the Ancient of Days is "the oldest man, our Father Adam, Michael, he will call his children together and hold a council with them to prepare them for the coming of the Son of Man. He (Adam) is the father of the human family, and presides over the spirits of all men, and all that have had the keys must stand before him in this grand council. . . . The Son of Man stands before him, and there is given him glory and dominion. Adam delivers up his stewardship to Christ, that which was delivered to him as holding the keys of the universe, but retains his standing as head of the human family."[13] This great meeting will take

---

[11]Discourse of 8 Apr. 1843, recorded by William Clayton; Ehat and Cook, p. 185; punctuation and spelling modernized. Also found in Smith, p. 291.

[12]Smith, p. 289.

[13]Smith, p. 157. For an extended explanation of this event, see Bruce R. McConkie, *The Millennial Messiah* (Salt Lake City: Deseret Book Co., 1982), beginning at p. 578.

place at Adam-ondi-Ahman in Missouri. "It is the place where Adam shall come to visit his people, or the Ancient of Days shall sit, as spoken of by Daniel the prophet" (D&C 116).

Daniel understood that until this event occurs, the Saints would be subject to the harassment of the world, but this great council would mark the beginning of their triumph over it. It would also mark Jehovah's personal direction of matters concerning this earth and particularly the preparation for his own millennial kingdom. "And the kingdom and dominion, and the greatness of the kingdom under the whole heaven, shall be given to the people of the saints of the most High, whose kingdom is an everlasting kingdom, and all dominions shall serve and obey him" (Dan. 7:27).

Chapter 8 depicts conflicts between beasts, representing kingdoms of the world. "Media" and "Persia" are mentioned, but it is not known whether the ancient lands by those names are intended. Even with the angelic interpretation, the vision was beyond Daniel's understanding. As a result of it, he "fainted, and was sick certain days." "I was astonished at the vision," he wrote, "but none understood it" (Dan. 8:27).

Chapter 9 records Daniel's prayer of grief and repentance at the sins of his people that had led to the destruction of Jerusalem and the temple and had brought them into exile in Babylon (Dan. 9:1–18). The angel Gabriel, responding to Daniel's prayer, delivered a message that is expressed in dramatic apocalyptic language. A specified period of time would be required for the forsaking of transgression, the reconciliation for iniquity, and the bringing in of the era of "everlasting righteousness" (Dan. 9:24). In the meantime, Jerusalem would be rebuilt, the Messiah would come but would be cut off, foreign troops would again destroy the city and the temple, and its sacrifices would cease amidst wars and desolating abominations (Dan. 9:25–27). Latter-day Saints will recognize what appears to be a striking parallel from Daniel's contemporary, the prophet Jacob, on the other side of the world: the Jews would return to Jerusalem, the Lord would come among them in the flesh, they would kill him, and they would then be "smitten and afflicted" (2 Ne. 6:8–10). Jesus referred explicitly to the afflictions foretold in Daniel 9:27 when he warned the Jews of "the abomination of desolation, spoken of by Daniel the prophet concerning the destruction of Jerusalem" (JS–M 1:12; Matt. 24:15). It would be God's great act of judgment against the Jews of that generation:

the destruction of Jerusalem and the temple at the hands of the Romans in A.D. 70.

Chapters 10 through 12 record the final revelation in the book of Daniel. It is the vision of a series of battles involving various kings and nations. Its apocalyptic tone puts it beyond our capacity to understand the details of its message, except to the point that it again shows the rule of the nations over the earth, the tribulations of the faithful, and the ultimate triumph of God. Michael would rise and lead God's forces at a time of unprecedented trouble. God's people would finally be delivered, and the resurrection would give them their reward of "everlasting life," in which they will "shine as the brightness of the firmament" (Dan. 12:1–3). Again, Daniel was commanded to seal the revelation so that its interpretation would not be known until "the time of the end" (Dan. 12:4).

Conclusion

Because of the sealed nature of the book of Daniel, the identities of kingdoms and symbols are not known. But what is abundantly clear and unmistakable throughout the book is the message of the visions: God's kingdom will prevail in the last days. It will grow until it consumes all other kingdoms, until it is the only kingdom on the face of the whole earth. Another theme is also very clear. During the reign of the beastly kingdoms, the Saints will have distress. Their troubles will continue until "the kingdoms of this world are become the kingdoms of our Lord, and of his Christ" (Rev. 11:15). The Saints must endure in faith and faithfulness until that time. Thus, God's people in the latter days will be much like the Jews of Daniel's day, strangers and foreigners serving for a time in an unfriendly land, waiting for the day of final deliverance. The task set before exiled Judah and modern Saints is to learn to do the will of God while living in an environment that opposes it. This message makes the book of Daniel relevant both then and now.

30

THE RETURN FROM EXILE

(Ezra 1–6)

Andrew C. Skinner

The book of Ezra is a historical work that continues the narrative of 2 Chronicles. That is apparent when one notices that the last two verses of 2 Chronicles are repeated almost word for word in the first two and one-half verses of Ezra. The book covers the period from 538 B.C. (Cyrus's Edict of Liberation) to approximately 458 B.C. (Ezra's commission). It tells the story of the beginnings of Judah's return from exile, chapters 1 through 6, and the career of the priest/scribe Ezra, whose memoirs are contained in chapters 7 through 10.

Cyrus the Great

The destruction of Jerusalem (587 B.C.) and the Babylonian exile (587–538 B.C.) were times of great sorrow for the kingdom of Judah, but the Lord had said that his city and his people would not be forgotten. He would raise up a deliverer to bring down Babylon and cause Jerusalem, along with the holy temple, to be rebuilt. That deliverer would be an instrument in God's hands, and his name would be Cyrus: "Thus saith the Lord, thy redeemer, . . . I am the Lord that maketh all things; . . . that saith to Jerusalem, Thou shalt be inhabited; and to the cities of Judah, Ye shall be built, and I will raise up the decayed places thereof: that saith of Cyrus, He is my shepherd, and shall perform all my pleasure:

Andrew C. Skinner is assistant professor of ancient scripture at Brigham Young University.

even saying to Jerusalem, Thou shalt be built; and to the temple, Thy foundation shall be laid" (Isa. 44:24, 26, 28).

Cyrus emerged in history around 559 B.C. as ruler of the province Anshan in Elam, east of Mesopotamia, succeeding his father, Cambyses I. Sometime between 559 B.C. and 549 B.C. he overthrew Astyages, king of the Medes, and established himself as master of the Median kingdom, which in due time included Persia (modern Iran), northern Assyria, and part of Asia Minor. With power and care Cyrus began organizing an empire that lasted two hundred years, until Alexander the Great,[1] and became the greatest the world had yet seen.[2] In 539 B.C. Cyrus moved against Babylon and in dramatic fashion conquered it, "without any battle."[3] His historical record, the Cyrus Cylinder, makes it clear that he was seen as a liberator, for when he advanced to the city its gates were opened to him and the entire population "bowed to him and kissed his feet" and "greeted him as a master through whose help they had come [again] to life from death."[4] Cyrus himself claimed to have followed an enlightened policy toward conquered or subjugated peoples. He said he abolished forced labor, improved housing conditions, and enjoyed the affection of the populace as a benevolent despot. This favorable view of Cyrus, though written as propaganda for the time, is not unjustified.

Apparently Cyrus understood the futility of trying to compel loyalty through violence and terror. He stated, "I did not allow anybody to terrorize [any place]."[5] Compared with other conquerors in ancient times, especially the Assyrians and Babylonians, Cyrus was extraordinarily humane and benevolent. Undoubtedly that was so because God had chosen him as an instrument to help bring about divine purposes, even though

---

[1]Alexander the Great, Macedonian king and military genius, conquered the Persian empire in 331 B.C. and used it as the foundation of his Hellenistic empire. Alexander admired Cyrus and was deeply moved after having visited his tomb at Pasargadae, in what is now Iran, while returning home from India. According to Plutarch, a Roman writer of the early Christian era, Cyrus's tomb bore the inscription: "O man, whosoever thou art and whencesoever thou comest, for I know that thou wilt come, I am Cyrus, and I won for the Persians their empire. Do not, therefore, begrudge me this little earth which covers my body."

[2]Cyrus is generally regarded as the de facto founder of the Achaemenid dynasty, which survived from roughly 550 B.C. to 330 B.C.

[3]James B. Pritchard, ed., *Ancient Near Eastern Texts Relating to the Old Testament*, 3d ed. with Supplement (Princeton: Princeton University, 1969), pp. 315–16.

[4]Pritchard, pp. 315–16

[5]Pritchard, pp. 315–16.

Cyrus did not cease to honor the deities of other nations. In the only Old Testament passage where the term "messiah" or "anointed one" is used to refer to a non-Israelite, the relationship between the Lord and Cyrus is described. According to Isaiah, Cyrus's success was a product of Jehovah's design: "Thus saith the Lord to his anointed [Hebrew, *māšîaḥ* or messiah], to Cyrus, whose right hand I have holden, to subdue nations before him; and I will loose the loins of kings, to open before him the two leaved gates; and the gates shall not be shut; I will go before thee, and make the crooked places straight: I will break in pieces the gates of brass, and cut in sunder the bars of iron: And I will give thee the treasures of darkness, and hidden riches of secret places, that thou mayest know that I, the Lord, which call thee by thy name, am the God of Israel" (Isa. 45:1–3).[6]

In the first century A.D., Jewish historian Flavius Josephus indicated that Isaiah's prophecies themselves had a great effect on Cyrus once he entered Babylon and was shown the sacred writings. In fact, Josephus portrayed the comments of Cyrus as a response motivated by the Lord's declarations in scripture:

> For he [the Lord] stirred up the mind of Cyrus, and made him write this throughout all Asia: — "Thus saith Cyrus the King: Since God Almighty hath appointed me to be king of the habitable earth, I believe that he is that God which the nation of the Israelites worship; for indeed he foretold my name by the prophets, and that I should build him a house at Jerusalem, in the country of Judea." This was known to Cyrus by his reading the book which Isaiah left behind him of his prophecies; for this prophet said that God had spoken thus to him in a secret vision: "My will is, that Cyrus, whom I have appointed to be king over many and great nations, send back my people to their own land, and build my temple." This was foretold by Isaiah one hundred and forty years before the temple was demolished. Accordingly, when Cyrus read this, and admired the Divine power, an earnest desire and ambition seized upon him to fulfil what was so written.[7]

---

[6]The Cyrus Cylinder, a clay barrel inscribed with the story of the king's conquest of Babylon, attributes the success of Cyrus to his having been chosen by the god Marduk, the chief god of the Babylonian pantheon. Cyrus may have been a polytheist, but it should be remembered that the Cyrus Cylinder was written as propaganda for the Babylonians and was probably the product of a Babylonian priest/scribe.

[7]Flavius Josephus, *Antiquities of the Jews*, 11.1.1–2, in *Josephus: Complete Works*, trans. William Whiston (Grand Rapids, Mich.: Kregel, 1960), p. 228.

Even though some have pointed out that Cyrus's acceptance of Jehovah's message was simply a reflection of his pantheistic approach to religion, it is still his receptivity to the idea of Judah's freedom and restoration that needs to be emphasized and remembered. President Ezra Taft Benson said, "God, the Father of us all, uses the men of the earth, especially good men, to accomplish his purposes."[8]

The Return

It is against the foregoing historical and theological background that the opening verses of the book of Ezra are to be understood. In Cyrus's first year as king of Babylon (538 B.C.), the Lord indeed "stirred up the spirit of Cyrus king of Persia, that he made a proclamation" (Ezra 1:1), a proclamation which has come to be known as the Edict of Liberation. The edict is preserved in the book of Ezra in two versions. One (Ezra 1:2–4) is written in Hebrew, the traditional biblical language of Israel and Judah. The other (Ezra 6:3–5) is written in Aramaic, the diplomatic language of the Persian Empire, which gradually became the common tongue of the Jewish people during the post-exilic period.[9]

Hebrew Version	*Aramaic Version*
Thus saith Cyrus king of Persia, The Lord God of heaven hath given me all the kingdoms of the earth; and he hath charged me to build him an house at Jerusalem, which is in Judah. Who is there among you of all his people? his God be with him, and let him go up to Jerusalem, which is in Judah, and build the house of the Lord God of Israel, (he is the God,) which is in Jerusalem. And whosoever remaineth in any place where he sojourneth, let the men of his place help him with	In the first year of Cyrus the king the same Cyrus the king made a decree concerning the house of God at Jerusalem, Let the house be builded, the place where they offered sacrifices, and let the foundations thereof be strongly laid; the height thereof threescore cubits, and the breadth thereof threescore cubits; With three rows of great stones, and a row of new timber: and let the expenses be given out of the king's house: And also let the golden and silver vessels of the house of God,

---

[8]Ezra Taft Benson, "Civic Standards for the Faithful Saints," *Ensign*, July 1972, p. 59.

[9]See the discussion in Bernhard W. Anderson, *Understanding the Old Testament*, 4th ed. (Englewood Cliffs, N.J.: Prentice Hall, 1986), pp. 508–9.

silver, and with gold, and with goods, and with beasts, beside the freewill offering for the house of God that is in Jerusalem (Ezra 1:2–4).

which Nebuchadnezzar took forth out of the temple which is at Jerusalem, and brought unto Babylon, be restored, and brought again unto the temple which is at Jerusalem, every one to his place, and place them in the house of God (Ezra 6:3–5).

Although there has been some discussion as to which version of the edict represents the original document and which is a translation, the historicity of Cyrus's decree is beyond doubt. The very fact that the edict is preserved in two versions speaks for its authenticity. It is probable that the Hebrew text (Ezra 1:2–4) represents the oral proclamation of the decree and the Aramaic text (Ezra 6:3–5) the official written decree. The edict is also substantiated by an independent source, the Cyrus Cylinder itself. In one passage of the Cylinder, Cyrus declared: "I returned to [these] sacred cities on the other side of the Tigris, the sanctuaries of which have been ruins for a long time, the images which [used] to live therein and established for them permanent sanctuaries. I [also] gathered all their [former] inhabitants and returned [to them] their habitations."[10]

To head up the return from exile, Cyrus appointed a leader named Sheshbazzar to be governor (Ezra 5:14). We know little else about him except that he was "the prince of Judah" (Ezra 1:8). His name is almost immediately replaced in the biblical text by that of Zerubbabel, who is identified in Haggai 2:2 as the governor of Judah and leader of the returning expedition.

Some commentators believe that the two names identify the same person.[11] Others hold that Sheshbazzar and Zerubbabel are two separate individuals, that Sheshbazzar is better identified with Shenazar (1 Chron. 3:18), the son of Jehoiachin (Jeconiah) and uncle of Zerubbabel (1 Chron. 3:19), and that Sheshbazzar, being older, was simply succeeded by the younger Zerubbabel at this crucial juncture.[12]

As Judah prepared to return home, the times would have been stressful and would have taken their toll emotionally and physically on everyone.

---

[10]Pritchard, pp. 315–16.

[11]See "Zerubbabel," Bible Dictionary, LDS Bible.

[12]See Anderson, p. 509; William F. Albright, *The Biblical Period from Abraham to Ezra* (New York: Harper and Row, 1963), p. 87.

The Jewish governor appointed by Cyrus would have been made responsible for overseeing the preparations and the journey, as well as the activities of the people once they reached their destination. The governor of the Jews was subordinate to the great governor or "satrap" who ruled over the district west of the Euphrates and who was responsible to the Persian emperor himself. Tatnai was such a satrap (Ezra 5:3, 6; 6:6, 13).

Zerubbabel, like Sheshbazzar before him, was chosen governor of the return because of his lineage and ability. He was a grandson of Jehoiachin, the king of Judah who had been taken into captivity in Babylon in 597 B.C. Zerubbabel was raised in the Chaldean capital and was of the royal Davidic line. He was also an ancestor of Jesus Christ ("Zorobabel" of Matt. 1:12–13 is the Greek form of the name) and was favorably regarded as Jehovah's servant by Haggai, the prophet of the second temple, which sometimes is also called Zerubbabel's temple.

A New Day—A New Culture

The preparations made by the returning exiles, with their collections of gold and silver temple vessels, is reminiscent of an earlier day when the children of Israel gathered together the precious items of Egypt (Ex. 12:35–36) as they made ready to embark upon their exodus. But here the parallel ends. This was a new day, and unlike the Israelites at the time of the Exodus, most of the expatriated Jews living in Babylon in 538 B.C. chose not to return to the lands of their inheritance. Years later the Talmudic rabbis wrote, "Many cities which were conquered by the Israelites who came up from Egypt were not reconquered by those who came up from Babylon."[13] As to the reasons why, W. F. Albright commented, "In the first place, the latter were in general becoming well established in their new homes, as vividly illustrated by Egyptian papyri beginning in the year 495 and by Babylonian contract tablets dating from various periods (but sporadic and often uncertain until 437 B.C., when Jewish names become abundant in the Nippur documents). In the second place, the journey was dangerous and expensive, while conditions in Judah were certainly very unsatisfactory."[14]

---

[13]Babylonian Talmud: *Seder Kodashim, Hullin* 1.7a.
[14]Albright, p. 87.

Much of Judah had been absorbed into the Babylonian way of life. Even the Babylonian name of the Jewish leader, Zerubbabel (*Zēr-Bābili*, "Offspring of Babylon"), reflects the degree to which Jewish life had been affected by Babylonian culture. As exiles gradually returned over the next century and more, beginning in Zerubbabel's day, they took back new ideas, culturally and religiously, to the land from which they or their ancestors had been deported. New institutions, new religious leaders, and a different religious orientation grew up in Babylon and gradually were brought to Palestine. In Babylon the religion of Israel began the transformation into what we recognize as Judaism. A summary of the most important developments that began there during this period would include the following:

1. The scriptures were preserved and honored, and the Law of Moses was exalted. Without the temple, the exiles were deprived of the sacrificial system of the Mosaic code, which resulted eventually in increased veneration of the Law.

2. The synagogue emerged as a center for religious observance, taking the place of the temple. The synagogue (literally "assembly" in Greek) was a place to meet, study, and reverence the Law. When the temple was rebuilt, the synagogue did not die out. Today, it is the most important community institution in Judaism.

3. A vast collection of oral traditions, later codified in the Mishnah and Talmud, began to be extremely important, eventually to achieve greater authority than the scriptures in Judaism.

4. A class of experts in scripture and in the Mosaic law evolved. These were the scribes, who would later have a profound effect on Judaism, as noted in the New Testament.

5. Aramaic began to replace Hebrew as the common language of the people. This process was completed during the post-Exilic period and contributed to the growing power of the scribes, who could read the sacred texts in Hebrew.

Chapter 2 of Ezra presents the principal list of each clan that returned from Babylon with Zerubbabel and other leaders of the Exile (Ezra 2:2). A parallel list is found in Nehemiah 7:7–63. This appears to be a genealogical register, the significance of which lies in its arrangement. Names are organized into two basic categories. The first is laymen according to family (Ezra 2:3–20) and city (Ezra 2:21–35). The second category is far more important and detailed; it is those names associated with the temple: priests (Ezra 2:36–39), Levites (Ezra 2:40), singers (Ezra 2:41), porters (Ezra 2:42), Nethinim — literally "given ones" or "dedicated ones" to the temple (Ezra 2:43–54), and sons of Solomon's servants (Ezra 2:55–58). Each of the clans in these classes of temple ministrants is relatively small in number compared with those of the laymen. But it was important for the author to be more exact in accounting for those groups who could function in a new temple. Thus chapter 2, besides being a genealogical survey, is really a foreshadowing of a primary aim of the returning exiles — the reconstruction of the temple — and also a disclosure of the centrality of the temple for the religious and theological system of the returning exiles.[15]

Related to the general category of temple ministrants is a group of individuals who claimed to be priesthood holders and thus eligible to participate in temple rites but whose genealogy could not be certified (Ezra 2:59–63). This group is discussed here in the genealogical register because of the danger they posed in possibly contaminating the temple and desecrating its prescribed rites. We are reminded that the Lord's kingdom is one of order and that all things associated with God's temples are to be done with exactness and propriety. Thus uncertified priests of Zerubbabel's day were forbidden to partake of "the most holy things" (Ezra 2:63) — special portions of food reserved for the male descendants of Aaron (Lev. 2:3; 7:31–33). It seems their exclusion was not intended to be permanent but only until a divine decision could be received through the use of Urim and Thummim.[16]

Building the Temple

Some time after the exiles were resettled in Palestine, they gathered together at Jerusalem under the direction of Zerubbabel, their political leader, and Jeshua, the Aaronic high priest and religious leader of the

---

[15]See also Robert H. Pfeiffer, *Introduction to the Old Testament* (New York: Harper & Brothers, 1941), pp. 822, 836.

[16]The Talmudic rabbis considered the exclusion mentioned in verse 63 to be in effect until the dead were resurrected or "until Elijah comes" in connection with the Messiah, when all difficult theological questions would be settled. *Tosephta Sota* 13.1; *Sota* 486; *Ketuboth* 24b; *Shebuoth* 16a.

community (Hag. 1:1). They first built an altar and resumed the offering of sacrifices to reinstate the official worship of Jehovah in Jerusalem and to prepare for the building of the temple (Ezra 3:2–6). The altar could exist legally without the temple and was greatly needed for the rehabilitation of the people and the religious system that was centered around the house of the Lord. Not until the second year of their repatriation did the former exiles begin actual construction on the temple, because of the preparations that had to be made (Ezra 3:7–8).

The shouting, singing, and praising that accompanied the completion of the temple foundation were in harmony with Davidic custom (1 Chron. 25) and must have been a joyous occasion for the younger sector of the population. Yet mingled with the sounds of happiness were sounds of sadness; for there were in Jerusalem in that day some older men — "many of the priests and Levites and chief of the fathers" (Ezra 3:12) — who had seen the first temple, which had been built by Solomon, and who now wept and wailed over the inferiority of this new house (Ezra 3:11–13; see also Hag. 2:3). Josephus wrote that they exhibited great grief as they saw how far they had sunk materially.[17] Undoubtedly the occasion accentuated some of the same sentiments expressed in Psalm 137:1, "Yea, we wept, when we remembered Zion."

Apparently it was not long after construction had commenced that work on the new temple was interrupted by the Samaritans, who wanted to participate with the Jews in rebuilding the house of the Lord (Ezra 4:1–4).[18] Under the direction of Zerubbabel and Jeshua, the returned exiles refused to allow Samaritan participation, whereupon the Samaritans took revenge and hindered the work of building. They also hired advocates to lobby against Judah at the court of Cyrus (who died in 529 B.C.) and the king who succeeded him (see Ezra 4:4–6). The phrase used in Ezra 4:4, which says the Samaritans "weakened the hands" of Judah, reflects a Hebrew idiom which means to cause someone to lose heart and become discouraged. The phrase was used in a nonbiblical source, a Hebrew ostracon from Lachish, in which a prophet was accused of

---

[17]Josephus, *Antiquities*, 11.4.2.

[18]See "Samaritans," Bible Dictionary, LDS Bible. See also Stephen D. Ricks, "No Prophet Is Accepted in His Own Country," in *Studies in Scripture, Volume Five: The Gospels*, ed. Kent P. Jackson and Robert L. Millet (Salt Lake City: Deseret Book Co., 1986), pp. 204–8.

lowering the morale of the country at a critical moment.[19] Thus, in their spiritually and emotionally weak state, the Jews, having little resolve, allowed harassment from the Samaritans to hinder their work on the new temple for several years.

Ezra 4:6–23 is apparently out of place in its present location in the book. It refers to a later attempt to rebuild the city and its walls. One fear of Judah's opponents was that if Jerusalem were rebuilt, its inhabitants would rebel and cease paying tribute to the Persian treasury (Ezra 4:13–16). When an investigation was conducted into the Persian archives, it was determined that Jerusalem had been a rebellious city in times past. Thus the decision was made not to allow the Jews to rebuild (Ezra 4:23). This event probably took place at least fifty years after the event described in Ezra 4:1–5, perhaps during the reign of Xerxes I (485–65 B.C.).[20] The prohibition against rebuilding the walls of Jerusalem was not lifted until the time of Nehemiah's first mission to Jerusalem in 445 B.C. (see Neh. 2).

Work on the house of the Lord remained dormant for seventeen years, until the second year (520 B.C.) of the reign of a new ruler — the second in succession after Cyrus — King Darius I of Persia. In that year, two of the great post-Exilic prophets, Haggai and Zechariah, rose up and provided the inspiration needed to get construction going again (Ezra 5:1–2).[21] More attempts were made to obstruct progress on the temple by Tatnai, the general governor over the region west of the Euphrates under whose jurisdiction the Jews fell, and by leaders of Samaria. This time, however, the resolve of the people was strong and work did not cease, because they heeded the prophetic counsel: "Be strong, all ye people of the land, saith the Lord, and work: for I am with you, saith the Lord of hosts" (Hag. 2:4). In fact, so tenacious and bold had the people become that when Tatnai the governor asked to know who had authorized the commencement of construction and who were the leaders of the project, the elders answered, "We are the servants of the God of heaven and earth, and build the house that was builded these many years

---

[19]As proposed in Jacob M. Myers, *Ezra-Nehemiah*, Anchor Bible 14 (Garden City, N.Y.: Doubleday, 1965), p. 34. See also Jer. 38:3–4.

[20]See the discussion in Raymond A. Bowman's exegesis of the book of Ezra in *The Interpreter's Bible*, 12 vols., ed. G. A. Buttrick, et al. (Nashville: Abingdon, 1952–57), 3:597.

[21]See my discussion on Haggai in Chap. 31 of this volume.

ago, which a great king of Israel builded and set up" (Ezra 5:11). Furthermore, the people of Judah requested that a search be made of the Persian archives to find the original decree issued by Cyrus that gave them legal right to build the temple. When the document was found, King Darius issued another proclamation not only to permit the continuation of construction but also to assist financially. All this was made effective by penalty of death for those who tried to alter the king's declaration. So work on the Lord's house continued until the second temple was finally finished in 515 B.C.

Those who had returned from Babylon to the now desolate, but once holy, city of Jerusalem observed the dedication of the new temple with joy. The priesthood holders who attended were seated in their proper divisions and courses much like the arrangement followed in solemn assemblies today, as one supposes (Ezra 6:15–22). Though inferior to Solomon's temple, the dedicated second temple meant that God would again personally come to Jerusalem to reveal his will.[22]

Some Lessons

The story of the rebuilding of the temple in the post-Exilic period (from 538 B.C. on) provides Latter-day Saints with some valuable lessons. We come to understand just how effective a weapon discouragement can be to material and spiritual progress. The work of the Lord is greatly hampered by attitudes of discouragement, but listening to our prophets can change people's attitudes and they, in turn, can change life's circumstances. Indeed, one of the great lessons of this episode is that the prophetic voice of encouragement is just as valuable as the prophetic voice of warning. Heeding the prophets produces prosperity: "Then rose up Zerubbabel the son of Shealtiel, and Jeshua the son of Jozadak, and began to build the house of God which is at Jerusalem: and with them were the prophets of God helping them. . . . And the elders of the Jews builded, and they prospered through the prophesying of Haggai the prophet and Zechariah the son of Iddo. And they builded, and finished

---

[22]James E. Talmage, *The House of the Lord* (Salt Lake City: Deseret Book Co., 1968), pp. 42–43.

it, according to the commandment of the God of Israel, and according to the commandment of Cyrus, and Darius, and Artaxerxes king of Persia" (Ezra 5:2; 6:14).

Another lesson for our day concerns the challenges to temple-building the returning exiles had to overcome. As seen by the people then, and as we know from recent experience, the adversary will go to great lengths and use any obstacle to keep temples from being built. The Lord's chosen people of every temple-building dispensation will always find it necessary to have faith and go to work (see Hag. 2:4).

History of the post-Exilic period begins with the book of Ezra, a fact obscured by its order of placement in English translations of the Bible. Ezra and Nehemiah are actually the last two historical books of the Old Testament. Zechariah and Haggai were among the prophets of the period and were among the last to have served Judah. We know only of Malachi and perhaps Joel who came after them. The books of Ezra and Nehemiah originally circulated as one book and told the story of Judah's history from the return to Jerusalem to the end of Nehemiah's second term as governor (538 B.C. to about 400 B.C.).

The era discussed in Ezra 1 through 6 witnessed profound changes for the remnant of Judah that returned to Jerusalem. Culturally these changes are evidenced by the fact that a large portion of Ezra (Ezra 4:8–6:18; 7:12–26) is preserved in Aramaic rather than Hebrew, which reflects the new cultural milieu out of which Judah came in 538 B.C. But the greatest changes were religious. Much of Israel was gone; only Judah remained. Prophecies of doom and destruction made before the Exile had been fulfilled. It had taken the disaster of the captivity and the destruction of Solomon's temple to humble a nation and awaken it to its responsibilities and transgressions. But out of that awakening something significant had come. Repentance had occurred, the temple had been rebuilt, and the Jews now had a second chance to live as the Lord's covenant people. They had the holy city Jerusalem, the leadership of a descendant of David,[23] and divine guidance through prophets. The task of the returned exiles would be to live in such a way that they could enjoy those blessings forever.

---

[23]Zerubbabel, though heir to the throne of David, is never called "king" in the Bible. It is likely that the Persians were not open to the idea of the reestablishment of Judah's Davidic monarchy.

31
THE BOOK OF HAGGAI

ANDREW C. SKINNER

Though not regarded with the great or well-known prophets such as Isaiah, Ezekiel, and Jeremiah, Haggai was an important prophet who performed valuable service in the Lord's kingdom. Along with Zechariah, he motivated the former Jewish exiles of Babylon to renew and redouble their efforts to start again building the second temple in Jerusalem after a long period of difficulty. His exhortations prepared the way for the Spirit of the Lord to stir the souls of the people (Hag. 1:13–14). Haggai worked to alleviate discouragement and restore faith in Jehovah, which led to the great accomplishment of 515 B.C.: the completion of a new house of the Lord.

After Cyrus conquered Babylon (539 B.C.) and became virtual master of the Near East, he issued a decree allowing the Jewish captives to return to their homeland. He also encouraged the rebuilding of the temple at Jerusalem and offered financial assistance (Ezra 1:1–4). By 520 B.C., however, all construction had ceased, little progress on the temple had been made, and all resolve had disappeared because of harassment by the Samaritans, who felt slighted after their offer to help with the building had been refused (Ezra 4:1–5).

Adding to the discouragement of the returning exiles was the desolate condition of the land of Judah and their own material poverty. This, plus the inescapable conclusion that the new temple would be far inferior to the old one, even when only the foundation of the new had been laid, caused many old leaders of the group (priests, Levites, and chiefs of the fathers) to weep as they remembered the comparative splendor of

---

Andrew C. Skinner is assistant professor of ancient scripture at Brigham Young University.

the first house of the Lord (Ezra 3:12; cf. Hag. 2:3). Continuing opposition from the Samaritans and other adversaries brought the morale of the repatriated exiles to a low ebb, and they began to say that the time to rebuild the temple had not yet come (Hag. 1:2). At this point the prophet Haggai entered onto the stage of post-Exilic history.

We know very little about Haggai. He is mentioned only in this short book (two chapters) that bears his name and in Ezra 5:1 and 6:14. His book is to be read in conjunction with Ezra 5 and 6. Haggai and Zechariah are the earliest known prophets of the post-Exilic restoration of Judah. It is generally assumed that Haggai was among the main contingent of returning exiles to come out of captivity after Cyrus issued his edict (538 B.C.). If that is the case, he probably witnessed the initial attempts to rebuild the temple and the subsequent hiatus caused by Samaritan and official Persian opposition.[1]

Some suggest that Haggai was an old man at the time of his preaching, owing to Haggai 2:3, which may indicate that the prophet had seen the splendor of the first temple. Others believe Haggai was a priest, based on Haggai 2:10–14. Such inferences are hazardous. What is known is that Haggai's recorded activity as a prophet was of short duration. All his messages that we know about were delivered over four months in 520 B.C., the second year of the reign of Darius I of Persia.

The Message

In 520 B.C. on the first day of the sixth month (corresponding to our August-September), Haggai presented the word of the Lord to the two leaders of the Jewish community: Zerubbabel, the governor, who was heir to the throne of David, and Joshua (Jeshua), the high priest.[2]

---

[1]In contrast to such other prophets as Isaiah, Ezekiel, Jeremiah, and even Zechariah, the parentage of Haggai is nowhere mentioned. Haggai's name in Hebrew means "Festive," and some postulate that it was given to him because he was born on a feast day. The birth of a child on such a day was considered a good omen that deserved to be preserved in a child's name. (A name of this type is Shabbethai [Ezra 10:15], meaning "born on the sabbath.") See the discussion in D. Winton Thomas, "Haggai: Introduction," in *The Interpreter's Bible*, 12 vols., ed. G. A. Buttrick, et al. (Nashville: Abingdon, 1952–57), 6:1037.

[2]For Zerubbabel's genealogy, see "Zerubbabel," Bible Dictionary, LDS Bible. Joshua (the Hebrew form, because the book of Haggai is written in Hebrew) is called Jeshua (Aramaic) in the book of Ezra (much of which is in Aramaic).

It was blunt: "Go up to the temple mount and finish construction on the house of the Lord!"

Material concerns and discouragement because of opposition were the two considerations with which the Lord dealt through his servant Haggai. He exhorted the people to consider their ways. Progress and prosperity were tied to the temple. Haggai asked if it was right for the people to be concerned with paneling their own houses ("ceiled houses") while the Lord's house remained in ruins (Hag. 1:4). He pointed out that material well-being was indeed elusive, just as it seemed to be, because the temple had been neglected (Hag. 1:6, 9–10). Even the occurrence of drought and famine was related to the temple. The Lord said that he had "called for a drought upon the land" (Hag. 1:11). The Hebrew word for "drought" is *hōreb,* whereas the word for "waste" or "ruin," the condition of the temple as described in Haggai 1:9, is *hāréb.* The play on words is intentional and inextricably links the temple to Judah's well-being. As long as the temple lay in ruins, the drought would continue (Hag. 1:10–11).

The Lord's message began to have its desired effect. Once the fear of the Lord (Hag. 1:12) began to replace the fear of men, the Spirit worked powerfully on the people, and "they came and did work in the house of the Lord of hosts, their God" (Hag. 1:14). We learn from the book of Ezra that Haggai's preaching was successful (see Ezra 5:1–6:15). Within five years the Jews finished the construction of what is called the second temple, or Zerubbabel's temple.

Haggai delivered another prophetic message on the twenty-first day of the seventh month (corresponding to our September-October). It began by exhorting the people to continue to be strong, faithful, and hardworking on the temple. He recalled the covenant made with the Lord at the time of the Exodus and concluded with a prophecy of a glorious future temple: "I will shake all nations, and the desire of all nations shall come: and I will fill this house with glory, saith the Lord of hosts. . . . The glory of this latter house shall be greater than of the former, saith the Lord of hosts: and in this place will I give peace, saith the Lord of hosts" (Hag. 2:7, 9). As beautiful as Solomon's temple had been—with which the humble, new second temple was compared—neither of them would be as glorious as a yet-future temple that would exist in the day when the Lord would "give peace" to his holy city. In that millennial day, the house of the Lord will be filled with glory, because the Lord himself will be there.

Haggai's final recorded messages were delivered on the twenty-fourth day of the ninth month (corresponding to our November-December). He taught the people an important lesson about the holiness of the temple. Under Mosaic law, as the people with whom Haggai spoke acknowledged, something unholy cannot be made holy merely by touching something that is holy (Hag. 2:12). But something ritually unclean would spread that uncleanliness by simple contact. So it was with the remnant of Judah in Haggai's day. Mere contact with or construction of the holy temple would not make the nation holy. In fact, an unholy or unclean people would defile or desecrate sacred ordinances as well as the Lord's sacred house. Sanctity and purity start with individual lives and individual worthiness; holiness works from the inside out, not from the outside in. Haggai exhorted the people to consider their status and their behavior as though it were the time before the temple foundation had ever been laid, as though it were a brand new era, a new day, or a time of planting—a time before the fruit is already set—so that they could make renewed commitments that would bring them the Lord's blessing from that very day onward (Hag. 2:19).

The book ends, significantly, with a prophecy in which the name *Zerubbabel* is used in a messianic context (Hag. 2:21–23). Its fulfillment, to be sure, would not be in Zerubbabel himself but in Jesus Christ, who would descend of his lineage more than five hundred years later (see Matt. 1:12) and who will rule as Israel's king in the Millennium. Ezekiel (37:21–25) had earlier referred to the millennial king by the name of his ancestor David, whom the Jews considered to be the very model of divinely appointed kingship. Now Haggai referred to the millennial Messiah by the name of another ancestor, Zerubbabel. Just as Zerubbabel presided over the returned exiles of Judah and their restoration to their promised land, so also—but on a much grander scale—will Christ preside over all the restored house of Israel in the Millennium.[3]

Though it is true that Haggai is classified as one of the Minor Prophets, his messages were of great value to post-Exilic Judah. With his help the

---

[3]See the discussion of Christ as the millennial king "David" in Chap. 27 of this volume.

temple was built and became the center of religious life for that remnant of Israel whom we call the Jews.

There is no more timely message for our own day than the one delivered by Haggai. Real progress and prosperity are connected with the house of the Lord. But not only do we need to build and attend temples, we need to live holy lives. As Haggai counseled: "Yet now be strong . . . and work" (Hag. 2:4).[4]

---

[4]Additional insights on Haggai and his times can be found in W. S. LaSor, D. A. Hubbard, and F. W. Bush, *Old Testament Survey* (Grand Rapids, Mich.: Eerdmans, 1982), pp. 480–88, 648–49; and John Bright, *A History of Israel*, 3d ed. (Philadelphia: Westminster, 1981), pp. 360–72. The most detailed and scholarly of recent commentaries available is C. L. Myers and E. M. Myers, *Haggai; Zechariah 1–8*, Anchor Bible 25B (Garden City, N.Y.: Doubleday, 1987).

32

THE BOOK OF ZECHARIAH

RICHARD D. DRAPER

Little is known about Zechariah. His grandfather was presumably the Iddo who was the head of a priestly family that came out of Babylon with Zerubbabel the governor and Joshua (called Jeshua in Ezra 3–5) the high priest about 537 B.C. (Ezra 5:1; 6:14; Neh. 12:4, 16). If that is the case, then Zechariah was both priest and prophet. He was called to declare God's word and assist Haggai around 520 B.C. in motivating the Jews to rebuild the temple. The visions recorded in Zechariah 1 through 8 are contemporary with the events described in Haggai 1 and 2 and Ezra 5 and 6, whereas those of Zechariah 9 through 14 perhaps come afterward.

The prophet's name means "Jehovah remembers," a fitting appellation for the one through whom these prophecies came.[1] The content of his writings reveals that Jehovah's word is ever before his eyes and that his purposes cannot be frustrated.

The prophecies of Zechariah have been described as the quintessence of prophetic utterance.[2] Though that may be a bit of an overstatement, it still accurately portrays the majesty of Zechariah's visions as well as his excellent acquaintance with the writings of the Israelite prophets since the time of Moses.[3] Indeed, the pure Hebrew, free from any taint

---

Richard D. Draper is assistant professor of ancient scripture at Brigham Young University.

[1]Sidney B. Sperry, *The Voice of Israel's Prophets* (Salt Lake City: Deseret Book Co., 1952), p. 403.

[2]D. Guthrie, *The New Bible Commentary* (Grand Rapids, Mich.: Eerdmans, 1970), p. 786. The term *quintessence* was used by ancient philosophers to denote that divine substance latent in all things. Thus, the idea expressed is that of essential nature in its refined and exact form.

[3]Some have suggested that there are allusions to, if not exact borrowings from, Exodus, Leviticus, Deuteronomy, Chronicles, Isaiah, Jeremiah, Ezekiel, Daniel, Hosea, Amos, and Micah. For an analysis, see Guthrie, p. 786.

of Aramaic, echoes the language of his prophetic ancestors and under-scores his direct prophetic succession.[4]

Yet of all the Minor Prophets, Zechariah is perhaps the most difficult to read. Following in the footsteps of Ezekiel and Daniel, he couched much of his teaching in apocalyptic style, thereby hiding his message in dramatic symbols (see "Apocalyptic Revelation" in Chap. 28 of this volume).[5] Out of that style has grown one major question that confronts any careful reader of this book: are the images Zechariah used reflections on his own day, or are they types of later events? When he described the activities of the high priest Joshua, was he referring to his contem-porary, or to a latter-day counterpart, or to both? History would suggest that Zechariah was using objects and people from his own day as types to represent millennial counterparts.[6] But though there are problems with understanding the writing, the broad outline of his message is plain and the breadth of his vision, clear.

The Eight Visions (Zech. 1–6)

Early in 520 B.C. Zechariah received a series of visions all on the same night. The first three focus on Zion and the glory that the Lord intends to bring to her. The next five focus on the work of the Messiah as the Priest-King and the steps he will take to bring about the promised glory. The most important of these steps are the gathering and purging of Israel from sin, the Savior's mediating her cause with God, and finally

---

[4]Nearly all of the Jewish writings after the Babylonian captivity, including those of the later prophets, contain Aramaic words and idioms. Zechariah carefully avoided these, and in so doing, tied his prophecies closely to the earlier prophetic traditions.

[5]The term *apocalypse* comes from the Greek word meaning "to disclose or uncover." The term is applied today to a genre of literature that began in Old Testament times and was especially popular among Jews from 200 B.C. to A.D. 100 and among Christians to around A.D. 300. That which sets this genre apart from other kinds of writing is the use of striking symbols as the major vehicle through which the message is delivered.

[6]The perspective that this book presents concerning Joshua, Zerubbabel, and the temple seems to be exaggerated (if not wrong) in light of historical developments. Within a generation, Malachi proclaimed the temple and the priesthood corrupt; Zerubbabel's royal line was never heard of again until Christ, more than five hundred years later; Joshua's family only briefly held the office of high priest and was out of power by the time of Ezra, only eighty years later. Most importantly, there was no glorious restoration as predicted by the prophet. In light of these things, it is most certain that these contemporary themes were used as types.

Christ's presidency over the final confrontation between the forces of good and evil. Satan will be totally overthrown, God's wrath appeased, and his kingdom established on the earth.

The First Vision:
The Outriders (Zech. 1:7–17)

In vision, the prophet saw four riders who had been observing conditions on the earth.[7] They found all at peace. Therefore, Judah had no excuse for not building the temple, a major step in the establishment of Zion. The Lord promised the Jews protection and abundance if they would begin building the temple, and he commanded them to build the city as well. Zechariah proclaimed the promised blessings which would come from doing the Lord's will.

The Second Vision:
The End of Gentile Supremacy (Zech. 1:18–21)

The prophet was shown four horns, symbols of powers that had participated in the scattering of Israel. It is probable that the prophet did not have four actual kingdoms in mind. Rather, he was alluding to those forces that did and would prevail against God's people from every quarter.

Along with these, he saw four craftsmen who had the capacity to terrify the great powers because of their ability to destroy them. The figure of craftsmen may suggest that the conquest over the scattering powers would be by peaceful means, growing out of the efforts of God's people to engage in the work of temple building.[8]

The Third Vision:
The Foreshadowing of the Future City (Zech. 2:1–13)

In the next vision, the prophet saw a young man who set out to measure the dimensions of the holy city. He was stopped for two reasons: first, because the future Zion, here symbolized by the center city of Jerusalem, was to be contained not in one city but many; and second,

---

[7]These likely represent angels of God. The number four was often used in apocalyptic literature to represent geographical scope rather than an actual number. The idea that seems to be stressed here is that the angels have charge over the whole earth.

[8]Guthrie, p. 790.

because her strength would be beyond measurement, it being the glory of God. Before Zion can come, however, Judah must break free from the spiritual bonds of Babylon (see D&C 45:66–70; 115:6; 133:14). Only then will the nations become one with her and Jehovah dwell in her.

The Fourth Vision:
The Coming of the Priest-King Mediator (Zech. 3:1–10)

Having seen the power and beauty of the future kingdom, Zechariah turned to the means by which it would come to pass. He saw the high priest, Joshua, standing before an angel of the Lord.[9] Joshua was cleansed of sin and given the priestly robe and miter with the promise that the Lord would be with him. His ordination became a type of that of a future high priest called the Branch. The term was sometimes used in a technical sense by the prophets to designate Christ in his role as the millennial Davidic King (Isa. 4:2–6; Jer. 23:3–6; 33:14–26).[10] To the Branch would rightly belong not only the keys of kingship, but also the keys of priesthood, as associated with the temple.[11] This description makes it clear that the Priest-King referred to is none other than the Savior himself (see Jer. 23:5–6; 33:15–16).

At the time of this Priest-King, the kingdom of God, symbolized by a stone being watched over with care, would have all iniquity removed from it.[12]

The Fifth Vision:
The Lamp-Stand and the Olive Trees (Zech. 4:1–14)

In the next vision, the prophet saw a lamp-stand positioned between two olive trees. The trees supplied the oil, which the lamp burned. It seems likely that the lamp symbolizes Israel, the oil the Holy Spirit, and the light the Savior, which Israel is to hold up to all the world. Though

---

[9]The name *Joshua* (*Jeshua* in Aramaic) is based on the Hebrew verb for "save" and means "Jehovah is salvation." The Greek equivalent is transliterated as "Jesus."

[10]Note Guthrie, p. 791.

[11]See Joseph Smith, *History of The Church of Jesus Christ of Latter-day Saints*, 7 vols., 2d ed. rev., edited by B. H. Roberts (Salt Lake City: Deseret Book Co., 1973), 6:253. See also Isa. 11:10; D&C 113:5–6.

[12]The stone reminds us of Dan. 2:34 and D&C 65:2; the seven eyes upon the stone (Israel) suggest the idea that all heaven is concerned and watching over it. The angels shall assist in the work of cleansing her. See Joseph Smith, *Teachings of the Prophet Joseph Smith,* sel. Joseph Fielding Smith (Salt Lake City: Deseret Book Co., 1938), p. 159.

the text seems to be imperfectly preserved and is, therefore, difficult to read, it appears that the imagery of the olive trees was picked up by John in his revelation and interpreted as the two prophets raised up in the last days to prophesy to Judah (see Rev. 11:3–4; D&C 77:15).[13]

Just as with Joshua in the previous vision (Zech. 3:5–8), now Zerubbabel, the Davidic ruler, becomes a type of Christ, the true King of Israel (Zech. 4:6–10).

The Sixth and Seventh Visions:
The Flying Scroll and the Barrel (Zech. 5:1–11)

These visions are closely related. In the sixth vision, Zechariah saw a flying scroll, which seems to represent the judgment of the Lord upon those who break his law (Zech. 5:3). The idea expressed by the vision is that Israel must be purged from sin. Only through judgment upon that house would this be possible (note D&C 112:24–26). Next, the prophet saw a barrel[14] with a heavy, leaden lid. Inside the barrel was a woman of filthiness. She was taken away to Shinar, Babylon, the symbolic seat of apostasy. In this way, the prophet illustrated that Judah must and would become rid of the evil of apostasy forevermore.

The Eighth Vision:
The Universal Sovereignty of the Lord (Zech. 6:1–15)

In this vision the prophet saw symbolic representations of the servants of the Lord subduing the nations in all corners of the earth (Zech. 6:1–8). Then came the command to crown Joshua in similitude of the future crowning of the Branch, the millennial High Priest, the great temple builder, the Savior who would establish Zion and then come in his glory. With this act, the first series of visions is brought to a dramatic close.

Zechariah's visions use images and individuals from his own time to point to the latter days. They teach us that the earth must be cleansed of all unrighteousness (Zech. 1:18–21; 5:1–11; 6:1–8), that Zion will be established and its temple built (Zech. 1:7–17; 2:1–13), and that Christ will rule as both Priest (symbolized by the high priest, Joshua; Zech. 3:6–8; 6:11–13) and King (symbolized by the Davidic heir, Zerubbabel; Zech.

---

[13]Sperry, pp. 414–15; Richard D. Draper, *Opening the Seven Seals: The Visions of John the Revelator* (Salt Lake City: Deseret Book Co., 1991), pp. 119–21.

[14]An ephah is a unit of measure, equivalent to one-half bushel or twenty-two liters.

4:6–8). He shall "rule upon his throne; and he shall be a priest upon his throne; and the counsel of peace shall be between them both" (Zech. 6:13).

Mercy, Truth, and Justice in Zion (Zech. 7–8)

In response to a question about fasting, the Lord instructed Zechariah to teach the Jews the true principles that underlie a righteous fast: "Execute true judgment [i.e., justice[15]], and shew mercy and compassions every man to his brother" (Zech. 7:9). "Speak ye every man the truth to his neighbour; execute the judgment [justice] of truth and peace in your gates. And let none of you imagine evil in your hearts against his neighbour" (Zech. 8:16–17). The Lord, through earlier prophets, had taught these things clearly to Israel (Zech. 7:7), "but they refused to hearken, and pulled away the shoulder, and stopped their ears, that they should not hear" (Zech. 7:11). Thus they were scattered, and their land was made desolate (Zech. 7:14).

As with many other Old Testament passages, a prophecy of hope follows the discussion of God's punishment against his rebellious children. God would not forsake his people forever. There would be a restoration to the promised land and a reconstruction of the holy city. Its streets would again be filled with old men, old women, and boys and girls (Zech. 8:1–8). God would be in their midst (Zech. 8:3), which would prompt people from other nations to seek them out and worship the Lord among them (Zech. 8:22–23). In that day, said the Lord, "they shall be my people, and I will be their God, in truth and in righteousness" (Zech. 8:8).

Zechariah lived in a day in which exiled Jews were returning to reestablish their city and their community. But the restoration of Israel that he saw was that of the latter days, and the holy city that he envisioned was that of the Millennium, in which the Lord himself, the "king over all the earth" (Zech. 4:9), "will be the glory in the midst of her" (Zech. 2:5).

---

[15]The Hebrew word mišpaṭ, translated as "judgment" in the KJV, is more accurately rendered "justice."

The Worldwide Rule of Zion's King (Zech. 9–14)

The visions discussed above were not the last of those seen by Zechariah. The second portion of his book records further details concerning the coming of the Messiah. Looking to a future day, the prophet saw judgment poured out against those who would fight against the Lord's chosen people (Zech. 9:1–8), and he witnessed the coming of Zion's king (Zech. 9:9–17). Before that day, however, he saw that Israel must be gathered. Using the symbols of shepherding, he envisioned the summons of scattered Israel (Zech. 10:1–12) and the wail of the shepherds, Israel's leaders, as they realize that they were greatly responsible for her loss (Zech. 11:1–3). Finally would come the purification of Jerusalem (Zech. 12:1–14), the cleansing of her lands of false prophecy (Zech. 13:1–6), and the separation of the wicked from the righteous (Zech. 13:7–9). Zechariah concluded his prophecy with the glorious vision of the coming of the Lord, who will rout his foes and dwell in glory within the holy city (Zech. 14:1–21). "In that day," he wrote, even the bells on the horses and the mundane pots and pans of Jerusalem would be consecrated to the Lord's service (Zech. 14:20–21). And all of God's children will be invited to the millennial feast (Zech. 14:16, 21).

Some Specific Prophecies of the Coming Messiah

In the breadth of his vision, the prophet alluded to events associated with both the first and the second comings of the Messiah. It seems well to conclude this discussion with specific mention of two of the former and one of the latter.

In chapter 9 Zechariah taught of the coming of the great king, not in glory with armies, but meek and humble, riding on a donkey colt, a symbol of royalty but expressing the Lord's essential peaceableness.[16] This prophecy clearly describes the first coming of the Lord as a man of peace and blessing and foreshadows his triumphal entry into Jerusalem, which many of his followers saw as a fulfillment of this prophecy (see Matt.

---

[16]See *The Interpreter's Dictionary of the Bible*, 5 vols., ed. G. A. Buttrick, et al. (Nashville: Abingdon, 1962–76), 1:260.

21:4–5; John 12:14–16).[17] But the fulfillment was not complete with that event alone, because the larger context of the passage is millennial (see Zech. 9:10). Like many messianic prophecies in the Old Testament, this one foresees both Christ's first and second comings.

In chapter 11 Zechariah presented the allegory of the good shepherd who tries to save the sheep but because of opposition cannot do it. Finally, he quits in anger, breaks his two staves, and demands his wages. He is paid the sum of thirty pieces of silver. These he throws down before the potter inside the Lord's house, in testimony before Jehovah of his wrongs and rejection. This allegory reflects the rejection of the true shepherd who was sold for thirty pieces of silver and delivered over to false brethren. This betrayer's ransom later bought a potter's field (Matt. 27:7–10).

Looking to the Second Coming, the prophet described the participation of the great King in a battle for the holy city (Zech. 12:1–4; 14:1–5). As nations mount against the covenant people, the Lord himself will intervene. He shall stand upon the Mount of Olives, which shall be split in two. His people shall rush to him in the newly formed valley and there learn his true identity. Amid tears of sorrow and rejoicing, they will acknowledge him as their Lord and King (cf. D&C 45:48–53; 133:20, 35). At that time he will subdue all enemies, and the earth shall rest under his divine power. Little wonder Zechariah rejoiced in the testimony of his King and worked so diligently to bring his people to him.

---

[17]See Joseph F. McConkie, "Triumphal Entry and a Day of Debate," in Kent P. Jackson and Robert L. Millet, eds., *Studies in Scripture, Volume Five: The Gospels* (Salt Lake City: Deseret Book Co., 1986), pp. 374–75.

33

THE BOOK OF JOEL

KENT P. JACKSON

The words preserved in the book of Joel give us no information about when the book was written. Its opening verses lack the customary reference to the ruling monarch, and its content provides no information about Joel's time. Given these difficulties, commentators have dated the book anywhere from the ninth to the fifth centuries B.C.[1] Recently, some scholars have turned to linguistic clues to establish the book's date. Over time, languages undergo change, as readers of the King James Version are aware. Some studies suggest that the dialect of Hebrew preserved in Joel is consistent with that of other documents from early in the post-Exilic period: Haggai, Zechariah, and Malachi.[2] If this is the case, Joel can then be dated to around 500 B.C., making it one of the latest of the prophetic books.[3] That is the conclusion accepted in this study.

The book of Joel seems to be completely removed from the context of the time and place in which it was written. This absence of contemporary references certainly seems to be deliberate; it is as though Joel wanted us to leave behind all thoughts of the here and now and join him in his visions of the future. And the future is clearly the book's focus. I believe that aside from the names of Joel and his father in Joel

---

Kent P. Jackson is professor of ancient scripture at Brigham Young University.

[1]For a good summary of the arguments, see Douglas Stuart, *Hosea-Jonah*, Word Biblical Commentary, vol. 31 (Waco, Texas: Word, 1987), pp. 224–26. See his bibliography, pp. 222–24.

[2]See Andrew E. Hill, *The Book of Malachi: Its Place in Post-Exilic Chronology Linguistically Reconsidered*. Unpublished dissertation, University of Michigan, 1981.

[3]Linguists are certainly aware of factors that could confuse the dating process, such as the deliberate use of older language (as with the use of "thee" and "thou" in Latter-day Saint prayers) and the possibility that Joel could have been written centuries earlier and then "translated" into a more modern dialect of Hebrew at a later date.

1:1, every word in the book refers to the latter days—from the time of the Prophet Joseph Smith into the Millennium. Joel's apocalyptic style makes his fundamental message very clear: in a dramatic way, God will bring judgment upon the world, destroying evil and blessing the righteous with millennial peace and happiness (see "Apocalyptic Revelation" in Chap. 28 of this volume).

A Day of Darkness and Gloominess (Joel 1:1–2:27)

As is typical in apocalyptic prophecy, vivid symbolic images are used to convey the Lord's message of great future events. Joel is best known for his image of a destructive army of insects that would invade the land. The waves of destroyers would leave nothing in their path: "That which the palmerworm hath left hath the locust eaten; and that which the locust hath left hath the cankerworm eaten; and that which the cankerworm hath left hath the caterpiller eaten" (Joel 1:4). While the precise meaning of the obscure insect vocabulary is not known,[4] the message is nonetheless quite clear: "If one doesn't get you, the next one will." As Joel's metaphor continues, the plague of insects becomes "a nation, . . . strong, and without number," with "the cheek teeth of a great lion" (Joel 1:6). They strip the bark off trees, dry up the vines, and wither "all the trees of the field" (Joel 1:7, 12). Seeds rot, grain withers, herds and flocks are decimated, and the rivers are dried up (Joel 1:17–20). In the destructive march of this unprecedented horde, fire devours all that it touches. Though the land was "as the garden of Eden before them," behind them it is "a desolate wilderness" (Joel 2:2–3). They look like horses, gallop like horse-warriors, sound like crackling fire, climb walls like men, never break ranks, and are immune to the weapons of those whom they attack. At their approach, the earth quakes, the heavens tremble, the sun and the moon become dark, and the stars cease to shine (Joel 2:4–10). Indeed, when they come, it is "a day of darkness and of gloominess, a day of clouds and of thick darkness" (Joel 2:2).

"Alas for the day! for the day of the Lord is at hand, and as a destruction from the Almighty shall it come" (Joel 1:15). "Let all the

---

[4] These terms perhaps represent different stages in the metamorphosis of one kind of insect.

inhabitants of the land tremble: for the day of the Lord cometh, for it is nigh at hand" (Joel 2:1). "The Lord shall utter his voice before his army: for his camp is very great: for he is strong that executeth his word: for the day of the Lord is great and very terrible; and who can abide it?" (Joel 2:11).

It should be clear by this point that Joel was describing neither bugs nor people with lion teeth. His words were meant to convey the awesome power, terror, and despair that will accompany the day of the Lord, that day in which the Lord will return to earth to bring judgment upon the wicked and peace to the righteous. The vivid images seem to represent the destruction that the Lord will unleash to cleanse the world. The tone of fear and doom suggests that the message was addressed primarily to those who need to change their lives.

As is typical in Old Testament prophecy, the words of despair are followed by words of hope, in this case an invitation to repent: "Turn ye even to me with all your heart, and with fasting, and with weeping, and with mourning: and rend your heart, and not your garments, and repent, and turn unto the Lord your God; for he is gracious and merciful, slow to anger, and of great kindness, and he will turn away the evil from you" (JST Joel 2:12–13). In due time, the house of Israel will indeed accept the Lord's invitation and come unto Christ. Then he will have compassion on them and restore their fortunes: those who oppress them will be removed, the fertility of the land will be restored, the storehouses will overflow with plenty, and the devastation of the locust, the cankerworm, the caterpiller, and the palmerworm will be undone. The Lord's covenant people will praise his name, "and ye shall know that I am in the midst of Israel, and that I am the Lord your God, and none else: and my people shall never be ashamed" (Joel 2:15–27).

Wonders in Heaven and Earth (Joel 2:28–32)

When Moroni appeared to Joseph Smith during the night of 21–22 September 1823, he introduced the young Prophet to his mission by teaching him from the scriptures.[5] Among the passages that Moroni

[5]For a discussion of Moroni's appearance and the scriptures he quoted, see Kent P. Jackson,

quoted was Joel 2:28–32, which begins with the following revelation: "And it shall come to pass afterward, that I will pour out my spirit upon all flesh; and your sons and your daughters shall prophesy, your old men shall dream dreams, your young men shall see visions: and also upon the servants and upon the handmaids in those days will I pour out my spirit" (Joel 2:28–29). Moroni told Joseph Smith that this revelation "was not yet fulfilled, but was soon to be" (JS–H 1:41). The Millennium will be the greatest era of fulfillment, since it will be the day in which "the earth shall be full of the knowledge of the Lord, as the waters cover the sea" (Isa. 11:9). But spiritual experiences are had among the Lord's Saints today, and it may be that the time of outpouring, which Moroni said "was soon to be," has now arrived. Perhaps it began on that same night, as the heavens were opened and the systematic restoration of sacred things commenced. Since that time, even greater things have been revealed.

What are the spiritual blessings of which Joel prophesied? Most often when we think of such things, we envision such miraculous events as visions, healings, and speaking in tongues. Though these are tremendous manifestations, the blessings of which Joel spoke are not restricted to these. Perhaps the greatest fulfillment of these words is in the quiet witness that faithful Saints receive in answer to their humble prayers concerning the truthfulness of the gospel and the divine mission of the Church. The most powerful manifestation of the Spirit today is the personal revelation that we call a testimony, which is granted freely by the Lord to the sons, daughters, old and young, servants and handmaids of the Church. God's Spirit is at work among the Latter-day Saints as they quietly "prophesy" — enjoy personal revelation in their lives — "dream dreams," "see visions," and otherwise enjoy the blessings of the gift of the Holy Ghost.

Moroni also quoted the rest of chapter 2, which foretells a time in which will be seen "blood, and fire, and pillars of smoke. The sun shall be turned into darkness, and the moon into blood, before the great and

---

"The Appearance of Moroni to Joseph Smith," in *Studies in Scripture, Volume Two: The Pearl of Great Price*, ed. Robert L. Millet and Kent P. Jackson (Salt Lake City: Randall Book, 1985), pp. 339–66. See also Kent P. Jackson, "Moroni's Message to Joseph Smith," *Ensign*, Aug. 1990, pp. 13–16.

the terrible day of the Lord come" (Joel 2:30–31). The scriptures testify that we will witness terrifying things as the earth is being cleansed for the coming of Christ (see also Matt. 24:29; D&C 29:14–21; 45:40–42; 88:88–91; JS–M 1:33). While the precise nature of these cosmic calamities is unclear, it seems safe to say that they have not yet happened, but that we will recognize them when they do. In any case, as Joel reminded us, those who "call on the name of the Lord shall be delivered" and will find safety among the Lord's Saints in Zion (Joel 2:32).

In the Valley of Judgment and Decision (Joel 3:1–16)

Joel foretold, in dramatic words, the Lord's day of reckoning against the nations of the world. He would gather them together and enter into judgment against them, contending with the oppressors on behalf of his covenant people (Joel 3:1–2).[6] The offenders would receive according to the evil that they had done, for the Lord would "return your recompence upon your own head," he warned them (Joel 3:3–8). In this symbolic scene, the nations would be roused to action. They would be called to convert their plowshares into swords and their pruning hooks into spears (Joel 3:10), in striking contrast to millennial circumstances (Isa. 2:4). They would be brought to one place, and the Lord would judge them all together (Joel 3:12).

In Joel's apocalyptic description, the place of God's reckoning is called "the valley of Jehoshaphat," a symbolic name meaning "the Lord judges" (Joel 3:2). Later, the site is called "the valley of decision" (Joel 3:14). The names have no geographical significance but punctuate the imagery by emphasizing the nature of the event.[7] Medieval tradition equates this scene with the final judgment, but it is clearly meant to be understood in a different context. Jehovah's great act of judgment against the world will be at the time of his second coming, when the earth will

---

[6]The KJV translation "plead with them" seems too weak a rendering of the Hebrew *špṭ*, in this particular construction. Some other translations have "enter into judgment" (New International Version; New Revised Standard Version) and "bring to judgement" (Revised English Bible).

[7]A belief from the Middle Ages, without the support of scripture, sees Jerusalem's Kidron Valley as the Valley of Jehoshaphat and anticipates that the resurrection will begin there. Thus for centuries it has served as a favorite burial ground for Jews, Muslims, and Christians. See Cecil Roth, ed., *Encyclopedia Judaica*, 17 vols. (Jerusalem: Keter, 1971), 9:1327–28.

be cleansed of all that is corrupt in it. It appears that this cleansing will result from upheaval in the forces of nature, from manmade calamities, particularly warfare, and from the burning of the earth that will attend the Lord's coming in his glory. In Joel's visionary scene, the nations are gathered together for war, but it does not appear that they fight — either against each other or against the Lord's Saints, who are not mentioned. Instead, it is the Lord alone who contends against the world. "Put ye in the sickle," Joel wrote, "for the harvest is ripe." He invites them to trample down the grapes in the overflowing winepress, "for their wickedness is great" (Joel 3:13). As was revealed to the Prophet Joseph Smith, when Christ returns he will be "red in his apparel, and his garments like him that treadeth in the wine-vat. . . . And his voice shall be heard: I have trodden the wine-press alone, and have brought judgment upon all people; and none were with me; and I have trampled them in my fury, and I did tread upon them in mine anger, and their blood have I sprinkled upon my garments, and stained all my raiment; for this was the day of vengeance which was in my heart" (D&C 133:48, 50–51).

The Lord Dwelleth in Zion (Joel 3:17–21)

As in all circumstances in which the nations rage against God's work, the Lord is the hope and the strength of his covenant people (Joel 3:16). Joel ends, like most of the prophetic books, with a lovely promise of millennial hope and blessing. In that day, Jerusalem will again be a "holy city"; none but the sanctified will be found there. The earth will be renewed to a level of fertility not experienced since the Fall (see A of F 10), which Joel describes poetically as the mountains dripping with new wine, the hills flowing with milk, and water coming forth from the house of the Lord to nourish the earth both physically and spiritually (Joel 3:18). When Christ reigns as king, all the world will be his domain. The nations will cease to be, and the Lord's covenant Saints will dwell in his presence (Joel 3:19–21).

34

THE BOOK OF MALACHI

RICHARD D. DRAPER

To the Nephites and Lamanites the risen Savior quoted sections of the prophecies of Malachi, stating that the Father himself had commanded him to do so. The reason, he stated, was "that they should be given unto future generations" (3 Ne. 24:1; 26:2). Those generations were the righteous children of Lehi who established the perfect society after the coming of the Lord.[1] Those people needed the words of Malachi in order to understand the new dimension which the work of the Lord took, now that he had fulfilled his mortal mission. Up to this time most of the preparation had been for his first coming. From that point on, it would be for his second. The words of Malachi reveal not only key events but also the nature of the work that would prepare for that coming. Therefore, the Savior used the words of Malachi as the basis on which he expounded "all things which should come upon the face of the earth, even until the elements should melt with fervent heat, and the earth should be wrapt together as a scroll, and the heavens and the earth should pass away" (3 Ne. 26:3).

Further emphasizing the importance of the writings of Malachi was the angel Moroni's use of them. When he instructed Joseph Smith during the night of 21–22 September 1823, he quoted portions of Malachi to

---

Richard D. Draper is assistant professor of ancient scripture at Brigham Young University.

[1]It is doubtful that the Lord was referring to any other people. For those living in the last days, the writings of Malachi have been preserved in the Bible. The essential purity of the biblical text of Malachi is attested in the Book of Mormon by Joseph Smith's translation of the Savior's quotations, which uses the same language as that in the KJV. It would seem, therefore, that the Savior intended his transmission of the text to be for the Nephites. The preservation of Malachi's text in two sets of scriptures, like that of Isaiah, underscores its importance.

introduce the extent and nature of the work which had to be accomplished before the Lord would come in glory. In doing so, he laid the foundation for the work in which the latter-day Church would be engaged. Thus, we see that Malachi's prophecies were necessary not only for the Nephites but for the Latter-day Saints as well.[2]

The exact dates of Malachi's ministry are not known. From his written work it is clear that the temple had been rebuilt and the ordinances involving animal sacrifice were being performed. This places his ministry after 515 B.C., the year when the temple was dedicated. The abuses he castigated were the among those that the reforms of Ezra and Nehemiah were designed to correct. Because those reforms do not appear to have been in effect yet in Malachi's day, it is likely that his writings precede them. Therefore, his ministry would fall before 458 B.C. and was probably closer to 500 B.C.[3] Malachi's name is unique in the Hebrew cannon. It means "my messenger," or "my angel," but it may be a shortened form of "the Lord's messenger."[4] Although we know very little about him and his life's history, latter-day revelation makes it clear that he was an important individual who labored with Judah as one of her great prophets (D&C 138:46).

The Dishonor of Israel (Mal. 1–2)

One of the main problems faced by Malachi was the lack of faith the Jews felt toward Jehovah. This problem expressed itself in four specific ways: questioning the Lord's love, offering impure sacrifices, marrying outside the covenant, and lack of diligence in keeping the commandments. The prophet addressed each of these.

The Lord gave the Jews evidence of his love for them. Judah's cousins, the Edomites (descendants of Esau), were among her most bitter enemies. They had even assisted Judah's other enemies from time to time and had

[2]For discussion, see Kent P. Jackson, "The Appearance of Moroni to Joseph Smith," in *Studies in Scripture, Volume Two: The Pearl of Great Price*, ed. Robert L. Millet and Kent P. Jackson (Salt Lake City: Randall Book, 1985), pp. 361–62.

[3]For a discussion of the dating of the ministry of Malachi, see R. K. Harrison, *Introduction to the Old Testament* (Grand Rapids, Mich.: Eerdmans, 1969), pp. 960–61.

[4]For discussion, see D. Guthrie, *The New Bible Commentary* (Grand Rapids, Mich.: Eerdmans, 1970), p. 806.

benefited greatly from Judah's fall in 587 B.C. by usurping part of her land. During the ministry of Zerubbabel, however, they had suffered a setback. Through Malachi, the Lord stated that this would actually prove their demise; they would never rise to power again.[5] Their empty land would be proof of the Lord's care for Israel and would vouchsafe his right to demand their love and loyalty in return (Mal. 1:2–5).

In the meantime, Judah was not excused for doubting God's love nor profaning the sacrifices which she was hypocritically offering the Lord. Sick and blemished animals were used, against the Levitical law. And the priests, who should have guarded the rights of the Lord, not only turned a blind eye to these infractions but seem to have fostered them, probably out of self-interest (Mal. 1:6–14). All this was but a symptom of the real problem: a faithlessness by which "ye have corrupted [i.e., broken] the covenant" (Mal. 2:8). This last charge was leveled especially against the priests, whose duty it was to declare the law of God and guard his rights. In this they had failed and now stood in danger of bringing cursings upon the people. The Lord castigated the Levites for breaking the "covenant of Levi" their father—that is, dishonoring the priesthood with which the Lord had blessed their family. Their Aaronic Priesthood calling could have been a covenant of "life and peace" (Mal. 2:5). Because they dishonored it, however, the Lord would curse them and their work (Mal. 2:2–3, 8–9).

It appears that Israel in general had lost the privilege of eternal marriage at Sinai (D&C 84:23–27). But they had not forfeited the responsibility to marry within the covenant. Marriage to non-Israelites had proven to be the seedbed of apostasy; for this reason the Lord had forbidden it.[6] In Malachi's day, the men of Judah and Levi had turned to foreign women and taken them as wives (Mal. 2:11, 13–15). Many had divorced their Israelite wives in order to accommodate their unrighteous desires. Malachi expressed well the Lord's hatred for this practice and its result: the rejection of all offerings made to him and the forfeiture of the consequent blessings (Mal. 2:12, 16–17).

---

[5]The Arabs were successful in taking over Edom by the fifth century and even began to mingle with those who had fled into southern Palestine. Eventually a new people, called the Nabateans, gained control of Edom. See Guthrie, p. 806.

[6]Jehovah had specifically forbidden the practice for this very reason (see Ex. 34:15–16; Deut. 7:3–4), and the history of Israel had proved his wisdom (e.g., 1 Kgs. 11:1–11).

The Coming Purification (Mal. 3:1–4)

The people had wearied the Lord with their claim that he delighted in evil because he had not come out against their enemies (Mal. 2:17). They ignored their own faithlessness and insisted that a good God would have done something to avenge them. Malachi warned them that the full vindication of the Lord's righteousness would be revealed in the Day of Judgment. But if the Jews expected the Day of Judgment to come in their own generation, they were very mistaken. Like so many Old Testament prophecies, Malachi's would take millennia to be fulfilled.

A key to understanding Malachi 3:1–4 is in identifying the messenger who would herald the day of judgment.[7] The Savior identified John the Baptist as that messenger: "For this is he, of whom it is written, Behold, I send my messenger before thy face, which shall prepare thy way before thee" (Matt. 11:10). John's excellent service during the Lord's mortal ministry fulfilled the prophecy but only in part, because the context of the prophecy is with Jesus' second coming. John seems to have understood that his role would extend beyond his mortal ministry. When asked who he was, he stated, "I am the voice of one crying in the wilderness, Make straight the way of the Lord, as said the prophet Esaias" (John 1:23), referring to Isaiah 40:3. The context of Isaiah's words, like Malachi's, does not correspond with the events of the first coming of the Lord. They speak, rather, of the second, when "the glory of the Lord shall be revealed, and all flesh shall see it together" (Isa. 40:5). John would thus be the Lord's messenger twice, once to prepare the way for his first coming and then again for his second. The latter-day fulfillment was when John bestowed his powers upon Joseph Smith and Oliver Cowdery, allowing them and those whom they commissioned to be further messengers in preparing the way for the Lord.[8] Perhaps the prophecy will be, or has been, fulfilled in other ways as well.[9]

Malachi noted that two important events would yet transpire: the

---

[7]See the discussion by Jackson, "The Appearance of Moroni," pp. 348–50, and "Teaching from the Words of the Prophets," in *Studies in Scripture, Volume Eight: Alma 30 to Moroni*, ed. Kent P. Jackson (Salt Lake City: Deseret Book Co., 1988), pp. 198–201.

[8]JS–H 2:68–72; D&C 13. Of these commissioned messengers, none would be greater than Joseph Smith himself, who was the prophet of the Restoration and was specifically commissioned to prepare the way for the second coming of the Lord.

[9]See Jackson, "Teaching from the Words of the Prophets," pp. 198–99.

Lord would come to his temple (Mal. 3:1), and the sons of Levi would be purified and then make an acceptable offering before the Lord (Mal. 3:3).

The Lord came suddenly to his temple on 3 April 1836, as described in Doctrine and Covenants 110.[10] His coming inaugurated the great latter-day work of the house of the Lord: "This is the beginning of the blessing which shall be poured out upon the heads of my people," he proclaimed (D&C 110:10). His appearance was followed by that of others, including Elijah, whose coming fulfilled another prophecy in Malachi (D&C 110:13–16; Mal. 4:5–6).

As seen in chapters 1 and 2, much of the message of Malachi concerns the unrighteousness of the Levites, who had violated the priesthood stewardship with which the Lord had blessed them and had brought their ministry under a curse (Mal. 2:2, 8). It is thus significant that a later son of Levi, John the Baptist, would be foretold in Malachi's record. John's ministry typified the lesser priesthood perfectly, since it would "prepare the way before" the greater ministry which was to come (Mal. 3:1).

But Malachi had more to say about the future of the sons of Levi. The Lord would yet purify them collectively and accept a righteous offering at their hand (Mal. 3:3–4). How will the sons of Levi be purified? In the same way that the sons of Ephraim, the sons of Lehi, and the Gentiles are purified: by forsaking their sins and the false traditions of their fathers, by accepting the gospel, and by being baptized into The Church of Jesus Christ of Latter-day Saints. How will they "offer unto the Lord an offering in righteousness"? (Mal. 3:3). Joseph Smith, speaking concerning Malachi 3:3, taught that in order for "the restitution of all things" to be complete, the ordinance of animal sacrifice must be "fully restored." It "will be continued when the Priesthood is restored with all its authority, power and blessings." "Then shall the sons of Levi offer an acceptable offering to the Lord." This will take place, he said, "when the Temple of the Lord shall be built, and the sons of Levi be purified."[11]

---

[10]See Joseph Fielding Smith, *Doctrines of Salvation*, 3 vols., comp. Bruce R. McConkie (Salt Lake City: Bookcraft, 1954–56), 3:12–13. It is likely that the prophecy in Mal. 3:1 is not limited solely to that appearance. See Bruce R. McConkie, *Mormon Doctrine*, 2d ed. (Salt Lake City: Bookcraft, 1966), pp. 693–94.

[11]Joseph Smith, *History of The Church of Jesus Christ of Latter-day Saints*, 7 vols., 2d ed. rev.,

The Prophet did not give further details concerning this ordinance, nor do the scriptures. But it is safe to conclude that it will be of sufficient duration to fulfill the prophecies and to signify that the sons of Levi acknowledge Jesus Christ as their Lord and are thus worthy again to be numbered among the covenant people.[12] And it will be of sufficient quality and sincerity to lift from them the curse of which Malachi wrote (Mal. 2:1–3, 8), which they received when their offerings were unworthy of the Lord's approbation.

The Lord's Challenge (Mal. 3:5–18)

After showing how the offerings of the sons of Levi will become acceptable to the Lord in the last days, Malachi turned to the evil practices of his own day. He promised Judah that in spite of any future blessings, Jehovah would come against them in fury for the grievous sins they were then committing. Only if they would immediately return to him would they stave off destruction (Mal. 3:5–6).

To the question, "Wherein shall we return?" the Lord responded by specifying that they start by offering unto him tithes, which are his due (Lev. 27:30; Num. 18:21). As in every dispensation, this was a demand for faith. Judah was to quit trusting in her own arm and place her trust fully in the Lord. In a rare instance of challenge, the Lord demanded that the people test him in this matter, and he promised that blessings would flow from heaven in great abundance (Mal. 3:8–11). The result would be that even the Gentile nations would have to proclaim that Judah was blessed of God (Mal. 3:12).

"With Healing in His Wings" (Mal. 4)

Malachi again turned to the future day of judgment. He noted that it would be a day of distress, devastation, and sorrow for the wicked

---

edited by B. H. Roberts (Salt Lake City: Deseret Book Co., 1957), 4:211. See also Joseph Smith, *Teachings of the Prophet Joseph Smith*, sel. Joseph Fielding Smith (Salt Lake City: Deseret Book Co., 1938), pp. 172–73.

[12]See Smith, *Doctrines of Salvation*, 3:93–94; McConkie, *Mormon Doctrine*, p. 666; Bruce R. McConkie, *The Mortal Messiah*, 4 vols. (Salt Lake City: Deseret Book Co., 1979–81), 1:128. For another interpretation, see Sidney B. Sperry, *The Voice of Israel's Prophets* (Salt Lake City: Deseret Book Co., 1952), pp. 438–39.

(Mal. 4:1). The major cause of the anguish would be that wickedness would no longer prevail. Indeed, the wicked will be consumed from off the face of the earth at the time of the Savior's great coming.[13] But for the righteous, it will be a great day of deliverance and joy in which they will at last prevail against those who oppress them (Mal. 4:2–3).

But once again the prophet noted that the great day would be preceded by the coming of one sent from God (Mal. 4:5–6). This was to be Elijah. His mission would be twofold: first, to restore certain priesthood keys, and second, to plant in the hearts of the children the promises made to their forefathers, such that the hearts of the children would be drawn to their fathers.[14] Elijah has already come to fulfill Malachi's words. He appeared in the Kirtland Temple on 3 April 1836 and conferred the keys of the sealing power upon Joseph Smith and Oliver Cowdery (D&C 110:13–16).

The keys which Elijah restored are most significant. They rounded out those already received so that the priesthood could then function in its fullness.[15] One of the blessings that grew out of this power was eternal marriage and the resultant blessing of the sealing of children to parents. By extension, it also allowed generations to be linked together back over the course of the history of the earth. The blessings of the gospel and the sealing power are thus granted to those righteous people who were born during periods of apostasy. A byproduct of this process is that those on the earth are sealed to those in heaven and can draw assistance from them.[16]

So important is this work that the whole purpose of the earth would be frustrated if it were not done. Modern revelation explains why. Each generation needs to be welded to the one before it, such that a whole,

---

[13]From the reading of this verse in JS–H 1:37, it appears that the wicked will be destroyed by the glory of those who come with Christ. This verse (Mal. 4:1) is referred to three times in the Doctrine and Covenants (29:9; 64:23; 133:64), which gives some indication of the importance of this event. See the discussion of Mal. 4:1–4 in Jackson, "The Appearance of Moroni," pp. 350–52.

[14]This verse was significantly altered by Moroni so that Joseph Smith would fully understand the teaching of Malachi (JS–H 1:38–39). See the discussion by Jackson, "Teaching from the Words of the Prophets," pp. 202–3.

[15]Joseph Smith taught that Elijah brought the power for revelation, ordinances, and endowments of the fulness of the Melchizedek Priesthood. See Smith, *History of the Church*, 6:250–51.

[16]Ibid., 6:252.

complete, and perfect union can be made. One of the first things necessary for that union is the organization of the righteous from every dispensation into one eternal family. In this way all the keys, powers, and glories from the days of Adam to the present are brought together to prepare the earth for the return of its great King (see D&C 128:18). In a very real way, the dead cannot be made perfect without their latter-day descendants doing the necessary temple work. Similarly, those living in the last days cannot receive all the power necessary for salvation until the links are fully complete. The fathers were promised that their posterity must save them in order to save themselves. As the children come to understand how dependent they are upon the fathers, their hearts turn to them. As the welding links are fully formed, the family of God is established and prepared for exaltation. In this way the earth fulfills its purpose.

The prophecies of Malachi show the responsibility that the prophets of the former day and the Saints of the latter day have in the work of the Lord. They testify to the dependence each generation of righteous people has on those who came before and those who will come after. But most of all, Malachi's words testify of the glorious work of God in the salvation of all his children.

35

THE WORK OF EZRA AND NEHEMIAH

(EZRA 7–10; NEHEMIAH)

ADAM D. LAMOREAUX

When Ezra arrived at Jerusalem from Babylon in 458 B.C., he found the Jews in a weak temporal and spiritual condition. Although the temple had been rebuilt, Jerusalem's walls and much of the city still lay in ruins, and few people lived there. The sorry state of the Holy City was paralleled by a general neglect of the Law of Moses, and the Jews were in danger of losing their former cultural and religious identity through intermarriage with the local non-Jewish population.

It was clear that the efforts of the prophets Haggai and Zechariah some sixty years earlier had failed to produce a permanent effect on the religious feeling of the Jews in Palestine, despite their success in motivating them to finish the reconstruction of the temple in 515 B.C. In addition, the ministry of the prophet Malachi probably fell between the completion of the temple and the coming of Ezra, and his writings contain a very negative picture of the Jews' religious devotion (see Mal. 1–2). With the era of the prophets already over, Ezra was left to do his best to keep the Jews in Palestine from assimilating into the surrounding environment and abandoning the law given to their fathers.

Ezra and Nehemiah both found favor in the eyes of the king of Persia, Artaxerxes I (465–424 B.C.), and came to Judah armed with royal authority to enforce strict observance of the Law of Moses and to strengthen the small Jewish community. Although scholars disagree over the dates

Adam D. Lamoreaux is an officer in the United States foreign service.

of their arrival in Jerusalem, this essay will adhere to the traditional view that Ezra arrived in 458 and Nehemiah in 445.[1]

Like other books in the Old Testament, the final version of the books of Ezra and Nehemiah probably represents the work of later editors, who arranged the records of these two men in the form in which we have them now. One indication of this process is the shift from first to third person that occurs in many places in the text (compare Ezra 7:6 with 7:28; 9:1 with 10:1; and Neh. 12:47 with 13:6). In addition, the record of Ezra's reading the law to the people is found in the middle of Nehemiah's record (Neh. 8–10) rather than with Ezra 7–10.[2] While these problems should be acknowledged, they do not justify the pessimistic conclusions of some critics that the Old Testament is historically untrustworthy as a whole.[3]

The books of Ezra and Nehemiah were originally considered one book, which constituted a continuation of the history of Israel given in 1 and 2 Chronicles. The last two verses of 2 Chronicles (2 Chron. 36:22–23) are repeated in Ezra 1:1–3. This repetition was "used to indicate an original connection between the two parts."[4] Chronicles was written some time after the return of the Jews from Babylon, and the records of Ezra and Nehemiah were added to it later, perhaps around 400 B.C.[5] Ezra 7–10 and Nehemiah constitute the last chapter in this history of Israel.

---

[1]See F. M. Cross, "A Reconstruction of the Judean Restoration," *Interpretation* 29 (1975): 187–203.

[2]The apocryphal book 1 Esdras and Josephus' history of the Jews (*Antiquities of the Jews*) both separate the activity of Ezra and Nehemiah and never mention them together. If their perspective is accurate, then the Ezra material in Nehemiah is out of place. For a more lengthy discussion of the textual history of Ezra and Nehemiah, see Jacob M. Myers, *Ezra-Nehemiah*, Anchor Bible 14 (Garden City, N.Y.: Doubleday, 1965), pp. xxxviii–lii.

[3]The Book of Mormon has gone through a similar process, with Mormon and Moroni selecting and editing the material that they wrote on the gold plates: sometimes they quoted their source directly (Alma 34), sometimes they summarized events in their own words (Alma 35), and sometimes they also inserted their own editorial comments into the record (Ether 4:4–6:1). Although this comparison is instructive, it is important to note that Latter-day Saints should have more confidence in the Book of Mormon, because the tasks of editing and translating always remained in prophetic hands, which is something that cannot be maintained in the case of the Bible. See Joseph Smith, *Teachings of the Prophet Joseph Smith*, sel. Joseph Fielding Smith (Salt Lake City: Deseret Book Co., 1938), pp. 9–10, 194, 327.

[4]Victor L. Ludlow, *Unlocking the Old Testament* (Salt Lake City: Deseret Book Co., 1981), p. 114.

[5]The authorship of the history from 1 Chronicles to Nehemiah is unknown, although Ezra is often given credit. It is most likely that this material is the work of more than one author. See Myers, pp. xl, lxviii–lxx, and Cross, p. 194.

Adam D. Lamoreaux

Although the Jews seemed determined to neglect the law and the prophets were taken from them, the work of these two pious men demonstrated that the Lord was still willing to grant his wayward people some degree of help and prosperity.

The Commission of Ezra (Ezra 7–8)

Ezra was of priestly descent, and his genealogy back to Aaron is given at the beginning of his record (Ezra 7:1–5). He is described as "a ready scribe in the law of Moses" (Ezra 7:6). A scribe was an instructor and interpreter of the Mosaic law. As such he was qualified to argue cases and render legal decisions from the Torah in a Jewish court. Subsequent generations of scribes and rabbinic leaders in Judaism looked back to Ezra as the great scribal prototype and the spiritual father of their tradition.[6]

However impressive Ezra's credentials appear, he is never described as a prophet either in Ezra or in Nehemiah. Despite the assumption of the text that the Lord was guiding him (Ezra 7:6), we have no indication that the Lord ever revealed his will to him. Although he was a pious man, interested in the spiritual welfare of his people, he did not enjoy the Spirit of the Lord that characterized the call of a prophet in Old Testament times.[7]

Because of Ezra's priestly lineage, his family was perhaps respected and influential in Babylon. That may explain why he gained the favor of King Artaxerxes, who "granted him all his request" in connection with his desire to go to Jerusalem (Ezra 7:6). Persian kings generally took an interest in the religions of their subject peoples, thereby gaining the respect and loyalty of their subjects and reducing the possibility of rebellion and dissent in their far-flung empire.[8]

Artaxerxes gave Ezra a letter detailing the terms of his commission (Ezra 7:12–26), which had three general directives: (1) Any Jews in the empire who wished to accompany Ezra to Jerusalem could do so. (2) Ezra

---

[6]See Matthew Black, "Scribe," in *The Interpreter's Dictionary of the Bible*, 5 vols., ed. G. A. Buttrick, et al. (Nashville: Abingdon, 1962–76), 4:246–48.

[7]See Gen. 41:38; 1 Sam. 10:10–11; Ezek. 11:5; Micah 3:8; 1 Ne. 11:1; and Jacob 7:8 for examples of the Spirit guiding the prophets.

[8]Myers, pp. lvii–lviii.

375

was given gold, silver, and precious vessels from the king's treasury to use in purchasing sacrifices and offerings for the temple and other aspects of temple worship, according to Ezra's discretion. He was also empowered to collect offerings from the Jews in Babylon for the same purpose and to draw money from the treasuries of local officials in Palestine, if necessary. (3) Ezra was given authority to order religious affairs in Judah and the power to punish those who did not cooperate with him. With the complete support of Artaxerxes, Ezra was now ready to depart on the Lord's errand.

Ezra was accompanied by a group of more than fifteen hundred men, thirty-eight Levites, and two hundred twenty temple attendants (see Ezra 8:1–20). With the addition of wives and children, the total number would have been considerably larger.[9] The group arrived at Jerusalem in the fifth month of the seventh year of the reign of Artaxerxes (Ezra 7:7–8) and "furthered the people, and the house of God" (Ezra 8:36).

The Prohibition of Intermarriage (Ezra 9–10)

Some time shortly after Ezra's arrival at Jerusalem, he was informed that many of the Jews had intermarried with the surrounding peoples (Ezra 9:1). The text hints that the Jews had begun to adopt the religious practices of these peoples (Ezra 9:1, 14), but the references to the "abominations" of the non-Jews may simply mean that their religious practices made them unsuitable as marriage partners because of the potential for apostasy in a mixed marriage.

The scriptural prohibition against intermarriage that Ezra quotes at Ezra 9:11–12 is not found in our Old Testament. It was evidently once part of the scriptures and has since been lost. Intermarriage with seven specific Canaanite peoples is prohibited in Deuteronomy 7:1–4, and the Pentateuch generally discourages marriage with foreigners (see Gen. 26:34–35; 27:46–28:2; see also JST 1 Kgs. 3:1). There are some notable exceptions, however, such as Joseph (Gen. 41:45), Moses (Num. 12:1), and Boaz (Ruth 4:13). It is possible that the passage that Ezra quoted

---

[9]See Myers, p. 70.

was given to a prophet some time after the ministry of Moses to clarify that the Lord did not want the Israelites to marry any foreigners.

The primary reason given in the Old Testament for discouraging intermarriage is that it would turn the Israelites away from the Lord to the worship of the false heathen gods of their spouses (Ex. 34:16; Deut. 7:4; 1 Kgs. 11:1–4). Ezra was no doubt aware of this, although it appears that his main concern was to avoid the Lord's retribution for breaking a commandment rather than the consequences of religious contamination (Ezra 9:10–15).

Ezra's strictness was in keeping with other post-Exilic instances of extreme concern for maintaining the separateness of the house of Israel (see Neh. 9:2). After the return of the Jews in 538 B.C., priests who could not prove their lineage were excluded from serving in the priesthood (Ezra 2:61–63), and the Samaritans, whose lineage was part Israelite and part foreign, were also excluded from association with the Jews (Ezra 4:1–3). Malachi also condemned the Jews for marrying outside of Israel (Mal. 2:11). These practices may seem extreme, but they need to be viewed in light of the near-destruction of Judah as a people and their need to follow the Lord's commandments strictly in order to avoid his further punishment and to obtain some measure of spiritual and temporal prosperity.[10]

The people were apparently convinced of their wrongdoing, and they agreed to take the extraordinary step of divorcing all of their foreign wives (Ezra 10:1–5, 9–12). Even if the people were against this decision, there was little they could do, because Ezra had royal authority to enforce his interpretation of the Law of Moses (Ezra 7:25–26). This decision was reached four months after Ezra's arrival (Ezra 10:9), and a list of the priests who had married foreign wives was recorded (Ezra 10:18–44).

The Renewal of the Covenant (Neh. 8–10)

Part of Ezra's commission from Artaxerxes was to teach the Jews "the laws of thy God" (Ezra 7:25–26). The account of Ezra's teaching efforts

---

[10]In New Testament times, Paul advised those married to a non-Christian spouse to remain married, because of the chance that the non-Christian spouse could be converted (1 Cor. 7:12–16).

is found in Nehemiah 8 through 10. Why were these events placed in the middle of the record of Nehemiah's activities? If the chronological sequence is preserved accurately, it would appear that Ezra did not read the law to the Jews until after Nehemiah arrived in 445. But it does not seem consistent that Ezra would wait thirteen years to get around to teaching the law to the Jews.[11] Whenever this reading occurred, it was a very significant event, for the Jews made a covenant to live the Law of Moses. However difficult Ezra and Nehemiah found it to keep the Jews from straying from the law, their efforts paid dividends in the long run, and subsequent generations of Jews sought to maintain their commitment to the Torah.

Several statements indicate that the Jews were not keeping the law and that they were ignorant of many of its commandments, such as those concerning the Sabbath day (Neh. 8:9–12). They were not keeping the Feast of Tabernacles, and the text even states that the Jews had not kept this feast since the days of Joshua (Neh. 8:14–17). The Jewish leaders admitted their guilt and included their own generation among the previous generations of disobedient Israelites (Neh. 9:33–34).

Ezra instructed the Jews on the first day of the seventh month from a platform that overlooked the street which was "before the water gate," in which the people were assembled (Neh. 8:1–2, 5). The law was read and explained by Ezra and the Levites, so that the people could clearly understand their duties and obligations. It is probable that the people could not understand the law in Hebrew because they spoke Aramaic, which was at that time the common language of Babylon and the *lingua franca* of the Near East. Their sojourn in Babylon would have placed them in an Aramaic-speaking environment, and because Aramaic is similar to Hebrew (like modern Spanish and Portuguese), it would have been relatively easy for the Jews to learn. It is also possible that they still spoke some Hebrew but that their speech had assimilated enough Aramaic words and phrases to make the law difficult to understand. This would explain why it was necessary that the Levites "gave the sense, and caused them to understand the reading" (Neh. 8:8).

Ezra read the law for two days (Neh. 8:13), and then the people

---

[11]Cross believes that Ezra read the law in 458 B.C., two months after he arrived in Palestine; see Cross, pp. 199–200.

celebrated the Feast of Booths (Tabernacles) after they had learned about it from what Ezra had read to them (Neh. 8:13–18; cf. Deut. 16:13–15). The Jews gathered together again on the twenty-fourth day of the seventh month clothed in sackcloth, with dirt on them (symbols of mourning and repentance), and in fasting (Neh. 9:1). After disassociating themselves from all non-Jews, hearing the law for a fourth of the day, and confessing their sins and worshiping the Lord for another fourth of the day, they made a covenant to obey the Law of Moses (Neh. 9:2–3, 38; 10:29). The covenant was made after the leaders of the Jews rehearsed the history of God's dealings with Israel (Neh. 9:4–35), which they rightly understood to be a history of disobedience on the part of their forefathers. The priests, Levites, and other family heads signed their names to this covenant, in addition to Nehemiah.[12]

The Old Testament contains several references to covenant-renewal ceremonies like the one described here. Moses originally instructed the children of Israel to read the law every seven years at the Feast of Tabernacles (Deut. 31:10–13). There is no evidence that this command was strictly observed, but in certain cases the Israelites did gather together and make a covenant to live the law. Moses received the law at Mount Sinai in the wilderness, and the children of Israel made a covenant there to obey it after Moses had read it to them (Ex. 24:1–8). Forty years later, he spoke to Israel on the east bank of the Jordan River before his death. This generation was not alive when the law was originally given at Sinai, and for this reason, as well as to encourage the Israelites to be obedient in the promised land, Moses reviewed the law (Deut. 4–27) and put the people under covenant again (Deut. 29). The covenant was renewed at the end of Joshua's life (Josh. 24:24–25), and centuries later Josiah put the people under covenant to obey the law after a period of apostasy (2 Kgs. 23:1–3). The last address of King Benjamin to the Nephites is also an excellent example of a covenant-renewal ceremony (Mosiah 1–6).[13]

---

[12]If the law was read by Ezra before Nehemiah's arrival, then Nehemiah's name was added later, perhaps by the editor who put the account of Ezra's reading the law in the middle of the book of Nehemiah. It is also curious that Ezra's name was not included. These issues point up the chronological problem that has been noted in the introduction.

[13]See Stephen D. Ricks, "The Treaty/Covenant Pattern in King Benjamin's Address (Mosiah 1–6)," BYU Studies 24 (1984): 151–62. This article also contains an overview of covenant-renewal ceremonies in the Old Testament and their ancient Near Eastern background.

Because some traditions and many scholars ascribe to Ezra the work of editing the Pentateuch and placing it in its present form,[14] we may ask to what extent Ezra interpreted the Law of Moses to apply to the Jews' current circumstances. Because there are no copies of the Pentateuch available that date from the time of Ezra or before, aside from scattered references from the Book of Mormon, this question cannot be answered with any degree of certainty. Ezra's reverence for the law in the books of Ezra and Nehemiah (Ezra 9:5–10; Neh. 8) seems to preclude the possibility that he would alter it in substantial ways, yet in all dispensations the scriptures have been applied by the Lord's servants to suit the current circumstances of the people (see 1 Ne. 19:23).

The Commission of Nehemiah (Neh. 1–2)

Whereas Ezra was a religious reformer, Nehemiah was primarily a political reformer: Artaxerxes gave Ezra power to reform and regulate Jewish worship, but Nehemiah was given authority to rebuild the city of Jerusalem. Nehemiah had the distinction of being the cupbearer of Artaxerxes (Neh. 1:11–2:1), which means that he served the king's drink and sampled it to ensure that it had not been poisoned before it was given to the king. This practice was common in Near Eastern courts to prevent the assassination of the king.

Nehemiah's record begins at Susa, one of the main royal residences in Persia (center of Map 12, LDS Bible), in the twentieth year of Artaxerxes' reign (445 B.C.). There at the court of Artaxerxes, Nehemiah learned that the Jews in Palestine were not faring well and that Jerusalem still lay in ruins (Neh. 1:1–3). Nehemiah then pleaded with the Lord on behalf of the Jews to deliver them from their suffering and to give him success in asking the king if he might go to Jerusalem and rebuild it (Neh. 1:4–2:5). The king granted Nehemiah's request, and an armed escort accompanied him to Jerusalem in 445 B.C. (Neh. 2:5–9).

Nehemiah is never called a prophet, nor does he appear to have been a priest or to have had any special religious credentials, as did Ezra.

---

[14]See Myers, pp. lxxiii–lxxiv. One of the first modern critics of the Bible to espouse this view was Benedict de Spinoza in 1670. See his *A Theologico-Political Treatise and a Political Treatise*, trans. R. H. M. Elwes (New York: Dover, 1951), pp. 129–30.

What he accomplished was done through royal authority, but he must have been a man of humble intentions in light of his prayer recorded in Nehemiah 1 and other statements wherein he asked the Lord to remember and bless him (Neh. 5:19; 13:31). There is one instance in Nehemiah's record where he mentioned receiving inspiration: "And my God put into mine heart to gather together the nobles, and the rulers, and the people, that they might be reckoned by genealogy" (Neh. 7:5). Nehemiah may have lacked religious credentials, but he was able to receive the Lord's inspiration and to receive answers to his prayers.

Nehemiah's letters of authorization are not written in the text (Neh. 2:7–9), but it appears that in addition to having authority to rebuild Jerusalem, he was made governor of the province of Judah as well (Neh. 10:1; 12:26). This circumstance helps explain the enmity of Sanballat, governor of Samaria, because the territory of Judah was probably under his jurisdiction until Nehemiah came.[15]

Rebuilding the Walls of Jerusalem (Neh. 3–7; 11–12)

Nehemiah faced a formidable task in rebuilding Jerusalem's walls, because of the opposition of other local officials. In addition to Sanballat, Tobiah, the governor of the province of Ammon, and Geshem, a prince from the province of Arabia to the south of Judah, opposed the rebuilding program (Neh. 2:19).[16] Their motives for opposing Nehemiah's work were political: they wanted the Jews to remain weak and feared that a strong province of Judah would erode their own power and influence.

Nehemiah inspected the walls of Jerusalem at night because he had kept his mission a secret, no doubt to avoid the immediate opposition of his enemies, who were not happy that Judah had a new governor (Neh. 2:10–16). When the nature of his mission did become public knowledge, the unholy alliance of Sanballat, Tobiah, and Geshem accused Nehemiah of sedition against Artaxerxes (Neh. 2:19). They knew that their charge was false, but it showed that they would make every effort to frustrate Nehemiah's plans. Nehemiah's reply is indicative of

---

[15]Myers, p. xxxiii.
[16]Myers, pp. 100–101, 125.

his faith: instead of producing his royal orders, he replied, "The God of heaven, he will prosper us" (Neh. 2:20). The work commenced despite these threats, and a list of those who repaired the walls, in addition to their location, appears in Nehemiah 3.[17]

The work went quickly because of the enthusiasm of the Jews, and soon half of the wall was restored (Neh. 4:6). The walls did not need to be completely rebuilt, as is evident from the statement "the breaches began to be stopped" (Neh. 4:7). The Jews would have built the wall from the foundation up in places where breaches had been made. This success enraged Sanballat and Tobiah, who made threats about attacking the Jews. Nehemiah responded by placing half of the Jews on guard duty during the day and by having the workers stay in Jerusalem at night to protect themselves and the walls (Neh. 4:7–23).

Through Nehemiah's able and energetic leadership, the breaches in the wall were all repaired (Neh. 6:1) and only the gates remained to be replaced. Nehemiah's enemies desperately continued their scheming. Sanballat and Geshem requested a meeting with Nehemiah away from Jerusalem, where they planned to kill him. He wisely refused all of their invitations (Neh. 6:1–4). That they would try such an obvious plan indicates their weakening position. Sanballat then sent a servant to Nehemiah with a letter that charged the Jews with planning a revolt against the king. The building of the wall was used as evidence for this rebellion, as well as false reports that the Jews had already appointed a king over them (presumably Nehemiah). Sanballat threatened to send the letter to the Persian king unless Nehemiah met with him. Nehemiah denied the charges and again refused to meet Sanballat, no doubt aware that he had the confidence of the king and that Sanballat's complaint would not be taken seriously (Neh. 6:5–9). A final effort to discredit Nehemiah also failed (Neh. 6:10–13).

Despite the machinations of Nehemiah's enemies, the work was completed (Neh. 6:15; 7:1). According to the text, it took only fifty-two days to reconstruct the walls and gates, although the later Jewish historian Josephus records that it took two years and four months, which is probably a more reliable figure for an undertaking of this kind.[18]

---

[17]For a discussion of the probable layout of the walls of Jerusalem at this time, including a map, see Myers, pp. 112–19.

[18]Josephus, *Antiquities* 11.5.8.

Nehemiah made provisions for guarding the walls and gates of Jerusalem and for shutting the gates at night.

Despite the Jews' triumph, the fact that there were many destroyed houses in the sparsely populated city overshadowed their success (Neh. 7:4). At this time, only the Jewish leaders and those associated with the functions of temple worship made their homes in Jerusalem. As a measure to increase the security of the city, or perhaps out of national pride, the Jews chose one-tenth of their population by lot to move into the city (Neh. 11:1–2). A list of the residents of Jerusalem follows, in addition to a description of the area of Judah settled by the Jews (Neh. 11:3–36). A record of the dedication ceremony for the walls is given (Neh. 12:27–43), and "the joy of Jerusalem was heard even afar off" (Neh. 12:43). Thanks to Nehemiah's efforts, Jerusalem now had a secure wall and many new residents, in addition to a temple. After almost 150 years, the visible reminders of the destruction of Jerusalem in 587 B.C. were finally being erased.

Nehemiah's Reforms (Neh. 13)

Nehemiah also undertook some social and religious reforms. As with Ezra, because of Nehemiah's political power, the Jews were not in a position to ignore his wishes. During the building of the walls, there was a general complaint brought to Nehemiah by the poorer people that they were heavily in debt to their richer brethren and that they were resorting to placing their children in bondage to pay their taxes and to buy food, because of famine. They were also paying usury, or interest, on their debts (Neh. 5:1–5). This situation angered Nehemiah, because charging interest on the debts of fellow Israelites was clearly against the Law of Moses (Ex. 22:25–27; Lev. 25:36–37; Deut. 23:19–20). After a hearty tongue-lashing by Nehemiah, the Jewish creditors covenanted to quit charging usury and to redeem the slaves and property that they held (Neh. 5:6–13). After these debts were canceled, Nehemiah spoke relative to his own benevolent conduct in being free with his money to support the Jews. He wanted it known that his motives were for the good of his people and not for financial gain (Neh. 5:14–19).

There are two genealogical lists in Nehemiah. One is a record of those who came to Judah from Babylon (Neh. 7:5–69), a copy of the list given in Ezra 2. The other is a list of priests and Levites who came from Babylon (Neh. 12:1–26). These lists are given to verify the genealogy of the people, because the law was apparently read at the dedication ceremony, in which it was discovered that Ammonites and Moabites were not to be part of the Jews' society (Neh. 13:1–2; cf. Deut. 23:3–6). Those who were apparently of any foreign lineage were expelled from the meeting and presumably from Jewish society and worship (Neh. 13:3). These lists may have had other functions as well. The general list of families in Nehemiah 7:5–69 may have been given to establish the family credentials of the Jews before the resettlement of Jerusalem was undertaken (see Neh. 11:1–36). The list of priestly and Levitical families was probably used to help in regulating the priesthood, because it was at this time that provisions were made for the collection of tithes and offerings and temple worship was ordered and regulated (Neh. 12:44–47).

Nehemiah left Jerusalem and returned to Artaxerxes' court after a twelve-year stay (445–433 B.C.). A short, unspecified period of time later, he returned to Jerusalem and found that the Law of Moses had been neglected in his absence. His steps to correct the situation included removing the irreverent Tobiah out of the temple chamber were he had made his home (Neh. 13:4–9), regulating temple rituals that had been neglected (Neh. 13:10–14, 30–31), prohibiting buying and selling on the Sabbath (Neh. 13:15–22), and dealing with intermarriage (Neh. 13:23–30). Unlike Ezra, who was more worried about God's punishment for marrying outside of Israel, Nehemiah was more concerned with assimilation and the loss of Jewish identity (see Neh. 13:24–26; cf. Ezra 9:14). This neglect of the law in Nehemiah's absence points out the continually lax attitude of the Jews toward obeying the Lord and the ever-present danger of assimilation. The record of Nehemiah ends with the humble request, "Remember me, O my God, for good" (Neh. 13:31). We are left without any further details concerning the life of this zealous cupbearer of Artaxerxes.

Conclusion

The work of Ezra and Nehemiah in the last half of the fifth century B.C. saved the Jewish community at Jerusalem from the dangers of cultural and religious assimilation and from a wholesale defection from the Law of Moses. They lived in a period of religious twilight, at a time when prophecy had ceased. They themselves were not prophets and never spoke in the name of the Lord. But as God-fearing men, they did their best to persuade the Jews to obey the law that their fathers had long neglected. Their success was due to their faith and their royal authority, with which they felt the Lord had mercifully blessed them (Ezra 7:6; Neh. 1:11; 2:18).

Ezra and Nehemiah constantly fought against the Jews' laxness regarding the law. It is remarkable that the Jews did not turn from the law again after these influential leaders died. Something happened in subsequent years to awaken in the people a burning desire to obey the Law of Moses. Perhaps they took the efforts and examples of Ezra and Nehemiah to heart. Perhaps they realized that their situation as a people was hopeless if they continued to disobey. Perhaps the absence of the prophets and the withdrawal of the Lord's Spirit helped them to recognize that their complete spiritual death was imminent. For whatever reason, the Jews clung to the only light and knowledge that the Lord had left them with, and that was the law and the records of the now-departed prophets. They looked back on the work of Ezra and Nehemiah with admiration and gratitude and maintained a hope that the Lord would not forget them. Their hope was not in vain, for the righteous Jews of a later generation recognized Jesus of Nazareth as their Lord and Messiah. After the mortal ministry of the Lord was finished, the believers among them fully understood that the law that their fathers had lived pointed to him and meant nothing without his atoning sacrifice and resurrection.

36

THE BOOK OF ESTHER

ROGER R. KELLER

The book of Esther is either deeply revered or virtually disregarded. It is one book of the Bible toward which one finds little neutrality. On the one hand, it has been said that there are more extant manuscripts of Esther among the Jews than of any other book of the Old Testament; and Maimonides, the great medieval Jewish philosopher (A.D. 1135–1204), ranked Esther just after the Pentateuch in value.[1] On the other hand, it is the only Old Testament book that was not found among the Dead Sea Scrolls; and Martin Luther, the Protestant Reformer, suggested that there would be no loss if Esther did not exist.[2] Thus, our task is to determine whether Esther has a message that can address the needs of Latter-day Saints.

Summary of Esther

Esther is set in ancient Persia during the reign of Ahasuerus, commonly identified with Xerxes I, who reigned 486 through 465 B.C.[3] The book of Esther begins with Ahasuerus giving a great banquet for dignitaries

---

Roger R. Keller is associate professor of Church history and doctrine at Brigham Young University.

[1]Reidar B. Bjornard, "Esther," in *The Broadman Bible Commentary*, 12 vols., ed. C. J. Allen (Nashville: Broadman, 1969–72), 4:1. It should be noted that there are Hebrew manuscripts and Greek manuscripts, the latter reflecting the Septuagint version. The Greek text is longer than the Hebrew and has additions that make the outwardly secular Hebrew story more acceptable in religious circles.

[2]Carey A. Moore, *Esther*, Anchor Bible 7B (Garden City, N.Y.: Doubleday, 1971), p. xvi.

[3]R. K. Harrison, *Introduction to the Old Testament* (Grand Rapids, Mich.: Eerdmans, 1969), p. 1087.

from across his empire. In a drunken stupor he ordered the beautiful Queen Vashti to dance for his guests. She refused and was deposed (Esth. 1:1–22), thereby opening the way for Esther, a beautiful Jewish girl, ultimately to be chosen as the new queen (Esth. 2:15–18). On the advice of her uncle, Mordecai, she had hidden her Jewish identity (Esth. 2:10).

After Esther became queen, Mordecai uncovered a plot to assassinate the king and warned him through Esther. Although Mordecai received no reward at that time, his action was recorded in the official annals (Esth. 2:19–23). Some time after that, Haman, an Amalekite, became prime minister, and Mordecai refused to bow before him as was the traditional practice, thereby infuriating Haman. Haman decided to exterminate Mordecai, as well as all Jews, and persuaded Ahasuerus to issue an edict permitting the destruction of those who did not abide by the laws of the realm (Esth. 3:1–15).

Learning of the threat to the Jews, Mordecai persuaded Esther to intercede on behalf of her people, even though it could mean the loss of her own life. Esther agreed but asked the Jews to fast with her for three days before she entered the king's presence uninvited, an act for which she could be summarily executed (Esth. 4:1–17). Upon entering the king's presence, she was graciously received and told she could have whatever she wanted (Esth. 5:1–3). In response, she invited the king and Haman to dinner. When the king at dinner again offered her whatever she wanted, all she did was invite Haman and the king to return the next night (Esth. 4:4–8).

Flushed with his apparent importance, Haman determined to hang Mordecai, who had once again refused to bow to him as Haman passed through the palace gate (Esth. 5:9–14). Meanwhile, the king was unable to sleep and ordered passages from the royal records read to him. The account of Mordecai's discovery of the assassination plot was read, and the king realized he had never rewarded him. He called Haman, who had been waiting outside to request Mordecai's execution. Ahasuerus asked Haman how one who had done a great favor for the king should be rewarded, and Haman, assuming he was the one worthy of such favor, suggested that such a person should be given royal robes, royal jewelry, and the king's own horse, and led through the streets by a high government official who would proclaim that this was the way in which the king honored faithful servants. Haman was immediately commanded to do this for Mordecai (Esth. 6:1–13).

That night at dinner, Esther revealed the plot against the Jews and Haman's part in it. The king, angered, left the room, and upon his return found Haman groveling before the queen, perhaps even touching her, and immediately ordered Haman hanged on the very gallows he had built for Mordecai (Esth. 6:14–7:10). Because he could not reverse the royal edict permitting the persecution of the Jews, the king issued another edict permitting the Jews to defend themselves (Esth. 8:1–17). On the 14th and 15th of Adar (the last month of the Jewish calendar), the Jews killed as many as seventy-five thousand Persians in response to attacks (Esth. 9:1–19). This caused a great celebration, which is still observed today, known as Purim (Esth. 9:20–32). The book of Esther ends with a final note on the greatness of Mordecai and the work that he did for his people (Esth. 10:1–3).

Historicity and Authorship

There is a broad range of opinion concerning the historicity of the book of Esther. Some scholars believe there is no historical basis at all but that the book is a fable encouraging faithfulness during persecution.[4] Others hold that the book is wholly historical; still others suggest that it has a historical core. Arguments for historicity center on the author's knowledge of Persia and its practices. For example, the empire of Xerxes I did stretch from Ethiopia to India, as indicated in Esther 1:1. The author had clear knowledge of the palace at Susa and of Xerxes' lavish parties, extravagant promises, and nasty temper. He also clearly portrayed the Persian government, as well as using a number of Persian and Aramaic words.[5]

The most serious argument against historicity is that no other record mentions either Vashti or Esther as a queen of Xerxes I. The queen mentioned by Herodotus is Amestris. Other arguments include doubt that the king would host a 180-day feast, that Vashti would refuse to

---

[4]E.g., D. Harvey, "Esther, Book of," in *The Interpreter's Dictionary of the Bible*, 5 vols., ed. G. A. Buttrick, et al. (Nashville: Abingdon, 1962–76), 2:149–51.

[5]Moore, p. xli. Aramaic was the official language of correspondence in the Persian empire.

dance, that a non-Persian (Haman) could be prime minister, that per-mission would be given a year in advance to attack the Jews, and that the king would permit his own people to be wiped out by foreigners. Amestris was undoubtedly not the only queen Xerxes had, because he had an extensive harem. Also, the king could not have entertained all his officials at once, and possibly the officials were rotated periodically. Vashti could have refused to dance and suffered the consequences. There is much evidence that many foreigners occupied high places, not only in Persia but in other kingdoms, not the least of whom was Joseph in Egypt.[6] Further, kings have been known to be brutal to their own people many times, and it is perfectly possible that Xerxes issued an edict a year ahead that would have prepared the machinery for a massive pogrom. In addition, the name *Mordecai* is well attested; a tablet from the time of Xerxes refers to one Mardukâ (Mordecai), an accountant, who was a member of an inspection team at Susa.[7] Given the above, it is possible that Esther may have a strong historical base.

The author of Esther is unknown but was probably a Persian Jew.[8] There is no agreement among Bible scholars concerning the date of authorship. Obviously, since Esther 10:1–3 implies that the Persian king was dead, the book could not have been written before 465 B.C. The language of the Hebrew text appears to be of the same general time period as that of Chronicles, Ecclesiastes, and Daniel.[9] The absence of Greek words would point to a date before 300 B.C., by which time the Persian empire had been overthrown by the Greeks and the hellenization of the Near East was underway. Together, these factors seem to suggest a date of composition somewhere near 400 B.C.

Purpose

The prime difficulty in explaining Esther is that nowhere in the text is God mentioned. Moreover, there is an aura of revenge surrounding

---

[6]F. B. Huey, Jr., "Esther," in *The Expositor's Bible Commentary*, 12 vols., ed. F. E. Gaebelein (Grand Rapids, Mich.: Zondervan, 1976): 4:791. Nehemiah and Daniel are other examples. See Neh. 1:11.

[7]Moore, p. l.

[8]Huey, 4:776.

[9]Moore, p. liv.

the book, and none of the characters is especially admirable. Yet there is still an overriding sense of the providence of God that preserves his people, even when they are less than lovely: it was no accident that Vashti was deposed, any more than it was an accident that Esther succeeded her, that Mordecai discovered the plot against the king, that the king graciously received Esther when she entered the throne room uninvited, that the king could not sleep, and that the story of Mordecai was read. Mordecai implied that even if Esther did not approach the king, things would still work out because of divine providence (Esth. 4:14). Thus on every page, despite the fact that God is not mentioned, he seems to be at work.

The book of Esther explains the origin of the Jewish feast Purim, the celebration that arises from the Jews' victory in Persia. Attempts to find an explanation for Purim other than this have provided no clear alternative.

This book causes its readers to consider the ways of God. God works in the midst of his children, often behind the scenes, to bring about their well-being. Sometimes he does this even when their behavior and motives are less than honorable.

It is clear that to a persecuted people, this book provided great strength. Like the book of Daniel, it taught the Jews that they could be steadfast in living their religion, despite exile or persecution. The Jews throughout their history have suffered persecution, and the message of Esther that they once came out victorious over their enemies gave courage to a people under siege. Perhaps only those who have experienced persecution can appreciate the power of this narrative.[10]

---

[10]Bjornard, 4:4; Huey, 4:776.

37

THE BOOK OF JOB

John S. Tanner

The Greek dramatist Aeschylus observed anciently that God "lays it down as law that we must suffer, suffer into truth."[1] Like a figure out of Greek tragedy, the biblical Job suffers into truth. The truth costs him his possessions, family, friends, health, everything: "Naked came I out of my mother's womb, and naked shall I return thither" (Job 1:21). Bereft of all, he tragically exclaims: "Man that is born of woman is of few days, and full of trouble" (Job 14:1). Yet Job's wisdom eventually exceeds even the tragic hero's dark insight that the world confronts us with inexplicable pain. For Job learns to hear God's voice, even in the whirlwind.

In a double sense, Job may be said to learn wisdom from the whirlwind. Job is taught first by the winds of adversity. A great wind collapses the roof of the eldest son's house (Job 1:19), crushing all Job's children. This disaster culminates a series of external calamities that lead Job to question why humans endure seemingly senseless suffering. Hence a literal desert storm hurls Job into a spiritual maelstrom. By corollary, Job's inquiry is ended by a whirlwind. The Lord reminds Job "out of the whirlwind" that human life is compassed about by unfathomable mysteries (Job 38:1).[2] Thus Job learns wisdom from the winds of affliction and of revelation. What Job and we learn from these whirlwinds is the topic of this essay.

John S. Tanner is professor of English at Brigham Young University.

[1]*Agamemnon,* in *The Oresteia,* trans. Robert Fagles (New York: Viking, 1975), p. 112.

[2]Biblical theophanies often are accompanied by storms. See, for example, Ex. 19:16–20 and Ezek. 1:2–4. Both Marvin H. Pope, *Job,* Anchor Bible 15 (Garden City, N.Y.: Doubleday, 1973), p. 290 n., and John E. Hartley, *The Book of Job,* New International Commentary on the Old Testament (Grand Rapids, Mich.: Eerdmans, 1988), p. 490 n., cite many more references.

Job the Man and the Text

Nothing is known about the man Job apart from the slender information contained in the first few verses of the book of Job. These explain only that Job was a righteous rich man from the land of Uz, which tells us even less than one may suppose, for Uz has not been identified with certainty.[3] Further, the text makes no reference to Job's genealogy, as is typical of biblical narratives treating the patriarchs, nor to the time when Job lived, as is the pattern with prophetic literature in the Old Testament. As a result, the Babylonian Talmud and the later Jewish sage Maimonides speculated that the book of Job is a parable.[4]

Clearly, the book of Job makes much slighter claims to be history than is characteristic of Old Testament books in general. Owing to this historical vagueness, there was anciently some disagreement about where the book of Job was to be located in the canon. This controversy is still reflected in differing placements of the book in various versions of the Bible. Yet despite Job's vague historical identification and in spite of the assault he levels against conventional notions of retributive justice, the book of Job has always been accepted as canonical.[5]

Modern scholars classify the book of Job as "wisdom literature," in concert with Proverbs and Ecclesiastes in the Bible and with Ecclesiasticus (also called the "Wisdom of Jesus Ben Sirach") in the Apocrypha.[6] Unlike prophetic and historical biblical texts, wisdom texts are less concerned with the unfolding history of a covenant people through time than they are with the timeless truths of the individual's relationship to moral and religious principles. Wisdom literature, moreover, belongs to an international movement; Egyptian and Babylonian sages also composed prudential maxims (such as Proverbs) and skeptical reflections on life (such as Ecclesiastes). There also exist Babylonian and Egyptian dialogues about suicide and divine justice similar to those in Job.[7]

---

[3]It is generally identified with either Edom to the southeast of Palestine or the Hauran to the north. See E. Dhorme, *A Commentary on the Book of Job,* trans. Harold Knight (London: Thomas Nelson and Sons, 1926; trans. and rpt., 1967), pp. xxi–xxiv; Hartley, pp. 65–66; Pope, pp. 3–5.

[4]Dhorme, p. xv.

[5]Dhorme, pp. vii–xii; Hartley, p. 3; Pope, pp. xlii–xliii.

[6]For a standard introduction, see Bernhard Anderson, *Understanding the Old Testament,* 4th ed. (Englewood Cliffs: Prentice-Hall, 1986), pp. 588–601.

[7]See, for example, in J. B. Pritchard, *Ancient Near Eastern Texts Relating to the Old Testament,*

Though most modern scholars regard the man Job as legendary, Job is mentioned twice in the Bible outside the book of Job and once again in the Doctrine and Covenants. Ezekiel listed Job together with Noah and Daniel as one of three worthies for whose sake the Lord would still not refrain from smiting the rebellious house of Israel with famine and plague (Ezek. 14:14, 20). In the New Testament, James praised the "patience of Job" (James 5:11) — though "patience" (which the King James translators likely used because it comes from the Latin "to suffer") might be better translated in modern English as "steadfastness" or "endurance." Certainly Job as we see him in the text is anything but passive and uncomplaining; indeed, his complaints compose most of the book. Lastly, modern scripture refers to Job when the Lord reminded Joseph Smith as he languished in Liberty Jail: "Thou art not yet as Job; thy friends do not contend against thee, neither charge thee with transgression, as they did Job" (D&C 121:10).

Together, these additional scriptural citations confirm important aspects of the book of Job. They portray Job as a blameless, long-suffering man, wrongfully accused by his friends when calamity befalls him. They are silent, we might note, about the problematical wager scene and about the neat restoration of Job's prosperity.[8] Do these allusions prove Job's story is more than a fable, that the book is historical? Not necessarily. It is possible to allude to Job's trials without intending to confirm their historicity — as one might speak of the beauty of Adonis or the folly of King Lear without intending to verify the reality of these figures.[9] Still, these scriptural allusions add plausibility to the thesis that Job was, as I

3d ed. with Supplement (Princeton: Princeton University, 1969): "Dispute over Suicide" (Egyptian; pp. 405–7), "I Will Praise the Lord of Wisdom" (Babylonian; pp. 434–37), and "A Dialogue about Human Misery" (Babylonian; pp. 438–40).

[8]For many readers these are the most fabulous and therefore troubling aspects of the text. It has recently occurred to me, however, that even these incidents might well reflect truths. The wager scene bears some resemblance to the council in heaven, wherein God determined to give Satan leave to tempt and try us, while the doubling of Job's prosperity at the end reminds us that God loves to bless his faithful servants and that he can do so in this life. I discuss these ideas more fully at the end of this essay.

[9]I am not persuaded by Keith Meservy's point of view that an allusion by the Lord to a fictional Job would constitute a cruel mockery of Joseph Smith's nonfictional suffering. The Lord's purpose here is simply to remind the Prophet that things could be worse, not to verify Job's existence. See Keith A. Meservy, "Job: 'Yet Will I Trust in Him,' " Sixth Annual Sperry Symposium, January 1978; as cited in *Old Testament Student Manual: 1 Kings-Malachi* (Salt Lake City: Church Educational System, 1981), p. 29.

believe, a real man — one who, though conspicuously upright, fell into great misfortune.

Whatever Job's actual experiences may have been, the book of Job clearly confers a literary shape upon them. Indeed, the book's symmetrical patterning is hard to miss. Broadly speaking, the book of Job comprises four major parts: a prose prologue, three cycles of poetic dialogues between Job and his comforters, the theophany (also poetry), and a prose epilogue. The central dialogues, moreover, observe further symmetries as Job responds to each of his three comforters individually and in the same order. The following outline of the book can profitably be used as a study tool to save the reader from becoming lost in verse-by-verse reading.

    I. Prologue [prose], chaps. 1–2
   II. Dialogues with the Comforters [poetry], chaps. 3–37
      A. First Cycle of Speeches (chaps. 3–14)
         1. Job's Complaint (chap. 3)
         2. Dialogue with Eliphaz (chaps. 4–7)
            a. Eliphaz (chaps. 4–5)
            b. Job (chaps. 6–7)
         3. Dialogue with Bildad (chaps. 8–10)
            a. Bildad (chap. 8)
            b. Job (chaps. 9–10)
         4. Dialogue with Zophar (chaps. 11–14)
            a. Zophar (chap. 11)
            b. Job (chaps. 12–14)
      B. Second Cycle of Speeches (chaps. 15–21)
         1. Dialogue with Eliphaz (chaps. 15–17)
            a. Eliphaz (chap. 15)
            b. Job (chaps. 16–17)
         2. Dialogue with Bildad (chaps. 18–19)
            a. Bildad (chap. 18)
            b. Job (chap. 19)
         3. Dialogue with Zophar (chaps. 20–21)
            a. Zophar (chap. 20)
            b. Job (chap. 21)
      C. Third Cycle of Speeches (chaps. 22–32)
         1. Dialogue with Eliphaz (chaps. 22–24)
            a. Eliphaz (chap. 22)
            b. Job (chaps. 23–24)

The text's literary patterning does not, of course, disprove the historicity of Job any more than Julius Caesar must be dismissed as fictional because he is the subject of a play. Furthermore, whether the book of Job is story or history, its message is still true in a deeper sense. For in every age, if not every life, Job's predicament is reenacted in events all too monstrously real. Good people suffer every day and for no discernible reason.

Wisdom about Retribution

Because scripture ordinarily correlates suffering with sin and righteousness with reward, that scriptural axiom, traditionally labeled the doctrine of "retributive justice," is debated many times between Job and his comforters. Each of Job's three comforters presumes that if Job were righteous, he would not have suffered such terrible affliction. It follows, according to their false moral arithmetic, that Job must be sinful. Eliphaz declares that if Job were blameless he need not fear either famine or death by the sword, for the righteous shall surely die of old age, with full barns and a great posterity (see Job 5:19–27). Bildad avers, "If thou wert pure and upright; surely now he [God] would awake for thee, and make the habitation of the righteous prosperous" (Job 8:6). While Zophar, confident that Job's suffering attests to unworthiness, observes:

"God exacteth of thee less than thine iniquity deserveth" (Job 11:6). But Job has heard all this before: "Who knoweth not such things as these?" (Job 12:3).

The comforters' rigid view of retribution has been the party line among uninspired dogmatists from Job's day to ours. That it is a common error owes to its origin in partial truth. The comforters might have derived their arguments, in part, from mistaken readings of such prophets as Isaiah, Jeremiah, Hosea, and Amos—all of whom threaten the people with doom because of wickedness. Equally, the comforters' counsel might have been extrapolated from such statements about rewards and retribution as this in Deuteronomy: "Behold, I set before you this day a blessing and a curse; A blessing, if ye obey the commandments of the Lord your God, which I command you this day: And a curse, if ye will not obey the commandments of the Lord your God, but turn aside out of the way which I command you this day, to go after other gods, which ye have not known" (Deut. 11:26–28). Similarly, the comforters' doctrine of retribution resembles teachings set forth in Latter-day Saint scripture. For example, like Deuteronomy, the Book of Mormon insists that the history of the promised land is balanced on a fulcrum of divine punishments and rewards according to the obedience or rebellion of the people (e.g., Alma 9:14; 38:1). Likewise, the Doctrine and Covenants confirms a correlation between blessings and obedience on the one hand, and punishment and transgression on the other. For example, "I, the Lord, am bound when ye do what I say" (D&C 82:10), and "There is a law, irrevocably decreed in heaven . . . upon which all blessings are predicated" (D&C 130:20).

So how can we understand Job's predicament in the light of these scriptures seeming to verify a doctrine of retribution? Were Job's comforters right? Is there a flat contradiction between Job's example and the scriptural doctrine of retribution? I think not. Rather, I believe Job's example can help us understand the true correlation between suffering and sin, in the following ways:

First and foremost, Job's example makes clear that though sometimes suffering is a sign of punishment, it is not so always. Though the book of Job "does not entirely answer the question as to why Job (or any human) might suffer . . . it does make it clear that affliction is not necessarily evidence that one has sinned."[10] That is a great comfort, especially for the many blameless souls who accuse themselves when tragedy befalls them. When an infant is born with birth defects or a loved one is killed in an auto accident, when cancer strikes or a job is lost — our immediate response often is, "What have I done to deserve this?" Job implies that there can be "no-fault" tragedy. This is a truth that pious, well-intentioned religionists have been ever prone to forget. Jesus had to remind those in his day of this lesson on more than one occasion (Luke 13:1–5; John 9:1–3). So, too, did Joseph Smith. The Prophet taught the Saints "that it is an unhallowed principle to say that such and such have transgressed because they have been preyed upon by disease or death, for all flesh is subject to death; and the Savior has said, 'Judge not, lest ye be judged.' "[11] The Old Testament underscores this same point through the unforgettable story of Job.

Second, Job's example warns us against trying to reason backwards from peoples' external circumstances to the condition of their souls. To do so traps us in an "if/then" fallacy, called in logic "affirming the consequent." "If/then" sequences are not reversible: If A then B does not permit the reverse conclusion B therefore A. If a man is a millionaire then he may live in a mansion on the hill. But if a man lives in a mansion, he is not necessarily a millionaire (he could be simply in debt). Or, to apply the same logic to Job: if a man is wicked, then he may suffer. But if a man suffers, he is not necessarily wicked. Sinfulness will ultimately result in suffering, but suffering does not necessarily imply sinfulness. The same holds true for the corollary: virtue may result in prosperity, but prosperity does not necessarily imply virtue. One cannot reason backwards from the fact of prosperity or suffering to the state of the soul, as Job's comforters try to do.

Job's example reminds us that neither prosperity nor suffering can be easily or routinely interpreted. In fact, *suffering* may be the blessing and *prosperity* the trial. Prosperity may test the faith of individuals as well as of nations, whereas suffering may ready them for salvation. Francis Bacon observed in his essay "Of Adversity": "Prosperity is the blessing of the Old Testament; Adversity is the blessing of the New."

---

[10]"Job, Book of," Bible Dictionary, LDS Bible.

[11]Joseph Smith, *Teachings of the Prophet Joseph Smith,* sel. Joseph Fielding Smith (Salt Lake City: Deseret Book Co., 1938), pp. 162–63.

And third, Job's example should caution us not to extrapolate from covenants made to whole peoples automatic promises of individual "success." Individuals often live out personal tragedies quite apart from the general prosperity and happiness of the larger community. The book of Job tells of the plight of a particular individual, not an entire covenant people. That is significant. Old Testament and Book of Mormon promises cited above, by contrast, pertain to an entire covenant community. Likewise, the Doctrine and Covenants promise that the Lord is bound refers specifically to the plural "ye." We should not speak glibly of our individual acts "binding the Lord" nor convey the impression that we hold the Lord of the universe to do our bidding. The nature of a covenant is that the Lord binds himself. He, not we, sets the terms, and he fulfills them in his own time and way.

If we look carefully at the Bible or the Book of Mormon or modern Church history, we can find many instances of good individuals who, like Job, suffer. To cite a few Book of Mormon examples, think of the martyred women and children who were burned before the eyes of Alma and Amulek, or of the wives and children in Moroni's day who were forced to feed upon the flesh of their husbands and fathers (Alma 14:7–11; Moro. 9:7–8). Complicating the comforters' simplistic view of retribution is that sometimes "the Lord suffereth the righteous to be slain that his justice and judgment may come upon the wicked" (Alma 60:13; cf. 14:11).

Job's example, then, corrects simplistic misapplication of the doctrine of retribution. It reminds us that the Lord's plan of rewards and punishment does not guarantee that only the wicked suffer while the righteous are insulated from adversity, if not positively assured material rewards in this life. As Christians, we need not look only to Job to refute these oversimplifications. The supreme refutation is Christ, who, though blameless, suffered more than has any man. The mortal Messiah intimately knew pain, hunger, thirst, fatigue, betrayal, and agonizing death (see Mosiah 3:7). If the Lord, who was perfect, had to endure such affliction, should we, who are imperfect, expect to be spared from it? As the Lord himself gently reminded the Prophet Joseph Smith, are we greater than He? (D&C 122:8). The only reward for righteousness that the Lord holds out unfailingly to individuals is "peace in this world, and eternal life in the world to come" (D&C 59:23) — and even this peace must be found *amid* persecutions, not in their absence (see John 14:27; 15:20).

Wisdom about Relationships

The whirlwind reveals valuable wisdom about human relationships — to God in our adversity and to others in theirs. Rather than an explanation of suffering, the book of Job supplies, as the apostle James said, an "example of suffering affliction" (James 5:10). Job's example instructs us in how to "suffer suffering,"[12] rather than in the reason for it. From the book of Job we gain no definitive answers to the philosophical problem of evil. In fact, the Lord never supplies Job with an explanation for his afflictions, much less for suffering in general. But Job's deepest need, as ours, is not for reasons but for revelation, not for theological precepts but for the divine presence. His crisis is spiritual.[13] His deepest anguish springs from his feeling of godforsakenness, which can be relieved only by the witness, borne on the whirlwind, that God has not forsaken him.

The Bible clearly focuses on Job's relationship with God and the comforters rather than on his physical suffering. Only a very few (albeit vivid) verses are devoted to a description of Job's physical pain, which he endures in silence. When, after abiding seven days and seven nights in complete silence, Job finally cries out, he complains not of boils but of betrayal (Job 3:20). However difficult to bear, his physical pain is most embittering for what it seems to him to betoken: a violated relationship. Job's relationship to God remains at issue throughout the ensuing dialogues, which make no further reference to his personal losses or boils.

Also at issue is Job's relation to his dogmatic comforters and their glib explanations about why he suffers. Job rejects their pious counsel that he accept his calamities as punishment for sin. To do so would force him to live a lie. He would have to confess that he feels deserving of

---

[12]Paul Ricoeur, *Essays on Biblical Interpretation*, ed. Lewis S. Mudge (Philadelphia: Fortress, 1980), pp. 86–87.

[13]Or existential. See Claus Westermann, *The Structure of the Book of Job*, trans. Charles A. Muenshow (Philadelphia: Fortress, 1977), for a similar interpretation of the book. Westermann argues that the book is a lament, not a treatise, and that an existential problem lies at its core, not a propositional one.

his affliction — which he does not, and should not, feel. Instead, Job stoutly maintains that weighed in the balance-scales of justice — one of his favorite images (Job 6:2; 31:6) — his suffering is disproportionate to any sin that could be laid to his charge.

Repeatedly, he cries out for an encounter with the Lord. He begs God to come into the dock so he might prove his own innocence: "Oh that I knew where I might find him! that I might come even to his seat! I would order my cause before him, and fill my mouth with arguments" (Job 23:3–4; see also 16:21; 31:35). In a shocking blend of effrontery and faith, Job intends to argue his case before God, though the Lord slay him for it (Job 13:13–16). Yet he trusts God, who, Job affirms, "shall be my salvation: for an hypocrite shall not come before him." Surely, the Lord of truth would not want him to accede to his comforters' doctrine, feigning to comprehend suffering that he cannot fathom.

We sense Job's powerful integrity and genuine depth of feelings for God, qualities seemingly absent from his coldly correct friends. Yet we also sense a measure of pride and even arrogance, that he, Job, a mere man, should think himself sufficient to prosecute a case against God. No wonder Job stands condemned by the Lord in the final chapters as one "that darkeneth counsel by words without knowledge." "Shall he that contendeth with the Almighty instruct him?" the Lord demands, "he that reproveth God, let him answer" (Job 38:2; 40:2). Humbled by the voice from the whirlwind, Job repents: "Behold, I am vile; what shall I answer thee? I will lay mine hand upon my mouth"; "therefore have I uttered that I understood not; things too wonderful for me, which I knew not" (Job 40:4; 42:3).

But Job is not only condemned by the Lord but also approved. His comforters, by contrast, are only condemned. Of Job's dogmatic comforters, so sure that they can read the Lord's hidden purposes in their friend's suffering, the Lord says: "My wrath is kindled against thee [Eliphaz], and against thy two friends: for ye have not spoken of me the thing that is right, as my servant Job hath" (Job 42:7). How has Job spoken the thing that is right? A narrow answer would point only to Job's speeches of repentance. But I wonder if Job also speaks that which is right throughout. He refuses to pretend he understood what he could not comprehend, yet he continues to look to the Lord, not to his friends, for answers. Job kept his integrity. He fought for answers from God himself. His relationship to God is more right than is that of his friends because it is more honest, searching, open to revelation. And how have the comforters *not* spoken that which is right? Many of their arguments that God punishes the wicked and blesses the faithful seem pious, even formally correct. Moreover, they think they are defending God's ways. But perhaps they are really defending an idol—their own tidy, programmatic view of God's ways.

From the Lord's condemnation of Job's comforters, we can learn much about how to comfort those suffering crises of faith. We learn that it is not enough to have all the "right" answers. We must also speak the truth in love, as Elder Russell M. Nelson has counseled.[14] With good cause Job complains to Eliphaz: "To him that is afflicted pity should be shewed from his friend" (Job 6:14; see also 19:21). We learn that we risk divine displeasure when we cease to truly comfort and start to accuse. The Prophet Joseph Smith warned the Saints that they should "judge not." On another occasion he taught that those who accuse place "themselves in the seat of Satan."[15] Significantly, the word *devil* derives from the Greek *diábolos,* meaning "slanderer, accuser." From the failure of Job's comforters, we further learn that the only abiding comfort must come from *the* Comforter. For Job, and those like him, the real problem is spiritual, not intellectual; the solution must also be spiritual. Job does not need a carefully argued treatise solving "the problem of evil." He needs a renewed witness that God has not forsaken him or ceased to be a God of justice.

Wisdom about Revelation

The witness that Job needs can only come from personal revelation. The comforters' inability to reason Job out of his anguish provides a striking illustration of the impotence of unaided human wisdom to resolve Job's anguish. Let no one mistake that the comforters' counsels, though perhaps derived from scripture, are really the product of their own wisdom. Eliphaz proudly discloses the source of his knowledge and in doing so

[14]Russell M. Nelson, *"Truth and More:" On the Lord's Errand,* address given at the Annual University Conference, Brigham Young University, Provo, Utah, 27 Aug. 1985.
[15]Smith, p. 212.

seems to speak for all the comforters: "Lo this, we have searched it, so it is; hear it, and know thou it [is] for thy good" (Job 5:27). They claim no revelation about Job's particular predicament, nor do they know God's specific intentions.

We should take heed from this. For sometimes we, like the comforters, may be tempted to offer our rationalizations about the Lord's purposes in allowing tragedies, as if they were gospel truth. If we do not know by revelation that someone's daughter died because she was needed in heaven more than here, that someone's son is born deformed so he himself could learn to be more compassionate, that God allowed a terrible war to devastate a nation in order that our missionaries could enter the country, etc., we should be reticent to promote our reasoning as the Lord's hidden will. Some comfort can be obtained only by personal revelation, usually to the aggrieved party rather than to a well-intentioned, self-appointed comforter. Unless we have both the revelation and the right to offer it, we should normally give comfort by mourning with those who mourn and by sharing with them our faith in the Lord's ultimate justice and mercy, however difficult to see in this life.

Sometimes, even having the right answers is not enough. Thus Job's fourth and final comforter, Elihu, utters speeches that echo those issuing forth from the whirlwind. Yet young Elihu's words have no effect on Job. For reason alone — even the correct doctrine — cannot provide Job the real comfort he needs. Elihu's answer remains "mere argument"; the Lord's is a revelation.

As a personal revelation from the Lord to the long-suffering, steadfast Job, the Lord's voice from the whirlwind has authority and meaning that no merely human voice can match. Apart from *what* the Lord says, simply *that* he speaks to Job at all fulfills Job's deepest need — his need to be reassured that God has not forsaken him. Theology can never provide this knowledge; only the witness of the Spirit can.

One writer recently observed that "for those who experience god-forsakenness there can be no answer except the stammeringly uttered truth that God himself keeps company with those who are oppressed."[16] In its way, this observation is very wise. But it does not go quite far enough. To our witness that God keeps company with the afflicted must

---

[16]Kenneth Surin, "Theodicy?" *Harvard Theological Review* 76.2 (1985): 246.

be added the witness of the Spirit that the Lord still keeps company with the aggrieved one, here and now, in his desperation. We can testify to the truth that the Lord loves and pities his children in the midst of their sharpest sorrows; we can offer scriptural insights about the various purposes served by suffering; but only the Lord can confirm his continuing love through the voice of the only unfailing comforter, *his* Comforter. Revelation is the essential comfort every Job requires.

The book of Job, then, is at bottom about the need for revelation. Revelation is the key to human crises of faith brought on by suffering. This interpretation, little recognized in biblical scholarship, fits Latter-day Saint teachings, which stress the need for both general and personal revelation. Indeed, "there is a mystery in the incidence of suffering that only a fresh revelation can solve."[17]

Wisdom about Divine Justice and Love

A final gem of wisdom from the book of Job concerns the nature of this mystery, as revealed in the voice from the whirlwind. The Lord's words overwhelm Job with a sense of creation's mysteries. He is reminded that humans live surrounded by a cosmos whose design and purpose we do not fully comprehend (chaps. 38–39). The reason for any number of tragedies is but one of many mysteries. Beyond recognizing the mystery of suffering, however, Latter-day Saints affirm the existence of a just and loving God. Bible scholars from other faiths sometimes fail to read the whirlwind this way. They see oracles uttered from the whirlwind as cutting loose the God of the Old Testament from concepts such as justice, reward, and punishment altogether.[18]

But does the Lord's speech to Job imply that the Almighty is so sovereign that he is divorced from the attributes of justice, order, and morality? Latter-day Saint doctrine, certainly, does not endorse this kind of sovereignty — which from a human vantage appears indistinguishable

---

[17]"Job, Book of," Bible Dictionary, LDS Bible.

[18]See, for example: Matitiahu Tsevat, "The Meaning of the Book of Job," in *Studies in Ancient Israelite Wisdom: The Library of Biblical Studies*, ed. James L. Crenshaw (New York: KTAV, 1976), p. 373; and James L. Crenshaw, *Old Testament Wisdom Literature: An Introduction* (Atlanta: John Knox, 1981), p. 125.

from caprice. The innate human demand for fairness, order, and law is doubtless a legacy from our divine parentage. In the words of the eminent Jewish scholar Abraham Heschel, "even the cry of despair—There is no justice in heaven!—is a cry in the name of justice that cannot come out of us and be still missing in the source of ourselves."[19]

We glimpse traces of a divine regard for order in the very questions the Lord asks Job from the whirlwind. The Lord's language recalls descriptions of creation in Genesis, when the Lord imbued form and light upon the immense deep, that heretofore was "without form and void" and dark (Gen. 1:2). "Where wast thou when I laid the foundations of the earth? . . . When the morning stars sang together, and all the sons of God shouted for joy?" (Job 38:4, 7). Such questions remind us that the voice in the whirlwind belongs to one who has brought order to the world. He is the God of Creation, not a capricious being who, in the words of one biblical scholar, rejects the "putative principle of order."[20]

Nor is justice absent from the voice in the whirlwind. As we have noted, the Lord's equity reaches so deep that it penetrates beneath the superficial morality of the comforters and probes beneath the pride and sometimes reckless cynicism of Job, in order to honor the one who is most truly faithful (Job) and rebuke those who are most proud and cynical (the comforters). This is the voice of one who "looketh [not] on the outward appearance, but . . . on the heart" (1 Sam. 16:7).

It is, furthermore, the voice of a God who clearly continues to care about human suffering. This is a crucial, but often overlooked, point. That the Lord responds at all assures us that he is not a permanently hidden God, as Job fears (Job 23:1–9). In his own time and way, the Lord condescends to reveal himself to his children. Often he manifests himself, as he does to Job, in our darkest hours of need. As one scholar so eloquently phrases it: "A God who concerns himself for man is a God who loves. There is no love without sharing and a God who loves is a God who suffers. Underneath the high notes a *De Profundis* of God's own agonies is audible."[21] Here the writer hints at a distinctively

---

[19]Quoted in Crenshaw, p. 303 n.

[20]Crenshaw, p. 125.

[21]Samuel Terrien, *Poet of Existence*, p. 241. On the whole issue of the Old Testament image of a suffering God, see Terrence E. Fretheim, *The Suffering of God* (Philadelphia: Fortress, 1984), and also Kazoh Kitamori, *Theology of the Pain of God*, trans. M. E. Brachten (Richmond: John Knox, 1965).

Latter-day Saint view regarding the Lord's outlook on the "problem of evil": namely, that evil is a problem for the Lord, too. In any world of both natural law (where apples *and* parachutists fall according to the same law of gravity) and of agency (where people are free to do good *and* evil), suffering will occur. But on the whole, God neither wants nor wills our suffering out of indifference or malice. In fact, he grieves over it; the heavens thunder and weep in emotional solidarity with the Saints (Moses 7:29–40). Enoch wondered how this can be so: "How is it that the heavens weep?" (Moses 7:28). But he finally came to share the Lord's view of human misery: "Wherefore Enoch . . . looked upon their wickedness, and their misery, and wept and stretched forth his arms, and his heart swelled wide as eternity; and his bowels yearned; and all eternity shook" (Moses 7:41).

Precisely because it verges on trivializing the Lord's compassion for human suffering and his relationship to the devil, many readers are disturbed by the wager story with which the book of Job begins. Similar reservations are often expressed about the final chapter too, in which Job's blessings are restored. If not literally true, however, these chapters may reflect truths about the nature of God's loving relation to us in this life. The wager story describes this life as a period of testing; a time when the Lord agrees to put all of us, like Job, temporarily in Satan's power; a time when he agrees not normally to intervene in our tests (see Job 1:12). All that is true of mortality. Latter-day Saint readers might discover in the wager story oblique reflections of agreements made in premortal councils. Moreover, if Job, too, agreed to such conditions, then he could be seen as more of a party and less of a pawn in the wager.

Similarly, the epilogue is often faulted for seeming to trivialize Job's loss (can new children ever replace the ones that were lost?) and for reintroducing the idea of retribution (Job ends up living a long and prosperous life, just as his comforters said all righteous men would; Job 42:10–17). I suspect, however, that these cavils miss the point. The book of Job corrects mistaken notions about the doctrine of retribution; it does not invalidate the idea of retribution altogether. The restoration of Job's blessings simply verifies the Lord's love for a long-suffering servant. That Job's blessings are restored reminds us that God delights to bless those who love him and also reaffirms the Lord's power to grace his children in this life as well as in the next.[22] The epilogue also reintegrates Job, formerly isolated by affliction, into the society of friends and family. He reenters his community, presumably, a changed man, as we do also if, by studying the book of Job, we learn wisdom from the whirlwind.

Wisdom from the Whirlwind

Refusing to offer ready-made answers for why Job or any one suffers, God acknowledges from the whirlwind how inexplicably cruel life can be. At the same time he points to a way of enduring, proposing "not a speculative answer . . . but a way of consecrated living" and presenting a world "not [wholly] intelligible, but livable."[23] From the whirlwind we learn indispensable lessons about honesty in our relationship with God, about compassion in comforting those in spiritual distress, and about tentativeness in offering them easy explanations. Foremost of all, we learn from the whirlwind that only personal revelation can resolve the crisis of faith that encompasses the problem of understanding, and we glimpse evidence that, however unfathomable, the God who reveals himself is a being of justice as well as of power. As Latter-day Saints, we should welcome a text that finally throws us back, just as it does Job, upon the necessity of seeking personal revelation from an occasionally inscrutable but nevertheless living and loving God. For finally the highest wisdom of Job is this: that only the divine voice from the whirlwind can answer the anguish that is borne to each of us upon the whirlwinds of affliction.

---

[22]For a sensitive treatment of the epilogue along these lines, see Hartley, especially pp. 22, 47, 540–45.

[23]Samuel Terrien, "Introduction and Exegesis to Job," *Interpreter's Bible*, 12 vols., ed. G. A. Buttrick, et al. (Nashville: Abingdon, 1952–57), 3:902; Terrien, *Poet of Existence*, p. 248.

38

THE HYMNAL OF ANCIENT ISRAEL

(PSALMS, PART 1)

R. SCOTT BURTON

The book of Psalms is a collection of ancient prayers and songs that has wielded enormous influence on the religious thought of both Judaism and Christianity. Not only have the psalms been used for significant didactic lessons, but many psalms — such as the Psalms of Ascent (120–34), which were recited during portions of the feast of Tabernacles — have been included in Judaism's liturgy for more than two thousand years. Many psalms may have been composed originally for the purpose of accompanying various rituals, sacrifices, and processions of ancient Israel; others were only later adopted into such uses. Post-Apostolic Christianity, seizing upon the popularity of the psalms during the New Testament period — the book of Psalms is the New Testament's most frequently quoted Old Testament book — incorporated the psalms into its own liturgy. Later, the Protestant movement adopted the psalms as part of their standard worship services. Jews, Catholics, and Protestants alike have found that the psalms speak a language that transcends the millennia since their composition.

Largely because the gospel has very little official liturgy, the psalms have found their way into Latter-day Saint thought, discourse, and worship to a more limited degree. Though it may appear that members of the Church do not share the widespread appreciation of the Old Testament psalms, it is important to note that the Psalm of Nephi (2 Ne. 4:15–35) is, for many Latter-day Saints, one of the most cherished and

---

R. Scott Burton is the director of the LDS Institute of Religion in Auburn, Alabama.

moving passages in the Book of Mormon. Not only does this "psalm" exhibit a good deal of indebtedness to the Old Testament psalmic imagery and phraseology — Nephi seems, at times, to be quoting Old Testament psalms — but the entire books of 1 and 2 Nephi often themselves express ideas that seem quite compatible with and even influenced by the "theology" of the Psalter. This is a hint that Nephi did indeed behold and understand "the things of the Jews" (see 2 Ne. 25:5).

A survey of the Joseph Smith Translation of the Old Testament reveals that the Prophet possessed a keen interest in the book of Psalms. Except for Genesis and Isaiah, no book of the Old Testament saw a greater proportion of its verses altered (7 percent of its verses were changed compared to 10 percent in Isaiah, 5 percent in Exodus, wholesale rewriting of parts of Genesis, and less than 1 percent in nearly every other book in the Old Testament). After reading the Hebrew texts of the Old Testament, one comes to believe that Isaiah and Psalms saw frequent revisions not because they contain more textual corruptions but because the material in them was of particular interest to the Prophet. His interest in the patriarchal narratives and his love of latter-day things is obvious and might, in part, explain the energy spent on Genesis and Isaiah. The psalms, on the other hand, speak to the shared experience of all religious people: to confidence in God and hope in the future, to physical suffering and spiritual trial, to exaltation in the victory of God over all enemies, and to the eventual triumph of all those who accept the rule of God. Those who spend time in this glorious book soon find that it merits all the reflection devoted to it by our forefathers.

The Joseph Smith Translation of the Psalms

Around two hundred verses in some fifty different psalms saw revision at the hands of Joseph Smith. Because he worked from the King James Version without reference to Hebrew or Greek texts, many of the changes have to do with KJV difficulties rather than difficulties arising from the original texts, though such difficulties certainly do exist. It is my perception that one-half to three-quarters of the changes made to the book of Psalms seek to clarify vague KJV readings — a much appreciated help indeed.

The changes made to the Psalter are of various types and of varying significance. Some, for example, are as mundane as changing "hath" to "has," "an" to "a," "mine" to "my," "shew" to "show," "that" to "who," "as" to "like," "thine" to "thy," etc. Other changes involve transference of words or phrases from one place to another for clarification or for a more smooth reading. For example Psalm 17:7 of the KJV reads in part, "O thou that savest by thy right hand them which put their trust in thee." This, being a bit awkward to the modern English reader, is changed in the JST to read "O thou that savest them which put their trust in thee, by thy right hand." Psalm 46:2 is changed from the KJV "Therefore will not we fear" to the JST "Therefore we will not fear."

While discussing Psalm 46, we should mention a change that is somewhat representative of changes made in several other places (Ps. 11, 12, and 24 contain such examples). The present tense of the verb found in Psalm 46:3–11 of the KJV is altered to the future tense in the JST. When one reads Psalm 46 in the KJV, the feeling is that the Psalmist is magnifying God because of a recent or even concurrent trial at the hands of "heathens." While reading the JST, on the other hand, one gets the feeling that it is a prophetic insight on the part of the Psalmist concerning some far-distant occurrence. This impression is confirmed upon arriving at the end of verse 8: "in the latter days" is added in the JST. What this means is that the Prophet read some psalms as prophetic oracles concerning the latter days which the KJV read as historical occurrences within ancient Israel.

One of the results of reading many psalms in this prophetic, latter-day-looking manner is that Joseph Smith found additional material concerning the founding of a latter-day Zion. It is clear, even from a cursory reading of the Doctrine and Covenants, that the formation of Zion was one of the main objects of Joseph Smith's ministry. Indeed, one could easily be justified in adding a subtitle to this latter-day collection of revelations: "A Guide for the Establishment and Maintenance of Zion." In Psalm 46:5 we read from the KJV of a very concrete, very present, city: "God is in the midst of her [the city of God]; she shall not be moved: God shall help her, and that right early." In the JST we read of a city not yet a reality: "For Zion shall come, and God shall be in the midst of her; she shall not be moved; God shall help her right early." Similarly, the KJV of Psalm 14:7 exclaims, "Oh that the salvation of Israel were come out of Zion! when the Lord bringeth back the captivity of his people, Jacob shall rejoice, and Israel shall be glad." This was changed to the yearning query, "Oh that Zion were established out of heaven, the salvation of Israel. O Lord, when wilt thou establish Zion? When the Lord bringeth back the captivity of his people, Jacob shall rejoice, Israel shall be glad." For the KJV translators, deliverance would come out of the midst of the holy city, presumably by means of some overt act on the part of God himself. For the JST the founding of some, as yet, unfounded holy city, which came from heaven itself, *was* the very deliverance for which Israel yearned.

A few words are in order concerning theological lessons that resulted from the Prophet's work on the book of Psalms. In Psalm 14:2, the KJV has God looking down from heaven in search of a man, any man, who might be in search of God. This is changed, reflecting the fact that God is omniscient and thus does not need to go around searching for knowledge which he already possesses. In the JST the passage reads: "For the Lord looked down from heaven upon the children of men, and by his voice said unto his servant, Seek ye among the children of men, to see if there are any that do understand God" (Ps. 14:2; cf. Jer. 5:1–5). After the servant's faithful search, he returns to the Lord with a list of those who say they are the Lord's, whereupon the Lord instructs the servant on the spiritual state of the community. God had known already what that state was—they are all gone aside, etc.—and wished to show his servant through this lesson what the real state of affairs was. The change made in the JST emphasizes the omniscience of God in a very direct way.

A simpler example is found in Psalm 22:2. There the KJV states that God does not "hear" the prayer of the tormented Psalmist. Lest there be any confusion on the point, the JST states that God does not choose to "answer" the plea at the time. He always hears but does sometimes forestall his answers.

In another place (Ps. 106:45), the JST points out what is taught elsewhere in the Old Testament; i.e., that God does not repent (this is actually a good example of a KJV problem that does not really exist in the original Hebrew text, inasmuch as the word translated as "repented" should properly be translated, in this instance, something like "was compassionate toward"). The JST informs us that God "spared" the people.

Finally, the Psalmist's sharp rebuke of God recorded in Psalm 82:2

in which he asks God how long he would "judge unjustly," according to the KJV, is changed to read "how long will ye suffer them [the wicked] to judge unjustly." No true prophet would accuse God of wrongful judgment!

Not only should we appreciate the Prophet's inspiration as he sought to understand the word of God more fully through his study and translation of the Bible but we should also appreciate his example of fearlessness and faith as he went about his pursuit of truth. "I want to come up into the presence of God, and learn all things; but the creeds set up stakes, and say, 'Hitherto shalt thou come, and no further'; which I cannot subscribe to."[1] At another time he stated, "I want to see truth in all its bearings and hug it to my bosom. I believe all that God ever revealed, and I never heard of a man being damned for believing too much; but they are damned for unbelief."[2]

Authorship and Date of Composition

Readers of the LDS edition of the Bible will find italicized chapter headings. These were supplied by the modern editors. Beneath them, in regular small type, are headings that date from ancient times. These headings specify eight traditional authors, or schools of authors, within the Psalter. There are seventy-two psalms attributed to David, ten to the sons of Korah, thirteen to Asaph, and one each to Solomon, Heman, Ethan, and Moses. The other fifty-one can be attributed to that most famous of all authors, "anonymous." The phrases, with their traditional translations, are respectively *ledāwid*, "of David;" *libnê qōraḥ*, "of the sons of Korah;" *le'āsāp*, "of Asaph;" *lišlōmōh*, "of Solomon;" *lehêmān*, "of Heman;" *le'êtān*, "of Ethan;" and *lemōšeh*, "of Moses." Although these personal names preceded by the *"le-"* are sometimes thought to indicate authorship, they could also indicate that a given psalm belonged to David in the sense that he owned it. Perhaps David, or his descendants, commissioned someone to compose the psalm for Israel's worship or for some royal occasion, such as a marriage. Or perhaps the psalm had been

---

[1]Joseph Smith, *Teachings of the Prophet Joseph Smith*, sel. Joseph Fielding Smith (Salt Lake City: Deseret Book Co., 1938), p. 327.

[2]Ibid., p. 374.

dedicated by the composer to David or his royal household. This grammatical construction may also indicate that a given psalm is "about David" or "about Solomon."

That is not to say that David, Asaph, Heman, and so forth, did not compose any of the psalms in question. The evidence is too strong to deny David's compositional skills (see 1 Sam. 16:16–18; 2 Sam. 1:17–27; 23:1); and, as we shall see below, Asaph, Ethan, and Heman were all associated with the musical priests of the temple. These individuals did, apparently, have the skills needed to compose both lyrics and accompaniment for psalms (see below, "The Musical Nature of the Psalms") and were therefore considered suitable candidates for authorship by later generations. The superscriptions are probably later additions to the text, however, thus they may contain little hard historical data that can be used to prove any given position concerning authorship.

When we turn to the question of an individual psalm's date of composition, we have very little more information. We now know that the writers of psalms used vocabulary and poetic devices which are of very ancient date. At times this ancient vocabulary and these ancient forms are the result of ancient composition. At other times they are the result of intentional archaizing, that is, intentionally using language older than the time the psalm was written. Additionally, written language changes more slowly than does colloquial, sometimes making a text appear much older than it may actually be. On the other hand, ancient texts may be updated and modernized through various means and thus appear younger than is actually the case. All of this must be considered as one attempts to date individual psalms.

The most useful criterion for determining the date of composition for any given psalm is the actual content of the psalm — historical allusions. Though this method is not foolproof or without its pitfalls, it appears to be the most reliable when coupled with considerations of vocabulary and form. If we use this method to determine the relative date of individual psalms, we can conclude with a fair degree of confidence that those included in the Psalter come from nearly every period of Israelite history: from the time of the United Monarchy — and possibly the early federation period — to the post-Exilic period.

For example, in Psalm 137 the author mentions the "rivers of Babylon" as a place of captivity and laments, "How shall we sing the Lord's song in a strange land?" (Ps. 137:1, 4). We can safely conclude that this psalm was not composed earlier than the beginning of the Babylonian captivity. The same is true of Psalm 74. Here the psalmist mourns that the enemy—most likely Babylon—burned and destroyed the temple, or holy place, and "every location where God was worshiped" (KJV, "synagogues of God," vv. 7 and 8).

On the other hand, Psalm 72 is almost definitely pre-Exilic and most likely was actually composed in Solomon's royal court. The language, according to Mitchell Dahood,[3] is very archaic, and many of the references are best understood on the assumption that it was composed during Solomon's lifetime or very shortly thereafter. The repeated emphasis on Sheba and gifts that come from there convinces the interpreter that Sheba was historically important at the time of the psalm's composition and hence that it was written during the United Monarchy.

Psalm 83 should be seen as having been composed during the Assyrian period. In it, numerous enemies are mentioned. Because Assyria is mentioned, it seems safe to assume that the psalm was written no earlier than around 750 B.C.—the time when Assyria began to be a threat to Israel's interests. Further, since Babylon is not mentioned, the psalm would appear to be written no later than around 630 B.C., the time of Babylon's grand entrance on the stage of international politics.

From these few examples, it can be seen that individual psalms can be dated from early, middle, and late periods of Israelite history. It must be remembered, however, that many of the psalms were composed for liturgical purposes within Israel's ceremonial worship. Ceremonial texts are notoriously difficult to date accurately.

The Musical Nature of the Psalms

The Hebrew title of the book of Psalms is *tehilîm*, "praises," "songs of praise," "sacred songs to be shouted/sung with rejoicing." Our English name *Psalms* originated from the Septuagint (the ancient Greek translation of the Old Testament) title of the book, *psalmoi*, plural of *psalmos*,

---

[3]Mitchell Dahood, *Psalms II*, Anchor Bible 17 (Garden City, N.Y.: Doubleday, 1968), pp. 179–80.

meaning "the twitching or twanging with fingers," associated mostly with the strings of a musical instrument. Later, *psalmos* came to mean "a song sung to the harp."

Superscriptions to the psalms, which are generally later than the composition of the psalms, attest to the musical nature of many psalms: *mizmôr ledāwid,* "a song or melody for/to/about David;" *bingînôt,* "with stringed instruments;" *šîr,* "a song;" etc. In addition to such linguistic evidence, there is direct and indirect historical testimony that the psalms were of a musical nature. Second Chronicles 29:30 states that Hezekiah, in the eighth century, commanded Levites to "sing praise [shout] unto the Lord with the words of David, and of Asaph the seer."[4] According to Chronicles, David originated the use of singing priests in Israel's worship. First Chronicles 6:31–32 states that David appointed Levites "over the service of song in the house of the Lord, after that the Ark had rest. And they ministered before the dwelling place of the tabernacle of the congregation with singing." (According to 1 Chron. 16:39, the ark was in Jerusalem while the tent was "in the high place which was at Gibeon.") These singers performed with "instruments of musick, psalteries and harps and cymbals, sounding, by lifting up the voice with joy" (1 Chron. 15:16, KJV). Today there is general agreement among scholars that the book of Psalms is a collection of ancient songs—the lyrics of those songs, anyway: "The Psalter is the hymnal of ancient Israel, compiled from older collections of lyrics for use in the temple."[5]

In its present form, Psalms preserves no understandable musical notation that might indicate what tunes accompanied the lyrics, what metrical measurements were used, where verses began and ended, etc. Although many of the unknown terms in the superscriptions, i.e., *šemînît, miktām, maśkîl,* etc. may very well provide such information, scholars have arrived at no general consensus about their meaning. The ancient traditions, where not entirely lacking, are of little help.

The book of Psalms itself speaks much of its own musical nature and of music and musical instruments. Consider the following examples. (All

---

[4]Asaph—and I would include in this designation the descendants of Asaph—is credited with having composed Ps. 50; 73–83.

[5]"Introduction to the Psalms," *The Oxford Annotated Bible* (London: Oxford University Press, 1962), p. 656. See "The Ceremonial Nature of the Psalms," below, for more discussion of the use of Psalms in temple ceremonies.

Old Testament quotations in this and the following chapter are my own translations, unless otherwise noted.)

> I shall turn my ear to a parable
>> I shall expound my riddle upon the lyre.
>>>>>> (Ps. 49:4)

The Psalmist then utters, with musical accompaniment, his riddle, which has to do with life, death, and redemption.

> It is good to give praise to the Lord,
>> and to sing to your name, O most High
> by telling, in the morning, of your faithfulness
>> and of your fidelity at night
> accompanied by a ten-stringed instrument
>> and the placid sound of the harp.
>>>>>> (Ps. 92:1–3)

> My resolve is firm, O God;
>> I shall sing and make music with all sincerity.
> Rouse yourselves, stringed instrument and harp
>> that I may awaken the dawn.
>>>>>> (Ps. 108:1–2)

> Sing praise to him accompanied by the sound of the trumpet;
>> Sing praise to him accompanied by the lyre and harp.
> Sing praise to him accompanied by the timbrel and with dancing;
>> Sing praise to him accompanied by strings and pipes.
> Sing praise to him accompanied by small cymbals;
>> Sing praise to him accompanied by large cymbals.
>>>>>> (Ps. 150:3–5)

> Sing praise to the Lord accompanied by the harp;
>> Sing to him accompanied by a ten-stringed instrument.
> Sing to him a new song.
>> Play well the stringed instrument with a shout of joy.
>>>>>> (Ps. 33:2–3)

The Poetic Nature of the Psalms

It is important that the reader realize that the lyrics of these ancient Israelite "hymns" have been written and preserved in poetic form. Although the King James Version in some ways hides the fact, Psalms is a book of collected poetry. Discovery of poetic texts at such places as Ras Shamra (Ugarit), Mari, and Southern Mesopotamia has demonstrated that the psalms use many of the same poetic devices used in other ancient Near Eastern cultures. The most important literary device, parallelism, is found throughout the psalms. Parallelism is of three primary types: synonymous (same thought expressed in two different ways), antithetic (contrasting thoughts expressed), and synthetic (second thought extends that of the first). An example of each might be useful to the reader. These occur repeatedly throughout the book of Psalms.

> *Synonymous:* The cords of Death enwrapped me,
> and the torrents of the swallower engulfed me.
> The cords of sheol wrapped around me,
> the snares of Death violently confronted me.
>
> (Ps. 18:4–5)

In this example Death, the swallower, and sheol (the world of the dead, or place of departed spirits) are all the same entity, similar to Nephi's "awful monster death and hell" (see 2 Ne. 9:10, 19). The instruments of this monster's terror are the same: cords, snares, and torrents — all constricting and threatening.

> *Antithetic:* Some commemorate that which is done through chariots
> and some that done through horses;
> but we commemorate that which is done through the name of the Lord, our God.
>
> (Ps. 20:7)
>
> *Synthetic:* As far as east is from west
> has God removed our sins from us.
>
> (Ps. 103:12)

Chiasm is also common.[6] Psalmic ideology, imagery, and metaphor

---

[6]The passage used above to exemplify synonymous parallelism (Ps. 18:4–5) can also exemplify chiasm. This translation, unlike the one given above, represents a syntactical literal translation:

> 4. They enwrapped me, cords of Death
> and the torrents of the swallower engulfed me.
> 5. The cords of sheol wrapped around me,
> they violently confronted me, snares of Death.

We are accustomed to seeing contextual chiasms such as Alma 36. The syntactical chiastic structure in the above example is, in verse 4: Verb/Subject — Subject/Verb, and in verse 5: Subject/Verb — Verb/Subject.

416

are also remarkably similar — in a few cases identical — to examples from other ancient cultures.[7] Though this "kindred" poetry has not shed much light on the musical nature of the psalms nor on the meter of the poetry — many scholars have spent a lifetime trying to uncover the Hebrew metrical system without producing a convincing solution — still, it has increased our understanding of the historical context and meaning of many psalms.

The Prophetic Nature of the Psalms

Modern scholarship has helped shed light on the prophetic nature of the psalms through literary and historical research into other Near Eastern cultures. One specialist in Hebrew poetry, David Noel Freedman, has affirmed:

> From time immemorial the language of heaven and of heroes has been poetic in form. . . . The basic and persistent medium of classic religion and revelation is poetry. . . . Poetry and prophecy in the biblical tradition share so many of the same features and overlap to such an extent that one cannot be understood except in terms of the other; in short, they are different aspects or categories of the same basic phenomenon, viz., the personal contact between God and man.[8]

The close association between the psalms and the prophetic tradition can be inferred from many of the historical narratives of the Old Testament. Chronicles records how David assigned the sons of Asaph, Heman, and Jeduthun to "prophecy [nb'] with harps, with psalteries, and with cymbals . . . which prophesied according to the order of the king . . . to give thanks and to praise the Lord" (1 Chron. 25:1–3). A prophet (nābî') is one who announces the will of God concerning the past, present, or future. Thus Asaph, Heman, and Jeduthun (and their descendants) were to announce divine oracles of God's will accompanied by the musical instruments of Israel's worship (cf. 2 Kgs. 3:13–19; 1 Sam.

---

[7]Psalm 29 is a parade example of Israelite imagery being borrowed from Canaanite imagery. In this psalm, as in other places in the psalms and the Old Testament, the Lord is described as the God of the thunderstorm, just as Baal is in the Ugaritic epic literature. See M. Dahood, *Psalms I*, Anchor Bible 16 (Garden City, N.Y.: Doubleday, 1966), pp. 174–80.

[8]D. N. Freedman, "Pottery, Poetry, and Prophecy," *Journal of Biblical Literature* 96.1 (March 1977): 15, 21.

10:5–6). Asaph, Heman, and Jeduthun, in addition, were known as "seers" (*rō'eh*, "one who sees," a "see-er"; see 1 Chron. 25:5; 2 Chron. 29:30; 35:15).

Freedman has pointed out that every biblical writer of poetry has been associated in some way with prophecy.[9] An example, in addition to Asaph, Heman, and Jeduthun, is a descendant of Asaph named Jahaziel. According to Chronicles, during the reign of Jehoshaphat the kingdom of Judah was seriously threatened by a united front consisting of Moabites and Ammonites.[10] After the people of Judah had fasted, assembled, and prayed "before the Lord," i.e., at the temple (2 Chron. 20:13), Jahaziel, almost certainly a singing/composing priest, stood in the assembly and proclaimed by the "Spirit of the Lord,"

> Give me your attention, all Judah, all those who dwell in Jerusalem and king Jehoshaphat.
> Thus has the Lord said to you:
>> Do not be afraid;
> do not be terrorized by this great threat.
>> For the battle is not yours but God's.
> You will not need to fight this battle!
>> Stand firm, Stand forth and see the Lord's saving act on your behalf.
> O Judah and Jerusalem, do not be afraid;
>> do not be terrorized.
> Tomorrow, Go out against them.
>> The Lord will be with you.
>
> (2 Chron. 20:15–17)

Jahaziel was probably acting here in the capacity of a priest-prophet, a Levite who officiated in Israel's ceremonial worship and received oracles from God for the congregation.[11] A number of psalms contain prophetic oracles. Psalm 20 provides an example. The psalm begins with a plea to the Lord (vv. 1–5), perhaps accompanied by some type of offering (v. 3), that he would protect the king, presumably from the armies of an

---

[9]Ibid., pp. 21–22.

[10]See H. G. M. Williamson, *1 and 2 Chronicles*, The New Century Bible Commentary (London: Marshall, Morgan, and Scott, 1982), pp. 293–94.

[11]See A. R. Johnson, *The Cultic Prophet and Israel's Psalmody* (Cardiff: University of Wales Press, 1979).

aggressor (see vv. 7–8). Verse 6 contains the oracle pronounced by the prophet/psalmist as the Spirit of God rested on him in the assembly:

> Now I know that the Lord has saved his anointed [mašîaḥ refers here to the king].
> He will answer him from his holy dwelling place
> With overpowering deliverance in his right hand.

Witnessing this divine edict, the king and assembly reaffirm their unwavering confidence in the Lord as captain of Israel's hosts (Ps. 20:7–8). The psalm ends with the assembly's united petition that the oracle received might indeed come to pass. This psalm may have been a part of a unique and spontaneous experience in Israel's military history or may represent a very common and rehearsed practice of Israel's ceremonial worship; we have examples of both.

Numerous other psalms contain possible oracles, e.g., Psalms 81 and 85 among others, but one more example should suffice. In Psalm 60 the congregation laments the fact that the Lord has allowed their enemies — in this case Moab, Edom, and Philistia — to defeat Israel and take some possessions in Transjordan (Ps. 60:1–5). They plead to God for deliverance. One can almost feel the anxious and expectant silence as the prophet stands to make his announcement:

> God has spoken from his Holy Place:
> "I shall go up and parcel out Shechem
>   and the valley of Succoth I shall measure off.
> Gilead is mine, and Manasseh is mine.
>   Ephraim is my helmet,
> Judah, my staff.
>   Moab is my washbasin,
> Upon Edom I shall cast my sandal.
>   Against Philistia shall I sound the alarm of battle."
>
> (Ps. 60:6–8)

Though the congregation remembers their dire condition (vv. 9–11), suddenly the comforting words of the prophet reach the hearts of all, and all exclaim:

> With God we are able to do anything,
>   and he will tread down our adversaries.
>
> (Ps. 60:12)

Christianity, seizing upon this prophetic aspect of the psalms, used the inspired utterances of these psalmic seers to evidence that the ministry, passion, death, and resurrection of Christ had been seen and foretold. We shall turn to this in the next chapter.

The Ceremonial Nature of the Psalms

As mentioned earlier, the book of Psalms is a "hymnal of ancient Israel . . . for use in the temple."[12] There is widespread agreement that many of the individual psalms were indeed written for and used in the temple ceremonies; that is the context in which they are best understood. They represent text that accompanied various rituals of the temple. Although this general statement is widely affirmed by scholars, the specific application of a particular psalm to a particular rite is not well understood.

As can be imagined, there is great difficulty involved in the attempt to uncover the specific setting of a particular psalm. Consider the task of a forty-fifth century A.D. anthropologist, who knows nothing of the gospel, and who discovers a small five-inch by seven-inch card with the text of our sacrament prayer. What will he think? Perhaps, he might hypothesize, the context of this prayer is to be found in the family meal; it is a blessing on the food. With considerable more research he might discover that the prayer accompanied some type of ritualistic meal, though he may never understand all the associations and subtle shades of meaning that even the most theologically unsophisticated current participant clearly understands and appreciates. Such is the task facing the modern Bible scholar. Although we may never fully appreciate all the associations, connections, and nuances that the ancient devotee easily grasped, yet, there is tremendous potential for greater understanding and appreciation in the attempt.

When the reader of the Old Testament reads of the many different sacrifices of the temple, perhaps he may wonder what was happening while the actual slaughters and sacrifices were taking place. Were they performed in stark and solemn silence? Were prayers being offered? What

---

[12]"Introduction to the Psalms," *The Oxford Annotated Bible*. Mowinckle was the pioneer into the investigation of Psalm use in Israel's temple. See his book, *The Psalms in Israel's Worship* (Oxford: Basil Blackwell, 1965).

about psalms? Consider the following historical evidence. Chronicles describes, among other things, how the Chronicler saw a burnt offering being conducted during the reign of Hezekiah (715–687 B.C.).

> And he [Hezekiah] set the Levites in the house of the Lord with cymbals, with psalteries, and with harps, according to the commandment of David, and of Gad the king's seer, and Nathan the prophet: for so was the commandment of the Lord by his prophets.
>
> And the Levites stood with the instruments of David, and the priests with the trumpets.
>
> And Hezekiah commanded to offer the burnt offering upon the altar. And when the burnt offering began, the song of the Lord began also with the trumpets, and with the instruments ordained by David king of Israel.
>
> And all the congregation worshipped, and the singers sang, and the trumpeters sounded: and all this continued until the burnt offering was finished.
>
> And when they had made an end of offering, the king and all that were present with him bowed themselves, and worshipped.
>
> Moreover Hezekiah the king and the princes commanded the Levites to sing praise unto the Lord with the words of David, and of Asaph the seer. And they sang praises with gladness, and they bowed their heads and worshipped (2 Chron. 29:25–30, KJV).

This is an impressive scene: a throng of Levites standing about the court raising their united voices in adoration to God the Most High; others playing their musical instruments; others, with the people, bowing and worshiping with their faces to the ground. But what would they be singing? What are the words to the music? What about other sacrifices? Were they accompanied by music? What was the text to the music? There is evidence from the psalms themselves that they were sometimes used in such ritual settings. In Psalm 27, the psalmist is threatened by dangerous enemies; however, he hopes that through God he will be victorious against them.

> Then he [God] will exalt my head
>> above my enemies who are surrounding me,
> and I *shall offer sacrifice* at his tabernacle:
>> sacrifices *with shouts of joy,*
> I *shall sing and make music to the Lord.*
>
>> (Ps. 27:6; emphasis added)

Perhaps the sacrifice mentioned in Psalm 27 is a thank offering. Psalm 107:22 suggests that singing accompanied thank offerings:

Let them offer thank offerings,
    and recount his deeds with joyful shouting.[13]

Psalm 116 may also be a text which accompanied a thank offering. There the author/composer relates how God delivered him from the "cords of death" and now wonders how he might "repay the Lord for all his goodness." At least part of the answer is to be found in the verses that follow:

I shall offer a thank offering to you:
    and shall call upon the name of the Lord
I shall fulfill my vows to the Lord
    in the presence of all his people
within the courts of the Lord's temple
    in the heart of Jerusalem.

(Ps. 116:17–19)

Was the text of this psalm, and others like it, performed as the offering was made, as might be suggested by 2 Chronicles 29:25–30 quoted above? Psalm 81 is another which may have its setting in an Israelite ritual context: the Feast of Tabernacles. The language of this psalm suggests that it could have been used in a covenant-renewal ceremony which, we now know, was an important part of the Feast of Tabernacles. Note Psalm 81:1–3:[14]

Cry out to God our source of strength;
    Shout aloud to the God of Jacob.
Begin a song and sound the timbrel,
    the lovely sounding harp with the lyre;
blow the ram's horn *at the new moon,*
    and at the full moon, *the day of our festival.*

(Ps. 81:1–3; emphasis added)

We now believe, through comparisons with other Near Eastern

---

[13]It must be remembered that what would be considered as singing by an Israelite may sound more like shouting to us. The Hebrew root used here, *rnn,* is closely associated with music in 2 Chron. 20:21–22, as in other places.

[14]Note that in the verses that follow there is a historical review of God's relationship with Israel. This is common in a covenant renewal.

cultures, that during the Feast of Tabernacles there were numerous special ritual performances, such as processions and assemblies.[15] One of these was the enthronement of God as Israel's true king.

> God has ascended [his throne] accompanied by shouts;
> the Lord [has ascended] accompanied by the sound of the ram's horn.
> Sing to God, Sing!
> Sing to our King, Sing!
> Because God is King over all the earth,
> Sing a skilled song
> God reigns over all nations;
> God is seated upon his holy throne.
>
> (Ps. 47:5–8)

Again, one must ask whether this text might not have been recited at the very time of the described action — in this case that of the Lord taking his throne. According to Psalm 80:1 and 99:1, the God of Israel was enthroned "between the cherubim" which were located in the most holy place of the tabernacle or temple. Psalm 24 may have been addressing the doors of the temple, or the porters thereof, during an enthronement ceremony when it urged:

> Lift up your heads, O gates,
> be lifted up, O eternal doors;
> that the King of glory may enter in
> Who is this King of glory?
> The Lord, strong and mighty.
> The Lord, mighty in battle.
> Lift up your heads, O gates,
> be lifted up, O eternal doors
> that the King of glory may enter in.
> Who is He, this King of glory?
> The Lord, captain of the host.
> He it is who is the King of glory!
>
> (Ps. 24:7–10)

Other psalms that may say nothing of sacrifice, enthronement,

---

[15]These processions and assemblies are used in many different contexts. Ps. 118:27; 42:4; and 68:24–27, among others, speak of processions; Ps. 109:30 and 149:1, among others, speak of assemblies. Ps. 136 may be an example of a text used in an assembly of some type. There, a line is recited and then a refrain is recited, most likely by the assembly of priests or the congregation.

procession, or assembly may still, with caution, be considered as possible ceremonial texts. For example, psalms such as 25, 38, or 130 might be associated with a guilt or sin offering.[16]

> Turn to me and show mercy to me
>> for I am alone and am afflicted
> The distress of my heart has grown large;
>> deliver me from my distresses.
> Look upon my afflictions and my sorrow,
>> and take away all my sins.
>
> (Ps. 25:16–18)

> If you should pay attention to iniquity, Oh Lord,
>> Lord, who could stand before you?
> But with you there is forgiveness;
>> therefore you are revered.
> I wait for the Lord, my soul waits;
>> I wait for his announcement.[17]
> My soul waits for my Lord
>> more than watchmen wait for the morning,
> more than watchmen wait for the morning.[18]
> Hope, O Israel, in the Lord
>> because He is faithful,
> and with him there is total redemption.
>> So will He redeem Israel from all his iniquities.[19]
>
> (Ps. 130:3–8)

Finally, a psalm such as Psalm 32 might express the joy and peace experienced by a worshiper immediately following such a guilt offering and its acceptance by God.

> Blessed is he
>> whose transgression is forgiven,
> whose sins are covered.
> Blessed is the man

---

[16]These psalms and others like them could also be associated with the even more solemn occasion of the Day of Atonement. On this day Israel's sins of the previous year were atoned for through the scapegoat and the goat whose blood was carried into the most holy place and sprinkled on the ark of the covenant.

[17]The pronouncement that the speaker is waiting for is one of forgiveness.

[18]These could be the words of a specific individual or the words of an officiating priest who is speaking for an individual or assembly.

[19]This could be the announcement of forgiveness made by an officiating priest. The Lord's forgiving disposition is one of the constant themes of the Psalter.

whose iniquity the Lord does not consider.
Now, there is no deception in this.[20]

(Ps. 32:1–2)

These utterances take on a new and vibrant life when viewed in this light. Could they represent ceremonial words which accompanied sacrifices offered with the hope of bringing forgiveness and redemption? Such words as these seem appropriate for that most solemn of all Israelite ceremonial occasions, the Day of Atonement. The possibility is real, exciting, and should be seriously investigated.

Conclusion

As can be seen from this brief survey, we are in possession of a wealth of information concerning the nature of the psalms, with hints of much more that we are now lacking and would very much like to see. The book of Psalms contains a rich gold mine of information concerning Israel's poetic, musical, and prophetic traditions. Further, perhaps nowhere else in the Old Testament is there more information (and potential information) concerning the temple. If we but possessed the keys to unlock the mystery, we would undoubtedly find that there are, as yet, undiscovered wonders awaiting those who investigate its hidden recesses.

As we shall see in the following chapter, however, there is much we can learn from its inspired pages in light of our present understanding. Above all, the Psalms will teach us of God—his nature, attributes, desires, requirements, and kingdom.

---

[20]This is a very badly damaged line of poetry. Commentators and translators have assumed this line continues to refer to the man whose sins are forgiven. I have, however, assumed here that it is a pronouncement of the faithfulness of God's word: the man's sins are covered and he is happy. Verses 1 and 2 could be the words of an officiating priest; verses 3 through 7 the words of the individual who has been pronounced forgiven; verses 8 through 10 the words of the officiating priest again. Verse 11 could be either the individual, the priest, an assembly of priests, or worshipers. The affirmation of God's faithfulness (verse 2c) to his promise and edicts, then, would not be unlike that found in Psalm 12. There the Lord promises to come to the aid of the needy who have been denied justice by the rich and powerful. Then it is affirmed:

The words of the Lord are pure [a pure word is true, faithful, to be counted on]
    as silver refined in a furnace of clay
refined seven times [and thus all the more faithful and real].

(12:6)

39

THE NATURE OF GOD IN THE PSALMS

(PSALMS, PART 2)

R. SCOTT BURTON

The Political Nature of the Psalms

The book of Psalms affirms, with the rest of the Old Testament, that the Lord is not only the God of Israel but also the King of Israel. The two are one, inseparable.[1] To him belong all the functions normally attributed to the state: protection of the citizenry from hostile parties outside the state (charge over the conducting of warfare), protection of individual citizens from hostile parties within the state (the legislation and enforcement of just laws that protect the rights of all citizens), and the overseeing of the state's economic well-being. These are the three functions of government, and, according to the Old Testament in general and the book of Psalms in particular, these belong to the Lord alone. This is no mere metaphoric or symbolic rule but actual, direct rule of God over the fortunes of his state, Israel.[2]

R. Scott Burton is the director of the LDS Institute of Religion in Auburn, Alabama.

[1]Note the response of Gideon when the Israelites wanted him to be their king: "I will not rule over you, neither shall my son rule over you: the Lord shall rule over you" (Judg. 8:22–23, KJV). The prophet Samuel taught this truth unmistakably when the children of Israel asked him to anoint a king to rule over them that they might be "like all the nations" (1 Sam. 8:20; see all of chaps. 8 and 12). That God is Israel's king is reaffirmed over and over in the Old Testament.

[2]God will rule among his people as directly as they will allow. It is strange to relate, as the Book of Mormon does, that such is the foolishness of men that "they do not desire that the Lord their God, who hath created them, should rule and reign over them; notwithstanding his great goodness and his mercy towards them, they do set at naught his counsels, and they will not that he should be their guide" (Hel. 12:6).

Warfare

In the previous chapter we have already seen hints of God's charge over warfare, but some more direct references may be helpful. (All Old Testament quotations in this chapter are my own translations, unless otherwise indicated.)

> For it was not by their sword that they took possession of the land
>> nor was it their own strength that gave them the victory,
> but it was your right hand and your strength
>> and your presence;[3] for you took delight in them.
> You are the one who is my King and God;
>> the one who decrees deliverance for Jacob.
> Through you we drive our foes;
>> through your name we tread down those who arise against us.
> It is not upon my bow that I rely;
>> my sword cannot deliver me,
> but it is you who delivers us from our foes,
>> it is you who humiliates our enemies.
> We boast of God at all times,
>> and praise his name forever.[4]
>
> (Ps. 44:3–8)

Regarding warfare, Israel and Judah needed to be reminded over and over again that,

> It is not in the strength of the horse that he delights;
>> nor is it in the power of man[5] that he is satisfied.
> The Lord is satisfied with those who fear him;
>> with those who hope in his unchanging faithfulness.
>
> (Ps. 147:10–11)

---

[3]Literally, "the light of your face."

[4]Before bringing Israel into the promised land, the Lord stated concerning the enemies which they would face: "Ye shall not fear them: for the Lord your God he shall fight for you" (Deut. 3:22, KJV). This truth is confirmed throughout the Old Testament, including in the Prophets. See Zech. 12:2–5; Isa. 26:1; 31:1–9; 49:25–26; Ps. 124; 68:17. See also n. 2, above.

[5]Both Ps. 118:8–9, which reminds us that trusting in man— either common or extraordinary (rulers)—is a gross error, and 60:11–12, which states that the "help of man is *worthless*," could have been part of the influence which persuaded Nephi to say: "I will not put my trust in the arm of flesh; for I know that cursed is he that putteth his trust in the arm of flesh" (2 Ne. 4:34). It is clear from the Old Testament that trusting in men is not only foolish and disappointing but also a most serious breach of the covenant relationship between God and Israel. See also Ps. 146:3.

Unless the Lord is guarding the city,
     guards keep watch in vain.

                                    (Ps. 127:1b)

There is not a single king who is delivered by possessing a large military force;
     a soldier does not deliver himself by possessing great strength.
Deliverance by horse is a lie;
     even in its great strength it cannot deliver.
                    (Ps. 33:16–17; see also 76:4–7; 147:10)

Even a cursory study of history clearly demonstrates that very few monarchs or heads of state have believed this. These "shepherds" always wish to have the latest in technological advances as they arm themselves for war, believing the age-old adage, Might makes right. The kings of Israel and Judah were, sadly, no exception to this rule. The prophets could never penetrate their thick skulls — or should we say, bend their stiff necks — with this unwanted message. Their administrations did, of course, give lip service to Jehovah's right to rule, but history demonstrates unequivocally that Isaiah's criticism was right on target: "This people draw near me with their mouth, and with their lips do honour me, but have removed their heart far from me" (Isa. 29:13). Israelite and Judahite kings alike were enamored with the latest in war technology; the horse and chariot are but two examples of such technological advances. The book of Psalms agrees with the Old Testament prophets in viewing such attitudes as faithless, destructive, and a blatant refusal to accept the rule of God. Israel so often and conveniently forgot that the Lord's great deliverance of Israel in battle was dependent upon Israel's faithfulness to covenant obligations, not upon her commitment to and diligence in armament.[6]

---

[6]Some have thought that the Book of Mormon refutes this position; however, it must be remembered that the Lord may bestow and revoke commandments according to the needs and faithfulness of his people. He may command one group of people to arm themselves under his direction, as was the case with Captain Moroni, but forbid another group at a different time to arm themselves, such as was the case with the people of Ammon. The Lord commanded Israel to trust in his ability to fight their battles rather than to trust in chariots, horses, armies, weapons, etc. Still the Book of Mormon affirms, consistent with the Old Testament, that even though Moroni armed and fortified his people against the Lamanites, it was the wickedness or righteousness of the people that ultimately determined the outcome of war. See, among others, Alma 44:3 (notice Zerahemnah's response to the Nephite victory in v. 9); 50:21–22; 57:26; 60:15, 28; Hel. 4:11–13.

Ephraim, though armed with bowmen,
    retreated in the day of battle;
They did not keep the covenant of God,
    but refused to follow his laws.

                    (Ps. 78:9–10)

O that my people would listen to me!
    O that Israel would walk in my ways!
I would quickly subdue their enemies,
    and would stretch my hand over their foes.

                    (Ps. 81:13–14)

Law

The psalms avow with the rest of the Old Testament that, as head of state, the Lord himself was Israel's lawgiver — Israel's only perfectly valid lawgiver. His laws were based on his righteousness and sense of justice.

He had declared his word to Jacob;
    His laws and decrees to Israel.
He has not done so for any other nation,
    for they do not know of his decisions.[7]

                    (Ps. 147:19–20)

For he decreed statutes in Jacob,
    and established the law in Israel
which he commanded our fathers
    to make known to their children.

                    (Ps. 78:5)

---

[7]The Lord confirmed this truth immediately before Israel's entrance into the promised land: "For what nation is there so great, who hath God so nigh unto them, as the Lord our God is in all things that we call upon him for? And what nation is there so great, that hath statutes and judgments so righteous as all this law, which I set before you this day?" (Deut. 4:7–8, KJV). Israel's rejection of the Lord as their king in Samuel's lifetime included this aspect of his rule. "Make us a king *to judge us* like all the nations" (1 Sam. 8:5, KJV; emphasis added). See also Isa. 33:22; 2:3; 3:13–15; Jer. 31:33–34; Zech. 7:8–12.

Righteousness[8] and justice are the foundation of your throne.[9]
Unfailing love and consistency are ever before you.

(Ps. 89:14)

Jehovah was also Israel's only perfectly capable judge, as he decided cases based on the laws he instituted and his own perfect sense of justice. His two most important functions as judge in Israel were to defend the vulnerable and reprove the powerful, prestigious, and wealthy who might, because of their position, take advantage of those less fortunate than themselves. He was not susceptible to the kinds of abuses of power so common among mortal leaders. His laws and his judgments were equitable and fair. He never sought advantage over the vulnerable but looked lovingly and ardently after their interests. Neither would he condone any evil use of power on the part of the wealthy, powerful, and prestigious. He could not be bought off by bribes or threats.[10]

The Lord is the everlasting king!
　Nations will perish from his land.
You are favorably inclined toward the afflicted.
　The desire of the deprived you hear, O Jehovah.
You encourage them, and pay heed to them
　to defend the orphan and the insignificant.
So that never again will a mortal person be viewed with awe.

(Ps. 10:16–18)

I know that the Lord gives heed to the plea of the deprived
　and dispenses justice to the needy.[11]

(Ps. 140:12)

---

[8]This is rightness. God acts according to what is right.

[9]God's throne — his right to rule — is based on his attributes of rightness and justness. The same is true of human government whether secular or sacred; when humans cease to govern by rightness and justice, they cease to rule. As the Doctrine and Covenants puts it, "Amen to the priesthood or the authority of that man" (D&C 121:37).

[10]He "never shows partiality and never takes bribes. He defends the rights of orphans and widows; and he loves foreigners, giving them food and clothing" (Deut. 10:17–18).

[11]This is very much different from the normal state of human affairs. Not only are the poor deprived of the economic necessities of life but they are often deprived of their legal rights because of their poverty. The Psalms with the Old Testament prophets lament such injustice against the poor. Compare Isa. 1:15–17, 23; 3:13–15; 5:7, 23; Jer. 5:26–28; 8:8, 22; Amos 2:6–8; 5:12; 8:4–6; Micah 3:1–3.

A father to the fatherless,
>and an advocate for the widowed
is God in his holy dwelling place.

(Ps. 68:5)

However, those who did not keep the laws of the kingdom could expect to be brought before the Great Judge, who would rule in their case in accordance with their actions.

Because of the ruin of the deprived;
>Because of the groan of the needy;
I shall now arise, says the Lord.
>I shall place them safely away from those who threaten them.

(Ps. 12:5)

God says to the wicked:
What do you mean by speaking of my laws,
>and making mention of my covenant;
When you hate my instruction,
>and cast my words behind you?
When you see a thief you aid him,
>and you throw in your lot with adulterers.
Your mouth is used for evil purposes.
>and your tongue for deceptive purposes.
You speak against your brother;
>You place guilt upon your mother's son.
You have done these things while I have kept quiet.
>You considered me to be just like you.[12]
I shall convict you,
>and I shall present the case against you.[13]

(Ps. 50:16–21)

The Lord did not ask much of his subjects. His laws, while creating a model community, were "not grievous" (see 1 Jn. 5:3). He only asked, as Jesus so succinctly taught the Pharisees: "Thou shalt love the Lord thy God with all thy heart, and with all thy soul, and with all thy mind, and with all thy strength: this is the first commandment. And the second is like, namely this, Thou shalt love thy neighbour as thyself. There is none other commandment greater than these" (Mark 12:30–31). Simply put, Israel's God asked only that they follow his example and walk in

---

[12]They created a god in their own image.

[13]The Lord here becomes the prosecuting attorney presenting the case against the guilty party.

rightness and justness with others and that they walk before him with the reverence due his person. As Micah stated so eloquently, "He hath shewed thee, O man, what is good; and what doth the Lord require of thee, but to do justly, and to love mercy, and to walk humbly with thy God" (Micah 6:8).[14]

Economy

The Lord's control over the economic welfare of Israel expressed itself in his control, as creator and maintainer, over nature. Rainfall, drought, wind, temperature, insect infestations, and so on, were all dependent upon him, and these in turn were dependant upon Israel's faithfulness to the covenant with her God.[15]

> You provide for the land and water it.
>> You enrich it greatly.
> A channel from God is filled with water.
>> You furnish the people with grain; for it is you who furnish it.
> You saturate the land's furrows with water;
>> making water to flow down the furrows,
> softening them with abundant showers,
>> and blessing their new growth.
> You crown the year with your blessings,
>> and from your carts drip abundance.
> Pastures of the wilderness are well watered.
>> Hills are clothed with joy.

---

[14]Ancient Israel inevitably tried to substitute ritual and legalistic behavior for the true ethical and moral behavior the Lord's law called for. See Jer. 7:4–11; Isa. 1:11–17; Amos 4:4–5; 5:21–25; Micah 6:6–8; 1 Sam. 15:22.

[15]This is not to say that good economy should be the motivating factor for covenant faithfulness. Nor does it mean that the righteous will have everything go their way. Individuals should fulfill their obligations toward their neighbors and their God because they are indebted to God to start with, not because they imagine they can have God indebted to them (see Mosiah 2:23–24). The deliverance of Israel from Egypt was the Lord's great saving act in Israelite history. Israel was under obligation to their God whether he ever did another thing for them or not—but of course he did and would. So it is today. We are already under obligation to our God and Redeemer for his deliverance from that awful monster, death and hell, and the power we receive through the Atonement to overcome sin and sickness. Our obedience to him should be based on our gratitude for the love expressed through his unselfish act and not on an attempt to put him under some imagined obligation to us—a kind of arm-twisting of Deity.

Pastures are covered with flocks,
    and valleys are covered with grain.
They shout for joy; yea, they sing.[16]

(Ps. 68:9–13)

No matter how talented her economists and government officials might be, they could only measure, analyze, index, and report. If they were to have any "control" over the economy, it could only be by means of their moral behavior toward others and their attitude toward God.

O that my people would listen to me!
    O that Israel would walk in my ways! . . .
I would feed them with the choicest of wheat,
    and I would satisfy them with honey from the mountains.

(Ps. 81:13, 16)

Just as the Lord looked after the legal interests of the underprivileged, so too did he look after their economic interests.

I shall truly bless her [Jerusalem's] provisions;
    her needy shall I satisfy with food.

(Ps. 132:15)

Who is like the Lord, our God;
    the one who is enthroned on high;
the one who comes down to look
    throughout the heavens and the earth;
Who raises up from the dust the poor;
    from the trash heap, he lifts up the needy.
He seats them with the noble;
    with the most noble of the people.

(Ps. 113:5–8)

God took the poor from the trash heap where they were searching for food and placed them in the company of those who had plenty. If those who had plenty were not generous with their means — and worse

---

[16]God promised Israel as they were ready to enter the promised land that he would provide for their economic needs: "I will give you the rain of your land in his due season, the first rain and the latter rain, that thou mayest gather in thy corn, and thy wine, and thine oil. And I will send grass in thy fields for thy cattle, that thou mayest eat and be full" (Deut. 11:12–15, KJV). Also, according to Deut. 8:18: "But thou shalt remember the Lord thy God: for it is he that giveth thee power to get wealth, that he may establish his covenant which he sware unto thy fathers, as it is this day." See also Isa. 30:23–24; 51:3; Jer. 5:24; Zech. 1:17; 8:12.

still, if they were tight-fisted and even sought to get gain through dishonest means — they might be altogether supplanted!

> Your tongue plans the ruin of others;
>   it is a sharpened razor.
> You practice fraud.
> You love doing evil more than doing right.
>   [You love] lies more than upright speech.
> You love every word [practice] that consumes,
>   O fraudulent tongue!
>
> (Ps. 52:2–4)

This is the motivation behind such corrupt behavior:

> Here is the strong man who did not make God his means of security,
>   but he relied upon his great wealth.
> He sought security through his fraud.
>
> (Ps. 52:7)

But a grim fate awaits such a rascal.

> God will pull you down from your eminence.
>   He will snatch you up and tear you away from your dwelling;
> and he will uproot you from among the living.
>
> (Ps. 52:5)

The reader may be wondering about the application of the Lord's charge over warfare, law, and economy to today's Church and current political conditions; after all, things have changed — right? Two points should be made. First, the Doctrine and Covenants does make direct application of these principles to the establishment of Zion in the latter days. For example, Doctrine and Covenants 105:14 states: "For behold, I do not require at their hands to fight the battles of Zion; for, as I said in a former commandment, even so will I fulfil — I will fight your battles" (see also D&C 45:74–75). Consider the Lord's statements concerning the law of the Church or Kingdom: "But, verily I say unto you that in time ye shall have no king nor ruler, for I will be your king and watch over you. . . . And ye shall have no laws but my laws when I come, for I am your lawgiver" (D&C 38:21–22). "For it must needs be that they be organized according to my laws; if otherwise, they will be cut off" (D&C 51:2).

The laws spoken of in this last passage are those pertaining to the economy of the kingdom of God and include the following important features: "They shall look to the poor and the needy, and administer to their relief that they shall not suffer" (D&C 38:35). "Thou wilt remember the poor, and consecrate of thy properties for their support" (D&C 42:30). "It is not given that one man should possess that which is above another, wherefore the world lieth in sin" (D&C 49:20). "Let every man deal honestly, and be alike among this people, and receive alike, that ye may be one" (D&C 51:9). "Wo unto you rich men, that will not give your substance to the poor. . . . Wo unto you poor men, . . . whose bellies are not satisfied, and whose hands are not stayed from laying hold upon other men's goods, whose eyes are full of greediness" (D&C 56:16–17). That was spoken to members of the Church, not to Babylon. "In your temporal things you shall be equal, and this not grudgingly, otherwise the abundance of the manifestations of the Spirit shall be withheld" (D&C 70:14). "I, the Lord, stretched out the heavens, and built the earth, my very handiwork; and all things therein are mine. And it is my purpose to provide for my saints, for all things are mine. But it must needs be done in mine own way; and behold this [consecration], is the way that I, the Lord, have decreed to provide for my saints, that the poor shall be exalted, in that the rich are made low. . . . Therefore, if any man shall take of the abundance which I have made, and impart not his portion, according to the law of my gospel, unto the poor and the needy, he shall, with the wicked, lift up his eyes in hell, being in torment" (D&C 104:14–16, 18).

The Lord is still the king of his people. His warfare, legislative, and economic laws are still in effect for those who wish to establish his kingdom on earth. The reader may ask, When? Orson Pratt posed the same question to a group of Saints in 1874 and answered it for them. He was speaking specifically of the Lord's economic law—the law of consecration: "Now, why is it, Latter-day Saints, that we have been tossed to and fro and smitten and persecuted for these many years? It is because we have disobeyed the law of heaven, we have not kept the commandments of the Most High God, we have not fulfilled his law; we have disobeyed the word which he gave through his servant Joseph, and hence the Lord has suffered us to be smitten and afflicted under the hands of our enemies. Shall we ever return to the law of God? Yes. When? Why, when we will. We are agents; we can abide his law or reject it, just as long as we please, for God has not taken away your agency nor mine."[17]

Furthermore, using warfare as our example, who can doubt that there is a furious and enveloping battle going on every day as individuals seek to overcome their own lusts, passions, evil desires, and sins, as well as the continual temptations of Lucifer with his hosts of demonic helpers? Who can doubt that the God of Israel will come to the aid of those fighting in these battles any less than to those who fought in the battles of Old Testament Israel? Who can doubt that he will send his "tens of thousands and thousands of thousands of chariots" (Ps. 68:17) forward to help us fight the "ten thousands of people [and demons] that have set themselves against [us] round about"? (Ps. 3:6). Who can question that he will "teach [our] hands to war," give us the "shield of [his] salvation," hold us up with his "right hand," and "enlarge [our] steps"? (see Ps. 18:34–36). Is not the Lord, who is the same yesterday, today, and forever, as much "a very present help in trouble" today as ever before? This is a God, who, as the Psalmist testified, "performs wonderful acts" and "manifests his power among the peoples" (see Ps. 77:14).

The Messianic Nature of the Psalms

The book of Psalms is the New Testament's most frequently quoted Old Testament book. More than seventy verses from the Psalms are directly quoted by the New Testament authors.[18] Of these, just over thirty are used as messianic prophecies by New Testament writers.[19] Most of the messianic allusions were either discovered in the Old Testament text after Jesus' death or were taught by Jesus himself, mostly after his death.[20] As two disciples were walking the road to Emmaus, Jesus

---

[17]In *Journal of Discourses*, 26 vols. (Liverpool: F. D. Richards, LDS Book Depot, 1855–86), 17:110–11. The Saints did not keep the Lord's laws and were denied opportunities they would otherwise have received. Cf. D&C 101; 104:1–6.

[18]These are traditionally Ps. 2:2, 7–9; 4:4; 5:9; 8:2, 3–6; 10:7; 14:3; 16:10–11; 18:49; 19:4; 22:1, 18, 22; 24:1; 31:5; 32:1–2; 34:12–16, 20; 35:19; 36:1; 40:6–8; 41:9; 44:22; 45:6–7; 51:4; 53:2–3; 62:12; 68:18; 69:4, 9, 22, 23, 25; 78:2, 23; 82:6; 91:11–12; 94:11; 95:7–11; 102:25–27; 104:4; 109:8; 110:1, 4; 112:9; 116:10; 117:1; 118:7, 22, 23, 26; 140:3.

[19]These are traditionally Ps. 2:2, 7–9; 8:2, 3–6; 16:10–11; 22:1, 18; 31:5; 34:20; 35:19; 40:6–8; 41:9; 45:6–7; 69:4, 9; 78:2; 91:11–12; 110:1, 4; 118:22–23, 26.

[20]See John 2:22; 12:16; Luke 24:25–27, 44–45.

instructed them concerning the Old Testament prophecies: "And he said unto them, These are the words which I spake unto you, while I was yet with you, that *all things must be fulfilled, which were written* in the law of Moses, and in the prophets, and *in the psalms, concerning me.* Then opened he their understanding, that they might understand the scriptures" (Luke 24:44–45, KJV; emphasis added).

Given that the psalms have, by nature, a prophetic aspect to them, it is not at all surprising that they should speak of that which is of greatest significance in history — the atonement of Jesus Christ. The prophets and patriarchs "saw [his] day" (John 8:56); the sacrifices and other rituals of Israel's temple were "types and shadows" of this infinite and eternal sacrifice (see Mosiah 3:15). Why should the writers of individual psalms not write of this most important event? As Alma the Younger stated: "For behold, I say unto you there be many things to come; and behold, there is one thing which is of more importance than they all — for behold, the time is not far distant that the Redeemer liveth and cometh among his people" (Alma 7:7).[21]

Just how important the Psalms were to New Testament authors for an understanding of the Savior's atonement can be seen from a study of the Gospel accounts of the crucifixion. For example, in Matthew's gospel, which was written for the purpose of convincing Jews that Jesus of Nazareth was the Messiah, allusions from the book of Psalms are numerous throughout the crucifixion narrative: Jesus was given "vinegar to drink mingled with gall" (see Ps. 69:21); Jesus' garments became the object of a gamblers game (see Ps. 22:18); and Jesus was mocked in the same way and with the same words as the Psalmist (see Ps. 22:7–8). In addition, Matthew recorded words uttered by Jesus as he suffered on the cross — "My God, my God, why hast thou forsaken me?" (see Ps. 22:1). Many other things undoubtedly occurred during those depressing hours which could have been related (see John 21:25); they did not find their way into the record because Matthew's narrative was, at least partly, influenced

---

[21]The Prophet Joseph Smith reminded us of the importance of the atonement of Jesus Christ: "The fundamental principles of our religion are the testimony of the Apostles and Prophets, concerning Jesus Christ, that He died, was buried, and rose again the third day, and ascended into heaven; and all other things which pertain to our religion are only appendages to it." *Teachings of the Prophet Joseph Smith,* sel. Joseph Fielding Smith (Salt Lake City: Deseret Book Co., 1938), p. 121.

and shaped by psalmic expectations. Many of the words of Matthew's narrative were word for word—or nearly so—direct quotations of psalms.

Luke added that Jesus cried out, "Father, into thy hands I commend my spirit" (see Ps. 31:5). John recorded an interesting item that may tell us something of Jesus' view of the psalms and their relationship to his earthly ministry: "After this, Jesus knowing that all things were now accomplished, *that the scripture might be fulfilled,* saith, I thirst. Now there was set a vessel full of vinegar: and they filled a spunge with vinegar, and put it upon hyssop, and put it to his mouth. When Jesus therefore had received the vinegar, he said, It is finished: and he bowed his head, and gave up the ghost" (John 19:28–30, KJV; emphasis added). It is as though Jesus waited until every prophecy of the Old Testament concerning him was fulfilled (here it seems that Ps. 69:21 was still wanting in fulfillment); then he was free to return to his Father who had sent him. As Jesus suffered so immeasurably—physically, emotionally, and spiritually—he choose the words of the Psalter to express his horror: "My God, my God, why hast thou forsaken me?" (Ps. 22:1).

There are many other passages from the psalms that might have been chosen to express Jesus' suffering in those last few hours, however inadequate those words might be. One of the reasons for the great power of the psalms is to be found in their imagery. Liken the following words to Jesus as he suffered, whether it be the suffering of Gethsemane or of Golgotha.

> Deliver me, O God;
> > for the water is right up to my neck.
> I am sinking in the mire at the bottom;[22]
> > I cannot keep my footing.
> I have fallen into deep water;
> > the current is sweeping me away.

---

[22]The water and mud here are the water and mud of the underworld—the world of the dead—or Hebrew "sheol," English "hell." Notice that in vv. 14–15 this theme continues. This time we read, in addition, of the "mouth" of the "pit" (see Ps. 88:3–5). This is again sheol, or hell, with its ferocious appetite for the dead (see Hab. 2:5). Cf. D&C 122:7; Ps. 18:4–5. Here the Psalmist is threatened by sheol but is rescued (vv. 7–17) by God himself from the grave. The superscription states that this psalm was written when David was delivered from Saul, *ša'ûl.* A slightly different pointing would allow us to read "sheol," *še'ôl,* which makes every bit as much sense, if not more, based upon the content of the psalm. I would suggest that we see in Psalm 18 a ritual text involved in dying and reviving, not unlike that of the Egyptian mortuary texts so well known.

I have grown weary from my calling out for help;
   my throat burns,
my eyesight fails,
   as I wait for my God.

                                        (Ps. 69:1–3)

This is an exquisite and beautifully crafted picture, even if it is a somewhat dispiriting one. The speaker, on the verge of drowning, has been calling out for help for so long and so intensely that his throat is now parched and hoarse and his eyesight has blurred from the prolonged shouting. He is in true need, but no one has so far heard his cry for help. Who has not been swimming and felt the sudden shocking panic and sheer horror that races through one's body at possible drowning? The psalmist asks us to remember such an experience in order that we may understand how desperate he felt at a given moment—at the moment when he seemed alone without God.

How long, O Lord? Are you forgetting me forever?
How long are you going to withhold your presence from me?[23]
                                        (Ps. 13:1)

Could not such statements typify what Jesus felt emotionally as he cried out "My God, my God, why hast thou forsaken me?" Jesus—who had always been heard by the Father (see John 11:42), who had the Father always with him (see John 8:29), and who had not the Spirit given him by measure (see John 3:34)—this same Jesus was left alone, feeling for the first time what it was to live without God in this world. Little wonder that Jesus asked that "if it be possible, let this cup pass from me" (Matt. 26:39). Little wonder that Jesus felt, as he related to the Prophet Joseph Smith, "Would that I might not drink the bitter cup, and shrink" (D&C 19:18). Perhaps these words of the Psalter entered Jesus' mind at some point:

---

[23]Literally, "hide your face from me." This is not to say that the Psalmist, or Jesus, ever truly doubted that God would come to his aid. But he found it perhaps more terrible than he had expected: "And he taketh with him Peter and James and John, and began to be sore amazed, and to be very heavy; And saith unto them, My soul is exceeding sorrowful unto death: tarry ye here, and watch" (Mark 14:33–34, KJV). This reminds us, humbly, of the Book of Mormon's statement that any of the rest of us—even the best of us—could not have survived such agony: "And lo, he shall suffer temptations, and pain of body, hunger, thirst, and fatigue, even more than man can suffer, except it be unto death" (Mosiah 3:7).

My heart is in anguish in my midst,[24]
    the terrors of Death have fallen upon me.
Fear and trembling have come upon me;
    horror has spread through me.
Then I said, "O that I had wings like a dove,
    that I might fly away and be at rest."

(Ps. 55:4–6)

The picture of a cool, calm Jesus as he suffered at Gethsemane and Golgotha is, I think, mistaken. The death by which he was threatened was, of course, not so much the physical—he knew he had power over the grave—but the spiritual. Could it be that as he took upon himself our sins, he was, as it were, cast out of the presence of God—"there cannot any unclean thing enter into the kingdom of God"? (1 Ne. 15:34). Could it be that as he took upon himself our sins, those very sins became in some incomprehensible way his sins and he experienced firsthand the emotional and spiritual contradiction[25] and anguish that accompany sin? Could it be that the Atonement was much more frightening an experience than any of us even care to ponder?

We are left to ourselves to go and search the psalms to see if perhaps they may teach us of the Atonement in a way we had not expected—in a more powerful way than we ever had imagined. After reading the psalms, and there finding the redeeming Christ at his glorious work, we may feel a more urgent need than ever before to confess with the penitent Ammon:

> Therefore, let us glory, yea, we will glory in the Lord; yea, we will rejoice, for our joy is full; yea, we will praise our God forever. Behold, who can glory too much in the Lord? Yea, who can say too much of his great power, and of his mercy, and of his long-suffering towards the children of men? Behold, I say unto you, I cannot say the smallest part which I feel (Alma 26:16).

---

[24]Literally, his heart is whirling within him.

[25]Jesus "is called the Son because of the flesh, and descended in suffering below that which man can suffer; or, in other words, suffered greater sufferings, and was *exposed to more powerful contradictions than any man can be*." *Lectures on Faith* 5:20 (Salt Lake City: Deseret Book Co., 1985), p. 59; emphasis added.

440

The Theology of the Book of Psalms

Joseph Smith stated in the King Follett discourse: "It is the first principle of the Gospel to know for a certainty the Character of God, and to know that we may converse with him as one man converses with another."[26] This sounds like a restatement of the Savior's well-known teaching: "And this is life eternal, that they might know thee the only true God, and Jesus Christ, whom thou hast sent" (John 17:3, KJV).

The study and knowledge of the character of God is what I mean by theology. Perhaps nowhere in scripture do we have more information concerning God's character in so little space than in the book of Psalms. We have already seen some of his attributes in the preceding passages. Let us expand on what the Psalter has to say about the character of God.

The Lord Is Loving, Compassionate, Merciful, and Forgiving

Lord, your unfailing love reaches to heaven;
   your faithfulness [dependability, fidelity], to the sky; . . .
How precious is your unfailing love.

(Ps. 36:5, 7a)

The Lord's every action is guided by love and faithfulness (Ps. 25:10). His love not only reaches to the heavens but is "higher than the heavens" (Ps. 108:4) and "fills the earth" (Ps. 33:5). His love is not only unfailing but is "from old"—as is his mercy (Ps. 25:6)—and "endures forever" (Ps. 107:1). His love can be counted on to remain unchanged throughout time and eternity; it is dependable, faithful, constant, firm, and unshakable. His unfailing love is "better than life itself" (Ps. 63:3). Men are to "hope" in his love (Ps. 147:11), "give thanks to" and "praise" him for his love (Ps. 107:21; 138:2), "meditate upon" his love (Ps. 48:9), and "declare" his love (Ps. 40:10).

The Lord is compassionate and merciful,
   slow to anger and of great love.

[26]Joseph Smith, *History of The Church of Jesus Christ of Latter-day Saints*, 7 vols., 2d ed. rev., edited by B. H. Roberts (Salt Lake City: Deseret Book Co., 1957), 6:305.

> The Lord is good to all;
> He is merciful to all his works.
>
> (Ps. 145:8–9)

His love and compassion, mercy and grace make themselves felt in many ways in the life of each Saint, but nothing is more deeply felt and fully appreciated than his willingness to forgive sin.[27]

> For you, O Lord, are good and forgiving;
> abounding in unfailing love toward all who call upon you.
>
> (Ps. 86:5)

> If you should pay attention to iniquity, Oh Lord,
> Lord, who could stand before you?[28]
> But with you there is forgiveness;
> therefore you are revered. . . .
> Hope, O Israel, in the Lord
> because he is faithfully loving,
> and with him there is total redemption.
> So will He redeem Israel from all his iniquities.
>
> (Ps. 130:3–4, 7–8)

Certainly the writer of the third Lecture on Faith agreed with the Psalter on the forgiving nature of the Divine Character:

> Unless he was merciful and gracious, slow to anger, long-suffering and full of goodness, such is the weakness of human nature, and so great the frailties and imperfections of men, that unless they believed that these excellencies existed in the divine character, the faith necessary to salvation could not exist; for doubt would take the place of faith, and those who know their weakness and liability to sin would be in constant doubt of salvation if it were not for the idea which they have of the excellency of the character of God, that he is slow to anger and long-suffering, and of a forgiving disposition, and does forgive iniquity,

---

[27]See also the discussion on the ceremonial nature of the Psalms in Chap. 38 of this volume.

[28]It is the atonement of Jesus Christ that makes this possible. Otherwise, as the Book of Mormon emphasizes, every sin would be counted, and all men would perish: "And we talk of Christ, we rejoice in Christ, we preach of Christ, we prophesy of Christ, and we write according to our prophecies, that our children may know to what source they may look for a remission of their sins" (2 Ne. 25:26). "For it is expedient that an atonement should be made; for according to the great plan of the Eternal God there must be an atonement made, or else all mankind must unavoidably perish" (Alma 34:9). "And my soul delighteth in proving unto my people that save Christ should come all men must perish" (2 Ne. 11:6). See also Alma 42:11–15; 2 Ne. 9:7–12.

transgression, and sin. An idea of these facts does away doubt, and makes faith exceedingly strong.[29]

So desirable is this love and devotion God has for his children that the Psalmist declared with eternal longing:

As a deer longs for streams of water,
    even so does my soul long for you, O God.
My soul thirsts for God,
    for the living God.

(Ps. 42:1–2)

The Lord Is Righteous, Good, Upright, Just, Holy, and Honorable

"Taste and see," declared the Psalmist, "that the Lord is good" (Ps. 34:8). "Good and upright is the Lord" (Ps. 25:8). "The Lord loves righteousness and justice" (Ps. 33:3). This rightness and justness is, as noted earlier, the "foundation of his throne;" they go before him in all his dealings with humankind. We can be assured that he will always make the correct and just decision as he deals with each of us.

My mouth will tell of your righteousness;
    [it will tell] of your deliverance all day long;
though I cannot appreciate its extent.

(Ps. 71:15)

The Lord is also "holy;" that is, he is something completely apart from all else—whether it be mortal or divine.

Extol the Lord, Our God;
    and bow down before his foot stool.
He is holy.

(Ps. 99:5)

For who, in all the heavens, is comparable to the Lord?
    Who, among the sons of God, is like the Lord?

---

[29]Lectures on Faith 3:20, p. 42.

God creates awe among those in the council of saints.
He is feared above all those round about him.

(Ps. 89:6–7)

The Lord Is Powerful, Majestic, and Strong

One thing has God spoken;
    These two things have I heard;
That might belongs to God,
    and unfailing love belongs to my Lord.

(Ps. 62:11)

The Psalmist assures us through his testimony that God has power and acts with power in the lives of those who love and honor him. "The Lord is great and worthy of praise" (Ps. 48:1); to him belongs "strength" (Ps. 89:13); he is "exceedingly great," and "clothed with splendor and majesty" (Ps. 104:1).

Splendor and majesty are before him;
    strength and glory are in his sanctuary.

(Ps. 96:6)

As mentioned earlier, it is from the Lord that strength unto deliverance comes, whether it be temporal or spiritual. The Psalmist calls his God by several epithets, all of which emphasize his power of deliverance: Shield, Refuge, Stronghold, Rock, Buckler, Horn, Fortress, and Strong Tower. Do you need protection? asks the Psalmist. Rely on the God who shields — the "Shield." Rely on the "inaccessibly high Stronghold." Rely upon the "firm and unmoving Rock."

Truly my soul finds peace through God;
    he is the ground of my hope.
He is my Rock and my deliverance;
    he is my stronghold, I shall not be shaken.
My deliverance and my honor depend upon God;
    he is my Rock of might, my refuge is in God.

(Ps. 62:5–7)

This is a God who, as the Psalmist testifies, "answers the righteous when they cry out to him" (Ps. 34:17), "performs wonderful acts," and "manifests his power among the peoples" (Ps. 77:14). This God is, as

Mormon would later testify, "a God of miracles"—always was and always would be (see Morm. 9:9–11).

> Who can relate the mighty acts of the Lord?
> Who can proclaim all his renown?
>
> (Ps. 106:2)

> Many, O Lord, my God
> are the wonders you have performed.
> Your plans for us
> none can describe.
> If I were to expound them and speak them
> they would be too numerous to count.
>
> (Ps. 40:5)

> Great is the Lord and more than worthy of the praise given him.
> His marvelous deeds are unfathomable.
> Each generation will boast of your deeds to the next,
> and tell of your might.
> Each generation will speak of your honor and splendor;
> they will meditate upon your wonderful works.
> They will speak of your mighty and astonishing deeds;
> they will recount your marvelous doings.
>
> (Ps. 145:3–6)

> Great is our Lord, and tremendously powerful.
> His understanding is without limit.
>
> (Ps. 147:5)

The Lord's Expectations of His People

Finally, we learn from the Psalmist's testimony concerning God what type of behavior and actions demonstrate our love and commitment to him and please him. God is pleased with those who are blameless, righteous (act rightly), upright, just, generous, gracious, compassionate, brokenhearted, humble, contrite, and pure. God is pleased with those who hope in him, rely on him, fear him (that is, are in awe of him, recognize his supremacy), and delight in his commands. God is pleased with those who speak the truth and keep a promise.

The Psalmist also warns against those things that God finds unpleasant. God is displeased with those who are proud, wicked, unjust, boasters, tight-fisted, selfish, and unfeeling. He is displeased with those who lie about and slander others, do wrong to their fellowmen, cast a slur upon their fellowmen, make a mock of their fellowmen, lend money at interest, accept bribes (show partiality), steal, cheat, scheme, murder, oppress, rely on themselves and their wealth rather than on him, do not recognize him as their ruler, and put his commands far from them.

The reader will, no doubt, recognize that all the positive attributes that God is pleased to see in his children are those attributes that he himself possesses. All those negative attributes, which God finds displeasing, are those which are contrary to his very nature. The Psalmist agrees with the Savior, "I would that ye should be perfect even as I, or your Father who is in heaven is perfect" (3 Ne. 12:48); "What manner of men ought ye to be? Verily I say unto you, even as I am" (3 Ne. 27:27).

Conclusion

Even this short survey of the Psalmist's views on the nature of God and his kingdom ought to demonstrate how much the psalms can instruct us on these important subjects. We speak much of the kingdom of God and can, through this inspired book, perhaps speak with a little more authority about the rule of God, what is required to make that rule become reality, what we must become, and what great expectations the Lord has for those of his people who accept him as their Eternal King.

We have viewed anew the boundless love and awesome power he possesses — a love and power most clearly seen through the atoning sacrifice of Jesus Christ (see 1 Jn. 3:16; Eph. 1:19–20) — and the faith we must develop. Perhaps we understand a bit better the reasons for the Psalmist's great confidence in the Lord's eventual triumph and the triumph of all those who diligently and faithful seek him. We may share more fully in the glorious vision of the Psalmist's prophetic mind when he announces:

Posterity will serve him.
Generations will be told of the Lord.

They shall come and declare his righteousness
    to a people yet to be born.
God shall bring this to pass.

(Ps. 22:30–31)

Religion is ultimately a very personal thing. It is about a relationship between an individual and God. Once God has revealed himself — once he has revealed his character and attributes and the character and attributes he desires mortal men and women to incorporate — the individual on whom God has bestowed this great gift will desire to tell others of this most desirable, most sweet, most beautiful, most pure Being. Perhaps, through a faithful study of the Psalter's testimony, we may be better prepared to enter into a more intimate relationship with the God of Heaven, and thus answer the challenging query of the Prophet Joseph Smith: "What kind of being is God?"[30]

---

[30]Smith, *Teachings*, p. 343.

40

THE PROVERBS

Dana M. Pike

The book of Proverbs is found in that portion of the Old Testament
known as the Writings (material not included in the Law or the Prophets),
and is categorized as Wisdom Literature.[1] It is a compilation of instructions
and sayings that has as its aim the social, moral, and ultimately, spiritual
betterment of people. As an anthology, Proverbs is designed for consultation and study in measured doses.

Wisdom Literature in Israel and the Ancient Near East

The appreciation of wise instruction and the value given to it, as
well as the collecting of it in written form, were not unique to the ancient
Israelites. Texts preserved from throughout the ancient Near East, especially from Egypt and Mesopotamia (Sumer, Babylonia, and Assyria),
demonstrate that wise men, or sages, were active and important in these
ancient societies. These sages are usually thought to have been the scribes
who were employed by royal courts and temples, the two major institutions
in the ancient Near Eastern world. Scribes, in the learning of the world,
were the most educated people in their societies (definitely more so than
most rulers).[2]

Dana M. Pike is assistant professor of ancient scripture at Brigham Young University.

[1]The biblical books of Proverbs, Job, and Ecclesiastes and the apocryphal books of Ecclesiasticus
and Wisdom of Solomon are classified as "wisdom literature." Wisdom themes are also found in
many other books of the Bible.

[2]For further discussion, see J. G. Gammie and L. G. Perdue, eds., *The Sage in Israel and the
Ancient Near East* (Winona Lake, Ind.: Eisenbrauns, 1990), pp. 95–184. For a discussion of the

The content of most ancient Near Eastern wisdom literature does not generally emphasize religious, or theological, themes but rather practical, social, and ethical ones. (It goes without saying that religion was an integral part of all ancient Near Eastern societies, Israel included, so that such judgments are somewhat relative and based on modern perceptions.) Although Mesopotamian and Egyptian wisdom literatures employ somewhat different forms and emphasize somewhat different themes, as part of a broad genre they do share many themes and forms with the wisdom literature preserved in the Bible. The various types of wisdom literature preserved from the ancient Near East include proverbs, parables and fables, dialogues and monologues, instructions, and admonitions.[3]

The formal wisdom texts in the Bible may have originated with sages in scribal circles and been preserved by them, but it is also evident that wisdom in general and proverbs in particular had roots in the common experiences of families and everyday life. The claims and teachings contained in wisdom literature did not derive from theory, nor were they attributed to revelation. They came primarily from observation: what worked and what did not.[4] Adherence to wise counsel produced, according to the sages, happiness, prosperity, and longevity:

> My son, forget not my law;
> but let thine heart keep my commandments:
> For length of days, and long life, and peace,
> shall they add to thee
>
> (Prov. 3:1–2; cf. 4:10; 13:18).

---

education of scribes, including excerpts from practice texts, see H. W. F. Saggs, *Civilization Before Greece and Rome* (New Haven: Yale University, 1989), pp. 98–113. The desire of kings to have wise counselors and the importance placed on their counsel are well illustrated in several biblical passages, e.g., 2 Sam. 16:20–23; 1 Kgs. 12:6–15.

[3]For further discussion of wisdom literature in the ancient Near East, see W. G. Lambert, *Babylonian Wisdom Literature* (Oxford: Clarendon, 1960); G. E. Bryce, *A Legacy of Wisdom: The Egyptian Contribution to the Wisdom of Israel* (Lewisburg, Pa.: Bucknell University, 1979); J. H. Walton, *Ancient Israelite Literature in Its Cultural Context* (Grand Rapids, Mich.: Zondervan, 1989), pp. 169–200; R. E. Murphy, *The Tree of Life: An Exploration of Biblical Wisdom Literature* (Garden City, N.Y.: Doubleday, 1990), pp. 151–79. While the term "wisdom literature" may be somewhat inadequate if pressed in specific cases, it has become the standard way of categorizing these sage scribal creations and compilations.

[4]For a fuller discussion, see Murphy, pp. 3–5; see also Sidney B. Sperry, *The Spirit of the Old Testament*, 2d ed. (Salt Lake City: Deseret Book Co., 1970), pp. 70–73.

What Is a Proverb?

A proverb is usually defined as "a maxim, an adage, a pithy saying." As such it represents an attempt to render concisely in words a lesson learned through experience. Therefore, a proverb arises from, and its interpretation is at least partially dependent on, a specific context. On the one hand, the strength of proverbial wisdom is that it is so applicable to the life experiences of so many. On the other hand, one must not place too much weight upon the wisdom of any one proverb nor apply such wisdom in a context too dissimilar from that in which the proverb originated.[5]

The Hebrew word *māšāl* is usually rendered "proverb" in the KJV, as it is in the title, "The Proverbs." Nevertheless, the "proverb [*māšāl*] against the king of Babylon" (Isa. 14:4–23) is not a "typical" proverb.[6] Additionally, the word *māšāl* is rendered as "parable" more than a dozen times in the KJV, in passages such as Numbers 23:7; Psalm 49:4; Ezekiel 20:49; and Micah 2:4.

The proverbs compiled in the book of Proverbs represent various literary forms. For the sake of convenience they may be viewed as (1) multiverse, poetic wisdom "poems," (2) wisdom "sayings," (3) "admonitions/prohibitions," and (4) "numerical" proverbs.[7] These designations will be illustrated below as the content of the book of Proverbs is discussed more fully.

The Book of Proverbs

It is with good reason that readers of the Bible usually think of King Solomon when they think of the book of Proverbs. We learn in 1 Kings 3 that Solomon sought and received the gift of wisdom from the Lord. It is recorded that many people came "to hear the wisdom of Solomon" and that "he spake three thousand proverbs" (1 Kgs. 4:32, 34). The

---

[5]See Murphy, pp. 10–11, for further discussion and examples.

[6]Footnote *a* to Isa. 14:4 in the LDS Bible rightly indicates that this passage is "a satirical song."

[7]For further discussion of these forms, including several subtypes of "sayings," see Murphy, pp. 7–13.

superscription, or introductory first verse, of the book of Proverbs reads: "The proverbs of Solomon the son of David, king of Israel."

Although many of the proverbs in the book of Proverbs may have originated with Solomon, it is certain that he is not the source of all of them. The expression "proverbs of Solomon" in Proverbs 1:1 may mean proverbs that originated with Solomon or proverbs belonging to — that is, collected by — Solomon. It is likely that Solomon both originated and collected many of these proverbs, but it may be that some of this material was later associated with his name because of his fame in this regard. Furthermore, a few of the several subheadings throughout the book of Proverbs indicate that some of this material originated with others besides Solomon:

1:1	"The proverbs of Solomon"	(1:1–9:18)
10:1	"The proverbs of Solomon"	(10:1–22:16)
22:17	"The words of the wise"	(22:17–24:22)[8]
24:23	"These things also belong to the wise"	(24:23–34)
25:1	"Proverbs of Solomon which the men of Hezekiah king of Judah copied out"	(25:1–29:27)
30:1	"The words of Agur"	(30:1–33)
31:1	"The words of king Lemuel"	(31:1–31)[9]

Whereas most of this anthology is attributed to Solomon, some is attributed to "the wise" (that is, wise ones, sages) and some to Agur and Lemuel, two otherwise unknown individuals. The notation in Proverbs 25:1 about the activity of Hezekiah's scribes indicates that the book of Proverbs, as we have it today, did not reach its final form before the reign of King Hezekiah (729–686 B.C.), who ruled Judah two centuries after the death of King Solomon. The material in the last two chapters (Prov. 30–31), attributed to Agur and Lemuel, may have been added later still. It is not really known when the collection reached its final form.[10]

---

[8]This is usually considered a separate subheading, although in the Hebrew Bible, known as the Masoretic Text, and in most English translations, this phrase is part of a proverb. In the Septuagint, a third century B.C. Greek translation of the Hebrew Bible, the phrase functions as a heading. In this heading, as well as in 24:23, the word *wise* renders a plural Hebrew form (*hakāmîm*) and is best understood as "wise ones."

[9]It is not clear whether the acrostic poem about the proverbial "virtuous woman" (Prov. 31:10–31; discussed below) should be considered part of "the words of king Lemuel."

[10]Although there is no clearly discernible pattern in the arrangement of the content of the

The book of Proverbs can best be appreciated when understood as containing instruction that mainly focuses on one facet of a multidimensional approach to achieving a happy and successful life. A wide range of topics is mentioned in Proverbs, including personal discipline, diligence, honesty, appropriate conduct and speech, the appropriate attitude towards wealth and possessions, and so on. What is immediately striking about the wisdom of Proverbs, however, is the lack of specific instructions to fulfill various requirements of the Law of Moses and the gospel (such as keeping the Sabbath day holy, attending the required holy-day festivals, or observing the laws of purity). Also, themes such as the house of Israel, the Exodus, Zion, or the Messiah, which receive attention in prophetic books, are not dealt with in Proverbs. The "wisdom approach" generally focuses attention on the *outcome* of faithful living, not on "how-to" specifics. It attempts to encourage and motivate by stating "the conclusion of the whole matter" (Eccl. 12:13):

> The sacrifice of the wicked is an abomination to the Lord:
> but the prayer of the upright is his delight (Prov. 15:8).

> The Lord is far from the wicked:
> but he heareth the prayer of the righteous (Prov. 15:29).

Thus, the purpose of Israelite wisdom is to supplement, and witness the benefits of, the teachings and covenants of the Lord, not to provide an alternative to them.

A quick or superficial reading of the content of Proverbs may give the impression that the Israelite sages thought they knew all the answers and that the problems of life could be dispatched in a few words. That is not the case, however. The number of proverbs dealing with any one topic and the occasional coupling of contradictory proverbs, such as in Proverbs 26:4–5, suggest that the sages realized that what is appropriate in one situation may not be so in another:

> Answer not a fool according to his folly,
> lest thou also be like unto him (Prov. 26:4).

---

book of Proverbs, it has been observed that the number of proverbs in certain sections of the book and the number of lines in the final form of the book correspond to the numerical value of some of the names (Hebrew letters were assigned numerical value; there are no Hebrew numerals) contained in various headings of the book (see Murphy, p. 28). Perhaps this is one of the "riddles" alluded to in Prov. 1:6.

Answer a fool according to his folly,
lest he be wise in his own conceit (Prov. 26:5).

The sages also recognized the Lord's (not always humanly predictable) influence:

There is no wisdom, no insight,
no plan that can succeed against the Lord.
The horse is made ready for the day of battle,
but victory rests with the Lord (Prov. 21:30–31, NIV).[11]

Three further observations will assist in appreciating the content of the book of Proverbs. First, "wisdom" is often used interchangeably with "understanding" and, to a lesser extent, "knowledge."[12] To know and understand the ways of the Lord is to have wisdom. Second, wisdom and wise people are regularly contrasted with foolishness and fools:

Every prudent [that is, wise] man dealeth with knowledge:
but a fool layeth open his folly (Prov. 13:16).[13]

A fool hath no delight in understanding (Prov. 18:2).

The truly wise recognize that their wisdom derives from the Lord and that it is not usually compatible with the wisdom of the world: "Trust in the Lord with all thine heart; and lean not unto thine own understanding. . . . Be not wise in thine own eyes" (Prov. 3:5–7). The wise also realize the value of true wisdom ("for wisdom is better than rubies"; Prov. 8:11; cf. 16:16). Fools, however, are those who "despise wisdom and instruction" (Prov. 1:7).

Finally, wisdom instruction is often depicted as teachings given from parents, usually a father to a son ("my son, hear the instruction of thy father, and forsake not the law of thy mother"; Prov. 1:8; cf. 1:10; 2:1; 3:1). It is thought that this parent-child imagery reflects the relationship between a teacher/sage and a student, but it is likely that sages employed family imagery because the family was the original source of learning and

[11]New International Version.

[12]For a discussion of the semantic field (both synonyms and antonyms) of "wisdom" (*hokmâ*) and the "wise" (*hākām; hakāmîm*), see G. J. Botterweck and H. Ringgren, eds., *Theological Dictionary of the Old Testament*, trans. D. E. Green (Grand Rapids, Mich.: Eerdmans, 1980), 4:371–73.

[13]Compare Paul's statement to the Ephesians: "See then that ye walk circumspectly, not as fools, but as wise [people]" (Eph. 5:15).

wisdom. The following proverb neatly combines the parent-child theme and the contrast between wisdom and foolishness:

> A wise son maketh a glad father:
> but a foolish man despiseth his mother (Prov. 15:20; cf. 17:25).

Obviously it is not possible to discuss every proverb in, or even every chapter of, the book of Proverbs, so the following comments focus on the main divisions of the book and will discuss some of the interesting forms and content within these divisions.

Proverbs 1 through 9

Proverbs 1:1 through 7

The first seven verses of the book of Proverbs can be viewed as an introduction to the whole book. Following the superscription (Prov. 1:1), verses 2 through 6 provide a statement of purpose: by studying the content of this book, the reader will be able "to know wisdom and instruction; to perceive the words of understanding; to receive the instruction of wisdom, justice and judgment, and equity; . . . to understand a proverb, and the interpretation; the words of the wise, and their dark sayings [that is, riddles]" (Prov. 1:2–3, 6). This statement is followed in verse 7 by the underlying principle of Israelite wisdom: "The fear of the Lord [that is, Jehovah] is the beginning of knowledge." For the ancient Israelites, as for the Saints of God in any age, true wisdom is attained only by those who "hate evil" (Prov. 8:13) and who revere and honor the Lord. This is no surprise, considering that wisdom is a gift of the Holy Spirit.[14] Job understood this concept and quoted the Lord as saying that "the fear of the Lord, that is wisdom; and to depart from evil is understanding" (Job 28:28).[15]

Proverbs 1:7 through 9:18

Verse 7 of Proverbs 1 represents the beginning of the first collection of proverbial material attributed to Solomon. The form of most of the

---

[14]See 1 Cor. 12:8; Moro. 10:9; D&C 46:17–18.

[15]See also Prov. 9:10; Ps. 111:10; Eccl. 12:13; and several passages in the Book of Mormon in which wisdom and acting wisely are equated with reverence and righteousness. Note, for example, Alma's instruction to his son Helaman: "O, remember, my son, and learn wisdom in thy youth; yea, learn in thy youth to keep the commandments of God" (Alma 37:35).

proverbs in this section is not that of a maxim but that of the multiverse "wisdom poem." The following three examples are typical of the type of proverbs contained in chapters 1 through 9. Proverbs 1:10–19 contains an exhortation to a "son" to avoid the ways of the greedy: "my son, if sinners entice thee, consent thou not." The instruction that begins in Proverbs 4:1 ("hear, ye children, the instruction of a father") and that includes such exhortations as "wisdom is the principle thing; . . . with all thy getting get understanding" extends through Proverbs 4:9 and extols the virtue of wisdom. An extended proverb for a lazy person ("go to the ant, thou sluggard; consider her ways, and be wise") is found in Proverbs 6:5–11.

It is this section of Proverbs, chapters 1 through 9, that contains most of the clearly gospel-oriented instructions in the book. As noted above, admonitions that equate specific religious practices with wisdom are rare at best in this book; however, the following passages illustrate the type of "religious" instruction that is included:

> For the upright shall dwell in the land. . . .
> But the wicked shall be cut off from the earth (Prov. 2:21–22).[16]

> Honour the Lord with thy substance,
> and with the firstfruits of all thine increase:
> So shall thy barns be filled with plenty,
> and thy presses shall burst out with new wine (Prov. 3:9–10).[17]

> My son, despise not the chastening of the Lord;
> neither be weary of his correction:
> For whom the Lord loveth he correcteth (Prov. 3:11–12).[18]

> I love them that love me;
> and those that seek me early shall find me (Prov. 8:17).[19]

This last example is especially interesting, because it is so similar to the Lord's statement in Doctrine and Covenants 88:83; however, in Proverbs 8:17 it is wisdom, personified as a woman, who makes this statement.

---

[16]See "Land" and "Lands of Inheritance," Topical Guide, LDS Bible.

[17]See "Tithing" and "Honor," Topical Guide, LDS Bible.

[18]See "Chastening," Topical Guide, LDS Bible.

[19]See "God, Access to," Topical Guide, LDS Bible. Cf. 1:24–33 (esp. v. 28), in which it is stated that the wicked who seek "early" will *not* receive divine assistance.

"Lady Wisdom"

Personification, especially in poetic texts, is commonly employed in scripture as a literary device for helping render abstract qualities or ideas more concretely. For example, "wine is a mocker" (Prov. 20:1) and "righteousness and peace have kissed" (Ps. 85:10). One of the most striking features of Israelite wisdom literature is the personification of wisdom as a woman. This is clearly evident in several passages in the first section of the book of Proverbs (including Prov. 1:20–33; 9:1–12; and especially chap. 8, where she speaks in the first person; see, for example, 8:17, quoted just above).[20] Although scholars have suggested that Lady Wisdom represents a pagan goddess in sanitized form, it is clear that in the biblical context "she" is both an attribute of and a gift from God:

> The Lord by wisdom hath founded the earth;
> by understanding hath he established the heavens (Prov. 3:19).

> For the Lord giveth wisdom (Prov. 2:6).

"Her" voice is the Lord's voice; "her" teachings are the Lord's teachings. To gain understanding and wisdom is to gain insight and inspiration through the Spirit of the Lord.

The female personification of wisdom is also preserved in the Book of Mormon. King Limhi contrasted the "marvellous works of the Lord" with the "blind and impenetrable . . . understandings" of people, noting that "they will not seek wisdom, neither do they desire that *she* should rule over them!" (Mosiah 8:20; emphasis added).

The Strange Woman

Consistent with the contrast between wisdom and foolishness, Lady Wisdom is contrasted in the book of Proverbs with the "strange" woman, someone who has sold herself physically or spiritually and thus has no part in "covenant Israel":

> Say unto wisdom, Thou art my sister;
> and call understanding thy kinswoman:
> that they may keep thee from the strange woman,

---

[20]See Murphy, pp. 133–49, for a well-balanced discussion of Lady Wisdom in all the relevant biblical and apocryphal texts.

456

from the stranger which flattereth with her words (Prov. 7:4–5).

For the lips of a strange woman drop as an honeycomb, . . .
But her end is bitter as wormwood (Prov. 5:3–4).

Many strong men have been slain by her.
Her house is the way to hell (Prov. 7:26–27).

As with any personification, we must realize that the "kiss of death" can come in many forms from either gender.

Proverbs 10 through 29

Proverbs 10 through 29 contains material attributed to Solomon (Prov. 10:1–22:16; 25:1–29:27) and to "the wise," unidentified sages (Prov. 22:17–24:34).

Literary Forms

Although the prominent literary form in chapters 1 through 9 is the multiverse wisdom poem, this portion of the book consists mainly of concise "sayings" and "admonitions." Most of these are a single verse and employ a poetic form known as "parallelism." The two most basic forms of parallelism, and the ones most frequently employed in Proverbs, are synonymous parallelism, in which a statement is made and then is reiterated using different words, and antithetic parallelism, in which the second line or thought represents the antithesis, or opposite, of the first line or thought.[21] These two types of parallelism will be evident in the examples that follow.

There is variety in the types of sayings preserved in the book of Proverbs (see n. 7, above), yet they all make a statement or express an observation. Note these examples:

Pride goeth before destruction,
and a haughty spirit before a fall (Prov. 16:18).

In the mouth of the foolish is a rod of pride:

---

[21]The technique of comparing contrasting situations or ideas for the purpose of emphasizing what is the best choice or approach is found many times in the Bible and the Book of Mormon. See, for example, Mormon's editorial use of this style in Hel. 6:34–38.

but the lips of the wise shall preserve them (Prov. 14:3).[22]

"Admonitions" may be positive or negative, in which case they are termed "prohibitions." They often employ an imperative verbal form, having the force of a command. An example of an admonition and a prohibition follow. Note that each proverb provides a reason for the behavior that is admonished:

> Train up a child in the way he should go:
> and when he is old, he will not depart from it (Prov. 22:6).

> Do not envy wicked men,
> do not desire their company;
> for their hearts plot violence,
> and their lips talk about making trouble (Prov. 24:1–2, NIV; cf. 3:31).[23]

Joseph Smith Translation

There is only one verse in the book of Proverbs for which Joseph Smith provided a substantive change as part of his inspired revision of the Bible:

> KJV: Whoso findeth a wife findeth a good thing,
>   and obtaineth favour of the Lord (Prov. 18:22).

> JST: Whoso findeth a good wife
>   hath obtained favor of the Lord.

The emphasis of the proverb is appropriately restored to the significance of a "good" spouse. It is not clear whether Joseph Smith thought there were no further changes to be made in the book of Proverbs, or whether this book, because it is less doctrinal in nature, received less attention from the Prophet. The latter possibility seems more likely.[24]

---

[22]Latter-day Saints will be familiar with the proverbial saying, in antithetic parallelistic form, which the Lord shared with Moroni: "Fools mock, but they shall mourn" (Ether 12:26).

[23]The NIV rendition of the first phrase is more accessible and accurate than the KJV's "be thou not envious against evil men."

[24]See Robert J. Matthews, "A Plainer Translation": Joseph Smith's Translation of the Bible, A History and Commentary (Provo, Utah: Brigham Young University Press, 1985), p. 375; and Joseph F. McConkie, "Joseph Smith and the Poetic Writings," in The Joseph Smith Translation: The Restoration of Plain and Precious Things, ed. Monte S. Nyman and Robert L. Millet (Provo, Utah: Religious Studies Center, Brigham Young University, 1985), p. 104.

Proverbs 22:17 through 24:22

During the first part of the twentieth century, an Egyptian text known as the Instruction of Amenemope(t), thought to have been composed about 1200 B.C., was published. Scholars have observed a relationship between this text and the so-called "words of the wise" contained in Proverbs 22:17–24:22. Much of the material in this portion of Proverbs, including headings and key words, is similar to, and may be dependent on, the Egyptian text.[25] If the Egyptian text is primary, however, "close comparison shows that the Israelite writer was quite independent; he adapted the Egyptian admonitions rather freely to suit his own purpose."[26] Such a situation is not particularly surprising, given the extent of the wisdom tradition throughout the ancient Near East and the universal nature of much of proverbial wisdom.

Proverbs 30

Agur, to whom the content of Proverbs 30 is attributed, claimed to be "more brutish than any man" and that he had "not the understanding of a man" (Prov. 30:2). Although that would seem to disqualify anything he said from inclusion in a wisdom book, this self-deprecating description may have been made in the same spirit as Paul's statement that "Jesus came into the world to save sinners; of whom I am chief" (1 Tim. 1:15). Interestingly, Agur's words are described as a "prophecy" or inspired pronouncement.[27] As noted above, nothing is known of Agur outside of this passage.

---

[25]Most scholars accept the primacy of the Egyptian text, based in part on the proposed date of composition, although surviving texts date several centuries later. Some suggest that the "Instruction of Amenemope(t)" and Prov. 22:17–24:22 both share a common source, whereas a few, such as Hugh Nibley, accept the primacy of this portion of Proverbs over the Egyptian text. See Nibley's semicryptic comment in *Since Cumorah*, 2d ed. (Salt Lake City: Deseret Book Co., 1988), pp. 52–53.

[26]Murphy, p. 24; see pp. 23–25 for a convenient discussion of the similarities. For an English translation of the "Instruction of Amenemope(t)," see Pritchard, pp. 421–25.

[27]Rather than translate it as "prophecy," as in the KJV, some scholars prefer to render the Hebrew word *maśśā'* as a place name; thus, "the words of Agur the son of Jakeh of Massa." The definite article attached to *maśśā'* makes that unlikely; however, compare Prov. 31:1, in which *maśśā'* also occurs but without the definite article. It is often rendered as a place name there as well.

After a few rhetorical questions reminiscent of the book of Job ("Who hath ascended up into heaven? . . . Who hath gathered the wind in his fists?"; Prov. 30:4), there is one clearly religious statement: "Every word of God is pure: he is a shield unto them that put their trust in him" (Prov. 30:5).[28] Nonetheless, this chapter mainly consists of multiverse "numerical" proverbs. For example:

> There be three things which are too wonderful for me,
> yea, four which I know not:
> The way of an eagle in the air;
> the way of a serpent upon a rock;
> the way of a ship in the midst of the sea;
> and the way of a man with a maid (Prov. 30:18–19).

The literary technique of numbering plus adding one more is an idiomatic means of expressing a cumulative affect. In the proverb just quoted, it is used to express the unfathomableness of some of the wondrous mysteries of the earth. Elsewhere in Proverbs, a list of sins is introduced by this numerical feature:

> These six things doth the Lord hate:
> yea, seven are an abomination unto him:
> A proud look, a lying tongue . . . (6:16–19).[29]

Proverbs 31

Verse 1 of Proverbs 31 indicates that the words that follow are not King Lemuel's but his mother's, given as instruction *to* Lemuel.[30] This mother instructs her son to avoid the entanglements of women (presumably to whom he was not married!) and wine (Prov. 31:2–7) and to "judge righteously" and stand up for the oppressed (Prov. 31:8–9).

As noted above, it is not clear whether the proverbial poem about a virtuous woman that follows should be regarded as a continuation of

---

[28]Some find the questions in v. 4 and the names of Agur and his father in v. 1 to be part of a riddle, the solution to which reaffirms that Jacob/Israel is the "son" of Jehovah. See Murphy, p. 25.

[29]An example of the use of this technique to represent the consequences of sin is found in the Lord's expression: "for three transgressions, . . . and for four" (Amos 1–2).

[30]See n. 27, above, concerning the term *prophecy*.

the preceding comments of Lemuel's mother or whether it is a separate text that was appended to the end of the book without any heading.

Although it is not evident in the KJV (or most other translations), this proverbial poem is acrostic in form, meaning that the first word in the first verse of the poem, verse 10, begins with the first letter of the Hebrew alphabet, and each succeeding verse begins with the succeeding letter. There are twenty-two letters in the Hebrew alphabet; there are twenty-two verses in this poem about a virtuous woman.[31]

The Hebrew phrase translated "a virtuous woman" in the KJV literally means "a woman of strength, ability" and it is often rendered as "a capable woman" in more recent English translations. The woman portrayed in this poem is, however, more than just capable. She represents an ideal, the epitome of a self-assured, productive, and successful woman. She is neither distant nor demure but energetic and involved. Above all, she is wise:

> She openeth her mouth with wisdom;
> and in her tongue is the law of kindness.
> Favour is deceitful,
> and beauty is vain:
> but a woman that feareth the Lord,
> she shall be praised (Prov. 31:26, 30).

The first phrase of this poem asks, "Who can find" such a woman? (Prov. 31:10). As was noted about the wisdom of Proverbs, the focus is more on the outcome than on the process. This portrait of a "virtuous woman" represents the end of a process, not the beginning.

It is probably no accident that this poem, the last passage in the book of Proverbs, represents a summation of the wisdom contained in the book, a final illustration of the benefits of a life founded on true wisdom. Not surprisingly, the attributes of this "virtuous woman" are the attributes of Wisdom herself: she is priceless (Prov. 31:10; cf. 3:15; 8:11), she is energetic, not lazy (v. 27; cf. 6:5), her spouse (thus all who embrace her) is happy and satisfied (Prov. 31:23, 28; cf. 3:13; 18:22), and when she speaks, she does so wisely, not foolishly (Prov. 31:26; cf. 8:7–9).

---

[31]Acrostics can also be found in the books of Psalms and Lamentations, although with the exception of Ps. 119, in which the Hebrew letter is indicated (apparently because groups of verses begin with the same Hebrew letter), these are not indicated or discernible in the KJV.

Final Thoughts

As with all the gifts of God, gaining wisdom usually proceeds "line upon line" and is not without effort. The Israelite sages understood this:

> Counsel in the heart of man is like deep water;
> but a man of understanding will draw it out (Prov. 20:5).

The quest for wisdom is the quest to know and understand and fear the Lord. It is a quest that involves a recognition of the wise and foolish choices available in life and the conscious selection of the Lord's way. With potent symbolism, Israel's wise ones depicted wisdom as "a fountain of life" (Prov. 13:14) and as "a tree of life to them that lay hold upon her" (Prov. 3:18). Well might the sages of Israel have admonished, as did Jacob, the brother of Nephi:

> O be wise;
> what can I say more? (Jacob 6:12).

41

ECCLESIASTES

DAVID ROLPH SEELY

Ecclesiastes is a unique and distinctive book in the Old Testament; in fact, there existed a great deal of dissension among the early rabbis whether it should be considered part of the scriptures at all.[1] That this book survived the ravages of time is probably because it did make it into the Jewish canon, where it is found in the Writings—one of the five *Megilloth,* "little scrolls," which, in the Jewish tradition, are read in the synagogue on the annual festivals. Ecclesiastes is read at the Feast of Tabernacles—its somber tone a marked contrast to the rejoicing of the festival and providing a solemn reminder of the transitory nature of mortality and of the need to fulfill one's vows (Eccl. 5:4–5).[2] In the Christian canon, following the Septuagint, Ecclesiastes is grouped with the Song of Solomon and Proverbs, as all three are attributed to Solomon.

The title of Ecclesiastes is taken from the first line, "the words of the Preacher" (Eccl. 1:1). *Ecclesiastes* is a Greek translation of Hebrew *qōhelet,* "one who convenes a congregation" and has often been translated "the Preacher." The book is attributed to Solomon, though his name does not occur in the book, because of the allusions to the author in chapters 1 and 12, which identify the Preacher as "the son of David, king in Jerusalem." Whether the book was written by Solomon is not

David Rolph Seely is assistant professor of ancient scripture at Brigham Young University.

[1]See the Mishnah, *Yadaim* 3.5; in Herbert Danby, *The Mishnah* (London: Oxford University, 1933), pp. 781–82.

[2]The other four books of the *Megilloth* are Song of Solomon, read at Passover; Ruth, read at Pentecost; Lamentations, read on the ninth of Ab to commemorate the destruction of the temple in 587 B.C. and A.D. 70; and Esther, read at Purim.

known, but the attribution is certainly one of the reasons it became part of the canon.

Ecclesiastes is often defined as pessimistic, cynical, or philosophical and thus is disregarded by many. It is all of those, and yet when scripture offends us, that is when we should take a careful look at its message. Perhaps one of the most common criticisms is that it is a human-centered work and not a statement of faith. Yet, though admittedly human-centered — that is, not explicitly given by revelation — it is most assuredly a statement of faith, and in many ways it is a profound and mature faith.

Ecclesiastes is part of a very important internal dialogue that takes place between various books in the Old Testament. In the Mosaic covenant the Lord states: "Behold, I set before you this day a blessing and a curse; A blessing, if ye obey the commandments of the Lord your God, which I command you this day: And a curse, if ye will not obey the commandments of the Lord your God" (Deut. 11:26–28). Job, on the other hand, learned that righteousness provides no escape from the trials and vicissitudes of mortality and vehemently protested his innocence to the Lord, seeking an understanding of his suffering. Based on their shallow religious understanding which they justify by the covenantal promises, Job's friends, seeing his suffering, assumed his guilt. The book of Proverbs, based on further interpretation of the covenantal principle, presents a whole series of aphorisms suggesting that correct behavior will bring results — stated in terms of health, wealth, prosperity, and success in life. Ecclesiastes is written by one who in the course of his life has come to the conclusion that such a connection between righteousness, wisdom, and worldly success is an abuse of religion and an oversimplified view of life. The Preacher's tone is often bitter and cynical, but his observations are timely and the issues he addresses are relevant to the world we live in today.[3]

"Vanity of vanities; all is vanity" (Eccl. 1:2). The Preacher continually reminds us of the transitory nature of mortality and warns us against trusting too much in the things of the flesh. He recounts his search for

---

[3]The relevance of Ecclesiastes to modern life has been eloquently expressed by Rabbi Harold Kushner in his thought-provoking best-seller based on an interpretation of Ecclesiastes: *When All You've Ever Wanted Isn't Enough: The Search for a Life That Matters* (New York: Summit Books, 1986). Likewise his book *When Bad Things Happen to Good People* (New York: Schocken Books, 1981) contains a perceptive discussion of the book of Job.

fulfillment in life, first devoting himself to pleasure and laughter (Eccl. 2:1–3), then wealth (Eccl. 2:4–11), and finally wisdom (Eccl. 2:12–17), but ultimately finding that all is "vanity and vexation of spirit" (Eccl. 2:11, 17, 26). The Preacher's solution is simple and profound: "There is nothing better for a man, than that he should eat and drink, and that he should make his soul enjoy good in his labour. This also I saw, that it was from the hand of God" (Eccl. 2:24). He is not advocating the moral abandon described in 2 Nephi 28:7–8, where committing sin is justified, but he is recognizing that there is much to be enjoyed in life. In fact the Preacher goes on to acknowledge God's power to give "to a man that is good in his sight wisdom, and knowledge, and joy: but to the sinner he giveth travail, to gather and to heap up" (Eccl. 2:26).

"To every thing there is a season, and a time to every purpose under the heaven" (Eccl. 3:1). Mortality presents us with a wide gamut of experiences: birth and death, weeping and laughing, war and peace. The Preacher warns us that we do not always know the mind of the Lord or the causes of these things: "No man can find out the work that God maketh from the beginning to the end" (Eccl. 3:11). The "gift of God" is that "every man should eat and drink, and enjoy the good of all his labour" (Eccl. 3:13). Ultimately all will die, at which time true "success" will be measured (Eccl. 3:16–17). In the meantime, it is allotted to mortals to find joy and meaning in their daily lives.

Some have put their faith in the power of acquisition to give meaning to their lives, but "he that loveth silver shall not be satisfied with silver; nor he that loveth abundance with increase: that is also vanity" (Eccl. 5:10–11).

The Preacher then asks the most difficult question—why do the righteous suffer? "There is a just man that perisheth in his righteousness, and there is a wicked man that prolongeth his life in his wickedness" (Eccl. 7:15). How then should one behave in order to have some control of one's mortal condition? The Preacher implicitly warns us that it is only with an eternal perspective that such a paradox can be understood and answers, "He that feareth God shall come forth of them all" (Eccl. 7:18).

The covenantal principle "if you are righteous you will prosper" is often only true in an eternal sense: "Let us hear the conclusion of the whole matter: Fear God, and keep his commandments: for this is the

465

whole duty of man. For God shall bring every work into judgment, with every secret thing, whether it be good, or whether it be evil" (Eccl. 12:13–14).[4] Such a sentiment may not bring immediate comfort to those who suffer, but such an understanding is essential to a spirituality that can endure trials.

In the end, the message of the Preacher is that we understand the precarious and transitory nature of mortality. While a mindless pursuit of earthbound priorities is "vanity of vanities" (Eccl. 1:2; 12:8), mortality is a great blessing which offers much to be enjoyed—to "eat and drink, and enjoy the good of all his labour" (Eccl. 3:13), to live and to die, to laugh and to cry, and to love those around us—each in its own season (Eccl. 3:1–11). Eternal perspective is essential to achieving peace of mind. Precisely because we understand that mortality will not last forever, we can endure its trials and enjoy its bounty.

---

[4]The final section of the book, Eccl. 12:9–14, was possibly added by someone other than the Preacher. Many scholars interpret verses 13 and 14, promising final judgment, as an "orthodox" conclusion inconsistent with the pessimistic tone of the rest of the book. They hypothesize that this ending was added by a later editor to make the book conform to covenantal theology. The addition of these two verses does significantly alter the tone of the book, but though the absoluteness of verses 13 and 14 is not apparent throughout Ecclesiastes, emphasis on the "fear of the Lord" is found in various passages (Eccl. 3:14; 8:12–13), and the ending is not as inconsistent as many believe.

42

THE SONG OF SOLOMON

David Rolph Seely

The Song of Solomon is a song of love. And a love poem in the Old Testament demands a response. Hence it has been the most praised, the most maligned, or the most ignored book in the Old Testament. It was preserved from antiquity in the Jewish canon, where it is found in the Writings—one of the five *Megilloth*, "little scrolls," which, in the Jewish tradition, are read in the synagogue on the annual festivals. The Song of Solomon is read at Passover, celebrating the Lord's love for his bride, the covenant people.[1] In addition it is joyfully sung by some Jewish congregations on Friday evening as they welcome "the bride"—the Sabbath. In the Christian canon, following the Septuagint, the Song of Solomon is grouped with the poetic books and follows Proverbs and Ecclesiastes, as all three are attributed to Solomon.

The Song of Solomon is an erotic love song celebrating the love between a woman and a man. It is rich with unforgettable imagery: "thy love is better than wine" (Song 1:2); "the voice of the turtle-dove is heard in our land" (Song 2:12, author's translation); "his eyes are as the eyes of doves" (Song 5:12); and "who is she that looketh forth as the morning, fair as the moon, clear as the sun, and terrible as an army with banners" (Song 6:10). The Hebrew title of this book is found in the first line: "Song of Songs," a superlative formed in Hebrew by placing the two words "song" and "songs" in juxtaposition—as in the term "holy of holies"—to indicate that it is a most sublime love song.

David Rolph Seely is assistant professor of ancient scripture at Brigham Young University.

[1]The other four books are Ruth, read at Pentecost; Lamentations, read on the ninth of Ab to commemorate the destruction of the temple in 587 B.C. and A.D. 70; Ecclesiastes, read at the Feast of Tabernacles; and Esther, read at Purim.

The book is attributed to Solomon because his name occurs in Song of Solomon 1:5; 3:7, 9, 11; and 8:11–12, though none of these passages is a statement of authorship, and because Solomon is known for his one thousand wives and concubines (1 Kgs. 11:3). Some have wondered how such an erotic and worldly book ever made it into the canon. Certainly the attribution to Solomon was a factor. The Mishnah records that the early rabbis debated long and hard whether this book should be admitted into the canon and were finally swayed by the impassioned Rabbi Akiba, who declared, "The whole world is not worth the day on which the Song of Songs was given to Israel; all the holy Writings are holy, and the Song of Songs is the holy of the holies."[2]

The Song of Solomon is a difficult book for a casual reader. The lack of a logical sequence or plot has led to great debate about the nature of the book. It is not even always certain who is speaking. Is it one poem or a collection of many? Scholars have identified anywhere from one to twenty-five different poems or fragments.

Likewise there are numerous interpretations of the book.[3] Some have seen it as simply a love song, others a drama, a collection of wedding songs, a pagan liturgy from a Tammuz cult, or a mystical text. The traditional Jewish and Christian interpretation is that the Song is an allegory of the covenantal relationship between God and his people, and many scholars believe it was canonized because of this allegorical interpretation. It is worth noting, however, that some believe it is in the canon simply because it is a celebration of the love between a man and a woman, and its inclusion symbolizes the Lord's approval of such relationships.[4] Such scholars would argue that the allegorical interpretation occurred after the book was canonized and not before.[5]

One ingenious scholar has attempted to reconstruct the story line of

---

[2]See the Mishnah, *Yadaim* 3.5; in Herbert Danby, *The Mishnah* (London: Oxford University, 1933), pp 781–82.

[3]The most comprehensive study of this book in English is undoubtedly Marvin H. Pope, *Song of Songs,* Anchor Bible 7C (Garden City, N.Y.: Doubleday, 1977). He systematically reviews all of the various interpretations of the book through the ages.

[4]For example, see B. S. Childs, *Introduction to the Old Testament as Scripture* (Philadelphia: Fortress, 1979), p. 578.

[5]For example, it is not clear if Rabbi Akiba considered the Song of Solomon symbolically. For a discussion, see N. K. Gottwald, "Song of Songs," in *The Interpreter's Dictionary of the Bible,* 5 vols., ed. G. A. Buttrick, et al. (Nashville: Abingdon, 1962–76), 4:421–22.

the poetry.[6] His reconstructions may be a bit fanciful in places, but such a suggested reconstruction may prove helpful to an interested reader who needs a story line to read poetry. Briefly, this reconstruction goes as follows: A young woman from Shulam (Song 6:13; or Shunam) is tending the family flocks when she meets a young shepherd with whom she starts a love affair resulting in espousal. Her brothers overhear her beloved inviting her to meet him in the fields (Song 2:8–17). In an attempt to keep her from meeting her beloved there, they assign her to the vineyard (Song 1:6), where she is working when she is seen by King Solomon, who is visiting the neighborhood (Song 3:6–11). Solomon is enamored with her exquisite beauty and takes her to his tent, where he attempts to gain her affection (Song 1:9–15) with flattery and promises and with the cajoling of the court ladies—to whom she continues to affirm her love for her shepherd (Song 1:1–8, 16–17; 2:1–7). Finally, Solomon takes her with him to his capital, Jerusalem, with the hope of dazzling her with its splendor. There she meets (or dreams about) her beloved shepherd for whom she longs and to whom she reaffirms her love and loyalty (Song 3:1–5; 5:1–5). The Shulamitess describes her beloved to the ladies of the court, who are amazed at her loyalty (Song 5:1–6:3). Her beloved invites her to flee with him (Song 4:1–16). Solomon then promises to elevate her to the highest rank, above all the other wives and concubines (Song 6:4–7:9)—an offer that she rejects because her love is promised to another (Song 7:10). In the end the maiden remains faithful to her true love (Song 7:11–8:4); they are reunited under the tree where they first met (Song 8:5–7); she reaffirms her faithfulness (Song 8:8–12); and finally he calls to her (Song 8:13), and she answers (Song 8:14). Thus it is a story of a woman's loyalty and virtue and the victory of true love.

The most prevalent interpretation, fostered by the rabbis as well as the church fathers of early Christianity, is that the Song is an allegory of the love that God has for his people. The image of God and his people as a husband and bride is well developed in the Old Testament prophets: Hosea (1–3), Isaiah (62:5; see also 66:5–13), and Jeremiah (2:1–4). In Ezekiel 16 the apostasy of Judah—the young bride turned harlot—is graphically described with imagery every bit as sexually explicit as that

---

[6]C. D. Ginsburg, *The Song of Songs*, 1857, as summarized by Pope, p. 137.

of the Song of Solomon. The intimacy of marriage is an effective image that includes many parallels to the relationship of God and his people: covenant, love, trust, loyalty, and tenderness. This same theme is prominent in the New Testament in the parable of the ten virgins (Matt. 25:1–13) and the supper of the Lord as a wedding feast (Matt. 22:1–14; Luke 14:16–24; D&C 58:6–12).

The best-known fact among Latter-day Saints about the Song of Solomon is that Joseph Smith wrote in the manuscript of the Joseph Smith Translation, "The Songs of Solomon are not inspired writings."[7] Nevertheless, we have a very significant allusion to a passage from it in modern revelation. The bride is referred to in the Song of Solomon as one "that looketh forth as the morning, fair as the moon, clear as the sun, and terrible as an army with banners" (Song 6:10). In the book of Revelation we find the symbol of a woman who "fled into the wilderness" (Rev. 12:5), who represents "the church of God," and who "brought forth the kingdom of our God and his Christ" (JST Rev. 12:7).[8] In the Doctrine and Covenants, Joseph Smith's inspired dedicatory prayer for the Kirtland Temple refers to the coming forth of the Church in the latter days with the same imagery, building on the language found in the Song of Solomon: "That thy church may come forth out of the wilderness of darkness, and shine forth fair as the moon, clear as the sun, and terrible as an army with banners; And be adorned as a bride for that day when thou shalt unveil the heavens, and cause the mountains to flow down at thy presence, and the valleys to be exalted, the rough places made smooth; that thy glory may fill the earth" (D&C 109:73–74; see also 105:31–32).

The Song of Solomon can be profitably read from many perspectives. It can be enjoyed simply for its delightful images, as a beautiful love poem exalting the relationship between a man and a woman, or it can be read as an allegory of the relationship between God and his children — a relationship that is used repeatedly in scripture to teach us about the covenant.

---

[7]See Robert J. Matthews, "A Plainer Translation": Joseph Smith's Translation of the Bible, A History and Commentary (Provo, Utah: Brigham Young University Press, 1975), pp. 87, 215.

[8]See Victor L. Ludlow, Unlocking the Old Testament (Salt Lake City: Deseret Book Co., 1981), pp. 142–44, who discusses the allusions to this imagery known in the Song of Solomon in the New Testament and the Doctrine and Covenants.

43

FROM MALACHI TO JOHN THE BAPTIST: THE DYNAMICS OF APOSTASY

M. Catherine Thomas

Three distinct features characterize the revealed religion of the Old Testament: scripture, temple, and prophecy. Each of these suffered corruption in the apostasy that ended the Old Testament period and ripened in the intertestamental period (ca. 500 B.C. to A.D. 30). We have no evidence that God sent any more prophets to Israel after Malachi, ca. 490 B.C. "The keys, the kingdom, the power, [and] the glory, had departed from the Jews," taught Joseph Smith, and "John, the son of Zachariah, by the holy anointing, and decree of heaven" would be the next legal administrator to hold the prophetic office.[1] Judaism, as it appeared in the intertestamental period, was not the revealed religion of the Old Testament. It had suffered mutation. The process followed this path: a steadily increasing rejection of living prophets (1200–500 B.C.), the cessation of revelation (ca. 490 B.C.), and changes that developed as the result of the absence of revelation, such as reliance on tradition and the interpretations of men, tampering with scripture, and the changing of doctrine. The loss of divine gifts in Judah had implications not only for the Jews but for the Christians as well, who would travel the same path of apostasy within a very few years of John's and Jesus's restoration. Because apostasy follows a discernible pattern, our purpose here is to analyze the dynamics of apostasy in general but specifically to identify its manifestations in doctrine, scripture, and sources of revelation between Malachi and John the Baptist.[2]

M. Catherine Thomas is a part-time instructor in ancient scripture at Brigham Young University.

[1]Sermon of 29 Jan. 1843, *Times and Seasons* 4 (15 May 1843): 200.

[2]This chapter deals with theological developments between the Old and the New Testaments.

The Nature of Apostasy

The purpose of the Church in any dispensation is to prepare the Saints through priesthood ordinances to acquire the divine nature and stand in God's presence. Jesus rebuked the Pharisees and scribes for thwarting that divine purpose: "Woe unto you, lawyers! for ye have taken away that key of knowledge: ye entered not in yourselves, and them that were entering in ye hindered" (Luke 11:52). The Joseph Smith Translation of this passage clarifies *knowledge* as "the fulness of the scriptures" (JST Luke 11:53). Apostasy changes doctrines, deletes covenants, and tampers with scripture to justify the positions of the apostates.

Scripture reveals fundamental principles about the corruption of truth. The underlying dynamic of apostasy is pride, as we see from the Lord's reproach in Luke: "Woe unto you, Pharisees! for ye love the uppermost seats in the synagogues, and greetings in the markets" (Luke 11:43). A scant seventy years later the apostle John would describe the apostasy developing in the Church of Jesus Christ: "I wrote unto the church: but Diotrephes, who loveth to have the preeminence among them, receiveth us not . . . prating against us with malicious words: and not content therewith, neither doth he himself receive the brethren, and forbiddeth them that would, and casteth them out of the church" (3 Jn. 1:9–10).

Apostasy, by its nature, takes place *within* the covenant people: "They [antichrists] went out from us, but they were not of us" (1 Jn. 2:18–19). The word *apostasy* comes from the Greek word *apostasía,* which means *rebellion.* Satan was the first apostate and the father of apostasy. He revealed the essential motive behind apostasy when he challenged God: "Wherefore give me thine honor" (Moses 4:1). Indeed, apostasy is a fruit of pride and is characterized by hatred. President Ezra Taft Benson spoke with penetrating insight on pride: "The central feature of pride is enmity—enmity toward God and enmity toward our fellowmen. *Enmity* means 'hatred toward, hostility to, or a state of opposition.' It is the power by which Satan wishes to reign over us."[3]

For a discussion of historical developments and circumstances during the same period, see Stephen E. Robinson, "The Setting of the Gospels," in *Studies in Scripture, Volume Five: The Gospels,* ed. Kent P. Jackson and Robert L. Millet (Salt Lake City: Deseret Book Co., 1986), pp. 10–37.

[3]"Beware of Pride," *Ensign,* May 1989, p. 4; see also C. S. Lewis, *Mere Christianity* (New York: Macmillan, 1960), p. 111.

Jesus highlighted the malice of apostates as he charged the Pharisees with the blood of all the martyred prophets and Saints shed from the foundation of the world (Luke 11:50–51). Luke recorded the Pharisees' hatred of Jesus, as they were "laying wait for him, and seeking to catch something out of his mouth, that they might accuse him" (Luke 11:54). These Pharisees who sought Jesus's life were the descendants of that apostasy that thrived in Old Testament times and into the succeeding period.

As apostasy ripens, it develops from individual and random wickedness to an increasingly sophisticated state of organization. The apostasy that brought prophecy to an end and later flourished in the intertestamental period probably began to assume an organizational structure in the days of Ezra (ca. 458 B.C.), who was a priest and scribe but also a political appointee of the Persian emperor, Artaxerxes I (Ezra 7:12–26). Ezra's objective was "to teach in Israel statutes and judgments" (Ezra 7:10). It was apparently from this time that the institution of the synagogue rose, the gathering place for instruction in the Law. The scribal tradition seems to have taken shape in this period also. Some of the educated Jews began to use knowledge of the scripture as a means of personal promotion (e.g., see Matt. 23:1–12). The scribes, professional scholars of the law, became the most prominent citizens of the community. From these beginnings rose the institutions of the Pharisees, scribes, and lawyers of Jesus' day. Along with the Sadducees—the priests and their allies—these groups were responsible for the dissemination of apostate ideas.

As awareness increased that God no longer worked among men, the Jews' spiritual leaders began to focus on the written word as if it were their messiah and vested it with the power of salvation.[4] Nephi wrote that to his people the Law was dead, that they only kept it because they were commanded to (2 Ne. 25:25). But he then foreshadowed the difficulty that the Jews would have in letting go of the Law: the Jews "need not harden their hearts" against Christ "when the law ought to be done away" (2 Ne. 25:27). Later, Abinadi found that the priests of Noah did indeed believe that salvation came not by Christ but by the Law of Moses (Mosiah 12:31–32).

---

[4]See John 5:39–40: "You search the scriptures because you *think* that in them you have eternal life; and [yet] it is they that testify on my behalf. Yet you refuse to come to me to have life" (New Revised Standard Version; emphasis added).

Among the Jews, then, prophecy had ceased, the canon of scripture was closed, and private interpretation of scripture supplanted divine revelation. Three things happened as a wave of darkness and confusion washed over the Jewish community: divine revelation withdrew, revealed doctrines began to change — especially the doctrine of God, and scriptural mutations appeared.

The Transformation of Scripture

That scripture tampering is a fundamental component of apostasy is revealed by the Book of Mormon. Nephi prophesied that evil men would deliberately take key passages from the prophets' records "that they might pervert the right ways of the Lord" (1 Ne. 13:23, 25–27, 29). Moses too learned from the Lord that men would esteem his words as naught and take many of them from the book that Moses would write (Moses 1:41). Just when these changes happened is not clear.

The Old Testament describes Ezra as "a ready scribe in the law [Torah][5] of Moses" (Ezra 7:6) who had "prepared his heart to seek [search, study, or interpret] the law of the Lord, and to do it" (Ezra 7:10). Not only did he "read in the book in the law of God distinctly," he "gave the sense, and caused them to understand the reading" (Neh. 8:8). This practice of interpreting the Law is what the scribes strove to do. The scribes were the lawyer class of Jewish life, the "doctors of the law." Educated intellectuals, trained in the practical or civil aspects of the Law of Moses, the scribes interpreted and applied the Law for everyday life.[6] In the absence of divine revelation, the Law became susceptible to fresh interpretations for each succeeding generation. To make applications to every aspect of life, the scribes developed a running commentary on the words of scripture. This method of teaching was known as Midrash (from Hebrew *drš*, meaning "to search," with the implication of searching out the true interpretation). In places where the Law was unclear, its meaning had to be interpreted and expounded. The scribes and later the rabbis

---

[5]Hebrew *law* or *teaching*; the Jews used the term to refer both to the law that God gave Moses on Sinai and to the first five books in the Old Testament, Genesis to Deuteronomy. These five books are also known as the Pentateuch.

[6]See Robinson, pp. 10–37.

(teachers who came after and continued the tradition of the scribes) built "a fence around the Law,"[7] which consisted of cautionary rules, such as that forbidding not simply the use but even the handling of tools on the Sabbath day. Thus by this "fence," a man would be halted before he found himself in danger of breaching the Law of God. These rules and interpretations of the Law constituted the "Oral Tradition." Therefore the Law was seen to have two parts: written and oral, and each was of equal authority. Each was also viewed to be of equal antiquity, for Moses himself, so they believed, had received the Law, written and oral, at Sinai, from which it had been handed down through successive generations of faithful men. It was in part a conflict over the authority of the oral tradition that led to the appearance of the two major parties of Jesus' day: the Pharisees and the Sadducees. The Pharisees were the inheritors, guardians, and perpetuators of the oral tradition; the Sadducees regarded the written Law alone as authoritative.[8]

As time went on, the oral tradition became disassociated from the text of the written scriptures and no longer needed to find its justification there. The oral tradition took on a life of its own. The Mishnah (from verbal teaching by repeated recitation; Hebrew root, *šnh*) is the collection of the rabbis' interpretations, or the oral tradition, written down about A.D. 200. The Talmud (literally, "learning") is a compilation consisting of the Mishnah, together with the subsequent discussions and commentaries (the *Gemara,* literally, "completion") which arose in the Jewish schools.[9] The Jews' scriptural tradition had become a mixing of scripture with the philosophies of men. They sought guidance from this source rather than from God. The inspired person sees scripture as a catalyst to revelation; apostasy founders in literalism.

From the time of Ezra onward, the Judaism that gradually developed attached great importance to the Law; the other sections of the scripture — the Prophets and the Writings — had less importance. And during the period 500–200 B.C., another gradual shifting of emphasis occurred from the Temple to the Law. By about 200 B.C., the religion of the Law was solidly established.[10] The attitude toward the structure of the Hebrew

---

[7]Herbert Danby, ed., *The Mishnah* (London: Oxford, 1983), p. 446; *Aboth* 1.1.

[8]See Robinson, pp. 22–25, 29.

[9]D. S. Russell, *Between the Testaments* (London: SCM, 1963), p. 60.

[10]Ibid., p. 68.

Bible itself reflects the Jewish consciousness of the ebbing away of spiritual power in Israel: the rabbis saw Moses' Law as the most sacred, the Prophets next, and the Writings they saw as least sacred.[11] Because God had spoken face to face with Moses, the Law was the holiest writing, in their view. The prophets received their revelation through the Holy Spirit, not directly from God; and the Writings came from individuals of lesser prophetic gifts. Thus the golden age of revelation in the mind of the Jews had been the age of Moses, and each succeeding age had diminished in splendor.

By about 250 B.C., many Jews who lived scattered throughout the Mediterranean area (in the Diaspora, or Dispersion) had lost a knowledge of Hebrew, the language of the Old Testament. Therefore, a Greek translation of the Hebrew scriptures was commissioned, called the Septuagint (often abbreviated as LXX). But with the translation of revealed religion into the Greek idiom, many Greek religious concepts slipped into the religion of the Jews.

The Corruption of the Doctrine of God

Hellenism, the Greek culture that grew to dominate the Near East after Alexander the Great's conquests of the fourth century B.C., had a profound effect on Jewish thought. One of the doctrines most affected by the hellenization of Judaism was the doctrine of the nature of God. This doctrine is one of the first to undergo modification in any apostasy. The object is generally to deprive God of his body and his feelings and thus to render him amorphous and distant. With these transformations, true religion loses the doctrine of the deification of men and the accompanying commitment to fidelity in marriage and to stable, nurturing families.[12] This loss of the knowledge of the true God happened early in Christianity as well. Alma found it among apostate Zoramite Nephites

---

[11]For a listing of the books in the order in which they appear in the Hebrew Bible, see Kent P. Jackson, "God's Testament to Ancient Israel," *Studies in Scripture, Volume Three: Genesis to 2 Samuel* (Salt Lake City: Randall Book, 1985), p. 7.

[12]For a full discussion of the effects of sexual asceticism on the doctrines of the deification of man, the nature of God, and the Atonement, see M. Catherine Thomas, "The Influence of Asceticism on the Rise of Text, Doctrine, and Practice in the First Two Christian Centuries," unpublished dissertation, Brigham Young University, 1989.

(Alma 31:15). The first knowledge restored to Joseph Smith in the First Vision was that God the Father and his Son Jesus Christ have separate bodies in the form of men, a doctrine that had been officially absent from Christianity since the Council of Nicea declared the consubstantiality of the Father and the Son (in A.D. 325). Hellenism and other forces influenced the shape and nature of God in apostate Judaism.

After Alexander's conquests (ca. 300 B.C.), the Jews were surrounded by Greek culture and civilization. Particularly in the Diaspora (the Jewish colonies outside Palestine), many of the Jews who adopted the Greek language were deeply influenced by their hellenistic environment. With the absorption of Greek language and culture, Jewish thinking began to take on an increasingly Greek tone. A proliferation of apocryphal literature appeared in this period, manifesting a mixture of Jewish and Greek thought. The hellenized Jew Philo, a contemporary of Jesus and Paul, embraced Greek ideas of an utterly transcendent God who had nothing to do with the material world because of its inferior nature and had even caused the world to be created by inferior beings.[13] These ideas would within a few years help to produce sexual asceticism and docetism (the doctrine that Christ only *seemed* to be flesh) in the earliest Christian church. Hellenization was an aggressive movement, and the pressure exerted by sophisticated Greek philosophical systems was more than many Jews could resist. Again pride was at work as Jews became ashamed of the plain, revealed religion of their Israelite forefathers (e.g., 1 Maccabees 1:11–15, which documents the "uncircumcising" of Jews).

In contrast, the doctrine of God in the Old Testament was simple. God had not simply wound up the world like a clock and retired. The revealed God of the Old Testament sought constant interaction with his children. He spoke in terms of bride and bridegroom when he expressed the loving and nourishing covenant relationship that he desired with Israel: "I will betroth thee unto me for ever; yea, I will betroth thee unto me in righteousness, and in judgment, and in lovingkindness, and in mercies. I will even betroth thee unto me in faithfulness: and thou shalt know the Lord" (Hosea 2:19–20).

The Old Testament abounds in anthropomorphic (pertaining to human form) expressions referring to God. The parts of the human body

---

[13]Philo, *Conf.* 179; *The Confusion of Tongues*, Loeb Classical Library 4 (Cambridge, Mass.: Harvard, 1930), p. 109.

frequently serve as descriptions of the acts of God. "The eyes of the Lord" and the "ears of the Lord" occur in the Prophets and in Psalms; "the mouth of the Lord" speaks both in the Law and the Prophets; the heavens are the work of his fingers (Ps. 8:3), and the tablets of the covenant are written by the finger of God (Ex. 31:18). We read of his "nose," that is, the wrath of God; "his countenance" which he causes to shine, or, alternatively, which he hides. We read of "his right hand," "his arm," and "his sword." In Genesis he "walks about in the garden" (Gen. 3:8); he "goes down" in order to see what is being done on the earth (Gen. 11:5; 18:21) or to reveal himself there (Ex. 19:18; 34:5), and he goes up again (Gen. 17:22; 35:13). He sits on a throne (Isa. 6:1) and causes his voice to be heard among the cherubim who hover over the ark of the tabernacle (Num. 7:89). The hair of his head is as wool (Dan. 7:9), and Moses sees "his back" (Ex. 33:23).[14]

Anthropopathisms (humanlike emotions) abound as well: God expresses love, joy and delight, regret and sadness, pity and compassion, disgust, anger, and other feelings. One scholar observed that the early Israelites preferred making God immediate rather than distant:

> Ultimately, every religious expression is caught in the dilemma between, on the one hand, the theological desire to emphasize the absolute and transcendental nature of the Divine, thereby relinquishing its vitality and immediate reality and relevance, and on the other hand, the religious need to conceive of the Deity and man's contact with Him in some vital and meaningful way. Jewish tradition has usually shown preference for the second tendency, and there is a marked readiness to speak of God in a very concrete and vital manner and not to recoil from the dangers involved in the use of apparent anthropomorphisms.[15]

In time, however, the more sophisticated people did recoil at an anthropomorphic God. At least by post-Old Testament times, the scribes and the rabbis who gave us the Mishnah found the anthropomorphisms offensive and took steps to make small textual changes which they described as "biblical modifications of expression."[16] In place of "I will dwell in your midst" (spoken by God) was substituted "I shall cause you

---

[14]See "Anthropomorphism," *Encyclopaedia Judaica*, 17 vols. (Jerusalem: Keter, 1982), 3:53.
[15]Ibid.
[16]Ibid.

to dwell."[17] To avoid an objectionable anthropomorphism, the text of Exodus 34:24 may have been changed from "to see the face of the Lord" (*lir'ôt 'et-penê yhwh*) to "to appear before the Lord" (*lērā'ôt 'et-penê yhwh*).[18] Early translations of scripture also changed such phrases as "he saw" or "he knew," referring to God, to "it was revealed before him." "He went down" became "he revealed himself;" "he heard" became "it was heard before him," etc.

The translators of the Septuagint went further than the scribes in spiritualizing the anthropomorphic or anthropopathic phrases of the Bible. The "image of God" became in the Septuagint "the glory of the Lord"; "the mouth of God" became "the voice of the Lord." They deprived God of human emotions in careful, nonhuman representations of God's wrath and pity.[19] Although the Israelites of Moses's time could accept an anthropomorphic God, the Jews of Jesus' time were ready to stone him for his proclamation that he was Jehovah (John 8:58–59), because they had long sought to obscure the doctrine of a God in human form.

Another means of distancing God was avoiding the use of his name. By the third century B.C., saying the name *Yahweh* (Jehovah) was avoided[20] and ultimately became illegal and blasphemous; *Adonai*, translated "the Lord," was substituted for it. But God had ordained his name as a key-word by which a covenant person could gain access to him (Moses 5:8; 1 Kgs. 8:28–29). Possession of the name through priesthood authority meant possession of priesthood power (Abr. 1:18–19). To forbid the name was to forbid access to the power to acquire the divine nature and thus to prevent access to God himself.[21]

Distancing God by making him amorphous and transcendent makes him less demanding. If the Jews wanted to place distance between them and God, they could do so, at least for the time being. Jacob taught in the Book of Mormon that the Jews "despised the words of plainness, and killed the prophets, and sought for things that they could not

---

[17]Ibid.

[18]Ibid.

[19]See also Bruce R. McConkie, *A New Witness for the Articles of Faith* (Salt Lake City: Deseret Book Co., 1985), p. 403.

[20]"God, Name of," *Encyclopaedia Judaica*, 7:680.

[21]For further discussion of the Name, see Elder Dallin H. Oaks, in Conference Report, Apr. 1985, p. 103.

understand.[22] . . . For God hath taken away his plainness from them, and delivered unto them many things which they cannot understand, *because they desired it.* And because they desired it God hath done it, that they may stumble" (Jacob 4:14; emphasis added).

Perhaps it is helpful to note here that in any apostasy there are always innocent and well-intentioned victims. Not all promoters of false ideas have malignant intent; most are to some extent the victims of those who have gone before. But the Lord has made it apparent that the initiators of apostasy set out to destroy the work of the Lord (see 1 Ne. 13:27), and that many subsequent perpetrators of apostasy had the same objective. Joseph Smith wrote that many errors in the Bible were done in ignorance or by accident, but that many were the work of "designing and corrupt priests."[23]

The Cessation of Divine Revelation

Malachi (ca. 490 B.C.) wrote the last prophetic book in the Old Testament. After his time, the Jews clearly understood that prophecy had ceased. Even in Israel's earlier wicked days, God had continued to strive with them through prophets. But for the word of God to cease altogether among men reflects abysmal spiritual conditions.

Later Jews looked back on this part of Israel's history and acknowledged that the spirit of prophecy and revelation had been withdrawn. In medieval rabbinic literature, three Hebrew terms were used to represent God's revelation of himself to his children: *Ru'ah ha-Qodesh* (the Holy Spirit), *Shekhinah* (God's presence), and *Bath-qol* (a small voice). According to the rabbis, these manifestations thrived in Israel prior to the destruction of Solomon's temple (587 B.C.); but later they had been withdrawn. The second temple, rebuilt by Zerubbabel, was viewed as inferior to the first on at least five points: the absence of (1) the ark of the covenant, (2) the divine fire, (3) the Urim and Thummim, (4) the

---

[22]That is, the Jews preferred the mysterious doctrines that they had created over plain doctrine. The Christians would do the same within a few years of Jesus' ascension.

[23]With "priests" presumably referring to any kind of religious leader; see Joseph Smith, *Teachings of the Prophet Joseph Smith,* sel. Joseph Fielding Smith (Salt Lake City: Deseret Book Co., 1938), p. 327.

Shekhinah (God's presence), and (5) the Holy Spirit.[24] The rabbis, finding themselves in a spiritual void, looked longingly back on the golden age of revelation of God to man and forward to the great messianic age, the "end of days," the culmination of which would be the restoration of the powers of the Holy Spirit.

Shekhinah is a rabbinic term that looks back on Old Testament times and refers to the presence of God's glory at such historic manifestations as Exodus 33:18, 22; Deuteronomy 5:22, 24; and 1 Kings 8:10–13. This majestic presence of God descended to "dwell" among men.[25] Israel constructed the tabernacle in order that this divine presence might dwell on earth and enter the Holy of Holies. The *Shekhinah* was often identified in rabbinic literature with the Holy Spirit and was frequently depicted in the form of a dove.[26]

The *Bath-qol*, translated "daughter of a voice" (implying a small voice), proclaimed God's will. In the Aramaic versions of the Bible, in the Midrash, and in the Talmud, the heavenly revelation is usually introduced with "A voice fell from heaven," "came from heaven," "was heard," or "proceeded from heaven." But the rabbis made a distinction between the *Bath-qol* and the Holy Spirit: whereas the prophets seemed to *possess* the Holy Spirit, the *Bath-qol* had no personal or persisting relationship with those who heard it. It could not be possessed.[27]

Even though a lesser gift than prophecy, the *Bath-qol*, according to the rabbis, had co-existed with prophecy in earlier times when the Spirit visited Israel. All three of these spiritual manifestations — the Holy Spirit, the *Shekhinah*, and the *Bath-qol* — were connected with the sign of the dove in rabbinic literature.

In Jewish tradition, three main views date the cessation of these manifestations of the Spirit and God's presence: (1) some date it as late as the destruction of Herod's temple (A.D. 70); (2) some date it from the destruction of the first temple (587 B.C.) when the Jews realized that the *Shekhinah* and the Holy Spirit of prophecy did not dwell in the second temple; (3) others point to the passing of the last three prophets (ca.

---

[24]Babylonian Talmud, *Yoma* 21b.

[25]"Shekhinah," *The Jewish Encyclopedia*, 12 vols. (New York: Funk and Wagnalls, 1901–6), 11:258.

[26]Ibid, 11:260.

[27]"Bath-qol," *Jewish Encyclopedia*, 2:589.

500 B.C.). The Mishnah has references to the ceasing of divine revelation: "When the last of the prophets, Haggai, Zechariah, and Malachi, died, the Holy Spirit departed from Israel; nevertheless they made use of the Bath-qol."[28] Another passage says, "At first, before Israel sinned against morality, the Shechinah abode with each individual; as it is said, 'For the Lord thy God walketh in the midst of thy camp' (Deut. 23:14). When they sinned, the Shekhinah departed from them."[29] The writers of the Talmud believed that the Spirit of prophecy vanished with the last prophets, and they acknowledged that thereafter the *Bath-qol* served instead. First Maccabees records, "Thus there was great trouble in Israel, such as had not been since the time when a prophet last appeared among them" (9:27). Another teacher declared, "In this world there is neither a prophet nor a Holy Spirit [Ps. 74:9], and even the *Shekhinah* has vanished on account of our sins [Isa. 59:2]; but in the future world a new revelation will be vouchsafed to them."[30]

It was at the baptism of Jesus Christ that the signal appeared that the restoration of the Spirit of prophecy had taken place. The Holy Spirit descending like a dove, proclaimed the reconnection of heaven and earth (John 1:32–33). The ancient sign of the Holy Spirit, the Presence, and the small voice was manifested to Israel. The medium was the message, and the message could not have been lost on a Jewish audience: here was clear evidence that the heavens were open again.

Conclusion

The apostasy of the Jews went right on, largely uninterrupted by the coming of Jesus Christ. After Jesus' and John's short ministries, those hellenistic influences that had produced the Jewish apostasy infiltrated the young Christian church as well; the same gospel mutations appeared in a remarkably short time, as we can see in the letters of Paul (e.g., Titus

---

[28]*Yoma* 9b and *Sotah* 48b.

[29]*Sotah* 3b.

[30]Arthur Marmorstein, *Studies in Jewish Theology* (Freeport, N.Y.: Books for Libraries Press, 1972), p. 125.

1:14). The doctrine of God suffered corruption almost immediately at the hands of hellenized Christians, as did the scriptures (see 1 Ne. 13:24–29). The temple was destroyed again in A.D. 70 as Jesus prophesied it would be (Matt. 24), and the Spirit of prophecy had again flown by the end of the first century A.D.

44

A CHRONOLOGY OF THE OLD TESTAMENT

Kent P. Jackson

The following charts include the names of most of the major figures of the Old Testament. The dates suggested are based on current understanding of the Old Testament text, biblical and related history, and archaeology.

Dating ancient events and people is one of the more difficult aspects of historical research.[1] Scholars endeavor, through examination of all available sources, to establish both *relative* dates and *absolute* dates. Relative dating consists of determining when something took place in relation to other events. In many cases in the Old Testament, the text itself provides enough clear evidence that this form of dating can be accomplished without much difficulty. For example, 2 Kings 14:1 tells us that King Amaziah of Judah began to rule in the second year of King Joash of Israel. With this one verse, we know the relative positions of these two kings.

In contrast, absolute dating, determining when things happened according to our modern calendar, is much more difficult. To determine absolute dates, one must usually rely on a series of relative dates, some of which cross ancient cultural boundaries. The firmest dates in Old Testament history are those that provide synchronisms with dates from the Assyrians and Babylonians, whose calendars often dated events on the basis of astronomical phenomena that can be determined scientifically. An example is 2 Kings 24:8, 12, which synchronizes the

---

Kent P. Jackson is professor of ancient scripture at Brigham Young University.

[1]An extensive scholarly discussion of Old Testament dating is found in Mordecai Cogan, "Chronology, Hebrew Bible," *The Anchor Bible Dictionary,* 6 vols., ed. David Noel Freedman (New York: Doubleday, 1992), 1:1002–11.

ill-fated rule of Jehoiachin with the reign of Nebuchadnezzar, which is established confidently in Babylonian sources. Starting with such synchronisms, then, relative dating is employed within biblical history to provide dates for other events. Needless to say, this is not a perfect system.

As dating from ancient sources necessarily involves varying degrees of historical reconstruction, the reader is advised to use caution when dealing with biblical dates. Much of the dating for the later periods, represented in charts III and IV, is based on good cross-references to Mesopotamian sources and is thus fairly reliable.[2] But for the earlier periods, represented in charts I and II, significant uncertainties continue to exist. No attempt is made here to date anything in the Bible prior to Abraham's time.

I. The Covenant People from Adam to Abraham

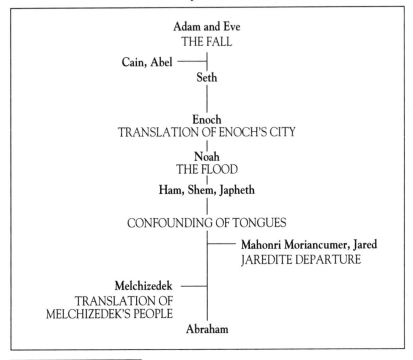

---

[2]All of the dates for the kings of Israel and Judah are taken from John Bright, *A History of Israel*, 3d ed. (Philadelphia: Westminster, 1981). Permission from the publisher is gratefully acknowledged.

II. The House of Israel to the Time of Solomon

Books		Egypt	Palestine	Other
Genesis	2000	MIDDLE KINGDOM (11th-12th Dynasties) 2040-1786	MIDDLE BRONZE AGE 2000-1550	
	1900		Melchizedek Abraham	
	1800		Isaac	Hammurapi (Babylon) 1792-1750
	1700	SECOND INTER-MEDIATE PERIOD (Hyksos) 1786-1558	Jacob	
	1600		Joseph	Mursilis I (Hittites) 1620-1595
Exodus		Ahmose 1558-1533		
	1500	Hatshepsut 1490-1469		
	1450	NEW KINGDOM (18th-20th Dynasties) 1558-1069	LATE BRONZE AGE 1550-1200	
	1400			
	1350	Akhenaten 1364-1347 Tutankhamun 1347-1338		Suppululiumas (Hittites) 1375-1335
	1300	Ramesses II 1290-1224		Muwatallis (Hittites) 1306-1282
Lev. Num. Deut. Josh.	1250		Moses The Exodus	Hattusilis III (Hittites) 1275-1250
	1200	Merneptah 1224-1214	Joshua The Conquest Incursions by the Sea Peoples (Philistines)	Fall of the Hittite Empire
Judges	1150		The Judges	
	1100			
Ruth				
1 Sam.	1050		Samuel Saul 1020-1000(?)	
	1000		David 1000-961(?)	
2 Sam. 1 Chron.	950	Shishak 935-914	Solomon 961-922(?)	Hiram I (Tyre) 969-936
1 Kings 2 Chron.	900			

ISRAELITES IN EGYPT

III. Israel and Judah 922-587 B.C.

Books		Judah	Israel	Assyria
1 Kings / 2 Chronicles	925	DIVISION OF THE KINGDOMS 922		
		Rehoboam 922-915	Jeroboam I 922-901	
		Abijah 915-913		
	900	Asa 913-873	Nadab 901-900	
			Baasha 900-877	
			Elah 877-876	Asshurnasirpal II 883-859
	875		Zimri 876	
		Jehoshaphat 873-849	Omri 876-869	
			Ahab 869-850 *Elijah*	
				Shalmaneser III 858-824
	850	Jehoram 849-843	Ahaziah 850-849	
		Ahaziah 843-842	Jehoram 849-843 *Elisha*	
		Athaliah 842-837	Jehu 843-815	
	825	Joash 837-800		
			Jehoahaz 815-802	
				Adadnirari III 810-783
	800	Amaziah 800-783	Jehoash 802-786	
			Jeroboam II 786-746	
		Uzziah/Azariah 783-742		
Jonah	775		*Jonah*	
Amos			*Amos*	
Hosea			*Hosea*	
	750	Jotham 742-735	Zechariah 746-745	Tiglath-pileser III (Pul)
			Shallum 745	744-727
			Menahem 745-737	
Micah		Ahaz 735-715 *Micah*	Pekahiah 737-736	Shalmaneser V 726-722
Isaiah	725	*Isaiah*	Pekah 736-732	Sargon II 721-705
			Hoshea 732-724	
		Hezekiah 715-687	Fall of Samaria 721	
	700			Sennacherib 704-681
		Manasseh 687-642		
	675			Esarhaddon 680-669
				Asshurbanipal 668-627
	650	Amon 642-640	Babylon	
		Josiah 640-609	(Neo-Babylonian Empire)	
Jer.	625	*Jeremiah*	Nabopolassar 625-605	
Zeph.		*Zephaniah*		
Nah.		Jehoahaz 609 *Nahum*		Fall of Assyrian Empire
		Jehoiakim 609-598	Nebuchadnezzar 604-562	
Hab.	600	Jehoiachin 598-597 *Habakkuk*		
		First Deportation to Exile 597		
1Ne. 1		Zedekiah 597-587 *Lehi*	*Ezekial*	
		Fall of Jerusalem 587	*Daniel*	
Obad.		*Obadiah*		

IV. Judah from the Time of Jeremiah 600-432 B.C.

Books			Judah		Babylon	Media/Persia
2 Chron. / 2 Kgs.	1Ne. 1	600	*Jeremiah*		**Nebuchadnezzar** 604-562	
	Ezek. Dan.		*Lehi* First Deportation to Exile 597 **Zedekiah** 597-587 Fall of Jerusalem 587 Second Deportation	*Ezekiel* *Daniel*		
	Obad.	575	*Obadiah*			
2 Chron.		550		JEWS IN EXILE	**Amel-marduk** 562-560 **Nabonidus** 556-539 (Belshazzar co-regent) Fall of Neo-Babylonian Empire 539	**Cyrus** 550-530
Ezra 1:1- 4:5, 24			**Zerubbabel** **Jeshua**	Edict of Liberation 538		
		525	*Haggai* *Zechariah* Temple Rebuilt 515			**Cambyses** 530-522 **Darius I** 522-486
Hag./Zech. Ezra 5-6						
Joel(?) Malachi		500	*Joel(?)* *Malachi*			
						Xerxes I 486-465
Ezra 4:6–23		475				
						Artaxerxes I 465-424
Ezra 7–10 Neh. 8-10		450	**Ezra's appointment 458**			
Neh. 1-7, 11-13			**Nehemiah's appointment 445**			
		425	**Nehemiah's second appointment 432**			

SCRIPTURE INDEX

18:8–9	226	25–26	201–2
18:18	232	25–29	197
18:18–23	231–32	25:3–4	201
18:20	232	25:10	201
18:23	232	25:11	201
19–20	224, 226–27	25:13	246
19:3	226	25:15–16	246
19:6	227	25:15–38	201, 208, 246
19:7	227	25:17–38	246
19:8	227	25:19	246
19:9	227	25:20	246
19:11	227	25:21	246
20	175, 224, 227, 232	25:22	246
20:1–2	227	25:23–24	246
20:2	39	25:25	246
20:3–6	227	25:26	246
20:7–9	232	25:34–38	218
20:7–13	232	26	200–202, 215–16,
20:11–13	232		220–21, 223–24
20:14–18	216, 232–34	26–35	197
21–24	197, 236	26:1	216
21–25	197	26:6	193
21:1–10	237–38	26:8–10	223
21:2	237	26:12–13, JST	223
21:4	237	26:18	68
21:5	237, 257	26:18–19	68
21:9	211, 217, 238	26:18–19, JST	72
21:11–22:9	238	26:20	224
21:11–22:30	238–39	26:24	209
21:12	238	27	175, 204
22	238	27–28	224
22:3	238	27–29	204–6
22:8–9	238	27:1	204
22:10–12	199, 238	27:2, 20	204
22:13–16	239	27:6–8	204
22:13–19	173, 200, 238	27:12–18	278
22:15–16	172, 199	27:14	204, 205
22:18–19	173, 200	27:16	205
22:19	239	28	175, 204
22:20–30	239	28:1	204
23	239	28:1–17	174, 278
23:1	294	28:9	205
23:1–4	218, 239	28:10–11	205
23:3–6	354	28:15–16	205
23:4	239	28:17	205
23:5	152, 240	29	175, 205
23:5–6	296, 354	29:5	205
23:7–8	228, 240	29:7–9	205
23:9–40	240	29:8–9	174
23:14	240	29:17	217
23:16	240	29:21	205
23:17	240–41	29:21–23	175
23:21	240	30	206, 242
23:25–27	240	30–31	197, 236, 242–43
23:27	241	30:3	212, 242
24:6–7	241	30:8	242
24:7	299, 241	30:9	242
24:8–10	241	30:14	242
24:10	217	30:20	242
25	201	30:22	299

95:6	158
96:1	155
98:12	123
101	436
101:12	93
101:25–34	101
101:26, 29	101
104	436
104:14–16, 18	435
105:14	434
105:31–32	470
109:29	191
109:73–74	470
110:11	103
110:11–16	102
110:13–16	26, 316, 369, 371
112:15, 32	102
112:24–26	355
112:25–26	91
113:1–2	101–2
113:3–4	102
113:5–6	102, 354
113:7–8	149
113:9–10	149
115:6	93, 354
116	322, 332
121:10	393
121:26–32	101
121:37	430
122:5–8	233–34
122:7	438
122:8	398
122:9	234
124:60–61	271
128:17	26
128:18	372
128:20	102
128:21	123
130:20	396
130:20–21	217
131:5	27
133:5, 7, 14	186
133:5, 12	252
133:9	155
133:14	354
133:20, 35	358
133:25–35	104
133:27	103
133:37–39	163
133:40–45	163
133:46–56	163
133:48, 50–51	364

133:64	371
135:4	230
138:30	138
138:44	322
138:46	26, 366

THE PEARL OF GREAT PRICE

MOSES
4:1	472
4:1–4	105
5:8	479
6:6	182
6:26	194
6:32	194
6:33–36	194
6:63	2, 96
7:13–17	93
7:16–19	90
7:28	67, 405
7:29–40	405
7:41	405
7:48–49, 61–64	101

ABRAHAM
1:18–19	479
2:9–11	136, 142
2:10	147
2:11	147
3:27	87
4:29–30	101

JOSEPH SMITH–MATTHEW
1:12	332
1:18	133
1:26	134
1:33	363

JOSEPH SMITH–HISTORY
1:37	371
1:38–39	371
1:40	138
1:40, 45–46, 49	102
1:41	362
1:63–65	123
2:68–72	368

ARTICLES OF FAITH
10	128, 130, 134, 296, 299, 306–7, 319, 364

SUBJECT INDEX

nations by, 110–13; apocalypse of, 118–21; six woes of, 121–27; messianic prophecies of, 126; message of repentance of, 126–27; on destruction, 129–30; on restoration, 130–31; on idolatry, 139, 157; sees the future, 140; wrote for future generations, 141; as a servant, 145; definition of, 146; Christ quotes, 151; describes the Atonement, 159; light motif in, 160–61; vengeance in, 162–63; obedience in, 223; symbolic acts of, 224; quoted in Book of Mormon, 261; themes in, 267; importance of, 346; warnings of, 396; marriage metaphor in, 469

Ishmael, 161, 176, 208–9

Israel: rebellion of, 2, 281–83; two histories of, 4; downfall of, 7; political position of Solomon's, 17–18; division of, 20–21; destruction of, 24–25, 305–6; fights Judah, 38–40; scattering of, 43, 228; prophecies of destruction of, 57–58; as God's servant, 136–37; gathering of, 155–56, 158, 161, 183, 242–43, 303; sins of, 157; restoration of, 301, 303–7; purification of, 368–70. See also Jerusalem; Judah; Kingdoms; Northern Kingdom; Southern Kingdom

Jacob, 2, 136, 143–44, 162, 262, 292–93, 462

Jahaziel, 418

James, 26, 393, 399

Jeduthun, 417–18

Jehoahaz (Shallum), 173, 199, 238, 281

Jehoiachin (Coniah or Jeconiah), 173–74, 176, 200, 212, 238–39, 241, 268–69, 273, 280–81, 338–39

Jehoiakim (Eliakim), 173, 196, 199–202, 210, 215–16, 221, 224, 238–39, 248, 281

Jehoida, 35–37

Jehoram (Joram), 34. See also Joram

Jehoshaphat, 10, 418

Jehosheba (Jehoshabeath), 35

Jehovah. See Jesus Christ

Jehu, 31–32, 44

Jephthah, 249

Jeremiah: oracles against nations by, 110; on the restoration, 142; mourns Josiah, 173; forced to flee Jerusalem, 176; lineage of, 193; receives prophetic call, 193–94; mission of, 195–96, 236; biography of, 197–98; admires Josiah, 199–200; denounces Jehoiakim, 200; persecution of, 201; warnings of, 201, 396; temple sermon of, 202; imprisonment of, 204, 207–8; buys land, 206; release of, 209; message of, 209–10; restoration prophecies of, 211–12; commitment of, 212–13; calling of, 214; messages of, 214–16; images of, 217–20; temple sermon of, 220–24; symbolic acts of, 224–27; laments of, 228–34; prophesies against kings, 238; as messianic oracle, 239–41; sees vision of figs, 241–42; on a new covenant, 243–45; oracles of, against foreign nations, 245–52; as author of Lamentations, 253–54; knew Obadiah, 264; themes in, 267; opposition to, 278; point of view of, 281; importance of, 346; marriage metaphor in, 469

Jeroboam I, 11, 43–44

Jeroboam II, 46, 52

Jeroboam, 18–23

Jerusalem: destruction of, 92, 116–17, 123, 133–34, 174–76, 208; rebuilding of, 159; destruction foretold of, 180–81; lamentations of, 254–55; pronouncements against, 283–85; rebuilding walls of, 381–83. See also Israel; Judah

Jeshua (Joshua), 341–42, 344, 347

Jesus Christ: as God of Old Testament, 1; message of, 2; prophets testify of, 2–3; Elijah and Elisha foreshadowed,